XENOP

OECONOMICUS

XENOPHON
OECONOMICUS

A Social and Historical Commentary

With a new English translation
by

SARAH B. POMEROY

CLARENDON PRESS · OXFORD

Oxford University Press, Walton Street, Oxford OX2 6DP

Oxford   New York
Athens   Auckland   Bangkok   Bombay
Calcutta   Cape Town   Dar es Salaam   Delhi
Florence   Hong Kong   Istanbul   Karachi
Kuala Lumpur   Madras   Madrid   Melbourne
Mexico City   Nairobi   Paris   Singapore
Taipei   Tokyo   Toronto
and associated companies in
Berlin   Ibadan

Oxford is a trade mark of Oxford University Press

Published in the United States
by Oxford University Press Inc., New York

British Library Cataloguing in Publication Data
Data available

Library of Congress Cataloging in Publication Data
Xenophon, Oeconomicus: a social and historical commentary, with a
new English translation by Sarah B. Pomeroy.
Greek text with English translation and commentary.
Includes bibliographical references.
1. Xenophon. Oeconomicus. 2. Home economics—Early works to
1800. 3. Home economics—Greece. I. Xenophon. Oeconomicus.
English & Greek. 1994. II. Title.
PA4494.O43P66   1944   330.15'12—dc20   93-34855
ISBN 0-19-815025-3

1   3   5   7   9   10   8   6   4   2

Printed in Great Britain on acid-free paper by
Biddles Ltd., Guildford and King's Lynn

To Lee

PREFACE

The *Oeconomicus* is unique in Greek literature in combining a discussion of the proper management of an oikos ('family', 'household', or 'estate') with didactic material on agriculture. I was drawn to this text because the subjects it comprises were those to which I have devoted my scholarly life. My doctoral dissertation, in papyrology, was largely a study of olive-culture in Graeco-Roman Egypt. In more recent years I have worked on the history of women and the family.

I began to write this book while I was the Blegen Distinguished Visiting Research Professor at Vassar College and continued while I was a fellow at the Humanities Research Centre in Canberra. The book was completed when I was a Fellow at St Hilda's College, Oxford. I wish to express my gratitude to these institutions. I am also grateful to the National Endowment for the Humanities for awarding me a Fellowship and to the Foundation Hardt pour l'Étude de l'Antiquité classique for its hospitality during the summer of 1989.

This book covers a wide range of subjects including agriculture, philosophy, and social, military, intellectual, and economic history. In it I have used methodologies, approaches, and data drawn from many disciplines, especially classics, history, anthropology, and art history. I am grateful to have been able to discuss some of the subjects with other scholars, though it should not be assumed that they concur with all my statements. I continue to be grateful to J. K. Anderson, Stanley Mayer Burstein, Jørgen Mejer, and Donald Russell for reading the entire manuscript; to Diskin Clay and David Harvey for their advice on the translation; to Lin Foxhall and Robin Osborne for reading the Commentary on cc. x–xx; and to Beatrice Gottlieb, Dorothy Helly, and Jo Ann MacNamara for their comments on the translation and on Chs. 4–6. I am also grateful to the participants in the Seminars for College Teachers, sponsored by the National Endowment for the

Humanities, that I directed in 1987 and 1989 and to colleagues in Europe, Australia, Canada, and the United States, who attended my lectures and discussed my work while it was in progress. Finally, I wish to thank Leofranc Holford-Strevens, who copy-edited the manuscript, for his enlightening comments.

The *Oeconomicus* is one of the richest primary sources for the social, economic, and intellectual history of classical Athens. It contains valuable information and raises questions of perennial interest on marriage, the innate moral, physical, and mental qualities of men and women, the functioning of the domestic and public economies, rural and urban life, Greek slavery, popular religion, the role of education, and many other topics. Despite the current widespread interest in the subjects discussed in the *Oeconomicus*, this text has been largely ignored, and only a few European dissertations (none in English) have been written on it.

With the exception of Chs. 2 and 7, the introductory chapters preceding the translation were written to be comprehensible both to readers who know ancient Greek and Greek history, and to readers who do not. Chs. 3 and 7 and the Commentary are more technical and specialized. However, Greekless readers can easily identify any part of the Commentary they wish to consult by locating the chapter- and paragraph-numbers in the Greek text. Many of the topics discussed in the Commentary are themselves the subjects of countless books and articles. This book is about the *Oeconomicus*: it is not an economic history of Greece or a monograph on the Greek family. Of necessity, I have limited my remarks and citations of secondary literature in the Commentary to what I deemed useful and enlightening to readers of the *Oeconomicus*. My translations are usually literal; but when it seemed necessary, I have strayed from literalness in order to make a passage intelligible to the Greekless reader.

'Pseudo-' (abbreviated to 'Ps.-') preceding an author's name indicates that scholars have cast doubt upon the attribution of a literary work to a particular author; it does not imply a t-classical forgery. Thus a work attributed to Pseudo-Demosthenes was probably written by one of Demosthenes' less gifted contemporaries, and one attributed to Pseudo-Aristotle actually written by a student of Aristotle or a slightly later Peripatetic. With the exception of those given in biblio-grapical references, lower-case roman numerals refer to the twenty-one chapters of the *Oeconomicus*.

The manuscript of this book was completed in January 1991, and I have been able to refer to only a few works published after that date.

S. B. P.

ACKNOWLEDGMENT

THE Greek text of the *Oeconomicus* is reproduced with the permission of the Oxford University Press.

CONTENTS

List of Illustrations   xii

1. Xenophon's Life and the Date of Composition
   of the *Oeconomicus*   I

2. Languge, Style, Structure, and Dramatic Date   9

3. Xenophon and Socrates   21

4. The Family in Classical Greece   31

5. The Domestic Economy   41

6. The *Oeconomicus* After Xenophon   68

7. The History of the Text   91

Remarks on the Translation   97

Sigla   103

TEXT AND TRANSLATION   104

COMMENTARY   213

Bibliography   347

Greek Index to Commentary   372

General Index   374

LIST OF ILLUSTRATIONS

Pl. 1. Persian king ploughing   239
Pl. 2. King Darius I hunting lions from a chariot   244
Pl. 3. Women working wool   307

Fig. 1. Houses at Priene   294

I

Xenophon's Life and the Date of Composition of the *Oeconomicus*

In addition to Xenophon's own works, the principal ancient source for his life is the biography in Diogenes Laertius (2. 48–9, early 3rd c. AD).[1] Like much ancient biography, this work is naïve and unreliable. Many statements in the biography can be traced back to Xenophon's own writings. Perhaps because Xenophon did not found a philosophical school, details of his life were of no interest to immediately succeeding generations.[2] The biography by Diogenes Laertius derived from one written in the first century BC by Demetrius of Magnesia.[3]

A. *Youth*

Judging from historical events that occurred during his life, we may surmise that Xenophon was born in Athens around 430 BC, or slightly later. The floruit of 401/0 BC given in

[1] The present discussion will concentrate on those aspects of Xenophon's life which may relate directly to the composition of the *Oeconomicus*. For a more complete modern survey of Xenophon's life and his work, see e.g. J. K. Anderson, *Xenophon* (London and New York, 1974). Édouard Delebecque, *Essai sur la vie de Xénophon* (Paris, 1957), gives a 532-page reconstruction of Xenophon's life, consisting in large part of the events described by Xenophon himself set in historical context and of Delebecque's psychohistorical speculations on his subject's private life. He refers to Ischomachus as 'cet autre Xénophon' or 'Xénophon-Ischomaque' in 'Sur la date et l'objet de l'Économique', *REG* 64 (1951), 29, 53. However, Ischomachus is rather what Xenophon might have aspired to be if he had lived earlier in the 5th c. It is true that in the *Anabasis* Xenophon had written an autobiographical war-memoir in which he does not disguise his own name and importance, but whether his life should be construed as a principal source for his other works is questionable.

[2] Jørgen Mejer, *Diogenes Laertius and his Hellenistic Background* (Wiesbaden, 1978), 39, 69, observes that the biography of Xenophon was not part of the Hellenistic biographical tradition.

[3] D.L. 2. 52, 56, 57 refers to Demetrius. See further U. von Wilamowitz-Moellendorff, *Antigonos von Karystus* (Berlin, 1881), 330–5.

Diogenes Laertius 2. 55 does not mean that he was 40 years old at that date; instead, as the rest of the sentence indicates, it probably refers to Xenophon's campaign with Cyrus that he undertook when he was still young (*Anab.* 3. 1. 14). His father's name was Gryllus, his mother's was Diodora, and he belonged to the inland deme Erchia of the tribe Aigeis.[4]

Xenophon's family was at least of equestrian rank (i.e. of the second highest census class). There is no evidence that they qualified for liturgical (i.e. 'wealthiest') status, but the evidence for such status is incomplete.[5] Xenophon's education, his ownership of a horse, and his relationships with Athenians and foreigners of high status strongly suggest that he belonged to the highest class (see on i. 8 ἵππον and ii. 5 ξένους). He thus enjoyed a privileged upbringing and was probably as wealthy as other young men (such as Critobulus) who listened to Socrates conversing and who are portrayed in the Socratic dialogues. According to Philostratus (*Lives of the Sophists* 1. 12) Xenophon was captured by the Boeotians in 406 BC before the battle of Arginusae. During his imprisonment he heard the discourses of Prodicus of Ceos, who was then lecturing in Thebes. However, this tradition, like much in ancient biography, may be fictional.[6]

Xenophon served in the cavalry during the last years of the Peloponnesian War (431–404 BC) and probably was involved in the political turmoil at the end. The cavalry had supported the Thirty (Xen. *Hell.* 2. 4. 8, 10, 3. 1. 4) and were thought to favour oligarchy.[7]

B. *Departure from Athens*

With other young men, but few other Athenians, Xenophon left Greece in 401 BC to serve as a mercenary in the army of

[4] Eugene Vanderpool, 'The Location of the Attic Deme Erchia', *BCH* 89 (1965), 21–6, located the deme centre at Pousiri near Spata, the find-spot of a stele inscribed with a sacrificial calendar (375–350 BC: *SEG* 21. 541 = *LSCG 18* and see below Ch. 4, Sect. B, and on ii. 5–6, xvii. 10).

[5] The family is not cited in J. K. Davies, *Athenian Propertied Families* (Oxford, 1971).

[6] H. R. Breitenbach, *Xenophon von Athen* (Stuttgart, 1966) = *RE*² ixA2, col. 1572, rejects this tradition. See Ch. 2, sect. D.

[7] See further P. Cloché, *La Restauration démocratique à Athènes* (Paris, 1915), 68, 84, 88, 407, 475, and most recently Barry Strauss, *Athens after the Peloponnesian War* (Ithaca, NY, 1987).

Cyrus the Younger, pretender to the Persian throne (*Anab.* 1. 2. 1, D.L. 2. 55). Although Xenophon, like his Greek compatriots, was originally a citizen-soldier, who served as required, when he became a mercenary he was a professional soldier. An analogous transformation from part-time country squire to professional farmer is recommended in the *Oeconomicus*. In each case the professional is to retain his versatility. As the history of the Hellenistic period made quite clear, service as a mercenary did not prevent a man from marrying and raising children. Marriage at approximately the age of thirty was normal for upper-class Athenian men. Xenophon may have married his wife Philesia shortly before leaving Athens. But judging from the ages of his two sons Gryllus and Diodorus, they were married while he was in Asia Minor.

Cyrus died at the battle of Cunaxa in 401 BC. Despite the brevity of their acquaintance, he had made such a favourable impression on Xenophon that in *Oec.* iv he could be described in the same terms as Cyrus the Great, who had become an almost legendary figure (see ad loc.).

After the deaths of Cyrus and of most of the original Greek generals, Xenophon was chosen by the Greeks to lead them from Persia back to the Greek world. He described the march of the Ten Thousand in the *Anabasis*. Owing to his associations with Persians and his lengthy sojourn in Asia, Xenophon acquired first-hand knowledge of the Persian Empire. His own interest in practical matters (such as supplying sustenance to the soldiers in his charge) is also evident in the *Oeconomicus*. In particular, the subject of leadership, which is a central concern in the *Oeconomicus*, the *Cyropaedia*, the *Hiero*, the *Cavalry Commander*, and *Agesilaus*, is certainly one of which Xenophon had first-hand knowledge. In the *Anabasis* he describes his own experience as a military leader.[8]

On their return to Greece, the remnants of the Ten Thousand took up service with Seuthes, king of Thrace, and in 399 BC they joined the Spartans in an effort to free the Ionian cities from Persia (Xen. *Hell.* 3. 1. 11–28). Thus Xenophon was not in Athens at the time of Socrates' trial and

[8] See further Anderson, *Xenophon*, ch. 10, and Marcel Caster, 'Sur l'*Économique* de Xénophon', in *Mélanges offerts à A.-M. Desrousseaux* (Paris, 1937), 49–57.

death. In 396 BC Xenophon met the Spartan king Agesilaus, who, like Cyrus the Younger, was in his view an exemplary leader. Xenophon and other Greek soldiers who had served with Agesilaus returned to Greece in his company in 395/4 BC. Agesilaus was victorious against Athens and her allies at Coronea in Boeotia.

C. Exile

Probably soon after the battle of Coronea, Xenophon was sentenced to exile by the Athenians for having favoured the Spartans.[9] In any event, he was absent from mainland Greece for approximately seven years. Therefore, although he represents himself as present at a conversation when Socrates mentioned the battle of Cunaxa, he could not have actually been there (see on iv. 18).[10]

Because of Xenophon's friendship with Agesilaus and other Spartans, he was granted an estate at Scillus in Triphylia, south of Olympia (Xen. *Anab.* 5. 3, D.L. 2. 52, Paus. 5. 6. 5). After the Spartans were defeated at Leuctra in 371 BC and Scillus was attacked by the Eleans, Xenophon moved to Corinth.

Around 365 BC Athens rescinded the decree of banishment. Xenophon may have returned to Athens permanently. Or he may have remained in and died at Corinth, as reported by D.L. 2. 56, while visiting Athens regularly and showing concern for his native city's political and economic condition. His son Gryllus was killed in 362 BC fighting on the Athenian side at Mantinea (see on vii. 1 στοᾷ). Judging from historical events (especially the Third Sacred War) apparently reflected in

---

[9] Peter J. Rahn, 'The Date of Xenophon's Exile' in G. S. Shrimpton and D. J. McCargar (eds.), *Classical Contributions: Studies in Honour of Malcolm Francis McGregor* (New York, 1981), 103–19, argues, on the basis of Athenian politics in the first decade of the 4th c. BC, that the decree banishing Xenophon from Athens must have been promulgated during the archonship of Eubulides, in late 394 or early 393, after Coronea. Anderson, *Xenophon*, 149, and others had supposed that the decree of exile followed closely after Xenophon's departure for Persia.

[10] During this period the testimony of Andocides implicated in scandal a certain Chrysilla, who may have been Ischomachus' wife (And. 1. 124–7; on Chrysilla and Ischomachus, see on vi. 17).

Revenues 5. 9, 12, Xenophon died at the end of 356 BC.[11] These allusions also suggest that the date of birth furnished by Diogenes Laertius is too early. Xenophon's grandson, a son of Diodorus named after his famous grandfather, seems to have carried on the family tradition of activity on an international scale: sometime in or just after 306 BC Ephesus awarded him citizenship.[12]

D. *Biographical Interpretation of the Composition of the* Oeconomicus

As we have mentioned, Xenophon grew up in a rural deme. Moreover, the sojourn in Scillus was probably influential on his views on estate management and fostered his enjoyment of rural life, although the *Oeconomicus* is set in Athens (see on xi. 14 κατὰ πόλιν). That Xenophon turned his attention to the subject of the domestic economy is not accidental. Disgust with politics, service as a mercenary rather than as a citizen-soldier, and life as an exile debarred from political activity may have induced him to turn away from the public sphere for some time to a consideration of the private realm, and inspired him to begin work on the *Oeconomicus*. He also continued to write about politics and probably continued to work on the *Oeconomicus* after he resumed political activity. At any rate, he displayed an interest in the private world and the individual that was to develop into a distinctive feature of the literature of the Hellenistic period (see Ch. 4).

All Xenophon's books are extant. According to D.L. 2. 52, he wrote his histories in Scillus. Because of the itinerant nature of the first half of his adult life, some scholars, including Delebecque and Anderson, have generalized from Diogenes' statement, and reasonably assumed that Xenophon began to write only when he was in exile.[13] Delebecque argues that the first five chapters of the *Oeconomicus* were written at Scillus

[11] According to D.L. 2. 56, who quotes from Demetrius of Magnesia, Xenophon died in Corinth in the first year of the 105th Olympiad, or 360/59 BC. This date can only be a *terminus post quem*.

[12] See *SEG* 33 (1983), 267–9, no. 932.

[13] Anderson, *Xenophon*, 175, is less certain about the date of composition but also finds memories of Scillus in the *Oeconomicus*.

because he believes he can detect some Spartan influence in the first part, but none thereafter. He concludes that the remainder of the work was written at Athens.[14] This hypothesis, however, is unacceptable, for it implies that Xenophon had forgotten Sparta after leaving Scillus (although he certainly remembered his march through Persia and other events that had taken place even earlier in his life). One aspect of alleged Spartan influence that Delebecque notes is the freedom of Ischomachus' wife. However, the fact that this feature actually appears in the portrait of the wife in what should be the Athenian phase of Delebecque's scenario certainly weakens his argument. Furthermore, the wealth of allusions to rural life need not indicate Spartan genesis. In the classical period most Athenians, like Xenophon himself, were familiar with both city and countryside (see Ch. 5). In support of his hypothesis, Delebecque also cites Luigi Castiglioni.[15] Castiglioni asserts that the *Oeconomicus* was written in two parts; he draws attention to repetitions and inconsistencies in the text and, in particular, notes that the list of topics in the review in c. vi did not correspond precisely in content or order with the previous five chapters, nor, he argues, does it look forward to the rest of the work. He speculates that Xenophon would have eliminated this section in a final revision.[16] In my opinion, the recapitulation in c. vi is adequate and appropriate (see on vi. 2–10). Moreover, Castiglioni argues that although the first five chapters imply that Socrates is knowledgeable about οἰκονομία, in the remainder of the work Ischomachus serves as the authority on this subject. Though Castiglioni makes some legitimate criticisms of Xenophon's prose style, he fails to prove his principal thesis. With a little encouragement from Ischomachus, Socrates does turn out to know something about οἰκονομία (see Ch. 3). Furthermore, Castiglioni is misguided in demanding that Xenophon write with the precision, economy, and smooth transitions expected of the best modern prose style. It should be recognized that the standards Greek prose authors imposed on themselves differ from those of

[14] *Essai*, 235, 368–70.
[15] 'Studi senofontei IV: intorno all'Economico', *Riv. di fil.* 48 (1920), 321–42.
[16] Ibid. 331.

6

authors in the twentieth century. For example, Xenophon (and Plato) do not hesitate to introduce anachronisms of which they surely were aware and which they could have avoided (see on i. 1 ἤκουσα). Moreover, some of the problems Castiglioni detected in the text may be artefacts of the chaotic state of the manuscripts (see Ch. 7). Castiglioni's arguments are similar to those of several scholars in the twentieth century who assert that the *Hellenica, Anabasis, Cyropaedia, Memorabilia,* and *Spartan Constitution* were each composed in at least two different parts, separated by considerable time-spans.[17] As far as the *Oeconomicus* is concerned, these arguments are not totally convincing. It seems more plausible that Xenophon began to write or, more probably, completed the first draft of the entire *Oeconomicus* while he was in exile in Scillus, and revised it or made some additions at least once before he died. Certainly at no time could he have intended that cc. i–v should stand alone, for they have no theme or purpose and would be too short to comprise an independent dialogue.

The analyses of Castiglioni and Delebecque do not take account of Xenophon's merits as an innovator in literary forms. They do not consider the possibility that he is representing a conversation in which Socrates may not have remembered the exact order or content of a past discussion when such precision was not essential to the development of his argument, or, what is more likely, that Xenophon, or previous Socratics, invented most of the conversation. (On the unity of the *Oeconomicus* see further Ch. 2, sect. E). A possible explanation for some of the inconsistencies is that Xenophon based the *Oeconomicus* on at least two earlier Socratic sources that he had in his library, but failed to eliminate a few irregularities that resulted (see on iii. 14 Ἀσπασίαν and Ch. 3). Earlier philosophers had discussed themes similar to some of those in the *Oeconomicus.* The Sophist Protagoras treated household management (Pl. *Prot.* 318 E) and the Socratic Antisthenes wrote an *Oeconomicus*

---

[17] See e.g. Hubert A. Holden, *The Oeconomicus of Xenophon* (London, 1884), 87, Malcolm MacLaren, Jr., 'On the Composition of Xenophon's *Hellenica*', *AJP* 55 (1934), 121–39, D. J. Mosley, 'Xenophon', in *Oxford Classical Dictionary*, 2nd edn. (Oxford, 1971), 1142, and Stephen Usher, *The Historians of Greece and Rome* (Norman, Okla., 1985), 99.

(D.L. 6. 16). Xenophon might have adapted large sections of the Socratics' works without rewriting them sufficiently for them to merge into a flawless whole. That researchers should either use quotation-marks or feel obliged to rewrite the work of others in their own words was, after all, not a familiar notion to Greek authors. The two parts are distinguished but unified in that the first part is devoted to the theory and the second part to the practice of οἰκονομία. We can only speculate about when Xenophon began to write the *Oeconomicus*, and whether he wrote it in two parts, separated by a considerable time-span.[18] But if he chose to set the conversation between Socrates and Ischomachus in the stoa of Zeus Eleutherius because of the depiction of his son Gryllus at the battle of Mantinea in that building, he was still working on the *Oeconomicus* after 362 BC (see on vii. 1 στοᾷ).

Though Xenophon was reared in Athens and died there, he was familiar with the two groups the Athenians themselves considered most antithetical to themselves: the Spartans and the barbarians (i.e. non-Greeks). He had lived in urban and rural settings. He had been a citizen-soldier, a mercenary, and an exile. Though he was a friend of kings, he respected slaves (see Ch. 5). His varied life is reflected in the diversity and novelty of his writing.

[18] According to Delebecque's reconstruction of Xenophon's life, the *Oeconomicus* was published in its final form after July 362 BC, when the Athenians were in need of food and money: 'Sur la date et l'objet de l'Économique', 58, and *Essai*, 235, 376. The dates assigned to Xenophon's works by Mosley 1142 are far too dogmatic: he writes that the *Oeconomicus* was perhaps published *c*.362/1 BC, but Socrates' conversation was perhaps written *c*.381 BC. On the appearance of agricultural treatises in the 4th c. BC see on v. 1, xvi. 1, xx. 22, and Ch. 5, sect. D.

2
Language, Style, Structure, and Dramatic Date

Xenophon's remarkable life profoundly and discernibly influenced his style of writing. In his travels and exile he encountered many non-Greeks; some of these, no doubt, had learnt to speak Greek, but also introduced him to foreign words for which there was no Greek equivalent. For example, Iranian *paridaiza was picked up orally and adjusted to Greek phonology and morphology to become παράδεισος. He met many Greeks who were not Athenians, and who spoke dialects other than Attic. Thus Xenophon would have talked with Ionians in Asia Minor, with Dorians in Scillus, Sparta, and Corinth, and with Greeks from a variety of states who served in the army of Cyrus.

A. *Audience*

Unlike Plato, Xenophon did not found a school, and unlike Socrates, he did not even have disciples. He spent nearly half his life away from Athens. It is doubtful that he wrote the *Oeconomicus* exclusively for Athenian readers or other philosophers. Rather, we assume that his words were intended for a broad international readership including Athenians and others. Because agriculture formed the basis of all ancient economies, estate management was not an esoteric subject (see Ch. 5).

If it is appropriate to extrapolate from the memoirs of soldiers in other times and places, then we may surmise that Xenophon formed some enduring relationships with non-Athenians while serving as a mercenary. We know, at least, of his friendship with Agesilaus. Although the Spartans were

9

notorious for their lack of literary culture, it is likely that the elite, who constituted Xenophon's circle, were literate.[1] We may speculate that various friends and acquaintances in Sparta and elsewhere read Xenophon's works because they knew the author. Some women who were literate, like Ischomachus' wife, may also have read the *Oeconomicus* (see viii. 36, ix. 10).

Other writers read Xenophon's books. In the *Laws* (694 c), Plato criticized Xenophon's portrayal of Cyrus in the *Cyropaedia*. Furthermore, Aristotle mentioned that in order, at least in part, to please Xenophon, many authors, including Isocrates, wrote encomia after the death of Xenophon's son Gryllus at Mantinea (D.L. 2. 55 = Arist. fr. 68 Rose = p. 7 Ross = fr. 38 Gigon). Aristotle apparently complimented Xenophon by entitling his first work on rhetoric *Gryllus* (Quint. 2. 17. 14).

B. *Language and Style*

Because Xenophon was absent from Athens for much of his life, he could not be an active participant in the growth of fourth-century prose style, including the periodic structure used initially by the sophist and rhetorician Thrasymachus of Chalcedon, but fully developed by the Athenian Isocrates. This structure was characterized by amplitude, balanced clauses, syntactical completeness in a complex whole, and avoidance of poetical diction in general. Although he probably read some current Athenian literature, Xenophon may not have known or cared that some critics regarded archaic and poetic words as inappropriate for prose.

The works of Socrates' contemporaries, to which Xenophon probably referred, were written in the earlier style. Xenophon also makes surprisingly frequent use of technical philosophical words which were not common in everyday speech: apparently he invented some of these (see on title Οἰκονομικός). In addition, in the years he spent outside Athens he heard non-Attic

---

[1] See further P. A. Cartledge, 'Literacy in the Spartan Oligarchy', *JHS* 98 (1978), 25–37. For the possibility that the *Oeconomicus* was composed at Sparta see Ch. 1, sect. D. According to Xen. *Sp. Const.* 1. 9 the Spartans had oikoi.

vocabulary, syntax, and noun and verb forms and used them in speech and in his written work.[2]

In his employment of vocabulary from various dialects and from poetry, Xenophon exhibits characteristics of the common language of the period, the koine. Xenophon was the first to use the literary koine.[3] Of course, because so much of Greek literature is no longer extant, it is not possible to estimate the extent of one author's influence upon the development of the common literary language. Xenophon's works may have helped to win currency and acceptance for the literary use of non-Attic words and syntax. For example, βασίλισσα (for βασίλεια 'queen') appears, perhaps for the first time, in *Oec.* ix. 15, but this term was commonly used in the Hellenistic period (see ad loc.). Xenophon also anticipates Hellenistic usage in his adoption of nouns in -τήρ.

C. *Criticism of Xenophon's Prose: Attic or un-Attic?*

Ancient and modern critics have failed to reach a consensus in evaluating Xenophon's style. Most critics admire the so-called Attic style, but, lacking a universal definition of this style, they are divided on whether Xenophon's work conforms to it. Some commentators have drawn attention to Xenophon's deviations from pure Attic vocabulary and, especially during the Second Sophistic (2nd c. AD), some condemned his usage. Hermogenes of Tarsus (*On Types* 405), for example, observed that Xenophon employs poetical expressions that differ from his normal vocabulary. Similarly, Phrynichus of Bithynia pointed out that Xenophon transgresses the rules of his paternal dialect by using ὀδμή instead of ὀσμή as the word for 'smell'.[4] Galen noted with disapproval Xenophon's use of foreign words and figurative expressions (ὀνόματα γλωσσηματικὰ

---

[2] Though some other scholars have been unfavourably impressed by the variety of Xenophon's vocabulary and use of synonyms derived from various dialects, as a translator I have observed that he is also very fond of repetition. (See further below, 'Remarks on the Translation'.)

[3] A. Thumb, 'Zur neugriechischen Sprachfrage', *NJbb* 17 (1906), 704–12.

[4] *Ecloge* 62 Fischer, s.v. ὀσμή. But Marchant iv. 21, v. 3 gives ὀσμή without further comment.

Language, Style, Structure,

καὶ τροπικά).[5] In the fourth century AD, Helladius mentioned the influence of Xenophon's absence from Athens on his style.[6] The ancient lexica contain numerous citations of Xenophon's un-Attic and unique vocabulary.[7] In the nineteenth century, F. W. Sturz, *Lexicon Xenophonteum*, provided a guide to Xenophon's vocabulary and G. Sauppe, *Lexilogus Xenophonteus*, analysed Xenophon's syntax in dictionary form.[8] These two descriptive works were followed by a spate of criticism and dissertations devoted to pointing out Xenophon's use of un-Attic words and poetic and rhetorical devices. For example, W. G. Rutherford castigated Xenophon for the inconsistency of his diction and for his use of such words as ἀλεξητήρ (iv. 3) and ὄψιμος (xvii. 4) that had appeared in the *Iliad* (20. 396, 2. 325) but are not found again—with the exception of Xenophon—until late Greek.[9]

Even in antiquity, some critics considered that not only was Xenophon's vocabulary anomalous but his style was artificial. Longinus (*On the Sublime* 4. 4) refers to Xenophon and Plato as heroes and admires them both, but he condemns them for frigidity (the use of insipid, inappropriate expression). In the nineteenth century some scholars elaborated Longinus' criticism and scrutinized rhetorical figures in Xenophon.[10]

---

[5] *Comm. on Hippocrates* Περὶ ἄρθρων 58. 1, 414–15 Kühn.

[6] In Photius, *Bibl.* 533 b25–8.

[7] For example, the *Suda* (s.v. ἀγλευκές, i. 29 Adler), and Photius (s.v. ἀγλευκές = p. 27, no. 200 Theodoridis, emended by Reitzenstein, 19, to 'Ρίνθωνι), drew attention to Xenophon's use of ἀγλευκές as a Sicilian word. However, because this word does not appear in any manuscript of the *Oeconomicus*, Marchant relegated it to the apparatus criticus (viii. 3).

[8] Unfortunately there are no more recent publications, and references in Sturz and Sauppe are to outdated numbers of chapters and sections.

[9] *The New Phrynichus* (London, 1881), 124, *et passim*. Among the words in the *Oeconomicus* that Rutherford also faulted as poetic or un-Attic were ἄλκιμος (iv. 15), ἀπερύκω (v. 6), ἀρήγω (v. 7), δάπεδον (viii. 17), δειπνίζω (ii. 5), δεσπόσυνος (ix. 16, xiv. 2), σαφηνίζω (xx. 13, etc.), τάραχος (viii. 10), and νέογνος (vii. 21). Similarly, Tycho Mommsen, *Beiträge zur Lehre der griechischen Präpositionen* (Frankfurt, 1887), 2, called Xenophon the worst practitioner of Attic style. J. Wackernagel referred to Xenophon as a 'demi-Atticist' (*Halbattiker*) in *Hellenistica* (Göttingen, 1907), 5 = *Kleine Schriften* (Göttingen, 1953), ii. 1036, and H. Richards, *Notes on Xenophon and Others* (London, 1907), 159, called Xenophon's diction 'bizarre'.

[10] J. A. Simon, *Xenophon-Studien* (Douren, 1887), discusses rhetoric and grammatical irregularities. Hans Schacht, *De Xenophontis studiis rhetoricis* (diss. Berlin, 1890), claimed to be able to trace the distinct influence of Gorgias on Xenophon's style. Gustav Eichler, *Die Redebilder in den Schriften Xenophons* (Dresden, 1894), 33, declared that

Although these monographs contain useful collections of examples, many of their conclusions are obvious, silly, and tendentious. All prose writers use poetic words and figures, and just because certain words and phrases had appeared in poetry, prose writers were not obliged to reject them (see below, Sect. D).

Some ancient criticism of Xenophon's style was favourable. Cicero pronounces Xenophon's style sweeter than honey[11] and calls him gentle and agreeable (*Orator* 32, *de Oratore* 20. 58). He also remarks upon the wit Socrates displays in the works of Plato, Xenophon, and Aeschines (*Brutus* 292); his description of Xenophon as the voice of the Muses (*Or.* 62) was reported by Quintilian (10. 1. 33). Cicero's judgement increases in importance because he must have read the *Oeconomicus* carefully when he translated the entire work (see Ch. 6). However, the ancient critics who discuss Xenophon's prose style do not actually quote from the *Oeconomicus*, but prefer to quote from longer works such as the *Anabasis* and *Cyropaedia*. Diogenes Laertius (2. 57) also must have approved of Xenophon, for he dubbed him the Attic Muse. Quintilian (10. 83) implies that his writings were without artifice by referring to Xenophon's *iucunditas inaffectata*. Hermogenes (*On Types* 404–6) also praises Xenophon for purity and simplicity, although, as we have mentioned, he does note the use of poetic expressions. Only in the Second Sophistic, when the pure Attic style was revered, was some criticism of Xenophon's style occasionally voiced. However, this opinion was not universal in the second century AD, nor, it seems, was there agreement about the definition of Attic style. Thus Plutarch (*Mor.* 79 D) writes of Xenophon's pure Attic style. In the *Discourses* and *Manual* Arrian compliments Xenophon's style by imitating it. Arrian also considers himself to be another Xenophon (*Peripl. M. Eux.* 1. 1, 12. 5, *On Hunting* 3. 5).

Some modern critics have also praised Xenophon's style.

Xenophon uses an abundance of poetic devices and similes, three-quarters of which begin with the word ὥσπερ ('as').

[11] Hermogenes (*On Types* 335, 405) and Tacitus (*Dial.* 31), also mention Xenophon's sweetness. Similarly, the *Suda* (s.v. Ξενοφῶν, iii. 496 Adler), refers to Xenophon's sweetness by calling him the Attic bee.

For example, Alfred Croiset eschewed the narrow definition of Atticism that measured authors according to their use of Attic vocabulary.[12] Instead he declared that Xenophon was a quintessential representative of Atticism. Lucian had called Xenophon 'honest' (δίκαιος, *Hist.* 39), indicating that he had written history without prejudice. For Croiset too, Xenophon's Atticism consisted in his being an honest man, not an orator or sophist, in avoiding the artifice of Gorgias and Antiphon, and evincing instead perfect grace and naturalness.[13] L. Gautier[14] also argued that Xenophon's written language was not highly rhetorical, but was close to his spoken language. But these views seem to emanate from an idealization of Xenophon as a simple soldier, and are not correct in asserting that he avoided artifice and sophistical diction.

As the preceding survey shows, both ancient and modern criticism of Xenophon's style has been highly subjective and inconsistent. Some critics draw attention to his use of rhetorical and poetical vocabulary and syntax; others, in contrast, emphasize his simplicity and lack of artifice. One conclusion is obvious: not being an orator, Xenophon does not observe the restrictions and rules that the orators show; his style is characterized by diversity rather than by uniformity. Indeed, Dio Chrysostom (18. 14–17) praises Xenophon's versatility and states that models for every kind of eloquence needed in public life can be found in his writings.

Modern analysis of Xenophon's prose has not essentially progressed beyond the observations of the ancient critics. Perhaps the chief problem in analysing Xenophon's prose style has been the lack of a comprehensive theoretical study of the development of Greek prose style buttressed by facts and examples. Even in the twentieth century, despite the bulk of Xenophon's prose, E. Norden[15] and J. D. Denniston[16] mention him only in passing. Assessments of Xenophon's style have not

[12] In A. and M. Croiset, *Histoire de la littérature grecque*, iv (Paris, 1895), 410.

[13] E. Norden, *Die antike Kunstprosa* (Leipzig and Berlin, 1909), 101, also admired Xenophon's harmonious blending of artifice and nature.

[14] *La Langue de Xénophon* (Geneva, 1911), esp. 109–10, 134, 142. In general, Gautier's analysis is the most sensible and thorough of modern works on Xenophon's language and style.

[15] *Kunstprosa*, 101.

[16] *Greek Prose Style* (Oxford, 1952).

14

been divorced from critics' judgement about content. Cicero was enthusiastic in his admiration of Xenophon's style doubtless, at least in part, because he was sympathetic to Xenophon's views. The attribution of the politically conservative *Athenian Constitution* to Xenophon and its inclusion in the manuscripts and editions of his work probably did not help his reputation in the opinion of many readers in the nineteenth and twentieth centuries, although as early as the first century BC Demetrius of Magnesia had denied that Xenophon was the author of the treatise (D.L. 2. 57).

Like some ancient critics, present-day readers are less concerned about the purity of the Attic style and are more appreciative of Xenophon's versatility, especially as a philosopher and historian, and of his innovations in the formation of Greek prose. Xenophon is just as experimental and wide-ranging in his use of prose genres as he is in his employment of vocabulary and prose styles. He wrote history, philosophical dialogue, a historical novel, a war memoir, an encomium, technical treatises, and essays ranging widely in subject-matter, length, and literary style. Diogenes Laertius and the *Suda* (s.v. Ξενοφῶν, iii. 496 Adler) credit Xenophon with being the first to write lives and reminiscences of the philosophers (see below, sect. G). The *Anabasis* is the first war memoir and the *Cyropaedia* the first historical novel. The *Oeconomicus* was among the first prose treatises to be written on agriculture and is the earliest one which is extant.

D. *Rhetoric in the* Oeconomicus

In his affinities with the koine Xenophon looks forward, but in his employment of classical rhetoric he looks back to an earlier period. His prose is studded with rhetorical modes of argument which he must have learnt in his youth at school from sophists or rhetoricians.[17] The same is true of other writers who were Xenophon's contemporaries. Oratory was ubiquitous in Athenian education and public life. Not only Ischomachus himself, but even his slaves can make accusations

[17] For examples principally from the *Anabasis*, see Gustav Lange, 'Xenophons Verhältnis zur Rhetorik', in *Natalicium Johannes Geffcken* (Heidelberg, 1931), 67–84.

or speeches for the defence and his wife can understand and serve as jury (xi. 23–5). Furthermore, according to biographical tradition, Xenophon was detained in Thebes during his youth (see Ch. 1). There, or in Athens, he may have heard the lectures of Prodicus, who was reputedly interested in determining the proper definitions of words. Xenophon was also probably influenced by Thucydides' prose, which is imbued with rhetoric.[18] Xenophon most likely had his own collection of books.[19] By reading texts written in the fifth century BC Xenophon had the prose style of an earlier period reimpressed upon him (see Ch. 3). With the works of the Sicilian Gorgias and the early works of the Athenian Antiphon serving as his models, Xenophon did not hesitate to use rhetorical devices.

Xenophon probably read Plato's earlier dialogues as well as the literature of preceding centuries (see above, sect. A, and Ch. 3). The dialogue form certainly permitted the use of poetical words in elevated passages and allowed characters to quote from poetry (see below, sect. G). Throughout antiquity Homeric epic continued to serve as the basis of the Greek literary curriculum: Homeric diction probably did not sound unfamiliar (as we, who have learnt Greek by memorizing paradigms constructed from classical Attic, might at first suppose) to authors who lived in the classical period. Though Plato's style differs from Xenophon's, like Xenophon Plato uses an abundance of poetical words and figurative language. It may well be that both Xenophon and Plato, feeling nostalgia for the fifth century BC and perhaps with some desire for verisimilitude in evoking the conversations of Socrates, deliberately avoided using the prose style of their own contemporaries.

Socrates, as depicted by both Xenophon and Plato, chose his words carefully, and delighted in word-play (see on i. 22). Some examples of rhetorical and poetical figures that Xenophon shows Socrates using in the *Oeconomicus* are:

personification: Mother Earth (v. 17, xx. 13–14); Farming (xv. 3, xix. 17–19);

asyndeton: ὁπλίτης ... ἄμαξα (viii. 4);

[18] See further Elisabeth Vorrenhagen, *De orationibus quae sunt in Xenophontis Hellenicis* (Elberfeld, 1926), esp. 137–8.

[19] Delebecque, *Essai*, 231, assumes that Xenophon had a library with him in Scillus.

anaphora: καλὸν ... καλὸν ... καλὸν ... καλὸν ... καλὸν ... καλόν (viii. 19);

homoioteleuton: ψυχεινά ... ἀλεεινά (ix. 4);

assonance: οἶκον οἰκονομοῦντα ... οἰκοδομοῦντα (i. 4), ἵππον ἱππασάμην ἱππασίαν (xi. 17), λιχνειῶν ... λαγνειῶν (i. 22);

word-play: χειρὶ ... χεῖρες (xxi. 8);

concinnity: πρόβατον ... ἵππος ... γυναικός (iii. 11);

variety: βοθύνους ... βόθρον (xix. 3, 7);

recurrent metaphors: e.g. of ship and army (viii, xxi).

In c. viii, Xenophon provides an excellent example of a purple patch in Ischomachus' eulogy on orderliness, especially in his description of the Phoenician ship with its obvious and heavy-handed use of asyndeton and anaphora. This elaborate prose is appropriate to the characterization of Ischomachus as indefatigable and pompous. (See also on the eulogy of rural life in c. v.)

E. Narrative Structure

Xenophon's skill in unifying a prose work is evident in his reiteration of themes, especially his linking the Persian king to the queen bee (see notes on c. iv) and his repeated use of the metaphors of ship and army (viii, xxi). He returns to the same themes, often using the very same words. In the present Commentary these repetitions are usually pointed out by cross-references. In addition the more formal reviews and previews in the openings of cc. iii and vi serve to unify the work. (On the unity of the *Oeconomicus* see further Ch. 1, sect. D.)

The time-frame also creates a series of connections throughout the work. It is elaborately constructed: stories are nested within stories with remarkable complexity. Xenophon tells his readers that he once heard Socrates and Critobulus talking (i. 1). In the course of the *Oeconomicus* Socrates presents two models to Critobulus: Cyrus and Ischomachus. Socrates reports a conversation of Cyrus' that he learnt of through a series of reporters: (1) a story (λέγεται), (2) a stranger at Megara, (3) Lysander (iv. 20).

Cyrus→Lysander→stranger at Megara→story→Soc.→Xen.→reader

At c. vii Socrates begins to relate to Critobulus a longer discussion that he once had with Ischomachus, who, in turn, had told him of several dialogues he had had with his wife when they were first married. During one of those early dialogues, Ischomachus and his wife recall what their father and mother respectively had once told them about σωφροσύνη (vii. 14–15, see diagram and notes on passages cited).

father→Ischomachus→Socrates→Critobulus→Xenophon→reader
　　　　　↑
mother→wife

F. *Dramatic Date*

The Socratics were notorious for disregarding historical chronology in their writings.[20] Although Xenophon wrote historical texts, he does not avoid anachronisms in his Socratic works. For example, probably in an attempt to enhance the veracity of his report, he represents himself as an auditor of conversations which, because of his age and circumstances, he could not have attended (i. 1 ἤκουσα). He also portrays Socrates making a more detailed comment on Cyrus' death than is plausible (iv. 18-19). He intended perhaps to increase the prestige of his friend Cyrus by showing that Socrates esteemed him. Other clues to the dramatic date of the *Oeconomicus* may be more reliable: at least, in these cases any motivation Xenophon may have had for tampering with the facts is not apparent. Approximate dates can be offered for the following circumstances:

(*a*) Critobulus is married, but probably not newly wed (i. 1). He married in 422 BC.

(*b*) Critobulus is reminded of his responsibility to contribute financially to the costs of war (ii. 6). These payments must have been especially burdensome during the Peloponnesian War. The dialogue, however, takes place at a period when

---

[20] On anachronisms in the Socratic texts see notes on individual passages cited in the present discussion. On vagueness in geographical location see on xi. 14 κατὰ πόλιν ... εἰς ἀγρόν. On anachronisms in the Socratics in general see Olof Gigon, *Sokrates: Sein Bild in Dichtung und Geschichte* (Berne, 1947), 284.

18

Athens is at peace, either during a temporary lull, or after 421 BC.

(*c*) When Socrates spoke with Ischomachus, the latter gentleman had been married for quite some time, long enough for his wife to have learnt to manage the estate so well that he has turned it over to her (vii. 3–4). She has also stopped using the cosmetics that she had used in the past (x. 2 ποτέ). When Ischomachus had had the conversation with his wife that he related to Socrates, they did not yet have children (vii. 12). Their daughter was born *c.* 435–430 (see on vi. 17). He died probably by 404 BC (see on vi. 17).

(*d*) The dialogue between Socrates and Ischomachus took place in the Stoa of Zeus Eleutherius. This building was constructed in the last third of the fifth century BC (see on vii. 1). The dates listed above indicate a dramatic date of *c.* 420–410 BC for Socrates' dialogue with Critobulus. Socrates' meeting with Ischomachus in the Stoa had taken place some time before that (vii. 1 ποτέ). It is neither essential nor possible to pinpoint the dates of the conversations reported in the *Oeconomicus*: their themes are appropriate to the last quarter of the fifth century BC. Xenophon did not fix the dates precisely, nor can the modern reader.

G. *Dialogue*

The primary source of the philosophical dialogue was the conversation of Socrates with his disciples and with strangers. The chief Socratics, namely Aeschines, Antisthenes, Plato, and Xenophon, all wrote dialogues in which Socrates played a major role (see further Ch. 3). Aristotle (*Poetics* 1447[b] 9–13) discusses the Socratic dialogues along with mimes and classifies both as poetry because of their use of mimesis ('imitation' or 'representation by means of art'). The *Oeconomicus* also conforms to the ancient definition of a dialogue as a discourse consisting of questions and answers on some philosophical or political subject, with due regard for the appropriate characterization of the personages introduced and for the style of diction.[21] The dialogue developed into a form in which long

---

[21] Albinus, *Eisagoge* 2, in C. F. Hermann, *Platonis Dialogi secundum Thrasylli Tetralogias Dispositi*, vi. 147; D.L. 3. 48.

speeches set forth different sides of a question, as in Plato's *Symposium*. In the *Oeconomicus*, however, there is really no debate between opposing views.

At times the dialogue form seems an awkward vehicle for conveying philosophical doctrine, not to mention information on farming. Like ordinary conversation, the dialogue meanders and charms instead of moving relentlessly toward a conclusion. In some of Plato's later work, the dramatic element has virtually disappeared and doctrine is presented as though in a lecture. Xenophon eschews the dialogue form entirely in favour of the essay for some of his short didactic works. The combination of ethical and practical agricultural instruction found in the *Oeconomicus* is unique in classical philosophical dialogue.

3
Xenophon and Socrates

The relationship between Xenophon's life and his literary
productions is relevant to a consideration of the verisimilitude
of his portrayal of Socrates in the *Oeconomicus*. In the following
discussion we shall concentrate on three questions: (1) How
well did Xenophon know Socrates? (2) How does Xenophon's
portrait compare with those of Plato and other Socratics? (3)
How accurate are the various portraits of Socrates?

A. *A Disciple of Socrates*

From approximately 412–410 BC and onwards Xenophon
would have had opportunities to get to know Socrates (see
Ch. 1). He could have been a disciple of Socrates between
404 BC, when his military obligations outside Attica ended,
and 401 BC, when he left to join Cyrus. Thus Xenophon could
have known him almost as long as Plato did, although he was
absent from Athens when Socrates was executed in 399 BC.
Diogenes Laertius tells a credible, though not necessarily true,
story of Xenophon's first confrontation with Socrates and his
decision to become a pupil of the philosopher:

They say that when Socrates met Xenophon in a narrow alley he
held out his walking-stick and prevented him from passing through,
while he asked him where various items that were available were sold.
After Xenophon had answered, Socrates asked him 'and where do
men become gentlemen [i.e. καλοὶ κἀγαθοί, literally "beautiful and
good"]?'[1] Xenophon was puzzled. 'Then follow me', said Socrates,
'and learn.' And from then on he was a pupil of Socrates. (2. 48.)

Greek and Roman authors did not question Xenophon's
affiliation with Socrates, nor did they hesitate to call him a

[1] On this expression see vi. 12.

21

philosopher. In fact, they classified him more often among philosophers than among historians. For example, Cicero (*Brutus* 292) states that Xenophon, Plato, and Antisthenes accurately portrayed Socratic irony.[2] Dionysius of Halicarnassus (*Comp.* 10) calls Xenophon a Socratic. Quintilian (10. 1. 75, 82–3) declines to discuss Xenophon as a historian and treats him as a Socratic philosopher. Tacitus (*Dial. Orat.* 31. 6) includes Xenophon in his discussion of philosophers, mentioning him just after Plato. Longinus (4. 4) states that Xenophon and Plato were both educated in Socrates' school. Aulus Gellius (14. 3. 7) refers to Xenophon and Plato as philosophers, and Columella (*RR* 1. 1. 7) calls Xenophon *Socraticus*. Hermogenes (*On Types* 404) treats Xenophon with other philosophers and ranks him after Plato and before Aeschines. Julian associates Xenophon with Plato and Antisthenes.[3] Diogenes Laertius (2. 64) quotes Panaetius' judgement that the only true (ἀληθεῖς) Socratic dialogues are those by Xenophon, Plato, Antisthenes, and Aeschines. Diogenes arranged his biographies of the philosophers so that the life of Xenophon follows that of Socrates in immediate succession.

B. *The 'Socratic Problem'*

Socrates never put his philosophic thought into written form (see on i. 1 ἤκουσα). Ideas attributed to him have been transmitted only through the works of followers who claim to have known him personally; principally Xenophon and Plato, but in addition, some fragments of the works of other Socratics such as Aeschines and Antisthenes are extant. Aristophanes' *Clouds* also supplies contemporary testimony, presented, of course, with the bias of comedy.

Socrates is depicted in four of Xenophon's fourteen works, the *Memorabilia*, the *Symposium*, the *Apology*, and the *Oeconomicus*; he is present in most of Plato's. Socrates' method of inquiry,

---

[2] For Philodemus' interpretation of Xenophon's portrayal of Socrates in the *Oeconomicus* see Ch. 6, sect. B.

[3] *Epist. ad Themist.* 10 (264 C–D) = G. Giannantoni, *Socraticorum reliquiae*, 4 vols. (Naples, 1983–5), I. 13, no. 12; *Orat.* 7. 4 (209 A), 7. 10 (215 C), 7. 11 (216 D–217 B) = Giannantoni ii. 336, no. 44.

his personality, and some of his ideas, as reported by Xenophon on the one hand and by Plato on the other are, in my view, essentially reconcilable. However, it is the differences between Xenophon's and Plato's views that have contributed arguments to the 'Socratic problem'. A long and vigorous debate over whether Xenophon or Plato paints a more realistic portrait of Socrates, or whether neither portrait is historically accurate, has raged among scholars. The present context permits only a brief review of several representative opinions and arguments that may affect our evaluation of historical and fictional (or literary) elements in the portrayal of Socrates in the *Oeconomicus*.[4]

In Germany,[5] the testimononies of Xenophon and Plato were considered equally valid until the middle of the eighteenth century, when Jacob Brucker gave priority to Xenophon.[6] Brucker declared that the *Memorabilia* give a much more accurate idea of the opinions of Socrates and of his manner of teaching than Plato's dialogues, for, he argued, Plato added his own notions and those of other philosophers. In support of his position, Brucker[7] cited criticisms of Plato's historical accuracy by Athenaeus (11. 505) and Diogenes Laertius (3. 35). F. Schleiermacher[8] reacted to Brucker's assessment by rejecting Xenophon's portrayal of Socrates in favour of Plato's. Schleiermacher argued that Xenophon was not a philosopher himself and therefore he was incapable of understanding Socrates. Schleiermacher attempted to discover what Socrates could have been, other than what we know of him from Xenophon, without being inconsistent with the character-

---

[4] For greater detail, see the 368-page list in A. Patzer, *Bibliographia Socratica* (Freiburg, 1985), and the 103-page list in Donald R. Morrison, *Bibliography of Editions, Translations, and Commentary on Xenophon's Socratic Writings, 1600–Present* (Pittsburgh, 1988).

[5] For a detailed history of the 'Socratic Problem', see Eduard Zeller, *Die Philosophie der Griechen*, 5th edn., 3 vols. (Leipzig, 1922), ii 1. 92.

[6] *Historia Critica Philosophiae*, 2nd edn. (Leipzig, 1767) 6. Mario Montuori, *De Socrate iuste damnato* (Amsterdam, 1981) locates the rise of the Socratic problem and the beginning of Socratic historiography in France in the 18th c. But he fails to prove his thesis that the works of Fréret and Garnier influenced historians of philosophy.

[7] *Historia Critica Philosophiae*, 556–9.

[8] 'Über den Werth des Sokrates als Philosophen', *Abhandlungen der Berl. Akad. Phil. Kl. aus den Jahren 1814–15* (1818), 53, 57–9, *et passim*.

istics and ethical maxims that Xenophon definitely transmitted as Socratic. What else must Socrates have been to provide Plato with the inspiration to present him as he does in his dialogues?

Since Brucker and Schleiermacher the pendulum has swung back and forth, but the current orthodox scholarly view is that Plato's early works give the most accurate picture of the essence of Socrates' originality of thought and modes of argument. Most historians of philosophy in the twentieth century argue that because Xenophon did not devote his working life to the study and development of Socrates' philosophical ideas, as Plato clearly did, he may have been able to recall less, in full detail, of Socrates' actual ideas and argumentations when he came to write Socratic dialogues.[9] However, Xenophon continued to enjoy some support. In the second half of the twentieth century Leo Strauss[10] and his followers have been among the most ardent partisans of Xenophon's portrayal.[11]

Socratic scholarship of the mid-twentieth century is noteworthy for the revisionist approachs of Olof Gigon[12] and of Anton-Hermann Chroust.[13] They argue that no ancient author actually intended to write about the historical Socrates, but

---

[9] Thus K. Joël, *Der echte und der Xenophontische Sokrates* (Berlin, 1893–1901); Zeller, *Die Philosophie der Griechen*, ii 1, p. vi; A. E. Taylor, *Varia Socratica* (Oxford, 1911), 8; John Burnet, *Greek Philosophy: Thales to Plato* (1914, repr. London, 1953), 127; Heinrich Maier, *Sokrates* (Tübingen, 1913), 20; G. Vlastos, 'Introduction: The Paradox of Socrates' in id. (ed.), *The Philosophy of Socrates* (Garden City, NY, 1971), 1–21; and F. H. Sandbach, 'Plato and the Socratic Work of Xenophon', in P. E. Easterling and B. M. Knox (eds.), *The Cambridge History of Classical Literature*, 2 vols. (Cambridge, 1982–5), i. 480.

[10] Strauss, *Xenophon's Socratic Discourse*, 86, assigned priority to Xenophon's representation of Socrates in the *Oeconomicus*, arguing that because Xenophon was a historian he must have portrayed the historical figure as he was. However, ancient historians were not journalists. Furthermore, Xenophon was not a historian when he was not writing history. For example, the *Oeconomicus* is not without anachronisms, even concerning events that occurred in Xenophon's own lifetime (See on i. 1 ἤκουσα and iv. 18 μαχούμενος).

[11] But Strauss does not enjoy universal respect as a historian of philosophy. Moreover, the fact that several of Strauss's disciples have been active in contemporary conservative politics in the United States has complicated the 'Socratic problem' and caused some other scholars to give short shrift to Straussian interpretations of Greek philosophy. H. von Arnim, *Xenophons Memorabilien und Apologie des Sokrates* (Copenhagen, 1923), also considered Xenophon the authoritative source on Socrates.

[12] *Sokrates* and *Kommentar zur ersten Buch von Xenophons Memorabilien* (Basle, 1953).

[13] *Socrates, Man and Myth* (London, 1957).

rather to depict a legendary figure. Both Gigon and Chroust draw attention to the essentially literary nature of the Socratic writings and stress Xenophon's and Plato's similarities to each other and their debts to the earlier Socratics. Chief among these sources were the works of Antisthenes, a contemporary of Socrates.[14] Although Antisthenes' work is known to us only through fragments and a list of titles in Diogenes Laertius, he apparently depicted a Socrates who was concerned with practical matters. The report (D.L. 6. 16) that Antisthenes also wrote a work with the word οἰκονομικός in the title, Περὶ νίκης· οἰκονομικός (*On Victory: A Work on Estate Management*) lends some support to the argument that Xenophon's portrayal of Socrates was consistent with that by earlier Socratics (but see further on the title Οἰκονομικός). It cannot, however, be demonstrated either that Xenophon's *Oeconomicus* was largely derived from Antisthenes' treatise or even that the earlier work gave a historically accurate depiction of Socrates.

While it is not possible here to solve a problem which has plagued generations of scholars, common sense, at least, suggests that it is not necessary to chose between the Socrates of Xenophon and the Socrates of Plato. The notion that one representation is true and the other false is naïve. Socrates was a great teacher. Such teachers know how to bring out the best in their pupils: they start with subjects which interest the pupil and then proceed to what the teacher believes ought to be taught. Inasmuch as Socrates did not seek to impart a systematic, all-embracing doctrine, there was ample opportunity for his followers to interject their own thoughts into the discussions. No doubt with Plato his discussions were more theoretical while with Xenophon they were more practical. Thus it is significant that at the first meeting of Socrates with Xenophon according to Diogenes Laertius (2. 48, quoted above) Socrates posed a question about gentlemen (καλοὶ κἀγαθοί) that was an important theme in the *Oeconomicus* (see on vi. 12). The charge that the student transformed the teacher into his *alter ego* can be levelled against Plato as well as against Xenophon. Furthermore, Socrates, Plato, and Xenophon all lived long

[14] For the possible influence of Aeschines and Antisthenes see also Ch. 6, sect. D, and notes on ii. 7, and iii. 14.

lives and their interests doubtless changed over the years. The *Clouds* and the *Phaedo* indicate that at some time in his long life Socrates, like several other philosophers who were his contemporaries, actually was interested in practical matters and in the physical world.

C. *Xenophon's Relationship to Plato*

The debate over the Platonic and Xenophontic Socrates is complicated by the question of Xenophon's relationship to Plato. As we have mentioned, Diogenes Laertius (2. 48) states that Xenophon was the first to write down and publish the words of Socrates, but he credits Plato with inventing the dialogue form because he perfected it (D.L. 3. 48 and see Ch. 2, sect. G).[15] However, the invention of a genre is not the same as the perfection of it. Whether or not Diogenes' statements are true, there is no reason to assume that when Xenophon and Plato touch on the same subjects, or employ the same literary form, or use similar language, Xenophon was copying from Plato.[16] This assumption arises, no doubt, from a scholarly consensus that Plato's intellectual gifts were superior to Xenophon's. In fact, the reverse could have been true and Plato may have borrowed from Xenophon, for, in the use of genres, Xenophon was more innovative than Plato (see Ch. 2, sect. C). Similarities might also arise if both Plato and Xenophon used the same Socratic sources and read each other's work. Xenophon and Plato were contemporaries and probably began writing at about the same time. Plato does seem to have read at least some of Xenophon's work, for in the *Laws* (3. 694 c–695 b) he is critical of Xenophon's portrayal of Cyrus in the *Cyropaedia* (see on iv. 5 γεωργίας).[17]

Athenaeus (11. 504 E–506 A) and Diogenes Laertius (3. 34,

[15] See further R. Hirzel, *Der Dialog*, 2 vols. (Leipzig, 1895; repr. Hildesheim, 1963), i. 208, who accepts the testimony of Diogenes Laertius.

[16] So e.g. W. K. C. Guthrie, *A History of Greek Philosophy*, 6 vols. (Cambridge, 1962–81), iii. 330, A. R. Lacey, 'Our Knowledge of Socrates', in G. Vlastos (ed.), *The Philosophy of Socrates*, 22–49, and J. Mitscherling, 'Xenophon and Plato', *CQ* NS 32 (1982), 468–9.

[17] P. Chantraine, *Xénophon: Économique* (Paris, 1949), 70 n. 1, sees an allusion to Pl. *Hp. Mi.* 288 D at viii. 19, but this seems far-fetched.

see also 2. 57) treat Plato's critical comment in the *Laws* as evidence of Plato's rivalry with Xenophon. Marcellinus (*Vita Thuc.* 27) refers to Xenophon's jealousy toward Plato, but Gellius (14. 3. 9–10) rejects the notion that the two were enemies and suggests that because they were equally eminent their partisans wrongly deduced that they were rivals.[18] Ancient biographers often used such rivalries as topoi, but, of course, sometimes there was some truth in the story.[19] Xenophon names Plato only in passing, but with an acknowledgment of a special relationship to Socrates (*Mem.* 3. 6. 1), while Plato never mentions Xenophon.

Plato and Xenophon agree on many aspects of the portrayal of Socrates (see Commentary, *passim*, for citations of parallels). Both wrote dramatic dialogues depicting eristic conversations between Socrates and young men who are eager to learn.[20] Both show Socrates' use of the elenctic method, though in Xenophon the discussions lead to a positive statement more often than they do in Plato. Xenophon's and Plato's depictions of Socrates' use of the maieutic method and anamnesis are reconcilable.[21] These techniques are particularly apparent in the *Oec.* xvi. 8–xix. Socrates' searches for definitions, for example, the attempts to define $οἰκονομία$ and $χρήματα$ in *Oec.* i, are paralleled by similar attempts in the opening of the *Memorabilia*, and many such efforts in the early chapters of Plato's dialogues. Both Xenophon and Plato supply abundant evidence to support Aristotle's view (*Metaph.* 1078[b]27) that Socrates' principal contribution was in inductive reasoning and general definition (see on i. 1–2 $ὄνομα$ ... $ἔργον$).

Xenophon and Plato concur in their description of Socrates' personality and physical characteristics: they are doubtless telling the truth. Their readers would have included men like themselves who had actually encountered Socrates. Both authors depict Socrates' control of his physical appetites and

[18] Gellius was reluctant to believe that philosophers could be capable of feuding. See further Leofranc Holford-Strevens, *Aulus Gellius* (London, 1988), 198–9.

[19] Chroust, *Socrates*, 318–19 n. 1398 *et passim* discusses rivalries between the Socratics, especially between Plato and Xenophon.

[20] See e.g. Xen. *Oec.* iv. 2, *Mem.* 4. 7, 3. 1, Pl. *Lach.* 180 C–D, *Apol.* 24 B–C, 26 B.

[21] See further Robert R. Wellman, 'Socratic Method in Xenophon', *JHI* 37 (1976), 307–18.

passions. Socrates' poverty is mentioned in the *Oec*. ii. 3, and *Mem*. 1. 6. 1, 10, as well as in Plato (e.g. *Apol*. 23 C, 31 C). In the works of both Plato (e.g. *Lach*. 180 C–D) and Xenophon (e.g. *Mem*. 3. 1), Socrates' followers are well-to-do young men and he himself reveals attitudes more characteristic of the aristocracy than of the son of a stonemason or sculptor, as, for example, in his scorn for banausic occupations (see further on iv. 2). If Xenophon's, Plato's (esp. *Apol*. 38 A–B), and Aristophanes' descriptions of Socrates' poverty reflect historical reality, Socrates' economic status had changed radically. The fact that he had qualified for service as a hoplite at Delium and Potidaea (Pl. *Symp*. 221 A) indicates that he had not been impoverished for his entire life. Sculptors in classical Athens might be quite successful financially.[22] Moreover, according to a law attributed to Solon, a father was obliged to teach his son a trade, and it was natural that Socrates should learn his father's.[23] According to the (albeit unreliable) testimony of Libanius (*Apol*. 17–18) Socrates had inherited not only his trade, but 80 minae as well, from his father (see also D.L. 2. 18–19). But perhaps he gave up his trade in the service of philosophy (cf. Pl. *Apol*. 31 B). By the time the second version of Aristophanes' *Clouds* was produced, he was poor (*c*.420–417 BC: see *Clouds* 103, 175, 362).

The *Oeconomicus* is typical of the Socratic works of Xenophon and Plato in showing Socrates using humour, irony and paradox, professing ignorance (ii. 9, iii. 1), and insulting, teasing, and embarrassing others as a prelude to their instruction and improvement (ii. 8). Other common features include portrayals of Socrates marshalling examples from the animal world as proofs (see on iii. 11), and expressing interest in the expertise of craftsmen (i. 1–2, vi. 13–16, *Mem*. 1. 2. 32–7, cf. Pl. *Apol*. 22 C–D, *Rep*. 1, *Gorg*. 490 E–491 F, *Symp*. 221 E), but professing modesty about his own store of knowledge. Perhaps in response to the charges levelled against Socrates at his trial, the *Oeconomicus*, like other works of Xenophon and Plato, shows

[22] The family of Praxiteles was wealthy: see Davies, *Athenian Propertied Families*, 286–90, no. 8334 Kephisodotos.

[23] Plut. *Sol*. 22, Galen, *Protrept*. 8, D.L. 1. 55, Aesch. 1. 28, cf. Ael. *HA* 9. 1.

Socrates displaying a conventional piety and exerting a beneficial influence on the young.

D. *Socrates, the Oikos, and the* Oeconomicus

Although there is much congruence between Plato and
Xenophon, Plato offers no counterpart to the portrayal of
Socrates in the *Oeconomicus*. Most scholars nowadays are more
comfortable with Plato's characterization of Socrates as a man
of thought than with the practical man portrayed by
Xenophon. Therefore, the Socrates of the *Oeconomicus*, examin-
ing clods of earth, appears most anomalous, or perhaps most
disturbing, for in fact this portrayal is reminiscent of the
Socrates who is depicted by Aristophanes in the *Clouds* as being
interested in natural philosophy. Even a scholar such as E. C.
Marchant, who devoted himself to editing and translating
Xenophon's complete works could write about the *Oeconomicus*:
'The thoughts and reflections, whether put into the mouth of
Socrates or Ischomachus, are so entirely Xenophon's own that
we may wonder why he did not frankly produce a treatise on
the management of an estate instead of a Socratic dialogue.'[24]
The answer to Marchant's question may lie both in the
literary traditions of the Socratics and in historical reality,
although explanations previously offered along each of these
lines have not been persuasive because they have favoured one
alternative while totally excluding the other. Some of those
who deny the veracity of Xenophon's portrayal of Socrates
argue that the philosopher was an urban person, who did not
care about agriculture, or military affairs, or Persia.[25]
However, Plato, as well as Xenophon, depicts Socrates as
open-minded, with a keen interest in matters pertaining to
everyday life in Athens (see on i. 1 οἰκονομίας). Even though
in Pl. *Phaedrus* 230 D, Socrates says that he never left the city
of his own free will, like other citizens he would have attended
rural festivals and certainly engaged in military exercises and
in active service beyond the city walls. City and countryside

---

[24] *Xenophon* (New York and London, 1923), iv, p. xxiv.
[25] Thus Lacey, 'Our Knowledge of Socrates', argues that the portrayal of Socrates
in the *Oeconomicus* is not historical, for Socrates was a townsman.

were not strictly demarcated in classical Athens, certainly not in the period of Socrates' youth. In the fifth century BC, even citizens who lived in the city often owned a plot of land. That Socrates questioned successful managers of estates about their work just as he questioned artists and craftsmen about theirs is perfectly credible. In *Mem.* 1. 2. 48, 64 Socrates also draws attention to the household economy. Furthermore, as Xenophon portrays him in the *Oeconomicus*, he does not pretend to be an authority in practical affairs, but quotes the testimony of a reputed expert. In the *Oeconomicus* the search for definitions and ethical issues predominates in the first six chapters of the treatise, when Socrates is the principal speaker; practical subjects come to the fore when Ischomachus directs the conversation. All our sources testify to Socrates' interest in the ethical aspects of everyday life and to his quest to find a context in which women and men could act in fulfilment of their appropriate virtues. It would be amazing if, in his long life and varied conversations, Socrates had never discussed the oikos, and in particular, the relationships among its human members, though none of the Socratics might have had an accurate or detailed memory of what he actually said in such conversations. Therefore in the present book I have adopted the view that the *Oeconomicus* should not be read as though it were based on verbatim stenographic notes taken at the time of Socrates' various conversations, but rather it should be understood as a literary reminiscence with a germ of historical reality.

4
The Family in Classical Greece and in the *Oeconomicus*

Oἰκονομία denotes the science of household or estate management. The oikos ('estate', 'household', or 'family') was a large entity embracing the members of the family, slaves, animals, the house itself, land, and all that was produced, consumed, and disbursed by the household. To the modern English-speaking reader, the translation of οἶκος as 'household' or 'estate' may seem to emphasize property while ignoring affective relationships, but such a translation does point immediately to differences between ancient and modern ideas of family. Inasmuch as the oikos was the basic unit of Greek society, it had been discussed or represented in Greek literature from the earliest time, but Xenophon's *Oeconomicus* is the earliest extant Greek didactic work to focus on this subject. (Because the property described in the *Oeconomicus* is large, I have usually preferred to translate οἶκος as 'estate'.)

A. *The Family in the Fourth Century* BC

In its concern with the oikos, the *Oeconomicus* is particularly a product of the fourth century. Social institutions tend to become a subject of study only when they are perceived as beginning to deteriorate or change. Legislation of the fifth century attempting to shore up the oikos indicates the early genesis of problems. The Peloponnesian War had subverted the old socio-economic substructure of the Athenian oikos, although the courts were actively defending it. Misogynistic remarks and complaints about marriage in Middle and New Comedy, while not quantifiable, seem abundant. The sale of family farms suggests diminution of family sentiment (see on

31

xx. 22). And because Xenophon lived as an exile in Sparta and wrote about the archaic legislation attributed to Lycurgus in the *Spartan Constitution*, he certainly was cognizant of the economic problems inherent in the structure of the Spartan family and state in the fourth century. Greek and Roman authors speak of excessively large dowries, landless Spartan men losing their rights as citizens, and a decline in population.[1] The Spartans' enjoyment of their victory in the Peloponnesian War was brief (see e.g. Xen. *Hell*. 3. 5.)

While it is true that our sources for the history of the Athenian family differ vastly from the fifth to the fourth century, the difference in the sources may be not so much the cause of the change in our perceptions as it is a symptom of the change we can perceive. In other words, the subtle shift from the communal concerns voiced in fifth-century Athenian drama and public addresses such as Pericles' Funeral Oration (Thuc. 2. 35–46) to the squabbles, financial problems, and self-interest expressed in the fourth century in inscriptions and private orations may not simply be an accident of the change in historical sources but may reflect actual social change.[2] Thus the fourth century would represent a stage in the transition to the focus on the private world and the individual that distinguished the Hellenistic period.

Of course, the relationship between art and life is always complex, but it is interesting to note that the visual arts, as well, to some extent reflect a change in gender-relationships within the family.[3] According to Robert Sutton, at the end of the fifth and the beginning of the fourth centuries, Attic red-figure vases begin to stress more romantic relationships between husbands and wives than had been portrayed on vases

[1] See e.g. Arist. *Pol.* 1269ª29–1270ᵇ6, Cic. *Tusc. Disp.* 2. 36, and for recent discussions see Stephen Hodkinson, 'Land Tenure and Inheritance in Classical Sparta', *CQ*, ns 36 (1986), 378–406, and Claude Mossé, 'Women in the Spartan Revolutions of the Third Century BC', in Sarah B. Pomeroy (ed.), *Women's History and Ancient History* (Chapel Hill, NC, 1991), 138–53.

[2] On factionalism and strife in the public sphere see most recently Barry Strauss, *Athens after the Peloponnesian War* (Ithaca, NY, 1987).

[3] J. J. Pollitt, *Art and Experience in Classical Greece* (Cambridge, 1972), 136–7, points out that although in its formal and stylistic features the art of the 4th c. is a continuation of the 5th, in its concern with the experiences of the individual rather than with the community it has more similarities with Hellenistic art.

of the preceding period.[4] However, there are very few representations on vases of family groups engaged in everyday activities. An exception is an epinetron of 430–420 BC showing a seated woman who is spinning as the master of the house walks in. Eros flies overhead. Sutton has suggested that the scene anticipates Xenophon's view of marriage as an economic union bound by Eros.[5] Grave stelai of the fourth century regularly display images of the deceased surrounded by family members and slaves. In some examples, the deceased sits and clasps the hand of a family member, spouse, or parent, while they gaze into one another's eyes. These stelai, although as yet not sufficiently studied from the viewpoint of social history, seem to indicate a concern for emotional relationships among family members.[6]

The *Oeconomicus* deals with many aspects of estate management including agricultural techniques and the care of slaves, but the marital relationship is viewed as fundamental to the success of an oikos. Thus, in c. vii Ischomachus begins his description of his own flourishing oikos by relating some conversations he had had with his young bride. For didactic purposes, at the start of its life-cycle Ischomachus' family is nuclear and consists of only one generation, the husband and the wife, although references are made to the parents of both spouses (vii. 11, 14–15, xx. 26), to the possibility that children will be born (vii. 11, 21, 24, 30, 34, 42, ix. 19), and to the distant future when the children will be grown and the wife will be old (vii. 42).

B. *Philosophical Views of the Oikos in the Fourth Century*

The *Oeconomicus* contains a medley of normative and idealistic thoughts on the Greek household. Like many traditional Mediterranean societies, that of the Greeks was separated into public and private or domestic spheres; the former was the world of men, the latter of women. More than was usual for

---

[4] 'The Interaction between Men and Women Portrayed on Attic Red-Figure Pottery' (Ph.D. diss., Univ. of North Carolina at Chapel Hill, 1981).

[5] Ibid., Cat. F 7, pp. 228–32.

[6] For the stelai, see C. W. Clairmont, *Gravestone and Epigram* (Mainz, 1970).

classical authors, Xenophon focuses on the relationship between men and women and on the private sphere.

In analysing gender-roles in the families described by Xenophon, it is instructive to look at another fourth-century view of the same institution. A brief review of Aristotle's description of the normative oikos will help to clarify what is utopian in Xenophon. Aristotle states that the basic relationships in the household are those between husband and wife, father and child, and master and slave (*Pol.* 1252^a 24^b–27, 1253^b–11, 1254^b 13–16). The man who is the head of the household is the authority figure in all three relationships. This patriarchal hierarchy exists by nature and therefore is unalterable. Thus Aristotle would never have cited as a model the household described by Xenophon in the *Oeconomicus* in which a wife who has learnt her lessons well can exercise authority over her husband. Aristotle admits of only one situation in which a wife may rule the husband: that is when she is an heiress. He reflects that in such circumstances the authority is allocated not to the one who has more virtue but to the one who possesses greater wealth (*Eth. Nic.* 1161^a 1–2 and see on Pseudo-Aristotle in Ch. 6, sect. A).

According to Aristotle (*Pol.* 1260^a 12–14), women's minds have the rational element (τὸ βουλευτικόν) but it is without authority (ἄκυρον). Therefore, it is not only natural but also beneficial for women to be ruled by men. Aristotle's view of women's capacity and of human relationships is static. He does not consider educating women so as to develop the rational part of their minds. Xenophon, in contrast, portrays the wife of Ischomachus as literate (ix. 10) and he can envisage a situation in which a woman's mental capacities can be cultivated to the point that she can be said to rule rightfully over her husband and to have a masculine intelligence (see on vii. 32 and x. 1). Her superiority redounds to her husband's credit as well as to her own, for he taught her a substantial part of what she knows.

Finally, Aristotle emphasizes reproduction of the species as the primary motive for the union of male and female. Ischomachus considers sexual intercourse as only one of several elements that marriage comprises. He recognizes that children are fundamental to the continuity of the human species, and serve as the support of parents in their old age. But in a household with slaves, a wife is not absolutely essential for the convenient satisfaction of a married man's sexual appetites. Ischomachus is fairly explicit about the sexual attractions of slaves and their availability to the master (see on ix. 5 τεκνο-ποιῶνται οἱ οἰκέται). But he acknowledges that slaves are less desirable as sexual partners, for they come to the master's bed by compulsion. He remarks that it is preferable to have intercourse with a wife, especially if she is physically attractive and willing. Husband and wife are joined to be partners in one another's bodies. The family, of course, is a social unit for both production and reproduction. Yet Ischomachus states that if sharing a bed were all that there is to marriage, it would be very easy to find a spouse, and talks instead in more general terms of the benefits of marriage (cc. vii–x).

Although in his description of Ischomachus' family Xeno-phon accepts the constraints of patriarchal society in which the double standard of sexual conduct is in force and in which a wife's power must be delegated to her by her husband, within this framework a woman exercises moral autonomy and proves to be superior to a man in important areas of knowledge. In contrast to the views of Ischomachus, most Greek thought tended to reduce the value of a wife to the primary function of sexual reproduction. Athenian marriage, indeed, was based on such a misogynistic concept. In the fourth century an Athenian orator (Ps.-Dem. 59. 122), disting-uished wives from other women with whom a man might have a sexual relationship by stating: 'Mistresses we have for pleas-ure, concubines for daily attention to our bodies, but wives to be the bearers of legitimate children and to be the faithful guardians of the household.' The marriage formula set forth only the procreative function of the wife: the father of the bride promised to give his daughter for the sowing of legitimate children.[7] Large families were rare. Therefore, after a woman had borne the requisite number of children she could be consid-ered as little more than a parasite, a consumer, like the first

---

[7] See LSJ s.v. ἄροτος.

human bride, Pandora (see Hes. *Theog.* 585–612, *WD* 53–82). Semonides (fr. 7) complains about wives who are like pigs, or asses, or mares, or so stupid that they seem to be made of earth: these women cannot control their appetites. None of them are concerned with the welfare of their husbands: such wives do nothing but eat, grow fat, and indulge in extra-marital sex. The sole favourable portrait is that of the rare wife who is like a bee. In a long misogynistic tirade, Hippo-lytus suggests that if men could purchase their children at temples there would be no need for wives at all (Eur. *Hipp.* 618–24).

In contrast to Greek philosophical and literary traditions, Xenophon is the first Greek author to give full recognition to the value of women's work (see Ch. 5 and cc. vii–x). Rather than polarizing husband and wife, he views their familial and economic roles as complementary; therefore they never cease to need one another. For this reason, the wife is completely incorporated into her husband's oikos at the start of the mar-riage and Ischomachus assumes that she will be a permanent member (vii. 43). He does not lock up his possessions; rather, he does not hesitate to give his wife access to his storerooms, even before he has taught her where everything is located (viii. 1). Xenophon assumes that the wife may be trained quickly to her domestic duties, if taught by a careful and persuasive husband like Ischomachus. It appears to have been more usual for an Athenian husband to test his wife for about a year until the birth of a child signalled that he might trust her to manage his (his, not their) affairs. This trial period is described as normal in Lys. 1. 6–14.

In order to support his idea that the division of labour is natural, Xenophon must argue that men and women have different aptitudes that make their distinct gender-roles in-evitable. He asserts that men are more capable in body and mind of enduring cold and heat; therefore they fare better on journeys and campaigns. Men are more courageous; but because women are more fearful, they are better at guarding the house. They also have a maternal instinct that makes them the suitable caretakers of infants. These qualities make it appropriate to assign indoor tasks to women and outdoor tasks to men.[8] This spatial division of labour remains traditional in Mediterranean society.[9]

However, like Plato in *Rep.* 5 (449 c–472), Xenophon makes it clear that the qualities of the soul are neither immutable nor predetermined by gender: men and women are equal in their ability to exercise memory, diligence, moderation, and discretion. Women are teachable and can even learn to exercise the kingly skill of command (cc. vii–x). Both parents participate in the education of children (vii. 12). This description of gender-construction is unique in Greek literature. In contrast to Xenophon, the Pseudo-Aristotelian *Oeconomica* (1343^b26–1344^a23) is consistent with Aristotle's conventional views on gender. Pseudo-Aristotle gives a briefer discussion of the capabilities of male and female, since the view presented is commonplace and needs no argumentation. That the Pseudo-Aristotelian text (1344^a8) assigns the education of children solely to the father and does not mention an equality of male and female in mental capabilities is also noteworthy (see Ch. 6, sect. F).

It is also instructive to compare Xenophon's radical views on gender difference with those of Plato. Both were students of Socrates and were equally dismayed at the situation in fourth-century Athens. Plato's *Republic*—like the *Oeconomicus*—has been dated to the 370s (see Ch. 3, sect. C). In the programme for the daily life of the guardian class that Plato sets forth mainly in *Rep.* 5 the traditional private sphere is eliminated. The nuclear family is abolished. Wives and children are held in common. Both Plato and Xenophon advocate eugenics and believe that opportunities for sexual intercourse should be granted as rewards for good behaviour. The best men among the guardians, like the best slaves in Ischomachus'

---

[8] The division between the sexes in classical Greece was so far-reaching that Ischomachus separates not only clothing and shoes according to whether they will be worn by men or women, but he also separates the bedding used in the women's quarters from the bedding used in the men's quarters (ix. 6–7). The sacrificial calendar of Erchia (*SEG* 21. 541) abides strictly by the principle that female victims are sacrificed to goddesses and male victims to gods.

[9] See e.g. Juliet Du Boulay, *Portrait of a Greek Mountain Village* (Oxford, 1974), and Lloyd A. and Margaret C. Fallers, 'Sex Roles in Edremit', in J. G. Peristiany (ed.), *Honour and Shame: The Values of Mediterranean Society* (Chicago, 1966), 243–60.

household, are accorded the most frequent opportunities to reproduce. In the *Republic* children are reared by the state. Domestic economy, dowries, and private property do not exist. Therefore Plato is obliged to integrate the female guardians into the public sphere. Like Xenophon, Plato grants that women are, in general, physically weaker, but he adds that some are athletic and warlike. Plato advocates a full programme of compulsory physical training for women, whereas Xenophon recommends housework for exercise (x. 10–11). Ischomachus tells his wife he would prefer that her cheeks became rosy naturally, and that she did not wear cosmetics. Nor should she try to look taller than she is by wearing platform shoes. This contrast between false perceptions and truth also appears in ii. 95, where Socrates had demonstrated to Critobulus that although his own possessions were of little value, they sufficed for his needs whereas Critobulus, who seemed to be very wealthy, was constantly pressed for funds. Plato, of course, develops an analogous distinction between seeming and being, most explicitly in the Theory of Ideas (*Rep.* 6).

Both Plato and Xenophon are interested in educating men and women for leadership. In the *Oeconomicus* and the *Republic* those in charge bear the heaviest responsibilities. Plato agrees with Xenophon that some women have intellectual powers equal or superior to those of men. Inasmuch as both advocate a meritocratic system, the best women may justly exercise authority over men. Like Xenophon, Plato relies upon education to prepare women for their proper function. Plato's curriculum begins virtually in the womb. In the *Oeconomicus*, the husband could not begin to educate the wife till after their marriage, but she came to him as virtually a *tabula rasa* (vii. 5–6). Whereas Xenophon's notion of education is what we might call 'vocational', Plato's version includes the liberal arts. In the *Republic* girls and boys are given the same education. They follow an educational programme derived from the model used for Greek boys in the classical period, although Plato adds a special emphasis on mathematics. Ischomachus received at least part of his education, and his bride all hers, at home from their respective parents (vii. 14–15) and they expect to be involved in the education of their own children (vii. 12). In contrast, in Plato's *Republic* education is handled by professional teachers and takes place outside the home (perforce, because the guardians do not have specific parents, spouses, or private homes). Although sexual division of labour is minimal in Plato's utopia, the result is not androgyny. Rather Plato has devised a society in which traditional women's work like nursing one's own babies and weaving is of minor importance or does not exist at all. Mothers do not know the identity of their babies; the babies are nursed by foster-mothers and tended by nurses. When not pregnant or nursing, the best women play male roles as both warriors and magistrates. Neither Xenophon nor Plato could totally free himself from his patriarchal biases, which made him consider the male as superior or as the norm to which the female should aspire. Thus in *Oec.* x. 1 the educated wife has a masculine mind.

Xenophon, in the *Oeconomicus*, and Plato, in the *Republic* attempted to regulate the behaviour of women and transform them into what they considered to be more productive members of society. These recommendations did not emanate from ideas about women's repression and need for liberation; it would be anachronistic to attribute such a programme to them. As Plato noted in the *Laws* (781 A) and as Aristotle (*Pol.* 1269^b 14–19) also pointed out a little later in his discussion of the decline of Sparta, when women are unregulated, half a country is ungoverned. Moreover, neither Xenophon nor Plato is consistent in his views about women throughout his various works. For example, in the *Laws* Plato observes that women are the weaker sex and inferior to men in ἀρετή ('virtue'). In the *Oeconomicus* Xenophon is sensitive to women's condition; for example, he writes that an older woman may be treated with dishonour in her own home (vii. 42), that a mother may participate in decisions regarding the education of children and the marriage of a daughter (vii. 11–12), and that a slave is not enthusiastic about sexual intercourse with a master (x. 12). Although in the *Oeconomicus* a wife may have a masculine mind (x. 1), in the *Symposium* (2. 9–12) the caveat that women's nature is inferior to men's in judgement is added.

C. *Slaves*

Slaves were not considered members of the Greek family as, in contrast, they were in the Roman *familia*, where they bore a form of the family name upon manumission and might be buried in the family tomb. Thus in the study of slaves in the Greek oikos (as often in the study of family groupings in later European history) family must be distinguished from household. Slaves, however, did constitute part of the property of the oikos, they will therefore be discussed in Ch. 5, sect. I, and in the note on i. 1.

5

The Domestic Economy

The *Oeconomicus* makes a major contribution to our understanding of the economy of ancient Greece, for it is the only extant Greek didactic work to draw attention to the importance of the oikos ('estate', 'household', or 'family') as an economic entity.[1] The earliest written evidence from the Greek world indicates that oikoi, both royal and common, were the basis of the Greek economy: they were the most common units of production and consumption.[2] The polis was a community of oikoi rather than of individual citizens. In Athens and elsewhere, public legislation and private custom concurred to perpetuate the oikoi: thus the oikoi were expected to remain in continuous operation, enduring longer than the lifespan of any individual member, and continuing to bear economic and social burdens imposed by the state.

A. *The Oikos in Economic Theory*

That the oikos was fundamental to the ancient economy would seem to be obvious. Yet, for the most part, economic historians of the Greek world have virtually ignored the domestic economy (except its agrarian aspect), and preferred to discuss industries, banking, and trade-routes. Thus Gustave Glotz in *Le Travail dans la Grèce ancienne*[3] presented a brief

[1] The material in this chapter was first presented at the University of Chicago, 10 Apr. 1986. It has since been presented at other seminars in the United States, Australia, England, Poland, and the Netherlands.

[2] Jon-Christian Billigmeier, 'Studies on the Family in the Aegean Bronze Age and in Homer', *Trends in History*, 3, 3/4 (1985), 14, points out that in Mycenaean Greek kinship terminology is not used to designate the extended family but is restricted to members of the immediate family. Of course, the fact that the sources are limited to government tallies may have produced this result.

[3] (Paris, 1920).

discussion of the family economy only in his opening chapters on the Homeric period, treating domestic production as part of a primitive world predating the formation of the polis. Neither M. I. Rostovtzeff in *The Social and Economic History of the Hellenistic World*[4] nor H. Michell in *The Economics of Ancient Greece*[5] treated domestic labour and its products. Their discussions distort our view of the Greek economy and other pre-capitalist economies to make it fit into categories appropriate to the analysis of bourgeois capitalism of the nineteenth and twentieth centuries and impose some distinctions between public and private that are artificial in the context of classical Greece.

The late M. I. Finley, whose work dominated the study of the Greek economy in the mid-twentieth century, asserted that the Greeks were ignorant of economic theory.[6] Finley grafted on to his study of the Greek economy modern definitions formulated by J. A. Schumpeter, who meant by economic analysis 'the intellectual efforts that men have made in order to *understand* [italics his] economic phenomena'.[7] Therefore, Finley deduced that in Xenophon 'there is not one sentence that expresses an economic principle or offers an economic analysis, nothing on efficiency of production. [or] rational choice...'.[8] Thus Finley proceeded to reject the work of the earliest Greek economist.

Finley also argued that part of the problem posed by Greek economics was the result not only of the lack of vocabulary for such notions as 'real property', but of the failure of scholars to devote adequate attention to the meanings of such common terms as χρήματα ('wealth', 'money', or 'property') and οἶκος.[9] But Finley unjustly imputed the failings of classical scholars to

---

[4] (Oxford, 1941).   [5] (New York, 1957).

[6] 'Aristotle and Economic Analysis', *Past and Present*, 47 (1970), 13, n. 44. See the rebuttal by Scott Meikle, 'Aristotle and the Political Economy of the Polis', *JHS* 99 (1979), 57–73. For additional criticism of Finley's theories see W. E. Thompson, 'The Athenian Entrepreneur', *AC* 51 (1982), 53–85, and S. Todd Lowry, *The Archaeology of Economic Ideas* (Durham, NC, 1987).

[7] *History of Economic Analysis* (New York, 1959), 54.

[8] *The Ancient Economy*, 2nd edn., (Berkeley and Los Angeles, 1985), 19.

[9] Review of *Xenophon: Économique*, ed. and trans. Pierre Chantraine, *CP* 46 (1951), 252–3, and 'Land, Debt, and the Man of Property in Classical Athens', *Political Science Quarterly*, 68 (1953), 261.

classical authors. In the *Oeconomicus*, especially in the opening chapter, Xenophon makes an unprecedented effort to establish definitions of words such as οἰκονομία, οἶκος, and χρήματα.

Finley criticized Xenophon for being 'interested in specialization of crafts rather than in division of labour'.[10] Though Finley does not mention Marx, he refers to the same passage in *Cyrop*. 8. 2. 5, where the development of τέχναι ('arts', 'crafts', or 'occupations') in large cities is described, as Marx did when he observed that Xenophon displayed a characteristic bourgeois instinct in his discussion of division of labour in the workshop. Marx had a better opinion of Xenophon than Finley did: in *Das Kapital* he comments that in the *Cyropaedia* passage Xenophon stressed the excellence to be attained in use-value, although he knew that the gradations of division of labour depend on the extent of the market.[11] Georges Sorel summarized Marx's comment and added that Xenophon, unlike Plato, shows an understanding of the importance of production.[12]

Finley's negative assessment of Xenophon resulted, in part, from an anachronistic view of economic theory that excluded, by definition, much of what the Greeks themselves regarded as the economy: he declared that 'what we call the economy was exclusively the business of outsiders'.[13] He thus failed to give full recognition to the private sphere and the contribution of women, both slave and free, to the economy. Beyond admitting that bakers and textile workers were productive, he paid little attention to the work of female domestics,[14] although it

---

[10] 'Aristotle and Economic Analysis', 4. This criticism might more justly be levelled at Plato, for example, in his description of the nascent city in *Rep.* 369 D–E.

[11] *Das Kapital*, 1 (1867) = Karl Marx and Friedrich Engels, *Werke*, xxiii (Berlin, DDR, 1969), 388 n. 81. Adam Smith had also seen a connection between the division of labour and the market. See Ronald L. Meek and Andrew S. Skinner, 'The Development of Adam Smith's Ideas on the Division of Labour', *Economic Journal*, 83 (1973), 1100.

[12] *Réflexions sur la violence*, 8th edn. (Paris, 1936), 366 n. 2.

[13] 'Aristotle and Economic Analysis', 25. P. Herfst, *Le Travail de la femme dans la Grèce ancienne* (Utrecht, 1922), 9, also states that the *Oeconomicus* fails to treat what we call the economy.

[14] This blindness about women mars Finley's analysis of ancient slavery, inasmuch as his distinction between slave and free—that no slave held public office or sat on the deliberative and judicial bodies (in 'Was Greek Civilization Based on Slave Labour?', *Historia*, 8 (1959), 147 = id. (ed.), *Slavery in Classical Antiquity* (Cambridge, 1960), 55—cannot be used to differentiate women's statuses.

is likely that females were numerous, perhaps, as A. W. Gomme suggested, even outnumbering male slaves within the city of Athens.[15]

Unlike Finley, G. E. M. de Ste. Croix did make some attempt to integrate women into his explanation of economy and society. He stated that all Greek wives should be regarded as a distinct economic class, because their role in human reproduction led to their being subjected to men, politically, economically, and socially. However, he devoted a mere twelve pages of *The Class Struggle*, out of a total of 732, to the class and status of women, and confessed that 'this needs a great deal of further thought'.[16]

With some adjustments, the theory of A. V. Chayanov can be made to accommodate the domestic economy, despite his observation that the Greek oikos did not correspond to any of the pure non-capitalist economic types he described.[17] Although he was studying Russian serfdom and peasant farms, his terminology can be adopted as a heuristic device. Chayanov's theory is based on three axioms that can be applied to our discussion of the domestic economy: (1) there are various types of economies and these must be analysed in terms appropriate specifically to them; (2) an economy must be understood by analysing its organization for production; and (3) the smallest production unit must be analysed first before the interconnections between all the units are understood.[18]

The oikos described by Xenophon combines features of the farm employing the labour of the family with the type of economic unit exploiting slave labour. Even when free leaseholders work the land, as they may do according to the provi-

---

[15] A. W. Gomme, *The Population of Athens in the Fifth and Fourth Centuries B.C.* (Oxford, 1933), 21 n. 3. On the population of Athens, see more recently Mogens Herman Hansen, *Demography and Democracy: The Number of Citizens in Fourth Century Athens* (Herning, 1985).

[16] G. E. M. de Ste. Croix, *The Class Struggle in the Ancient Greek World* (London and Ithaca, NY, 1981), 101.

[17] 'On the Theory of Non-Capitalist Economic Systems', trans. C. Lane in D. Thorner, B. Kerblay, and R. E. F. Smith (eds.), *The Theory of Peasant Economy*, (Homewood, Ill., 1966), 1–28.

[18] For a discussion of Chayanov see Nicola Tannenbaum, 'Chayanov and Economic Anthropology', in P. Durrenberger (ed.), *Chayanov, Peasants, and Economic Anthropology* (Orlando, Fla., 1984), 27–38.

sions of land-leases (see on xii. 3), Chayanov's models remain relevant: the sources of labour remain the same even if the ownership is, so to speak, temporary. Because the economic unit based on the family does not include wages for individuals, it is not essential to calculate net profit per worker. Thus we find Ischomachus making general (rather than specific) remarks about the contributions of husband and wife to the domestic economy (see below, sect. G). In contrast, the profitability of the economic unit based on slave labour may be calculated by taking into consideration quantifiable factors such as the cost of purchasing and maintaining a slave or of rearing one from birth, the interest on the capital thus invested, the product of slave labour, and the net profit. Ischomachus does keep account of these factors, though they are embedded in various places in the dialogue rather than set forth concisely and systematically (see below, sect. E). The slave labour unit is more flexible than the family, for slaves can be bought or sold, or (in Greece) leased as required. Ischomachus does not buy or sell slaves for profit, but excess numbers are sent away from the main house (vii. 34). The kind of intensification of land exploitation described by Ischomachus is possible with slave labour and managerial skill (see on ix. 5 and xii. 3). In order to increase their labour supply wealthy landowners like Ischomachus would not have compelled family members to work harder. Moreover, at the dramatic time of the conversation afterwards related in the *Oeconomicus* the family consists of only two members, Ischomachus and his wife, and their roles are largely supervisory.

B. *Xenophon as Economist*

Xenophon's concern with economic matters is apparent not only in the *Oeconomicus* and *Revenues*, which focus directly on the economy, but also in his other works, especially the *Cyropaedia* and the *Anabasis*. His interest in material things and his experience as a general lead him to theorize about the laws of supply and demand, the value of silver and gold, and the division of labour.[19] When he was in exile, as he probably was

[19] See further Claude Mossé, 'Xénophon économiste', in J. Bingen, G. Cambier, and G. Nachtergael (eds.), *Le Monde grec: Hommages à Claire Préaux* (Brussels, 1975), 69–76.

when he wrote the *Oeconomicus*, he could neither observe nor influence the public economy of Athens (see Ch. 1, sect. D). Therefore, in the *Oeconomicus* he pays particular attention to the sexual division of labour and to the notion of private profit. Xenophon was one of the first authors to display an interest in the domestic economy. This new focus, however, should not be interpreted as mere selfishness and abandonment of civic duties. The oikoi constituted the foundation of the polis and served to reproduce the citizen population; therefore strengthening the individual oikoi would result in a more stable and vigorous polis. The oikoi and their members, in turn, were sustained by agriculture. Thus a strong agricultural economy was vital to the health of the polis.

C. *Agriculture in Attica in the Fourth Century* BC

The economy of Attica was typical of that of pre-capitalist Mediterranean societies. Aristotle (*Pol.* 1256^{a}38–40) observes that the majority of men made their living from the land and crops; according to Ps.-Arist. *Oec.* 1345^{b}32–3 agriculture was the most important source of revenue for the state. In the context of a discussion on procuring wealth, Aristotle (*Pol.* 1258^{b}39–1259^{a}2) reports that authors from several cities had written manuals on agriculture (see on xvi. 1. λόγῳ). The appearance of these treatises in the fourth century is attributable to several factors. The Peloponnesian War had demonstrated that the Athenians could survive within their walls without relying on farming and could gain their livelihood from the sea (Xen. *Hell.* 7. 1. 4 and see on xvi. 1). The authors of the treatises mentioned by Aristotle hailed from mainland Greece and the islands. It is reasonable to assume that the war had disrupted agriculture and created new opportunities for ambitious farmers in many parts of the Greek world, although most of our information, both textual and archaeological, comes from Attica. Ways of making money had grown increasingly specialized so that a wealthy man like Demosthenes' father, who owned workshops of knife-makers and couchmakers, might have had all his capital invested in manufacturing and finance and own no land at all,[20] while another, following the model of Ischomachus, might have treated land management as a profession and sought not mere subsistence from his estate, but rather profits substantial enough to enable him to pay for the liturgies (compulsory public benefactions) for which his capital made him eligible.[21] The existence of the word οἰκονομικός indicates that estate management had become a science (see on title Οἰκονομικός). Land cultivation was intensified, for according to the historian of the *Hellenica Oxyrhynchia* (17. 5), the Athenians actually did improve their methods of land cultivation in the first half of the fourth century. Such intensification may be observed in the employment of slaves on the land, short fallow and consequent decrease in pasturage, application of liquid manure, and reclamation of underproductive land (see on xvi. 10, 12, xx. 11–12, 22).

The devastation of farmland during the Peloponnesian War may have also inspired the production of handbooks on agriculture, at least in part (see xvi. 1). Scholars continue to disagree over the effect the war had on agriculture in Attica: there is little certainty and substantial latitude for speculation. W. G. Hardy had argued that although much lasting and irreversible damage to agriculture was inflicted during the Decelean War, the olive-trees were spared.[22] Several ancient historians have recently revived Hardy's position and assert that agricultural damage during the Peloponnesian War was minimal. They claim that the effort required to destroy olive-trees was prohibitive;[23] therefore the war did not produce a

---

[20] Other Athenians of liturgical status whose wealth derived from manufacture include Cleon and his father Cleaenetus, who owned workshops of slave tanners (Ael. *VH* 10. 17). Mining was a major source of wealth for some, including Callias and his descendants (Nepos, *Alcib.* 2. 1, *Cim.* 1. 3, *And.* 1. 130, *Isoc.* 16. 31, Xen. *Revenues* 15) and Nicias (Plut. *Nic.* 4. 2, Xen. *Mem.* 2.5. 2, *Revenues* 4. 14). See J. K. Davies, *Wealth and the Power of Wealth in Classical Athens* (Salem, NH, 1984), 41–3, for a list of wealthy Athenians whose income was derived primarily from industry rather than from agriculture.

[21] It would appear, especially from Ps.-Dem. 42. 18–23, that a landowner might be burdened with liturgies even if he was not prosperous.

[22] 'The *Hellenica Oxyrhynchia* and the Devastation of Attica', *CP* 21 (1926), 346–55.

[23] Thus Victor Davis Hanson, *Warfare and Agriculture in Classical Greece* (Pisa, 1983), 47–56, 142–3.

long-term or widespread crisis in agriculture.[24] They also assert that the cavalry was effective in protecting agriculture in Attica. The primary sources do not give a clear picture. According to Thucydides (2. 55. 1–2) Pericles' strategy was to protect urban Athens and to treat the city as though it were an island by relying on the navy for defence. However, his advice probably did not prevail without opposition even at the beginning of the war, and certainly not throughout its duration. At the outbreak of the war the majority of Athenians lived outside the city walls in rural areas. In the first year of the war, Pericles thought it necessary to send the cavalry to defend the land near the city (Thuc. 2. 22. 2) and the cavalry continued to defend the land. Thucydides mentions a few specific occasions on which the cavalry rode out to defend rural Attica, and states that this activity was customary (3. 1. 1, see also 7. 27. 5). Xenophon doubtless bases his generalization on historical fact when he states in *Oec.* vi. 6–7 that farmers prefer to defend the land rather than the city walls (see also v. 7, 13). Unlike Thucydides, Xenophon lived in Athens for the duration of the war and served in the cavalry (see Ch. 1, sect. A). He indicates that Pericles' original plan was retained and that the efforts of the cavalry alone were not totally successful in preventing serious devastation, though he implies they could have been more effective under different circumstances. In *Cav. Comm.* 7. 3–4 he states: 'if the city turns to its navy and if it is content to defend the city walls as happened when the Spartans invaded with the aid of all the Greeks, and if the city decides that the cavalry should defend what is beyond the city walls and should do this alone against all the assembled enemy...'.

Other ancient testimony, including Thuc. 2. 20, Aesch. 2. 175, Pl. *Menex.* 242c, Lys. 7. 6–7, and the *Hellenica Oxyrhynchia* 17. 5, confirms Xenophon's statement. According to Diodorus 12. 45. 4 trees were cut down as early as 430 BC. There is certainly no doubt that agriculture in Attica was

---

[24] Thus Josiah Ober, 'Thucydides, Pericles, and the Strategy of Defense', in *The Craft of the Ancient Historian: Studies in Honor of Chester G. Starr* (Lanham, Md., and London, 1985), 171–88, and I. G. Spence, 'Perikles and the Defence of Attika during the Peloponnesian War', *JHS* 110 (1990), 91–109.

disrupted especially after the Spartan occupation of Deceleia in 413 BC, although some scholars may have exaggerated the extent and duration of the agrarian problems that the war produced. Because olive-trees require forty years to reach maturity, if the Spartans did destroy the Athenians' olive-trees, the production of olives would have been interrupted for a generation. Grain crops recover rapidly. However, the long war surely depleted the number of able-bodied men available to perform agricultural labour, but it did not similarly reduce the numbers of the other inhabitants of Athens who needed sustenance. Thus the Peloponnesian War must have had a serious effect on Athenian agriculture. Owing to the uncertainties of war and the diminution in the population, the price of land probably fluctuated, falling at first owing to a lack of demand, but rising after the loss of the Athenian Empire. The value of the historical Ischomachus' estate may have declined as a result of raids on his farmland during the Deceleian War (see on vi. 17).[25]

Some scholars, perhaps, have exaggerated the extent and duration of the damage the war inflicted on Athenian agriculture, and in turn provoked other scholars to minimalize it. M. I. Finley had pointed out that his predecessors, including Ehrenberg, Oertel, Michell, Pohlmann, Kornemann, and Busolt, misinterpreted the horoi inscriptions (recording debt on mortgaged property) in supposing that they gave evidence for small farms' being abandoned owing to debt: actually the horoi record hypothecation of land by well-to-do citizens (see on xx. 22).[26] Nevertheless, the pendulum swung back and Ephraim David asserted that the owners of small farms suffered losses grave enough to produce a social and economic crisis. Although the crisis David postulates is too enormous to be credible,[27] there certainly were major social changes in the fourth century.[28] For example, the Peloponnesian War was a

---

[25] See further J. K. Davies, *Athenian Propertied Families*, 268.

[26] *Studies in Land and Credit in Ancient Athens, 500–200 B.C.* (New Brunswick, NJ, 1952), 252 n. 13.

[27] *Aristophanes and Athenian Society of the Early Fourth Century B.C.* (Leiden, 1984).

[28] See further Claude Mossé, 'La vie économique d'Athènes au IVe siècle, crise ou renouveau?', in Franco Sartori (ed.), *Praelectiones Patavinae* (Rome, 1972), 135–44, modifying the picture of radical change she expressed in *La Fin de la démocratie athénienne*

watershed in the history of Athenian women.[29] That Xenophon
at times expresses nostalgia for the fifth century indicates that
the fourth century was different (see on iv. 5). Jean Luccioni
suggested that Xenophon wrote the *Oeconomicus* with the intention of criticizing young aristocrats of Athens, some of whom,
such as Critobulus, were irresponsible and inept at managing
their property, and others were devoted to commerce and
industry rather than to the old-fashioned way of life spent as
a soldier and gentleman farmer.[30] According to Luccioni the
Oeconomicus provides the first glimpse of the re-emergence of
the aristocratic ideal, which was revived by the Macedonians.
However, he is not persuasive. This ideal was alive and well,
even in the classical period (see on vi. 12 καλός τε κἀγαθός).
Furthermore, the *Oeconomicus* does not read like a work of
criticism. Surely Xenophon envisaged a wider audience than
Luccioni suggests (see Ch. 2, sect. A).

An economic or social crisis need not be of long duration to
inspire a literary work. Growing up during the war, viewing
the problems created by it, personally affected by the execution
of Socrates and by his own exile, Xenophon could not comfort
himself with the certainty displayed by some contemporary
scholars that the crises would be temporary, or last no more
than forty years. There is no doubt that the supply of grain
to Athens posed a larger problem in the fourth century than
it had in the fifth (see on xx. 27 ἔμποροι). Xenophon may
have wished to demonstrate to landowners that by improving
domestic food production they could simultaneously perform
a public service and increase their own profits. Thus it is
certainly reasonable to suppose that concern about the state of
Athenian agriculture after the Peloponnesian War served, at
least in part, to motivate Xenophon to write the *Oeconomicus*.

(Paris, 1962), 55–6, and in *Athens in Decline* (London, 1973), 12–14. See also works
cited in J. Pečírka, 'The Crisis of the Athenian Polis in the Fourth Century BC', *Eirene*,
14 (1976), 5–29.

[29] See further Sarah B. Pomeroy, *Goddesses, Whores, Wives, and Slaves* (New York,
1975), 80–1, and 'Technikai kai Mousikai', *AJAH* 2 (1977), 51–68, and on the
possible effects of the long war on Aspasia and Chrysilla see on iii. 14 Ἀσπασίαν and
vi. 17 Ἰσχόμαχον.

[30] *Les Idées politiques et sociales de Xénophon* (Paris, 1947), 72.

D. *Estate Management in Classical Athens*

Although in some aspects of the position of the wife, the treatment of slaves, and the importance accorded to education the household attributed to Ischomachus is more an idealistic, albeit attainable, vision than a description of reality, other historical sources indicate that it is normative in many respects (see Ch. 4). Certainly, Roman agronomists considered Xenophon's advice practicable (see Ch. 6). Furthermore, no other historical source gives such a wide range of detailed practical information on an oikos. Therefore it is reasonable to attempt to glean some information about the economic structure of the normal oikos from the *Oeconomicus*. Because all Athenian citizens belonged to an oikos, and many men owned some land, the experiences of Ischomachus were relevant to them (see Ch. 2, sect. A). In the present discussion and in the Commentary information about Greek agriculture derived from archaeological evidence, augmented by some inferences from contemporary Greek farming practices, will be used to illuminate the text of the *Oeconomicus*.

Most Athenians did not belong to an oikos as extensive or wealthy as Ischomachus' (see on vii. 1), whose oikos was so large that his family alone could not supply the requisite labour or the necessary supervision. His wealth is apparent in that he owned an unspecified number of both male and female slaves, an unspecified amount of land, and so much movable property that a census was needed to keep track of it (ix. 10). But Xenophon (v. 4) does not distinguish the small farmer who works with his own hands from the man who supervises other labourers. Because Ischomachus' holdings were fragmented as a result of buying and selling plots which were probably not adjacent, his property may be thought of as consisting of a number of small farms rather than a vast single plantation. Hence he used some agricultural techniques appropriate to cultivating relatively small plots, such as employing human labour armed with hoes and mattocks to pulverize the soil instead of constantly using ploughs drawn by large draught animals (xvi. 12, xvii. 12).

According to the *Oeconomicus*, profit is the chief goal of estate management. Some men, it is true, mismanage their estates so badly that they produce only loss (iii. 5, xx. 9, 21, 29). Other estates, no doubt, are little more than self-sufficient: clothing is manufactured at home and farming produces the food and other necessities that are consumed (vii. 20, 22). If a small farmer does not raise grain, he will need to sell some of his other produce in order to purchase it as well as other items. But in classical Greece the domestic economy is linked to the political structure. The dichotomy between public and private that appears in industrialized societies is not characteristic of the Greek economy. Not only does the family farm provide an opportunity for citizens to practice their military skills (v. 8, xi. 17), but in order for an oikos to assume its proper share of civic responsibility a surplus of wealth must also be created. It is not sufficient for Ischomachus merely to earn money (i. 4 μισθοφορεῖν) by estate management. Large profits are the goal (i. 4-5 πολύν ... μισθόν ... περιουσίαν ... αὔξειν). The emphasis throughout is on increasing the estate (αὔξειν i. 5, 15, 16, ii. 1). Οἰκονομία is a dynamic science by which people can make estates increase (vi. 4 οἴκους αὔξειν).

To be wealth, what is produced must be used or sold, i.e. exchanged for cash (i. 11). Such cash will enable the propertied oikos to meet expenses imposed by the state. Xenophon mentions paying for sacrifices, public banquets and benefactions, entertaining guests (ξενία), maintaining horses, and other liturgies (ii. 5–6, vii. 3, ix. 9–10). Private citizens also make demands of the wealthy, for example, expecting loans of money (ii. 8). In addition, the oikos must be able to provide dowries for its daughters (as for the bride of Ischomachus in vii. 13) so that a new generation of citizens may be produced.

Because of the Athenian system of taxation, which, by means of liturgies and other public evidence of generosity, provided a direct link between private prosperity and public welfare, the quest to increase the family fortune was not regarded as selfish. Xenophon draws attention to this link by embedding practical advice on estate management in an ethical treatise.[31] The number of oikoi in the liturgical class were relatively

---

[31] Similarly Thuc. 1.2 considers economic and technical progress as the prerequisites for the existence of the civilized polis.

few.[32] Thus Demosthenes (27. 64) attempted to win the sympathy of the jury when he stated that owing to his guardians' fraudulent machinations, his estate was no longer capable of contributing generously to tax levies (μεγάλας εἰσφοράς) and affording liturgies. The reputation of Ischomachus as a gentleman (καλὸς κἀγαθός) would not have been compromised by accusations of greed (see on vi. 12).[33] In winning a higher return on his investments, Ischomachus did not exploit or deceive other Athenians. Rather, he demonstrated by means of his own example his contention that virtue and diligence produce wealth (ix. 13, xi. 12, xii. 15, xiv. 7, 9), while laziness results in loss (xx. 21–2). Socrates' position in this argument is ambivalent: because he was poor, he can only conceive of borrowing rather than lending; but he does assert that his wealth suffices for his needs (ii. 2, 8 and see Ch. 2). In xi. 6, Socrates goes so far as to suggest that even a poor man may be good. However, this statement runs counter to Ischomachus' assertions and is inconsistent with the view previously expressed by Socrates in i. 22, where, in an effort to persuade Critobulus to abandon his puerile indulgences, he stated that penury results from lack of virtue.

The wife's dowry plus the husband's contribution constituted the foundation of the oikos at the start of a marriage. Dowries consisted of cash and movables (see below, sect. G.) The husband provided the land and the house with most of its contents, as Ischomachus does. The sources of ongoing income for an oikos based on an agricultural economy are numerous. The *Oeconomicus* mentions income (πρόσοδοι) from the sale of horses (ii. 11, iii. 9). Slaves, sheep, cash, and other items are also potential sources of income (i. 9, ii. 11, iii. 15, v. 3, 6, 18, 20, vii. 41, xx. 23). Slaves are profitable for what they produce (vii. 41, xvi. 1, and see below, sect. I). Ischomachus, at least, does not buy or sell them, but remarks in the dialogue indicate that other owners do.

Athens conforms to the pattern of other pre-industrial

---

[32] Davies, *Wealth*, 33–4.
[33] On the popular attitude towards wealth see on ii. 5–6 and see K. J. Dover, *Greek Popular Morality in the Time of Plato and Aristotle* (Oxford, 1974), 175–80.

societies: peasant farmers sold their produce in the agora.[34] In addition there were probably local secondary markets in the demes. Thus the manager of an oikos like that of Pericles, who converted produce to cash rather than storing it for future consumption, would have frequented such markets (see on vii. 36 διανεμητέον). It also appears likely that merchants, such as those mentioned in *Oec*. xx. 27, would have purchased substantial quantities of agricultural produce (e.g. olive oil) from large landowners such as Ischomachus and sold it wherever prices were high. Furthermore, the land itself could be a principal source of income and the one which was most deserving of the estate manager's concern (iii. 5, v. 1, vi. 11, xv. 1, xxi. 10). From the enthusiasm of Ischomachus, it appears that there might be an enormous profit in improving land and selling it (xx. 26). The result of such entrepreneurship was that a single owner such as Ischomachus would own parcels of non-contiguous land. Fragmentation of landed property was not unusual in Attica.[35] Prudent owners would assign slaves to guard these scattered properties (see on vii. 34). The variety of locations could encourage the raising of varied crops, which in turn would tend to increase the self-sufficiency of the oikos and provide some insurance against natural disasters. Despite their fragmentary nature, land leases from classical and Hellenistic Greece show that growing several crops, even on unfragmented property, was normal in antiquity. For example, *SIG*[3] 963 mentions cereals, vines, and figs; *IG* ii[2]. 1241 mentions grain, vines, figs, and perhaps olives; *IG* ii[2]. 2492 mentions grain, vines, and olives; *IG* ii[2]. 2493 mentions grain, figs, and, perhaps, olives; *IG* ii[2]. 2494 mentions grain, olives, and figs.[36] Intensive working of the soil to conserve moisture even around trees prepared such land to receive seed, and crops could be planted in orchards (see on c. xvi).

The appropriateness and profitability of Ischomachus' tech-

---

[34] Finley, 'The Study of the Ancient Economy: Further Thoughts', *Opus*, 3 (1984), 8, wrote of a lack of information in the sources about how farmers sold or used their produce. However, Victor Ehrenberg, *The People of Aristophanes*, 2nd edn. (1951; pb. repr. New York, 1962), 130, gives many examples from Attic comedy.

[35] Davies, *Wealth*, 52–4 and Robin Osborne, *Demos* (Cambridge, 1985).

[36] See the convenient table of the provisions in agricultural leases in Robin Osborne, *Classical Landscape with Figures* (London, 1987), 42–3.

niques of land management are confirmed by their use in Greece nowadays. One of the chief characteristics of Ischomachus' agricultural enterprise is versatility. Like Ischomachus, farmers today raise a variety of fruits and crops. Diversification also means that labour resources can be employed over a period of time, rather than used intensively and then left idle.[37] Greek farmers today combine agriculture with some pastoralism. Though animal husbandry can be an excellent source of cash through the sale of wool and milk products, it is also a higher-risk operation than agriculture (see on v. 20).[38] Thus prudent farmers may effectively exploit their resources by creating a symbiosis between flora and fauna, for example by allowing livestock to graze under their olive-trees or feeding the livestock the prunings from their vines. Similarly, though farming scattered plots of land reduces profitability, through time lost by travel and by the need to duplicate implements, land fragmentation is thought to increase stability by reducing natural risk. Nowadays, despite the advice of agronomists, farmers resist attempts to integrate their holdings.[39]

E. *Record-Keeping*

Greek farmers calculated their profits or losses. In *Revenues* 4. 5 Xenophon states that landowners know how many workers and animals are required to cultivate a given property and understand that using more than are required is simply wasteful. In *Oec.* xx. 16 he draws attention to the losses incurred by permitting a worker to work too slowly or to quit work ahead of the proper time. According to A. Jardé's calculations, based on figures in a lawsuit (Ps.-Dem. 42), the large estate of

[37] Hamish A. Forbes, '"We Have a Little of Everything"', in Muriel Dimen and Ernestine Friedl (eds.), *Regional Variation in Modern Greece and Cyprus* (New York, 1976), 236–50, points out that although diversification appears less profitable, it provides more stability.

[38] On the profitability of animal husbandry and its relationship to agriculture see Stephen Hodkinson, 'Animal Husbandry in the Greek Polis', in C. R. Whittaker (ed.), *Pastoral Economies in Classical Antiquity* (Cambridge, 1988), 35–74.

[39] J. L. Bintliff and A. M. Snodgrass, 'The Cambridge/Bradford Boeotian Expedition: The First Four Years', *JFA* 12 (1985), 154–5, and Forbes, 'We have a Little of Everything'.

Phaenippus produced an income of 12 drachmas daily, or a yield of about 9.5 per cent on the capital invested.[40] Even if the numbers supplied by the speaker are exaggerated in order to win his case, the fact that he gives figures which he expects the jury to believe suggests that landowners did make such calculations.

G. Mickwitz argued that, even lacking modern accounting techniques, ancient landowners could calculate income and capital and have a good idea of profits that might accrue from farming.[41] In contrast, G. E. M. de Ste. Croix asserted that because of their inefficient methods of accounting, ancient landowners could not have an accurate idea about which agricultural activities were profitable.[42] Probably as a result of his familiarity with papyri, Mickwitz properly credited Greek landowners with a firm grasp of their financial situation. Some papyrus accounts not only keep track of receipts and expenditures but also reveal efforts to analyse the overall financial status of an estate. Ischomachus and his wife probably kept financial records as Zenon did, on a larger scale, in Egypt in the middle of the third century BC. Zenon's accounts show, *inter alia*, a monthly distribution of grain to slaves and other workers.[43] Ischomachus' wife also regulates her budget on a

---

[40] For Phaenippus, see Davies, *Athenian Propertied Families*, no. 14734. A. Jardé, *Les Céréales dans l'antiquité grecque* (Paris, 1925), 151–6, had estimated the yield on the estate. G. E. M. de Ste. Croix, 'The Estate of Phaenippus (Ps.-Dem., xlii)', in E. Badian (ed.), *Ancient Society and Institutions: Studies Presented to Victor Ehrenberg* (Oxford, 1966), 109–14, argues that the estate was smaller than modern scholars have thought, but that it was still the largest estate of which we know in Athens. He questions Jardé's calculations of the yield, since they are based on the controversial figures supplied by Phaenippus and his opponent (111–12).

[41] 'Economic Rationalism in Graeco-Roman Agriculture', *English Historical Review*, 52 (1937), 577–89.

[42] 'Greek and Roman Accounting', in A. C. Littleton and B. S. Yamey (eds.), *Studies in the History of Accounting* (Homewood, Ill., 1956), 14–74, esp. 37 n. 14. In his second edition of *The Ancient Economy* (180–91), Finley continued to accept de Ste. Croix's views emphasizing the inadequacies of ancient accounting. But Richard H. Macve, 'Some Glosses on "Greek and Roman Accounting"', in P. A. Cartledge and F. D. Harvey (eds.), *Crux: Essays Presented to G. E. M. de Ste. Croix on his 75th Birthday* (Exeter, 1985), 235 n. 11, commented that de Ste. Croix had exaggerated the importance of modern accounting techniques in computing agricultural profit.

[43] Claire Préaux, 'L'économie lagide: 1933–1958', *Proceedings of the IX International Congress of Papyrology, Oslo, 19th–22nd August, 1958* (Oslo, 1961), 232, suggested that there was a direct link between the financial apparatus of mainland Greek cities in the 4th c. BC and the financial practices of Greeks in Ptolemaic Egypt. On the system

monthly basis (ix. 8, see also on vii. 36). At least two systems of income management were practised in the Greek world. Ischomachus advises his wife to do the budgeting in the Spartan or Persian manner by dividing the supplies allocated for a year into monthly instalments (see on vii. 36, ix. 8).

The finances of a well-managed oikos such as that of Ischomachus and his wife were not subject to caprice but were managed according to a predetermined plan (ix. 8, iii. 15). Written accounts were kept (vi. 3), and income and expenditures noted (i. 4, iii. 15, vii. 13, 33, 36, sim. Ar. *Clouds* 18–24, 30–1, Lys. 32. 19–22 and see above, sect. E, on sources of income). Whether husband or wife contributed more could be determined (vii. 13–14). It is clear that Ischomachus believes that he and his wife are keeping track of their estate's financial gains and losses.

F. *The Economics of Patriarchy*

Because, as I have argued at the beginning of this chapter, the *Oeconomicus* with its focus on the domestic economy, does not fit readily into any modern conceptual framework, whether Marxist or non-Marxist, it is questionable whether existing approaches have sufficiently illuminated the economy of ancient Greece. Despite their attention to division of labour, and their acknowledgement that Xenophon understood the division of labour among men in workshops, Marx, Sorel, and Finley all failed to realize that in the *Oeconomicus*, Xenophon discusses the sexual division of labour that is fundamental to Greek society. (See above, sect. A).[44] In societies characterized by strict sexual division of labour, where most women are excluded from the labour market, cash economy, and ownership of the means of production, the categories that have been applied by economic historians are relevant almost exclusively to males who participate in the cash economy.

employed by Zenon, see T. Reekmans, *La Sitométrie dans les archives de Zénon* (Brussels, 1966), and C. Orrieux, 'Les comptes privés de Zénon à Philadelphie', *CE* 56 (1981), 314–40, esp. 315–18.

[44] On the division of labour as the principal incentive for human marriage see Claude Lévi-Strauss, e.g. *The Elementary Structures of Kinship* (London, 1969), 40.

In the following discussion I shall analyse the *Oeconomicus* primarily from the perspective of women, the same perspective that Xenophon himself emphasizes in cc. iii and vii–x (see Ch. 6, sect. F). Work will be defined as productive activity for household use or for exchange.[45] I shall concentrate particularly on those aspects of the domestic economy that have been overlooked by previous historians and argue for an understanding of the Greek economy that I believe to be more historically accurate than the interpretations of my predecessors. I shall also attempt to redefine the productivity of the household and of its members. Patriarchy literally means 'the rule of fathers'; I shall explain how patriarchy functions not only as a social system, but also as an economic system in which the male who heads the oikos appropriates the labour of his wife, children, and slaves. Finally, I shall show that in the *Oeconomicus* Xenophon expresses economic principles that are suitable to the analysis of the Greek economy.

G. *Marriage*

Marriage constituted the economic basis of the oikos. The *Oeconomicus* presents a view of marriage as an economic partnership whose goal is the increase of property (vii. 2, 11). The fourth century was a period of increasing education for women, a time when education was responsible for the entrance of women into the liberal arts and professions, when women began to appear as artists, physicians, and philosophers.[46] The *Oeconomicus* is also largely about women's education: it elevates the role of housewife to the status of a profession with important economic consequences.

Xenophon's extensive discussion of married life appears in two passages. The first (i–vi. 16) records a conversation between Socrates and Critobulus, a member of the liturgical (i.e. wealthiest) class. Critobulus asks Socrates for advice in managing his affairs. Socrates points out that some men reap profit and others loss from the same assets, and that some

---

[45] For this terminology, see Louise A. Tilly and Joan W. Scott, *Women, Work, and Family* (New York, 1978), 3.

[46] Pomeroy, 'Technikai kai Mousikai'.

marriages, through the joint efforts of husband and wife, turn out to be productive, while the treatment other men accord their wives leads to disaster. Moreover, the wife who handles household affairs competently as her husband's partner is his peer in contributing to the financial success of the oikos.

In a subsequent, longer section (vii–x) Socrates tells Critobulus about a discussion on marriage that he once had with Ischomachus. Like Critobulus, Ischomachus is a member of the liturgical class, but, in contrast to Critobulus, Ischomachus enjoys a reputation for managing his household profitably. Socrates' relationship with his own wife and the poverty of his household were so notorious that he could scarcely claim expertise in the domestic realm; his report indicates that he simply asked Ischomachus questions and accepted his responses without contradiction.

Ischomachus begins his exposition with a description of the early days of his marriage when his bride was not yet 15. By his account, she had lived such a protected life that she knew little when she married him except how to control her appetite, how to weave, and how to assign spinning to the slaves. These accomplishments were not negligible. Inasmuch as women were in charge of the kitchen, and gluttony was portrayed in misogynistic and humorous texts as a vice to which females were prone, control over the appetite was worth mentioning. In order to prevent theft, the mistress of the house needed to know how to weigh out wool for spinning. Ischomachus' wife could also read and write. Her literacy would have been a decided advantage in keeping track of the household possessions and financial records (vii. 36).

In the *Oeconomicus* Xenophon treats the family as a social relationship for production. He is the first Greek author to give full recognition to the use-value of women's work, and to understand that domestic labour has economic value even if it lacks exchange-value. This idea was radical in the formal literature of classical Greece, and has yet to gain acceptance in modern times. Ischomachus compares his wife to a queen bee (see on vii. 32). The analogy between the good housekeeper and the bee can be traced as far back as Semonides fr. 7. 83–93 West. The poet makes a direct connection between the virtuous wife, domestic economy, and prosperity. The good wife increases her husband's wealth. But while Semonides merely compliments the good wife, Xenophon goes much further. In the *Oeconomicus* the married couple's property and its disposition are shared. The wife's labour in the house becomes the basis of her autonomy, of her status as queen bee, and of the possibility that she will rule over her husband if she proves to be a better manager than he is. This turns out to be the case in Ischomachus' household (see Ch. 4).

By means of her dowry, the wife contributed capital to the oikos. Ischomachus says to his wife: 'I go on paying into the common fund everything I have and you deposited everything you brought with you' (vii. 13). Some anthropologists have postulated that the dowry is usually found in societies where women are considered economic liabilities.[47] As Medea stated brutally, a woman needed a dowry to buy a husband (Eur. *Med.* 232–4). Ischomachus, however, does not regard his wife's dowry as simply a sort of trust fund to be used for the support of a person who is nothing but a parasite. Although his own payments into the household accounts are tangible and continual, Ischomachus values not only his wife's dowry, but her future contributions as well. He goes on to point out that an industrious woman will be honoured for her work, even in old age while other women are despised, presumably because their child-bearing years are past and they are considered useless (vii. 42). In Greek literature before Xenophon, weaving was women's only productive activity that was regularly accorded some recognition (see below, sect. H). Ischomachus' wife will probably be too busy to weave (see on vii. 6.) In fact, he acknowledges that his wife's contribution to the household may exceed his own (vii. 13–14 ὁπότερος ... συμβάλλεται). In other words, her potential contribution is no paltry sum; by being a prudent manager, she can be responsible for more than half the income of an oikos in the liturgical class.

The interest on an investment in education is not simple, but compound. Owing to her husband's instruction,

---

[47] For a review of the anthropological and historical literature see Diane Owen Hughes, 'From Brideprice to Dowry in Mediterranean Europe', *Journal of Family History*, 3 (1978), 262–96, repr. in *Women and History*, 10 (1985), 13–58.

Ischomachus' wife not only increased her own contribution to the household, but became capable of teaching others in turn. Ischomachus tells his wife that she can make her slaves twice as valuable by teaching them to be productive, and she protects the investment in human capital by nursing the slaves who are ill (vii. 37, 41).

H. *Profit and Work*

All the human members of an oikos may contribute to its successful operation or produce losses. Xenophon pays particular attention to those in authority, both male and female as well as slave and free. The husband and the wife can increase the estate (iii. 10, vii. 13–14). The housekeeper (ix. 12) and the bailiff, by producing a surplus, can create a profit ($\pi\epsilon\rho\iota\text{ov}$-$\sigma\acute{\iota}\alpha\nu$ xv. 1, xxi. 10). Even ordinary female slaves can increase the worth of the estate by doubling their own value when they learn to spin (vii. 41). Thus their work will contribute directly to the capital of the oikos.

Textile manufacture was the sole productive activity by women that the Greeks traditionally recognized as making an economic contribution. For example, the Law Code of Gortyn (inscribed in the 5th c. BC, but including earlier laws) directs that in case of divorce a woman might take with her half of what she had woven,[48] and weaving is the only work of respectable women to be depicted on classical vases. But, as Xenophon indicates in *Mem.* 2. 7, men were reluctant to regard such work, when done by family members rather than by slaves, as effectively producing cash, because working for money compromised the status of a free, respectable woman (see on vii. 6).[49] Historians, as well, have not given textile manufacture the attention it deserves. Among skilled workers listed on Linear B tablets from Cnossus and Pylos, large numbers of female and male textile workers are recorded.[50] The females

[48] *Inscr. Creticae*, iv. 72, col. 2. 48–52, col. 3. 17–24.

[49] Pomeroy, *Goddesses, Whores, Wives, and Slaves*, 71–3.

[50] For detailed discussion see John T. Killen, 'The Wool Industry of Crete in the Late Bronze Age', *ABSA* 59 (1964), 1–15; id., 'The Textile Industries at Pylos and Knossos', in C. W. Shelmerdine and T. G. Palaima (eds.), *Pylos Comes Alive: Industry and Administration in a Mycenaean Palace* (New York, 1984), 49–63. For some titles of

are more than twice as numerous as the males. That these women received the same food-rations as the men suggests that their work was considered both equally laborious and equal in value. The picture painted by the Homeric epics is consistent with the evidence of the tablets. In the *Iliad* and the *Odyssey*, female slaves were valued for their handiwork.[51] Their products were a significant commodity in the gift-exchange system.[52] For example, the ransom of Hector included twelve each of robes, mantles, blankets, cloaks, and tunics (*Il.* 24. 229–31), and Odysseus tells Laertes that he was once given twelve each of cloaks, blankets, robes, and tunics (*Od.* 24. 273–9). The Phaeacians gave Odysseus thirteen robes and thirteen tunics (*Od.* 8. 390–3). When we consider the amount of labour that must have been required to produce these textiles, we must reject Finley's view that female slaves were useful primarily for sexual purposes and that domestic slavery and products manufactured by women were important only for household consumption.[53]

Even after the introduction of a moneyed economy, textiles continued to function as liquid wealth, for they could be readily converted to cash. Textiles are recorded in temple inventories, for example that of Artemis Brauronia (*IG* ii². 1514–29). Articles of clothing (ἱμάτια) are inventoried individually on the Attic stelai listing confiscated property (*IG* i³. 421, col. 4.222–49). Demosthenes (27. 10) includes clothing as part of his inheritance and mentions that clothing and bedding (στρώματα) served as security for a loan (49. 22). In manumission inscriptions from classical Athens ταλασιουργοί ('spinners') constitute the largest group by far of manumitted workers whose special job is recorded. It should be assumed

specialized jobs see Pierre Carlier, 'La femme dans la société mycénienne d'après les archives en linéaire B', in E. Lévy (ed.), *La Femme dans les sociétés antiques: Actes des colloques de Strasbourg (mai 1980 et mars 1981)* (Strasburg, 1983), 29 n. 53. According to Arist. *HA* 5. 19, and Pliny, *NH* 11. 76, a Greek woman invented the weaving of silk.

[51] e.g. Agamemnon's expectation that Chryseis will both weave and serve as a sexual partner, *Il.* 1. 31.

[52] On textiles as part of the guest-friendship alliance system see most recently Beate Wagner-Hasel, 'Geschlecht und Gabe: Zum Brautgütersystem bei Homer', *ZRG* 105 (1988), 32–73.

[53] *Slavery in Classical Antiquity*, 58, '... domestic slaves, often an unproductive element...'.

that they purchased their freedom and were able to pay the 100 drachmas required for the dedication of a φιάλη ('cup') as a result of their work.[54] That female slaves were considered as productive as males is suggested by the fact that the average price of females and males listed in the Attic stelai was the same.[55] Doubtless, those slave women whose primary job was not wool-working were also expected to spin if they had any spare time. Xenophon may be referring to such activities when he mentions doubling a slave's value by teaching her to spin (see on viii. 41).

In the *Oeconomicus* (vii. 33–8), Ischomachus compares the estate to a beehive. Though Greek philosophers were uncertain about the sex of the leader of the bees, there was general agreement that the workers were female. According to the metaphor, then, female slaves function as worker-bees. They change raw materials into textiles. Similarly worker-bees weave combs and produce honey, a valuable commodity that can be sold. (Pliny, *NH* 11. 22 uses the words *textum* ['woven fabric'] and *tela* ['web'] in describing the building of the hive.) Ischomachus displays the stores of textiles belonging to his oikos: some are valuable enough to be locked in the master bedroom (θάλαμος ix. 3, 6). This hoard is a portion of the wealth of the oikos. An anthropological study of Sicily supplies information about how such textiles might have functioned as wealth in many spheres of exchange.[56] Until the middle of the twentieth century, brides brought to marriages substantial quantities of textiles which they had made and embroidered. These trousseaux were not totally designated for personal use: rather a portion was kept in reserve and regarded as capital, to be exchanged for food or cash in hard times. In classical Greece women of all social classes could weave and earn cash

---

[54] *IG* ii². 1553–8 in the new edition by D. M. Lewis, 'Attic Manumissions', *Hesperia*, 28 (1959), 208–38; id., 'Dedications of Phialai at Athens', ibid. 37 (1968), 368–80, and Helen McClees, *A Study of Women in Attic Inscriptions* (New York, 1920), 31. Davies, *Wealth*, 48, focuses on the few male industrial slaves in this document as a source of wealth, and ignores the numerous female wool-workers.

[55] See on vii. 41 ἀνεπιστήμονα ταλασίας ... διπλασίου and W. Kendrick Pritchett, 'The Attic Stelai: Part II', *Hesperia*, 25 (1956), 178–317.

[56] Jane Schneider, 'Trousseau as Treasure: Some Contradictions of Late Nineteenth-Century Change in Sicily', in Eric Ross (ed.), *Beyond the Myths of Culture* (Orlando, Fla., 1980), 323–56, republished in *Women and History*, 10 (1985), 81–119.

by this activity if necessary. Aeschines (1. 97) enumerates the skilled slaves inherited by Timarchus. Amongst them he makes specific and detailed mention of a woman skilled in working flax, who produced sheer textiles for the market. The scholion comments that these goods were very valuable (πολύτιμα). Ar. *Frogs* 1346–51 refers to what must have been a common situation: a poor woman in the agora, selling what she had woven. In Xen. *Mem.* 2. 7. 2–12 a large number of upper-class women are forced to move in with their relative Aristarchus, who cannot afford to maintain them; capital (ἀφορμή) was provided for the purchase of wool and the women became able to contribute to their own support by weaving. Weaving was so much a woman's job that Aristarchus is the only member of his household who continues to be idle (§ 12). In persuading Aristarchus to put his relatives to work for profit, Socrates reminds him that most of the Megarians make their living from the sale of textiles.[57] According to Xenophon (§ 6), the Megarians bought foreign slaves. They also harboured slaves who had run away from Athens. Thucydides 1. 139. 2, 7. 27. 5, refers to the slaves as ἀνδράποδα (at. 7. 27. 5 also as χειροτέχναι), but does not specify their sex. Ar. *Ach.* 524 supplies the information that the slaves were female; though we do not have to believe Dicaeopolis' allegation that they were prostitutes who had belonged to Aspasia, his statement indicates that women were among the runaways.[58] In any event, at Megara slaves manufactured inexpensive woollen clothing for export. With the proceeds, their masters were able to purchase the grain that was essential for their survival. The Athenian embargo against importing Megarian textiles and other products was a significant cause of the Peloponnesian War.[59] In other words,

---

[57] The Megarians had no fertile land, or harbours, or mines (Isoc. 8. 117): see Ronald P. Legon, *Megara* (Ithaca, NY, 1981), 280–2.

[58] Even if Aspasia ran a brothel, how many slaves could she have owned? See on iii. 14. De Ste. Croix, *The Class Struggle*, 506, assumes that the cheirotechnai were '*skilled* [itals. his] men'. A. W. Gomme, *A Historical Commentary on Thucydides*, i (Oxford, 1945), on 1. 139. 2, does discuss the female flax-worker in And. 1. 93.

[59] For the decree see Thuc. 1. 42. 2, 67. 4, 139. 1, Ephorus F 196 (=Diod. 12. 38. 4), Plut. *Per.*, 29–30. For references to textiles in the Megarian decree see e.g. Ar. *Ach.* 519, *Peace* 1002 (reading 'κ Μεγάρων in 1000).

the economy of an important Greek city was largely supported by the work of female slaves.

I. *Slaves in the* Oeconomicus

Whether slavery in general was hostile to the accumulation of capital, because of the slaves' supposed lack of energy and lack of interest in the creation and preservation of capital, has often been debated. Ischomachus and his wife, however, seek to avoid such a problem by incorporating slaves into their oikos more than was common in Athens, where slaves belonging to wealthy owners were considered as little more than property (see on i. 1 Οἰκονομικός). Ischomachus' treatment of the housekeeper and farm foremen parallels his treatment of his wife. At first all three are outsiders, who must be transformed into insiders so that they will be as concerned as he is about the success of the oikos. Ischomachus selects his wife, his housekeeper, and his foremen carefully, and trains them (see Ch. 4). Evidently he expects them all to remain permanently: at least he never mentions that the slaves will be manumitted or sold. Nor will they run away. They must be trustworthy so that they can be sent to work on Ischomachus' scattered properties or lead his valuable horse from the farm to the city (xi. 18 and see above, sect. D). Indeed, they will prefer to stay with their master and mistress, for they are well treated (vii. 38). The mistress looks after the health of the slaves personally (vii. 37) and the master hesitates to make sexual advances to an unwilling slave (x. 12).

Ischomachus and his wife also employ a system of rewards and incentives. Slaves are loyal because they are given various forms of partnerships. The loyalty of slaves such as the housekeeper and foremen, who work in a supervisory capacity, is ensured by making them partners in the losses and gains of the oikos. They are even given a share of the profits (ix. 11–13, xii. 9, 16). Good slaves are differentiated from their inferiors by the clothing allocated to them (xiii. 10). As vase-painting indicates and as the Old Oligarch complains (Ps.-Xen. *Const. of Ath.* 1. 10), it was impossible to distinguish slaves from free people by their appearance. Therefore the allocation of clothing according to merit implies that good slaves may be rewarded by decent clothing. According to Ps.-Arist. *Oec.* (1344^a35), the lot of slaves consists of work, punishments, and food. In contrast, while Ischomachus mentions the possibility of bad slaves, he usually emphasizes rewarding the good ones, rather than punishing the bad. Furthermore, the Pseudo-Aristotelian text advocates allowing slaves to reproduce so that the children shall serve as hostages for their parents' good behaviour and replace them when they are manumitted (1344^b17-18; Arist. *Pol.* 1330^a32-3 also recommends manumission as a reward). Ischomachus considers children a reward for slaves who have demonstrated their virtues, rather than forbidding procreation or using children as a potential means of disciplining the parents (ix. 5). He does not allude to manumission or sale; therefore slave families will not be dissolved.

In his attitude towards slaves, as in his views of women, Xenophon appears liberal, or even radical. Slaves are usually seen as rational and behaving as well as their owners; but occasionally they are assimilated to animals in an unflattering comparison (xiii. 9), are said to need severe punishment, and are described as given to vices such as drunkenness, sloth, and lechery (xii. 11–13).

Xenophon's views on slaves are consistent with his ideas about women and non-Greeks. In the *Oeconomicus*, there is no natural hierarchy among human beings according to gender, race, or class. Men and women, slave and free, potentially have the same virtues, vices, and talents (e.g., vii. 15, x. 1, xii). Obedience is not demeaning.[60] In fact, if the wife of Ischomachus demonstrates that she is superior to her husband, he will gladly become her servant (vii. 42). Like women, slaves are teachable and can learn to exercise the kingly skill of command (xiii. 4).[61] Furthermore, slaves are not demeaned simply on the basis of the work they perform. Xenophon does not distinguish slave labour from free. Although some kinds of employment are rejected as mechanical (iv. 2 βαναυσικαί),

---

[60] For a different attitude towards being subject to the will of another, see on xii. 3 and the views of Eutherus in Xen. *Mem.* 2. 8. 3.

[61] Similarly, in *Revenues* 4. 39, 42, Xenophon suggests that slaves serve in the military. Evidently he does not fear rebellion or desertion.

Ischomachus and his wife, like the female relatives of Aristarchus in the *Memorabilia*, often do the very same agricultural and domestic work as slaves. They are ennobled by such work and ennoble it for slaves as well.

Xenophon was by no means a conservative in his views on slavery. The slaves of Ischomachus and his wife were probably not of Greek descent (see on ix. 5). However, there is no natural mental or physical difference between free Greeks and their slaves. Xenophon uses the same language to describe them (see on iii. 10 and iv. 15). Slaves who are given positions of authority possess the same moral qualities as their master and mistress. They might even rule over other slaves as kings rule their subjects (xxi. 10). They do not, as an inevitable consequence of their social class, manifest the psychic inferiority that Aristotle imputes to the natural slave (*Pol.* 1252ª31–4, 1254ᵇ17–19, 1260ª12, 1280ª33–4). The fact that Ischomachus expects his slaves to understand that it is in their interest to obey reveals his belief that they will be guided by their own rationality (xiii. 9–10). The bailiff is taught to be able to take his master's place (xiii. 4). Both the bailiff and the housekeeper, like Ischomachus and his wife, are to be temperate in their appetites, loyal, and enthusiastic about increasing the family's property (vii. 30). Ischomachus treats his slaves according to laws applicable to citizens rather than those governing slaves (xiv. 4). The master and mistress reward the housekeeper for meritorious behaviour by granting her greater wealth and freedom (ix. 13), and reward the bailiff by honouring him (xii. 16) and by treating him as a gentleman (xiv. 9 ὥσπερ ἐλευθέροις and καλούς τε κἀγαθούς). In contrast, some people of the highest economic class are metaphorically deemed to be slaves by their own volition owing to their ignoble character (i. 17, x. 10). Although Xenophon, like his contemporaries, took slavery for granted and assumed the system could be lucrative, he did not have a theory of natural slavery.

6

The *Oeconomicus* after Xenophon

A. *Greece*

The earliest extant adaptation of Xenophon's *Oeconomicus* is the *Oeconomica* included among the works of Aristotle.[1] According to Philodemus (Περὶ οἰκονομίας, col. 7. 38, 44, col. 27. 14), the author was actually Theophrastus; modern scholars attribute it to a student of Theophrastus or to another student of Aristotle, and some posit more than one author.[2] Books 1 and 3 deal with the relationship of husband and wife, and the differences between it and its predecessor draw attention to the radical ideas in Xenophon's work. Consistent with Peripatetic thinking, expressed most succinctly in Arist. *Pol.* 1, the Pseudo-Aristotelian text assumes that the oikos will be managed according to principles of hierarchy and inequality, and that the wife will obey the husband. (For a brief synopsis of Aristotle's views on the family, see Ch. 4. On differences between Xenophon and Pseudo-Aristotle in the treatment of slaves see Ch. 5, sect. I.) He is to have the supreme authority

[1] Karl Münscher, *Xenophon in der griechisch-römischen Literatur* (*Philologus*, Supplementband 13 2; Leipzig, 1920), cites echoes of Xenophon in later literature. His survey, though useful, is not complete: he traces Xenophon's influence primarily as a literary phenomenon and does not discuss the various historical contexts in which his works were revived or discussed. E. Richter, *Xenophon in der römischen Literatur* (Berlin, 1905), is also useful. Significant parallel passages from other classical authors will be cited in the Commentary below.

[2] See further Chr. Jensen, *Philodemi Περὶ οἰκονομίας* (Leipzig, 1906), p. xxx n. 1, and Renato Laurenti, *Studi sull'Economico attribuito ad Aristotele* (Milan, 1968), 29. B. A. van Groningen and André Wartelle, *Aristote: Économique* (Paris, 1968), date the work to 325–275 BC. Ulrich Victor, [*Aristoteles*] *Oikonomikos: Das erste Buch der Ökonomik—Handschriften, Text, Übersetzung und Kommentar—und seine Beziehungen zur Ökonomikliteratur* (Königstein im Taurus, 1983), compares the language of select portions of Xenophon and Pseudo-Aristotle; he suggests (pp. 188–92) that both derive from a lost work by Antisthenes (on which see i. 1), but this is not persuasive. The models for Pseudo-Aristotle are Xenophon's *Oeconomicus* and the works of Aristotle (see this chapter and the Commentary, *passim*).

regarding the allocation of food, considered a slave's salary (1344^a36-^b4), and he alone educates the children (1344^a8). In Xen. *Oec.* vii. 11–12, the mother shares in educating the children and giving the daughter in marriage, while in Pseudo-Aristotle (1344^a7), she only nurtures the children. Contrary to custom, the husband is to confine his sexual activities to his own household (1344^a12). A similar but more detailed restriction appears as well in Pl. *Laws* 841 D, but Pseudo-Aristotle may also have been influenced by Stoic or Neo-Pythagorean ideas.

Along with the interest in the private sphere and the individual, marriage and the proper conduct of husband and wife became a common theme in philosophical literature in the Hellenistic period.[3] Perhaps it was because Xenophon did not found a philosophical school that, with the exception of the Pseudo-Aristotelian *Oeconomica*, the *Oeconomicus* does not seem to have had much direct influence in the generations immediately following his death. That Claude Vatin devotes only half a sentence to Xenophon in a wide-ranging survey of this literature suggests that he was of little significance to the authors of extant Hellenistic treatises on domestic conduct and the household economy (including Neo-Pythagoreans and Plutarch), who paid closer attention to the writings of members of the philosophical schools.[4] The following survey is confined to those works in which Xenophon is actually named or where his influence can be detected.

B. *Rome*

Surviving quotations and paraphrases leave no doubt that Romans read Xenophon's *Oeconomicus* and, for the most part, approved of it. The elder Cato, who did not usually admire Greek literature, is represented by Cicero (*De Sen.* 59) as

---

[3] For this literature, see Pomeroy, *Goddesses, Whores, Wives, and Slaves*, 132–6; ead., *Women in Hellenistic Literature*, 67–71; and Claude Vatin, *Recherches sur le mariage et la condition de la femme mariée à l'époque hellénistique*, esp. ch. 1.

[4] Ibid. 21. For a review of the development of economic ideas in Greek philosophical literature see Albert Augustus Trever, *A History of Greek Economic Thought* (Chicago, 1916).

recommending the books of Xenophon and finding the
Oeconomicus particularly useful.

The extant text of Philodemus' Περὶ οἰκονομίας (1st c. BC),
opens with a discussion of Xenophon's views.[5] Philodemus is
highly critical of Xenophon's materialism and criticizes him
for using Socrates in a work on economics because, he asserts,
the philosopher did not exhibit any need of money (col. 5).
Philodemus does not approve of Xenophon's idealism, either,
and criticizes him for what he considered to be the impractical
application of philosophical principles in his system of education, inasmuch as the historical reality of classical Athens was
so different from Xenophon's recommendations (col. 7). As an
Epicurean, he questions whether a wife is necessary for the
management of the household and the peaceful life which suits
a philosopher (col. 27). He also asks whether a woman is
capable of learning her proper duties and whether a husband
is responsible for his wife's errors (col. 2. 4).[6]

Cicero, who was a contemporary of Philodemus, considered
Xenophon's ethical teachings so useful that he translated the
Oeconomicus around 85 BC, when he was 20 (*De Off.* 2. 87). His
translation seems to have circulated widely: Varro, Columella,
Pliny, and Quintilian quote or paraphrase from Cicero's version, rather than from the Greek.[7] Surviving quotations indicate that Cicero did not make a literal translation, according
to modern standards, but rather a paraphrase with some
additions.[8]

The *Oeconomicus* was so easily transported to the world of
Rome that Servius (*Georg.* 1.43) could say of it: *praecepta habet*

[5] For the text see Jensen. For reconstructions and discussion see e.g. Renato
Laurenti, *Filodemo e il pensiero economico degli epicurei* (Milan, 1973), and Marcello
Gigante, *Ricerche filodemee* 2nd edn. (Naples, 1983), 105–7.
[6] According to Knut Kleve, 'Scurra Atticus: The Epicurean view of Socrates', in
G. Pugliese Caratelli (ed.), *Suzetesis: Studi sull'epicureismo greco e romano offerti a Marcello
Gigante* (Naples, 1983), i. 233–4, 238–42, Philodemus was actually criticizing Socrates,
rather than Xenophon.
[7] For the testimony and fragments see G. Garbarino, *M. Tulli Ciceronis Fragmenta
ex libris philosophicis, ex aliis libris deperditis, ex scriptis incertis,* (Florence, 1984) 15–17,
65–83, differing considerably from the earlier collection by V. Lundström, 'Ciceros
öfversättning af Xenophons Oikonomikos', *Eranos,* 12 (1912), 1–31.
[8] *Contra* Luigi Alfonsi, 'La traduzione ciceroniana dell'Economico di Senofonte',
Ciceroniana, 3–6 (1961–4), 7–17, who argues that the translation was faithful to the
Greek original. See also below, 'Remarks on the Translation'.

quemadmodum debeat materfamilias domi agere ('it contains instructions on the domestic conduct of the mistress of the household'). Cicero's first-hand knowledge of women, such as his own wife Terentia, who were competent in business and managed vast amounts of money and real property, will have led him to find the authority vested in the wife of Ischomachus within the realm of reality. In a period of civil war and sexual freedom, Xenophon's text appealed to Roman nostalgia for 'the good old days' when marriage was a natural union in which mothers were honoured and actively involved in educating their children, and wives were happy to be rewarded for thrift, industry, and chastity.[9] In that Golden Age, a rural husband and wife performed the work which later Romans delegated to a *vilicus* ('slave foreman on an estate') and *vilica* ('slave "wife" of slave foreman'; Col., *RR* 11. 1. 5, 12 pr., and see on cc. vii–x, esp. vii. 32 ἡ τῶν μελιττῶν ἡγεμών). Columella contrasts his own time, when women did not even supervise wool-making, nor would they wear home-made clothing, or enjoy a visit to the country. Marriage was no longer a partnership; instead, by employing *sine manu* marriage, husband and wife kept their property separate. The vices of indolent and wealthy women which Columella enumerates at length are similar to those about which Ischomachus had warned his wife.

The greatest differences between the Greek original and the Roman versions appear in the discussion of slaves (see Ch. 5, sect. I). Xenophon could mould the slaves who held positions of leadership according to the models of their own master and mistress for whom they were able to serve as surrogates; whereas Columella was obliged to invoke exemplars from the remote past. Other Roman agronomists readily adopted Xenophon's ideas about slaves in positions of authority. Cato (*De Agr.* 5. 2) specifically recommends that the *vilicus* reward slaves for good work and that he himself be temperate (*ne sit ambulator, sobrius siet semper . . .*). Columella declares that the *vilicus* should be abstemious in respect to drinking, sleep, and sexual activity (*RR* 11. 1. 13). He ascribes the virtues of Ischomachus' wife to the *vilica*, foreman's wife, who was a

---

[9] On the Roman ideal see Suzanne Dixon, *The Roman Mother* (Norman, Okla., and London, 1988).

slave, and also (*RR* 12. 2) transfers to her some of the particularly female duties which the bee-wife had performed in Xenophon's *Oeconomicus* (see on xii. 11–13). The good *vilica* is what the epitaphs regularly call a *custos* ('guardian'). She stores the estate's possessions and provisions in an orderly fashion and supervises the expenditures. Her sexual conduct is beyond reproach. In Rome, the norm for both male and female slaves is heterosexuality and 'marriage' (*contubernium*, i.e. *de facto* marriage, though without legal force). The 'marriage' of the *vilicus* and *vilica* has the potential to be excessively passionate, with the result that the *vilicus* will spend too much time indoors in order to enjoy his wife's embraces. In contrast, the slaves in Ischomachus' household are segregated by sex. One criterion for the selection of the housekeeper is that she can control her sexual appetite (ix. 11); she does not hold her position by virtue of any quasi-marriage or other relationship with a man. Well-behaved slaves are permitted to have heterosexual intercourse, but this relationship is said to be for the purpose of reproduction (τεκνοποιῶνται ix. 5). Whereas Columella (*RR* 12. 1. 2–3) is concerned lest the *vilicus* become too lecherous toward the *vilica*, Ischomachus worries that his foremen may be distracted by affairs with boys (παιδικά xii. 14).

Cicero (*De Inv.* 1. 51–2), describes a brief conversation between Aspasia, Xenophon, and Xenophon's wife; he cites Aeschines as his source. This anecdote evidently derived from Aeschines' dialogue *Aspasia*.[10] Aeschines may have also served as Xenophon's source for the first part of the *Oeconomicus*, which ends with the promise to bring in Aspasia (see on iii. 14 Ἀσπασίαν). Xenophon certainly knew Aeschines' work, but it is not improbable that Aeschines also knew Xenophon's. Therefore we should not eliminate the possibility that the *Oeconomicus* was written first, and served as Aeschines' source. Such a hypothesis would explain the interest in conjugal relations attributed to Xenophon by Aeschines. In any event, after a few questions on marriage, to which Xenophon's wife gives responses which are shown to be absurd, Aspasia—now a moralist—gives her the correct answers, culminating in an

---

[10] So H. Dittmar, *Aischines von Sphettos: Studien zur Literaturgeschichte der Sokratiker* (Berlin, 1912), 32–4.

assertion that a wife should prefer her own husband despite
the superior attractions of other men. Quintilian (5. 11. 28–9)
quotes the passage from Cicero as an example of Socratic
inductive reasoning.[11]

Among the twenty-six papyrus fragments of Xenophon are
two fragments of the *Oeconomicus* (see Ch. 7, sect. A). The lack
of popularity may be attributable to mere chance or to the
fact that the oikos system was not established in Egypt and
that farming methods were not the same as in mainland
Greece. However, many other works of classical Greek literature were read despite their inappropriateness to local
conditions.

C. *Middle Ages*

Cicero's version of the *Oeconomicus* was known to Jerome[12]
and the original was cited in Greek lexica (see Ch. 7, sect. A).
However, by the seventh century both may have become rare,

---

[11] The anecdote is mentioned by Alcuin, *Disputatio de rhetorica et de virtutibus* 30
(p. 540 Halm). Alcuin substitutes *philosophus quidam* ('some male philosopher') for
Aspasia and expands the interview so that the philosopher poses similar questions to
both Xenophon and his wife. A meeting between Aspasia and Xenophon's wife was
chronologically improbable inasmuch as the last datable event in Aspasia's life was
her marriage to Lysicles and the birth of their son Poristes around 428 BC (see Davies,
APF 458). If she was at that time in her early thirties at the very least, she probably
did not survive until Xenophon's marriage in the 390s. Therefore the meeting may
be yet another instance of the anachronisms of the Socratics. Moreover, it was unlikely
that an upper-class Greek husband would allow his young wife to converse with a
woman who had been a hetaira, even if she was quite old, although some conventions
were breached towards the end of the Peloponnesian War and following it, and
Aspasia was surely an unusual enough woman to have become an exception to rules.
(See Pomeroy, *Goddesses, Whores, Wives, and Slaves*, 66, 119.) In Cicero's own time
respectable women were not secluded and distinctions between *matronae* and courtesans
were less carefully drawn; nevertheless, courtesans were not socially acceptable: the
notion of a courtesan giving advice to a legitimate wife would have seemed bizarre
in Rome as it was in classical Athens. The anecdote displays features of a fictional
biography which was derived from the subject's own work, in this case the *Oeconomicus*.
Following this pseudo-biographical tradition Marius Victorinus (pp. 240–1 Halm)
explains that Xenophon and his wife quarrelled frequently and that Aspasia was
invited to reconcile their differences.

[12] Jerome, preface to Pentateuch; *Epp.* 57. 5. 2, 106. 3. 3, 121. 6. 6–7 (CSEL
54. 508, 55. 250, 56. 22); *Adv. Rufin.* 2. 25 (CCSL 79. 63). Garbarino 69–70 includes
an eleven-word passage in Priscian (fr. 4) and a nine-word sentence in Donatus
(fr. 5), but the sentiments are too commonplace and the passages too brief to be
definitely attributed to Cicero's translation.

for Isidore of Seville fails to mention the *Oeconomicus* in a list of works on agriculture.[13] Among the works of Hugo of Saint-Victor appears a brief Latin paraphrase of Xenophon's idea that the man should work outdoors and the woman indoors, but he is probably quoting from Columella as he does in the succeeding sentence.[14] Petrarch mentions that he learnt about Xenophon's *Oeconomicus* from Cicero's *De Senectute* and *De Officiis* (*Fam.* 3. 18). In a fictional letter to Cicero, Petrarch laments the loss of his translation (*Fam.* 24. 4). Of course, much of classical literature failed to survive. The Byzantine tradition of the *Oeconomicus* is no worse than that of Xenophon's *opera minora*.

D. *The Renaissance: Italy*

Although Roman agronomists were interested in the entire text of the *Oeconomicus*, most commentators have lavished far more attention on the sections which deal with the relationships of wives and husbands than on Xenophon's discussion of agriculture. Because of its focus on women, marriage, and gender roles, the vicissitudes of the *Oeconomicus* after the death of Xenophon shed some light on later attitudes toward these subjects.[15] During the Renaissance in Italy, the views of Plutarch and the Pseudo-Aristotelian *Oeconomica* were influential on Francesco and Ermolao Barbaro, Giovanni Caldiera, Leon Battista Alberti, and other fifteenth-century humanists who wrote about the family.[16] Leonardo Bruni's translation of the first two books of the Pseudo-Aristotelian work circulated widely after its publication in 1420 and was extremely influential. Two hundred and twenty-three copies are extant.[17]

---

[13] *Etym.* 17. 1. 1. Arévalo does not draw attention to the omission of Xenophon: 'Ad S. Isidori Etymologias Arevali Notae' (PL 82. 1003–16).

[14] *De nuptiis* 1. 1 (PL 176. 1206 A), printed without ascription among spurious works.

[15] The following brief survey is not intended to be a complete review of the *Nachleben* of Xenophon's *Oeconomicus*. Rather it provides a context in which to discuss the remarkable phenomenon of the popularity of this work in Renaissance England.

[16] I am grateful to Barbara Harris, Margaret Leah King, Benjamin G. Kohl, and Margaret Lael Mikesell for their comments on the humanists.

[17] Josef Soudek, 'Leonardo Bruni and his Public: A Statistical and Interpretative Study of his Annotated Latin Version of the (Pseudo-) Aristotelian *Economics*', *Studies in Medieval and Renaissance History*, 5 (1968), 52, mentions an additional six copies which are known to have existed.

Xenophon's *Oeconomicus* was much less popular and influential than Pseudo-Aristotle's *Oeconomica*. The first Italian to translate it into Latin was Lampus Biragus;[18] his translation, dedicated to Pope Nicholas V (1447–55) was never printed and has survived in only four copies.[19] According to the Italian humanists of the fifteenth century, marriage was to be as hierarchical as the governmental, religious, and social structures in their own world. As Caldiera makes clear in *De iconomica*, the paterfamilias is to rule the family. The wife obeys him, the children obey the parents, next come the servants, with animals occupying the lowest rank. The wife is considered principally as an instrument for reproduction.[20]

The reiteration of selected themes which also appear in Xenophon's *Oeconomicus*—such as references to the beehive, the army, and the chorus, and to the laws of Lycurgus banning the wearing of cosmetics (see on x. 2)—but do not appear in Pseudo-Aristotle's *Oeconomica* shows that Alberti and Francesco Barbaro had read Xenophon but chose to recommend the family structure in the Pseudo-Aristotelian text.[21] Barbaro, more than the other civic humanists who dealt with marriage, was influenced by Xenophon: he writes in praise of marriage, citing the companionship, intimacy, and mutual respect that a married couple may enjoy.[22]

[18] On Biragus, see M. Miglio in *Dizionario biografico degli italiani* (Rome, 1968), x. 595–7. Aurispa had visited Byzantium in 1422 and returned with all the works of Xenophon: see J. Gil, *Jenofonte: Económico* (Madrid, 1966), 141.

[19] A Latin translation of the *Oeconomicus* (by Raphael Maffei of Volterra) was not printed in Italy until the 16th c. The earliest published commentaries were those by Joachim Camerarius (Leipzig, 1564) and Franciscus Portus (Paris, 1586). I am grateful to D. Marsh for sending me a preliminary draft of his article 'Xenophon', in Virginia Brown (ed.), *Mediaeval and Renaissance Latin Translations*, vii (Washington, DC, forthcoming).

[20] See further Margaret Leah King, 'Caldiera and the Barbaros on Marriage and the family: Humanist Reflections of Venetian Realities', *Journal of Medieval and Renaissance Studies*, 6 (1976), 19–50.

[21] See Benjamin G. Kohl, introduction and notes to his translation of Francesco Barbaro, *De re uxoria*, in Benjamin G. Kohl and Ronald G. Witt (eds.), *The Earthly Republic* (Philadelphia, 1978), 179–228, and Joan Kelly-Gadol, *Leon Battista Alberti: Universal Man of the Early Renaissance* (Chicago, 1969), esp. 225–6, on *De familia*, 'in which Alberti was imitating Xenophon in the person of the good bourgeois, Gianozzo'.

[22] Barbaro makes direct reference to the *Oeconomicus* in *De re uxoria*, 17. 5, written in 1416. Percy Gothein, *Das Buch von der Ehe* (Berlin, 1933), notes, *passim*, draws attention to his debts to Xenophon and other classical authors. David Herlihy and Christiane Klapisch-Zuber, *Tuscans and their Families* (New Haven, Conn., 1985),

E. *The Renaissance: England*

The picture was different a century later in England, where humanists at Cambridge held Xenophon in high esteem and were influential in gaining a wider readership for the *Oeconomicus* than it had probably enjoyed at any time in the past. Sir John Cheke, Provost of King's College, who became Regius Professor in 1540 and then tutor to Prince Edward, was accustomed to giving texts of Xenophon to students to encourage their study of Greek.[23] Roger Ascham considered that Cheke was the principal influence on his own education and agreed with Cheke's preferences among Greek authors. Both preferred prose. Ascham thought that Xenophon was particularly useful for student and schoolmaster alike: 'But chefely I wolde wisshe and (if I were of authoritie) I wolde counsel al the yong gentlemen of this realme, neuer to lay out of theyr handes .ii. authors Xenophon in Greke, and Cęsar in Latyn.'[24] Ascham considered himself well qualified to write a historical report on politics in Germany, for he had the guidance of Xenophon and Caesar: 'What better commoditie to know the trouth any writer in Greeke Latine or other toung hath had, I can not perceiue, except onely Xenophon, Cæsar, and Phillip Comines.'[25] From the frequency and manner in which Ascham refers to the *Anabasis* and the *Cyropaedia* in

229–31, distinguish Barbaro from the more 'patriarchal' civic humanists. Similarly, in post-Reformation Germany, the Aristotelian view of the family, which had been fundamental to scholasticism, was not rejected. Moreover, the legacy of Roman law served to enhance the view of the father as all-powerful paterfamilias. See Dieter Schwab, 'Familie', in Otto Brunner, Werner Conze, and Reinhart Koselleck (eds.), *Geschichtliche Grundbegriffe* (Stuttgart, 1975), ii. 259.

[23] Richard Mulcaster, *Positions concerning the Training Up of Children* (London, 1581; repr. Amsterdam, 1971), 244. A British Library copy (525 c. 26) of a Spanish translation of the *Oeconomicus*, together with philosophical works by Cicero, licensed by the inquisitors on 10 Oct. 1545 and reprinted at Antwerp together with other works in or after 1549, appears in the handwritten catalogue of the Old Royal Library and bears on its spine, albeit after rebinding, the device E.VI.R. The original binding may well have indicated Edward's ownership. (Information kindly supplied by the Reading Room Information and Admission Section, British Library.)

[24] Ascham, *Toxophilus* (London, 1545; repr. Menston, 1971), A, fos. 24ᵛ–25ʳ; at *The Scholemaster* (London, 1570; repr. Menston, 1967), 2, fo. 52ʳ, Ascham reports that Cheke considered the Bible, Cicero, Plato, Aristotle, Xenophon, Isocrates, and Demosthenes sufficient to make 'an excellent man'.

[25] Ascham, *A Report and Discourse of the affaires and state of Germany* (London, *c.*1570). fo. 2ʳ.

Toxophilus and *The Scholemaster* we may surmise that these two were his special favourites.

A study of the popularity of ancient historians from 1450 to 1700 in Europe based on vernacular editions shows the *Cyropaedia* to be the most widely circulated of Xenophon's writings and the fourth most popular Greek historical work in this period.[26] The popularity of the *Cyropaedia* was probably inspired, at least in part, by Renaissance interest in the education of the ideal prince who would reign with justice and wisdom. The popularity of the *Cyropaedia* may have inspired interest in the *Oeconomicus*, inasmuch as Cyrus the Great appears in both (see on iv. 18). The *Cyropaedia*, like Plato's *Republic*, described the training of the virtuous ruler. However, Tudor England had to confront the possibility that the ruler might be female and that the system of education devised for a boy might not be totally appropriate for a girl. Ascham was appointed tutor to Princess Elizabeth in 1548 and they studied together, with intervals, for over twenty years.[27] Among the Greeks, they read mostly prose authors. Elizabeth herself is said to have translated Xenophon's *Hiero*.[28]

Owing largely to the patronage of educated women, several humanistic works dealing with women and the family, and showing the influence of Xenophon, became popular in Renaissance England. Catherine of Aragon was a highly educated woman who became largely responsible for bringing Xenophon's ideas about estate management back into currency. Daughter of Isabella of Castile, who knew Latin, Catherine began to read and write Latin as a child. As an

[26] Peter Burke, 'A Survey of the Popularity of Ancient Historians, 1450–1700', *History and Theory*, 5 (1966), 135–52. I am grateful to Joan Todd for this reference.

[27] Gloria Kaufman, 'Juan Luis Vives on the Education of Women', *Signs*, 3 (1978), 893–4, suggests that Catherine Parr, who read Greek and Latin, was responsible for Elizabeth's early knowledge of the classics.

[28] See J. Nichols, *The Progresses and Public Processions of Queen Elizabeth* (London, 1823), i, p. x n. 3. T. W. Baldwin, *William Shakespere's small Latine & lesse Greeke* (Urbana, Ill., 1944), i. 282, argues that Elizabeth made this translation under the tutelage of Sir Henry Savile, because Xenophon appears to have been Savile's Greek favourite, but he underestimates the widespread enthusiasm for Xenophon prevalent in the period. However, according to L. Bradner, 'The Xenophon Translation Attributed to Queen Elizabeth I', *JWI* 7 (1964), 324–6, the translation of *Hiero* (MS Ff. 6. 3) in the Cambridge University Library which Tanner had attributed to Elizabeth is not in her hand or style.

adult, she was a patron of scholars. One of her beneficiaries was her countryman Juan Luis Vives, who was born at Valencia in 1492. Catherine became his patron while he was studying in Leuven with Erasmus.[29] She invited him to come to England to supervise the education of Princess Mary. In 1523 Vives published *De institutione feminae christianae*, which he wrote for Mary and dedicated to Catherine. She commissioned Sir Thomas More to translate Vives's treatise, but More delegated the assignment to Richard Hyrde, whom he had employed as a tutor for his family. The first English translation was published by Thomas Berthelet[30] under the title *A very frutefull and pleasant boke called the Instruction of a Christen Woman* in 1529, followed by at least eight more editions.[31] Vives's treatise was also translated into French, German, and Italian in the 1540s. This book was the first, and for a long time, the only full-length work of the English Renaissance written specifically on women's education, and it remained the most authoritative sixteenth-century treatise on this subject. Not only did it constitute part of the curriculum for women, but it served to advocate their education. Although Vives more consistently adopts the views of Aristotle, Xenophon's influence can be detected in his positive views of women's capabilities.

The Preface to the translation mentions that 'Xenophon and Aristotle, gyuyng rules of house kepyng, and Plato, makyng preceptes of orderyng the common weale, spake many thynges appertaynyng vnto the womans office and dewte.' Vives declares that Xenophon was the most important of the authors who wrote on οἰκονομική.[32] Xenophon, Aristotle,

[29] On Vives and his circle see further Foster Watson, *Vives and the Renascence Education of Women* (London, 1912).

[30] On Berthelet, who was one of the most prolific Elizabethan printers, see H. S. Bennett, *English Books and Readers 1475 to 1557* (Cambridge, 1952), *passim*.

[31] W. A. Jackson, F. S. Ferguson, and Katherine F. Pantzer, *A Short-Title Catalogue of Books Printed in England, Scotland, and Ireland and of English Books Printed Abroad, 1475–1640*, rev. edn., 3 vols. (Oxford, 1976–91). ii, 429, give the date of the first edition (*STC* 24856, 24856.5) as 1529?, with further editions: 24857, 1531?; 24858, 1541; 24859, 1547 (1541); 24860 and 24861, 1557; 24862, 1585; and 24863, 1592. According to David Cressy, *Literacy and the Social Order* (Cambridge, 1980), 47, an edition usually consisted of 1,500 copies, at most. Kenneth Charlton, *Education in Renaissance England* (London, 1965), 108, gives 1,250 as the usual size.

[32] *De tradendis disciplinis*, 5. 3 (*Opera omnia*, ed. G. Mayans, vi [Valencia, 1785], 406).

Plutarch, and Plato are the pagan Greek authors he specifically includes in curricula designed for girls, but this list is not exhaustive, for Vives adds *et similibus*.[33]

In 1529, a year after his departure from England, Vives published *De officio mariti*, a companion work to his *De institutione feminae christianae*. In his writings on domestic conduct, he exhibits his debt to Xenophon. He emphasizes the importance of domestic harmony, the value of marriage, and the woman's role in creating the proper domestic milieu so that the man's home may be to him a haven from the worries and anxieties of life: *neque vero sic vituperare ullus ausus est muliebre genus, quin rem optimam, auspicatissimam, prosperrimam, fateretur esse bonam mulierem; et, quemadmodum Xenophon in Oeconomicis inquit: maximum ad viri felicitatem momentum* ('And truly no man durste euer so farre dispreyse woman kynd: but he must nedes confesse, that a good woman is the beste treasure, and most lucky and prosperous thynge that can be. And as Xenophon saythe, she is the grettest cause of mans felicite').[34] Vives explicitly rejects the heathen view that equated caring for the household with preserving wealth.[35] Nevertheless, each member of the household must have a special, appropriate function, so that no one may be lazy, nor must anyone intrude on the duty of another, or consult the interest of his convenience only. The wife is to be trained in pharmacology so that she can cure common ailments like stomach-ache, headache, and worms, and plan the proper diet for her family. She should be skilled in all aspects of housewifery, especially cooking and textile manufacture, and should apply herself to wool-working to fill her idle moments.[36] Reproduction and the sexual side of marriage are scarcely mentioned.

The husband is the authority, even in the domestic sphere. Beginning with the *Oeconomicus*, all books on domestic conduct assume that men start out by knowing more than women about managing a household. As Xenophon had invoked royal

---

[33] Vives, *De institutione feminae Christianae* 1. 5, (*Opera omnia*, iv [1783], 89), and *De officio mariti*, 3 (ibid. 369).

[34] Vives, *De institutione feminae Christianae*, 2. 1 (*Opera omnia*, iv. 173).

[35] *De tradendis disciplinis*, 5, 3 (*Opera omnia*, vi. 406).

[36] Vives, *De institutione feminae Christianae*, 2. 10 (*Opera omnia*, iv. 249–52).

paradigms in the instruction of Ischomachus' wife (vii. 32), Vives uses Catherine as his model. However, perhaps in response to Xenophon, Vives insists upon the dominance of the man over the woman in all circumstances, citing St Paul (1 Tim. 2. 12–13): But I gyue no lycence to a woman to be a techer, nor to haue authorite of the man, but to be in silence. For Adam was the fyrst made, and after Eue...'.[37] Vives, like other Renaissance authors, and like Xenophon himself, cites Sparta as an example to be emulated, noting that Lycurgus banished all cosmetics, preferring women to be regarded by their virtue, and not their ornaments.[38] Citing Socrates' statement in Xenophon's *Symposium* (2. 9) that 'the womans witte is no lesse apte to al thinges, then the mans is: she wanteth but counsell and strengthe',[39] Vives argues that women are teachable. Moreover, education strengthens virtue: paradigms of womanhood including Cornelia, Laelia, Porcia, Cleobulina, and Theano demonstrate that no learned woman was ever evil.[40] Vives asserts that one of the husband's Christian duties is to be his wife's teacher, and gives further advice about a wife's curriculum. She is to learn 'that, whiche parteyneth vnto the ornament of her soule, and the keping and ordring of an house'; his recommendations for women's reading include Aristotle's and Xenophon's works on household economy.[41]

With the exception of extremely privileged women such as Lady Jane Grey and the daughters of Sir Thomas More, few women, even in Catherine's circle, could read Greek. If girls could read at all, they read only the vernacular. (On the literacy of English women see below.) In 1532 Gentian Hervet

---

[37] *De institutione feminae Christianae*, 1. 4, *et sim. passim*, (*Opera omnia*, iv. 84–5).

[38] *De institutione feminae Christianae*, 1. 8, sim. 2. 8 (*Opera omnia*, iv. 106, 228–34). On cosmetics see *Oec.* x. 2–9. On Xenophon's admiration of Sparta and the Spartan ideal see Elizabeth Rawson, *The Spartan Tradition in European Thought* (Oxford, 1969), 47–53, 130. For Renaissance criticism of women who wear cosmetics see Louis B. Wright, *Middle-Class Culture in Elizabethan England* (Chapel Hill, NC, 1935), 491–2; Chilton Latham Powell, *English Domestic Relations, 1487–1653* (New York, 1917), 106; and Linda Woodbridge, *Women and the English Renaissance* (Urbana, Ill., 1984), 27, 60.

[39] *De officio mariti*, 3 (*Opera omnia*, iv. 366).

[40] *De institutione feminae Christianae*, 1. 4 (*Opera omnia*, iv. 80).

[41] *De institutione feminae Christianae*, 1. 3 (*Opera omnia*, iv. 73), and *De officio mariti*, 3 (ibid. 369).

translated Xenophon's *Oeconomicus* at the request of Sir Geoffrey Pole. Hervet had been a member of the household of Sir Geoffrey's mother, Lady Margaret, Countess of Salisbury, who was Catherine's friend and governess and god-mother of Princess Mary. The work, which was titled *Xenophon's Treatise of Householde,* was the first direct translation of any work from Greek to English which can be dated and was the first English translation of any of Xenophon's works to be published.[42] It was reprinted in at least six editions, being the only English translation of a Greek philosophical work to achieve such popularity at this time.[43]

The *Oeconomicus* was easily transferred by Hervet to a con-temporary Christian setting. The dialogue takes place in the porch of St Paul's Church at the Sign of the Lamb rather than in the Stoa of Zeus Eleutherius. Slaves are transformed into servants. Ischomachus and his wife are as pious as they are in the original, but in the translation they swear by 'the faith I owe to God' instead of by Zeus. Early in the dialogue Socrates promises that he will bring in his wife (*sic!*), Aspasia, who was more capable of showing everything than he was. It is easy to understand a judgement that the learned Aspasia was a far more suitable wife than the shrewish and emotional Xanthippe. Socrates' wife has often been an embarrassment to those who revere the philosopher. In Xen. *Symp.* 2. 9–10, Antisthenes asks Socrates why, since he believed that women were teachable, he had not begun by instructing his own wife? Socrates responds that managing Xanthippe provides a chal-lenge which prepares him to deal with the rest of humanity. In mulling over this discrepancy between theory and practice, Vives had admitted that some women are intractable and characterized Socrates as a wise father of a family who is to be compared to Job and Tobit for the fortitude and patience

---

[42] Jackson, Ferguson, and Pantzer, *A Short-Title Catalogue,* ii. 481, give the following dates: (from Berthelet) 26069, 1532; 26071, 1537; 26072, 1544; 26073, 1550 (top border dated 1534); and (not from Berthelet) 26074, 1557 and 26075, 1573.

[43] Henry Burrowes Lathrop, *Translations from the Classics into English from Caxton to Chapman (1477–1620)* (Madison, Wis., 1933), 49–50. For a description of the various editions see Eustace F. Bosanquet, 'Three Little Tudor Books', *The Library,* 4th ser. 14 (1934), 178–92.

he displayed in his conjugal relationship.[44] Writers much later than Xenophon and Plato had implied that there was an erotic connection between Socrates and Aspasia.[45] Unless he simply made a mistake, Hervet may have regularized the relationship between Socrates and Aspasia in order to make his translation appropriate reading for young ladies.

Renaissance England experienced major changes not only in religion, but also in education, and class structure.[46] A brief review of the historical context in which the *Oeconomicus* became popular and a consideration of whether women might have read this book will be of interest to historians of women and the family. These remarks must be tentative inasmuch as literacy is just now the subject of intense scrutiny and debate among English historians and detailed studies begin with the second half of the sixteenth century, some thirty years after

[44] *De officio mariti*, 8 (*Opera Omnia*, iv. 407). We may note in passing that Xanthippe also merits praise for enduring marriage with Socrates. See Pomeroy, *Goddesses, Whores, Wives, and Slaves*, 79–80.

[45] Three figures on a Hellenistic terracotta relief and a bronze copy of it from the Roman period—both in Naples—have been identified as Socrates, Eros, and Aspasia. On this and other joint portrayals in sculpture of Socrates and Aspasia see C. C. Vermeule, 'Socrates and Aspasia', *CJ* 54 (1958), 49–55. G. M. A. Richter, *The Portraits of the Greeks* (London, 1966), i. 117, expresses doubts about this interpretation of the scene on the grounds that the figure of Socrates is coarse and the face of Aspasia not a distinctive portrait. In any case these sculptures do not constitute reliable historical evidence. Nor does the written tradition that links the two in an erotic context. This tradition appears in Maximus of Tyre (18. 4 Hobein) and Athenaeus (5. 219 D, quoting Herodicus of Babylon; for the poem, although the attribution is uncertain, see Hugh Lloyd-Jones and Peter Parsons, *Supplementum Hellenisticum* (Berlin, 1983), 248, no. 495, late 2nd c. BC). Athenaeus states that Aspasia was Socrates' ἐρωτοδιδάσκαλος ('teacher about love') and further, quoting Clearchus, hints at an amorous relationship between the two (13. 589 D = fr. 30 Wehrli). Athenaeus 13. 599 A–B quotes from the 'Leontion' of Hermesianax of Colophon (3rd c. BC) alluding to Socrates' unquenchable passion for Aspasia. (Text in J. U. Powell, *Collectanea Alexandrina* (Oxford, 1925), 98–104, Hermesianax fr. 7. 91–4.) Interestingly enough, Charles Burton Gulick, the translator of the Loeb volume (p. 229), refers to Xen. *Oec.* iii. 14 and *Mem.* 2. 6. 36 in a footnote as classical parallels for the passage in Athen. 13. 599 A–B. Athenaeus may have simply confused Aspasia with Diotima, the priestess whom Socrates, in Pl. *Symp.* 201 D, names as his mentor, though not sexual partner, in matters of love. (So Dittmar, *Aischines*, 40–1, followed by Barbara Ehlers, *Eine vorplatonische Deutung des sokratischen Eros* [Munich, 1966], 135–6.)

[46] For these social changes see e.g. Lawrence Stone, 'The Educational Revolution in England, 1560–1640', *Past and Present*, 28 (1964), 41–80, id., 'Social Mobility in England, 1500–1700', ibid. 33 (1966), 16–55.

the first printing of Hervet's translation.[47] Moreover, the reasons for historical changes are always complex; but at present I shall merely draw attention to a few factors that appear relevant.

The evidence for women's literacy is poor, but there is no doubt that far fewer women than men were literate. However, some popular books were directed towards women. In the Renaissance there was a marked increase in the number of educated people. Even for women, education was not limited to members of the royal court, or to those whose families could afford private tutors. Among gentry, parents sent their children to other families for an education that might include learning how to read and write.[48] The development of the printing-press made books available to large audiences. Studies of book-ownership show that the gentry, the clergy, schoolmasters, professionals, and the commercial élite were most likely to own books and that book-ownership was correlated with wealth.[49] Women, of course, could have read the books in their family's library, even if they are not listed as owners.

Education was based on the classics, which contained information that was of obvious practical value for doctors, clergy, and lawyers. Some members of the aristocracy endeavoured to ensure that classical learning was transmitted even to those who could read only the vernacular by engaging scholars to write translations.[50] The reason for fostering the reading of the classics was not only to preserve humanistic values but also to improve humanity by exposure to this body of knowledge. In so far as women were less likely than men to be able to read classical languages, some of these translations were directed towards them. Berthelet declares in his Preface

[47] On education and literacy, see e.g. id., 'Literacy and Education in England, 1640–1900', ibid. 42 (1969), 69–139; Cressy, *Literacy and the Social Order, passim*; and Peter Clark, 'The Ownership of Books in England, 1560–1640: The Example of Some Kentish Townsfolk', in Lawrence Stone (ed.), *Schooling and Society* (Baltimore and London, 1976), 95–111.

[48] See Charlton, *Education in Renaissance England*, 209–10, Wright, *Middle-Class Culture in Elizabethan England*, 103–18, and Stone, 'The Educational Revolution in England, 1560–1640', 42–3.

[49] See Cressy, *Literacy and the Social Order*, 123. Clark, 'The Ownership of Books in England, 1560–1640', 99, studying a small sample, stated that, before 1600, 14 per cent of women owned books.

[50] Bennett, *English Books and Readers 1475 to 1557*, 156–7 n. 33.

to Hervet's translation of the *Oeconomicus* that the book 'for the welth of this realme, I deme very profitable to be red', and Hyrde dedicated his translation of Vives to Catherine because of her gracious zeal 'to the virtuous education of the woman-kind of this realm'.

The recipients of this largess were avid consumers. The English Renaissance was a time of rapid social mobility and demographic change in which the numbers of the urban and rural propertied classes increased. These people had the funds to invest in educating their children and in purchasing books, and printing now made it possible for many more people to have them. The *nouveaux riches* had profound faith in the power of education to improve their social position. The moral theory of the middle classes treated marriage as a financial partnership in which the wife was responsible for household management.[51] The *Oeconomicus* provided an explicit model of how a gentleman and his wife conducted their life and how education could serve as the principal avenue to success. Handbooks on self-improvement as well as on practical matters were popular at this time.[52] Therefore it is no surprise to discover that the *Oeconomicus* is often bound with books on surveying and hus-bandry.[53] The secular spirit which pervades the *Oeconomicus* corresponded to the interests of this segment of English society, which increasingly comprised a literate audience. Ischomachus is an ἀνὴρ χρηματιστικός ('businessman'), who manages to remain a thorough gentleman. Both husband and wife are thrifty, self-disciplined, impatient of leisure, insatiable when it comes to work, and dedicated to increasing their capital.[54]

[51] See Linda T. Fitz [Woodbridge], '"What Says the Married Woman?"': Marriage Theory and Feminism in the English Renaissance', *Mosaic*, 13/2 (1980), 1–22.

[52] See Louis B. Wright, 'Handbook Learning of the Renaissance Middle Class', *Studies in Philology*, 28 (1931), 58–86, and Cressy, *Literacy and the Social Order*, 7.

[53] Bodleian Library 70 c. 103, Antiq. f. E. 85, and Huntington Library, RB 59725–7 all exhibit Hervet's translation (respectively *STC* 26072, 26072, 26073) bound together with John Fitzherbert, *The boke of husbandry* (*STC* 10996, 10997, 10999) and id., *Surueyinge* (*STC* 11011, 11009, 11011). The first-named volume also contains: *A glasse for householders* (*STC* 11917) and the beginning of *The maner of kepynge a courte Baron and a Lete* (*STC* 7717). For another combined copy see reference to *The Papers of Benjamin Franklin*, below, n. 59.

[54] Powell, *English Domestic Relations, 1487–1653*, 114, mistakes the social class of Ischomachus, of Xenophon, and of his readers when he states that 'the household described is that of a simple Greek husbandman'.

Perhaps the most important reason for the popularity of the *Oeconomicus* is that it provides instruction on marriage. It is the first book in English entirely devoted to household management. As the sixteenth century progressed, marriage manuals, including translations of treatises on marriage by humanists and original works in English, proliferated.[55] Under Catholicism, it had only been better to marry than to burn. But Protestants rejected celibacy. With the closing of the nunneries marriage provided the only vocation for respectable women. A substantial number of English books for women give instruction on domestic matters. Like the *Oeconomicus*, these books were often written in dialogue form and outline the mutual duties of the members of the family towards one another, as well as the duties of master and mistress towards servants and of servants towards master and mistress. Hervet's translation of the *Oeconomicus* was read by both men[56] and women. The autographed copies that I have examined in the British Library, the Bodleian Library, and the Butler Library of Columbia University all bear the signatures of men.[57] A copy in the Huntington library was owned by Ann, daughter of Sir William Browne, Lord Mayor of London, who was married to Sir William Petre, Secretary to Queen Elizabeth, and died in 1581; her inscription reads: 'Thys boke ys myne/Ane petre Given/me by my husband/Sr Wyllyam petre.' Her book was bound with two that were of interest to men.[58]

---

[55] For marriage manuals see Powell, *English Domestic Relations, 1487–1653,* and John K. Yost, 'The Value of Married Life for the Social Order in the Early English Renaissance', *Societas,* 6 (1976), 25–39.

[56] Suzanne W. Hull, *Chaste, Silent, and Obedient* (San Marino, Calif., 1982), 48, considers the possibility that guidebooks ostensibly written for women were actually intended for men, but on p. 67 she includes the *Oeconomicus* in her list of practical books for women. On the Renaissance debate over women see e.g. Katherine Usher Henderson and Barbara McManus, *Half Humankind: Contexts and Texts of the Controversy about Women in England 1540–1640* (Urbana, Ill., and Chicago, 1985), and Woodbridge, *Women and the English Renaissance.*

[57] British Library G. 16783 belonged to the Hon. Thos. Grenville and 449. a. 48 to Doncun R. Farmer and Jos. Banks. Bodleian Antiq. f. E. 1557. 1 is inscribed 'Wm Herbert. 1782.' Bodleian Antiq. f. E. 85(3) bears the name of Thomas Roland on the inside front cover and marginalia in verse giving advice about dealing with a shrewish wife. The faded autograph in the inscribed copy in Columbia University (Phoenix BP 888. 3) indicates that the volume belonged to 'John'.

[58] Huntington Library, RB 59726: see above, n. 53.

The eighteenth-century bookplate of Robert James Lord Petre is pasted inside the front cover.[59]

A sophisticated and educated public debated major social problems such as the proper conduct of marriage and the position of women. Official Protestant doctrine affirmed the traditional belief in woman's subservience to man. In a sermon preached to Queen Elizabeth, Bishop Aylmer borrowed a theme from Plato's *Republic* in maintaining that 'some women be wiser, better learned, discreater, constanter, then a number of men'; contrary to John Knox's assertions, biblical condemnation of female rule (Isa. 3:12) was directed not at all women, 'but such as women be of the wurst sort, fond, folish, wanton, flibbergibbes, tatlers, triflers, wauering, witles, without counsell, feable, careles, rashe, proude, deintie, nise, tale bearers, euesdroppers, rumor raisers, euell tonged, worse minded, and in euerye wise doltefied with the dregges of the Deuils dounge hill.'[60] Edmund Tilney wrote in 1568: 'For indeede both diuine, & humaine lawes, in our religion giueth the man absolute authoritie, ouer the woman in all places' and stated that only barbarians might practise equality in marriage. Yet he admitted that although the skill, experience, wisdom, strength, patience, and courage which the sovereign must possess are commonly found in men, a rare woman may also have these virtues.[61] Whether Tilney liked it or not, sixteenth-century Englishmen experienced rule by a queen to whom indeed his treatise was dedicated. Thus the unique feature of the *Oeconomicus*—the possibility of governance by an educated, well-qualified woman—became a reality.[62]

59 In a letter to Benjamin Franklin dated 11 Feb. 1777, Georgiana Shipley wrote: 'I have been at length fortunate enough to procure the Economics, which I have read with great attention, as indeed everything else I can meet with relative to Socrates.' W. B. Willcox, in *The Papers of Benjamin Franklin*, xxiii. 305 n. 9, suggests that she was referring to the treatise published in Robert Vansittart, *Certain Ancient Tracts concerning the Management of Landed Property Reprinted* (London, 1767), in which the first item is Hervet's translation. Whether Franklin had directed her attention to this work cannot be ascertained.

60 J. Aylmer, *An Harborowe for Faithfull and Trewe Subjectes* ('Strasborowe' [London], 1959; repr. Amsterdam, 1972), fo. G3ᵛ.

61 'The office or duetie of the married woman', in *A Brief and Pleasant Discourse of Duties in Mariage, Called the Flower of Friendshippe* (London, 1568), fo. E1ʳ.

62 See e.g. Petrus Frarinus, *An Oration against the Unlawfull Insurrection of Protestantes of Our Time*, trans. J. Fowler (Antwerp, 1566; repr. Ilkley, 1975), fos. 35ʳ–36ʳ, who

The number of translations into the vernaculars and their many editions indicates that the *Oeconomicus* has continued to enjoy a noteworthy popularity.[63] There have been six translations in German in seven editions; eight in French in eleven editions;[64] fourteen in Italian in fourteen editions; two in Spanish in four editions; one in modern Greek; one in Portuguese; and nine in English in twenty-four editions. Hervet's translation was the most popular in its time.[65] The second most popular English translation was one with a Preface by John Ruskin, published, like Hervet's, when England was ruled by a queen.[66]

F. *Feminism and the* Oeconomicus

Because ideas about gender vary according to historical context the *Oeconomicus* has been accorded vastly different receptions over the years. In the modern era, Xenophon's *Oeconomicus* has been persistently misunderstood, by feminist as well as by traditional scholars. Caroline Dall, a feminist who participated in Margaret Fuller's 'Conversations' on classical mythology and who knew some Greek herself, was angry that Xenophon represented Ischomachus' wife as not tame enough to speak to her husband when she was a young bride. But Dall did not give Xenophon due credit, for she goes on

reports that the Puritan preacher Christopher Goodman (whom Frarinus conflates with Knox) had railed unjustifiably 'against the monstruouse raygne of women...'.

[63] Cited in Donald R. Morrison, *Bibliography*, 84–8. To Morrison's list of Italian translations, now add Carlo Natali, *Senofonte: L'amministrazione della casa (Economico)* (Venice, 1988), and Fabio Roscalla, *Senofonte: Economico* (Milan, 1991). In this count I have not included translations of the *Oeconomicus* in volumes of collected works of Xenophon.

[64] A. Espinas, *Histoire des doctrines économiques* (Paris, 1891), 128–33, points out that the first French translation, *La mesnagerie de Xenophon*, by Estienne de La Boëtie (Paris, 1571), was influential on Sully's *Économies royales*.

[65] Interestingly enough, Charles Butler, in *The feminine Monarchie, or a Treatise concerning Bees and the due Ordering of Bees* (Oxford, 1609), announced his discovery that the leader of the beehive was a queen rather than a king. Until this time Aristotle's view that the hive was ruled by a king had prevailed (see on vii. 32 ἡ τῶν μελιττῶν ἡγεμων).

[66] *The Economist of Xenophon*, trans. A. D. O. Wedderburn and W. G. Collingwood (London, 1876; repr. New York, 1971). According to Albert Augustus Trever, *A History of Greek Economic Thought*, 64, the *Oeconomicus* was the basis for Ruskin's economic theories.

to misquote him as follows: 'When Iscomachus [*sic*] ... asked his wife if she knew whether he had married her for love, "I know nothing," she replied, "but to be faithful to you, and to learn what you teach." He responded by an exhortation on "staying at home," ... and left her, with a kiss, for the saloon of Aspasia!'[67]

In more recent years, Xenophon has also been misunderstood by feminist as well as traditional scholars. For example, in an analysis of the influence of Greek thought on Alberti, Joan Kelly-Gadol was wrong to debit Xenophon with distinguishing 'an inferior domestic realm of women from the superior public realm of men'.[68] A careful reading of the *Oeconomicus* will show that Xenophon by no means considered the domestic realm as inferior (see Ch. 4 and notes to cc. vii–x). Xenophon asserts that women and men are complementary in their biological nature and therefore in their contributions to the domestic economy, but this difference does not imply inequality. Like Plato in the *Republic*, Xenophon makes it clear that the soul has no sex; men and women are endowed with a potential for moral equality. Kelly-Gadol was measuring the feminism of Xenophon by the standard of androgyny. When measured by the standard of 'separate but equal' rather than by that of androgyny the views of Xenophon and his Renaissance successors[69] on women may appear more acceptable to contemporary feminists. However, because of their political stances in favour of monarchy or aristocracy and because of the patriarchal framework of their society, which they never totally expunge, they cannot, of course, be called 'feminists'; but insofar as Xenophon emphasizes gender difference and the value of women's work his thinking does coincide with that of domestic feminists of the nineteenth century who

[67] Caroline H. Dall, *The College, the Market, and the Court: or Woman's Relation to Education, Labor, and Law* (1867, repr. New York, 1972), 52–3.

[68] 'Did Women Have a Renaissance?', in Renate Bridenthal and Claudia Koonz (eds.), *Becoming Visible* (Boston, Mass., 1977), 141, 161 n. 2.

[69] Similarly Kaufman, 'Juan Luis Vives on the Education of Women', 892, criticized Vives, for she defined 'feminist' (or 'profeminist') 'in the narrow sense of advocating the same humanistic education for women and men ... the question centers on the curriculum and texts presented to a girl. Does her course of studies differ from a boy's in academic content?'

found an identity for women and a means of incorporating them into industrialized society through their domestic labour.[70] Catherine Beecher and Harriet Beecher Stowe aimed to render women's true profession as desirable and respected and 'to elevate both the honor and the remuneration of all the employments that sustain the many difficult and sacred duties of the family state, and thus to render each department of woman's true profession as much desired and respected as are the most honored professions of men'.[71] Beecher also endorsed the doctrine of separate spheres. Whereas previous thinkers had asserted that men were the authorities in the household, according to Beecher women were to rule the home.

Modern feminists are beginning to react against the monolithic theories expressed by the founders of post-war feminism in the earliest and most influential works. Simone de Beauvoir[72] and Betty Friedan[73] had considered the traditional family to be an oppressive institution, and housekeeping and maternity nothing but monotonous burdens. More radical thinkers found that gender distinctions themselves created a biological tyranny.[74] In utopias not vastly different from Plato's *Republic*, androgyny rather than gender difference would be emphasized: the private sphere would be abolished, and cybernetics would provide the means of liberating women from biological oppression. In the eighties, however, some feminist thinkers reacted against the brave new worlds of their predecessors and moved closer to the world of Xenophon's *Oeconomicus*, endorsing women's uniqueness and difference from men.[75] They argue that denying gender difference undervalues women and look for a way for women to fulfil traditional female roles without handicaps.

Another twentieth-century interpretation of the status of Ischomachus' wife that has been suggested to me occasionally

---

[70] On domestic feminism, Catherine Beecher, and Harriet Beecher Stowe, see Dolores Hayden, *The Grand Domestic Revolution* (Cambridge, Mass., and London 1981).

[71] Harriet Beecher Stowe, *American Woman's Home* (1869, repr. Hartford, Conn., 1975), 13.

[72] *Le Deuxième Sexe* (Paris, 1949).

[73] *The Feminine Mystique* (New York, 1963).

[74] e.g. Shulamith Firestone, *The Dialectic of Sex* (New York, 1970).

[75] e.g. Carol Gilligan, *In a Different Voice* (Cambridge, Mass., and London, 1982).

after I have presented my own in a lecture is one which acknowledges that her position relative to that of her husband is unusually prestigious, but argues that inasmuch as that is the case Xenophon cannot be serious. It is true that Xenophon is occasionally humorous, but I doubt whether his extensive description of the relationship between Ischomachus and his wife (cc. vii–x) can be ignored by arguing that Xenophon was merely being humorous. In such a way, Allan Bloom dismissed book 5 of Plato's *Republic* (which deals with the education of the female guardians) as intentionally preposterous, and argued that Socrates expected it to be ridiculed.[76] But Bloom's hypothesis is absurd. In the *Laws* 804 D–805 A, Plato also makes serious recommendations concerning women's education. Extremely long jokes may be the basis of comedy, but they are unprecedented in Xenophon and Plato. At any rate, most readers from the Romans to the present have not believed Xenophon and Plato are joking, but rather taken them at their word.

[76] *The Republic of Plato* (New York, 1978), 380–1.

7
The History of the Text

A. *Ancient Texts*

Two papyrus fragments of the *Oeconomicus* are known:
P. Oxyrhynchus II. 227, of the end of the first or beginning of
the second century AD, and *P. Tebtunis* II. 682 of the third
century AD.[1] The Oxyrhynchus fragment gives the text of
viii. 17 ἰσχυρῶς–ix. 2 ἑκάστῳ. B. P. Grenfell and A. S. Hunt,
its original editors, declared the text corrupt.[2] In fact, a second
hand had entered corrections on the papyrus itself. In contrast,
Axel W. Persson argued that the differences between the
papyrus and the manuscripts indicated failures in the manuscript tradition.[3] Persson postulated that both the
Oxyrhynchus papyrus and Cicero's translation showed that
there was another recension different from those of our manuscripts.[4] But Persson's argument is not compelling: inasmuch
as Cicero did not intend to make a literal translation, quotations from his work cannot be used without caution in support
of Persson's view (see Ch. 6, sect. B and 'Remarks on the
Translation'). In 1974, long after the publication of any edition
of the *Oeconomicus*, Jean Lenaerts identified *P. Tebtunis* II. 682
as belonging to it. This fragment gives the text of xviii. 9 from
ἐννοῶ to γεωργεῖν. Within eight lines it shows three variations
from the manuscripts: one is a variation in orthography, in
the other two the grammatical construction is altered. None

---

[1] R. A. Pack, *The Greek and Latin Literary Texts from Roman Egypt*, 2nd edn. (Ann
Arbor, Mich., 1965), 90, No. 1563; P. Lit. Lond. 151; Wilhelm Crönert, 'Litterarische
Texte mit Ausschluß der christlichen', *Archiv für Papyrusforschung*, 1 (1901), 520–1;
and Pack adespoton 2905 now identified by Jean Lenaerts, 'Un Papyrus de l'*Économie*
de Xénophon', as a text of the *Oeconomicus* (see Ch. 6, sect. B).

[2] *The Oxyrhynchus Papyri*, II, p. 120.

[3] *Zur Textgeschichte Xenophons* (Lund, 1915), 48–9, followed by H. Hunger, *Geschichte
der Textüberlieferung* (Zurich, 1961), i, 272.

[4] *Textgeschichte*, 49, 168.

of the variations affects the meaning of the text. The first variation is the participle [ἐν]νοῶν where the manuscripts give the first person singular. The second variation is in spelling ζωιγραφε[ῖν] whereas the standard spelling is ζωγραφεῖν. The final variation [ἐδίδαξ]ε γὰρ ἐμὲ [οὔτε τα]ῦτα seems an improvement on the manuscripts' readings (though some readers might object that the emphatic pronoun is inappropriate and the word-order more pedestrian), but there is no proof that it is what Xenophon actually wrote. In any case, the two papyrus fragments indicate that the papyri descend from a different tradition from that of the manuscripts. The indirect tradition also includes Philodemus, Columella, and brief citations in ancient lexica, such as that of Stobaeus. It is at least as murky as that of the manuscripts. E. C. Marchant confesses doubt and uncertainty as to whether citations from Stobaeus should always be preferred to those in our manuscripts.[5]

B. *Medieval and Renaissance Texts*

All the manuscripts of the *Oeconomicus* are late. The oldest, Codex Reginensis 96 (H), is no earlier than the twelfth or thirteenth century. The principal manuscripts are dated to the fourteenth and fifteenth centuries. Karl Schenkl divided the manuscripts into two families, one headed by Codex Laurentianus 80. 13 (E) of the fourteenth century, the other by the Codex Reginensis 96 (H), with two manuscripts in a middle category. Both families descend from a common archetype that itself must have often been corrupt. Schenkl's work on the manuscript tradition was significant,[6] but despite his efforts, Wilamowitz declared the situation hopeless, for he thought that the corruptions of the entire paradosis were too numerous for even the boldest conjectural critic to discover, let alone emend.[7]

Since Schenkl, the standard work on the manuscripts of

---

[5] *Xenophontis Opera Omnia* ii, 2nd edn. (Oxford, 1921), 149.

[6] 'Xenophontische Studien, 3: Beiträge zur Kritik des Oikonomikos, des Symposion und der Apologie', *SB k. Akad. Wiss.* (Vienna), 83 (1876), 103–78.

[7] Review of *The Oxyrhynchus Papyri.* Part II, ed. Grenfell and Hunt, *Göttingische gelehrte Anzeigen,* 162 (1900), 47.

Xenophon has become Axel W. Persson, *Zur Textgeschichte Xenophons*. As Persson's index of passages cited demonstrates, he treats textual problems in individual works only briefly. After Persson, little important progress was made on the entire manuscript tradition of Xenophon's minor works and much remains to be done.[8]

The *Oeconomicus* is always found in manuscripts with other works of Xenophon. Because these works appear in varying order, it would be necessary to study the transmission of them all to clarify the manuscript tradition of the *Oeconomicus*. Meanwhile, considering the lack of uniformity and un-Attic nature of much of Xenophon's prose, rigorous editing to make Xenophon's work conform to that of his contemporaries must be avoided (see Ch. 2). Paradoxically, the manuscripts that at first glance appear least corrupt, inasmuch as they present little vocabulary and syntax that is unique to Xenophon, may have actually suffered an early revision by some Atticizing hand. Many words cited in the ancient lexica do not appear in our manuscripts.[9] Because of the welter of problems described above, I have usually declined to comment on purely lexicographical problems in the Commentary.

C. *The Relationship of the* Oeconomicus *to Xenophon's Other Works*

Galen (*Περὶ ἄρθρων*, Kühn xviii/1. 301) thought that the *Oeconomicus* was intended to be the final chapter of the *Memorabilia*. This notion has found some support among later scholars. For example, K. Lincke suggests that the *Memorabilia*, *Oeconomicus*, and *Apology* are continuous.[10] (He omits the *Symposium*, because he questions whether Xenophon is the author.) Although Xenophon's Socratic works appear in the manuscripts in varying order, the *Symposium* is often paired with the *Oeconomicus*. The distribution of the two works in

---

[8] D. O. Haltinner and E. A. Schmoll, 'The Older Manuscripts of Xenophon's *Hiero*', *RHT* 10 (1980), 231–6, claim to have identified 'many errors' in the work of Thalheim, Pierleoni, and Marchant on the texts of Xenophon's minor works.

[9] Nevertheless, C. P. Schulze, *Quaestiones grammaticae ad Xenophontem pertinentes* (Berlin, 1888), defended the manuscripts on these grounds.

[10] *De Xenophontis libris Socraticis* (Jena, 1890), 12.

manuscripts does not support the thesis that the *Oeconomicus* is a continuation of the *Memorabilia*. Nor does the use in the first sentence of the particle δέ ('and') and of the pronoun αὐτοῦ ('him'). Xenophon opens many of his works with a phrase implying earlier writing on the same subject (see on i. 1 δέ ... αὐτοῦ). Therefore I conclude that the *Memorabilia* and the *Oeconomicus* comprise a unity, but never were a single work.[11]

D. *Principal Editions From the Renaissance to the Twentieth Century*[12]

1516	*Editio princeps* of complete works. Intro. by Eufrosino Bonini (Florence: Ph. Junta).
1525	Asulanus, Complete works (Venice: Aldus).
1561, 1581	H. Stephanus, Works in Greek and Latin (Geneva).
1782	J. K. Zeune, *Xenophontis Oeconomicus, Apologia Socratis, Symposium, Hiero, Agesilaus* (Leipzig: Fritsch).
1812	J. G. Schneider, *Xenophontis Oeconomicus, Convivium, Hiero, Agesilaus* (Oxford: Clarendon).
1824, 1849, 1873	L. Dindorf, *Xenophontis scripta minora* (Leipzig: Teubner).
1842	L. Breitenbach, *Xenophontis Oeconomicus* (Gotha: Hemmings).
1865–7	Gust. Sauppe, *Xenophontis opera* (Leipzig: Tauchnitz).
1869, 1876	K. Schenkl, *Xenophontis opera*, ii. *Libri Socratici* (Berlin: Weidmann).
1878, 1884	Ch. Graux, *Xénophon: Économique. Chaptres I à XI*. Text and translation (Paris: Hachette).
1883	Ex recensione C. Schenkl, curavit S. R. Winans, *Xenophontis libri Socratici* (New York: Harper).

[11] In agreement with other scholars in the 20th c., including Axel Persson, *Zur Textgeschichte Xenophons*, 86 n. 3, Rainer Nickel, *Xenophon* (Darmstadt, 1979), 73, Sandra Taragna Novo, *Economia ed etica nell'Economico di Senofonte* (Turin, 1968), 3–4, and H. R. Breitenbach, *Xenophon von Athen*, cols. 1837–8.

[12] This list is not complete. See further Donald R. Morrison, *Bibliography*, 21–4, 82–4. When I have not been able to examine the title-page of a volume cited here, I have followed Morrison.

1884, 1885, 1886, H. A. Holden, *The Economicus of Xenophon*
 1889, 1895   (London: Macmillan).

1886, 1905   Ch. Graux and A. Jacob, *Xénophon:*
                  Économique (Paris: Hachette).

E. *Principal Twentieth-Century Editions*

The first noteworthy edition of the twentieth century was Th. Thalheim's revision of Dindorf's Teubner text.[13] Thalheim worked in the style of nineteenth-century text-editors: without adequate justification he bracketed huge portions of the text, for example iii. 1 to vi. 11, xiv. 1 to xv. 4, all c. xxi, and several shorter sections. Although he consulted Schenkl's work on the manuscripts, his apparatus reveals that he relied heavily on Lincke's judgement and his own. His text remains useful for citations of parallel, or translated passages in other classical authors including Pseudo-Aristotle, Philodemus, Plutarch, and Columella.

E. C. Marchant wisely exercised more caution than Thalheim. In his edition for the Loeb Classical Library,[14] Marchant used Sauppe's text with a few exceptions pointed out in his footnotes. Marchant's Oxford Classical Text,[15] which is reproduced with modifications in the present volume, is largely indebted to K. Schenkl's study of the manuscripts. Marchant considered the oldest manuscript, Codex Reginensis 96 (H), as the most reliable. Because he was uncertain whether the indirect tradition represented chiefly by *P. Oxy.* II. 227 and by quotations in Stobaeus was superior to the manuscripts, he usually prefers the manuscript readings.

Chantraine's Budé text[16] is conservative, showing only minor divergences from Marchant; as he himself states, he did not do additional work on the manuscripts.[17] Chantraine employs fewer square brackets than Thalheim or Marchant and his

---

[13] *Xenophontis scripta minora*, fasc. prior (Leipzig, 1910).

[14] *Xenophon 7 vols.: Memorabilia and Oeconomicus* (New York and London, 1923) = vol. iv of Loeb Classical Library edn., 7 vols. (1914–25).

[15] E. C. Marchant, *Xenophontis opera omnia*, ii, 2nd edn. (Oxford: Clarendon, 1921), 143–219, and Addenda et Corrigenda, no pagination.

[16] *Xénophon: Économique* (Paris: Les Belles Lettres, 1949).

[17] Ibid. 26.

apparatus criticus is imprecise.[18] Chantraine's major contribution has been lexicographical, particularly in determining the correct French translations of Greek technical terms.[19] Thus the standard modern text remains Marchant's, despite Chantraine's more recent edition.

[18] See further L. Castiglioni's review, *Gnomon*, 21 (1949), 339–42.
[19] As pointed out by M. I. Finley in his review, *CP* 46 (1951), 252–3.

Remarks on the Translation

This translation is designed to bring the *Oeconomicus* back into currency as a text for students, scholars, and amateurs of social and economic history, family history, and Greek philosophy and literature.

One of the reasons for the relative obscurity of the *Oeconomicus* nowadays, at least in the English-speaking world, is the lack of a modern translation that is both attractive and accurate. Of the three twentieth-century English translations currently in print, that by E. C. Marchant in the Loeb edition of 1923 is more fluent and polished than the Greek, while that by Carnes Lord, published in Leo Strauss, *Xenophon's Socratic Discourse: An Interpretation of the Oeconomicus*, is more crude and pedestrian. The translation by Robin Waterfield, published in 1990 in the Penguin series, is more readable, but less accurate, than Carnes Lord's.

Marchant and Waterfield both transformed the character of Ischomachus into an Englishman in a companionate marriage who addresses his wife as 'my dear'. The Greek word γύναι lacks this affective quality. Carnes Lord's translation of the same word as 'woman', however, is excessively literal and impolite. I have translated γύναι as 'wife', throughout. Despite its specific status connotations in British history, I have translated καλὸς κἀγαθός as 'gentleman', because I wanted to retain some flavour of rank, and reasoned that most contemporary English speakers would not be misled by this term. Waterfield's 'truly good' ignores the aristocratic connotation of the phrase. Oaths like 'by Zeus!' present a problem. Although when they are translated literally they often sound stilted, modern equivalents rarely work and quickly become outdated. I have usually translated oaths literally. Marchant and Waterfield simply omit them. In Waterfield's version, as in Marchant's, anachronisms abound, for example, 'God' for 'a god' and 'servant' for 'slave'. Waterfield also misidentifies the Elder Cyrus as the Younger Cyrus in iv. 16 and obscures the eminent role of Ischomachus' wife as her husband's partner in ix. 16 by translating the plural δεσποσύνων χρημάτων as 'master's assets' when the words actually refer to the property of both master and mistress. Finally, Waterfield's translation is more prudish than Marchant's: ἑταίρα is mistranslated as 'concubine'; the personification of Earth and Farming as female is suppressed (v; xix); and it is impossible to deduce from his translation 'loved one' that both παιδικῶν and ἐρωμένων (xii. 14) refer to homosexual eros.

I rejected the possibility of rendering the *Oeconomicus* throughout in gender-neutral language, inasmuch as the language of the Greeks reflects their patriarchal society. For example, Xenophon does not use the phrase καλὸς κἀγαθός ('gentleman') of women (see on vi. 12). Therefore it would not be correct to assume that he intended to include women when he uses the phrase in the masculine plural. In classical Athens women did not own land, nor, as Xenophon himself states, did they work out of doors (vii. 30). Therefore, it is clear that the references to agricultural affairs apply only to men.

Most previous translators endeavoured to use a variety of English words to translate the same Greek word. For example, in the first English translation Gentian Hervet had Ischomachus call his wife 'good bedfelowe' in his first direct statement to her in vii. 10, but in c. viii he addresses her as 'swete wyfe', and in x. 3 as 'good wyfe' (see Ch. 6, sect. E). Wedderburn and Collingwood use 'good wife', 'dear wife', and 'wife'.[1] I found the repetition of ἔφη (he said), required by the dialogue form in the *Oeconomicus*, to be acceptable stylistically in Greek, but monotonous if translated the same way throughout into English. Furthermore, the narrative frame in which some statements are repeated at seven removes from the reader is a *tour de force* in Greek, a language which renders subtle

---

[1] In John Ruskin, *The Economist of Xenophon*.

distinctions in quoted statements readily intelligible. But a literal translation would have created in English an intolerable web of 'he said that he said that she said ...' (see Ch. 2, sect. E). For the sake of vividness, in cc. i–vi I have turned the dialogue into a play, thereby suppressing one level of the time-frame; cc. vii–xxi, Socrates' report of his conversation with Ischomachus, has been rendered as a continuous narrative.

Some abstract words whose importance is emphasized in the commentary are usually represented by the same English word throughout the translation so that their repeated appearances may be located by the Greekless reader. For example, one of the principal themes in the *Oeconomicus* is the art of ruling: those in a supervisory position are obliged to be concerned about their bodies, their possessions, their subordinates, their families, friends, cities, and gods. To alert the reader to this persistent theme, compounds in ἐπιμελ- are usually translated by some variant of 'concern'. Where the suffix -ικός appears it is usually rendered by 'skilled in' (see on i. 1). Consistency has not been elevated to a principle at the expense of meaning. The translation of some other abstract nouns varies according to context, where repetition might cause the meaning of the text to be ambiguous. However, repetition is characteristic of Xenophon's style. Thus in iv. 21, I have rendered the three appearances of θαυμάζ- with two forms of 'amaze-', making the repetition as awkward in English as it was in Greek.

Commentators have stigmatized as un-Attic some Greek words and syntactical features which may have been common in spoken, rather than in literary, usage (see Ch. 2, sect. B). These words and usages have not been rendered as quaint and dialectal, for we do not know that they would have seemed so to Xenophon's contemporaries. On the other hand, I have retained infelicities such as abrupt changes from plural to singular or vice versa within a sentence (iii. 5–6, ll. 3–4, xv. 10, ll. 10–11). Sentences that were ponderously long in Greek have usually been rendered as remarkably long English sentences.

The young Cicero, who was the first translator of the *Oeconomicus*, evidently took more liberties in paraphrasing than any responsible translator would nowadays. Perhaps Cicero trusted his readers to consult the original text if required (see Ch. 6, sect. B). Classical authors usually did not feel obliged to render the words of other writers verbatim. However, the present translation was made primarily as an aid for an audience who, unlike Cicero's, cannot read the original Greek. Therefore, I have tried to remain as faithful to the text as possible.

For the Loeb edition (1923), Marchant translated the text of G. Sauppe (Leipzig, 1865–7), although it predated what he regarded (p. xxix) as the substantial improvements by K. Schenkl. Carnes Lord and Waterfield translated the second edition of Marchant's Oxford Classical Text (1921). Carnes Lord does not state whether he reviewed the addenda and corrigenda to Marchant's second edition, but his translation indicates that he did not adopt them. Waterfield adopts a few readings that differ from those preferred by Marchant. Inasmuch as the present work is principally a historical rather than a philological commentary, textual problems are not usually discussed in detail. The distribution of the dialogue which is sometimes debatable (e.g. i. 10. 25–6), does, of course, affect the translation. The conversations of Socrates in the *Oeconomicus* are not characterized by the thrust and parry of most of Plato's dialogues, but, instead, the speakers progress in agreement. Nor is Socrates the undisputed protagonist throughout, but rather Ischomachus often assumes the lead in the discussion. Therefore, attribution of a brief remark can occasionally be difficult. The dialogue form that I have adopted should prevent confusion. Rather than break up sentences by references to the paragraph-numbers of the Greek text, I have inserted them in the margin.

Although the dialogue is presented as filtered through Xenophon's recollection, the principal speakers are appropriately characterized. In 420–410 BC (see Ch. 2, sect. F) Socrates was a lively man in his mid-fifties. Ischomachus, though younger than Socrates by about ten years, is more serious, even pompous perhaps, owing to his role as an authority on the topics discussed. Critobulus is in his late twenties; in contrast to Ischomachus he behaves more immaturely than his age would suggest. In my translation I have attempted to convey the force of their personalities. In some places in his dialogue with Ischomachus I have added 'please' to Socrates' requests and questions, although there is no equivalent in the Greek original. Socrates seemed rude, otherwise, and I think that Xenophon intended to portray him in a favourable light.

The following translation is of Marchant's Oxford edition. The text has been modified by some of Marchant's addenda and corrigenda to his second edition (1921), by one suggestion by J. Gil,[2] and one by me as follows:

i. 10–11,	*Εἰ μὴ ἀποδιδοῖτό γε αὐτούς* Critobulo tribuit
ll. 16–17	Thalheim recte. *Τοῦτ᾽ αὖ* igitur servandum
iii. 14, l. 10	*δέ σοι*] *δὲ* recte Castalio
iv. 6, l. 22	*καὶ* del. Richards recte
iv. 15, l. 33	fort. ⟨*λέγοντα*⟩ *ὅτι*
iv. 18, l. 15	*ὅτε* Nitsche recte
iv. 21, l. 28	*τὰ* del. Schneider recte
vi. 13, l. 14–15	lege *ἀγαθοὺς χαλκέας, ἀγαθοὺς ζωγράφους, ἀγαθοὺς ἀνδριαντοποιούς* cum Stob.
vii. 8, l. 33	lege *πολλά, ὑπισχνουμένη μέν, εὐχομένη δὲ πρὸς*
viii. 4, l. 18–19	*πορευθείησαν, ἔχοντες οὕτως; ἐπικωλύσουσιν* Thalheim, Gil
viii. 13, l. 26	*ἐν* ⟨*ἐν*⟩*δεκακλίνῳ* Pomeroy
viii. 23, l. 6	lege *ἔκαστον κεῖται* cum *Π*
xii. 17, l. 11	*περὶ τοῦ παιδεύεσθαι* del. Schneider recte
xvi. 4, l. 22	*αὐτὴ* Hartman

[2] *Jenofonte: Económico.*

SIGLA

Π^1 = P. Oxy. II 227 (capp. viii. 17–ix. 2), saec. i vel ii
Π^2 = P. Tebt. II 682 (cap. xviii. 9), saec. iii
H = Reginensis 96, saec. xii vel xiii
G = Laurentianus pl. lv, 21, saec. xiv
N = Guelferbytanus 71, 19, saec. xv
B = Parisinus 2955 (desinit in v. λοιπόν i. 23), saec. xv
K = Palatinus 184. saec. xv
L = Vaticanus 128, saec. xv
Q = Ambrosianus A, 157 sup., scriptus a. 1426
R = Ambrosianus E, 119 sup., saec. xv
Z = consensus codicum H G N B K L Q R
H al. = consensus codicum H aliorumque ex his codd.
D = Parisinus 1647, saec. xvi
C = Parisinus 1646, saec. xvi
A = Parisinus 1643, saec. xv
E = Laurentianus pl. lxxx, 13, saec. xiv
P = Vindobonensis xxxvii, 70, saec. xv
F = Laurentianus pl. lxxxv, 9, saec. xiii
M = Lipsiensis 96 (desunt omnia inde a cap. xii. 8
usque ad cap. xix. 16), saec. xiv
Y = consensus codicum D C A E P F M
D al. = consensus codicum D aliorumque ex his codd.
Ven. 368 = Venetus Marcianus 368, saec. xv
Ven. 511 = Venetus Marcianus 511, saec. xii vel xiii
Ven. 513 = Venetus Marcianus 513, saec. xv
H^a = Britannicus 5110, saec. xv
J = Vrbinas 93 (desinit in v. καταβάλλειν xvi. 15)
saec. xv
O = Vindobonensis xcv, 48, saec. xv
Stobaei codd.:
Vind. = Vindobonensis lxvii, saec. xi
Esc. = Escorialensis lxxxx, saec. xi vel xii
Paris.(A) = Parisinus 1984, saec. xiv

ΞΕΝΟΦΩΝΤΟΣ

ΟΙΚΟΝΟΜΙΚΟΣ

I Ἤκουσα δέ ποτε αὐτοῦ καὶ περὶ οἰκονομίας τοιάδε
διαλεγομένου· Εἰπέ μοι, ἔφη, ὦ Κριτόβουλε, ἀρά γε ἡ οἰκονομία
ἐπιστήμης τινὸς ὄνομά ἐστιν, ὥσπερ ἡ ἰατρικὴ καὶ ἡ χαλκευτικὴ
2 καὶ ἡ τεκτονική; Ἔμοιγε δοκεῖ, ἔφη ὁ Κριτόβουλος. Ἦ καὶ ὥσπερ
τούτων τῶν τεχνῶν ἔχοιμεν ἂν εἰπεῖν ὅ τι ἔργον ἑκάστης, οὕτω 5
καὶ τῆς οἰκονομίας δυναίμεθ' ἂν εἰπεῖν ὅ τι ἔργον αὐτῆς ἐστι;
Δοκεῖ γοῦν, ἔφη ὁ Κριτόβουλος, οἰκονόμου ἀγαθοῦ εἶναι εὖ οἰκεῖν
3 τὸν ἑαυτοῦ οἶκον. Ἦ καὶ τὸν ἄλλου δὲ οἶκον, ἔφη ὁ Σωκράτης, εἰ
ἐπιτρέποι τις αὐτῷ, οὐκ ἂν δύναιτο, εἰ βούλοιτο, εὖ οἰκεῖν, ὥσπερ
καὶ τὸν ἑαυτοῦ; ὁ μὲν γὰρ τεκτονικὴν ἐπιστάμενος ὁμοίως ἂν καὶ 10
ἄλλῳ δύναιτο ἐργάζεσθαι ὅ τι περ καὶ ἑαυτῷ, καὶ ὁ οἰκονομικός
4 γ' ἂν ὡσαύτως. Ἔμοιγε δοκεῖ, ὦ Σώκρατες. Ἔστιν ἄρα, ἔφη ὁ
Σωκράτης, τὴν τέχνην ταύτην ἐπισταμένῳ, καὶ εἰ μὴ αὐτὸς τύχοι
χρήματα ἔχων, τὸν ἄλλου οἶκον οἰκονομοῦντα ὥσπερ καὶ
οἰκοδομοῦντα μισθοφορεῖν; Νὴ Δία καὶ πολύν γε μισθόν, ἔφη ὁ 15
Κριτόβουλος, φέροιτ' ἄν, εἰ δύναιτο οἶκον παραλαβὼν τελεῖν τε
5 ὅσα δεῖ καὶ περιουσίαν ποιῶν αὔξειν τὸν οἶκον. Οἶκος δὲ δὴ τί
δοκεῖ ἡμῖν εἶναι; ἀρα ὅπερ οἰκία, ἢ καὶ ὅσα τις ἔξω τῆς οἰκίας
6 κέκτηται, πάντα τοῦ οἴκου ταῦτά ἐστιν; Ἐμοὶ γοῦν, ἔφη ὁ
Κριτόβουλος, δοκεῖ, καὶ εἰ μηδ' ἐν τῇ αὐτῇ πόλει εἴη τῷ 20
κεκτημένῳ, πάντα τοῦ οἴκου εἶναι ὅσα τις κέκτηται. Οὐκοῦν καὶ
ἐχθροὺς κέκτηνταί τινες; Νὴ Δία καὶ πολλούς γε ἔνιοι. Ἦ καὶ
κτήματα αὐτῶν φήσομεν εἶναι τοὺς ἐχθρούς; Γελοῖον μεντἂν εἴη,
ἔφη ὁ Κριτόβουλος, εἰ ὁ τοὺς ἐχθροὺς αὔξων προσέτι καὶ μισθὸν
7 τούτου φέροι. Ὅτι τοι ἡμῖν ἐδόκει οἶκος ἀνδρὸς εἶναι ὅπερ κτῆσις. 25
Νὴ Δί', ἔφη ὁ Κριτόβουλος, ὅ τι γε τις ἀγαθὸν κέκτηται· οὐ μὰ

---

3 ἡ ante χαλκευτικὴ F L Hᵃ: om. cet.   4 ἡ om. A B O   6 δυνάμεθ' ἂν
codd. multi: δυνάμεθα R *Ven.* 513   8 δὲ] γε Heindorf   9 αὐτῷ; ἢ οὐκ Heindorf
11 ὁ add. G: om. cet.   16 φέροιτ' ἂν H al.: φέρειν τ' ἂν D al. et G: φέρει τ' ἂν A
P: φέροι τἂν Schenkl: φέροι ἂν Mehler   19 κέκτηται K: ἐκέκτητο cet.   25 ὅπερ
καὶ D L

104

XENOPHON

DISCOURSE ON THE SKILL OF ESTATE MANAGEMENT

And I once heard him discussing estate management also as follows: I

SOCRATES. Tell me, Critobulus, is estate management the name of some
  branch of knowledge, as medicine, smithing, and carpentry are?
CRITOBULUS. I certainly think so.   2
SOCRATES. And just as we could say what the function of each of these
  occupations is, could we say what the function of estate management is?
CRITOBULUS. Well, it is my opinion that the function of a good estate
  manager is to manage his own estate well.
SOCRATES. And if someone entrusted another person's estate to him,   3
  wouldn't he, if he wished, be able to manage it just as well as his own?
  For the person who knows the skill of carpentry should be able to
  perform the same work for another as he does for himself, and the estate
  manager should, too, on the same principle.
CRITOBULUS. I certainly think so, Socrates.   4
SOCRATES. Is it then possible for a person who knows this occupation,
  even if he does not actually have property himself, to make money by
  managing the estate of another, just as he might do by building a house?
CRITOBULUS. By Zeus,[1] he would certainly make a lot of money, if he
  were able to take over an estate, make the necessary payments, and by
  making a surplus, increase the estate.
SOCRATES. Well then, an estate—what do we think it is? Is it the same as 5
  a house or does it include whatever a person possesses outside the house,
  as well? Is all this part of the estate?
CRITOBULUS. I certainly think that even if it is not in the same city as 6
  the possessor, everything a person possesses is part of his estate.
SOCRATES. Don't some people also possess enemies?
CRITOBULUS. Yes, by Zeus, and some even have a great many.
SOCRATES. Then shall we also include enemies among their possessions?
CRITOBULUS. It would certainly be ridiculous, if someone increased the
  number of a man's enemies and then were paid money for doing so,
  as well.
SOCRATES. Yet, you know, we thought a man's estate was the same as his 7
  property.
CRITOBULUS. That's true, by Zeus, at least of any good thing he possesses;

---

[1] An oath by Zeus interjected into the conversation was mild.

Δι' οὐκ εἴ τι κακόν, τοῦτο κτῆμα ἐγὼ καλῶ. Σὺ δ' ἔοικας τὰ ἑκάστῳ ὠφέλιμα κτήματα καλεῖν. Πάνυ μὲν οὖν, ἔφη· τὰ δέ γε
8 *βλάπτοντα ζημίαν ἔγωγε νομίζω μᾶλλον ἢ χρήματα. Κἂν ἄρα γέ τις ἵππον πριάμενος μὴ ἐπίστηται αὐτῷ χρῆσθαι, ἀλλὰ καταπίπτων ἀπ' αὐτοῦ κακὰ λαμβάνῃ, οὐ χρήματα αὐτῷ ἐστιν ὁ ἵππος; Οὔκ,* 5
εἴπερ τὰ χρήματά γ' ἐστὶν ἀγαθόν. Οὐδ' ἄρα γε ἡ γῆ ἀνθρώπῳ ἐστὶ χρήματα, ὅστις οὕτως ἐργάζεται αὐτὴν ὥστε ζημιοῦσθαι ἐργαζόμενος. Οὐδὲ ἡ γῆ μέντοι χρήματά ἐστιν, εἴπερ ἀντὶ τοῦ
9 *τρέφειν πεινῆν παρασκευάζει. Οὐκοῦν καὶ τὰ πρόβατα ὡσαύτως, εἴ τις διὰ τὸ μὴ ἐπίστασθαι προβάτοις χρῆσθαι ζημιοῖτο, οὐδὲ τὰ* 10
πρόβατα χρήματα τούτῳ εἴη ἄν; Οὔκουν ἔμοιγε δοκεῖ. Σὺ ἄρα, ὡς ἔοικε, τὰ μὲν ὠφελοῦντα χρήματα ἡγῇ, τὰ δὲ βλάπτοντα οὐ
10 *χρήματα. Οὕτως. Ταὐτὰ ἄρα ὄντα τῷ μὲν ἐπισταμένῳ χρῆσθαι αὐτῶν ἑκάστοις χρήματά ἐστι, τῷ δὲ μὴ ἐπισταμένῳ οὐ χρήματα· ὥσπερ γε αὐλοὶ τῷ μὲν ἐπισταμένῳ ἀξίως λόγου αὐλεῖν χρήματά* 15
εἰσι, τῷ δὲ μὴ ἐπισταμένῳ οὐδὲν μᾶλλον ἢ ἄχρηστοι λίθοι. Εἰ μὴ
11 *ἀποδιδοῖτό γε αὐτούς. τοῦτ' αὖ φαίνεται ἡμῖν, ἀποδιδομένοις μὲν οἱ αὐλοὶ χρήματα, μὴ ἀποδιδομένοις δὲ ἀλλὰ κεκτημένοις οὔ, τοῖς μὴ ἐπισταμένοις αὐτοῖς χρῆσθαι. Καὶ ὁμολογουμένως γε, ὦ Σώκρατες, ὁ λόγος ἡμῖν χωρεῖ, ἐπείπερ εἴρηται τὰ ὠφελοῦντα* 20
χρήματα εἶναι. μὴ πωλούμενοι μὲν γὰρ οὐ χρήματά εἰσιν οἱ αὐλοί·
12 *οὐδὲν γὰρ χρήσιμοί εἰσι· πωλούμενοι δὲ χρήματα. πρὸς ταῦτα δ' ὁ Σωκράτης εἶπεν· Ἂν ἐπίστηταί γε πωλεῖν. εἰ δὲ πωλοίη αὖ πρὸς τοῦτο ᾧ μὴ ἐπίσταιτο χρῆσθαι, οὐδὲ πωλούμενοί εἰσι χρήματα κατά γε τὸν σὸν λόγον. Λέγειν ἔοικας, ὦ Σώκρατες, ὅτι οὐδὲ τὸ* 25
13 *ἀργύριόν ἐστι χρήματα, εἰ μή τις ἐπίσταιτο χρῆσθαι αὐτῷ. Καὶ σὺ δέ μοι δοκεῖς οὕτω συνομολογεῖν, ἀφ' ὧν τις ὠφελεῖσθαι δύναται, χρήματα εἶναι. εἰ γοῦν τις χρῷτο τῷ ἀργυρίῳ ὥστε πριάμενος οἷον ἑταίραν διὰ ταύτην κάκιον μὲν τὸ σῶμα ἔχοι, κάκιον δὲ τὴν ψυχήν, κάκιον δὲ τὸν οἶκον, πῶς ἂν ἔτι τὸ ἀργύριον* 30
αὐτῷ ὠφέλιμον εἴη; Οὐδαμῶς, εἰ μή πέρ γε καὶ τὸν ὑοσκύαμον καλούμενον χρήματα εἶναι φήσομεν, ὑφ' οὗ οἱ φαγόντες

---

1 δ' K et M s.v.: om. cet.   4 ἐπίστηται F K: ἐπίσταται. vel ἐπίσταιτο cet.
6 γ' om. H al. R   8 χρῆμα Y al.   16 ἐστι(ν) A P   ἄχρηστοι del. Herwerden
16–17 *Εἰ μὴ ἀποδιδοῖτό γε αὐτούς* Critobulo vindicavit Thalheim   17 αὖ] οὖν O:
αὐτὸ Weiske   18 post τοῖς add. γε Schneider   19 ὁμολογουμένως] δι'
ὁμολογουμένων Hirschig   23 εἰ ἐπίσταται Ven. 513   24 τούτο Ven. 513: τούτου
cet.   ᾧ Cobet: ὃς codd.   ἐπίσταιτο K: ἐπίσταται R Ven. 513: ἐπίστητο J: ἐπίσταιται
vel ἐπιστῆται cet.   26 ἢν μή τις ἐπίστηται Q R Ven. 513   32 φαγόντες B K
L M: φαγόντες αὐτὸ vel αὐτὸν vel αὐτοὶ cet.

if something is bad, by Zeus, I don't call it a possession.

SOCRATES. You seem to be calling 'property' whatever is beneficial to its owner.

CRITOBULUS. I most certainly do, and I consider what is harmful to be loss rather than wealth.

SOCRATES. And so if someone has bought a horse and does not know how 8 to use it, but keeps falling off and is injured, the horse doesn't count as wealth for him, I suppose?

CRITOBULUS. Not on the assumption that wealth is a good thing.

SOCRATES. Similarly, land is not wealth for a man who cultivates it in such a way that by its cultivation he incurs loss.

CRITOBULUS. No, not even land is wealth, then, if instead of nourishment it produces hunger.

SOCRATES. Isn't the principle the same with sheep: if someone incurred 9 loss through not knowing how to deal with sheep, the sheep wouldn't be wealth for him?

CRITOBULUS. Certainly not, in my opinion.

SOCRATES. Therefore, it seems, you consider what is beneficial as wealth and what is harmful as not wealth.

CRITOBULUS. Exactly.   10

SOCRATES. Things that are the same, then, can be wealth for the person who knows how to use each of them, but not wealth for one who does not know. On the same principle, flutes are wealth for the person who knows how to play the flute reasonably well, but about as useful as stones for one who does not know how to play.

CRITOBULUS. Yes, unless he sells them.

SOCRATES. Furthermore, this is our conclusion: for those who do not know 11 how to use them flutes are wealth if they sell them, but not wealth if they do not sell them but keep them.

CRITOBULUS. And our argument is progressing consistently, Socrates, because we have said that what is beneficial is wealth. For if flutes are not sold they are not wealth, for they aren't useful; but when they are 12 sold, they become wealth.

SOCRATES (*replying*). If, that is, a person knows how to sell them. But then again, if he should sell them in exchange for something he does not know how to use, even when sold they do not constitute wealth, at least according to your argument.

CRITOBULUS. You appear to be saying, Socrates, that even money isn't wealth unless a person knows how to use it.

SOCRATES. And you seem to agree with me, then, on this point, that what 13 a person can derive benefits from is wealth. If, at any rate, someone were to use wealth to buy a hetaira,[2] for example, and because of her he becomes worse in body, worse in soul, and worse in regard to his estate, how could money be beneficial to him in that case?

CRITOBULUS. In no way at all, unless we go so far as to say that the weed

---

[2] Perhaps 'hired or purchased bed-partner'. Modern English-speaking society has no counterpart, hence no precise word. See note on this passage.

14 παραπλῆγες γίγνονται. Τὸ μὲν δὴ ἀργύριον, εἰ μή τις ἐπίσταιτο
αὐτῷ χρῆσθαι, οὕτω πόρρω ἀπωθείσθω, ὦ Κριτόβουλε, ὥστε μηδὲ
χρήματα εἶναι. οἱ δὲ φίλοι, ἄν τις ἐπίστηται αὐτοῖς χρῆσθαι ὥστε
ὠφελεῖσθαι ἀπ' αὐτῶν, τί φήσομεν αὐτοὺς εἶναι; Χρήματα νὴ Δί',
ἔφη ὁ Κριτόβουλος, καὶ πολύ γε μᾶλλον ἢ τοὺς βοῦς, ἂν 5
15 ὠφελιμώτεροί γε ὦσι τῶν βοῶν. Καὶ οἱ ἐχθροί γε ἄρα κατά γε
τὸν σὸν λόγον χρήματά εἰσι τῷ δυναμένῳ ἀπὸ τῶν ἐχθρῶν
ὠφελεῖσθαι. Ἐμοὶ γοῦν δοκεῖ. Οἰκονόμου ἄρα ἐστὶν ἀγαθοῦ καὶ
τοῖς ἐχθροῖς ἐπίστασθαι χρῆσθαι ὥστε ὠφελεῖσθαι ἀπὸ τῶν
ἐχθρῶν. Ἰσχυρότατά γε. Καὶ γὰρ δὴ ὁρᾷς, ἔφη, ὦ Κριτόβουλε, 10
ὅσοι μὲν δὴ οἶκοι ἰδιωτῶν ηὐξημένοι εἰσὶν ἀπὸ πολέμου, ὅσοι δὲ
16 τυράννων. Ἀλλὰ γὰρ τὰ μὲν καλῶς ἔμοιγε δοκεῖ λέγεσθαι, ὦ
Σώκρατες, ἔφη ὁ Κριτόβουλος· ἐκεῖνο δ' ἡμῖν τί φαίνεται, ὁπόταν
ὁρῶμέν τινας ἐπιστήμας μὲν ἔχοντας καὶ ἀφορμὰς ἀφ' ὧν δύνανται
ἐργαζόμενοι αὔξειν τοὺς οἴκους, αἰσθανώμεθα δὲ αὐτοὺς ταῦτα μὴ 15
θέλοντας ποιεῖν, καὶ διὰ τοῦτο ὁρῶμεν ἀνωφελεῖς οὔσας αὐτοῖς
τὰς ἐπιστήμας; ἄλλο τι ἢ τούτοις αὖ οὔτε αἱ ἐπιστῆμαι χρήματά
17 εἰσιν οὔτε τὰ κτήματα; Περὶ δούλων μοι, ἔφη ὁ Σωκράτης,
ἐπιχειρεῖς, ὦ Κριτόβουλε, διαλέγεσθαι; Οὐ μὰ Δί', ἔφη, οὐκ ἔγωγε,
ἀλλὰ καὶ πάνυ εὐπατριδῶν ἐνίων γε δοκούντων εἶναι, οὓς ἐγὼ ὁρῶ 20
τοὺς μὲν πολεμικάς, τοὺς δὲ καὶ εἰρηνικὰς ἐπιστήμας ἔχοντας,
ταύτας δὲ οὐκ ἐθέλοντας ἐργάζεσθαι, ὡς μὲν ἐγὼ οἶμαι, δι' αὐτὸ
18 τοῦτο ὅτι δεσπότας οὐκ ἔχουσιν. Καὶ πῶς ἄν, ἔφη ὁ Σωκράτης,
δεσπότας οὐκ ἔχοιεν, εἰ εὐχόμενοι εὐδαιμονεῖν καὶ ποιεῖν βουλόμενοι ἀφ' ὧν ⟨ἂν⟩ ἔχοιεν ἀγαθὰ ἔπειτα κωλύονται ποιεῖν ταῦτα 25
ὑπὸ τῶν ἀρχόντων; Καὶ τίνες δὴ οὗτοί εἰσιν, ἔφη ὁ Κριτόβουλος,
19 οἳ ἀφανεῖς ὄντες ἄρχουσιν αὐτῶν; Ἀλλὰ μὰ Δί', ἔφη ὁ Σωκράτης,
οὐκ ἀφανεῖς εἰσιν, ἀλλὰ καὶ πάνυ φανεροί. καὶ ὅτι πονηρότατοί γέ
εἰσιν οὐδὲ σὲ λανθάνουσιν, εἴπερ πονηρίαν γε νομίζεις ἀργίαν τ'
20 εἶναι καὶ μαλακίαν ψυχῆς καὶ ἀμέλειαν. καὶ ἄλλαι δ' εἰσὶν ἀπατηλαί 30
τινες δέσποιναι προσποιούμεναι ἡδοναὶ εἶναι, κυβεῖαί τε καὶ
ἀνωφελεῖς ἀνθρώπων ὁμιλίαι, αἳ προϊόντος τοῦ χρόνου καὶ αὐτοῖς
τοῖς ἐξαπατηθεῖσι καταφανεῖς γίγνονται ὅτι λῦπαι ἄρα ἦσαν
ἡδοναῖς περιπεπεμμέναι, αἳ διακωλύουσιν αὐτοὺς ἀπὸ τῶν

---

3 ἐπίσταιτο H al.   9 ὠφελεῖσθαι καὶ conicio coll. Plut. *Mor.* p. 86 C   10 post
γε lacunam statuit Cobet   12 τυραννιῶν G: ἀπὸ τυράννων D: ἀπὸ τυραννιῶν cet.:
corr. Weiske: καὶ τυράννων Schneider   17 post ἐπιστήμας add. καὶ τὰς ἀφορμάς
Bock   18 τὰ om. H al.   21 post μὲν add. καὶ Y al.   23 ἔχουσιν Schäfer:
ἔχοιεν codd.   25 ἂν add. Richards   34 περιπεπλεγμέναι H al.

called henbane, which drives people mad if they eat it, is wealth.

SOCRATES. So if someone does not know how to use money, he should 14
thrust it so far away, Critobulus, that it doesn't even count as wealth
any more. Now, as for friends, if someone knows how to use them so as
to benefit from them, what shall we say they are?

CRITOBULUS. Wealth, by Zeus, and much more so than cattle, if they
actually are more beneficial than cattle.

SOCRATES. And enemies, at least according to your argument, are wealth 15
to anyone who can benefit from enemies.

CRITOBULUS. That is my opinion.

SOCRATES. Consequently, knowing how to use enemies so as to derive
benefit from them is a characteristic of a good estate manager.

CRITOBULUS. Most definitely.

SOCRATES. In fact, Critobulus, you see how many estates of private individuals have been increased by war, and of tyrants, too.

CRITOBULUS. Yes, I think what we have just said is right, Socrates, 16
but what is our view about the following question? Sometimes
we observe people who have the knowledge and the resources with
which they are able to increase their estates, provided they work;
yet we perceive that they do not want to do so, and we see that
their knowledge is therefore useless to them. Are we not forced to
conclude that for such people neither their knowledge nor their
property is wealth?

SOCRATES. Are you trying to discuss slaves with me, Critobulus? 17

CRITOBULUS. No, by Zeus, I'm not, but I'm talking about men, including,
it seems, those of the noblest birth, some of whom, I see, are skilful in
the arts of war, and others in those of peacetime. But they do not want
to make use of these skills, I believe, precisely because they have no
masters.

SOCRATES. And how can they be said to have no masters, if despite their 18
prayers for success and their wish to do something which will result in
good for them, they are nevertheless prevented from doing so by their
rulers?

CRITOBULUS. And who on earth are these? They rule them, yet are
invisible.

SOCRATES. No, by Zeus, they are not invisible, but very obvious 19
indeed! And even you must have noticed that they are most vicious, if,
that is, you think that idleness and moral weakness and carelessness
are vices. And there are also some deceptive mistresses who pretend 20
to be pleasures: gambling, and keeping unprofitable company. As
time goes by, it becomes obvious, even to those who had been
initially deceived, that they are really pains disguised as pleasures,
which, by dominating them, prevent them from engaging in profitable
occupations.

21 ὠφελίμων ἔργων κρατοῦσαι. Ἀλλὰ καὶ ἄλλοι, ἔφη, ὦ Σώκρατες,
ἐργάζεσθαι μὲν οὐ κωλύονται ὑπὸ τούτων, ἀλλὰ καὶ πάνυ σφοδρῶς
πρὸς τὸ ἐργάζεσθαι ἔχουσι καὶ μηχανᾶσθαι προσόδους· ὅμως δὲ
22 καὶ τοὺς οἴκους κατατρίβουσι καὶ ἀμηχανίαις συνέχονται. Δοῦλοι
γάρ εἰσι καὶ οὗτοι, ἔφη ὁ Σωκράτης, καὶ πάνυ γε χαλεπῶν 5
δεσποτῶν, οἱ μὲν λιχνειῶν, οἱ δὲ λαγνειῶν, οἱ δὲ οἰνοφλυγιῶν, οἱ
δὲ φιλοτιμιῶν τινων μώρων καὶ δαπανηρῶν, ἃ οὕτω χαλεπῶς ἄρχει
τῶν ἀνθρώπων ὧν ἂν ἐπικρατήσωσιν, ὥσθ' ἕως μὲν ἂν ὁρῶσιν
ἡβῶντας αὐτοὺς καὶ δυναμένους ἐργάζεσθαι, ἀναγκάζουσι φέρειν
ἃ ἂν αὐτοὶ ἐργάσωνται καὶ τελεῖν εἰς τὰς αὐτῶν ἐπιθυμίας, ἐπειδὰν 10
δὲ αὐτοὺς ἀδυνάτους αἴσθωνται ὄντας ἐργάζεσθαι διὰ τὸ γῆρας,
ἀπολείπουσι τούτους κακῶς γηράσκειν, ἄλλοις δ' αὖ πειρῶνται
23 δούλοις χρῆσθαι. ἀλλὰ δεῖ, ὦ Κριτόβουλε, πρὸς ταῦτα οὐχ ἧττον
διαμάχεσθαι περὶ τῆς ἐλευθερίας ἢ πρὸς τοὺς σὺν ὅπλοις
πειρωμένους καταδουλοῦσθαι. πολέμιοι μὲν οὖν ἤδη ὅταν καλοὶ 15
κἀγαθοὶ ὄντες καταδουλώσωνταί τινας, πολλοὺς δὴ βελτίους
ἠνάγκασαν εἶναι σωφρονίσαντες, καὶ ῥᾶον βιοτεύειν τὸν λοιπὸν
χρόνον ἐποίησαν· αἱ δὲ τοιαῦται δέσποιναι αἰκιζόμεναι τὰ σώματα
τῶν ἀνθρώπων καὶ τὰς ψυχὰς καὶ τοὺς οἴκους οὔποτε λήγουσιν,
ἔστ' ἂν ἄρχωσιν αὐτῶν. 20

II Ὁ οὖν Κριτόβουλος ἐκ τούτων ὧδέ πως εἶπεν· Ἀλλὰ περὶ μὲν
τῶν τοιούτων ἀρκούντως πάνυ μοι δοκῶ τὰ λεγόμενα ὑπὸ σοῦ
ἀκηκοέναι· αὐτὸς δ' ἐμαυτὸν ἐξετάζων δοκῶ μοι εὑρίσκειν ἐπιεικῶς
τῶν τοιούτων ἐγκρατῆ ὄντα, ὥστ' εἴ μοι συμβουλεύοις ὅ τι ἂν
ποιῶν αὔξοιμι τὸν οἶκον, οὐκ ἄν μοι δοκῶ ὑπό γε τούτων ὧν σὺ 25
δεσποινῶν καλεῖς κωλύεσθαι· ἀλλὰ θαρρῶν συμβούλευε ὅ τι ἔχεις
ἀγαθόν· ἢ κατέγνωκας ἡμῶν, ὦ Σώκρατες, ἱκανῶς πλουτεῖν καὶ
2 οὐδὲν δοκοῦμέν σοι προσδεῖσθαι χρημάτων; Οὔκουν ἔγωγε, ἔφη ὁ
Σωκράτης, εἰ καὶ περὶ ἐμοῦ λέγεις, οὐδέν μοι δοκῶ προσδεῖσθαι
χρημάτων, ἀλλ' ἱκανῶς πλουτεῖν· σὺ μέντοι, ὦ Κριτόβουλε, πάνυ 30
μοι δοκεῖς πένεσθαι, καὶ ναὶ μὰ Δί' ἔστιν ὅτε καὶ πάνυ οἰκτίρω σε
3 ἐγώ. καὶ ὁ Κριτόβουλος γελάσας εἶπε· Καὶ πόσον ἂν πρὸς τῶν
θεῶν οἴει, ὦ Σώκρατες, ἔφη, εὑρεῖν τὰ σὰ κτήματα πωλούμενα,
πόσον δὲ τὰ ἐμά; Ἐγὼ μὲν οἶμαι, ἔφη ὁ Σωκράτης, εἰ ἀγαθοῦ

3 τῷ(ι) B F al.: cf. xii. 16   4 ἀμηχανία B K L Q R Ven. 513   6 δεσποινῶν
Weiske   7 ἃ … ἄρχει] αἴ … ἄρχουσι Hirschig   10 αὐτῶν Sauppe: αὑτῶν
codd.   15 οὖν] γ' οὖν vel γοῦν codd. multi   17 σωφρονίσαντες G:
σωφρονίσαντας H N pr.: σωφρονήσαντε(vel α)ς cet.   λοιπὸν] hic desinit B   33 ἔφη
om. F

110

CRITOBULUS. But there are also others, Socrates, who are not prevented 21
from working by such masters, but are seriously disposed to work and
contrive to make an income; nevertheless they dissipate their estates and
are entangled in difficulties.

SOCRATES. And these, too, are slaves, and they are ruled by extremely 22
harsh masters. Some are ruled by gluttony, some by fornication, some
by drunkenness, and some by foolish and expensive ambitions which
rule cruelly over any men they get into their power, as long as they see
that they are in their prime and able to work; so cruelly indeed, that
they force them to bring whatever they have earned by working and to
spend it on their desires. But when they perceive that they are unable
to work because of age, they abandon them to a wretched old age and
they try to use others as their slaves, in turn. But, Critobulus, we must 23
constantly fight for our freedom against these influences even more than
against armed men trying to enslave us. For, in fact, whenever enemies
who are gentlemen try to enslave people, they force many of them to
become better by bringing them to their senses and make them live a
less strenuous life in the future. Whereas mistresses such as I have
described perpetually attack the bodies and souls and estates of men all
the time that they dominate them.

After this, Critobulus spoke more or less as follows: II

Well, I think I have listened enough to what you have said about such
influences. When I examine myself I believe I find that I am pretty well
in control of such things. Therefore if you give me advice about what
to do to increase my estate, I don't think I shall be stopped by those
things that you call 'mistresses'. So, then, take courage and give me
whatever good advice you can. Or have you judged, Socrates, that we
are rich enough and that we do not need additional wealth?

SOCRATES. If you're talking about me too, I, at least, don't think I need 2
additional wealth; I'm rich enough. However, you, Critobulus, seem to
me very poor, and, by Zeus, there are times when I greatly pity you.

CRITOBULUS (*laughing*): By the gods, how much do you think your property 3
would bring in if it were sold, and how much would mine?

SOCRATES. I think, if I came across a good buyer, all my property including

ὠνητοῦ ἐπιτύχοιμι, εὑρεῖν ἄν μοι σὺν τῇ οἰκίᾳ καὶ τὰ ὄντα πάντα
πάνυ ῥᾳδίως πέντε μνᾶς· τὰ μέντοι σὰ ἀκριβῶς οἶδα ὅτι πλέον ἂν
4 εὗροι ἢ ἑκατονταπλασίονα τούτου. Κᾆτα οὕτως ἐγνωκὼς σὺ μὲν
οὐχ ἡγῇ προσδεῖσθαι χρημάτων, ἐμὲ δὲ οἰκτίρεις ἐπὶ τῇ πενίᾳ; Τὰ
μὲν γὰρ ἐμά, ἔφη, ἱκανά ἐστιν ἐμοὶ παρέχειν τὰ ἐμοὶ ἀρκοῦντα· 5
εἰς δὲ τὸ σὸν σχῆμα ὃ σὺ περιβέβλησαι καὶ τὴν σὴν δόξαν, οὐδ᾽ εἰ
τρὶς ὅσα νῦν κέκτησαι προσγένοιτό σοι, οὐδ᾽ ὡς ἂν ἱκανά μοι δοκεῖ
5 εἶναί σοι. Πῶς δὴ τοῦτ᾽; ἔφη ὁ Κριτόβουλος. ἀπεφήνατο ὁ
Σωκράτης· Ὅτι πρῶτον μὲν ὁρῶ σοι ἀνάγκην οὖσαν θύειν πολλά
τε καὶ μεγάλα, ἢ οὔτε θεοὺς οὔτε ἀνθρώπους οἶμαί σε ἂν 10
ἀνασχέσθαι· ἔπειτα ξένους προσήκει σοι πολλοὺς δέχεσθαι, καὶ
τούτους μεγαλοπρεπῶς· ἔπειτα δὲ πολίτας δειπνίζειν καὶ εὖ ποιεῖν,
6 ἢ ἔρημον συμμάχων εἶναι. ἔτι δὲ καὶ τὴν πόλιν αἰσθάνομαι τὰ μὲν
ἤδη σοι προστάττουσαν μεγάλα τελεῖν, ἱπποτροφίας τε καὶ
χορηγίας καὶ γυμνασιαρχίας καὶ προστατείας, ἂν δὲ δὴ πόλεμος 15
γένηται, οἶδ᾽ ὅτι καὶ τριηραρχίας [μισθοὺς] καὶ εἰσφορὰς τοσαύτας
σοι προστάξουσιν ὅσας σὺ οὐ ῥᾳδίως ὑποίσεις. ὅπου δ᾽ ἂν ἐνδεῶς
δόξῃς τι τούτων ποιεῖν, οἶδ᾽ ὅτι σε τιμωρήσονται Ἀθηναῖοι οὐδὲν
7 ἧττον ἢ εἰ τὰ αὑτῶν λάβοιεν κλέπτοντα. πρὸς δὲ τούτοις ὁρῶ σε
οἰόμενον πλουτεῖν, καὶ ἀμελῶς μὲν ἔχοντα πρὸς τὸ μηχανᾶσθαι 20
χρήματα, παιδικοῖς δὲ πράγμασι προσέχοντα τὸν νοῦν, ὥσπερ ἐξόν
σοι. ὧν ἕνεκα οἰκτίρω σε μή τι ἀνήκεστον κακὸν πάθῃς καὶ εἰς
8 πολλὴν ἀπορίαν καταστῇς. καὶ ἐμοὶ μέν, εἴ τι καὶ προσδεηθείην,
οἶδ᾽ ὅτι καὶ σὺ γιγνώσκεις ὡς εἰσὶν οἳ καὶ ἐπαρκέσειαν ἂν ὥστε
πάνυ μικρὰ πορίσαντες κατακλύσειαν ἂν ἀφθονίᾳ τὴν ἐμὴν δίαιταν· 25
οἱ δὲ σοὶ φίλοι πολὺ ἀρκοῦντα σοῦ μᾶλλον ἔχοντες τῇ ἑαυτῶν
κατασκευῇ ἢ σὺ τῇ σῇ ὅμως ὡς παρὰ σοῦ ὠφελησόμενοι
9 ἀποβλέπουσι. καὶ ὁ Κριτόβουλος εἶπεν· Ἐγὼ τούτοις, ὦ
Σώκρατες, οὐκ ἔχω ἀντιλέγειν· ἀλλ᾽ ὥρα σοι προστατεύειν ἐμοῦ,
ὅπως μὴ τῷ ὄντι οἰκτρὸς γένωμαι. ἀκούσας οὖν ὁ Σωκράτης εἶπε· 30
Καὶ οὐ θαυμαστὸν δοκεῖς, ὦ Κριτόβουλε, τοῦτο σαυτῷ ποιεῖν, ὅτι
ὀλίγῳ μὲν πρόσθεν, ὅτε ἐγὼ ἔφην πλουτεῖν, ἐγέλασας ἐπ᾽ ἐμοὶ
ὡς οὐδὲ εἰδότι ὅ τι εἴη πλοῦτος, καὶ πρότερον οὐκ ἐπαύσω πρὶν
ἐξήλεγξάς με καὶ ὁμολογεῖν ἐποίησας μηδὲ ἑκατοστὸν μέρος τῶν

---

1 μοι] μου Mehler   σὺν τῇ οἰκίᾳ] τὴν οἰκίαν Mehler   ὄντα] ἐνόντα Mehler
3 ἑκατονταπλάσια Hertlein   8 ἀπεφήνατο codd.: ἀπεκρίνατο Dind.: ἀπεφήνατο ὁ
Σωκράτης del. Cobet   10 οὔτε θεοὺς Stephanus: ὅσους codd.   12 τούτους]
ταῦτα cit. Richards   16 μισθοὺς del Cobet   19 τὰ αὑτῶν L: τὰ αὐτῶν, ταὐτῶν,
τ᾽ αὑτῶν cet.   21 πράγμασι susp. Leonclavio   24 ἂν D K: om. cet.   27 ὡς
F G: om. cet.   32 ὀλίγον K L

the house would very easily bring in five minae; but I know for sure that yours would bring in more than a hundred times as much.

CRITOBULUS. And although you recognize this, you think you don't need 4 any more wealth, and you pity me for my poverty?

SOCRATES. Yes, for my property is enough to provide me with all I need. Considering the style of life you have assumed and your reputation, I think that even if three times what you now have were added to your possessions, it wouldn't be enough for you.

CRITOBULUS. What do you mean? 5

SOCRATES. Because, first of all, I see that you need to offer many large sacrifices, or, I suppose, neither gods nor men would put up with you. Then you are expected to entertain many foreign guests, and generously at that. Thirdly, you must give feasts for the citizens and be a benefactor to them, or else you won't have anyone on your side. Furthermore, I 6 perceive that the state even now orders you to make large payments for keeping horses, and for training choruses for the festivals, and for athletic competitions and presidencies. And if there should be a war I know that they will order you to pay for the maintenance of triremes and to contribute to the cost of the war to an extent that you will find difficult to bear. If they think that you are fulfilling any of these obligations inadequately, I know the Athenians will punish you no less than if they had caught you stealing their property. In addition to this, I see that 7 you think you are wealthy and are negligent about contriving to make money, and you pay attention to boys' affairs as though it were within your means. Therefore I pity you and I'm afraid that you may suffer some irreversible misfortune and find yourself reduced to abject poverty. As for me, if I should possibly need anything else, you know, as I do, 8 that there are people who would help me so that by furnishing very little they would make my life overflow with abundance. But your friends, although they have means far more adequate for their style of life than you have for yours, look towards you in the hope that they will receive benefits from you.

CRITOBULUS. I cannot deny that, Socrates, but it is time for you to take 9 charge of me so that I don't really become an object of pity.

SOCRATES. Doesn't it seem to you that you're behaving in an amazing way, Critobulus? For a little while ago when I said I was rich, you laughed at me as though I didn't even know what wealth was, and you didn't stop until you had proved me wrong? And you forced me to agree that my possessions were less than a hundredth part of yours; but

σῶν κεκτῆσθαι, νῦν δὲ κελεύεις προστατεύειν μέ σου καὶ
10 ἐπιμελεῖσθαι ὅπως ἂν μὴ παντάπασιν ἀληθῶς πένης γένοιο· Ὁρῶ
γάρ σε, ἔφη, ὦ Σώκρατες, ἕν τι πλουτηρὸν ἔργον ἐπιστάμενον
περιουσίαν ποιεῖν. τὸν οὖν ἀπ᾽ ὀλίγων περιποιοῦντα ἐλπίζω ἀπὸ
11 πολλῶν γ᾽ ἂν πάνυ ῥᾳδίως πολλὴν περιουσίαν ποιῆσαι. Οὔκουν 5
μέμνησαι ἀρτίως ἐν τῷ λόγῳ ὅτε οὐδ᾽ ἀναγρύζειν μοι ἐξουσίαν
ἐποίησας, λέγων ὅτι τῷ μὴ ἐπισταμένῳ ἵπποις χρῆσθαι οὐκ εἴη
χρήματα οἱ ἵπποι οὐδὲ ἡ γῆ οὐδὲ τὰ πρόβατα οὐδὲ ἀργύριον οὐδὲ
ἄλλο οὐδὲ ἓν ὅτῳ τις μὴ ἐπίσταιτο χρῆσθαι; εἰσὶ μὲν οὖν αἱ
πρόσοδοι ἀπὸ τῶν τοιούτων· ἐμὲ δὲ πῶς τινι τούτων οἴει ἂν 10
ἐπιστηθῆναι χρῆσθαι, ᾧ τὴν ἀρχὴν οὐδὲν πώποτ᾽ ἐγένετο τούτων;
12 Ἀλλ᾽ ἐδόκει ἡμῖν, καὶ εἰ μὴ χρήματά τις τύχοι ἔχων, ὅμως εἶναί
τις ἐπιστήμη οἰκονομίας. τί οὖν κωλύει καὶ σὲ ἐπίστασθαι; Ὅπερ
νὴ Δία καὶ αὐλεῖν ἂν κωλύσειεν ἄνθρωπον ἐπίστασθαι, εἰ μήτε
αὐτὸς πώποτε κτήσαιτο αὐλοὺς μήτε ἄλλος αὐτῷ παράσχοι ἐν τοῖς 15
13 αὐτοῦ μανθάνειν· οὕτω δὴ καὶ ἐμοὶ ἔχει περὶ τῆς οἰκονομίας. οὔτε
γὰρ αὐτὸς ὄργανα χρήματα ἐκεκτήμην, ὥστε μανθάνειν, οὔτε ἄλλος
πώποτέ μοι παρέσχε τὰ ἑαυτοῦ διοικεῖν ἀλλ᾽ ἢ σὺ νυνὶ ἐθέλεις
παρέχειν. οἱ δὲ δήπου τὸ πρῶτον μανθάνοντες κιθαρίζειν καὶ τὰς
λύρας λυμαίνονται· καὶ ἐγὼ δὴ εἰ ἐπιχειρήσαιμι ἐν τῷ σῷ οἴκῳ 20
μανθάνειν οἰκονομεῖν, ἴσως ἂν καταλυμηναίμην ἄν σου τὸν οἶκον.
14 πρὸς ταῦτα ὁ Κριτόβουλος εἶπε· Προθύμως γε, ὦ Σώκρατες,
ἀποφεύγειν μοι πειρᾷ μηδέν με συνωφελῆσαι εἰς τὸ ῥᾷον ὑποφέρειν
τὰ ἐμοὶ ἀναγκαῖα πράγματα. Οὐ μὰ Δί᾽, ἔφη ὁ Σωκράτης, οὐκ
15 ἔγωγε, ἀλλ᾽ ὅσα ἔχω καὶ πάνυ προθύμως ἐξηγήσομαί σοι. οἶμαι 25
δ᾽ ἂν καὶ εἰ ἐπὶ πῦρ ἐλθόντος σου καὶ μὴ ὄντος παρ᾽ ἐμοί, εἰ ἄλλοσε
ἡγησάμην ὁπόθεν σοι εἴη λαβεῖν, οὐκ ἂν ἐμέμφου μοι, καὶ εἰ ὕδωρ
παρ᾽ ἐμοῦ αἰτοῦντί σοι αὐτὸς μὴ ἔχων ἄλλοσε καὶ ἐπὶ τοῦτο
ἤγαγον, οἶδ᾽ ὅτι οὐδ᾽ ἂν τοῦτό μοι ἐμέμφου, καὶ εἰ βουλομένου
μουσικὴν μαθεῖν σου παρ᾽ ἐμοῦ δείξαιμί σοι πολὺ δεινοτέρους ἐμοῦ 30
περὶ μουσικὴν καί σοι χάριν ⟨ἂν⟩ εἰδότας, εἰ ἐθέλοις παρ᾽ αὐτῶν
μανθάνειν, τί ἂν ἔτι μοι ταῦτα ποιοῦντι μέμφοιο; Οὐδὲν ἂν δικαίως
16 γε, ὦ Σώκρατες. Ἐγὼ τοίνυν σοι δείξω, ὦ Κριτόβουλε, ὅσα νῦν
λιπαρεῖς παρ᾽ ἐμοῦ μανθάνειν πολὺ ἄλλους ἐμοῦ δεινοτέρους

8 τἀργύριον R Ven. 513   11 οὐδὲν (ν s.v.) A: οὐδὲ cet. (μηδὲ O)   16 αὑτοῦ
codd.: corr. Stephanus   17 χρήματα del. Hartman   23 μοι susp. Schneidero
26 εἰ del. Cobet   28 αἰτοῦντά σε cit. Hartman   post ἔχων add. παρέχειν
Richards   29 ἤγαγον] ἡγησάμην Platt   30 prius ἐμοῦ K L: ἡμῶν cet.
31 ἂν add. Heindorf   33 γε om. H al.   34 ἐμοῦ om. D C

now you ask me to take charge of you and be concerned that you avoid falling into real and utter poverty?

CRITOBULUS. Socrates, I see that you know one particular way of making 10 wealth: the creation of a surplus. So I expect that the man who can make a surplus out of small resources can very easily produce a large surplus from large resources.

SOCRATES. Don't you remember that recently during our discussion when 11 you didn't allow me to get a word in edgeways, you said that horses do not constitute wealth to a man who does not know how to use horses, nor land, nor sheep, nor money, nor anything else which a person does not know how to use? For it is from such sources that revenues come. How do you think I know how to use any of these, since I have never owned any of them at all?

CRITOBULUS. But we agreed that even if someone didn't actually have 12 wealth, nevertheless there is a branch of knowledge concerned with estate management. What prevents you from knowing about it?

SOCRATES. That which, by Zeus, would prevent a man from knowing how to play the flute, if he himself never owned flutes, and if no one else lent him instruments so that he had an opportunity to learn to play. That's 13 just how it is with me when it comes to estate management. For neither have I possessed wealth that I could learn on like an instrument, nor has anyone ever offered me his own to manage, except that just now you were prepared to make an offer. Surely those who are first beginning to learn how to play the lyre actually damage the instruments. And certainly if I were to try to learn estate management by practising on your estate, I might well destroy it totally.

CRITOBULUS (*replying to this*). Socrates, you are eagerly trying to avoid 14 helping me bear my unavoidable burdens more easily.

SOCRATES. No, I'm not, by Zeus, but I'm very eager to explain to you as much as I can. I think that if you came to get fire and I did not have 15 any in my house, you wouldn't blame me if I led you to some other place where you could get it; or again, if you had asked me for water and I didn't have any, I'm sure that you would not have blamed me if I had directed you to some other place for this, too. And if you wanted to learn music from me, and I could show you people far more skilled in music than I am, who would be grateful to you if you wished to learn from them, again, why should you blame me for doing this?

CRITOBULUS. I couldn't rightly do so, Socrates.

SOCRATES. Well now, Critobulus, I will show you others far more skilled 16 than I in the subjects you are now begging to learn from me. I confess

[τοὺς] περὶ ταῦτα. ὁμολογῶ δὲ μεμεληκέναι μοι οἵτινες ἕκαστα
17 ἐπιστημονέστατοί εἰσι τῶν ἐν τῇ πόλει. καταμαθὼν γάρ ποτε ἀπὸ
τῶν αὐτῶν ἔργων τοὺς μὲν πάνυ ἀπόρους ὄντας, τοὺς δὲ πάνυ
πλουσίους, ἀπεθαύμασα, καὶ ἔδοξέ μοι ἄξιον εἶναι ἐπισκέψεως ὅ
τι εἴη τοῦτο. καὶ ηὗρον ἐπισκοπῶν πάνυ οἰκείως ταῦτα γιγνόμενα. 5
18 τοὺς μὲν γὰρ εἰκῇ ταῦτα πράττοντας ζημιουμένους ἑώρων, τοὺς
δὲ γνώμῃ συντεταμένῃ ἐπιμελουμένους καὶ θᾶττον καὶ ῥᾷον καὶ
κερδαλεώτερον κατέγνων πράττοντας. παρ᾽ ὧν ἂν καὶ σὲ οἶμαι, εἰ
βούλοιο, μαθόντα, εἴ σοι ὁ θεὸς μὴ ἐναντιοῖτο, πάνυ ἂν δεινὸν
χρηματιστὴν γενέσθαι. 10

III   Ἀκούσας ταῦτα ὁ Κριτόβουλος εἶπε· Νῦν τοι, ἔφη, ἐγώ σε οὐκέτι
ἀφήσω, ὦ Σώκρατες, πρὶν ἄν μοι ἃ ὑπέσχησαι ἐναντίον τῶν φίλων
τουτωνὶ ἀποδείξῃς. Τί οὖν, ἔφη ὁ Σωκράτης, ὦ Κριτόβουλε, ἄν
σοι ἀποδεικνύω πρῶτον μὲν οἰκίας τοὺς μὲν ἀπὸ πολλοῦ ἀργυρίου
ἀχρήστους οἰκοδομοῦντας, τοὺς δὲ ἀπὸ πολὺ ἐλάττονος πάντα 15
ἔχουσας ὅσα δεῖ, ἦ δόξω ἕν τί σοι τοῦτο τῶν οἰκονομικῶν ἔργων
2 ἐπιδεικνύναι; Καὶ πάνυ γ᾽, ἔφη ὁ Κριτόβουλος. Τί δ᾽ ἂν τὸ τούτου
ἀκόλουθον μετὰ τοῦτό σοι ἐπιδεικνύω, τοὺς μὲν πάνυ πολλὰ καὶ
παντοῖα κεκτημένους ἔπιπλα, καὶ τούτοις, ὅταν δέωνται, μὴ
ἔχοντας χρῆσθαι μηδὲ εἰδότας εἰ σῶά ἐστιν αὐτοῖς, καὶ διὰ ταῦτα 20
πολλὰ μὲν αὐτοὺς ἀνιωμένους, πολλὰ δὲ ἀνιῶντας τοὺς οἰκέτας·
τοὺς δὲ οὐδὲν πλέον ἀλλὰ καὶ μείονα τούτων κεκτημένους ἔχοντας
3 εὐθὺς ἕτοιμα [ὅταν] ὧν ἂν δέωνται χρῆσθαι. Ἄλλο τι οὖν τούτων
ἐστίν, ὦ Σώκρατες, αἴτιον ἢ ὅτι τοῖς μὲν ὅπου ἔτυχεν ἕκαστον
καταβέβληται, τοῖς δὲ ἐν χώρᾳ ἕκαστα τεταγμένα κεῖται; Ναὶ μὰ 25
Δί᾽, ἔφη ὁ Σωκράτης· καὶ οὐδ᾽ ἐν χώρᾳ γ᾽ ἐν ᾗ ἔτυχεν, ἀλλ᾽ ἔνθα
προσήκει, ἕκαστα διατέτακται. Λέγειν τί μοι δοκεῖς, ἔφη, καὶ
4 τοῦτο, ὁ Κριτόβουλος, τῶν οἰκονομικῶν. Τί οὖν, ἄν σοι, ἔφη, καὶ
οἰκέτας αὖ ἐπιδεικνύω ἔνθα μὲν πάντας ὡς εἰπεῖν δεδεμένους,
καὶ τούτους θαμινὰ ἀποδιδράσκοντας, ἔνθα δὲ λελυμένους καὶ 30
ἐθέλοντάς τε ἐργάζεσθαι καὶ παραμένειν, οὐ καὶ τοῦτό σοι δόξω
ἀξιοθέατον τῆς οἰκονομίας ἔργον ἐπιδεικνύναι; Ναὶ μὰ Δί᾽, ἔφη ὁ
5 Κριτόβουλος, καὶ σφόδρα γε. Ἂν δὲ καὶ παραπλησίους γεωργίας
γεωργοῦντας, τοὺς μὲν ἀπολωλέναι φάσκοντας ὑπὸ γεωργίας καὶ

---

1 τοὺς om. Q; ὄντας Leonclavius   5 οἰκείως] εἰκότως Herwerden   7 συν-
τεταγμένῃ H al. D al.   14 ἐπιδεικνύω Schneider   16 ἦ Ven. 368 et 511: οὐ
R Ven. 513: ἦ cet.   23 ὅταν codd., sed αν cum corruptelae signo A: del. Dind.:
ὅτων ἂν Koen.   ἄλλο τι Weiske: ἀλλὰ τί codd.   24 ὅποι Sauppe   31 δόξω
Q R Ven. 368, 511₂, 513: δείξω cet.   33 παραπλησίως H al.   34 ἀπὸ H G N

that I have been interested in learning who in the city are most knowledgeable about each occupation. For once when I learned that in the 17
same work some were very poor while others were very wealthy, I was
quite amazed, and I thought it was worth investigating just why this
should be so. And upon investigation I found that this happens quite
naturally. For I saw that some who do these jobs carelessly incur loss, 18
while I discovered that those who are seriously concerned accomplish
them more quickly and easily and profitably. I think that if you wished
to learn from them—if some god does not stand in your way—you
would become an extremely clever businessman.

CRITOBULUS. Now, Socrates, you know I shan't let you go before you III
have shown me what you promised in front of our friends here.

SOCRATES. Then, Critobulus, what if I show you first something about
houses, that some build useless ones at great expense, and others at
much less expense build houses that provide them with everything they
need? Will you think that in this I am showing you one of the principles
of estate management?

CRITOBULUS. Yes, certainly. 2

SOCRATES. What if I show you another principle that follows that one:
there are some who possess many furnishings of all kinds, but when they
need them, cannot use them and do not even know whether they are in
good condition, and for this reason they are often in torment, and they
often torment their slaves too. But others who possess not more, but less,
than these people, have everything that they need to use ready in no time.

CRITOBULUS. Yes, but what is the reason for this, Socrates? Isn't it just 3
that the first group toss their belongings all over the place, but the
others arrange everything in a designated place?

SOCRATES. Yes, by Zeus, everything is arranged where it belongs, not just
at random.

CRITOBULUS. I think that here you are stating another principle of estate
management.

SOCRATES. What if I also show you something about slaves: in some 4
households they are nearly all chained, but run away again and again,
while in others they are unchained and want to stay and work? Wouldn't
you think that in this too I'd be demonstrating to you a principle of
estate management worth examining?

CRITOBULUS. Yes, by Zeus, very well worth examining!

SOCRATES. And what if I also show you farmers cultivating similar farms, 5
yet some of them say they are being ruined by farming and are without

ἀποροῦντας, τοὺς δὲ ἀφθόνως καὶ καλῶς πάντα ἔχοντας ὅσων
δέονται ἀπὸ τῆς γεωργίας; Ναὶ μὰ Δί᾽, ἔφη ὁ Κριτόβουλος. ἴσως
γὰρ ἀναλίσκουσιν οὐκ εἰς ἃ δεῖ μόνον, ἀλλὰ καὶ εἰς ἃ βλάβην φέρει
6 αὐτῷ καὶ τῷ οἴκῳ. Εἰσὶ μέν τινες ἴσως, ἔφη ὁ Σωκράτης, καὶ
τοιοῦτοι. ἀλλ᾽ ἐγὼ οὐ τούτους λέγω, ἀλλ᾽ οἳ οὐδ᾽ εἰς τἀναγκαῖα 5
ἔχουσι δαπανᾶν, γεωργεῖν φάσκοντες. Καὶ τί ἂν εἴη τούτου αἴτιον,
ὦ Σώκρατες; Ἐγώ σε ἄξω καὶ ἐπὶ τούτους, ἔφη ὁ Σωκράτης· σὺ
δὲ θεώμενος δήπου καταμαθήσῃ. Νὴ Δί᾽, ἔφη, ἂν δύνωμαί γε.
7 Οὐκοῦν χρὴ θεώμενον σαυτοῦ ἀποπειρᾶσθαι εἰ γνώσῃ. νῦν δ᾽ ἐγὼ
σὲ σύνοιδα ἐπὶ μὲν κωμῳδῶν θέαν καὶ πάνυ πρῲ ἀνιστάμενον καὶ 10
πάνυ μακρὰν ὁδὸν βαδίζοντα καὶ ἐμὲ ἀναπείθοντα προθύμως
συνθεᾶσθαι· ἐπὶ δὲ τοιοῦτον οὐδέν με πώποτε ἔργον παρεκάλεσας.
8 Οὐκοῦν γελοῖός σοι φαίνομαι εἶναι, ὦ Σώκρατες. Σαυτῷ δὲ πολὺ
νὴ Δί᾽, ἔφη, γελοιότερος. ἂν δὲ καὶ ἀφ᾽ ἱππικῆς σοι ἐπιδεικνύω
τοὺς μὲν εἰς ἀπορίαν τῶν ἐπιτηδείων ἐληλυθότας, τοὺς δὲ διὰ τὴν 15
ἱππικὴν καὶ πάνυ εὐπόρους ὄντας καὶ ἅμα ἀγαλλομένους ἐπὶ τῷ
κέρδει; Οὐκοῦν τούτους μὲν καὶ ἐγὼ ὁρῶ καὶ οἶδα ἑκατέρους, καὶ
9 οὐδέν τι μᾶλλον τῶν κερδαινόντων γίγνομαι. Θεᾷ γὰρ αὐτοὺς ᾗπερ
τοὺς τραγῳδούς τε καὶ κωμῳδούς, οὐχ ὅπως ποιητὴς οἴομαι γένῃ,
ἀλλ᾽ ὅπως ἡσθῇς ἰδών τι ἢ ἀκούσας· καὶ ταῦτα μὲν ἴσως οὕτως 20
ὀρθῶς ἔχει (οὐ γὰρ ποιητὴς βούλει γενέσθαι), ἱππικῇ δ᾽
ἀναγκαζόμενος χρῆσθαι οὐ μῶρος οἴει εἶναι εἰ μὴ σκοπεῖς ὅπως
μὴ ἰδιώτης ἔσει τούτου τοῦ ἔργου, ἄλλως τε καὶ τῶν αὐτῶν ἵππων
ἀγαθῶν εἴς τε τὴν χρῆσιν καὶ κερδαλέων εἰς πώλησιν ὄντων;
10 Πωλοδαμνεῖν με κελεύεις, ὦ Σώκρατες; Οὐ μὰ Δί᾽ οὐδέν τι μᾶλλον 25
ἢ καὶ γεωργοὺς ἐκ παιδίων ὠνούμενον κατασκευάζειν, ἀλλ᾽ εἶναί
τινές μοι δοκοῦσιν ἡλικίαι καὶ ἵππων καὶ ἀνθρώπων, αἳ εὐθύς τε
χρήσιμοί εἰσι καὶ ἐπὶ τὸ βέλτιον ἐπιδιδόασιν. ἔχω δ᾽ ἐπιδεῖξαι καὶ
γυναιξὶ ταῖς γαμεταῖς τοὺς μὲν οὕτω χρωμένους ὥστε συνεργοὺς
ἔχειν αὐτὰς εἰς τὸ συναύξειν τοὺς οἴκους, τοὺς δὲ ᾗ ὅτι πλεῖστον 30
11 λυμαίνονται. Καὶ τούτου πότερα χρή, ὦ Σώκρατες, τὸν ἄνδρα
αἰτιᾶσθαι ἢ τὴν γυναῖκα; Πρόβατον μέν, ἔφη ὁ Σωκράτης, ὡς ἐπὶ
τὸ πολὺ ἂν κακῶς ἔχῃ, τὸν νομέα αἰτιώμεθα, καὶ ἵππος ὡς ἐπὶ τὸ
πολὺ ἂν κακουργῇ, τὸν ἱππέα κακίζομεν· τῆς δὲ γυναικός, εἰ μὲν

---

3 post ἃ add. μὴ Hartman   4 αὐτοῖς Cobet   10 σὲ Cobet: σοι codd.:
σοί … ἀνισταμένῳ … βαδίζοντι … ἀναπείθοντι Camerarius   14 ἀφ᾽] ὑφ᾽ Cobet
17 ἀμφοτέρους H al. J   21 βούλῃ C G   23 ἔσει Dind.: ἔσῃ(ι) codd.
24 ὄντων del Hirschig   28 χρήσιμοί A: χρήσιμαί cet.   30 οἱ πλεῖστα G: ὡς
πλεῖστα Stephanus   31 π(ρ)ότερον H al. M

resources, while others have a generous supply of all they need from farming?

CRITOBULUS. By Zeus, perhaps they are spending not only on necessities, but also on what brings harm to master and estate, as well.

SOCRATES. Perhaps there are also some people of that description. But I 6 don't mean them, rather those who are not even able to afford the basic necessities, even though they claim to be farmers.

CRITOBULUS. What could be the reason for that, Socrates?

SOCRATES. I shall lead you to these, too. No doubt, when you watch them you will find out.

CRITOBULUS. By Zeus, I shall! At least if I can.

SOCRATES. Then you must watch and test yourself to see whether you will 7 learn. But at present I notice that when there is a performance of comedies you get up very early, walk a very long distance, and eagerly urge me to join you in watching them. But you have never yet summoned me to a work such as you mentioned just now.

CRITOBULUS. Do you think I'm a fool, Socrates? 8

SOCRATES. Yes, but I'm sure you think yourself an even bigger fool, by Zeus. And, again, what if I show you that some people have reached the point where they are without basic necessities because they keep horses, while others, because they keep horses, have become wealthy and, what's more, are enjoying the profit?

CRITOBULUS. Well, I see these people, too, and I know both kinds, yet that doesn't help me in any way at all to become one of those who make a profit.

SOCRATES. Yes, because you watch them in the same way as you watch 9 tragic and comic actors, not, I imagine, in order to become a poet, but to enjoy yourself seeing or hearing something. And this no doubt is how it should be (for you don't want to become a poet); but, since you are forced to deal with horses don't you think you're stupid if you don't try to find out how to avoid being no more than a layman in this business, especially since it's the same horses that are good to use and profitable to sell?

CRITOBULUS. Are you asking me to break in colts, Socrates? 10

SOCRATES. No, by Zeus, no more than I am telling you to buy farmers and train them from childhood. But there seem to be certain stages in life for horses and men when they suddenly become useful and tend to improve. And I can show you men who treat their wives so as to have fellow workers in improving their estates, while others treat them in such a way that they cause utter disaster.

CRITOBULUS. And should the husband or the wife be blamed for this? 11

SOCRATES. Whenever a sheep is in a bad way, we usually blame the shepherd, and whenever a horse is vicious, we usually find fault with its rider. As for a wife, if she manages badly although she was taught what

διδασκομένη ὑπὸ τοῦ ἀνδρὸς τἀγαθὰ κακοποιεῖ, ἴσως δικαίως ἂν
ἡ γυνὴ τὴν αἰτίαν ἔχοι· εἰ δὲ μὴ διδάσκων τὰ καλὰ κἀγαθὰ
ἀνεπιστήμονι τούτων χρῷτο, ἆρ᾽ οὐ δικαίως ἂν ὁ ἀνὴρ τὴν αἰτίαν
12 ἔχοι; πάντως δ᾽, ἔφη, ὦ Κριτόβουλε (φίλοι γάρ ἐσμεν οἱ παρόντες)
ἀπαληθεῦσαι δεῖ πρὸς ἡμᾶς. ἔστιν ὅτῳ ἄλλῳ τῶν σπουδαίων πλείω 5
ἐπιτρέπεις ἢ τῇ γυναικί; Οὐδενί, ἔφη. Ἔστι δὲ ὅτῳ ἐλάττονα
13 διαλέγῃ ἢ τῇ γυναικί; Εἰ δὲ μή, οὐ πολλοῖς γε, ἔφη. Ἔγημας δὲ
αὐτὴν παῖδα νέαν μάλιστα καὶ ὡς ἐδύνατο ἐλάχιστα ἑωρακυῖαν
καὶ ἀκηκουῖαν; Μάλιστα. Οὐκοῦν πολὺ θαυμαστότερον εἴ τι ὧν
14 δεῖ λέγειν ἢ πράττειν ἐπίσταιτο ἢ εἰ ἐξαμαρτάνοι. Οἷς δὲ σὺ λέγεις 10
ἀγαθὰς εἶναι γυναῖκας, ὦ Σώκρατες, ἦ αὐτοὶ ταύτας ἐπαίδευσαν;
Οὐδὲν οἷον τὸ ἐπισκοπεῖσθαι. συστήσω δέ σοι ἐγὼ καὶ Ἀσπασίαν,
15 ἢ ἐπιστημονέστερον ἐμοῦ σοι ταῦτα πάντα ἐπιδείξει. νομίζω δὲ
γυναῖκα κοινωνὸν ἀγαθὴν οἴκου οὖσαν πάνυ ἀντίρροπον εἶναι τῷ
ἀνδρὶ ἐπὶ τὸ ἀγαθόν. ἔρχεται μὲν γὰρ εἰς τὴν οἰκίαν διὰ τῶν τοῦ 15
ἀνδρὸς πράξεων τὰ κτήματα ὡς ἐπὶ τὸ πολύ, δαπανᾶται δὲ διὰ
τῶν τῆς γυναικὸς ταμιευμάτων τὰ πλεῖστα· καὶ εὖ μὲν τούτων
γιγνομένων αὔξονται οἱ οἶκοι, κακῶς δὲ τούτων πραττομένων οἱ
16 οἶκοι μειοῦνται. οἶμαι δὲ καὶ τῶν ἄλλων ἐπιστημῶν τοὺς ἀξίως
λόγου ἑκάστην ἐργαζομένους ἔχειν ἂν ἐπιδεῖξαί σοι, εἰ τι 20
προσδεῖσθαι νομίζεις.

IV   Ἀλλὰ πάσας μὲν τί σε δεῖ ἐπιδεικνύναι, ὦ Σώκρατες; ἔφη ὁ
Κριτόβουλος· οὔτε γὰρ κτήσασθαι πασῶν τῶν τεχνῶν ἐργάτας
ῥᾴδιον οἵους δεῖ, οὔτε ἔμπειρον γενέσθαι αὐτῶν οἷόν τε, ἀλλ᾽ αἳ
δοκοῦσι κάλλισται τῶν ἐπιστημῶν καὶ ἐμοὶ πρέποι ἂν μάλιστα 25
ἐπιμελομένῳ, ταύτας μοι καὶ αὐτὰς ἐπιδείκνυε καὶ τοὺς
πράττοντας αὐτάς, καὶ αὐτὸς δὲ ὅ τι δύνασαι συνωφέλει εἰς ταῦτα
2 διδάσκων. Ἀλλὰ καλῶς, ἔφη, λέγεις, ὦ Κριτόβουλε. καὶ γὰρ αἵ γε
βαναυσικαὶ καλούμεναι καὶ ἐπίρρητοί εἰσι καὶ εἰκότως μέντοι πάνυ
ἀδοξοῦνται πρὸς τῶν πόλεων. καταλυμαίνονται γὰρ τὰ σώματα 30
τῶν τε ἐργαζομένων καὶ τῶν ἐπιμελομένων, ἀναγκάζουσαι
καθῆσθαι καὶ σκιατραφεῖσθαι, ἔνιαι δὲ καὶ πρὸς πῦρ ἡμερεύειν.
τῶν δὲ σωμάτων θηλυνομένων καὶ αἱ ψυχαὶ πολὺ ἀρρωστότεραι
3 γίγνονται. καὶ ἀσχολίας δὲ μάλιστα ἔχουσι καὶ φίλων καὶ πόλεως

4 δ'] δεῖ cit. Sauppe   5 ἀπαλήθευσον Stephanus   δεῖ R Ven. 513: om.
cet.   9 καί J K: ἢ καί cet.   10 εἰ Ven. 368: om. cet.   δέ σοι codd.: corr.
Castalio   17 τούτων ... οἶκοι om. Philodemus Oec. p. 42, 17   19 ἀξίους H
al. Y   20 σοι] τοι Richards   26 ἐπιμελομένῳ αὐτῶν Hartman   28 αἵ γε]
αἱ Stob.   29 εἰσι Stob.: τέ εἰσι codd.   μέντοι] μὲν δὴ Stob.   30 ἀδοξοῦσι
cit. Holden   31 posterius τῶν om. Stob.   34 ἔχουσι Stob.: ἔχουσαι codd.

is right by her husband, perhaps it would be proper to blame her. But if he doesn't teach her what is right and good and then discovers that she has no knowledge of these qualities, wouldn't it be proper to blame the husband? Anyhow, Critobulus, you must tell us the truth, for we are all friends here. Is there anyone to whom you entrust a greater number of serious matters than to your wife? 12

CRITOBULUS. No one.

SOCRATES. Is there anyone with whom you have fewer conversations than with your wife?

CRITOBULUS. No one, or at least not very many. 13

SOCRATES. And you married her when she was a very young child who had seen and heard virtually nothing of the world?

CRITOBULUS. Yes.

SOCRATES. Wouldn't it be much more remarkable if she had any knowledge at all about what she ought to say or do than if she made mistakes?

CRITOBULUS. What about those who you say have good wives, Socrates? 14 Did they educate them themselves?

SOCRATES. There is nothing like personal investigation. I will introduce Aspasia to you; she is much more knowledgeable in this matter than I am, and she will show you all this far more expertly than I should. I 15 think that a wife who is a good partner in the estate carries just as much weight as her husband in attaining prosperity. Property generally comes into the house through the exertions of the husband, but it is mostly dispensed through the housekeeping of the wife. If these activities are performed well, estates increase, but if they are managed incompetently, estates diminish. And I think I could also point out men who practise 16 each of the other branches of knowledge in a competent way, if you think you need any further demonstration.

CRITOBULUS. But why must you show all of them, Socrates? It is not very IV easy to procure workers who are competent in all the occupations, nor is it possible to become experienced in all of them. But show me the branches of knowledge which are considered to be most honourable and which I might must suitably concern myself with. Show me these and those who practise them, and you yourself, too—to the best of your ability—instruct me and help me to learn them.

SOCRATES. Very well said, Critobulus. In fact, the so-called 'banausic' 2 occupations are both denounced and, quite rightly, held in very low esteem by states. For they utterly ruin the bodies of those who work at them and those of their supervisors, by forcing them to lead a sedentary life and to stay indoors, and some of them even to spend the whole day by the fire. When their bodies become effeminate, their souls too become much weaker. Furthermore, the so-called 'banausic' occupations leave 3 a man no spare time to be concerned about his friends and city.

συνεπιμελεῖσθαι αἱ βαναυσικαὶ καλούμεναι. ὥστε οἱ τοιοῦτοι
δοκοῦσι κακοὶ καὶ φίλοις χρῆσθαι καὶ ταῖς πατρίσιν ἀλεξητῆρες
εἶναι. καὶ ἐν ἐνίαις μὲν τῶν πόλεων, μάλιστα δὲ ἐν ταῖς εὐπολέμοις
δοκούσαις εἶναι, οὐδ' ἔξεστι τῶν πολιτῶν οὐδενὶ βαναυσικὰς τέχνας
4 ἐργάζεσθαι. Ἡμῖν δὲ δὴ ποίαις συμβουλεύεις, ὦ Σώκρατες, 5
χρῆσθαι; Ἄρ', ἔφη ὁ Σωκράτης, μὴ αἰσχυνθῶμεν τὸν Περσῶν
βασιλέα μιμήσασθαι; ἐκεῖνον γάρ φασιν ἐν τοῖς καλλίστοις τε καὶ
ἀναγκαιοτάτοις ἡγούμενον εἶναι ἐπιμελήμασι γεωργίαν τε καὶ τὴν
πολεμικὴν τέχνην τούτων ἀμφοτέρων ἰσχυρῶς ἐπιμελεῖσθαι. καὶ ὁ
5 Κριτόβουλος ἀκούσας ταῦτα εἶπε· Καὶ τοῦτο, ἔφη, πιστεύεις, ὦ 10
Σώκρατες, βασιλέα τὸν Περσῶν γεωργίας τι συνεπιμελεῖσθαι;
Ὧδ' ἄν, ἔφη ὁ Σωκράτης, ἐπισκοποῦντες, ὦ Κριτόβουλε, ἴσως ἂν
καταμάθοιμεν εἴ τι συνεπιμελεῖται. τῶν μὲν γὰρ πολεμικῶν ἔργων
ὁμολογοῦμεν αὐτὸν ἰσχυρῶς ἐπιμελεῖσθαι, ὅτι ἐξ ὁπόσωνπερ ἐθνῶν
λαμβάνει ⟨τι⟩, τέταχε τῷ ἄρχοντι ἑκάστῳ εἰς ὁπόσους δεῖ διδόναι 15
τροφὴν ἱππέας καὶ τοξότας καὶ σφενδονήτας καὶ γερροφόρους,
οἵτινες τῶν τε ὑπ' αὐτοῦ ἀρχομένων ἱκανοὶ ἔσονται κρατεῖν καὶ ἂν
πολέμιοι ἐπίωσιν, ἀρήξουσι τῇ χώρᾳ, χωρὶς δὲ τούτων φύλακας
6 ἐν ταῖς ἀκροπόλεσι τρέφει· καὶ τὴν μὲν τροφὴν τοῖς φρουροῖς
δίδωσιν ὁ ἄρχων ᾧ τοῦτο προστέτακται, βασιλεὺς δὲ κατ' ἐνιαυτὸν 20
ἐξέτασιν ποιεῖται τῶν μισθοφόρων καὶ τῶν ἄλλων οἷς ὡπλίσθαι
προστέτακται, πάντας ἅμα συνάγων πλὴν τοὺς ἐν ταῖς
ἀκροπόλεσιν ἔνθα δὴ ὁ σύλλογος καλεῖται· καὶ τοὺς μὲν ἀμφὶ τὴν
ἑαυτοῦ οἴκησιν αὐτὸς ἐφορᾷ, τοὺς δὲ πρόσω ἀποικοῦντας πιστοὺς
7 πέμπει ἐπισκοπεῖν· καὶ οἳ μὲν ἂν φαίνωνται τῶν φρουράρχων καὶ 25
τῶν χιλιάρχων καὶ τῶν σατραπῶν τὸν ἀριθμὸν τὸν τεταγμένον
ἔκπλεων ἔχοντες, καὶ τούτους δοκίμοις ἵπποις τε καὶ ὅπλοις
κατεσκευασμένους παρέχωσι, τούτους μὲν τοὺς ἄρχοντας καὶ ταῖς
τιμαῖς αὔξει καὶ δώροις μεγάλοις καταπλουτίζει, οὓς δ' ἂν
εὕρῃ τῶν ἀρχόντων ἢ καταμελοῦντας τῶν φρουραρχιῶν ἢ 30
κατακερδαίνοντας, τούτους χαλεπῶς κολάζει καὶ παύων τῆς ἀρχῆς

---

1 αἱ βαναυσικαὶ καλούμεναι susp. Schenkl.   ὥστε εἰκότως σοι δοκοῦσι κακοὶ ἂν
καὶ Stob.   2 κακοὶ Stob.: κακὸν codd.   3 εὐπολέμοις Stob.: ἐν πολέμοις
codd.   6 Ἀλλ' ... μιμήσασθαι. cit. Richards   μὴ fort. spurium   τὸν A E K
L O P: τὸν τῶν F: τῶν cet.   11 τὸν K L: τῶν cet.   14 post ἐθνῶν add.
δασμοὺς Stephanus   15 λαμβάνειν codd.: corr. Castalio   τι add. Tournier
18 φυλακὰς G   19 τρέφειν codd.: corr. Castalio   22 καὶ πάντας codd.:
corr. Richards   23 καὶ om. Q   27 δοκίμοις Stephanus: δοκίμους codd.
28 τοὺς ἄρχοντας del. Cobet   30 τῶν ἀρχόντων del. Cobet   φρουράρχων codd.:
φρουρῶν Schäfer: fort. φρουραρχιῶν

Consequently such men seem to treat their friends badly and to defend their countries badly too. In fact, in some cities, especially in those reputed to excel in war, none of the citizens is permitted to work at the banausic occupations.

CRITOBULUS. Then, Socrates, which occupations do you advise us to 4 practise?

SOCRATES. Surely we ought not to be ashamed to imitate the king of the Persians? For they say that he classifies farming and the art of war among the noblest and most essential concerns, and he is seriously concerned about both of them.

CRITOBULUS. Do you really believe, Socrates, that the king of the Persians 5 is concerned at all about farming?

SOCRATES. If we look at it in the following way, Critobulus, perhaps we may learn whether he is concerned at all about it. We agree that he is seriously concerned about military matters, because he gives orders to each man who is in charge of the countries from which he receives tribute to supply provisions for a specified number of horsemen, archers, slingers, and light-armed troops who will be capable of controlling his subjects and of protecting the country if an enemy should attack. And besides these, he maintains guards in the citadels. And the official to 6 whom this duty has been assigned supplies provisions for the guards. The king holds an annual review of the mercenaries and the other troops who have been ordered to be under arms, assembling all of them, except those in the citadels, at the 'place of muster'. He personally inspects the troops near his own residence and he sends men whom he trusts to review those who live further away. And those garrison commanders 7 and chiliarchs[3] and satraps who show up with the full complement of soldiers assigned to them and present them equipped with horses that are well groomed and weapons that are well maintained he promotes with honours and rewards with valuable gifts. But those commanders whom he finds either showing a lack of concern for their garrisons or making a private profit from them, he punishes severely, removing them from office and appointing other men to take charge. Because he does

---

[3] Literally 'commanders of a thousand'.

ἄλλους ἐπιμελητὰς καθίστησι. τῶν μὲν δὴ πολεμικῶν ἔργων ταῦτα
8 ποιῶν δοκεῖ ἡμῖν ἀναμφιλόγως ἐπιμελεῖσθαι. ἔτι δὲ ὁπόσην μὲν
τῆς χώρας διελαύνων ἐφορᾷ αὐτός, καὶ δοκιμάζει, ὁπόσην δὲ μὴ
αὐτὸς ἐφορᾷ, πέμπων πιστοὺς ἐπισκοπεῖται. καὶ οὓς μὲν ἂν
αἰσθάνηται τῶν ἀρχόντων συνοικουμένην τε τὴν χώραν 5
παρεχομένους καὶ ἐνεργὸν οὖσαν τὴν γῆν καὶ πλήρη δένδρων τε
ὧν ἑκάστη φέρει καὶ καρπῶν, τούτοις μὲν χώραν τε ἄλλην
προστίθησι καὶ δώροις κοσμεῖ καὶ ἕδραις ἐντίμοις γεραίρει, οἷς δ᾽
ἂν ὁρᾷ ἀργόν τε τὴν χώραν οὖσαν καὶ ὀλιγάνθρωπον ἢ διὰ
χαλεπότητα ἢ δι᾽ ὕβριν ἢ δι᾽ ἀμέλειαν, τούτους δὲ κολάζων καὶ 10
9 παύων τῆς ἀρχῆς ἄρχοντας ἄλλους καθίστησι. ταῦτα ποιῶν δοκεῖ
ἧττον ἐπιμελεῖσθαι ὅπως ἡ γῆ ἐνεργὸς ἔσται ὑπὸ τῶν κατοικούντων
ἢ ὅπως εὖ φυλάξεται ὑπὸ τῶν φρουρούντων; καὶ εἰσὶ δ᾽ αὐτῷ οἱ
ἄρχοντες διατεταγμένοι ἐφ᾽ ἑκάτερον οὐχ οἱ αὐτοί, ἀλλ᾽ οἱ μὲν
ἄρχουσι τῶν κατοικούντων τε καὶ τῶν ἐργατῶν, καὶ δασμοὺς ἐκ 15
τούτων ἐκλέγουσιν, οἱ δ᾽ ἄρχουσι τῶν ὡπλισμένων ⟨τε καὶ τῶν⟩
10 φρουρῶν. κἂν μὲν ὁ φρούραρχος μὴ ἱκανῶς τῇ χώρᾳ ἀρήγῃ, ὁ τῶν
ἐνοικούντων ἄρχων καὶ τῶν ἔργων ἐπιμελούμενος κατηγορεῖ τοῦ
φρουράρχου, ὅτι οὐ δύνανται ἐργάζεσθαι διὰ τὴν ἀφυλαξίαν, ἂν δὲ
παρέχοντος τοῦ φρουράρχου εἰρήνην τοῖς ἔργοις ὁ ἄρχων 20
ὀλιγάνθρωπόν τε παρέχηται καὶ ἀργὸν τὴν χώραν, τούτου αὖ
11 κατηγορεῖ ὁ φρούραρχος. καὶ γὰρ σχεδόν τι οἱ κακῶς τὴν χώραν
ἐργαζόμενοι οὔτε τοὺς φρουροὺς τρέφουσιν οὔτε τοὺς δασμοὺς
δύνανται ἀποδιδόναι. ὅπου δ᾽ ἂν σατράπης καθιστῆται, οὗτος
12 ἀμφοτέρων τούτων ἐπιμελεῖται. ἐκ τούτων ὁ Κριτόβουλος εἶπεν· 25
Οὐκοῦν εἰ μὲν δὴ ταῦτα ποιεῖ βασιλεύς, ὦ Σώκρατες, οὐδὲν ἔμοιγε
δοκεῖ ἧττον τῶν γεωργικῶν ἔργων ἐπιμελεῖσθαι ἢ τῶν πολεμικῶν.
13 Ἔτι δὲ πρὸς τούτοις, ἔφη ὁ Σωκράτης, ἐν ὁπόσαις τε χώραις
ἐνοικεῖ καὶ εἰς ὁπόσας ἐπιστρέφεται, ἐπιμελεῖται τούτων ὅπως
κῆποί τε ἔσονται, οἱ παράδεισοι καλούμενοι, πάντων καλῶν τε 30
κἀγαθῶν μεστοὶ ὅσα ἡ γῆ φύειν θέλει, καὶ ἐν τούτοις αὐτὸς τὰ
14 πλεῖστα διατρίβει, ὅταν μὴ ἡ ὥρα τοῦ ἔτους ἐξείργῃ. Νὴ Δί᾽, ἔφη
ὁ Κριτόβουλος, ἀνάγκη τοίνυν, ὦ Σώκρατες, ἔνθα γε διατρίβει
αὐτός, καὶ ὅπως ὡς κάλλιστα κατεσκευασμένοι ἔσονται οἱ
παράδεισοι ἐπιμελεῖσθαι δένδρεσι καὶ τοῖς ἄλλοις ἅπασι καλοῖς

---

2 πόσην ... αὐτὸς καὶ Herwerden, ut sit exclamatio   3 ante καὶ add. αὐτὸς
Camerarius   5 τε Schneider: γε codd.   7 τε J: τὴν cet.   12 οὐχ
ἧττον sine interrog. signo Castalio   16 τε καὶ τῶν add. Graux   29 ἐπιμελεῖσθαι
codd. (ἐπιμελεῖται A s.v.)   30 fort. ἔσονται καὶ   34 κάλλιστα L O: κάλλιστοι cet.

these things, we think there can be no doubt at all that he is concerned with military matters. Furthermore, he himself examines all of the land 8 that he sees as he rides through it, and by sending men whom he trusts he surveys the land he does not examine personally. And those governors whom he observes presenting densely populated land and fields under cultivation stocked with the trees and crops that grow in that region, to these he gives additional territory and he lavishes gifts on them and rewards them with seats of honour; but those whose land he sees uncultivated and sparsely populated, because of the governor's harshness or arrogance or lack of concern, he punishes, removing them from office and appointing other governors. Since he does these things, does he 9 seem to be less concerned that the earth be well cultivated by the inhabitants than that it be well protected by the garrisons? Separate officials are appointed by him for each of these activities, not the same men: some are in charge of the inhabitants and the workers, and collect tribute from them; others command the armed troops and the garrisons. If the garrison commander does not adequately defend the country, the 10 official concerned with the inhabitants and agricultural production brings an accusation against the commander on the grounds that the people are not able to do their work because they are not properly protected. But if the garrison commander provides peace for farming, whereas the civil governor presents underpopulated, unproductive land, the garrison commander, in turn, brings an accusation against him. For, 11 on the whole, those who cultivate the land poorly are unable to support garrisons or pay tribute. But wherever a satrap is appointed, he is concerned with both areas of activity.

CRITOBULUS. Well, Socrates, if the king really does all this, he seems to 12 me to be concerned as much about agriculture as he is about military matters.

SOCRATES. And furthermore in whichever of his territories he lives and 13 whichever he visits, he is concerned that there should be gardens—the *paradeisoi*,[4] as they are called—full of all the fine and beautiful plants that the earth naturally produces. And he spends most of his time in these, except when the time of year prevents him.

CRITOBULUS. By Zeus, then Socrates, the king must be concerned that 14 the *paradeisoi*[4] in which he himself spends time should be furnished in the finest manner possible with trees and all the other fine things that the earth produces.

[4] i.e. parks.

15 ὅσα ἡ γῆ φύει. Φασὶ δέ τινες, ἔφη ὁ Σωκράτης, ὦ Κριτόβουλε,
καὶ ὅταν δῶρα διδῷ ὁ βασιλεύς, πρῶτον μὲν εἰσκαλεῖν τοὺς πολέμῳ
ἀγαθοὺς γεγονότας, ὅτι οὐδὲν ὄφελος πολλὰ ἀροῦν, εἰ μὴ εἶεν οἱ
ἀρήξοντες· δεύτερον δὲ τοὺς κατασκευάζοντας τὰς χώρας ἄριστα
καὶ ἐνεργοὺς ποιοῦντας, λέγοντα ὅτι οὐδ' ἂν οἱ ἄλκιμοι δύναιντο 5
16 ζῆν, εἰ μὴ εἶεν οἱ ἐργαζόμενοι. λέγεται δὲ καὶ Κῦρός ποτε, ὅσπερ
εὐδοκιμώτατος δὴ βασιλεὺς γεγένηται, εἰπεῖν τοῖς ἐπὶ τὰ δῶρα
κεκλημένοις ὅτι αὐτὸς ἂν δικαίως τὰ ἀμφοτέρων δῶρα λαμβάνοι·
κατασκευάζειν τε γὰρ ἄριστος εἶναι ἔφη χώραν καὶ ἀρήγειν τοῖς
17 κατεσκευασμένοις. Κῦρος μὲν τοίνυν, ἔφη ὁ Κριτόβουλος, ὦ 10
Σώκρατες, καὶ ἐπηγάλλετο οὐδὲν ἧττον, εἰ ταῦτα ἔλεγεν, ἐπὶ τῷ
χώρας ἐνεργοὺς ποιεῖν καὶ κατασκευάζειν ἢ ἐπὶ τῷ πολεμικὸς
18 εἶναι. Καὶ ναὶ μὰ Δί', ἔφη ὁ Σωκράτης, Κῦρός γε, εἰ ἐβίωσεν,
ἄριστος ἂν δοκεῖ ἄρχων γενέσθαι· καὶ τούτου τεκμήρια ἄλλα τε
πολλὰ παρέσχηται καὶ ὅτε περὶ τῆς βασιλείας τῷ ἀδελφῷ 15
ἐπορεύετο μαχούμενος, παρὰ μὲν Κύρου οὐδεὶς λέγεται
αὐτομολῆσαι πρὸς βασιλέα, παρὰ δὲ βασιλέως πολλαὶ μυριάδες
19 πρὸς Κῦρον. ἐγὼ δὲ καὶ τοῦτο ἡγοῦμαι μέγα τεκμήριον ἄρχοντος
ἀρετῆς εἶναι, ᾧ ἂν ἑκόντες πείθωνται καὶ ἐν τοῖς δεινοῖς παραμένειν
ἐθέλωσιν. ἐκείνῳ δὲ καὶ οἱ φίλοι ζῶντί τε συνεμάχοντο καὶ 20
ἀποθανόντι συναπέθανον πάντες περὶ τὸν νεκρὸν μαχόμενοι πλὴν
Ἀριαίου· Ἀριαῖος δ' ἔτυχεν ἐπὶ τῷ εὐωνύμῳ κέρατι τεταγμένος.
20 οὗτος τοίνυν ὁ Κῦρος λέγεται Λυσάνδρῳ, ὅτε ἦλθεν ἄγων αὐτῷ
τὰ παρὰ τῶν συμμάχων δῶρα, ἄλλα τε φιλοφρονεῖσθαι, ὡς αὐτὸς
ἔφη ὁ Λύσανδρος ξένῳ ποτέ τινι ἐν Μεγάροις διηγούμενος, καὶ 25
21 τὸν ἐν Σάρδεσι παράδεισον ἐπιδεικνύναι αὐτὸν ἔφη. ἐπεὶ δὲ
ἐθαύμαζεν αὐτὸν ὁ Λύσανδρος ὡς καλὰ μὲν τὰ δένδρα εἴη, δι' ἴσου
δὲ πεφυτευμένα, ὀρθοὶ δὲ οἱ στίχοι τῶν δένδρων, εὐγώνια δὲ
πάντα καλῶς εἴη, ὀσμαὶ δὲ πολλαὶ καὶ ἡδεῖαι συμπαρομαρτοῖεν
αὐτοῖς περιπατοῦσι, καὶ ταῦτα θαυμάζων εἶπεν· Ἀλλ' ἐγώ τοι, ὦ 30
Κῦρε, πάντα μὲν ⟨ταῦτα⟩ θαυμάζω ἐπὶ τῷ κάλλει, πολὺ δὲ μᾶλλον
ἄγαμαι τοῦ καταμετρήσαντός σοι καὶ διατάξαντος ἕκαστα τούτων·

2 ὁ del. Dind.   ἐν πολέμῳ Cobet   3 fort. ⟨λέγοντα⟩ ὅτε
9 ἔφη del. Cobet   11 καὶ del Weiske   ἐπηγ(γ)έ(vel ε ἱ)λ(λ)ετο codd.: corr.
Stephanus   13 omnia a § 18 ad finem capitis spuria putat Nitsche   Κῦρός γε ὁ
Δαρείου cit. Graux   ἐβίω Graux: ἐπεβίω Cobet: εἰ ἐβίωσεν fort. delendum   15 ὁπότε
codd.: corr. Nitsche   17 τοῦ βασιλέως codd. praeter Η Ν J   19 πείθωνται]
ἔπωνται Stob.   20 καὶ del. Dind   21 πλὴν γε Η Ν₂ J. πλὴν cet. et Anab. 1. 9,
31   27 αὐτὸν] αὐτοῦ Mehler   28 τὰ πεφυτευμένα codd.: corr. Schneider
31 ταῦτα add. Stephanus

SOCRATES. And, Critobulus, some people say too that whenever the king 15
bestows gifts, first he summons those who have proved themselves brave
in war, because it would be useless to plough many acres if there were
no men to defend them. Secondly, he rewards those who cultivate their
lands best and make them productive, and tells them that even the
valiant could not live unless workers existed too. And it is said that 16
Cyrus, who was without any doubt the most illustrious of all the Persian
kings, once told those who had been summoned to receive rewards that
he himself had a right to receive the rewards in both categories: for, he
said, he was best both at cultivating land and at defending the land he
had cultivated.

CRITOBULUS. Well, Socrates, if Cyrus said that, he was just as proud of 17
making the land productive and cultivated as he was of his military skills.

SOCRATES. Yes, by Zeus, to be sure, if Cyrus had lived, he would, I think, 18
have proved himself an excellent ruler. He has given many indications
that this might be so, most strikingly, when he was marching to meet
his brother in battle for the throne: they say that no one deserted from
Cyrus to the king, whereas many thousands deserted from the king to
Cyrus. I consider it to be a substantial indication of a ruler's merit, if 19
men obey him willingly and volunteer to stand by him in dangerous
circumstances. His friends fought side by side with him as long as he
was alive, and after he was killed all died at his side fighting around his
corpse, except Ariaeus. Ariaeus, as it happened, had been posted on the
left wing. Furthermore, they say that when Lysander came to him with 20
the gifts from the allies, this Cyrus was very friendly toward him, as
Lysander himself once related to a friend in Megara, adding, in particular, that Cyrus had personally shown him the *paradeisos* at Sardis. When 21
Lysander had expressed amazement at the beauty of the trees in it (for
they were planted at equal intervals in straight rows and all at regular
angles), and many sweet fragrances wafted about them as they strolled
around, he exclaimed, in amazement, 'Cyrus, I certainly am amazed at
all these things for their beauty, but I admire even more the man who
measured out each of the trees for you and arranged each one of them
in order.' When Cyrus heard this, he was pleased and replied, 'Lysander,

22 ἀκούσαντα δὲ ταῦτα τὸν Κῦρον ἡσθῆναί τε καὶ εἰπεῖν· Ταῦτα
τοίνυν, ὦ Λύσανδρε, ἐγὼ πάντα καὶ διεμέτρησα καὶ διέταξα, ἔστι
23 δ᾽ αὐτῶν, φάναι, ἃ καὶ ἐφύτευσα αὐτός. καὶ ὁ Λύσανδρος ἔφη,
ἀποβλέψας εἰς αὐτὸν καὶ ἰδὼν τῶν τε ἱματίων τὸ κάλλος ὧν εἶχε
καὶ τῆς ὀσμῆς αἰσθόμενος καὶ τῶν στρεπτῶν καὶ τῶν ψελίων τὸ 5
κάλλος καὶ τοῦ ἄλλου κόσμου οὗ εἶχεν, εἰπεῖν· Τί λέγεις, φάναι,
ὦ Κῦρε; ἦ γὰρ σὺ ταῖς σαῖς χερσὶ τούτων τι ἐφύτευσας; καὶ τὸν
24 Κῦρον ἀποκρίνασθαι· Θαυμάζεις τοῦτο, [ἔφη,] ὦ Λύσανδρε;
ὄμνυμί σοι τὸν Μίθρην, ὅτανπερ ὑγιαίνω, μηπώποτε δειπνῆσαι
πρὶν ἱδρῶσαι ἢ τῶν πολεμικῶν τι ἢ τῶν γεωργικῶν ἔργων μελετῶν 10
25 ἢ ἀεὶ ἕν γέ τι φιλοτιμούμενος. καὶ αὐτὸς μέντοι ἔφη ὁ Λύσανδρος
ἀκούσας ταῦτα δεξιώσασθαί τε αὐτὸν καὶ εἰπεῖν· Δικαίως μοι
δοκεῖς, ὦ Κῦρε, εὐδαίμων εἶναι· ἀγαθὸς γὰρ ὢν ἀνὴρ εὐδαιμονεῖς.

V Ταῦτα δέ, ὦ Κριτόβουλε, ἐγὼ διηγοῦμαι, ἔφη ὁ Σωκράτης, ὅτι
τῆς γεωργίας οὐδ᾽ οἱ πάνυ μακάριοι δύνανται ἀπέχεσθαι. ἔοικε 15
γὰρ ἡ ἐπιμέλεια αὐτῆς εἶναι ἅμα τε ἡδυπάθειά τις καὶ οἴκου
αὔξησις καὶ σωμάτων ἄσκησις εἰς τὸ δύνασθαι ὅσα ἀνδρὶ ἐλευθέρῳ
2 προσήκει. πρῶτον μὲν γὰρ ἀφ᾽ ὧν ζῶσιν οἱ ἄνθρωποι, ταῦτα ἡ γῆ
φέρει ἐργαζομένοις, καὶ ἀφ᾽ ὧν τοίνυν ἡδυπαθοῦσι, προσεπιφέρει·
3 ἔπειτα δὲ ὅσοις κοσμοῦσι βωμοὺς καὶ ἀγάλματα καὶ οἷς αὐτοὶ 20
κοσμοῦνται, καὶ ταῦτα μετὰ ἡδίστων ὀσμῶν καὶ θεαμάτων
παρέχει· ἔπειτα δὲ ὄψα πολλὰ τὰ μὲν φύει, τὰ δὲ τρέφει· καὶ γὰρ
ἡ προβατευτικὴ τέχνη συνῆπται τῇ γεωργίᾳ, ὥστε ἔχειν καὶ θεοὺς
4 ἐξαρέσκεσθαι θύοντας καὶ αὐτοὺς χρῆσθαι. παρέχουσα δ᾽
ἀφθονώτατα τἀγαθὰ οὐκ ἐᾷ ταῦτα μετὰ μαλακίας λαμβάνειν, ἀλλὰ 25
ψύχη τε χειμῶνος καὶ θάλπη θέρους ἐθίζει καρτερεῖν. καὶ τοὺς μὲν
αὐτουργοὺς διὰ τῶν χειρῶν γυμνάζουσα ἰσχὺν αὐτοῖς προστίθησι,
τοὺς δὲ τῇ ἐπιμελείᾳ γεωργοῦντας ἀνδρίζει πρῷ τε ἐγείρουσα καὶ
πορεύεσθαι σφοδρῶς ἀναγκάζουσα. καὶ γὰρ ἐν τῷ χώρῳ καὶ ἐν
5 τῷ ἄστει ἀεὶ ἐν ὥρᾳ αἱ ἐπικαιριώταται πράξεις εἰσίν. ἔπειτα ἄν 30
τε σὺν ἵππῳ ἀρήγειν τις τῇ πόλει βούληται, τὸν ἵππον ἱκανωτάτη
ἡ γεωργία συντρέφειν, ἄν τε πεζῇ, σφοδρὸν τὸ σῶμα παρέχει·

4 τὸ κάλλος del Cobet   6 post κάλλος add. ἀγάμενος Zeune   8 ἔφη del.
Schenkl   11 ἕν Stephanus: ὧν codd.   13 δοκεῖς F K L: δοκεῖς ἔφη cet.
17 ὅσα] ἃ Stob.   19 προσεπιφέρει Stob.: προσέτι φέρει codd.   20 ὅσοις N
s.v.: ὅσοι vel ὅσα cet.: καὶ θεοὺς Stob.   post κοσμοῦσι add. καὶ Stob.   οἵοις Stob.
23 θεοὺς Cobet: θεοῖς codd.   25 ἀφθονώτατ᾽ FG al.   τἀγαθὰ Ven. 511: ἀγαθὰ
cet.   28 ἀνδρίζει Stob.: ἀνδρίζεσθαι codd.   τε Stob.: om. codd.   29 χωρίῳ
H G N Stob.   30 ἐπικαιρότατοι Stob. Paris.   ἔπειτα δ᾽ Stob.   31 βουληθῇ Stob.

I myself measured and arranged everything and I even planted some of 22
the trees myself.' Lysander relates that gazing at Cyrus, and seeing the 23
beauty of the robes that he wore, and smelling his perfume, and seeing
the beauty of his necklaces and anklets and other ornaments that he
wore, he said, 'What do you mean, Cyrus? Did you really plant any of
these with your own hands?' And Cyrus replied, 'Lysander, are you 24
amazed at this? I swear to you by Mithras that whenever I'm in good
health I never dine before working up a sweat either by practising some
military skill or doing some agricultural work or, at times, engaging in
some competitive activity.' Lysander himself said that when he heard 25
this, he congratulated him and said 'Cyrus, I think you deserve your
good fortune, for your good fortune is a result of your virtue.'

Critobulus, I am telling you this because not even those most favoured V
by the gods can do without farming. For concerning oneself with it
seems to be simultaneously a pleasant experience, a means of increasing
one's estate, and exercise for the body so that it may be capable of all
those things that are suitable for a free man. First of all, for those who 2
cultivate her the earth bears the food that human beings need in order
to live and provides their sources of enjoyment as well. Secondly, she 3
supplies what they use to decorate altars and statues and to adorn
themselves, and these are most pleasant to look at and to smell, too.
And then there are edible delicacies: some she produces, for others she
provides the means of sustenance; for the occupation of breeding livestock
is closely connected with farming, so that men may propitiate the gods
with sacrifices and make use of the animals for themselves. Although 4
the earth offers her goods most generously, she does not allow men to
take them without work, but she makes them accustomed to enduring
winter's cold and summer's heat. Through exercise she gives increased
strength to those who work the land with their own hands, and those
who farm by supervising their labourers she makes manly by waking
them up early and forcing them to move about energetically. For both
in the country and in the city most urgent operations occur at a fixed
time. Furthermore, if a man wishes to defend his city by serving in the 5
cavalry, farming is best suited for providing the horse with food; if he
serves in the infantry, it makes his body energetic. The earth encourages

θήραις τε ἐπιφιλοπονεῖσθαι συνεπαίρει τι ἡ γῆ καὶ κυσὶν εὐπέτειαν
6 τροφῆς παρέχουσα καὶ θηρία συμπαρατρέφουσα. ὠφελούμενοι δὲ
καὶ οἱ ἵπποι καὶ αἱ κύνες ἀπὸ τῆς γεωργίας ἀντωφελοῦσι τὸν
χῶρον, ὁ μὲν ἵππος πρῴ τε κομίζων τὸν κηδόμενον εἰς τὴν
ἐπιμέλειαν καὶ ἐξουσίαν παρέχων ὀψὲ ἀπιέναι, αἱ δὲ κύνες τά τε 5
θηρία ἀπερύκουσαι ἀπὸ λύμης καρπῶν καὶ προβάτων καὶ τῇ ἐρημίᾳ
7 τὴν ἀσφάλειαν συμπαρέχουσαι. παρορμᾷ δέ τι καὶ εἰς τὸ ἀρήγειν
σὺν ὅπλοις τῇ χώρᾳ καὶ ἡ γῆ τοὺς γεωργοὺς ἐν τῷ μέσῳ τοὺς
8 καρποὺς τρέφουσα τῷ κρατοῦντι λαμβάνειν. καὶ δραμεῖν δὲ καὶ
βαλεῖν καὶ πηδῆσαι τίς ἱκανωτέρους τέχνη γεωργίας παρέχεται; 10
τίς δὲ τοῖς ἐργαζομένοις πλείω τέχνη ἀντιχαρίζεται; τίς δὲ ἥδιον
τὸν ἐπιμελόμενον δέχεται προτείνουσα προσιόντι λαβεῖν ὅ τι
9 χρῄζει; τίς δὲ ξένους ἀφθονώτερον δέχεται; χειμάσαι δὲ πυρὶ
ἀφθόνῳ καὶ θερμοῖς λουτροῖς ποῦ πλείων εὐμάρεια ἢ ἐν χώρῳ τῳ;
ποῦ δὲ ἥδιον θερίσαι ὕδασί τε καὶ πνεύμασι καὶ σκιαῖς ἢ κατ᾽ 15
10 ἀγρόν; τίς δὲ ἄλλη θεοῖς ἀπαρχὰς πρεπωδεστέρας παρέχει ἢ ἑορτὰς
πληρεστέρας ἀποδεικνύει; τίς δὲ οἰκέταις προσφιλεστέρα ἢ γυναικὶ
11 ἡδίων ἢ τέκνοις ποθεινοτέρα ἢ φίλοις εὐχαριστοτέρα; ἐμοὶ μὲν
θαυμαστὸν δοκεῖ εἶναι εἴ τις ἐλεύθερος ἄνθρωπος ἢ κτῆμά τι τούτου
ἥδιον κέκτηται ἢ ἐπιμέλειαν ἡδίω τινὰ ταύτης ηὕρηκεν ἢ 20
12 ὠφελιμωτέραν εἰς τὸν βίον. ἔτι δὲ ἡ γῆ θεὸς οὖσα τοὺς δυναμένους
καταμανθάνειν καὶ δικαιοσύνην διδάσκει· τοὺς γὰρ ἄριστα
13 θεραπεύοντας αὐτὴν πλεῖστα ἀγαθὰ ἀντιποιεῖ. ἐὰν δ᾽ ἄρα καὶ ὑπὸ
πλήθους ποτὲ στρατευμάτων τῶν ἔργων στερηθῶσιν οἱ ἐν τῇ
γεωργίᾳ ἀναστρεφόμενοι καὶ σφοδρῶς καὶ ἀνδρικῶς παιδευόμενοι, 25
οὗτοι εὖ παρεσκευασμένοι καὶ τὰς ψυχὰς καὶ τὰ σώματα, ἂν μὴ
θεὸς ἀποκωλύῃ, δύνανται ἰόντες εἰς τὰς τῶν ἀποκωλυόντων
λαμβάνειν ἀφ᾽ ὧν θρέψονται. πολλάκις δ᾽ ἐν τῷ πολέμῳ καὶ
ἀσφαλέστερόν ἐστι σὺν τοῖς ὅπλοις τὴν τροφὴν μαστεύειν ἢ σὺν
14 τοῖς γεωργικοῖς ὀργάνοις. συμπαιδεύει δὲ καὶ εἰς τὸ ἐπαρκεῖν 30
ἀλλήλοις ἡ γεωργία. ἐπί τε γὰρ τοὺς πολεμίους σὺν ἀνθρώποις δεῖ

---

1 τι ἡ γῆ Stephanus: τε ἡ γῆ Stob.: τῇ(ῇ, η) γῇ(η) codd.   2 ὠφελούμενοι Stob.:
ὠφελούμεναι codd.   3 οἱ Stob.: om. D A: αἱ cet.   5 ὀψὲ] τοῦ (sic)
δείλης Stob.   6 τῇ Hᵃ Stob.: τῇ τε cet.   7 συμπαρορμᾷ Stob.   8 καὶ
susp. Schneidero: καὶ ... γεωργοὺς om. Stob. Paris. γῇ] γεωργία Stob. Vind.
10 βαλεῖν] βάδην ἰέναι cit. Schenkl   τέχνη del. Heindorf   12 ἐπιμελούμενον D C
Stob.   14 ποῦ Stob.: ποῦ πολύ codd.   εὐχέρεια Stob.   ἢ om G F al. Stob. Paris.
χώρῳ τῳ ω, ῷ, ο) codd.: χωρίῳ Stob.   18 εὐχαριτωτέρα Hertlein   21 θεὸς
οὖσα Stob.: θέ(λ)ουσα codd.   26 τὰ om. H al. D al.   27 κωλύῃ Stob.
τὰς codd.: τὰ Stob.   κωλυόντων Stob.   30 ἐπαρκεῖν ἀλλήλοις] ἄρχειν Stob.
31 πολεμίους Stob.: πολέμους codd.   πριυσ σὺν ἀνθρώποις] μετ᾽ ἀνθρώπων Stob.

him to take rather more pleasure in the activity of hunting, providing easy access to nourishment for the hounds and nourishing the prey at the same time. And as horses and hounds reap benefits from farming, 6 so, too, they in their turn bestow benefits on the land: the horse carries his master to his work of supervision early and makes it possible for him to return late, and the hounds prevent the wild beasts from damaging the crops and livestock and provide safety in deserted places as well. And the earth provides some incentive for farmers to defend the land 7 by force of arms, because the crops it produces are out in the open, so that it is the winner who takes them. And what occupation makes men 8 more suited for running, throwing, and jumping than farming? What occupation provides greater pleasure in return to those who work at it? What occupation welcomes the man who is concerned with it more graciously, inviting him to come and take what he needs? What occupa- 9 tion welcomes friends more generously? Where is it more comfortable to spend the winter than on a farm with a generous fire and warm baths? Where is it more pleasant to spend the summer than in the countryside with streams and breezes and shade? What other occupation 10 provides more appropriate first-fruits for the gods or produces festivals with a greater abundance of offerings? What occupation is more popular with slaves, or sweeter to a wife, or more attractive to children, or more agreeable to friends? I think it would be remarkable if any free man has 11 ever come to possess any property more pleasant than a farm, or has discovered any object of concern more pleasant or more useful for making a living. Furthermore, because the earth is divine, she teaches 12 justice to those who have the ability to learn from her. She gives the greatest benefits in return to those who cultivate her best. Moreover, if 13 those who are engaging in farming and receiving an energetic and manly training are sometime deprived of their lands by successive invading armies, because they are well prepared mentally and physically, they are able to attack the territory of the men who are keeping them out of their own, and take what they need to support themselves—unless some god prevents them. Often in war it is safer to search for food with weapons than with farm implements. Furthermore, farming helps train 14 people to collaborate with each other. For attacking the enemy requires co-operation and the cultivation of the earth requires co-operation.

15 ἰέναι, τῆς τε γῆς σὺν ἀνθρώποις ἐστὶν ἡ ἐργασία. τὸν οὖν μέλλοντα
εὖ γεωργήσειν δεῖ τοὺς ἐργαστῆρας καὶ προθύμους παρασκευάζειν
καὶ πείθεσθαι θέλοντας· τὸν δὲ ἐπὶ πολεμίους ἄγοντα ταὐτὰ δεῖ
μηχανᾶσθαι δωρούμενόν τε τοῖς ποιοῦσιν ἃ δεῖ ποιεῖν τοὺς ἀγαθοὺς
16 καὶ κολάζοντα τοὺς ἀτακτοῦντας. καὶ παρακελεύεσθαι δὲ πολλάκις 5
οὐδὲν ἧττον δεῖ τοῖς ἐργάταις τὸν γεωργὸν ἢ τὸν στρατηγὸν τοῖς
στρατιώταις· καὶ ἐλπίδων δὲ ἀγαθῶν οὐδὲν ἧττον οἱ δοῦλοι τῶν
17 ἐλευθέρων δέονται, ἀλλὰ καὶ μᾶλλον, ὅπως μένειν ἐθέλωσι. καλῶς
δὲ κἀκεῖνος εἶπεν ὃς ἔφη τὴν γεωργίαν τῶν ἄλλων τεχνῶν μητέρα
καὶ τροφὸν εἶναι. εὖ μὲν γὰρ φερομένης τῆς γεωργίας ἔρρωνται 10
καὶ αἱ ἄλλαι τέχναι ἅπασαι, ὅπου δ' ἂν ἀναγκασθῇ ἡ γῆ χερσεύειν,
ἀποσβέννυνται καὶ αἱ ἄλλαι τέχναι σχεδόν τι καὶ κατὰ γῆν καὶ
κατὰ θάλατταν.

18 Ἀκούσας δὲ ταῦτα ὁ Κριτόβουλος εἶπεν· Ἀλλὰ ταῦτα μὲν ἔμοιγε,
ὦ Σώκρατες, καλῶς δοκεῖς λέγειν· ὅτι δὲ τῆς γεωργικῆς τὰ 15
πλεῖστά ἐστιν ἀνθρώπῳ ἀδύνατα προνοῆσαι, ⟨δῆλον·⟩ καὶ γὰρ
χάλαζαι καὶ πάχναι ἐνίοτε καὶ αὐχμοὶ καὶ ὄμβροι ἐξαίσιοι καὶ
ἐρυσῖβαι καὶ ἄλλα πολλάκις τὰ καλῶς ἐγνωσμένα καὶ πεποιημένα
ἀφαιροῦνται· καὶ πρόβατα δ' ἐνίοτε κάλλιστα τεθραμμένα νόσος
19 ἐλθοῦσα κάκιστα ἀπώλεσεν. ἀκούσας δὲ ταῦτα ὁ Σωκράτης εἶπεν· 20
Ἀλλ' ᾤμην ἔγωγέ σε, ὦ Κριτόβουλε, εἰδέναι ὅτι οἱ θεοὶ οὐδὲν
ἧττόν εἰσι κύριοι τῶν ἐν τῇ γεωργίᾳ ἔργων ἢ τῶν ἐν τῷ πολέμῳ.
καὶ τοὺς μὲν ἐν τῷ πολέμῳ ὁρᾷς, οἶμαι, πρὸ τῶν πολεμικῶν
πράξεων ἐξαρεσκομένους τοὺς θεοὺς καὶ ἐπερωτῶντας θυσίαις καὶ
20 οἰωνοῖς ὅ τι τε χρὴ ποιεῖν καὶ ὅ τι μή· περὶ δὲ τῶν γεωργικῶν 25
πράξεων ἧττον οἴει δεῖν τοὺς θεοὺς ἱλάσκεσθαι; εὖ γὰρ ἴσθι, ἔφη,
ὅτι οἱ σώφρονες καὶ ὑπὲρ ὑγρῶν καὶ ξηρῶν καρπῶν καὶ βοῶν καὶ
ἵππων καὶ προβάτων καὶ ὑπὲρ πάντων γε δὴ τῶν κτημάτων τοὺς
θεοὺς θεραπεύουσιν.

VI Ἀλλὰ ταῦτα μέν, ἔφη, ὦ Σώκρατες, καλῶς μοι δοκεῖς λέγειν 30
κελεύων πειρᾶσθαι σὺν τοῖς θεοῖς ἄρχεσθαι παντὸς ἔργου, ὡς τῶν
θεῶν κυρίων ὄντων οὐδὲν ἧττον τῶν εἰρηνικῶν ἢ τῶν πολεμικῶν
ἔργων. ταῦτα μὲν οὖν πειρασόμεθα οὕτω ποιεῖν. σὺ δ' ἡμῖν ἔνθεν
λέγων περὶ τῆς οἰκονομίας ἀπέλιπες, πειρῶ τὰ τούτων ἐχόμενα
διεκπεραίνειν, ὡς καὶ νῦν μοι δοκῶ ἀκηκοὼς ὅσα εἶπες μᾶλλόν τι 35

---

3 τόν τε codd. et Stob.: corr. Zeune   ταὐτὰ Camerarius: ταῦτα codd. et Stob.
8 θέλωσι Y al.   16 lac. stat. Reisig   24 ἐξαρεσκομένους A L: ἐξαρεσκευομένους
cet.   τοὺς θεοὺς Cobet: τοῖς θεοῖς codd.

Therefore the man who is going to be a successful farmer must make 15
his labourers eager and disposed to be obedient. And the man who leads
his men against the enemy must contrive to produce the same result by
giving gifts to those who behave as brave men should and punishing
those who disobey commands. On many occasions the farmer must 16
encourage his workers no less than the general encourages his soldiers.
Slaves need some good thing to look forward to no less, in fact, even
more than free men so that they may be willing to stay. The man who 17
said that farming is the mother and nurse of the other arts spoke truly.
When farming is successful, all the other arts prosper, but wherever the
earth is forced to lie barren, the other arts, both on earth and sea, are
virtually extinguished.

CRITOBULUS. Well, Socrates, I believe that what you have said is right. 18
But it is impossible for a man to foresee most of what happens in farming.
Sometimes hail and frosts, droughts, and excessively heavy rain, blight,
and other catastrophes repeatedly destroy what has been well planned
and well accomplished. And sometimes disease attacks the best-raised
cattle and destroys them in a most dreadful manner.

SOCRATES. Yes, Critobulus, but I thought that you knew that the gods 19
control farming matters no less than the matters of war. No doubt you
have noticed that men who are engaged in war propitiate the gods
before joining combat, and try to discover through sacrifices and omens
what they should or should not do. Do you think it is any less essential 20
to propitiate the gods for agricultural matters? Take my word for it,
sensible men pay respect to the gods for the good of their fruits and
crops and cattle and horses and sheep and indeed of all their possessions.

CRITOBULUS. Well, Socrates, I think you're giving me good advice when VI
you tell me to try to begin every activity with the help of the gods,
because, as you say, they control the activities of peace no less than
those of war. We shall try, then, to do so. But please start from where
you left off when you were telling us about estate management, and try
to explain in detail the topics that follow on from what you said, since
having listened to what you were saying, I think that even now I already

2 ἤδη διορᾶν ἢ πρόσθεν ὅ τι χρὴ ποιοῦντα βιοτεύειν. Τί οὖν, ἔφη ὁ
Σωκράτης, ἆρα, εἰ πρῶτον μὲν ἐπανέλθοιμεν ὅσα συνομολογοῦντες
διεληλύθαμεν, ἵν᾽, ἄν πως δυνώμεθα, πειραθῶμεν οὕτω καὶ τὰ
3 λοιπὰ διεξιέναι συνομολογοῦντες; Ἡδὺ γοῦν ἐστιν, ἔφη ὁ
Κριτόβουλος, ὥσπερ καὶ χρημάτων κοινωνήσαντας ἀναμφιλόγως 5
διελθεῖν, οὕτω καὶ λόγων κοινωνοῦντας περὶ ὧν ἂν διαλεγώμεθα
4 συνομολογοῦντας διεξιέναι. Οὐκοῦν, ἔφη ὁ Σωκράτης, ἐπιστήμης
μέν τινος ἔδοξεν ἡμῖν ὄνομα εἶναι ἡ οἰκονομία, ἡ δὲ ἐπιστήμη αὕτη
ἐφαίνετο ᾗ οἴκους δύνανται αὔξειν ἄνθρωποι, οἶκος δ᾽ ἡμῖν ἐφαίνετο
ὅπερ κτῆσις ἡ σύμπασα, κτῆσιν δὲ τοῦτο ἔφαμεν εἶναι ὅ τι ἑκάστῳ 10
εἴη ὠφέλιμον εἰς τὸν βίον, ὠφέλιμα δὲ ὄντα ηὑρίσκετο πάντα
5 ὁπόσοις τις ἐπίσταιτο χρῆσθαι. πάσας μὲν οὖν τὰς ἐπιστήμας οὔτε
μαθεῖν οἷόν τε ἡμῖν ἐδόκει, συναπεδοκιμάζομέν τε ταῖς πόλεσι
τὰς βαναυσικὰς καλουμένας τέχνας, ὅτι καὶ τὰ σώματα
6 καταλυμαίνεσθαι δοκοῦσι καὶ τὰς ψυχὰς καταγνύουσι. τεκμήριον 15
δὲ σαφέστατον γενέσθαι ἂν τούτου ἔφαμεν, εἰ πολεμίων εἰς τὴν
χώραν ἰόντων διακαθίσας τις τοὺς γεωργοὺς καὶ τοὺς τεχνίτας
χωρὶς ἑκατέρους ἐπερωτῴη πότερα δοκεῖ ἀρήγειν τῇ χώρᾳ ἢ
7 ὑφεμένους τῆς γῆς τὰ τείχη διαφυλάττειν. οὕτως γὰρ ἂν τοὺς μὲν
ἀμφὶ γῆν ἔχοντας ᾠόμεθ᾽ ἂν ψηφίζεσθαι ἀρήγειν, τοὺς δὲ τεχνίτας 20
μὴ μάχεσθαι, ἀλλ᾽ ὅπερ πεπαίδευνται καθῆσθαι μήτε πονοῦντας
8 μήτε κινδυνεύοντας. ἐδοκιμάσαμεν δὲ ἀνδρὶ καλῷ τε κἀγαθῷ
ἐργασίαν εἶναι καὶ ἐπιστήμην κρατίστην γεωργίαν, ἀφ᾽ ἧς τὰ
9 ἐπιτήδεια ἄνθρωποι πορίζονται. αὕτη γὰρ ἡ ἐργασία μαθεῖν τε
ῥᾴστη ἐδόκει εἶναι καὶ ἡδίστη ἐργάζεσθαι, καὶ τὰ σώματα 25
κάλλιστά τε καὶ εὐρωστότατα παρέχεσθαι, καὶ ταῖς ψυχαῖς ἥκιστα
ἀσχολίαν παρέχειν φίλων τε καὶ πόλεων συνεπιμελεῖσθαι.
10 συμπαροξύνειν δέ τι ἐδόκει ἡμῖν καὶ εἰς τὸ ἀλκίμους εἶναι ἡ
γεωργία ἔξω τῶν ἐρυμάτων τὰ ἐπιτήδεια φύουσά τε καὶ τρέφουσα
τοὺς ἐργαζομένους. διὰ ταῦτα δὲ καὶ εὐδοξοτάτη εἶναι πρὸς τῶν 30
πόλεων αὕτη ἡ βιοτεία, ὅτι καὶ πολίτας ἀρίστους καὶ εὐνουστάτους
11 παρέχεσθαι δοκεῖ τῷ κοινῷ. καὶ ὁ Κριτόβουλος· Ὅτι μέν, ὦ

2 ἆρα codd. plurimi: del. Schenkl   συνομολογοῦντες Graux: μὲν ὁμολογοῦντες
codd.   3 ἵν᾽ et πειραθῶμεν del. Cobet: πειραθῶμεν om. R. Ven. 513   6 διελεῖν
Orelli   8 ἐδόκει Stob.   9 οἱ ἄνθρωποι L O: ἄνθρωποι Schenkl   13 συναπεδοκιμάζομέν Stob.: συναποδοκιμάζειν codd.   15 καταγνύναι Stob.   §§ 6–7 ab hac loco
alienas esse viderunt multi coll. c. iv   16 φαίνεται Camerarius
19 ἀφεμένους Cobet   οὕτω K L F   20 οἰόμεθ᾽ Camerarius   24 ἄνθρωποι
Schenkl   27 πόλεων codd.: πόλεως Dind.   29 τε del. Weiske   30 εὐδοξοτάτη
Hasse: ἐνδοξοτάτη codd.

perceive somewhat more clearly than before what I must do to earn
a living.

SOCRATES. Well, suppose we begin by reviewing the points of our discussion 2
on which we reached agreement, so that we may try to go through the
remaining points in similar agreement.

CRITOBULUS. Yes, certainly, for just as it is pleasant for business associates 3
to go through their accounts without argument, so it is for us who are
associates in a dialogue to go through our discussion in agreement.

SOCRATES. Well, we thought that estate management was the name of 4
some branch of knowledge. This knowledge appeared to be the science
by which men can increase their estates. And an estate seemed to be
identical with the total of a person's property. We said that property is
what is beneficial to each person for a livelihood. And we discovered
that everything which a person knows how to use is beneficial. We 5
thought that it was impossible to learn all the branches of knowledge.
And we agreed with the cities in rejecting the so-called 'banausic'
occupations on the grounds that we thought that they ruin men's bodies
and weaken their minds. We asserted that the clearest proof of this 6
would be evident during an enemy attack against the land, if the farmers
were to be separated from the craftsmen and asked whether they preferred to defend the land or to retreat from the open country to guard
the city walls. We thought that in such a situation those who are 7
occupied with the land would vote to defend it, but the craftsmen would
vote not to fight but to remain sitting down, as they have been trained
to do, and to avoid exertion and danger. We decided that for a true 8
gentleman, the best line of work and the best branch of knowledge is
farming, by which human beings obtain the necessities of life. This line 9
of work seemed to be very easy to learn and most enjoyable to practise,
to make men's bodies most handsome and strong, and to provide their
minds with the greatest amount of leisure to devote to their friends and
their cities. We thought that farming, to some extent, stimulated those 10
who work at it to be brave, because crops and cattle are raised outside
the city walls. Therefore this way of making a living, we thought, enjoys
the best reputation among cities; for they believe that it creates citizens
who are both extremely brave and most loyal to the community.

CRITOBULUS. I am quite convinced, Socrates, that farming is the best, 11

Σώκρατες, κάλλιστόν τε καὶ ἄριστον καὶ ἥδιστον ἀπὸ γεωργίας
τὸν βίον ποιεῖσθαι πάνυ μοι δοκῶ πεπεῖσθαι ἱκανῶς· ὅτι δὲ ἔφησθα
καταμαθεῖν τὰ αἴτια τῶν τε οὕτω γεωργούντων ὥστε ἀπὸ τῆς
γεωργίας ἀφθόνως ἔχειν ὧν δέονται καὶ τῶν οὕτως ἐργαζομένων
ὡς μὴ λυσιτελεῖν αὐτοῖς τὴν γεωργίαν, καὶ ταῦτ᾽ ⟨ἂν⟩ μοι δοκῶ 5
ἡδέως ἑκάτερα ἀκούειν σου, ὅπως ἃ μὲν ἀγαθά ἐστι ποιῶμεν, ἃ
12 δὲ βλαβερὰ μὴ ποιῶμεν. Τί οὖν, ἔφη ὁ Σωκράτης, ὦ Κριτόβουλε,
ἄν σοι ἐξ ἀρχῆς διηγήσωμαι ὡς συνεγενόμην ποτὲ ἀνδρί, ὃς ἐμοὶ
ἐδόκει εἶναι τῷ ὄντι τούτων τῶν ἀνδρῶν ἐφ᾽ οἷς τοῦτο τὸ ὄνομα
δικαίως ἐστὶν ὃ καλεῖται καλός τε κἀγαθὸς ἀνήρ; Πάνυ ἄν, ἔφη ὁ 10
Κριτόβουλος, βουλοίμην ἂν οὕτως ἀκούειν, ὡς καὶ ἔγωγε ἐρῶ
13 τούτου τοῦ ὀνόματος ἄξιος γενέσθαι. Λέξω τοίνυν σοι, ἔφη ὁ
Σωκράτης, ὡς καὶ ἦλθον ἐπὶ τὴν σκέψιν αὐτοῦ. τοὺς μὲν γὰρ
ἀγαθοὺς τέκτονας, ἀγαθοὺς χαλκέας, ἀγαθοὺς ζωγράφους, ἀγαθοὺς
ἀνδριαντοποιούς, καὶ τἆλλα τὰ τοιαῦτα, πάνυ ὀλίγος 15
μοι χρόνος ἐγένετο ἱκανὸς περιελθεῖν τε καὶ θεάσασθαι τὰ
14 δεδοκιμασμένα καλὰ ἔργα αὐτοῖς εἶναι. ὅπως δὲ δὴ καὶ τοὺς
ἔχοντας τὸ σεμνὸν ὄνομα τοῦτο τὸ καλός τε κἀγαθὸς ἐπισκεψαίμην,
τί ποτε ἐργαζόμενοι τοῦτ᾽ ἀξιοῖντο καλεῖσθαι, πάνυ μου ἡ ψυχὴ
15 ἐπεθύμει αὐτῶν τινι συγγενέσθαι. καὶ πρῶτον μὲν ὅτι προσέκειτο 20
τὸ καλὸς τῷ ἀγαθῷ, ὄντινα ἴδοιμι καλόν, τούτῳ προσῄειν καὶ
ἐπειρώμην καταμανθάνειν εἴ που ἴδοιμι προσηρτημένον τῷ καλῷ
16 τὸ ἀγαθόν. ἀλλ᾽ οὐκ ἄρα εἶχεν οὕτως, ἀλλ᾽ ἐνίους ἐδόκουν
καταμανθάνειν τῶν καλῶν τὰς μορφὰς πάνυ μοχθηροὺς ὄντας τὰς
ψυχάς. ἔδοξεν οὖν μοι ἀφέμενον τῆς καλῆς ὄψεως ἐπ᾽ αὐτῶν τινα 25
17 ἐλθεῖν τῶν καλουμένων καλῶν τε κἀγαθῶν. ἐπεὶ οὖν τὸν
Ἰσχόμαχον ἤκουον πρὸς πάντων καὶ ἀνδρῶν καὶ γυναικῶν καὶ
ξένων καὶ ἀστῶν καλόν τε κἀγαθὸν ἐπονομαζόμενον, ἔδοξέ μοι
τούτῳ πειραθῆναι συγγενέσθαι.

VII Ἰδὼν οὖν ποτε αὐτὸν ἐν τῇ τοῦ Διὸς τοῦ ἐλευθερίου στοᾷ 30
καθήμενον, ἐπεί μοι ἔδοξε σχολάζειν, προσῆλθον αὐτῷ καὶ
παρακαθιζόμενος εἶπον· Τί, ὦ Ἰσχόμαχε, οὐ μάλα εἰωθὼς
σχολάζειν κάθησαι; ἐπεὶ τά γε πλεῖστα ἢ πράττοντά τι ὁρῶ σε ἢ

5 ταῦτ᾽ ἂν Schäfer: ταῦτα codd.   11 ἂν om. Stob.   οὕτως σου Stob.: τοῦτό
σου Hertlein   14 ἀγαθοὺς χαλκεῖς, ἀγαθοὺς ζωγράφους, ἀγαθοὺς ἀνδριαντοποιούς
Stob.: χαλκέας ἀγαθούς, ζωγράφους ἀγαθούς, ἀνδριαντοποιούς codd.   15 τἆλλα]
πάντα Stob.   16 ἱκανὸς F N: ἱκανῶς cet.: om. Stob.   18 τὸ καλόν τε
κἀγαθὸν codd. (καλὸς κἀγαθὸς A in mg.): καλὸς τε κἀγαθὸς Stob. om. τὸ   19 ἐργασά-
μενοι Stob.   ἀξιοῦνται Stob.   μοι C et Stob.   21 τὸ κάλλος H N D C: ὁ καλὸς
Stob. Vind.   22 κάλλει Stob.   27 ἀνδρῶν A O: ἀνδρῶν τε cet.

noblest, and most pleasant way of making a living. But you told me that you had discovered the reasons why some farmers manage to farm in such a way that they get all they need in abundance, whereas others farm in such a way that their farming does not produce any profit for them. It would be a pleasure to hear from you about the reasons in each case so that we shall be able to do what is right and avoid what is disadvantageous.

SOCRATES. Critobulus, suppose I tell you from the beginning how I once 12 met a man who in my opinion really deserved that phrase we use 'a true gentleman'.[5]

CRITOBULUS. I should very much like to hear about it, for I myself have a great passion to be worthy of that title.

SOCRATES. Then I will tell you how I came to make enquiries about him. 13 I needed very little time to go around visiting the good smiths, good painters, good sculptors, and so on, and to view what were considered their finest works. My soul very much desired to become acquainted 14 with one of those who are called by that dignified title 'gentleman', so that I might consider what kind of behaviour it was that led people to think that such men deserved it. And first of all, because in this phrase 15 the word 'beautiful' was added to the word 'good' I approached every beautiful-looking man and tried to discover whether I could see virtue attached to beauty in any of them. But I found that things were not 16 like that at all. I discovered that some who were beautiful in appearance were, in my view, utterly depraved in their souls. So I decided to give up the notion of physical beauty and to approach one of those who are called 'gentlemen'. When I heard that Ischomachus was called a 'gentle- 17 man' by everyone, men and women, and foreigners and citizens, I decided to try to meet him.

[The following conversation (cc. vii–xxi) is related by Socrates to VII Critobulus. ἔφη φάναι 'he told me he said to her' and similar formulae have not been translated since they interrupt the flow of the narrative.]

One day, I saw him sitting in the Stoa of Zeus Eleutherius, apparently unoccupied, so I went up to him and sat next to him, and said, 'What's happening, Ischomachus? It's not like you to sit around unoccupied. Usually when I see you, you are busy with something or, at any rate, not

---

[5] Literally 'beautiful and good'.

2 οὐ πάνυ σχολάζοντα ἐν τῇ ἀγορᾷ. Οὐδὲ ἄν γε νῦν, ἔφη ὁ
Ἰσχόμαχος, ὦ Σώκρατες, ἑώρας, εἰ μὴ ξένους τινὰς συνεθέμην
ἀναμένειν ἐνθάδε. Ὅταν δὲ μὴ πράττῃς τι τοιοῦτον, πρὸς τῶν
θεῶν, ἔφην ἐγώ, ποῦ διατρίβεις καὶ τί ποιεῖς; ἐγὼ γάρ τοι πάνυ
βούλομαί σου πυθέσθαι τί ποτε πράττων καλὸς κἀγαθὸς κέκλησαι, 5
ἐπεὶ οὐκ ἔνδον γε διατρίβεις οὐδὲ τοιαύτη σου ἡ ἕξις τοῦ σώματος
3 καταφαίνεται. καὶ ὁ Ἰσχόμαχος γελάσας ἐπὶ τῷ τί ποιῶν καλὸς
κἀγαθὸς κέκλησαι, καὶ ἡσθείς, ὥς γ' ἐμοὶ ἔδοξεν, εἶπεν· Ἀλλ' εἰ
μὲν ὅταν σοι διαλέγωνται περὶ ἐμοῦ τινες καλοῦσί με τοῦτο τὸ
ὄνομα οὐκ οἶδα· οὐ γὰρ δή, ὅταν γέ με εἰς ἀντίδοσιν καλῶνται 10
τριηραρχίας ἢ χορηγίας, οὐδείς, ἔφη, ζητεῖ τὸν καλόν τε κἀγαθόν,
ἀλλὰ σαφῶς, ἔφη, ὀνομάζοντές με Ἰσχόμαχον πατρόθεν
προσκαλοῦνται. ἐγὼ μὲν τοίνυν, ἔφη, ὦ Σώκρατες, ὅ με ἐπήρου,
οὐδαμῶς ἔνδον διατρίβω. καὶ γὰρ δή, ἔφη, τά γε ἐν τῇ οἰκίᾳ μου
4 πάνυ καὶ αὐτὴ ἡ γυνή ἐστιν ἱκανὴ διοικεῖν. Ἀλλὰ καὶ τοῦτο, ἔφην, 15
ἔγωγε, ὦ Ἰσχόμαχε, πάνυ ἂν ἡδέως σου πυθοίμην, πότερα αὐτὸς
σὺ ἐπαίδευσας τὴν γυναῖκα ὥστε εἶναι οἵαν δεῖ ἢ ἐπισταμένην
ἔλαβες παρὰ τοῦ πατρὸς καὶ τῆς μητρὸς διοικεῖν τὰ προσήκοντα
5 αὐτῇ. Καὶ τί ἄν, ἔφη, ὦ Σώκρατες, ἐπισταμένην αὐτὴν παρέλαβον,
ἢ ἔτη μὲν οὔπω πεντεκαίδεκα γεγονυῖα ἦλθε πρὸς ἐμέ, τὸν δ' 20
ἔμπροσθεν χρόνον ἔζη ὑπὸ πολλῆς ἐπιμελείας ὅπως ὡς ἐλάχιστα
6 μὲν ὄψοιτο, ἐλάχιστα δ' ἀκούσοιτο, ἐλάχιστα δ' ἔροιτο; οὐ γὰρ
ἀγαπητόν σοι δοκεῖ εἶναι, εἰ μόνον ἦλθεν ἐπισταμένη ἔρια
παραλαβοῦσα ἱμάτιον ἀποδεῖξαι, καὶ ἑωρακυῖα ὡς ἔργα ταλάσια
θεραπαίναις δίδοται; ἐπεὶ τά γε ἀμφὶ γαστέρα, ἔφη, πάνυ καλῶς, 25
ὦ Σώκρατες, ἦλθε πεπαιδευμένη· ὅπερ μέγιστον ἔμοιγε δοκεῖ
7 παίδευμα εἶναι καὶ ἀνδρὶ καὶ γυναικί. Τὰ δ' ἄλλα, ἔφην ἐγώ, ὦ
Ἰσχόμαχε, αὐτὸς ἐπαίδευσας τὴν γυναῖκα ὥστε ἱκανὴν εἶναι ὧν
8 προσήκει ἐπιμελεῖσθαι; Οὐ μὰ Δί', ἔφη ὁ Ἰσχόμαχος, οὐ πρίν γε
καὶ ἔθυσα καὶ ηὐξάμην ἐμέ τε τυγχάνειν διδάσκοντα καὶ ἐκείνην 30
μανθάνουσαν τὰ βέλτιστα ἀμφοτέροις ἡμῖν. Οὐκοῦν, ἔφην ἐγώ, καὶ
ἡ γυνή σοι συνέθυε καὶ συνηύχετο ταῦτα ταῦτα; Καὶ μάλα γ', ἔφη
ὁ Ἰσχόμαχος, πολλά ὑπισχνουμένη μέν, ⟨εὐχομένη δὲ⟩ πρὸς τοὺς
θεοὺς γενέσθαι οἵαν δεῖ, καὶ εὔδηλος ἦν ὅτι οὐκ ἀμελήσει τῶν
9 διδασκομένων. Πρὸς θεῶν, ἔφην ἐγώ, ὦ Ἰσχόμαχε, τί πρῶτον 35

1 γε del. Cobet   5 καλός τε D al. P   14 διατρίβω L: καταρτίβω cet.
21 πολλῇ ἐπιμελείᾳ Hartman   ὡς del. Cobet   22 ἐρήσοιτο Hartman
25 δίδονται D C K pr.   32 ταὐτὰ Heindorf: αὐτὰ vel αὐτῷ(ῶ) codd.   33 ὑπισχνουμένη H N: ὑπισχομένη(ν O) vel ὑποσχομένη cet. εὐχομένη δὲ add. Marchant

totally unoccupied in the marketplace.'

Ischomachus replied, 'You wouldn't have seen me behaving like this 2 now, only I have agreed to meet some guests here.'

'When you're not doing something of that kind,' I asked, 'where do you spend your time by the gods, and what do you do? I should very much like you to tell me what exactly it is that you do to be called a "gentleman", since you don't spend your time indoors, and your physical condition does not suggest that you do so.'

Ischomachus laughed at the question: 'What do you do to be called a 3 "gentleman"?' But he was evidently pleased, and replied, 'I don't know whether people use this title when they are talking to you about me. Certainly whenever they challenge me to an exchange of property to pay for the maintenance of a trireme or for training choruses for the festivals, no one sets about looking for the "gentleman", but they summon me simply by the name Ischomachus together with that of my father. And, Socrates, in reply to your question, I certainly do not spend time indoors, for my wife is more than capable of managing everything inside the house, even by herself.'

I said, 'I should very much like you to tell me, Ischomachus, whether 4 you yourself trained your wife to become the sort of woman that she ought to be, or whether she already knew how to carry out her duties when you took her as your wife from her father and mother.'

'What could she have known when I took her as my wife, Socrates? She 5 was not yet fifteen when she came to me, and had spent her previous years under careful supervision so that she might see and hear and speak as little as possible. Don't you think it was adequate if she came to me knowing 6 only how to take wool and produce a cloak, and had seen how spinning tasks are allocated to the slaves? And besides, she had been very well trained to control her appetites, Socrates,' he said, 'and I think that sort of training is most important for man and woman alike.'

'Ischomachus,' I asked, 'did you train your wife yourself in other respects 7 so that she would be competent to deal with matters that concern her?'

'No, by Zeus,' said Ischomachus, 'at least, not until I had sacrificed to 8 the gods and prayed that I might be successful in teaching and she in learning what was best for both of us.'

'Did your wife sacrifice along with you and offer the same prayers?', I asked.

'Oh, yes, very much so, and she vowed and prayed fervently to the gods that she might become the sort of woman that she ought to be, and she made it clear that she would not neglect what she had been taught.'

'By the gods, Ischomachus,' I said, 'tell me what you began by teaching 9

διδάσκειν ἤρχου αὐτήν, διηγοῦ μοι· ὡς ἐγὼ ταῦτ᾽ ἂν ἥδιόν σου
διηγουμένου ἀκούοιμι ἢ εἴ μοι γυμνικὸν ἢ ἱππικὸν ἀγῶνα τὸν
10 κάλλιστον διηγοῖο. καὶ ὁ Ἰσχόμαχος ἀπεκρίνατο· Τί δ᾽; ἔφη, ὦ
Σώκρατες, ἐπεὶ ἤδη μοι χειροήθης ἦν καὶ ἐτετιθάσευτο ὥστε
διαλέγεσθαι, ἠρόμην αὐτὴν ὧδέ πως· Εἰπέ μοι, ὦ γύναι, ἆρα ἤδη 5
κατενόησας τίνος ποτὲ ἕνεκα ἐγώ τε σὲ ἔλαβον καὶ οἱ σοὶ γονεῖς
11 ἔδοσάν σε ἐμοί; ὅτι μὲν γὰρ οὐκ ἀπορία ἦν μεθ᾽ ὅτου ἄλλου
ἐκαθεύδομεν ἄν, οἶδ᾽ ὅτι καὶ σοὶ καταφανὲς τοῦτ᾽ ἐστί.
βουλευόμενος δ᾽ ἔγωγε ὑπὲρ ἐμοῦ καὶ οἱ σοὶ γονεῖς ὑπὲρ σοῦ τίν᾽
ἂν κοινωνὸν βέλτιστον οἴκου τε καὶ τέκνων λάβοιμεν, ἐγώ τε σὲ 10
ἐξελεξάμην καὶ οἱ σοὶ γονεῖς, ὡς ἐοίκασιν, ἐκ τῶν δυνατῶν ἐμέ.
12 τέκνα μὲν οὖν ἂν θεός ποτε διδῷ ἡμῖν γενέσθαι, τότε βουλευσόμεθα
περὶ αὐτῶν ὅπως ὅτι βέλτιστα παιδεύσομεν αὐτά· κοινὸν γὰρ ἡμῖν
καὶ τοῦτο ἀγαθόν, συμμάχων καὶ γηροβοσκῶν ὅτι βελτίστων
13 τυγχάνειν· νῦν δὲ δὴ οἶκος ἡμῖν ὅδε κοινός ἐστιν. ἐγώ τε γὰρ ὅσα 15
μοι ἔστιν ἅπαντα εἰς τὸ κοινὸν ἀποφαίνω, σύ τε ὅσα ἠνέγκω πάντα
εἰς τὸ κοινὸν κατέθηκας. καὶ οὐ τοῦτο δεῖ λογίζεσθαι, πότερος ἄρα
ἀριθμῷ πλείω συμβέβληται ἡμῶν, ἀλλ᾽ ἐκεῖνο εὖ εἰδέναι, ὅτι
ὁπότερος ἂν ἡμῶν βελτίων κοινωνὸς ᾖ, οὗτος τὰ πλείονος ἄξια
14 συμβάλλεται. ἀπεκρίνατο δέ μοι, ὦ Σώκρατες, πρὸς ταῦτα ἡ γυνή· 20
Τί δ᾽ ἂν ἐγώ σοι, ἔφη, δυναίμην συμπρᾶξαι; τίς δὲ ἡ ἐμὴ δύναμις;
ἀλλ᾽ ἐν σοὶ πάντα ἐστίν· ἐμὸν δ᾽ ἔφησεν ἡ μήτηρ ἔργον εἶναι
15 σωφρονεῖν. Ναὶ μὰ Δί᾽, ἔφην ἐγώ, ὦ γύναι, καὶ γὰρ ἐμοὶ ὁ πατήρ.
ἀλλὰ σωφρόνων τοί ἐστι καὶ ἀνδρὸς καὶ γυναικὸς οὕτω ποιεῖν, ὅπως
τά τε ὄντα ὡς βέλτιστα ἕξει καὶ ἄλλα ὅτι πλεῖστα ἐκ τοῦ καλοῦ τε 25
16 καὶ δικαίου προσγενήσεται. Καὶ τί δή, ἔφη, ὁρᾷς, ἡ γυνή, ὅ τι ἂν
ἐγὼ ποιοῦσα συναύξοιμι τὸν οἶκον; Ναὶ μὰ Δί᾽, ἔφην ἐγώ, ἅ τε οἱ
θεοὶ ἔφυσάν σε δύνασθαι καὶ ὁ νόμος συνεπαινεῖ, ταῦτα πειρῶ ὡς
17 βέλτιστα ποιεῖν. Καὶ τί δὴ ταῦτ᾽ ἐστιν; ἔφη ἐκείνη. Οἶμαι μὲν
ἔγωγε, ἔφην, οὐ τὰ ἐλαχίστου ἄξια, εἰ μή πέρ γε καὶ ἡ ἐν τῷ σμήνει 30
18 ἡγεμὼν μέλιττα ἐπ᾽ ἐλαχίστου ἀξίοις ἔργοις ἐφέστηκεν. ἐμοὶ γάρ
τοι, ἔφη φάναι, καὶ οἱ θεοί, ὦ γύναι, δοκοῦσι πολὺ διεσκεμμένως
μάλιστα τὸ ζεῦγος τοῦτο συντεθεικέναι ὃ καλεῖται θῆλυ καὶ ἄρρεν,
19 ὅπως ὅτι ὠφελιμώτατον ᾖ αὑτῷ εἰς τὴν κοινωνίαν. πρῶτον μὲν γὰρ

3 τί δέ ... εἰ μὴ ἐπεὶ Hartman   4 ἐτετιθάσευτο Schäfer: ἐπετιθασσεύετο,
ἐτιθάσσευτο, ἐτιθασ(σ)εύετο codd.   5 αὐτὴν ἔφη codd. multi   9 ἔγωγε]
ἐγώ τε Dind.   10 οἴκου A s.v.: οἴκοι cet.   14 ἀγαθόν Dobree: τἀγαθόν codd.
18 εὖ H G N: δεῖ εὖ cet.   26 δή L: δέ cet.   28 ἔφυσάν J O
P N Ven. 511: ἔφησάν, ἔφασάν, ἐφύτευσάν cet.   34 ὅτι F: ἔτι cet.   αὑτῷ F L:
αὐτῷ cet.

her, since I would rather hear you describing that than giving an account of the most splendid athletic competition or horse-race.'

Ischomachus replied, 'Well, Socrates, as soon as she was sufficiently 10 tamed and domesticated so as to be able to carry on a conversation, I questioned her more or less as follows: "Tell me, wife, have you ever thought about why I married you and why your parents gave you to me? It must be quite obvious to you, I am sure, that there was no shortage of 11 partners with whom we might sleep. I, on my part, and your parents, on your behalf, considered who was the best partner we could choose for managing an estate and for children. And I chose you, and your parents, apparently, chose me, out of those who were eligible. Now if some day the 12 god grants us children, then we shall consider how to train them in the best way possible. For this will be a blessing to us both, to obtain the best allies and support in old age. But at present we two share this estate. I go 13 on paying everything I have into the common fund; and you deposited into it everything you brought with you. There is no need to calculate precisely which of us has contributed more, but to be well aware of this: that the better partner is the one who makes the more valuable contribution."

'In reply to this, Socrates, my wife answered, "What should I be able 14 to do to help you? What ability have I got? Everything depends on you. My mother told me that my duty is to practise self-control."

'"By Zeus, wife," I said, "my father said the same to me. But self-control 15 for both man and woman means behaving so that their property will be in the very best condition and that the greatest possible increase will be made to it by just and honourable means."

'"And what do you envisage that I might do to help improve our estate?", 16 asked my wife.

'"By Zeus," I said, "try to do as well as possible what the gods have given you the natural ability to do, and which the law encourages, as well."

'"And what is that?", she asked.   17

'"I suppose," I said, "that they are not trivial matters, unless, of course, the activities that the queen bee presides over in the hive are trivial. Wife, 18 the gods seem to have shown much discernment in yoking together female and male, as we call them, so that the couple might constitute a partnership that is most beneficial to each of them. First of all, so that the various 19

τοῦ μὴ ἐκλιπεῖν ζώων γένη τοῦτο τὸ ζεῦγος κεῖται μετ᾽ ἀλλήλων
τεκνοποιούμενον, ἔπειτα τὸ γηροβοσκοὺς κεκτῆσθαι ἑαυτοῖς ἐκ
τούτου τοῦ ζεύγους τοῖς γοῦν ἀνθρώποις πορίζεται· ἔπειτα δὲ καὶ
ἡ δίαιτα τοῖς ἀνθρώποις οὐχ ὥσπερ τοῖς κτήνεσίν ἐστιν ἐν ὑπαίθρῳ,
20 ἀλλὰ στεγῶν δεῖται δῆλον ὅτι. δεῖ μέντοι τοῖς μέλλουσιν ἀνθρώποις 5
ἕξειν ὅ τι εἰσφέρωσιν εἰς τὸ στεγνὸν τοῦ ἐργασομένου τὰς ἐν τῷ
ὑπαίθρῳ ἐργασίας. καὶ γὰρ νεατὸς καὶ σπόρος καὶ φυτεία καὶ
νομαὶ ὑπαίθρια ταῦτα πάντα ἔργα ἐστίν· ἐκ τούτων δὲ τὰ ἐπιτήδεια
21 γίγνεται. δεῖ δ᾽ αὖ, ἐπειδὰν ταῦτα εἰσενεχθῇ εἰς τὸ στεγνόν, καὶ
τοῦ σώσοντος ταῦτα καὶ τοῦ ἐργασομένου δ᾽ ἃ τῶν στεγνῶν ἔργα 10
δεόμενά ἐστι. στεγνῶν δὲ δεῖται καὶ ἡ τῶν νεογνῶν τέκνων
παιδοτροφία, στεγνῶν δὲ καὶ αἱ ἐκ τοῦ καρποῦ σιτοποιίαι δέονται·
22 ὡσαύτως δὲ καὶ ἡ τῆς ἐσθῆτος ἐκ τῶν ἐρίων ἐργασία. ἐπεὶ δ᾽
ἀμφότερα ταῦτα καὶ ἔργων καὶ ἐπιμελείας δεῖται τά τε ἔνδον καὶ
τὰ ἔξω, καὶ τὴν φύσιν, φάναι, εὐθὺς παρεσκεύασεν ὁ θεός, ὡς ἐμοὶ 15
δοκεῖ, τὴν μὲν τῆς γυναικὸς ἐπὶ τὰ ἔνδον ἔργα καὶ ἐπιμελήματα,
23 ⟨τὴν δὲ τοῦ ἀνδρὸς ἐπὶ τὰ ἔξω.⟩ ῥίγη μὲν γὰρ καὶ θάλπη καὶ
ὁδοιπορίας καὶ στρατείας τοῦ ἀνδρὸς τὸ σῶμα καὶ τὴν ψυχὴν
μᾶλλον δίνασθαι καρτερεῖν κατεσκεύασεν· ὥστε τὰ ἔξω ἐπέταξεν
αὐτῷ ἔργα· τῇ δὲ γυναικὶ ἧττον τὸ σῶμα δυνατὸν πρὸς ταῦτα 20
φύσας τὰ ἔνδον ἔργα αὐτῇ, φάναι ἔφη, προστάξαι μοι δοκεῖ ὁ θεός.
24 εἰδὼς δὲ ὅτι τῇ γυναικὶ καὶ ἐνέφυσε καὶ προσέταξε τὴν τῶν νεογνῶν
τέκνων τροφήν, καὶ τοῦ στέργειν τὰ νεογνὰ βρέφη πλέον αὐτῇ
25 ἐδάσατο ἢ τῷ ἀνδρί. ἐπεὶ δὲ καὶ τὸ φυλάττειν τὰ εἰσενεχθέντα τῇ
γυναικὶ προσέταξε, γιγνώσκων ὁ θεὸς ὅτι πρὸς τὸ φυλάττειν οὐ 25
κάκιόν ἐστι φοβερὰν εἶναι τὴν ψυχὴν πλέον μέρος καὶ τοῦ φόβου
ἐδάσατο τῇ γυναικὶ ἢ τῷ ἀνδρί. εἰδὼς δὲ ὅτι καὶ ἀρήγειν αὖ δεήσει,
ἐάν τις ἀδικῇ, τὸν τὰ ἔξω ἔργα ἔχοντα, τούτῳ αὖ πλέον μέρος τοῦ
26 θράσους ἐδάσατο. ὅτι δ᾽ ἀμφοτέρους δεῖ καὶ διδόναι καὶ λαμβάνειν,
τὴν μνήμην καὶ τὴν ἐπιμέλειαν εἰς τὸ μέσον ἀμφοτέροις κατέθηκεν. 30
ὥστε οὐκ ἂν ἔχοις διελεῖν πότερα τὸ ἔθνος τὸ θῆλυ ἢ τὸ ἄρρεν
27 τούτων πλεονεκτεῖ. καὶ τὸ ἐγκρατεῖς δὲ εἶναι ὧν δεῖ εἰς τὸ μέσον
ἀμφοτέροις κατέθηκε, καὶ ἐξουσίαν ἐποίησεν ὁ θεὸς ὁπότερος ἂν
ᾖ βελτίων, εἴθ᾽ ὁ ἀνὴρ εἴθ᾽ ἡ γυνή, τοῦτον καὶ πλέον φέρεσθαι
28 τούτου τοῦ ἀγαθοῦ. διὰ δὲ τὸ τὴν φύσιν μὴ πρὸς πάντα ταῦτα 35

1 τοῦ Zeune: τὸ vel τῷ codd.   5 στεγνῶν Stephanus   6 εἰσοίσουσιν
Sauppe   τοῦ ἐργασομένου *Ven.* 513: τοὺς ἐργασ(vel ζ)ομένους cet.   10 δ᾽ ἃ
Weiske: ἃ QR *Ven.* 513: τὰ cet.   17 τὴν ... ἔξω add. Stephanus   19 παρεσκεύασεν
D al. J O   35 ταὐτὰ Schneider: ταῦτα codd.

species of living creatures may not become extinct, this pair sleeps together for the purpose of procreation. Then this pairing provides offspring to support the partners in their old age, at least in the case of human beings. And finally, human beings do not live outdoors like cattle, but obviously have need of shelter.

'"Those who intend to obtain produce to bring into the shelter need 20 someone to work at the outdoor jobs. For ploughing, sowing, planting, and herding is all work performed outdoors, and it is from these that our essential provisions are obtained. As soon as these are brought into the 21 shelter, then someone else is needed to look after them and to perform the work that requires shelters. The nursing of newborn children requires shelters, and so does the preparation of bread from grain, and likewise, making clothing out of wool. Because both the indoor and the outdoor 22 tasks require work and concern, I think the god, from the very beginning, designed the nature of woman for the indoor work and concerns and the nature of man for the outdoor work. For he prepared man's body and 23 mind to be more capable of enduring cold and heat and travelling and military campaigns, and so he assigned the outdoor work to him. Because the woman was physically less capable of endurance, I think the god has evidently assigned the indoor work to her. And because the god was aware 24 that he had both implanted in the woman and assigned to her the nurture of newborn children, he had measured out to her a greater share of affection for newborn babies than he gave to the man. And because the god had 25 also assigned to the woman the duty of guarding what had been brought into the house, realizing that a tendency to be afraid is not at all disadvantageous for guarding things, he measured out a greater portion of fear to the woman than to the man. And knowing that the person responsible for the outdoor work would have to serve as defender against any wrong doer, he measured out to him a greater share of courage.

'"Because it is necessary for both of them to give and to take, he gave 26 both of them equal powers of memory and concern. So you would not be able to distinguish whether the female or male sex has the larger share of these. And he gave them both equally the ability to practise self-control too, when it is needed. And the god granted the privilege to whichever one 27 is superior in this to gain a larger share of the benefit accruing from it, whether man or woman. So, because they are not equally well endowed 28 with all the same natural aptitudes, they are consequently more in need of

ἀμφοτέρων εὖ πεφυκέναι, διὰ τοῦτο καὶ δέονται μᾶλλον ἀλλήλων
καὶ τὸ ζεῦγος ὠφελιμώτερον ἑαυτῷ γεγένηται, ἃ τὸ ἕτερον
29 ἐλλείπεται τὸ ἕτερον δυνάμενον. ταῦτα δέ, ἔφην, δεῖ ἡμᾶς, ὦ γύναι,
εἰδότας, ἃ ἑκατέρῳ ἡμῶν προστέτακται ὑπὸ τοῦ θεοῦ, πειρᾶσθαι
ὅπως ὡς βέλτιστα τὰ προσήκοντα ἑκάτερον ἡμῶν διαπράττεσθαι. 5
30 συνεπαινεῖ δέ, ἔφη φάναι, καὶ ὁ νόμος αὐτά, συζευγνὺς ἄνδρα καὶ
γυναῖκα· καὶ κοινωνοὺς ὥσπερ τῶν τέκνων ὁ θεὸς ἐποίησεν, οὕτω καὶ
ὁ νόμος ⟨τοῦ οἴκου⟩ κοινωνοὺς καθίστησι. καὶ καλὰ δὲ εἶναι ὁ νόμος
ἀποδείκνυσιν ⟨ἃ⟩ καὶ ὁ θεὸς ἔφυσεν ἑκάτερον μᾶλλον δύνασθαι.
τῇ μὲν γὰρ γυναικὶ κάλλιον ἔνδον μένειν ἢ θυραυλεῖν, τῷ δὲ ἀνδρὶ 10
31 αἴσχιον ἔνδον μένειν ἢ τῶν ἔξω ἐπιμελεῖσθαι. εἰ δέ τις παρ' ἃ ὁ
θεὸς ἔφυσε ποιεῖ, ἴσως τι καὶ ἀτακτῶν τοὺς θεοὺς οὐ λήθει καὶ
δίκην δίδωσιν ἀμελῶν τῶν ἔργων τῶν ἑαυτοῦ ἢ πράττων τὰ τῆς
32 γυναικὸς ἔργα. δοκεῖ δέ μοι, ἔφην, καὶ ἡ τῶν μελιττῶν ἡγεμὼν
τοιαῦτα ἔργα ὑπὸ τοῦ θεοῦ προστεταγμένα διαπονεῖσθαι. Καὶ ποῖα 15
δή, ἔφη ἐκείνη, ἔργα ἔχουσα ἡ τῶν μελιττῶν ἡγεμὼν ἐξομοιοῦται
33 τοῖς ἔργοις οἷς ἐμὲ δεῖ πράττειν; Ὅτι, ἔφην ἐγώ, ἐκείνη γε ἐν τῷ
σμήνει μένουσα οὐκ ἐᾷ ἀργοὺς τὰς μελίττας εἶναι, ἀλλ' ἃς μὲν δεῖ
ἔξω ἐργάζεσθαι ἐκπέμπει ἐπὶ τὸ ἔργον, καὶ ἃ ἂν αὐτῶν ἑκάστη
εἰσφέρῃ οἶδέ τε καὶ δέχεται, καὶ σῴζει ταῦτα ἔστ' ἂν δέῃ χρῆσθαι. 20
ἐπειδὰν δὲ ἡ ὥρα τοῦ χρῆσθαι ἥκῃ, διανέμει τὸ δίκαιον ἑκάστῃ.
34 καὶ ἐπὶ τοῖς ἔνδον δ' ἐξυφαινομένοις κηρίοις ἐφέστηκεν, ὡς καλῶς
καὶ ταχέως ὑφαίνηται, καὶ τοῦ γιγνομένου τόκου ἐπιμελεῖται ὡς
ἐκτρέφηται· ἐπειδὰν δὲ ἐκτραφῇ καὶ ἀξιοεργοὶ οἱ νεοττοὶ γένωνται,
35 ἀποικίζει αὐτοὺς σὺν τῶν ἐπιγόνων τινὶ ἡγεμόνι. Ἦ καὶ ἐμὲ οὖν, 25
ἔφη ἡ γυνή, δεήσει ταῦτα ποιεῖν; Δεήσει μέντοι σε, ἔφην ἐγώ,
ἔνδον τε μένειν καὶ οἷς μὲν ἂν ἔξω τὸ ἔργον ᾖ τῶν οἰκετῶν, τούτους
συνεκπέμπειν, οἷς δ' ἂν ἔνδον ἔργον ἐργαστέον, τούτων σοι
36 ἐπιστατητέον, καὶ τά τε εἰσφερόμενα ἀποδεκτέον καὶ ἃ μὲν ἂν
αὐτῶν δέῃ δαπανᾶν σοὶ διανεμητέον, ἃ δ' ἂν περιττεύειν δέῃ, 30
προνοητέον καὶ φυλακτέον ὅπως μὴ ἡ εἰς τὸν ἐνιαυτὸν κειμένη
δαπάνη εἰς τὸν μῆνα δαπανᾶται. καὶ ὅταν ἔρια εἰσενεχθῇ σοι,
ἐπιμελητέον ὅπως οἷς δεῖ ἱμάτια γίγνηται. καὶ ὅ γε ξηρὸς σῖτος

---

3 ἐλλείπεται Schneider: ἐκλείπεται codd.   5 ὅπως om. G: del. Leonclavius:
cf. Hell. VI. ii. 32   8 τοῦ οἴκου add. Stephanus   9 ἃ καὶ Leonclavius:
καὶ ἃ A in marg.: καὶ cet.   μᾶλλον Hᵃ: μᾶλλον ἂν vel ἂν μᾶλλον cet.   12 ἴσως τι
corrupta videntur   16 δή Dind.: om. R Ven. 513: δὲ vel δ' cet.   17 γε
H F: τε cet (μὲν M: τε s.v.)   23 τὸν γιγνόμενον τόκον codd.: corr. Stephanus
25 ἐπιγόνων Stephanus: ἐπομένων codd.   31 φυλακτέον καὶ προνοητέον Stephanus

each other, and the bond is more beneficial to the couple, since one is capable where the other is deficient.

'"Well, wife, because we know what has been assigned to each of us by 29 the god, we must each try to perform our respective duties as well as possible. The law encourages this, for it yokes together husband and wife, 30 and just as the god made them partners in children, so the law has appointed them partners in the estate. And the law declares honourable those duties for which the god has made each of them more naturally capable. For the woman it is more honourable to remain indoors than to be outside; for the man it is more disgraceful to remain indoors than to attend to business outside. If someone behaves in a way contrary to the 31 nature the god has given him, perhaps his disobedience will not escape the notice of the gods, and he will pay a penalty for neglecting his proper business or for performing his wife's work. It seems to me", I added, "that 32 the queen bee toils constantly at such work appointed by the god."

'My wife asked, "How does the work of the queen bee resemble that which I must perform?"

'I replied, "She remains in the hive and does not allow the bees to be 33 idle, but those who ought to work outside she dispatches to their job, and she knows and receives what each brings in, and keeps it until it is necessary to use it. And when the time comes to use it, she distributes a fair share to each. She supervises the construction of the combs inside the hive, so that 34 they are woven beautifully and quickly, and she is concerned that the offspring shall be reared to maturity. When the little ones have been reared and are capable of working, she sends them out to found a colony with someone to lead the new generation."

'My wife asked, "Shall I have to do this too?" 35

'"Certainly," I replied, "you will have to stay indoors and send forth the group of slaves whose work is outdoors, and personally supervise those whose work is indoors. Moreover, you must receive what is brought inside 36 and dispense as much as should be spent. And you must plan ahead and guard whatever must remain in reserve, so that the provisions stored up for a year are not spent in a month. And when wool is brought in to you, you must see that clothes are produced for those who need them. And you must also be concerned that the dry grain is in good condition for eating.

37 ὅπως καλῶς ἐδώδιμος γίγνηται ἐπιμελητέον. ἐν μέντοι τῶν σοὶ
προσηκόντων, ἔφην ἐγώ, ἐπιμελημάτων ἴσως ἀχαριστότερον δόξει
εἶναι, ὅτι, ὃς ἂν κάμνῃ τῶν οἰκετῶν, τούτων σοι ἐπιμελητέον
πάντων ὅπως θεραπεύηται. Νὴ Δί᾽, ἔφη ἡ γυνή, ἐπιχαριτώτατον
μὲν οὖν, ἂν μέλλωσί γε οἱ καλῶς θεραπευθέντες χάριν εἴσεσθαι 5
38 καὶ εὐνούστεροι ἢ πρόσθεν ἔσεσθαι. Καὶ ἐγώ, ἔφη ὁ Ἰσχόμαχος,
ἀγασθεὶς αὐτῆς τὴν ἀπόκρισιν εἶπον· Ἆρά γε, ὦ γύναι, διὰ τοιαύτας
τινὰς προνοίας καὶ τῆς ἐν τῷ σμήνει ἡγεμόνος αἱ μέλιτται οὕτω
διατίθενται πρὸς αὐτήν, ὥστε, ὅταν ἐκείνη ἐκλίπῃ, οὐδεμία οἴεται
39 τῶν μελιττῶν ἀπολειπτέον εἶναι, ἀλλ᾽ ἕπονται πᾶσαι; καὶ ἡ γυνή 10
μοι ἀπεκρίνατο· Θαυμάζοιμ᾽ ἄν, ἔφη, εἰ μὴ πρὸς σὲ μᾶλλον τείνοι
τὰ τοῦ ἡγεμόνος ἔργα ἢ πρὸς ἐμέ. ἡ γὰρ ἐμὴ φυλακὴ τῶν ἔνδον
καὶ διανομὴ γελοία τις ἄν, οἶμαι, φαίνοιτο, εἰ μὴ σύγε ἐπιμελοῖο
40 ὅπως ἔξωθέν τι εἰσφέροιτο. Γελοία δ᾽ αὖ, ἔφην ἐγώ, ἡ ἐμὴ εἰσφορὰ
φαίνοιτ᾽ ἄν, εἰ μὴ εἴη ὅστις τὰ εἰσενεχθέντα σῴζοι. οὐχ ὁρᾷς, ἔφην 15
ἐγώ, οἱ εἰς τὸν τετρημένον πίθον ἀντλεῖν λεγόμενοι ὡς οἰκτίρονται,
ὅτι μάτην πονεῖν δοκοῦσι; Νὴ Δί᾽, ἔφη ἡ γυνή, καὶ γὰρ τλήμονές
41 εἰσιν, εἰ τοῦτό γε ποιοῦσιν. Ἄλλαι δέ τοι, ἔφην ἐγώ, ἴδιαι
ἐπιμέλειαι, ὦ γύναι, ἡδεῖαί σοι γίγνονται, ὁπόταν ἀνεπιστήμονα
ταλασίας λαβοῦσα ἐπιστήμονα ποιήσῃς καὶ διπλασίου σοι ἀξία 20
γένηται, καὶ ὁπόταν ἀνεπιστήμονα ταμείας καὶ διακονίας
παραλαβοῦσα ἐπιστήμονα καὶ πιστὴν καὶ διακονικὴν ποιησαμένη
παντὸς ἀξίαν ἔχῃς, καὶ ὁπόταν τοὺς μὲν σώφρονάς τε καὶ
ὠφελίμους τῷ σῷ οἴκῳ ἐξῇ σοι εὖ ποιῆσαι, ἐὰν δέ τις πονηρὸς
42 φαίνηται, ἐξῇ σοι κολάσαι· τὸ δὲ πάντων ἥδιστον, ἐὰν βελτίων 25
ἐμοῦ φανῇς, καὶ ἐμὲ σὸν θεράποντα ποιήσῃ, καὶ μὴ δέῃ σε
φοβεῖσθαι μὴ προϊούσης τῆς ἡλικίας ἀτιμοτέρα ἐν τῷ οἴκῳ γένῃ,
ἀλλὰ πιστεύσῃς ὅτι πρεσβυτέρα γιγνομένη ὅσῳ ἂν καὶ ἐμοὶ κοινωνὸς
καὶ παισὶν οἴκου φύλαξ ἀμείνων γίγνῃ, τοσούτῳ καὶ τιμιωτέρα ἐν
43 τῷ οἴκῳ ἔσει. τὰ γὰρ καλά τε κἀγαθά, ἐγὼ ἔφην, οὐ διὰ τὰς 30
ὡραιότητας, ἀλλὰ διὰ τὰς ἀρετὰς εἰς τὸν βίον τοῖς ἀνθρώποις
ἐπαύξεται. τοιαῦτα μέν, ὦ Σώκρατες, δοκῶ μεμνῆσθαι αὐτῇ τὰ
πρῶτα διαλεχθείς.

VIII Ἦ καὶ ἐπέγνως τι, ὦ Ἰσχόμαχε, ἔφην ἐγώ, ἐκ τούτων αὐτὴν
κεκινημένην μᾶλλον πρὸς τὴν ἐπιμέλειαν; Ναὶ μὰ Δί᾽, ἔφη ὁ 35
Ἰσχόμαχος, καὶ δηχθεῖσάν γε οἶδα αὐτὴν καὶ ἐρυθριάσασαν σφόδρα

---

2 ἀχαριτώτερον Cobet   15 σώσοι cit. Richards   29 φύλαξ ἀμείνων F₂
K L: φυλαξαμένων vel φυλαξομένων cet.   30 ἔσῃ(ι) codd.   καλά τε] καλὰ Stob.
31 τὰς ἐν τῷ βίῳ ἀρετὰς Stob.: εἰς ... ἀνθρώποις om. C

However," I said, "one of your proper concerns, perhaps, may seem to 37 you rather thankless: you will certainly have to be concerned about nursing any of the slaves who becomes ill."

'"Oh, no," exclaimed my wife, "it will be most gratifying if those who are well cared for will prove to be thankful and more loyal than before."'

Ischomachus went on: 'I was delighted with her response and said, 38 "Wife, because of such thoughtful actions on the part of the queen bee, isn't the relationship of the bees to her, too, of such a kind that when she deserts the hive, not one of the bees considers staying behind, but all follow her?"

'My wife replied, "It would surprise me if the leader's activities did not 39 apply more to you than to me. For if you were not concerned that supplies were brought in from outside, surely my guarding the things indoors and my budgeting would seem pretty ridiculous."

'And I replied: "Yes, but my bringing in supplies would appear just as 40 ridiculous if there were not someone to look after what has been brought in. Don't you see how people pity those who draw water in a leaky jar, as the saying goes, because they seem to labour in vain?"

'"Yes, by Zeus," said my wife, "they are truly miserable if they do that."

'"But, wife, your other special concerns turn out to be pleasant: whenever 41 you take a slave who has no knowledge of spinning, and teach her that skill so that you double her value to you: and whenever you take one who does not know how to manage a house or serve, and turn her into one who is a skilled and faithful servant and make her invaluable; and whenever it is in your power to reward the helpful and reasonable members of your household and to punish any of them who appears to be vicious. But the 42 sweetest experience of all will be this: if you prove to be better than I am and make me your servant. Then you will have no need to fear that as your years increase you will be less honoured in the household; but you may be confident that when you become older, the better partner you have been to me, and the better guardian of the estate for the children, the greater the respect you will enjoy in the household. For it is not because 43 of youthful grace that beautiful and good things increase for human beings, but rather because of their virtues," I said. As far as I can recall, those are the kind of subjects, Socrates, that I believe I discussed with her first.'

I asked, 'Did you also notice, Ischomachus, that as a result of these VIII discussions she was stimulated about the things that concern her?'

Ischomachus replied: 'Certainly, by Zeus. I know she was quite upset and that she blushed when she could not give me one of the things that

ὅτι τῶν εἰσενεχθέντων τι αἰτήσαντος ἐμοῦ οὐκ εἶχέ μοι δοῦναι.
2 καὶ ἐγὼ μέντοι ἰδὼν ἀχθεσθεῖσαν αὐτὴν εἶπον· Μηδέν τι, ἔφην,
ἀθυμήσῃς, ὦ γύναι, ὅτι οὐκ ἔχεις δοῦναι ὅ σε αἰτῶν τυγχάνω. ἔστι
μὲν γὰρ πενία αὕτη σαφής, τὸ δεόμενόν τινος μὴ ἔχειν χρῆσθαι·
ἀλυποτέρα δὲ αὕτη ἡ ἔνδεια, τὸ ζητοῦντά τι μὴ δύνασθαι λαβεῖν, 5
ἢ τὴν ἀρχὴν μηδὲ ζητεῖν εἰδότα ὅτι οὐκ ἔστιν. ἀλλὰ γάρ, ἔφην
ἐγώ, τούτων οὐ σὺ αἰτία, ἀλλ' ἐγὼ οὐ τάξας σοι παρέδωκα ὅπου
χρὴ ἕκαστα κεῖσθαι, ὅπως εἰδῇς ὅπου τε δεῖ τιθέναι καὶ ὁπόθεν
3 λαμβάνειν. ἔστι δ' οὐδὲν οὕτως, ὦ γύναι, οὔτ' εὔχρηστον οὔτε
καλὸν ἀνθρώποις ὡς τάξις. καὶ γὰρ χορὸς ἐξ ἀνθρώπων 10
συγκείμενός ἐστιν· ἀλλ' ὅταν μὲν ποιῶσιν ὅ τι ἂν τύχῃ ἕκαστος,
ταραχή τις φαίνεται καὶ θεᾶσθαι ἀτερπές, ὅταν δὲ τεταγμένως
ποιῶσι καὶ φθέγγωνται, ἅμα οἱ αὐτοὶ οὗτοι καὶ ἀξιοθέατοι
4 δοκοῦσιν εἶναι καὶ ἀξιάκουστοι. καὶ στρατιά γε, ἔφην ἐγώ, ὦ
γύναι, ἄτακτος μὲν οὖσα ταραχωδέστατον, καὶ τοῖς μὲν πολεμίοις 15
εὐχειρωτότατον, τοῖς δὲ φίλοις ἀκλεέστατον ὁρᾶν καὶ
ἀχρηστότατον, ὄνος ὁμοῦ, ὁπλίτης, σκευοφόρος, ψιλός, ἱππεύς,
ἅμαξα· — πῶς γὰρ ἂν πορευθείησαν, ἔχοντες οὕτως; ἐπι-
κωλύσουσιν ἀλλήλους, ὁ μὲν βαδίζων τὸν τρέχοντα, ὁ δὲ τρέχων
τὸν ἑστηκότα, ἡ δὲ ἅμαξα τὸν ἱππέα, ὁ δὲ ὄνος τὴν ἅμαξαν, ὁ δὲ 20
5 σκευοφόρος τὸν ὁπλίτην; εἰ δὲ καὶ μάχεσθαι δέοι, πῶς ἂν οὕτως
ἔχοντες μαχέσαιντο; οἷς γὰρ ἀνάγκη αὐτῶν τοὺς ἐπιόντας φεύγειν,
οὗτοι ἱκανοί εἰσι φεύγοντες καταπατῆσαι τοὺς ὅπλα ἔχοντας·
6 τεταγμένη δὲ στρατιὰ κάλλιστον μὲν ἰδεῖν τοῖς φίλοις,
δυσχερέστατον δὲ τοῖς πολεμίοις. τίς μὲν γὰρ οὐκ ἂν φίλος ἡδέως 25
θεάσαιτο ὁπλίτας πολλοὺς ἐν τάξει πορευομένους, τίς δ' οὐκ ἂν
θαυμάσειεν ἱππέας κατὰ τάξεις ἐλαύνοντας, τίς δὲ οὐκ ἂν πολέμιος
φοβηθείη ἰδὼν διηυκρινημένους ὁπλίτας, ἱππέας, πελταστάς,
τοξότας, σφενδονήτας, καὶ τοῖς ἄρχουσι τεταγμένως ἑπομένους;
7 ἀλλὰ καὶ πορευομένων ἐν τάξει, κἂν πολλαὶ μυριάδες ὦσιν, ὁμοίως 30
ὥσπερ εἷς ἕκαστος καθ' ἡσυχίαν πάντες πορεύονται· εἰς γὰρ τὸ
8 κενούμενον ἀεὶ ⟨οἱ⟩ ὄπισθεν ἐπέρχονται. καὶ τριήρης δέ τοι ἡ
σεσαγμένη ἀνθρώπων διὰ τί ἄλλο φοβερόν ἐστι πολεμίοις ἢ φίλοις
ἀξιοθέατον ἢ ὅτι ταχὺ πλεῖ; διὰ τί δὲ ἄλλο ἄλυποι ἀλλήλοις εἰσὶν

---

1 ὅτι] ὅτε Schneider: εἴ τι K L N   2 εἶπον om. A   ἔφην] εἶπον A
7 post σοι add. ἃ R *Ven.* 513   8 εἰδῇς] εἰδείης Platt: ᾔδεις Postgate   τε Hᵃ: γε
cet.   ὁπόθεν Schneider: ὅπου vel ὅποι codd.   10 ἡ τάξις K L   12 ἀτερπές]
ἀγλευκές Orelli ex Suida   16 εὐχειρότατον vel εὐχειροτότατον codd.: corr. Stephanus
ἀκλεέστατον] ἀηδέστατον Wyttenbach   18 distinxit Gil   ἐπικωλύσωσιν codd.:
corr. Thalheim   32 οἱ add. Camerarius   ἡ del. Castalio

had been brought into the house when I asked for it. However, I could see 2 that she was annoyed with herself, so I said, "Don't be so miserable, wife, just because you aren't able to give me what I happen to ask for. It's obviously poverty when you haven't got something for use when you need it; but this shortcoming, that is, looking for something without being able to find it, is less painful than not looking for it at all because you know it's not there. It's not your fault, but mine, because when I put the household into your hands, I failed to give you any instructions about where everything was to be put, so that you might know where you ought to put them away, and where to take them from. For there is nothing, wife, as useful or good 3 for people as order. For instance, a chorus is composed of people. But whenever every member does whatever he likes, there is simply chaos, and it is not a pleasant spectacle. But when they act and sing in an orderly manner, these same persons seem to be both worth watching and worth hearing.

"'Wife,' I said, "an army in disorder is a most chaotic thing, both very 4 easily overcome by its enemies and a most disgraceful sight for its allies, and most useless, too, with mule, hoplite, baggage-carrier, light-armed troops, cavalry, and wagons all mixed together. How could they march in such a state? They will impede each other, the marching man the runner, the runner the soldier who is standing at his post, the wagon the cavalry-man, the mule the wagon, and the baggage-carrier the hoplite. If they 5 should actually need to fight as well, how could they in such a state? For those of them who were forced to flee in the face of an attack would be in just the right position, in their flight, to trample on the men who had kept their arms. But an orderly army is a most noble sight for its allies to see, 6 and most odious for its enemies. For what ally would not be pleased to see a mass of hoplites marching in order? Who would not admire cavalry advancing in squadrons? What enemy would not be afraid at the sight of hoplites, cavalry, peltasts, archers, and slingers carefully drawn up in separate groups and following their commanders in an orderly manner? When they march in order, even if there are tens of thousands of them, 7 they all proceed smoothly as one man, for those behind continually move up to fill the space that the others have vacated.

"'And why is a trireme which is crammed with men a frightening 8 spectacle to enemies and a pleasant sight to allies? Is it not because it sails quickly? Why do the men on board not get in each other's way? Is it not

οἱ ἐμπλέοντες ἢ διότι ἐν τάξει μὲν κάθηνται, ἐν τάξει δὲ
προνεύουσιν, ἐν τάξει δ᾽ ἀναπίπτουσιν, ἐν τάξει δ᾽ ἐμβαίνουσι καὶ
9 ἐκβαίνουσιν; ἡ δ᾽ ἀταξία ὅμοιόν τί μοι δοκεῖ εἶναι οἷόνπερ εἰ
γεωργὸς ὁμοῦ ἐμβάλοι κριθὰς καὶ πυροὺς καὶ ὄσπρια, κἄπειτα,
ὁπότε δέοι ἢ μάζης ἢ ἄρτου ἢ ὄψου, διαλέγειν δέοι αὐτῷ ἀντὶ τοῦ 5
10 λαβόντα διηυκρινημένοις χρῆσθαι. καὶ σὺ οὖν, ὦ γύναι, ⟨εἰ⟩ τοῦ μὲν
ταράχου τούτου μὴ δέοιο, βούλοιο δ᾽ ἀκριβῶς διοικεῖν τὰ ὄντα
εἰδέναι καὶ τῶν ὄντων εὐπόρως λαμβάνουσα ὅτῳ ἂν δέῃ χρῆσθαι,
καὶ ἐμοί, ἐάν τι αἰτῷ, ἐν χάριτι διδόναι, χώραν τε δοκιμασώμεθα
τὴν προσήκουσαν ἑκάστοις ἔχειν καὶ ἐν ταύτῃ θέντες διδάξωμεν 10
τὴν διάκονον λαμβάνειν τε ἐντεῦθεν καὶ κατατιθέναι πάλιν εἰς
ταύτην· καὶ οὕτως εἰσόμεθα τά τε σῶα ὄντα καὶ τὰ μή· ἡ γὰρ
χώρα αὐτὴ τὸ μὴ ὂν ποθήσει, καὶ ⟨τὸ⟩ δεόμενον θεραπείας ἐξετάσει
ἡ ὄψις, καὶ τὸ εἰδέναι ὅπου ἕκαστόν ἐστι ταχὺ ἐγχειριεῖ, ὥστε μὴ
11 ἀπορεῖν χρῆσθαι. καλλίστην δέ ποτε καὶ ἀκριβεστάτην ἔδοξα 15
σκευῶν τάξιν ἰδεῖν, ὦ Σώκρατες, εἰσβὰς ἐπὶ θέαν εἰς τὸ μέγα
πλοῖον τὸ Φοινικικόν. πλεῖστα γὰρ σκεύη ἐν σμικροτάτῳ ἀγγείῳ
12 διακεχωρισμένα ἐθεασάμην. διὰ πολλῶν μὲν γὰρ δήπου, ἔφη,
ξυλίνων σκευῶν καὶ πλεκτῶν ὁρμίζεται ναῦς καὶ ἀνάγεται, διὰ
πολλῶν δὲ τῶν κρεμαστῶν καλουμένων πλεῖ, πολλοῖς δὲ 20
μηχανήμασιν ἀνθώπλισται πρὸς τὰ πολέμια πλοῖα, πολλὰ δὲ ὅπλα
τοῖς ἀνδράσι συμπεριάγει, πάντα δὲ σκεύη ὅσοισπερ ἐν οἰκίᾳ
χρῶνται ἄνθρωποι τῇ συσσιτίᾳ ἑκάστῃ κομίζει· γέμει δὲ παρὰ
13 πάντα φορτίων ὅσα ναύκληρος κέρδους ἕνεκα ἄγεται. καὶ ὅσα
λέγω, ἔφη, ἐγώ, πάντα οὐκ ἐν πολλῷ τινι μείζονι χώρᾳ ἔκειτο ἢ 25
ἐν ⟨ἐν⟩δεκακλίνῳ στέγῃ συμμέτρῳ. καὶ οὕτω κείμενα ἕκαστα
κατενόησα ὡς οὔτε ἄλληλα ἐμποδίζει οὔτε μαστευτοῦ δεῖται οὔτε
ἀσυσκεύαστά ἐστιν οὔτε δυσλύτως ἔχει, ὥστε διατριβὴν παρέχειν,
14 ὅταν τῳ ταχὺ δέῃ χρῆσθαι. τὸν δὲ τοῦ κυβερνήτου διάκονον, ὃς
πρῳρεὺς τῆς νεὼς καλεῖται, οὕτως ηὗρον ἐπιστάμενον ἑκάστων 30
τὴν χώραν ὡς καὶ ἀπὼν ἂν εἴποι ὅπου ἕκαστα κεῖται καὶ ὁπόσα
ἐστὶν οὐδὲν ἧττον ἢ ὁ γράμματα ἐπιστάμενος εἴποι ἂν Σωκράτους
15 καὶ ὁπόσα γράμματα καὶ ὅπου ἕκαστον τέτακται. εἶδον δέ, ἔφη ὁ
Ἰσχόμαχος, καὶ ἐξετάζοντα τοῦτον αὐτὸν ἐν τῇ σχολῇ πάντα

---

2 προνεύουσιν Eustathius: προσνεύουσιν codd. (πορεύουσιν A et in marg. ante corr.
προσνεύουσιν: προνεύουσιν A corr. in marg.)   6 εἰ add. Ernesti   7 δέει
et βούλει cit. Richards   8 ἂν δέοι D al. E   13 αὐτῇ J: αὕτη cet.   ὂν] ἐνὸν
cit. Richards   τὸ add. Hirschig   16 τὸ μέγα πλοῖον τὸ οὐ μέγα πλοῖόν τι Nitsche
17 Φοινικικόν Sturz: φοινικόν odd.   μικροτάτῳ G K M   26 ⟨ἐν⟩δεκακλίνῳ
Pomeroy   28 ἐστιν A in marg. G: εἰσιν cet.   30 ἑκάστων K: ἑκάστην cet.

because they sit on the benches in order, moving their bodies forward and backward in order, and embarking and disembarking in order? I think a rough parallel to disorder is what would result if a farmer tossed barley, 9 wheat, and beans into one bin, and then when he needed barley-cake or bread or something to go with it, had to pick it out grain by grain, instead of taking them ready for use when they had been already carefully arranged in separate groups.

'"And so, you too, wife, if you wish to avoid such confusion, and instead 10 wish to know exactly how to manage our property and to put your hands easily on whatever we need to use and to please me by giving me whatever I request, let us decide on the appropriate place for each item, and when we put it there, let us teach the maid to take it from that place and to put it back there again. That way we will know how much of our property is safe, and how much of it is not. For the place itself will indicate what is missing, and a glance will detect anything that needs attention. And if we know where each thing is, we can put our hands on it quickly so that we will never be unable to make use of it."

'I believe that the most beautiful and meticulous arrangement of equip- 11 ment that I ever saw, Socrates, was when I boarded the great Phoenician merchant ship to see what it was like. For I saw an enormous amount of equipment arranged in separate places in the smallest receptacle. For, you 12 know,' he said, 'a ship needs many pieces of wooden equipment and ropes when she anchors or puts out to sea, and much rigging, as they call it, when she sails. She is armed with many devices to use against enemy ships, and she carries around with her many weapons for the crew. She also carries all the same utensils that people use at home for the various meals they eat together. In addition to all this, she is laden with all the cargo the owner takes with him to make a profit. I'm telling you from my personal 13 experience,' he said, 'that all the items I am mentioning were stored in a space not much bigger than a dining-room large enough for eleven couches. I noticed that everything was stored in such a manner that nothing got in the way of anything else, and there was no need for anyone to go and search for it. Nothing was disarranged or difficult to untie so as to cause delay when something was required for immediate use. I found that the 14 pilot's mate, who is called the "look-out man", knew exactly where everything was, so that even when he wasn't on board he could say where each thing was stored and how many of them there were, just as accurately as a literate man can say how many letters there are in the word "Socrates" and what order they occur in.' Ischomachus went on: 'I saw the same man 15 in his spare time personally inspecting everything that was likely to be

ὁπόσοις ἄρα δεῖ ἐν τῷ πλοίῳ χρῆσθαι. θαυμάσας δέ, ἔφη, τὴν
ἐπίσκεψιν αὐτοῦ ἠρόμην τί πράττοι. ὁ δ' εἶπεν· Ἐπισκοπῶ, ἔφη,
ὦ ξένε, εἴ τι συμβαίνοι γίγνεσθαι, πῶς κεῖται, ἔφη, τὰ ἐν τῇ νηί,
16 ἢ εἴ τι ἀποστατεῖ ἢ εἰ δυστραπέλως τι σύγκειται. οὐ γάρ, ἔφη,
ἐγχωρεῖ, ὅταν χειμάζῃ ὁ θεὸς ἐν τῇ θαλάττῃ, οὔτε μαστεύειν ὅτου 5
ἂν δέῃ οὔτε δυστραπέλως ἔχον διδόναι. ἀπειλεῖ γὰρ ὁ θεὸς καὶ
κολάζει τοὺς βλᾶκας. ἐὰν δὲ μόνον μὴ ἀπολέσῃ τοὺς μὴ
ἁμαρτάνοντας, πάνυ ἀγαπητόν· ἐὰν δὲ καὶ πάνυ καλῶς
17 ὑπηρετοῦντας σῴζῃ, πολλὴ χάρις, ἔφη, τοῖς θεοῖς. ἐγὼ οὖν κατιδὼν
ταύτην τὴν ἀκρίβειαν τῆς κατασκευῆς ἔλεγον τῇ γυναικὶ ὅτι πάνυ 10
ἂν ἡμῶν εἴη βλακικόν, εἰ οἱ μὲν ἐν τοῖς πλοίοις καὶ μικροῖς οὖσι
χώρας εὑρίσκουσι, καὶ σαλεύοντες ἰσχυρῶς ὅμως σῴζουσι τὴν
τάξιν, καὶ ὑπερφοβούμενοι ὅμως εὑρίσκουσι τὸ δέον λαμβάνειν,
ἡμεῖς δὲ καὶ διῃρημένων ἑκάστοις θηκῶν ἐν τῇ οἰκίᾳ μεγάλων καὶ
βεβηκυίας τῆς οἰκίας ἐν δαπέδῳ, εἰ μὴ εὑρήσομεν καλὴν καὶ 15
εὑεύρετον χώραν ἑκάστοις αὐτῶν, πῶς οὐκ ἂν πολλὴ ἡμῶν
18 ἀσυνεσία εἴη; ὡς μὲν δὴ ἀγαθὸν τετάχθαι σκευῶν κατασκευὴν καὶ
ὡς ῥᾴδιον χώραν ἑκάστοις αὐτῶν εὑρεῖν ἐν οἰκίᾳ θεῖναι ὡς ἑκάστοις
19 συμφέρει εἴρηται· ὡς δὲ καλὸν φαίνεται, ἐπειδὰν ὑποδήματα ἐφεξῆς
κέηται, κἂν ὁποῖα ᾖ, καλὸν δὲ ἱμάτια κεχωρισμένα ἰδεῖν, κἂν ὁποῖα 20
ᾖ, καλὸν δὲ στρώματα, καλὸν δὲ χαλκία, καλὸν δὲ τὰ ἀμφὶ
τραπέζας, καλὸν δὲ καὶ ὃ πάντων καταγελάσειεν ἂν μάλιστα οὐχ
ὁ σεμνὸς ἀλλ' ὁ κομψός, [ὅτι] καὶ χύτρας [φησὶν] εὔρυθμον
20 φαίνεσθαι εὐκρινῶς κειμένας-τὰ δὲ ἄλλα ἤδη που ἀπὸ τούτου
ἅπαντα καλλίω φαίνεται κατὰ κόσμον κείμενα· χορὸς γὰρ σκευῶν 25
ἕκαστα φαίνεται, καὶ τὸ μέσον δὲ πάντων τούτων καλὸν φαίνεται,
ἐκποδὼν ἑκάστου κειμένου· ὥσπερ καὶ κύκλιος χορὸς οὐ μόνον
αὐτὸς καλὸν θέαμά ἐστιν, ἀλλὰ καὶ τὸ μέσον αὐτοῦ καλὸν καὶ
21 καθαρὸν φαίνεται-εἰ δὲ ἀληθῆ ταῦτα λέγω, ἔξεστιν, ἔφην, ὦ γύναι,
καὶ πεῖραν λαμβάνειν αὐτῶν οὔτε τι ζημιωθέντας οὔτε τι πολλὰ 30
πονήσαντας. ἀλλὰ μὴν οὐδὲ τοῦτο δεῖ ἀθυμῆσαι, ὦ γύναι, ἔφην
ἐγώ, ὡς χαλεπὸν εὑρεῖν τὸν μαθησόμενόν τε τὰς χώρας καὶ

1 πλοίῳ] πλῷ Cobet   6 ἀπειλεῖ] ἐπείγει Richards   12 ἰσχυρῶς]
incipit Π¹   14 διειρημενων Π¹   15 εἰ et 2 πῶς ... εἴη del. Cobet   16 ευρετον
Π¹: εὐάρεστον H al.   17 ἀγαθὸν A in marg. *Ven.* 511₂: ἀγαθῶν cet.   18 εὑρεῖν
καὶ A in marg.   prius ὡς om. Π¹   23 ὅτι om. Π¹   φημὶ Iacobs: φησὶ(ν) codd.
[Π¹]   24 τα δε αλλ απο τουτου παντα Π¹ om. ἤδη που: ἀπὸ τούτου
om. K L   25 ἅπαντα ἕκαστα H al.   κατὰ ... κείμενα post φαίνεται transp. Graux
26 παντων Π¹: om. codd.   27 ὥσπερ] ωστε Π¹   και Π¹: om. codd.   29 ἔφην
om., ut videtur, Π¹   30 ζημιωθέντες et ποιήσαντες A   τι susp. Schäfero

needed on the boat. I was surprised by his inspection,' he said, 'and so I asked him what he was doing. He answered, "My friend, I am inspecting the way in which the articles in the ship are stored, in case of any accident, or in case something is missing, or has been put away in the wrong place together with other equipment. For when the god raises a storm at sea, 16 there is no time to search for what is needed nor to hand out something that's in the wrong place. The god threatens and punishes the lazy. If he only fails to destroy the innocent, then we should be content enough; but if he also spares those who perform their work extremely well, then", he said, "great thanks are due to the gods."

'Having seen the meticulous arrangement of the equipment that I've just 17 described, I said to my wife: "Sailors on ships which are comparatively small find places for their equipment, and even when they are violently tossed about they still keep them in order, and even when they are terrified they can still find what they need to get. What about us? We have large storerooms in the house so that we can keep things separately in them, and the house rests on a firm foundation. Wouldn't it be sheer stupidity on our part if we don't find some good place where each thing can be easily found? I have already told you that it is good for equipment to be arranged in 18 order and that it is easy to find a place in the house that is suitable for each piece of it. How beautiful it looks, when shoes are arranged in rows, 19 each kind in its own proper place, how beautiful to see all kinds of clothing properly sorted out, each kind in its own proper place, how beautiful bed-linens, bronze pots, table-ware! And what a facetious man would laugh at most of all, but a serious man would not: even pots appear graceful when they are arranged in a discriminating manner. It follows from this that all 20 other things somehow appear more beautiful when they are in a regular arrangement. Each of them looks like a chorus of equipment, and the interval between them looks beautiful when each item is kept clear of it, just as a chorus of dancers moving in a circle is not only a beautiful sight in itself, but the interval between them seems pure and beautiful, too. Without going to any trouble or inconvenience, wife, we can check whether 21 these statements of mine are true. Moreover, wife, there is no need to be despondent either about the difficulty of finding someone who will learn where the proper places are and remember to put each thing back where

22 μεμνησόμενον καταχωρίζειν ἕκαστα. ἴσμεν γὰρ δήπου ὅτι
μυριοπλάσια ἡμῶν ἅπαντα ἔχει ἡ πᾶσα πόλις, ἀλλ' ὅμως, ὁποῖον
ἂν τῶν οἰκετῶν κελεύσῃς πριάμενόν τί σοι ἐξ ἀγορᾶς ἐνεγκεῖν,
οὐδεὶς ἀπορήσει, ἀλλὰ πᾶς εἰδὼς φανεῖται ὅποι χρὴ ἐλθόντα λαβεῖν
ἕκαστα. τούτου μέντοι, ἔφην ἐγώ, οὐδὲν ἄλλο αἴτιόν ἐστιν ἢ ὅτι 5
23 ἐν χώρᾳ ἕκαστον κεῖται τεταγμένῃ. ἄνθρωπον δέ γε ζητῶν, καὶ
ταῦτα ἐνίοτε ἀντιζητοῦντα, πολλάκις ἄν τις πρότερον, πρὶν εὑρεῖν,
ἀπείποι. καὶ τούτου αὖ οὐδὲν ἄλλο αἴτιόν ἐστιν ἢ τὸ μὴ εἶναι
τεταγμένον ὅπου ἕκαστον δεῖ ἀναμένειν. περὶ μὲν [γὰρ] δὴ τάξεως
σκευῶν καὶ χρήσεως τοιαῦτα αὐτῇ διαλεχθεὶς δοκῶ μεμνῆσθαι. 10

IX   Καὶ τί δή; ἡ γυνὴ ἐδόκει σοι, ἔφην ἐγώ, ὦ Ἰσχόμαχε, πώς τι
ὑπακούειν ὧν σὺ ἐσπούδαζες διδάσκων; Τί δέ, εἰ μὴ ὑπισχνεῖτό
γε ἐπιμελήσεσθαι καὶ φανερὰ ἦν ἡδομένη ἰσχυρῶς, ὥσπερ ἐξ
ἀμηχανίας εὐπορίαν τινὰ ηὑρηκυῖα, καὶ ἐδεῖτό μου ὡς τάχιστα
2 ᾗπερ ἔλεγον διατάξαι. Καὶ πῶς δή, ἔφην ἐγώ, ὦ Ἰσχόμαχε, 15
διέταξας αὐτῇ; Τί δ', εἰ μὴ τῆς γε οἰκίας τὴν δύναμιν ἔδοξέ μοι
πρῶτον ἐπιδεῖξαι αὐτῇ. οὐ γὰρ ποικίλμασι κεκόσμηται, ὦ
Σώκρατες, ἀλλὰ τὰ οἰκήματα ᾠκοδόμηται πρὸς αὐτὸ τοῦτο
ἐσκεμμένα, ὅπως ἀγγεῖα ὡς συμφορώτατα ᾖ τοῖς μέλλουσιν ἐν
αὐτοῖς ἔσεσθαι· ὥστε αὐτὰ ἐκάλει τὰ πρέποντα εἶναι ἐν ἑκάστῳ. 20
3 ὁ μὲν γὰρ θάλαμος ἐν ὀχυρῷ ὢν τὰ πλείστου ἄξια καὶ στρώματα
καὶ σκεύη παρεκάλει, τὰ δὲ ξηρὰ τῶν στεγνῶν τὸν σῖτον, τὰ δὲ
ψυχεινὰ τὸν οἶνον, τὰ δὲ φανὰ ὅσα φάους δεόμενα ἔργα τε καὶ
4 σκεύη ἐστί. καὶ διαιτητήρια δὲ τοῖς ἀνθρώποις ἐπεδείκνυον αὐτῇ
κεκαλλωπισμένα τοῦ μὲν θέρους ἔχειν ψυχεινά, τοῦ δὲ χειμῶνος 25
ἀλεεινά. καὶ σύμπασαν δὲ τὴν οἰκίαν ἐπέδειξα αὐτῇ ὅτι πρὸς
μεσημβρίαν ἀναπέπταται, ὥστε εὔδηλον εἶναι ὅτι χειμῶνος μὲν
5 εὐήλιός ἐστι, τοῦ δὲ θέρους εὔσκιος. ἔδειξα δὲ καὶ τὴν γυναικωνῖτιν
αὐτῇ, θύρᾳ βαλανωτῇ ὡρισμένην ἀπὸ τῆς ἀνδρωνίτιδος, ἵνα μήτε
ἐκφέρηται ἔνδοθεν ὅ τι μὴ δεῖ μήτε τεκνοποιῶνται οἱ οἰκέται ἄνευ 30
τῆς ἡμετέρας γνώμης. οἱ μὲν γὰρ χρηστοὶ παιδοποιησάμενοι
εὐνούστεροι ὡς ἐπὶ τὸ πολύ, οἱ δὲ πονηροὶ συζυγέντες εὐπορώτεροι
6 πρὸς τὸ κακουργεῖν γίγνονται. ἐπεὶ δὲ ταῦτα διήλθομεν, ἔφη, οὕτω
δὴ ἤδη κατὰ φυλὰς διεκρίνομεν τὰ ἔπιπλα. ἠρχόμεθα δὲ πρῶτον,

4 ελθοντας Π¹   6 εκαστον Π¹: om. codd.   8 αὖ et 9 γὰρ
om. Π¹   11 πώς Stephanus: πῶς codd.   12 ὑπακούειν Dind.: ἐπακούειν codd.
[Π¹]   15 εγωγ εφ[ην Π¹   16 γε Π¹: om. codd.   17 πολλοις
κεκοσμη[ται Π¹   19 ἐσκεμμένως Camerarius   20 ειναι εν Π¹: εἶναι codd.
εκασ] desinit Π¹   22 στεγνῶν Stephanus   25 ἔχειν Ven. 511: om. cet.
29 θύραν βαλανείῳ(ω) codd.: corr. Hermann

it belongs," I said. "For surely we know that the city as a whole has ten 22
thousand times as many things as we, but still you can order any of the
slaves to buy anything you want from the market and bring it to you, and
not one will be uncertain what to do. All of them clearly know where to
go to get each item. The only reason for this", I continued, "is that each
thing is arranged in its proper place. But when someone is looking for a 23
person, especially when that person is also out looking for him, often he
gives up the search before he finds him. The only reason for this is that no
arrangement has been made about where each one should wait." As far as
I can remember, that is more or less the discussion I had with her about
the arrangement and use of our equipment.'

'Then what?', I asked. 'Did you think, Ischomachus, that your wife paid IX
any attention to the lessons that you were so eagerly teaching her?'

'Of course. She promised she would be concerned. She was obviously
very pleased that she had found a solution to her problem, and she begged
me to arrange things as quickly as possible in the way I had described.'

'And how did you arrange things for her, Ischomachus?' 2

'Well, I thought it was best to show her the possibilities of our house
first. It is not elaborately decorated, Socrates, but the rooms are constructed
in such a way that they will serve as the most convenient places to contain
the things that will be kept in them. So the rooms themselves invited what
was suitable for each of them. Thus the bedroom, because it was in the 3
safest possible place, invited the most valuable bedding and furniture. The
dry storerooms called for grain, the cool ones for wine, and the bright ones
for those products and utensils which need light. I continued by showing 4
her living rooms for the occupants, decorated so as to be cool in summer
and warm in winter. I pointed out to her that the entire house has its
façade facing south, so that it was obviously sunny in winter and shady in
summer. I also showed her the women's quarters, separated from the men's 5
quarters by a bolted door, so that nothing might be removed from them
that should not be, and so that the slaves would not breed without our
permission. For, generally, honest slaves become more loyal when they
have produced children, but when bad ones mate, they become more
troublesome. After we had gone through these rooms,' he said, 'we sorted 6
the contents by type. We first began by putting together the things that

ἔφη, ἀθροίζοντες, οἷς ἀμφὶ θυσίας χρώμεθα. μετὰ ταῦτα κόσμον
γυναικὸς τὸν εἰς ἑορτὰς διηροῦμεν, ἐσθῆτα ἀνδρὸς τὴν εἰς ἑορτὰς
καὶ πόλεμον, καὶ στρώματα ἐν γυναικωνίτιδι, στρώματα ἐν
7 ἀνδρωνίτιδι, ὑποδήματα γυναικεῖα, ὑποδήματα ἀνδρεῖα. ὅπλων
ἄλλη φυλή, ἄλλη ταλασιουργικῶν ὀργάνων, ἄλλη σιτοποιικῶν, 5
ἄλλη ὀψοποιικῶν, ἄλλη τῶν ἀμφὶ λουτρόν, ἄλλη ἀμφὶ μάκτρας,
ἄλλη ἀμφὶ τραπέζας. καὶ ταῦτα πάντα διεχωρίσαμεν, οἷς τε ἀεὶ
8 δεῖ χρῆσθαι καὶ τὰ θοινητικά. χωρὶς δὲ καὶ τὰ κατὰ μῆνα
δαπανώμενα ἀφείλομεν, δίχα δὲ καὶ τὰ εἰς ἐνιαυτὸν
ἀπολελογισμένα κατέθεμεν. οὕτω γὰρ ἧττον λανθάνει ὅπως πρὸς 10
τὸ τέλος ἐκβήσεται. ἐπεὶ δὲ ἐχωρίσαμεν πάντα κατὰ φυλὰς τὰ
9 ἔπιπλα, εἰς τὰς χώρας τὰς προσηκούσας ἕκαστα διηνέγκαμεν. μετὰ
δὲ τοῦτο ὅσοις μὲν τῶν σκευῶν καθ᾽ ἡμέραν χρῶνται οἱ οἰκέται,
οἷον σιτοποιικοῖς, ὀψοποιικοῖς, ταλασιουργικοῖς, καὶ εἴ τι ἄλλο
τοιοῦτον, ταῦτα μὲν αὐτοῖς τοῖς χρωμένοις δείξαντες ὅπου δεῖ 15
10 τιθέναι, παρεδώκαμεν καὶ ἐπετάξαμεν σῶα παρέχειν· ὅσοις δ᾽ εἰς
ἑορτὰς ἢ ξενοδοκίας χρώμεθα ἢ εἰς τὰς διὰ χρόνου πράξεις, ταῦτα
δὲ τῇ ταμίᾳ παρεδώκαμεν, καὶ δείξαντες τὰς χώρας αὐτῶν καὶ
ἀπαριθμήσαντες καὶ γραψάμενοι ἕκαστα εἴπομεν αὐτῇ διδόναι
τούτων ὅτῳ δέοι ἕκαστον, καὶ μεμνῆσθαι ὅ τι ἄν τῳ διδῷ, καὶ 20
ἀπολαμβάνουσαν κατατιθέναι πάλιν ὅθενπερ ἂν ἕκαστα λαμβάνῃ.
11 Τὴν δὲ ταμίαν ἐποιησάμεθα ἐπισκεψάμενοι ἥτις ἡμῖν ἐδόκει
εἶναι ἐγκρατεστάτη καὶ γαστρὸς καὶ οἴνου καὶ ὕπνου καὶ ἀνδρῶν
συνουσίας, πρὸς τούτοις δὲ ἢ τὸ μνημονικὸν μάλιστα ἐδόκει ἔχειν
καὶ τὸ προνοεῖν μή τι κακὸν λάβῃ παρ᾽ ἡμῶν ἀμελοῦσα, καὶ 25
σκοπεῖν ὅπως χαριζομένη τι ἡμῖν ὑφ᾽ ἡμῶν ἀντιτιμήσεται.
12 ἐδιδάσκομεν δὲ αὐτὴν καὶ εὐνοϊκῶς ἔχειν πρὸς ἡμᾶς, ὅτ᾽
εὐφραινοίμεθα, τῶν εὐφροσυνῶν μεταδιδόντες, καὶ εἴ τι λυπηρὸν
εἴη, εἰς ταῦτα παρακαλοῦντες. καὶ τὸ προθυμεῖσθαι δὲ συναύξειν
τὸν οἶκον ἐπαιδεύομεν αὐτήν, ἐπιγιγνώσκειν αὐτὴν ποιοῦντες καὶ 30
13 τῆς εὐπραγίας αὐτῇ μεταδιδόντες. καὶ δικαιοσύνην δ᾽ αὐτῇ
ἐνεποιοῦμεν τιμιωτέρους τιθέντες τοὺς δικαίους τῶν ἀδίκων καὶ
ἐπιδεικνύοντες πλουσιώτερον καὶ ἐλευθεριώτερον βιοτεύοντας τῶν
14 ἀδίκων· καὶ αὐτὴν δὲ ἐν ταύτῃ τῇ χώρᾳ κατετάττομεν. ἐπὶ δὲ
τούτοις πᾶσιν εἶπον, ἔφη, ὦ Σώκρατες, ἐγὼ τῇ γυναικὶ ὅτι πάντων 35

8 θοινατικά Y al.   12 διηνέγκαμεν K L: διηνέγκομεν cet.   15 τοιοῦτον
H N: τοιοῦτο cet.   17 ξενοδοχίας codd.: corr. Cobet   20 ὅταν τί τῳ vertere
videtur Cicero ap. Colum. xii. 3   26 τὸ σκοπεῖν Hartman   34 ταύτῃ H O
pr.: αὐτῇ cet.

we use for sacrifices. After that we separated the fancy clothing that women wear at festivals, the men's clothing for festivals and for war, bedding for the women's quarters, bedding for the men's quarters, women's shoes, and men's shoes. Another type consisted of weapons, another of spinning imple- 7 ments, another of bread-making implements, another of implements used for other food, another of bathing implements, another of kneading implements, another of dining implements. And we divided all this equipment into two sets, those that are used daily and those used only for feasts. We 8 set aside the things that are consumed within a month, and stored separately what we calculated would last a year. That way we shall be less likely to make a mistake about how it will turn out at the end of the year. When we divided all the contents by types, we carried each thing to its proper place. After this, we showed the slaves where they should keep the utensils 9 they use every day—for example, those needed for baking, cooking, spinning, and so forth, and we handed these over to them and told them to keep them safe. Whatever we use for festivals or entertaining guests or at 10 rare intervals we handed over to the housekeeper; and when we had shown her where they belong, and had counted and made an inventory of each thing, we told her to give every member of the household what he or she required, but to remember what she had given to each of them and when she got it back, to return it to the place from which she takes things of that kind.

'Now, when we appointed our housekeeper, we looked for the one who 11 seemed to have the greatest degree of self-control in eating, drinking wine, sleeping, and intercourse with men, and who, furthermore, seemed to have memory and the foresight both to avoid being punished by us for negligence and to consider how, by pleasing us in any way, she might be rewarded by us in return. We taught her to be loyal to us by giving her a share of 12 our joy when we were happy, and if we had any trouble, we called on her to share it too. We trained her to be eager to improve the estate by taking her into our confidence and by giving her a share in our success. We 13 instilled a sense of justice in her by giving more honour to the just than to the unjust, and showing her that the just live lives that are richer and better suited to a free citizen than the unjust. And so we appointed her to this post.'

He went on: 'Besides all this, Socrates, I told my wife that there would 14 be no point in all these arrangements unless she personally was concerned

τούτων οὐδὲν ὄφελος, εἰ μὴ αὐτὴ ἐπιμελήσεται ὅπως διαμένῃ
ἑκάστῳ ἡ τάξις. ἐδίδασκον δὲ αὐτὴν ὅτι καὶ ἐν ταῖς εὐνομουμέναις
πόλεσιν οὐκ ἀρκεῖν δοκεῖ τοῖς πολίταις, ἂν νόμους καλοὺς
γράψωνται, ἀλλὰ καὶ νομοφύλακας προσαιροῦνται, οἵτινες
ἐπισκοποῦντες τὸν μὲν ποιοῦντα τὰ νόμιμα ἐπαινοῦσιν, ἂν δέ τις 5
15 παρὰ τοὺς νόμους ποιῇ, ζημιοῦσι. νομίσαι οὖν ἐκέλευον, ἔφη, τὴν
γυναῖκα καὶ αὐτὴν νομοφύλακα τῶν ἐν τῇ οἰκίᾳ εἶναι, καὶ ἐξετάζειν
δέ, ὅταν δόξῃ αὐτῇ, τὰ σκεύη, ὥσπερ ὁ φρούραρχος τὰς φυλακὰς
ἐξετάζει, καὶ δοκιμάζειν εἰ καλῶς ἕκαστον ἔχει, ὥσπερ ἡ βουλὴ
ἵππους καὶ ἱππέας δοκιμάζει, καὶ ἐπαινεῖν δὲ καὶ τιμᾶν ὥσπερ 10
βασίλισσαν τὸν ἄξιον ἀπὸ τῆς παρούσας δυνάμεως, καὶ λοιδορεῖν
16 καὶ κολάζειν τὸν τούτων δεόμενον. πρὸς δὲ τούτοις ἐδίδασκον
αὐτήν, ἔφη, ὡς οὐκ ἂν ἄχθοιτο δικαίως, εἰ πλείω αὐτῇ πράγματα
προστάττω ἢ τοῖς οἰκέταις περὶ τὰ κτήματα, ἐπιδεικνύων ὅτι τοῖς
μὲν οἰκέταις μέτεστι τῶν δεσποσύνων χρημάτων τοσοῦτον ὅσον 15
φέρειν ἢ θεραπεύειν ἢ φυλάττειν, χρῆσθαι δὲ οὐδενὶ αὐτῶν ἔξεστιν,
ὅτῳ ἂν μὴ δῷ ὁ κύριος· δεσπότου δὲ ἅπαντά ἐστιν †ῷ ἂν βούληται
17 ἕκαστα† χρῆσθαι. ὅτῳ οὖν καὶ σῳζομένων μεγίστη ὄνησις καὶ
φθειρομένων μεγίστη βλάβη, τούτῳ καὶ τὴν ἐπιμέλειαν μάλιστα
18 προσήκουσαν ἀπέφαινον. Τί οὖν; ἔφην ἐγώ, ὦ Ἰσχόμαχε, ταῦτα 20
ἀκούσασα ἡ γυνὴ πῶς σοι ὑπήκουε; Τί δέ, ἔφη, εἰ μὴ εἶπέ γέ μοι,
ὦ Σώκρατες, ὅτι οὐκ ὀρθῶς γιγνώσκοιμι, εἰ οἰοίμην χαλεπὰ
ἐπιτάττειν διδάσκων ὅτι ἐπιμελεῖσθαι δεῖ τῶν ὄντων. χαλεπώτερον
γὰρ ἄν, ἔφη φάναι, εἰ αὐτῇ ἐπέταττον ἀμελεῖν τῶν ἑαυτῆς ἢ εἰ
19 ἐπιμελεῖσθαι δεήσει τῶν οἰκείων ἀγαθῶν. πεφυκέναι γὰρ δοκεῖ, 25
ἔφη, ὥσπερ καὶ τέκνων τὸ ἐπιμελεῖσθαι τῇ σώφρονι τῶν ἑαυτῆς ἢ
ἀμελεῖν, οὕτω καὶ τῶν κτημάτων ὅσα ἴδια ὄντα εὐφραίνει ἥδιον
τὸ ἐπιμελεῖσθαι νομίζειν ἔφη εἶναι τῇ σώφρονι τῶν ἑαυτῆς ἢ
ἀμελεῖν.

X   Καὶ ἐγὼ ἀκούσας, ἔφη ὁ Σωκράτης, ἀποκρίνασθαι τὴν γυναῖκα 30
αὐτῷ ταῦτα, εἶπον· Νὴ τὴν Ἥραν, ἔφην, ὦ Ἰσχόμαχε, ἀνδρικήν
γε ἐπιδεικνύεις τὴν διάνοιαν τῆς γυναικός. Καὶ ἄλλα τοίνυν, ἔφη
ὁ Ἰσχόμαχος, θέλω σοι πάνυ μεγαλόφρονα αὐτῆς διηγήσασθαι, ἅ
μου ἅπαξ ἀκούσασα ταχὺ ἐπείθετο. Τὰ ποῖα; ἔφην ἐγώ· λέγε· ὡς
ἐμοὶ πολὺ ἥδιον ζώσης ἀρετὴν γυναικὸς καταμανθάνειν ἢ εἰ Ζεῦξίς 35

---

1 διαμένει D: διαμενεῖ Mehler   2 ἑκάστων H G N   10 ὥσπερ καὶ A
17–18 ὡς ... ἑκάστῳ Stephanus: ᾧ ... ἑκάστῳ Camerarius: ᾧ ... ἑκάστοτε Hartman:
ὅ τι ... ἑκάστῳ Kerst   21 πῶς Dind.: πῶς codd.   26 ἔφη om. vulg.   post
τέκνων add. ῥᾷον Stephanus: fort. τέκνων ἥδιον

constantly to maintain the order that we had established. I taught her that in well-governed cities the citizens do not believe that it is sufficient to pass good laws, but they also choose guardians of the laws who, acting in their capacity of supervisors, praise the law-abiding and punish the law-breakers.'

He said, 'I therefore told my wife to consider herself as guardian of the 15 household laws, and to examine the equipment whenever she saw fit, just as the garrison commander inspects the guard, and to check whether each item is in good condition, as the Council examines horses and cavalry. And I told her that she should praise and honour a worthy member of the household to the best of her ability, like a queen, and scold and punish anyone who deserves it.' He continued: 'In addition I taught her that she 16 would not be justified in feeling annoyed if I assign more duties to her than to the slaves in connection with our possessions, because, as I pointed out, slaves are involved with their owners' property only to the extent that they carry, look after, or guard it; but they cannot use any of it unless the head of the household gives it to them; whereas everything belongs to the owner to use each thing as he or she wishes. I tried to prove to her that it was 17 incumbent upon the person who derives the greatest benefit from their preservation and the greatest harm from their destruction to show the most concern for them.'

'Well, what happened, Ischomachus?' I asked. 'When your wife heard 18 this did she pay any attention to you?'

'Certainly,' he replied, 'she even told me that I was mistaken if I thought I was imposing a difficult task on her when I was teaching her that she must be concerned about our things. She said it would have been more difficult for her if my instructions had been that she should neglect her possessions than if she were required to be concerned about her own goods. "For," she added, "just as it seems natural for a decent woman to be 19 concerned about her children and not to neglect them, so too, it gives a decent woman more happiness to be concerned about her own possessions, inasmuch as they belong to her, rather than to neglect them."'

When I heard the answer that his wife had given him, I said, 'By Hera, X Ischomachus, you show that your wife has a masculine intelligence.'

'Yes,' said Ischomachus, 'and I should like to tell you about some other occasions that demonstrate the unusual nobility of her mind, when she obeyed as soon as she had heard what I'd said.'

'What are they?' I asked. 'Do tell me, for it would give me much more pleasure to learn about the virtue of a real woman than to have Zeuxis

2 μοι καλὴν εἰκάσας γραφῇ γυναῖκα ἐπεδείκνυεν. ἐντεῦθεν δὴ λέγει
ὁ Ἰσχόμαχος· Ἐγὼ τοίνυν, ἔφη, ἰδών ποτε αὐτήν, ὦ Σώκρατες,
ἐντετριμμένην πολλῷ μὲν ψιμυθίῳ, ὅπως λευκοτέρα ἔτι δοκοίη
εἶναι ἢ ἦν, πολλῇ δ' ἐγχούσῃ, ὅπως ἐρυθροτέρα φαίνοιτο τῆς
ἀληθείας, ὑποδήματα δ' ἔχουσαν ὑψηλά, ὅπως μείζων δοκοίη εἶναι 5
3 ἢ ἐπεφύκει, Εἰπέ μοι, ἔφην, ὦ γύναι, ποτέρως ἄν με κρίναις
ἀξιοφίλητον μᾶλλον εἶναι χρημάτων κοινωνόν, εἴ σοι αὐτὰ τὰ ὄντα
ἀποδεικνύοιμι, καὶ μήτε κομπάζοιμι ὡς πλείω τῶν ὄντων ἔστι
μοι, μήτε ἀποκρυπτοίμην τι τῶν ὄντων μηδέν, ἢ εἰ πειρῴμην σε
ἐξαπατᾶν λέγων τε ὡς πλείω ἔστι μοι τῶν ὄντων, ἐπιδεικνύς τε 10
ἀργύριον κίβδηλον [δηλοίην σε] καὶ ὅρμους ὑποξύλους καὶ
4 πορφυρίδας ἐξιτήλους φαίην ἀληθινὰς εἶναι; καὶ ὑπολαβοῦσα εὐθύς,
Εὐφήμει, ἔφη· μὴ γένοιο σὺ τοιοῦτος· οὐ γὰρ ἄν ἔγωγέ σε δυναίμην,
εἰ τοιοῦτος εἴης, ἀσπάσασθαι ἐκ τῆς ψυχῆς. Οὐκοῦν, ἔφην ἐγώ,
συνεληλύθαμεν, ὦ γύναι, ὡς καὶ τῶν σωμάτων κοινωνήσοντες 15
5 ἀλλήλοις; Φασὶ γοῦν, ἔφη, οἱ ἄνθρωποι. Ποτέρως ἄν οὖν, ἔφην
ἐγώ, τοῦ σώματος αὖ δοκοίην εἶναι ἀξιοφίλητος μᾶλλον κοινωνός,
εἴ σοι τὸ σῶμα πειρῴμην παρέχειν τὸ ἐμαυτοῦ ἐπιμελόμενος ὅπως
ὑγιαινόν τε καὶ ἐρρωμένον ἔσται, καὶ διὰ ταῦτα τῷ ὄντι εὔχρως
σοι ἔσομαι, ἢ εἴ σοι μίλτῳ ἀλειφόμενος καὶ τοὺς ὀφθαλμοὺς 20
ὑπαλειφόμενος ἀνδρεικέλῳ ἐπιδεικνύοιμί τε ἐμαυτὸν καὶ συνείην
ἐξαπατῶν σε καὶ παρέχων ὁρᾶν καὶ ἅπτεσθαι μίλτου ἀντὶ τοῦ
6 ἐμαυτοῦ χρωτός; Ἐγὼ μέν, ἔφη ἐκείνη, οὔτ' ἄν μίλτου ἁπτοίμην
ἥδιον ἢ σοῦ οὔτ' ἄν ἀνδρεικέλου χρῶμα ὁρῴην ἥδιον ἢ τὸ σὸν οὔτ'
ἄν τοὺς ὀφθαλμοὺς ὑπαληλιμμένους ἥδιον ὁρῴην τοὺς σοὺς ἢ 25
7 ὑγιαίνοντας. Καὶ ἐμὲ τοίνυν νόμιζε, εἰπεῖν ἔφη ὁ Ἰσχόμαχος, ὦ
γύναι, μήτε ψιμυθίου μήτε ἐγχούσης χρώματι ἥδεσθαι μᾶλλον ἢ
τῷ σῷ, ἀλλ' ὥσπερ οἱ θεοὶ ἐποίησαν ἵπποις μὲν ἵππους, βουσὶ δὲ
βοῦς ἥδιστον, προβάτοις δὲ πρόβατα, οὕτω καὶ οἱ ἄνθρωποι
8 ἀνθρώπου σῶμα καθαρὸν οἴονται ἥδιστον εἶναι· αἱ δ' ἀπάται αὗται 30
τοὺς μὲν ἔξω πως δύναιντ' ἄν ἀνεξελέγκτως ἐξαπατᾶν, συνόντας
δὲ ἀεὶ ἀνάγκη ἁλίσκεσθαι, ἄν ἐπιχειρῶσιν ἐξαπατᾶν ἀλλήλους. ἢ
γὰρ ἐξ εὐνῆς ἁλίσκονται ἐξανιστάμενοι πρὶν παρασκευάσασθαι ἢ
ὑπὸ ἱδρῶτος ἐλέγχονται ἢ ὑπὸ δακρύων βασανίζονται ἢ ὑπὸ

3 δοκοίη H G N: δοκοῖ A corr.: δοκεῖ vel δοκῇ cet.   9 τι del. Cobet   εἰ om.
H al. D C   πειρώμην Heindorf: ἐπειρώμην codd.   11 δηλοίην σε del. Stephanus
(σοι Q): δολοίην σε Graux: κηλοίην σε Orelli   12 ἐξιτήλας H al. J M O
30 ἀνθρώπου Q R Ven. 513: om. cet.   31 πως] ἴσως Naber   33 ἐξανιστάμεναι
D al.

160

show me a beautiful portrait of a woman that he'd painted.'

So Ischomachus said in reply: 'Well, Socrates, once I saw that she had 2 made up her face with a great deal of white powder so that she might appear paler than she was, and with plenty of rouge so that she might seem to have a more rosy complexion than she truly had. And she wore platform shoes so that she might seem taller than she naturally was. "Tell 3 me, wife," I said, "suppose I showed you my property just as it is, and neither boasted that I had more than I really have nor concealed any of it, or suppose I tried to deceive you by saying that I had more than I really have, showing you counterfeit money and necklaces of gilded wood and clothes dyed with purple that would fade, and claiming that they were genuine: would you think that I was more deserving of your love as a partner in our goods in the first case or the second?"

'She immediately interrupted and said, "Hush! Don't behave like that! 4 If you were like that I certainly shouldn't be able to love you from my heart."

'I said, "Wife, were we not joined in marriage to share our bodies in intercourse with each other too?"

'"That's what people say," she replied. 5

'"Should I seem more deserving of your love as a partner in intercourse if I tried to offer my body to you after taking care that it was strong and vigorous and therefore glowing with a genuinely healthy complexion? Or if I presented myself to you smeared with red lead and wearing flesh-coloured eye make-up and had intercourse with you like that, deceiving you and offering you red lead to see and touch instead of my own skin?", I asked.

'"Personally, I had not rather touch red lead than you, nor see flesh- 6 coloured eye make-up than your own complexion; nor your eyes covered with make-up than naturally healthy," she said.'

Ischomachus reported, 'I said, "Wife, you must understand that I too 7 do not prefer the colour of white powder and rouge to your own, but just as the gods have made horses most attractive to horses, cattle to cattle, and sheep to sheep, so human beings consider the human body most attractive when it is unadorned. These tricks might perhaps succeed in deceiving 8 strangers without being detected, but those who spend their whole lives together are bound to be found out if they try to deceive each other. Either they are found out when they get out of bed before they have got dressed, or they are detected by a drop of sweat, or convicted when they cry, or

9 λουτροῦ ἀληθινῶς κατωπτεύθησαν. Τί οὖν πρὸς θεῶν, ἔφην ἐγώ,
πρὸς ταῦτα ἀπεκρίνατο; Τί δέ, ἔφη, εἰ μὴ τοῦ ⟨γε⟩ λοιποῦ τοιοῦτον
μὲν οὐδὲν πώποτε ἔτι ἐπραγματεύσατο, καθαρὰν δὲ καὶ πρεπόντως
ἔχουσαν ἐπειρᾶτο ἑαυτὴν ἐπιδεικνύναι. καὶ ἐμὲ μέντοι ἠρώτα εἴ
τι ἔχοιμι συμβουλεῦσαι ὡς ἂν τῷ ὄντι καλὴ φαίνοιτο, ἀλλὰ μὴ 5
10 μόνον δοκοίη. καὶ ἐγὼ μέντοι, ὦ Σώκρατες, ἔφη, συνεβούλευον
αὐτῇ μὴ δουλικῶς ἀεὶ καθῆσθαι, ἀλλὰ σὺν τοῖς θεοῖς πειρᾶσθαι
δεσποτικῶς πρὸς μὲν τὸν ἱστὸν προσστᾶσαν ὅ τι μὲν βέλτιον ἄλλου
ἐπίσταιτο ἐπιδιδάξαι, ὅ τι δὲ χεῖρον ἐπιμαθεῖν, ἐπισκέψασθαι δὲ
καὶ σιτοποιόν, παραστῆναι δὲ καὶ ἀπομετρούσῃ τῇ ταμίᾳ, 10
περιελθεῖν δ' ἐπισκοπουμένην καὶ εἰ κατὰ χώραν ἔχει ᾗ δεῖ ἕκαστα.
11 ταῦτα γὰρ ἐδόκει μοι ἅμα ἐπιμέλεια εἶναι καὶ περίπατος. ἀγαθὸν
δὲ ἔφην εἶναι γυμνάσιον καὶ τὸ δεῦσαι καὶ μάξαι καὶ ἱμάτια καὶ
στρώματα ἀνασεῖσαι καὶ συνθεῖναι. γυμναζομένην δὲ ἔφην οὕτως
ἂν καὶ ἐσθίειν ἥδιον καὶ ὑγιαίνειν μᾶλλον καὶ εὐχρωτέραν 15
12 φαίνεσθαι τῇ ἀληθείᾳ. καὶ ὄψις δέ, ὁπόταν ἀνταγωνίζηται διακόνῳ
καθαρωτέρα οὖσα πρεπόντως τε μᾶλλον ἠμφιεσμένη, κινητικὸν
γίγνεται ἄλλως τε καὶ ὁπόταν τὸ ἑκοῦσαν χαρίζεσθαι προσῇ ἀντὶ
13 τοῦ ἀναγκαζομένην ὑπηρετεῖν. αἱ δ' ἀεὶ καθήμεναι σεμνῶς πρὸς
τὰς κεκοσμημένας καὶ ἐξαπατώσας κρίνεσθαι παρέχουσιν ἑαυτάς. 20
καὶ νῦν, ἔφη, ὦ Σώκρατες, οὕτως εὖ ἴσθι ἡ γυνή μου
κατεσκευασμένη βιοτεύει ὥσπερ ἐγὼ ἐδίδασκον αὐτὴν καὶ ὥσπερ
νῦν σοι λέγω.

XI   Ἐντεῦθεν δ' ἐγὼ εἶπον· Ὦ Ἰσχόμαχε, τὰ μὲν δὴ περὶ τῶν τῆς
γυναικὸς ἔργων ἱκανῶς μοι δοκῶ ἀκηκοέναι τὴν πρώτην, καὶ ἄξιά 25
γε πάνυ ἐπαίνου ἀμφοτέρων ὑμῶν. τὰ δ' αὖ σὰ ἔργα, ἔφην ἐγώ,
ἤδη μοι λέγε, ἵνα σύ τε ἐφ' οἷς εὐδοκιμεῖς διηγησάμενος ἡσθῇς
κἀγὼ τὰ τοῦ καλοῦ κἀγαθοῦ ἀνδρὸς ἔργα τελέως διακούσας καὶ
2 καταμαθών, ἂν δύνωμαι, πολλήν σοι χάριν εἰδῶ. Ἀλλὰ νὴ Δί', ἔφη
ὁ Ἰσχόμαχος, καὶ πάνυ ἡδέως σοι, ὦ Σώκρατες, διηγήσομαι ἃ 30
ἐγὼ ποιῶν διατελῶ, ἵνα καὶ μεταρρυθμίσῃς με, ἐάν τί σοι δοκῶ
3 μὴ καλῶς ποιεῖν. Ἀλλ' ἐγὼ μὲν δή, ἔφην, πῶς ἂν δικαίως
μεταρρυθμίσαιμι ἄνδρα ἀπειργασμένον καλόν τε κἀγαθόν, καὶ
ταῦτα ὢν ἀνὴρ ὃς ἀδολεσχεῖν τε δοκῶ καὶ ἀερομετρεῖν καί, τὸ

---

1 ἀληθινῶς susp. Schneidero   2 λοιποῦ γε cit. Schenkl   8 προσστᾶσαν
Schneider: προστᾶσαν codd.   10 τὴν σιτοποιόν Schneider   11 ἥν D al. L E O
16 fort. καὶ ὄψις δὲ δεσποίνης   26 τἀμφοτέρων cit. Schenkl   31 δοκῶ μή] μὴ
δοκῶ K L Q R Ven. 513   34 ἀεροβατεῖν L

are revealed as they truly are when they take a bath."

'By the gods,' I asked, 'what did she reply to that?' 9

'What do you think?', he replied. 'She never did anything like that in the future, but tried to present herself in an unadorned and becoming manner. However, she asked me if I had any advice to give her about how she might look really beautiful and not merely seem to be so. And, Socrates, 10 I advised her not to spend her time sitting around like a slave, but, with the help of the gods, to try to stand before the loom as a mistress of a household should, and furthermore to teach anything that she knew better than anyone else, and to learn anything that she knew less well; to supervise the baker, and to stand next to the housekeeper while she was measuring out provisions, and also to go around inspecting whether everything was where it ought to be. These activities, I thought, combined her domestic 11 concerns with a walk. I said that mixing flour and kneading dough were excellent exercise, as were shaking and folding clothes and linens. I said that after she had exercised in that way she would enjoy her food more, be healthier, and truly improve her complexion. For compared with a 12 slave, the appearance of a wife who is unadorned and suitably dressed becomes a sexual stimulant, especially when she is willing to please as well, whereas a slave is compelled to submit. But women who spend all their 13 time sitting around proudly lay themselves open to being judged by a comparison with women who are deceivers and wear make-up. And now, Socrates,' he said, 'take it from me that my wife still lives in accordance with the practices which I taught her and which I have just described to you.'

At that point I said, 'Ischomachus, I think I've heard all I need to know XI about your wife's activities for now. For a start, both of you deserve the highest praise. But now please tell me about your own activities, so that you can have the pleasure of giving a full account of why you have such an excellent reputation, and so that I may be truly grateful to you, as a result of listening attentively and learning from beginning to end, if I can, about the activities of a gentleman.'

'By Zeus!', exclaimed Ischomachus, 'I'd be delighted to describe my 2 routine activities to you, Socrates, so that you may put me on the right track if you think I'm doing anything wrong.'

I replied, 'As far as that goes, how could I properly put a perfect 3 gentleman on the right track, especially when I've gained the reputation of being an idle chatterer who measures the air, and am called "poverty-

πάντων δὴ ἀνοητότατον δοκοῦν εἶναι ἔγκλημα, πένης καλοῦμαι;
4 καὶ πάνυ μεντἂν, ὦ Ἰσχόμαχε, ἦν ἐν πολλῇ ἀθυμίᾳ τῷ ἐπικλήματι
τούτῳ, εἰ μὴ πρώην ἀπαντήσας τῷ Νικίου τοῦ †ἐπηλύτου ἵππῳ
εἶδον πολλοὺς ἀκολουθοῦντας αὐτῷ θεατάς, πολὺν δὲ λόγον
ἐχόντων τινῶν περὶ αὐτοῦ ἤκουον· καὶ δῆτα ἠρόμην προσελθὼν 5
5 τὸν ἱπποκόμον εἰ πολλὰ εἴη χρήματα τῷ ἵππῳ. ὁ δὲ προσβλέψας
με ὡς οὐδὲ ὑγιαίνοντα τῷ ἐρωτήματι εἶπε· Πῶς δ' ἂν ἵππῳ
χρήματα γένοιτο; οὕτω δὴ ἐγὼ ἀνέκυψα ἀκούσας ὅτι ἐστὶν ἄρα
θεμιτὸν καὶ πένητι ἵππῳ ἀγαθῷ γενέσθαι, εἰ τὴν ψυχὴν φύσει
6 ἀγαθὴν ἔχοι. ὡς οὖν θεμιτὸν καὶ ἐμοὶ ἀγαθῷ ἀνδρὶ γενέσθαι διηγοῦ 10
τελέως τὰ σὰ ἔργα, ἵνα, ὅ τι ἂν δύνωμαι ἀκούων καταμαθεῖν,
πειρῶμαι καὶ ἐγώ σε ἀπὸ τῆς αὔριον ἡμέρας ἀρξάμενος μιμεῖσθαι.
7 καὶ γὰρ ἀγαθή ἐστιν, ἔφην ἐγώ, ἡμέρα ὡς ἀρετῆς ἄρχεσθαι. Σὺ
μὲν παίζεις, ἔφη ὁ Ἰσχόμαχος, ὦ Σώκρατες, ἐγὼ δὲ ὅμως σοι
διηγήσομαι ἃ ἐγὼ ὅσον δύναμαι πειρῶμαι ἐπιτηδεύων διαπερᾶν 15
8 τὸν βίον. ἐπεὶ γὰρ καταμεμαθηκέναι δοκῶ ὅτι οἱ θεοὶ τοῖς
ἀνθρώποις ἄνευ μὲν τοῦ γιγνώσκειν τε ἃ δεῖ ποιεῖν καὶ ἐπιμελεῖσθαι
ὅπως ταῦτα περαίνηται οὐ θεμιτὸν ἐποίησαν εὖ πράττειν, φρονίμοις
δ' οὖσι καὶ ἐπιμελέσι τοῖς μὲν διδόασιν εὐδαιμονεῖν, τοῖς δ' οὔ,
οὕτω δὴ ἐγὼ ἄρχομαι μὲν τοὺς θεοὺς θεραπεύων, πειρῶμαι δὲ 20
ποιεῖν ὡς ἂν θέμις ᾖ μοι εὐχομένῳ καὶ ὑγιείας τυγχάνειν καὶ
ῥώμης σώματος καὶ τιμῆς ἐν πόλει καὶ εὐνοίας ἐν φίλοις καὶ ἐν
9 πολέμῳ καλῆς σωτηρίας καὶ πλούτου καλῶς αὐξομένου. καὶ ἐγὼ
ἀκούσας ταῦτα· Μέλει γὰρ δή σοι, ὦ Ἰσχόμαχε, ὅπως πλουτῇς
καὶ πολλὰ χρήματα ἔχων πολλὰ ἔχῃς πράγματα τούτων 25
ἐπιμελόμενος; Καὶ πάνυ γ', ἔφη ὁ Ἰσχόμαχος, μέλει μοι τούτων
ὧν ἐρωτᾷς· ἡδὺ γάρ μοι δοκεῖ, ὦ Σώκρατες, καὶ θεοὺς μεγαλείως
τιμᾶν καὶ φίλους, ἄν τινος δέωνται, ἐπωφελεῖν καὶ τὴν πόλιν μηδὲν
10 ⟨τὸ⟩ κατ' ἐμὲ χρήμασιν ἀκόσμητον εἶναι. Καὶ γὰρ καλά, ἔφην
ἐγώ, ὦ Ἰσχόμαχε, ἐστὶν ἃ σὺ λέγεις, καὶ δυνατοῦ γε ἰσχυρῶς 30
ἀνδρός· πῶς γὰρ οὔ; ὅτε πολλοὶ μὲν εἰσὶν ἄνθρωπος οἳ οὐ δύνανται
ζῆν ἄνευ τοῦ ἄλλων δεῖσθαι, πολλοὶ δὲ ἀγαπῶσιν, ἂν δύνωνται τὰ
ἑαυτοῖς ἀρκοῦντα πορίζεσθαι. οἱ δὲ δὴ δυνάμενοι μὴ μόνον τὸν
ἑαυτῶν οἶκον διοικεῖν, ἀλλὰ καὶ περιποιεῖν ὥστε καὶ τὴν πόλιν

1 ἀνοητότατον D al. J: ἀνοητότερον cet.: ἀνονητότατον Naber   3 ἐπηλύτου]
ἐπιλύτου H G N: ἱππολύτου Ven. 513: Νικηράτου Cobet: ἱππηλάτου Naber: τῷ ἱππηλύτῃ
cit. Richards   7 ἐπὶ τῷ cit. Schenkl   10 θεμιτὸν ὂν M (sed ὂν punctis
suppositis) et A marg.   13 πᾶσα ἡμέρα Tournier   20 θεραπεύων F:
θεραπεύειν cet.   29 τὸ add. Weiske

stricken"—a charge which I reckon is the most senseless of all? I should 4
have been very depressed by this accusation, Ischomachus, if I hadn't come
across the horse belonging to Nicias the foreigner the other day. I saw a
crowd of spectators following it, and I heard some of them engaged in a
lengthy discussion about it. Well, I went up to the groom and asked him
whether the horse had many possessions. He looked at me as if I were mad 5
to ask a question like that, and said, "How could a horse come to own
possessions?"

'It really cheered me up to hear that it was quite all right for even a
poor horse to become a good one, if it was endowed by nature with a good
spirit. For in that case it is quite all right for me also to become a good 6
man. So please describe your activities from beginning to end so that I
may listen and learn to the best of my ability, and try to follow your
example, starting from tomorrow. For that's a good day to embark on a 7
path of virtue.'

'Although you're teasing me, Socrates,' Ischomachus replied, 'nevertheless I will describe to you the principles that I try to follow, to the best of
my ability, in the course of my life. For I believe I've learnt that the gods 8
do not think it right that people should succeed unless they understand
their duties and are concerned that they are accomplished, but grant their
favour to some who are prudent and careful, while denying it to others.
Therefore I start by cultivating the good will of the gods. And I try to
behave so that it may be right for me when I pray, to acquire good health,
physical strength, distinction in the city, good will among my friends,
survival with honour in war, and wealth that has been increased by
honest means.'

Hearing this, I asked, 'Ischomachus, are you really concerned about 9
being rich and having many possessions, when you will also have many
problems taking care of them?'

Ischomachus replied, 'Yes, certainly I am concerned about the things
you're asking about. For, Socrates, I think it's a pleasure to honour the
gods magnificently, and to help my friends if they need anything, and to
see to it that, as far as I am responsible, the city never lacks adornments
through shortage of funds.'

I replied, 'The principles that you have mentioned are excellent, 10
Ischomachus, and are typical of an extremely influential man. There's no
doubt of that, because there are many men who cannot live without
requiring help from others, and also many who are quite content if they
are able to provide for their own needs. Those who are able not only to
manage their own estates but also to accumulate a surplus so that they can
adorn the city and support their friends well, such men must certainly be

κοσμεῖν καὶ τοὺς φίλους ἐπικουφίζειν, πῶς τούτους οὐχὶ βαθεῖς τε
11 καὶ ἐρρωμένους ἄνορας χρὴ νομίσαι; ἀλλὰ γὰρ ἐπαινεῖν μέν, ἔφην
ἐγώ, τοὺς τοιούτους πολλοὶ δυνάμεθα· σὺ δέ μοι λέξον, ὦ
Ἰσχόμαχε, ἀφ' ὧνπερ ἤρξω, πῶς ὑγιείας ἐπιμελῇ; πῶς τῆς τοῦ
σώματος ῥώμης; πῶς θέμις εἶναί σοι καὶ ἐκ πολέμου καλῶς 5
σῴζεσθαι; τῆς δὲ χρηματίσεως πέρι καὶ μετὰ ταῦτα, ἔφην ἐγώ,
12 ἀρκέσει ἀκούειν. Ἀλλ' ἔστι μέν, ἔφη ὁ Ἰσχόμαχος, ὥς γε ἐμοὶ
δοκεῖ, ὦ Σώκρατες, ἀκόλουθα ταῦτα πάντα ἀλλήλων. ἐπεὶ γὰρ
ἐσθίειν τις τὰ ἱκανὰ ἔχει, ἐκπονοῦντι μὲν ὀρθῶς μᾶλλον δοκεῖ μοι
ἡ ὑγίεια παραμένειν, ἐκπονοῦντι δὲ μᾶλλον ἡ ῥώμη προσγίγνεσθαι, 10
ἀσκοῦντι δὲ τὰ τοῦ πολέμου κάλλιον σῴζεσθαι, ὀρθῶς δὲ
ἐπιμελομένῳ καὶ μὴ καταμαλακιζομένῳ μᾶλλον εἰκὸς τὸν οἶκον
13 αὔξεσθαι. Ἀλλὰ μέχρι μὲν τούτου ἕπομαι, ἔφην ἐγώ, ὦ Ἰσχόμαχε,
ὅτι ἐκπονοῦντα φὴς καὶ ἐπιμελόμενον καὶ ἀσκοῦντα ἄνθρωπον
μᾶλλον τυγχάνειν τῶν ἀγαθῶν, ὁποίῳ δὲ πόνῳ χρὴ πρὸς τὴν· 15
εὐεξίαν καὶ ῥώμην καὶ ὅπως ἀσκεῖς τὰ τοῦ πολέμου καὶ ὅπως
ἐπιμελεῖ τοῦ περιουσίαν ποιεῖν ὡς καὶ φίλους ἐπωφελεῖν καὶ πόλιν
14 ἐπισχύειν, ταῦτα ἂν ἡδέως, ἔφην ἐγώ, πυθοίμην. Ἐγὼ τοίνυν,
ἔφη, ὦ Σώκρατες, ὁ Ἰσχόμαχος, ἀνίστασθαι μὲν ἐξ εὐνῆς εἴθισμαι
ἡνίκ' ⟨ἂν⟩ ἔτι ἔνδον καταλαμβάνοιμι, εἴ τινα δεόμενος ἰδεῖν 20
τυγχάνοιμι. κἂν μέν τι κατὰ πόλιν δέῃ πράττειν, ταῦτα
15 πραγματευόμενος περιπάτῳ τούτῳ χρῶμαι· ἂν δὲ μηδὲν ἀναγκαῖον
ᾖ κατὰ πόλιν, τὸν μὲν ἵππον ὁ παῖς προάγει εἰς ἀγρόν, ἐγὼ δὲ
περιπάτῳ χρῶμαι τῇ εἰς ἀγρὸν ὁδῷ ἴσως ἄμεινον, ὦ Σώκρατες, ἢ
16 εἰ ἐν τῷ ξυστῷ περιπατοίην. ἐπειδὰν δὲ ἔλθω εἰς ἀγρόν, ἄν τέ μοι 25
φυτεύοντες τυγχάνωσιν ἄν τε νειοποιοῦντες ἄν τε σπείροντες ἄν τε
καρπὸν προσκομίζοντες, ταῦτα ἐπισκεψάμενος ὅπως ἕκαστα
17 γίγνεται, μεταρρυθμίζω, ἐὰν ἔχω τι βέλτιον τοῦ παρόντος. μετὰ
δὲ ταῦτα ὡς τὰ πολλὰ ἀναβὰς ἐπὶ τὸν ἵππον ἱππασάμην ἱππασίαν
ὡς ἂν ἐγὼ δύνωμαι ὁμοιοτάτην ταῖς ἐν τῷ πολέμῳ ἀναγκαίαις 30
ἱππασίαις, οὔτε πλαγίου οὔτε κατάντους οὔτε τάφρου οὔτε ὀχετοῦ
ἀπεχόμενος, ὡς μέντοι δυνατὸν ταῦτα ποιοῦντα ἐπιμέλομαι μὴ
18 ἀποχωλεῦσαι τὸν ἵππον. ἐπειδὰν δὲ ταῦτα γένηται, ὁ παῖς ἐξαλίσας

---

4 ἐπιμελεῖν G   5 post θέμις add. οἴει Stephanus   6 περὶ (sic) A
marg.: om. cet.   7 ἀρκέσει] ἀρέσκει Bock   9 ἔχει H pr. M: ἔχοι cet.
10 προσγίγνεσθαι Stephanus: παραγίγνεται D: προσγίγνεται cet.   20 ἂν post
ἡνίκα add. Schäfer   δεόμενος A in marg. K M₂: δεόμενον cet.   23 εἰς ἀγρόν del.
Naber   24 ἀμείνονι Heindorf   27 εἰσκομίζοντες cit. Schenkl:
συγκομίζοντες Cobet   31 ὀχετοῦ] ὄχθου Courier   32 ποιῶν Hirschig
33 fort. ἀποχωλῶσαι

considered men of strength and abundance. But, in fact, many of us can 11
praise such men. However, what I want you to do, Ischomachus, is to
return to what you were beginning to tell me. How do you take care of
your health? How can it be right for you to survive with honour even in
war? After that there will be plenty of time to hear about your money-
making.'

'But, Socrates,' said Ischomachus, 'I think all these matters depend on 12
each other. For when someone has enough to eat and works it off properly
I think his health remains stable, and, in fact, the more he works it off,
the greater his strength becomes. If he practises military exercises, he will
survive with more honour, and by remaining careful and not letting himself
grow soft he is more likely to increase his estate.'

'I follow you so far, Ischomachus,' I replied. 'You are saying that by 13
working off meals, by taking good care, and by practice a person is more
likely to obtain a greater share of good things. However, I'd like you to
tell me what kind of work is conducive towards maintaining a good state
of health and physical strength, how you practise military exercises, and
how you take care to make a surplus so that you can benefit your friends
and strengthen the city.'

'Well, Socrates,' replied Ischomachus, 'I usually get out of bed early 14
enough that if there's anyone I need to see, I can find him still at home.
And if I have any business to transact in town, I also use this business
appointment as an opportunity to take a walk. If I haven't any urgent 15
business in town, then my slave leads my horse to the farm, and I make
the trip to the country serve as a walk, and maybe that's better, Socrates,
than if I'd strolled around in the arcade. Once I have arrived at the farm, 16
whether I find them planting, or working the fallow, or sowing, or gathering
in the crops, I always inspect how each of these jobs is being done, and
put them on the right track if I know of any method superior to the one
in use. Afterwards, I generally get on my horse and practise a horseman's 17
manoeuvres resembling the horseman's manoeuvres that are required in
war as closely as I can manage them, avoiding neither hillside nor steep
descent nor ditch nor stream, though, of course, I take as much care as
possible not to lame the horse while performing these exercises. When I 18
have finished, the slave gives the horse a roll and leads him back home,

τὸν ἵππον οἴκαδε ἀπάγει, ἅμα φέρων ἀπὸ τοῦ χώρου ἄν τι δεώμεθα
εἰς ἄστυ. ἐγὼ δὲ τὰ μὲν βάδην τὰ δὲ ἀποδραμὼν οἴκαδε
ἀπεστλεγγισάμην. εἶτα δὲ ἀριστῶ, ὦ Σώκρατες, ὅσα μήτε κενὸς
19 μήτε ἄγαν πλήρης διημερεύειν. Νὴ τὴν Ἥραν, ἔφην ἐγώ, ὦ
Ἰσχόμαχε, ἀρεσκόντως γέ μοι ταῦτα ποιεῖς. τὸ γὰρ ἐν τῷ αὐτῷ 5
χρόνῳ συνεσκευασμένοις χρῆσθαι τοῖς τε πρὸς τὴν ὑγίειαν καὶ τοῖς
πρὸς τὴν ῥώμην παρασκευάσμασι καὶ τοῖς εἰς τὸν πόλεμον
ἀσκήμασι καὶ ταῖς τοῦ πλούτου ἐπιμελείαις, ταῦτα πάντα ἀγαστά
20 μοι δοκεῖ εἶναι. καὶ γὰρ ὅτι ὀρθῶς ἑκάστου τούτων ἐπιμελῇ ἱκανὰ
τεκμήρια παρέχῃ· ὑγιαίνοντά τε γὰρ καὶ ἐρρωμένον ὡς ἐπὶ τὸ 10
πολὺ σὺν τοῖς θεοῖς σε ὁρῶμεν καὶ ἐν τοῖς ἱππικωτάτοις τε καὶ
21 πλουσιωτάτοις λεγόμενόν σε ἐπιστάμεθα. Ταῦτα τοίνυν ἐγὼ ποιῶν,
ἔφη, ὦ Σώκρατες, ὑπὸ πολλῶν πάνυ συκοφαντοῦμαι, σὺ δ᾽ ἴσως
22 ᾤου με ἐρεῖν ὡς ὑπὸ πολλῶν καλὸς κἀγαθὸς κέκλημαι. Ἀλλὰ καὶ
ἔμελλον δὲ ἐγώ, ἔφην, ὦ Ἰσχόμαχε, τοῦτο ἐρήσεσθαι, εἴ τινα καὶ 15
τούτου ἐπιμέλειαν ποιῇ, ὅπως δύνῃ λόγον διδόναι καὶ λαμβάνειν,
ἄν τινί ποτε δέῃ. Οὐ γὰρ δοκῶ σοι, ἔφη, ὦ Σώκρατες, αὐτὰ ταῦτα
διατελεῖν μελετῶν, ἀπολογεῖσθαι μὲν ὅτι οὐδένα ἀδικῶ, εὖ δὲ ποιῶ
πολλοὺς ὅσον ἂν δύνωμαι, κατηγορεῖν δὲ οὐ δοκῶ σοι μελετᾶν
ἀνθρώπων, ἀδικοῦντας μὲν καὶ ἰδίᾳ πολλοὺς καὶ τὴν πόλιν 20
23 καταμανθάνων τινάς, εὖ δὲ ποιοῦντας οὐδένα; Ἀλλ᾽ εἰ καὶ
ἑρμηνεύειν τοιαῦτα μελετᾷς, τοῦτό μοι, ἔφην ἐγώ, ἔτι, ὦ
Ἰσχόμαχε, δήλωσον. Οὐδὲν μὲν οὖν, ὦ Σώκρατες, παύομαι, ἔφη,
λέγειν μελετῶν. ἢ γὰρ κατηγοροῦντός τινος τῶν οἰκετῶν ἢ
ἀπολογουμένου ἀκούσας ἐλέγχειν πειρῶμαι, ἢ μέμφομαί τινα πρὸς 25
τοὺς φίλους ἢ ἐπαινῶ, ἢ διαλλάττω τινὰς τῶν ἐπιτηδείων
πειρώμενος διδάσκειν ὡς συμφέρει αὐτοῖς φίλους εἶναι μᾶλλον ἢ
24 πολεμίους, ⟨ἢ⟩ ἐπιτιμῶμέν τινι στρατηγῷ συμπαρόντες, ἢ
ἀπολογούμεθα ὑπέρ του, εἴ τις ἀδίκως αἰτίαν ἔχει, ἢ κατηγοροῦμεν
πρὸς ἀλλήλους, εἴ τις ἀδίκως τιμᾶται. πολλάκις δὲ καὶ 30
βουλευόμενοι ἃ μὲν ἂν ἐπιθυμῶμεν πράττειν, ταῦτα ἐπαινοῦμεν, ἃ
25 δ᾽ ἂν μὴ βουλώμεθα πράττειν, ταῦτα μεμφόμεθα. ἤδη δ᾽, ἔφη, ὦ
Σώκρατες, καὶ διειλημμένως πολλάκις ἐκρίθην ὅ τι χρὴ παθεῖν ἢ
ἀποτεῖσαι. Ὑπὸ τοῦ, ἔφην ἐγώ, ὦ Ἰσχόμαχε; ἐμὲ γὰρ δὴ τοῦτο

1 τοῦ K L: om. cet.   2 δραμὼν R Ven. 513   οἴκαδε ἐλθὼν cit. Schenkl
6 συνεσκευασμένοις G: συνεσκευασμένως (vel ων) cet.   9 ἐπιμελεῖ H
10 παρέχει H N pr. (?)   12 καταλεγόμενόν Cobet   15 δὲ] σε cit.
Richards   16 ποιεῖ H   19 οὐ ... μελετᾶν del. Schenkl   28 ante
ἐπιτιμῶμεν aliquid excidisse sensit Weiske   31 ἃ H K L R Ven. 513: τὰ cet.
33 διειλημμένος Schneider

taking the opportunity at the same time to bring from the country anything we might need in town. I walk part of the way back and run the rest, and when I have arrived home, I scrape myself clean with a strigil. Then I eat enough lunch, Socrates, to get me through the day feeling neither empty nor too full.'

'By Hera, Ischomachus!', I exclaimed. 'Your way of life is very much to 19 my liking. To employ methods which improve your health and physical strength, provide training for war, and consideration for your fortune, and all at the same time, too, seems to me totally admirable. And besides, you 20 have given convincing proofs that your concern for each of these is proper. For we can see that with the help of the gods you are nearly always healthy and strong. And we know that people say that you are one of the most skilled horsemen and wealthiest men.'

'Yes, Socrates, but although that is how I behave,' he said, 'I am 21 subjected to false accusations by many people, whereas I imagine you thought that I should say I was called a gentleman by many people.'

I said, 'I was about to ask you, Ischomachus, whether you are concerned 22 about this too, the ability to defend yourself in court and to prosecute a man, if necessary.'

'Don't you realize, Socrates, that I am constantly practising precisely that: defending myself by proving that I do no wrong to anyone and that I confer benefits on many people to the best of my ability? And don't you realize that I practise making accusations when I observe people wronging the city as well as many private citizens, and doing no good to anyone?'

'Please explain to me, Ischomachus,' I said, 'whether you actually prac- 23 tise delivering such speeches.'

'I never cease to practise public speaking, Socrates. For when I hear one of our slaves making an accusation or defending himself, I try to conduct a cross-examination; or else I either criticize or praise someone before my friends; or else I reconcile some of my acquaintances, trying to explain that it is more profitable for them to be friends than enemies. Or else some of us get together and censure a general, or we defend someone who has been 24 unjustly accused, or we take turns with each other making accusations when someone who doesn't deserve it has been honoured. Often we deliber- ate, praising those things that we desire to do and criticizing what we do 25 not want to do.' He added, 'Often before now, Socrates, I've been con- demned to suffer a specific punishment or to pay a specific fine.'

'By whom, Ischomachus?' I asked, for I had no idea what this meant.

ἐλάνθανεν. Ὑπὸ τῆς γυναικός, ἔφη. Καὶ πῶς δή, ἔφην ἐγώ,
ἀγωνίζει; Ὅταν μὲν ἀληθῆ λέγειν συμφέρῃ, πάνυ ἐπιεικῶς· ὅταν
δὲ ψευδῇ, τὸν ἥττω λόγον, ὦ Σώκρατες, οὐ μὰ τὸν Δία οὐ δύναμαι
κρείττω ποιεῖν. καὶ ἐγὼ εἶπον· Ἴσως γάρ, ὦ Ἰσχόμαχε, τὸ ψεῦδος
οὐ δύνασαι ἀληθὲς ποιεῖν.   5

XII   Ἀλλὰ γάρ, ἔφην ἐγώ, μή σε κατακωλύω, ὦ Ἰσχόμαχε, ἀπιέναι
ἤδη βουλόμενον. Μὰ Δί', ἔφη, ὦ Σώκρατες· ἐπεὶ οὐκ ἂν ἀπέλθοιμι
2 πρὶν ⟨ἂν⟩ παντάπασιν ἡ ἀγορὰ λυθῇ. Νὴ Δί', ἔφην ἐγώ, φυλάττῃ
γὰρ ἰσχυρῶς μὴ ἀποβάλῃς τὴν ἐπωνυμίαν, τὸ ἀνὴρ καλὸς κἀγαθὸς
κεκλῆσθαι. νῦν γὰρ πολλῶν σοι ἴσως ὄντων ἐπιμελείας δεομένων,   10
ἐπεὶ συνέθου τοῖς ξένοις, ἀναμένεις αὐτούς, ἵνα μὴ ψεύσῃ. Ἀλλά
τοι, ὦ Σώκρατες, ἔφη ὁ Ἰσχόμαχος, οὐδ' ἐκεῖνά μοι ἀμελεῖται ἃ
3 σὺ λέγεις· ἔχω γὰρ ἐπιτρόπους ἐν τοῖς ἀγροῖς. Πότερα δέ, ἐγὼ
ἔφην, ὦ Ἰσχόμαχε, ὅταν δεηθῇς ἐπιτρόπου, καταμαθὼν ἄν που ᾖ
ἐπιτροπευτικὸς ἀνήρ, τοῦτον πειρᾷ ὠνεῖσθαι, ὥσπερ, ὅταν τέκτονος   15
δεηθῇς, καταμαθὼν εὖ οἶδ' ὅτι ἄν που ἴδῃς τεκτονικόν, τοῦτον
4 πειρᾷ κτᾶσθαι, ἢ αὐτὸς παιδεύεις τοὺς ἐπιτρόπους; Αὐτὸς νὴ Δί',
ἔφη, ὦ Σώκρατες, πειρῶμαι παιδεύειν. καὶ γὰρ ὅστις μέλλει
ἀρκέσειν, ὅταν ἐγὼ ἀπῶ, ἀντ' ἐμοῦ ἐπιμελόμενος, τί αὐτὸν καὶ δεῖ
ἄλλο ἐπίστασθαι ἢ ἅπερ ἐγώ; εἴπερ γὰρ ἱκανός εἰμι τῶν ἔργων   20
προστατεύειν, κἂν ἄλλον δήπου δυναίμην διδάξαι ἅπερ αὐτὸς
5 ἐπίσταμαι. Οὐκοῦν εὔνοιαν πρῶτον, ἔφην ἐγώ, δεήσει αὐτὸν ἔχειν
σοὶ καὶ τοῖς σοῖς, εἰ μέλλει ἀρκέσειν ἀντὶ σοῦ παρών. ἄνευ γὰρ
εὐνοίας τί ὄφελος καὶ ὁποίας τινὸς οὖν ἐπιτρόπου ἐπιστήμης
γίγνεται; Οὐδὲν μὰ Δί', ἔφη ὁ Ἰσχόμαχος, ἀλλά τοι τὸ εὐνοεῖν   25
6 ἐμοὶ καὶ τοῖς ἐμοῖς ἐγὼ πρῶτον πειρῶμαι παιδεύειν. Καὶ πῶς,
ἐγὼ ἔφην, πρὸς τῶν θεῶν εὔνοιαν ἔχειν σοὶ καὶ τοῖς σοῖς διδάσκεις
ὅντινα ἂν βούλῃ; Εὐεργετῶν νὴ Δί', ἔφη ὁ Ἰσχόμαχος, ὅταν τινὸς
7 ἀγαθοῦ οἱ θεοὶ ἀφθονίαν διδῶσιν ἡμῖν. Τοῦτο οὖν λέγεις, ἔφην
ἐγώ, ὅτι οἱ ἀπολαύοντες τῶν σῶν ἀγαθῶν εὐνοί σοι γίγνονται καὶ   30
ἀγαθόν τί σε βούλονται πράττειν; Τοῦτο γὰρ ὄργανον, ὦ Σώκρατες,
8 εὐνοίας ἄριστον ὁρῶ ὄν. Ἂν δὲ δὴ εὔνους σοι γένηται, ἔφην, ὦ
Ἰσχόμαχε, ἦ τούτου ἕνεκα ἱκανὸς ἔσται ἐπιτροπεύειν; οὐχ ὁρᾷς
ὅτι καὶ ἑαυτοῖς εὖνοι πάντες ὄντες ὡς εἰπεῖν ἄνθρωποι, πολλοὶ

---

8 ἂν add. Schenkl   ἡ H al.: om. cet.   λυθείη Platt   φυλάττει H   9 ἀποβάλῃ
codd.: corr. Stephanus   10 post ὄντων add. τῶν Cobet   11 ἀναμένεις L M₂:
ἀναμένειν cet., quod tuetur Bock, post δεομένων inserto ἀμελεῖς   16 καταμαθὼν
del. Hartman: καταμαθεῖν H al. F   18 ἔφη om. K L   19 ἐπιμελόμενος K L:
ἐπιμελούμενος cet.   22 δεήσει A cor. Q: δεήσειν cet.   34 ὄντες om. K L:
ὄντες πάντες Jacob

'By my wife!', he said.

'And how do you get on when you plead your case?', I asked.

'Reasonably well, when it is expedient to speak the truth. But when I need to tell a lie, by Zeus, I cannot convert the worse cause into the better.'

And I commented, 'Perhaps, Ischomachus, you cannot convert a lie into truth.'

'But I'm afraid I'm detaining you, Ischomachus, and you want to be XII going now,' I said.

'By Zeus, no, Socrates,' he replied, 'I certainly shouldn't want to go 2 before the market closes.'

'By Zeus,' I rejoined, 'you take very strong precautions not to lose that title of "gentleman" that people have given you. For now, though there are many matters, I'm sure, that have a claim on your attention, because you made an arrangement with some guests, you're waiting for them so that you don't break your promise.'

'But, Socrates, I am not neglecting the matters which you mention,' said Ischomachus. 'I have foremen in the fields.'

'When you need a foreman,' I said, 'do you find out if there is a skilled 3 supervisor anywhere around and try to buy him, just as when you need a carpenter, you find out, I'm sure, where you can see a man with building skills and try to get him? Or do you train your foremen yourself?'

'By Zeus, Socrates,' he answered, 'I try to train them myself. If someone 4 is going to be capable of taking charge in my place when I'm away, what else does he need to know other than what I do? If I am capable of supervising the various types of work, surely I can teach someone else what I myself know.'

'First of all,' I said, 'he should be loyal towards you and yours if he is 5 to be capable of representing you in your absence. For what is the use of a foreman's having any kind of knowledge at all, if he has no loyalty?'

'None, by Zeus,' replied Ischomachus. 'So, you see, the first lesson I try to teach him is to be loyal to me and mine.'

'And how on earth do you teach loyalty to you and yours to the man 6 you've chosen?', I asked.

'By Zeus,' said Ischomachus, 'by rewarding him whenever the gods grant us an abundance of some good thing.'

'Do you mean to say,' I asked, 'that by getting some pleasure from your 7 good things, they become loyal to you and want to do some good to you?'

'Yes, Socrates, for I have come to see that this is the best device for securing loyalty.'

'Well, suppose he is loyal to you, Ischomachus,' I continued. 'Will that 8 be enough to make him a competent foreman? Don't you see that although nearly all human beings are loyal to their own interests, yet there are many

αὐτῶν εἰσὶν οἳ οὐκ ἐθέλουσιν ἐπιμελεῖσθαι ὅπως αὐτοῖς ἔσται ταῦτα
9 ἃ βούλονται εἶναί σφισι τὰ ἀγαθά; Ἀλλὰ ναὶ μὰ Δί᾽, ἔφη ὁ
Ἰσχόμαχος, τοιούτους ὅταν ἐπιτρόπους βούλωμαι καθιστάναι, καὶ
10 ἐπιμελεῖσθαι διδάσκω. Πῶς, ἔφην ἐγώ, πρὸς τῶν θεῶν; τοῦτο γὰρ
δὴ ἐγὼ παντάπασιν οὐ διδακτὸν ᾤμην εἶναι, τὸ ἐπιμελῆ ποιῆσαι. 5
Οὐδὲ γάρ ἐστιν, ἔφη, ὦ Σώκρατες, ἐφεξῆς γε οὕτως οἷόν τε πάντας
11 διδάξαι ἐπιμελεῖς εἶναι. Ποίους μὲν δή, ἐγὼ ἔφην, οἷόν τε; πάντως
μοι σαφῶς τούτους διασήμηνον. Πρῶτον μέν, ἔφη, ὦ Σώκρατες,
τοὺς οἴνου ἀκρατεῖς οὐκ ἂν δύναιο ἐπιμελεῖς ποιῆσαι· τὸ γὰρ
12 μεθύειν λήθην ἐμποιεῖ πάντων τῶν πράττειν δεομένων. Οἱ οὖν 10
τούτου ἀκρατεῖς μόνοι, ἐγὼ ἔφην, ἀδύνατοί εἰσιν ἐπιμελεῖσθαι ἢ
καὶ ἄλλοι τινές; Ναὶ μὰ Δί᾽, ἔφη ὁ Ἰσχόμαχος, καὶ οἵ γε τοῦ
ὕπνου· οὔτε γὰρ ἂν αὐτὸς δύναιτο καθεύδων τὰ δέοντα ποιεῖν οὔτε
13 ἄλλους παρέχεσθαι. Τί οὖν; ἐγὼ ἔφην, οὗτοι αὖ μόνοι ἀδύνατοι
ἡμῖν ἔσονται ταύτην τὴν ἐπιμέλειαν διδαχθῆναι ἢ καὶ ἄλλοι τινὲς 15
πρὸς τούτοις; Ἔμοιγέ τοι δοκοῦσιν, ἔφη ὁ Ἰσχόμαχος, καὶ οἱ τῶν
ἀφροδισίων δυσέρωτες ἀδύνατοι εἶναι διδαχθῆναι ἄλλου τινὸς
14 μᾶλλον ἐπιμελεῖσθαι ἢ τούτου· οὔτε γὰρ ἐλπίδα οὔτ᾽ ἐπιμέλειαν
ἡδίονα ῥᾴδιον εὑρεῖν τῆς τῶν παιδικῶν ἐπιμελείας, οὐδὲ μήν, ὅταν
παρῇ τὸ πρακτέον, τιμωρίαν χαλεπωτέραν εὐπετές ἐστι τοῦ ἀπὸ 20
τῶν ἐρωμένων κωλύεσθαι. ὑφίεμαι οὖν καὶ οὓς ἂν τοιούτους γνῶ
15 ὄντας μηδ᾽ ἐπιχειρεῖν ἐπιμελητὰς τούτων τινὰς καθιστάναι. Τί δέ,
ἔφην ἐγώ, οἵτινες αὖ ἐρωτικῶς ἔχουσι τοῦ κερδαίνειν, ἢ καὶ οὗτοι
ἀδύνατοί εἰσιν εἰς ἐπιμέλειαν τῶν κατ᾽ ἀγρὸν ἔργων παιδεύεσθαι;
Οὐ μὰ Δί᾽, ἔφη ὁ Ἰσχόμαχος, οὐδαμῶς γε, ἀλλὰ καὶ πάνυ εὐάγωγοί 25
εἰσιν εἰς τὴν τούτων ἐπιμέλειαν· οὐδὲν γὰρ ἄλλο δεῖ ἢ δεῖξαι μόνον
16 αὐτοῖς ὅτι κερδαλέον ἐστὶν ἡ ἐπιμέλεια. Τοὺς δὲ ἄλλους, ἔφην ἐγώ,
εἰ ἐγκρατεῖς τέ εἰσιν ὧν σὺ κελεύεις καὶ πρὸς τὸ φιλοκερδεῖς εἶναι
μετρίως ἔχουσι, πῶς ἐκδιδάσκεις ὧν σὺ βούλει ἐπιμελεῖς γίγνεσθαι;
Ἁπλῶς, ἔφη, πάνυ, ὦ Σώκρατες. ὅταν μὲν γὰρ ἐπιμελομένους 30
ἴδω, καὶ ἐπαινῶ καὶ τιμᾶν πειρῶμαι αὐτούς, ὅταν δὲ ἀμελοῦντας,
17 λέγειν τε πειρῶμαι καὶ ποιεῖν ὁποῖα δήξεται αὐτούς. Ἴθι, ἐγὼ
ἔφην, ὦ Ἰσχόμαχε, καὶ τόδε μοι παρατραπόμενος τοῦ λόγου περὶ

---

2 τὰ Brodaeus: τι codd.   5 τὸ ἐπιμελῆ ποιῆσαι del. Heindorf   8 ἔφη
om. K L   9 ἐπιμελεῖς K L: ἐπιμελεῖσθαι cet.   10 πράττεσθαι Dind.:
του πράττειν Jacob   11 μόνοι F: μόνον cet.   ἐπιμέλεσθαι Cobet: ἐπιμελεῖς ἔσεσθαι
codd.   13 post δύναιτο add. ὁ Cobet   19 ἐπιμελείας del. Schenkl
20 παρείη codd.: corr. Schneider   28 τὸ H N H Hᵃ: τῶ cet.   29 ὅπως codd.:
corr. Weiske   ὧν Brodaeus: ὡς codd.   30 ἐπιμελομένους G N: ἐπιμελουμένους cet.
33 λόγου τοῦ Jacob

of them who are not willing to concern themselves with acquiring the good things they want for themselves?'

'By Zeus,' replied Ischomachus, 'when I want to appoint men of that 9 sort as foremen, I also teach them to concern themselves about such things.'

'How on earth do you do that?' I asked. 'I thought that concern of this 10 kind was something which could not possibly be taught.'

'No, Socrates, it is not possible to teach every single one in succession to be concerned about such things,' he said.

'What sort of people can be taught, then?', I asked. 'Please give me a 11 clear idea of them, at any rate.'

'Well, for a start, Socrates,' he replied, 'you can't make those who drink too much wine into men who will show proper concern about things; for drunkenness makes them forget everything that they should do.'

'Are drunkards the only people who are incapable of showing proper 12 concern then, or are there also some other types?'

'There are, by Zeus,' answered Ischomachus, 'those who sleep too much. When asleep, such a man could not do his own work, nor make others do theirs.'

'Well then,' I asked, 'are these the only ones whom we shall find incapable 13 of being taught to show proper concern, or are there even more besides these?'

'I think,' replied Ischomachus, 'those who are love-sick cannot be taught to concern themselves about anything other than their love. For it is not 14 easy to find any hope or concern that gives greater pleasure than concern for darling boys, nor, I can assure you, when the thing to be done has passed by, is it easy to find any harsher punishment than separating him from his beloved. So I've given up even trying to appoint as foremen any of those in whom I recognize such symptoms.'

'Then what about those who are passionately in love with making a 15 profit?', I asked. 'Are these, too, incapable of being trained so that they can concern themselves with the work on a farm?'

'No, not at all,' responded Ischomachus, 'in fact, they can easily be led to concern themselves about such things. You need do nothing but show them that taking proper concern is profitable.'

'What about the others?', I asked. 'If they show self-control in the areas 16 in which you demand it, and are moderately interested in making a profit, how do you teach them to be concerned in the way you require?'

'Very simply, Socrates,' he answered. 'When I see them showing proper concern, I praise them and try to reward them, as well; but when they are not, I try to say and do things that will hurt their feelings.'

'Come, Ischomachus,' I said, 'let's change the subject, and instead of 17 discussing the people who are educated to take proper concern, tell me—

τῶν παιδευομένων εἰς τὴν ἐπιμέλειαν δήλωσον, εἰ οἷόν τέ ἐστιν
18 ἀμελῆ αὐτὸν ὄντα ἄλλους ποιεῖν ἐπιμελεῖς. Οὐ μὰ Δί', ἔφη ὁ
Ἰσχόμαχος, οὐδέν γε μᾶλλον ἢ ἄμουσον ὄντα αὐτὸν ἄλλους
μουσικοὺς ποιεῖν. χαλεπὸν γὰρ τοῦ διδασκάλου πονηρῶς τι
ὑποδεικνύοντος καλῶς τοῦτο ποιεῖν μαθεῖν, καὶ ἀμελεῖν γε 5
ὑποδεικνύοντος τοῦ δεσπότου χαλεπὸν ἐπιμελῆ θεράποντα
19 γενέσθαι. ὡς δὲ συντόμως εἰπεῖν, πονηροῦ μὲν δεσπότου οἰκέτας
οὐ δοκῶ χρηστοὺς καταμεμαθηκέναι· χρηστοῦ μέντοι πονηροὺς
ἤδη εἶδον, οὐ μέντοι ἀζημίους γε. τὸν δὲ ἐπιμελητικοὺς βουλόμενον
ποιήσασθαί τινας καὶ ἐφορατικὸν δεῖ εἶναι τῶν ἔργων καὶ 10
ἐξεταστικὸν καὶ χάριν θέλοντα τῶν καλῶς τελουμένων ἀποδιδόναι
τῷ αἰτίῳ, καὶ δίκην μὴ ὀκνοῦντα τὴν ἀξίαν ἐπιθεῖναι τῷ ἀμελοῦντι.
20 καλῶς δέ μοι δοκεῖ ἔχειν, ἔφη ὁ Ἰσχόμαχος, καὶ ἡ τοῦ βαρβάρου
λεγομένη ἀπόκρισις, ὅτε βασιλεὺς ἄρα ἵππου ἐπιτυχὼν ἀγαθοῦ
παχῦναι αὐτὸν ὡς τάχιστα βουλόμενος ἤρετο τῶν δεινῶν τινα ἀμφ' 15
ἵππους δοκούντων εἶναι τί τάχιστα παχύνει ἵππον· τὸν δ' εἰπεῖν
λέγεται ὅτι δεσπότου ὀφθαλμός. οὕτω δ', ἔφη, ὦ Σώκρατες, καὶ
τἆλλά μοι δοκεῖ δεσπότου ὀφθαλμὸς τὰ καλά τε κἀγαθὰ μάλιστα
ἐργάζεσθαι.

XIII   Ὅταν ⟨δὲ⟩ παραστήσῃς τινί, ἔφην ἐγώ, τοῦτο καὶ πάνυ 20
ἰσχυρῶς, ὅτι δεῖ ἐπιμελεῖσθαι ὧν ἂν σὺ βούλῃ, ἦ ἱκανὸς ἤδη ἔσται
ὁ τοιοῦτος ἐπιτροπεύειν, ἤ τι καὶ ἄλλο προσμαθητέον αὐτῷ ἔσται,
2 εἰ μέλλει ἐπίτροπος ἱκανὸς ἔσεσθαι; Ναὶ μὰ Δί', ἔφη ὁ Ἰσχόμαχος,
ἔτι μέντοι λοιπὸν αὐτῷ ἐστι γνῶναι ὅ τι τε ποιητέον καὶ ὁπότε
καὶ ὅπως, εἰ δὲ μή, τί μᾶλλον ἐπιτρόπου ἄνευ τούτων ὄφελος ἢ 25
ἰατροῦ ὃς ἐπιμελοῖτο μὲν κάμνοντός τινος πρῴ τε ἰὼν καὶ ὀψέ, ὅ
3 τι δὲ συμφέρον τῷ κάμνοντι ποιεῖν εἴη, τοῦτο μὴ εἰδείη; Ἐάν γε μὴν
καὶ τὰ ἔργα μάθῃ ὡς ἔστιν ἐργαστέα, ἔτι τινός, ἔφην ἐγώ,
προσδεήσεται, ἢ ἀποτετελεσμένος ἤδη οὗτός σοι ἔσται ἐπίτροπος;
4 Ἄρχειν γε, ἔφη, οἶμαι δεῖν αὐτὸν μαθεῖν τῶν ἐργαζομένων. Ἦ 30
οὖν, ἔφην ἐγώ, καὶ σὺ ἄρχειν ἱκανοὺς εἶναι παιδεύεις τοὺς
ἐπιτρόπους; Πειρῶμαί γε δή, ἔφη ὁ Ἰσχόμαχος. Καὶ πῶς δή, ἔφη
ἐγώ, πρὸς τῶν θεῶν τὸ ἀρχικοὺς εἶναι ἀνθρώπων παιδεύεις;
Φαύλως, ἔφη, πάνυ, ὦ Σώκρατες, ὥστε ἴσως ἂν καὶ καταγελάσαις

1 περὶ τοῦ παιδεύσθαι post δήλωσον codd.: del. Schneider   3 γε om. H N
14 ἵππῳ et ἀγαθῷ Y al. J O   17 λέγεται H G N: om. cet.: λέγεται ὅτι om.
Ven. 513   20 δὲ add. Castalio   27 ἐάν γε μὴν Q R P Ven. 513: ἐὰν δὲ μὴ
cet. (μὲν A in marg.): ἐὰν δὲ δὴ Camerarius   28 τινὸς Ven. 513: τίνος cet.
30 ἔφη om. K L   31 καὶ σὺ] σὺ καὶ Hertlein

is it possible for a person who lacks concern to make others show concern?'

'No, by Zeus,' replied Ischomachus, 'no more than a person who is 18 himself unskilled in the arts could make others artistic. For it is difficult to learn to do anything well if the teacher demonstrates it badly. And when the master shows that he lacks concern, it is difficult for a slave to be concerned. In short, I don't think I've ever come across a bad master with 19 good slaves: on the other hand, I've seen bad slaves belonging to a good master; however, they, at least, didn't escape punishment. But the master who wants to make his men be concerned must be in the habit of supervising their work and inspecting it, be prepared to reward any slave who is responsible for work that's well performed, and not hesitant to impose the due punishment on any slave who lacks concern. 'I think', he added, 'that 20 the well-known reply of the foreigner is very relevant: I mean, when the king had acquired a good horse and wanted to fatten him up as quickly as he could, he asked one of those who had a reputation as an expert on horses "What fattens a horse most quickly?" They say that he replied, "his master's eye". This applies to everything, I think, Socrates: the master's eye produces beautiful and good work.'

'When you have got this very firmly into a man's head, that he needs XIII to be properly concerned about those things that you want him to, will such a person then be qualified to be a supervisor immediately, or is there something else he must he learn if he is to be a qualified supervisor?'

'Of course, by Zeus,' Ischomachus answered, 'it still remains for him to 2 learn what he must do, and when, and how. If he didn't know these things, you wouldn't get any more benefit from a foreman than from a doctor who was concerned about a patient and visited him morning and night, but didn't know what treatment would do him good, would you?'

'Well, suppose he has learnt simply how farm work should be done, will 3 he need any more, or will he now, in your view, be a thoroughly accomplished foreman?', I asked.

'I think he must learn how to govern the workers,' he replied.   4

'And do you yourself teach your foremen to be capable of governing?', I asked.

'Well, I do my best,' answered Ischomachus.

'How on earth do you teach them to have the skills required to govern men?', I asked.

'In a ridiculously simple way, Socrates—so simple that you may well laugh at me when you hear about it,' he replied.

5 ἀκούων. Οὐ μὲν δὴ ἄξιόν γ', ἔφην ἐγώ, τὸ πρᾶγμα καταγέλωτος,
ὦ Ἰσχόμαχε. ὅστις γάρ τοι ἀρχικοὺς ἀνθρώπων δύναται ποιεῖν,
δῆλον ὅτι οὗτος καὶ δεσποτικοὺς ἀνθρώπων δύναται διδάσκειν,
ὅστις δὲ δεσποτικοὺς δύναται ποιεῖν, καὶ βασιλικούς. ὥστε οὐ
καταγέλωτός μοι δοκεῖ ἄξιος εἶναι ἀλλ' ἐπαίνου μεγάλου ὁ τοῦτο 5
6 δυνάμενος ποιεῖν. Οὐκοῦν, ἔφη, ὦ Σώκρατες, τὰ μὲν ἄλλα ζῷα ἐκ
δυοῖν τούτοιν τὸ πείθεσθαι μανθάνουσιν, ἔκ τε τοῦ ὅταν ἀπειθεῖν
ἐπιχειρῶσι κολάζεσθαι καὶ ἐκ τοῦ ὅταν προθύμως ὑπηρετῶσιν
7 εὖ πάσχειν. οἵ τε γοῦν πῶλοι μανθάνουσιν ὑπακούειν τοῖς
πωλοδάμναις τῷ ὅταν μὲν πείθωνται τῶν ἡδέων τι αὐτοῖς 10
γίγνεσθαι, ὅταν δὲ ἀπειθῶσι πράγματα ἔχειν, ἔστ' ἂν ὑπηρετήσωσι
8 κατὰ γνώμην τῷ πωλοδάμνῃ· καὶ τὰ κυνίδια δὲ πολὺ τῶν
ἀνθρώπων καὶ τῇ γνώμῃ καὶ τῇ γλώττῃ ὑποδεέστερα ὄντα ὅμως
καὶ περιτρέχειν καὶ κυβιστᾶν καὶ ἄλλα πολλὰ μανθάνει τῷ αὐτῷ
τούτῳ τρόπῳ. ὅταν μὲν γὰρ πείθηται, λαμβάνει τι ὧν δεῖται, ὅταν 15
9 δὲ ἀμελῇ, κολάζεται. ἀνθρώπους δ' ἔστι πιθανωτέρους ποιεῖν καὶ
λόγῳ, ἐπιδεικνύοντα ὡς συμφέρει αὐτοῖς πείθεσθαι, τοῖς δὲ δούλοις
καὶ ἡ δοκοῦσα θηριώδης παιδεία εἶναι πάνυ ἐστὶν ἐπαγωγὸς πρὸς
τὸ πείθεσθαι διδάσκειν· τῇ γὰρ γαστρὶ αὐτῶν ἐπὶ ταῖς ἐπιθυμίαις
προσχαριζόμενος ἂν πολλὰ ἀνύτοις παρ' αὐτῶν. αἱ δὲ φιλότιμοι 20
τῶν φύσεων καὶ τῷ ἐπαίνῳ παροξύνονται. πεινῶσι γὰρ τοῦ ἐπαίνου
οὐχ ἧττον ἔνιαι τῶν φύσεων ἢ ἄλλαι τῶν σίτων τε καὶ ποτῶν.
10 ταῦτά τε οὖν, ὅσαπερ αὐτὸς ποιῶν οἶμαι πιθανωτέροις ἀνθρώποις
χρῆσθαι, διδάσκω οὓς ἂν ἐπιτρόπους βούλωμαι καταστῆσαι καὶ
τάδε συλλαμβάνω αὐτοῖς· ἱμάτιά τε γὰρ ἃ δεῖ παρέχειν ἐμὲ τοῖς 25
ἐργαστῆρσι καὶ ὑποδήματα οὐχ ὅμοια πάντα ποιῶ, ἀλλὰ τὰ μὲν
χείρω, τὰ δὲ βελτίω, ἵνα ᾖ τὸν κρείττω τοῖς βελτίοσι τιμᾶν, τῷ
11 δὲ χείρονι τὰ ἥττω διδόναι. πάνυ γάρ μοι δοκεῖ, ἔφη, ὦ Σώκρατες,
ἀθυμία ἐγγίγνεσθαι τοῖς ἀγαθοῖς, ὅταν ὁρῶσι τὰ μὲν ἔργα δι'
αὐτῶν καταπραττόμενα, τῶν δὲ ὁμοίων τυγχάνοντας ἑαυτοῖς τοὺς 30
12 μήτε πονεῖν μήτε κινδυνεύειν ἐθέλοντας, ὅταν δέῃ. αὐτός τε οὖν
οὐδ' ὁπωστιοῦν τῶν ἴσων ἀξιῶ τοὺς ἀμείνους τοῖς κακίοσι
τυγχάνειν, τούς τε ἐπιτρόπους, ὅταν μὲν εἰδῶ διαδεδωκότας τοῖς
πλείστου ἀξίοις τὰ κράτιστα, ἐπαινῶ, ἂν δὲ ἴδω ἢ κολακεύμασί
τινα προτιμώμενον ἢ καὶ ἄλλῃ τινὶ ἀνωφελεῖ χάριτι, οὐκ ἀμελῶ, 35

9 καταμανθάνουσιν H al.   19 διδάσκειν del. Cobet   ἐπὶ] καὶ Hartman
20 ἀνύτοις ἂν Q   23 ταῦτά Bäumlein   τε del. Hertlein   24 διδάσκων
codd.: corr. Weiske   25 ἃ] ὅσα K L   30 αὐτῶν F Ven. 368: αὐτῶν cet.
33 εἰδῶ] ἴδω Dind.

'It certainly is no laughing matter, Ischomachus,' I said. 'You know, 5
whoever can make people skilled in governing men can obviously also make
them skilled masters of men; and whoever can make people skilled masters
can also make people skilled to be kings. So the person who can do this
seems to me to deserve great praise, not laughter.'

'Well, Socrates,' he said, 'other living creatures learn obedience in two 6
ways as follows: by being punished when they try to disobey, and by being
rewarded when they are eager to do as they are told. Colts, for instance, 7
learn to submit to the men who break them in by being given something
sweet when they obey them, but when they are disobedient, they get into
trouble, until they serve their trainer according to his wishes. Puppies, too, 8
are far inferior to human beings in sense and speech; still, they learn in the
same way to run in a circle, turn somersaults, and perform many other
tricks. For when they obey, they get something they want, but when they
show no concern, they are punished.

'And in the case of human beings it is possible to make them more 9
obedient merely by talking to them, pointing out that it is to their advantage
to obey. But for slaves the method of training that is accepted for wild
animals is very effective in teaching obedience. For if you gratify their
desires by filling their bellies, you may get a great deal out of them. Those
who are naturally ambitious become even keener with praise; for some
natures hunger for praise as much as others do for food and drink. These 10
methods, then, are exactly the ones that I use myself, because I believe
that I shall have more obedient people in my employ as a result, and I
teach them to those I wish to appoint as foremen. And I also help them in
the following ways: I make sure that the clothing and the shoes which I
must supply for the workers are not identical, but some are of inferior
quality, and others superior, so that I can reward the better workers with
superior garments and give the inferior ones to the less deserving. For, 11
Socrates,' he continued, 'I'm convinced that good workers become very
discouraged when they see that although they have done all the work,
nevertheless those who are unwilling to work or, when necessary, to run
risks, earn rewards equal to their own. I, myself, then, by no means think 12
that better workers should receive the same treatment as worthless ones.
And when I know that the foremen have distributed the best things to the
most deserving workers, I praise them; but when I see someone favoured
beyond the rest as a result of flattery or some other worthless service, I am
not unconcerned, but I reprimand the foreman, and try to teach him,

ἀλλ' ἐπιπλήττω καὶ πειρῶμαι διδάσκειν, ὦ Σώκρατες, ὅτι οὐδ'
αὑτῷ σύμφορα ταῦτα ποιεῖ.

XIV   Ὅταν δέ, ὦ Ἰσχόμαχε, ἔφην ἐγώ, καὶ ἄρχειν ἤδη ἱκανός σοι
γένηται ὥστε πειθομένους παρέχεσθαι, ἦ ἀποτετελεσμένον τοῦτον
ἡγῇ ἐπίτροπον, ἢ ἔτι τινὸς προσδεῖται ὁ ταῦτα ἔχων ἃ σὺ εἴρηκας; 5
2 Ναὶ μὰ Δί', ἔφη ὁ Ἰσχόμαχος, τοῦ γε ἀπέχεσθαι τῶν δεσποσύνων
καὶ μὴ κλέπτειν. εἰ γὰρ ὁ τοὺς καρποὺς μεταχειριζόμενος τολμώη
ἀφανίζειν ὥστε μὴ λείπειν λυσιτελοῦντας τοῖς ἔργοις, τί ἂν ὄφελος
3 εἴη τὸ διὰ τῆς τούτου ἐπιμελείας γεωργεῖν; Ἦ καὶ ταύτην οὖν,
ἔφην ἐγώ, τὴν δικαιοσύνην σὺ ὑποδύει διδάσκειν; Καὶ πάνυ, 10
ἔφη ὁ Ἰσχόμαχος· οὐ μέντοι γε πάντας ἐξ ἑτοίμου εὑρίσκω
4 ὑπακούοντας τῆς διδασκαλίας ταύτης. καίτοι τὰ μὲν καὶ ἐκ τῶν
Δράκοντος νόμων, τὰ δὲ καὶ ἐκ τῶν Σόλωνος πειρῶμαι, ἔφη,
λαμβάνων ἐμβιβάζειν εἰς τὴν δικαιοσύνην τοὺς οἰκέτας. δοκοῦσι
γάρ μοι, ἔφη, καὶ οὗτοι οἱ ἄνδρες θεῖναι πολλοὺς τῶν νόμων ἐπὶ 15
5 δικαιοσύνης τῆς τοιαύτης διδασκαλίᾳ. γέγραπται γὰρ ζημιοῦσθαι
ἐπὶ τοῖς κλέμμασι καὶ δεδέσθαι ἄν τις ἁλῷ ποιῶν καὶ θανατοῦσθαι
τοὺς ἐγχειροῦντας. δῆλον οὖν, ἔφη, ὅτι ἔγραφον αὐτὰ βουλόμενοι
6 ἀλυσιτελῆ ποιῆσαι τοῖς ἀδίκοις τὴν αἰσχροκέρδειαν. ἐγὼ οὖν καὶ
τούτων, ἔφη, προσφέρων ἔνια καὶ ἄλλα τῶν βασιλικῶν νόμων 20
προφερόμενος πειρῶμαι δικαίους περὶ τὰ διαχειριζόμενα
7 ἀπεργάζεσθαι τοὺς οἰκέτας. ἐκεῖνοι μὲν γὰρ οἱ νόμοι ζημίαι μόνον
εἰσὶ τοῖς ἁμαρτάνουσιν, οἱ δὲ βασιλικοὶ νόμοι οὐ μόνον ζημιοῦσι
τοὺς ἀδικοῦντας, ἀλλὰ καὶ ὠφελοῦσι τοὺς δικαίους· ὥστε ὁρῶντες
πλουσιωτέρους γιγνομένους τοὺς δικαίους τῶν ἀδίκων πολλοὶ καὶ 25
8 φιλοκερδεῖς ὄντες εὖ μάλα ἐπιμένουσι τῷ μὴ ἀδικεῖν. οὓς δ' ἂν
αἰσθάνωμαι, ἔφη, ὅμως καὶ εὖ πάσχοντας ἔτι ἀδικεῖν πειρωμένους,
τούτους ὡς ἀνηκέστους πλεονέκτας ὄντας ἤδη καὶ τῆς χρήσεως
9 ἀποπαύω. οὓς δ' ἂν αὖ καταμάθω μὴ τῷ πλέον ἔχειν μόνον διὰ
τὴν δικαιοσύνην ἐπαιρομένους δικαίους εἶναι, ἀλλὰ καὶ τοῦ 30
ἐπαινεῖσθαι ἐπιθυμοῦντας ὑπ' ἐμοῦ, τούτοις ὥσπερ ἐλευθέροις ἤδη
χρῶμαι, οὐ μόνον πλουτίζων ἀλλὰ καὶ τιμῶν ὡς καλούς τε
10 κἀγαθούς. τούτῳ γάρ μοι δοκεῖ, ἔφη, ὦ Σώκρατες, διαφέρειν ἀνὴρ
φιλότιμος ἀνδρὸς φιλοκερδοῦς, τῷ ἐθέλειν ἐπαίνου καὶ τιμῆς ἕνεκα

6 γε Heindorf: τε codd.   12 καὶ om. Q   16 δικαιοσύνη(η)
... διδασκαλίας codd.: corr. Heindorf   18 νύκτωρ ἐγχειροῦντας Richards
coll. Dem. c. Timocr. § 113   20 ἔφη del. Schenkl: ἔφη καὶ τούτων K L Q R
προσφέρων del. Heindorf: προφέρων L   21 προφερόμενος D Hᵃ: προσφερόμενος
cet.: del. Hermann   26 ἐμμένουσι Cobet   30 τοῦ G s.v.: τῷ cet. (τὸ F)
33 τοῦτο Y G J O R Ven. 513   34 τῷ L: τοῦ cet.

Socrates, that favouritism is not beneficial, not even to himself.'

'Ischomachus,' I said, 'when he has become capable of ruling, so that XIV he can make them obedient, do you think he is a perfect foreman, or is there anything else that the man who has the qualities you mentioned needs to have?'

'Yes, by Zeus,' responded Ischomachus. 'He must keep his hands off his 2 masters' property and not steal. For if the man who handles the crops dares to abscond with them, so that there is not enough left for the work to create a profit, what benefit would result from running a farm under his care?'

'Then do you undertake to teach this kind of honesty too?', I asked. 3

'Certainly,' replied Ischomachus. 'However, I don't find that everyone is prepared to learn from my teaching at first. Nevertheless,' he continued, 4 'by applying some provisions from the laws of Draco and some from the laws of Solon, I try to put my slaves on the path of honesty. Because', he said, 'I believe these men enacted many of their laws in order to teach honesty such as this.

'For it is enacted that offenders should be punished for acts of theft, and 5 that anyone convicted of attempted theft should be imprisoned, and even killed if caught in the act. It is clear', he continued, 'that they enacted these laws because they wanted to make greed unprofitable for the unjust. By applying some of these laws,' he said, 'and by adding other enactments 6 from the laws of the kings of Persia, I attempt to make my slaves honest in their handling of property. For the former laws only contain penalties 7 for wrongdoers, but the laws of the kings not only penalize the dishonest, but also reward the honest. So, because they see that the honest become wealthier than the dishonest, many lovers of profit continue firmly to refrain from dishonesty. However, when I perceive that people attempt to act 8 dishonestly, despite good treatment, I refuse to have anything more to do with them, on the grounds that they are incorrigibly greedy. On the other 9 hand, if I learn of some who are induced to be honest not only because of the advantages they gain through being honest, but because of a desire to be praised by me, I treat them as if they were free men, not only do I make them wealthy, but I even honour them like gentlemen. For, Socrates,' 10 he said, 'I think an ambitious man differs from a greedy one in that, for the sake of praise and honour, he is willing to work hard and to run risks

καὶ πονεῖν ὅπου δεῖ καὶ κινδυνεύειν καὶ αἰσχρῶν κερδῶν ἀπέχεσθαι.

XV   Ἀλλὰ μέντοι ἐπειδάν γε ἐμποιήσῃς τινὶ τὸ βούλεσθαί σοι εἶναι
τἀγαθά, ἐμποιήσῃς δὲ τῷ αὐτῷ τούτῳ ⟨τὸ⟩ ἐπιμελεῖσθαι ὅπως
ταῦτά σοι ἐπιτελῆται, ἔτι δὲ πρὸς τούτοις ἐπιστήμην κτήσῃ αὐτῷ
ὡς ἂν ποιούμενα ἕκαστα τῶν ἔργων ὠφελιμώτερα γίγνοιτο, πρὸς 5
δὲ τούτοις ἄρχειν ἱκανὸν αὐτὸν ποιήσῃς, ἐπὶ δὲ τούτοις πᾶσιν
ἤδηταί σοι τὰ ἐκ τῆς γῆς ὡραῖα ἀποδεικνύων ὅτι πλεῖστα ὥσπερ
σὺ σαυτῷ, οὐκέτι ἐρήσομαι περὶ τούτου εἰ ἔτι τινὸς ὁ τοιοῦτος
προσδεῖται· πάνυ γάρ μοι δοκεῖ ἤδη πολλοῦ ἂν ἄξιος εἶναι
ἐπίτροπος ὢν τοιοῦτος. ἐκεῖνο μέντοι, ἔφην ἐγώ, ὦ Ἰσχόμαχε, μὴ 10
2 ἀπολίπῃς, ὃ ἡμῖν ἀργότατα ἐπιδεδράμηται τοῦ λόγου. Τὸ ποῖον;
ἔφη ὁ Ἰσχόμαχος. Ἔλεξας δήπου, ἔφην ἐγώ, ὅτι μέγιστον εἴη
μαθεῖν ὅπως δεῖ ἐξεργάζεσθαι ἕκαστα· εἰ δὲ μή, οὐδὲ τῆς
ἐπιμελείας ἔφησθα ὄφελος οὐδὲν γίγνεσθαι, εἰ μή τις ἐπίσταιτο ἃ
3 δεῖ καὶ ὡς δεῖ ποιεῖν. ἐνταῦθα δὴ εἶπεν ὁ Ἰσχόμαχος· Τὴν τέχνην 15
με ἤδη, ὦ Σώκρατες, κελεύεις αὐτὴν διδάσκειν τῆς γεωργίας;
Αὕτη γὰρ ἴσως, ἔφην ἐγώ, ἤδη ἐστὶν ἡ ποιοῦσα τοὺς μὲν
ἐπισταμένους αὐτὴν πλουσίους, τοὺς δὲ μὴ ἐπισταμένους πολλὰ
4 πονοῦντας ἀπόρως βιοτεύειν. Νῦν τοίνυν, ἔφη, ὦ Σώκρατες, καὶ
τὴν φιλανθρωπίαν ταύτης τῆς τέχνης ἀκούσῃ. τὸ γὰρ 20
ὠφελιμωτάτην οὖσαν καὶ ἡδίστην ἐργάζεσθαι καὶ καλλίστην καὶ
προσφιλεστάτην θεοῖς τε καὶ ἀνθρώποις, ἔτι πρὸς τούτοις καὶ
ῥάστην εἶναι μαθεῖν πῶς οὐχὶ γενναῖόν ἐστι; γενναῖα δὲ δήπου
καλοῦμεν καὶ τῶν ζῴων ὁπόσα καλὰ καὶ μεγάλα καὶ ὠφέλιμα ὄντα
5 πραέα ἐστὶ πρὸς τοὺς ἀνθρώπους. Ἀλλὰ ταῦτα μὲν ἐγώ, ἔφην, ὦ 25
Ἰσχόμαχε, ἱκανῶς δοκῶ καταμεμαθηκέναι ᾗ εἶπας, καθ᾿ ἃ δεῖ
διδάσκειν τὸν ἐπίτροπον· καὶ γὰρ ᾗ ἔφησθα εὔνουν σοι ποιεῖν αὐτὸν
6 μαθεῖν δοκῶ, καὶ ᾗ ἐπιμελῆ καὶ ἀρχικὸν καὶ δίκαιον. ὃ δὲ εἶπας
ὡς δεῖ μαθεῖν τὸν μέλλοντα ὀρθῶς γεωργίας ἐπιμελεῖσθαι καὶ ἃ
δεῖ ποιεῖν καὶ ὡς δεῖ καὶ ὁπότε ἕκαστα, ταῦτά μοι δοκοῦμεν, ἔφην 30
7 ἐγώ, ἀργότερόν πως ἐπιδεδραμηκέναι τῷ λόγῳ· ὥσπερ εἰ εἴποις
ὅτι δεῖ γράμματα ἐπίστασθαι τὸν μέλλοντα δυνήσεσθαι τὰ
ὑπαγορευόμενα γράφειν καὶ τὰ γεγραμμένα ἀναγιγνώσκειν. ταῦτα

3 τὸ add. Heindorf   4 ἐπιτελεῖται codd. plerique   κτήσῃ corruptum
videtur   7 ἤδηταί H: ἤ(ἤ)δη τέ cet.   10 ὤν] ὁ R Ven. 513: ὢν ὁ Q
11 τῷ λόγῳ Bock   14 εἰ μή ... ποιεῖν del. Cobet   15 §§ 3–4 post § 9
transp. Ernesti   17 ἴσως Stephanus: ὡς codd.: om. R Ven. 513   18 ante
πολλὰ add. καὶ Reisig   23 γενναῖα ... ἀνθρώπους post § 12 transp. Schneider: del.
Schenkl   25 fort. ταῦτα μέν, ἐγὼ ἔφην   29 ἐπιμελήσεσθαι H N
30 δοκοῦμεν Camerarius: δοκῶμεν vel δοκῶ μὲν codd.

when necessary and to abstain from dishonest gains.'

'But when you have instilled in someone the desire that you should XV
prosper, and you have also made him concerned that you should actually
do so, and, in addition, have provided him with knowledge about how
each job may be performed more profitably, and, further, have made him
capable of ruling, and over and above all this, he delights as much as you
would in showing you the greatest quantities of the fruits of the earth in
their season, then I shall no longer ask whether there is any other quality
that such a man lacks. I think such a man would be a very valuable
foreman. But, Ischomachus,' I said, 'please don't leave out the point we
have run over very superficially in our discussion.'

'Which one?', Ischomachus asked.   2

'You stated, I believe,' I said, 'that the most important lesson to learn is
how to perform each job, and that unless a man understands what should
be done and how to do it, no good will come of his concern.'

At this point Ischomachus said, 'Are you asking me now to teach the 3
occupation of farming, Socrates?'

'Yes,' I answered, 'for that, presumably, is precisely what makes the men
who understand it rich, but makes those who do not understand it live in
abject poverty, even though they work hard.'

'In that case, Socrates,' he said, 'I will tell you now about the friendliness 4
of this occupation towards mankind. For it is most beneficial and pleasant
to work at, and most lovely and most dear to gods and men, and, in
addition, it is very easy to learn. So, how could it fail to be noble? For
surely we call "noble" those living creatures which are lovely, large, and
beneficial, yet gentle to human beings.'

'But, Ischomachus,' I said, 'I think I have understood sufficiently the 5
drift of what you've been saying—that is, the principle of instructing a
foreman. I believe I understand your suggestions about making him loyal
to you, and making him be concerned, capable of ruling, and honest. But 6
as to your statement that the person who is going to be concerned about
farming successfully must learn how and when to do each job—these
matters,' I said, 'we seem to have discussed somewhat superficially: it is as 7
if you were to say that anyone who is going to be able to write from
dictation and to read what he has written must know the alphabet. If I

γὰρ ἐγὼ ἀκούσας, ὅτι μὲν δεῖ γράμματα ἐπίστασθαι ἠκηκόη ἄν,
τοῦτο δὲ εἰδὼς οὐδέν τι οἶμαι μᾶλλον ἂν ἐπισταίμην γράμματα.
8 οὕτω δὲ καὶ νῦν ὅτι μὲν δεῖ ἐπίστασθαι γεωργίαν τὸν μέλλοντα
ὀρθῶς ἐπιμελεῖσθαι αὐτῆς ῥᾳδίως πέπεισμαι, τοῦτο μέντοι εἰδὼς
9 οὐδέν τι μᾶλλον ἐπίσταμαι ὅπως δεῖ γεωργεῖν. ἀλλ᾿ εἴ μοι αὐτίκα 5
μάλα δόξειε γεωργεῖν, ὅμοιος ἄν μοι δοκῶ εἶναι τῷ περιιόντι ἰατρῷ
καὶ ἐπισκοποῦντι τοὺς κάμνοντας, εἰδότι δὲ οὐδὲν ὅ τι συμφέρει
τοῖς κάμνουσιν. ἵν᾿ οὖν μὴ τοιοῦτος ὦ, ἔφην ἐγώ, δίδασκέ με αὐτὰ
10 τὰ ἔργα τῆς γεωργίας. Ἀλλὰ μήν, ἔφη, ὦ Σώκρατες, οὐχ ὥσπερ
γε τὰς ἄλλας τέχνας κατατριβῆναι δεῖ μανθάνοντας πρὶν ἄξια τῆς 10
τροφῆς ἐργάζεσθαι τὸν διδασκόμενον, οὐχ οὕτω καὶ ἡ γεωργία
δύσκολός ἐστι μαθεῖν, ἀλλὰ τὰ μὲν ἰδὼν ἂν ἐργαζομένους, τὰ δὲ
ἀκούσας εὐθὺς ἂν ἐπίσταιο, ὥστε καὶ ἄλλον, εἰ βούλοιο, διδάσκειν.
οἴομαι δ᾿, ἔφη, πάνυ καὶ λεληθέναι πολλά σε αὐτὸν ἐπιστάμενον
11 αὐτῆς. καὶ γὰρ δὴ οἱ μὲν ἄλλοι τεχνῖται ἀποκρύπτονταί πως τὰ 15
ἐπικαιριώτατα ἧς ἕκαστος ἔχει τέχνης, τῶν δὲ γεωργῶν ὁ κάλλιστα
μὲν φυτεύων μάλιστ᾿ ἂν ἥδοιτο, εἴ τις αὐτὸν θεῷτο, ὁ κάλλιστα
δὲ σπείρων ὡσαύτως· ὅ τι δὲ ἔροιο τῶν καλῶς πεποιημένων, οὐδὲν
12 ὅ τι ἄν σε ἀποκρύψαιτο ὅπως ἐποίησεν. οὕτω καὶ τὰ ἤθη, ὦ
Σώκρατες, ἔφη, γενναιοτάτους τοὺς αὐτῇ συνόντας ἡ γεωργία 20
13 ἔοικε παρέχεσθαι. Ἀλλὰ τὸ μὲν προοίμιον, ἔφην ἐγώ, καλὸν καὶ
οὐχ οἷον ἀκούσαντα ἀποτρέπεσθαι τοῦ ἐρωτήματος· σὺ δέ, ὅτι
εὐπετές ἐστι μαθεῖν, διὰ τοῦτο πολύ μοι μᾶλλον διέξιθι αὐτήν. οὐ
γὰρ σοὶ αἰσχρὸν τὰ ῥᾴδια διδάσκειν ἐστίν, ἀλλ᾿ ἐμοὶ πολὺ αἴσχιον
μὴ ἐπίστασθαι ἄλλως τε καὶ εἰ χρήσιμα ὄντα τυγχάνει. 25

XVI Πρῶτον μὲν τοίνυν, ἔφη, ὦ Σώκρατες, τοῦτο ἐπιδεῖξαι βούλομαί
σοι ὡς οὐ χαλεπόν ἐστιν ὃ λέγουσι ποικιλώτατον τῆς γεωργίας
εἶναι οἱ λόγῳ μὲν ἀκριβέστατα αὐτὴν διεξιόντες, ἥκιστα δὲ
2 ἐργαζόμενοι. φασὶ γὰρ τὸν μέλλοντα ὀρθῶς γεωργήσειν τὴν φύσιν
χρῆναι πρῶτον τῆς γῆς εἰδέναι. Ὀρθῶς γε, ἔφην ἐγώ, ταῦτα 30
λέγοντες. ὁ γὰρ μὴ εἰδὼς ὅ τι δύναται ἡ γῆ φέρειν, οὐδ᾿ ὅ τι
3 σπείρειν οἶμαι οὐδ᾿ ὅ τι φυτεύειν δεῖ εἰδείη ἄν. Οὐκοῦν, ἔφη ὁ
Ἰσχόμαχος, καὶ ἀλλοτρίας γῆς τοῦτο ἔστι γνῶναι, ὅ τι τε δύναται
φέρειν καὶ ὅ τι μὴ δύναται, ὁρῶντα τοὺς καρποὺς καὶ τὰ δένδρα.
ἐπειδὰν μέντοι γνῶ τις, οὐκέτι συμφέρει θεομαχεῖν. οὐ γὰρ ἄν, 35
ὅτου δέοιτο αὐτός, τοῦτο σπείρων καὶ φυτεύων μᾶλλον ἂν ἔχοι τὰ

---

1 ἠκηκόην C₁: ἠκηκόειν cet.   6 εἶναι L: om. cet.   8 ἵν᾿ Q: ἢν cet.
11 τὸν διδασκόμενον del. Bock   14 ἔοικεν H G N   πολλά σε αὐτὸν Jacob:
πολλὰ σεαυτὸν codd.   23 εὐπετές Wyttenbach: εὐπρεπές codd.

had been told this, I should, it is true, have heard that I must know the alphabet, but when I had understood that, I do not think I should know the alphabet any better. So too, in the present case I am readily convinced 8 that a man must understand farming if he is going to be concerned about farming successfully, but although I understand that, I don't know any more about farming. If I were to decide to become a farmer immediately, 9 I think I should be like a physician who went around examining patients without knowing what is good for the patients. So please teach me the actual jobs involved in farming so that I shall not be like him,' I said.

'Well, Socrates,' he replied, 'I can assure you that it is not necessary, as 10 it is in the case of other occupations, for people to wear themselves out studying before the student can earn his keep by working, for farming is not so troublesome to learn. By watching the workers perform some of the chores and by hearing about others, you can immediately know what to do, so that you could teach someone else if you wanted to. And I think,' he said, 'you know a great deal without realizing it. For other skilled 11 workers tend to conceal the most vital pieces of information about their occupation, but among farmers, the one who is best at planting would be particularly pleased if someone were watching him; so too would the one who is best at sowing. If you were to ask him about any of the things he does well, he would not conceal from you the way in which he does them. So, Socrates,' he stated, 'very noble are the characters of those who engage 12 in farming.'

'A fine introduction, and not such as to discourage the listener from the 13 inquiry,' I said. 'But since farming is easy to learn, that is all the more reason for you to give me a full account of it. For it is no disgrace for you to teach what is easy, but it is far more disgraceful for me to fail to understand it, especially if it happens to be useful.'

'Well, to begin with, Socrates,' he said, 'there is one aspect of farming XVI that authors who give a very accurate theoretical account of it, but who lack practical experience, say is extremely complicated. I want to show you that it is not really difficult at all. For they assert that the man who is 2 going to be a successful farmer must first understand the nature of the soil.'

'Yes, and they are quite right, too,' I replied, 'for anyone who does not know what the soil is capable of producing, I imagine, would not know what he ought to plant or to sow.'

Ischomachus said, 'Yes, but you can learn simply by looking at the crops 3 and the trees on another man's soil what it can produce and what it can't. When a man has learnt this, there is no point in persisting in struggling against the decrees of the gods; he is not likely to obtain provisions by sowing and planting what he wants, rather than what the soil prefers to

4 ἐπιτήδεια ἢ ὅ τι ἡ γῆ ἥδοιτο φύουσα καὶ τρέφουσα. ἂν δ᾿ ἄρα δι᾿
ἀργίαν τῶν ἐχόντων αὐτὴ μὴ ἔχῃ τὴν ἑαυτῆς δύναμιν ἐπιδεικνύναι,
ἔστι καὶ παρὰ γείτονος τόπου πολλάκις ἀληθέστερα περὶ αὐτῆς
5 γνῶναι ἢ παρὰ γείτονος ἀνθρώπου πυθέσθαι. καὶ χερσεύουσα δὲ
ὅμως ἐπιδείκνυσι τὴν αὐτῆς φύσιν· ἡ γὰρ τὰ ἄγρια καλὰ φύουσα 5
δύναται θεραπευομένη καὶ τὰ ἥμερα καλὰ ἐκφέρειν. φύσιν μὲν δὴ
γῆς οὕτως καὶ οἱ μὴ πάνυ ἔμπειροι γεωργίας ὅμως δύνανται
6 διαγιγνώσκειν. Ἀλλὰ τοῦτο μέν, ἔφην ἐγώ, ὦ Ἰσχόμαχε, ἱκανῶς
ἤδη μοι δοκῶ ἀποτεθαρρηκέναι, ὡς οὐ δεῖ φοβούμενον μὴ οὐ γνῶ
7 τῆς γῆς φύσιν ἀπέχεσθαι γεωργίας. καὶ γὰρ δή, ἔφην, ἀνεμνήσθην 10
τὸ τῶν ἁλιέων, ὅτι θαλαττουργοὶ ὄντες καὶ οὔτε καταστήσαντες
ἐπὶ θέαν οὔθ᾿ ἥσυχοι βαδίζοντες, ἀλλὰ παρατρέχοντες ἅμα τοὺς
ἀγρούς, ὅταν ὁρῶσι τοὺς καρποὺς ἐν τῇ γῇ, ὅμως οὐκ ὀκνοῦσιν
ἀποφαίνεσθαι περὶ τῆς γῆς ὁποία τε ἀγαθή ἐστι καὶ ὁποία κακή,
ἀλλὰ τὴν μὲν ψέγουσι, τὴν δ᾿ ἐπαινοῦσι. καὶ πάνυ τοίνυν τοῖς 15
ἐμπείροις γεωργίας ὁρῶ αὐτοὺς τὰ πλεῖστα κατὰ ταὐτὰ
8 ἀποφαινομένους περὶ τῆς ἀγαθῆς γῆς. Πόθεν οὖν βούλῃ, ἔφη, ὦ
Σώκρατες, ἄρξωμαί σε τῆς γεωργίας ὑπομιμνήσκειν; οἶδα γὰρ ὅτι
9 ἐπισταμένῳ σοι πάνυ πολλὰ φράσω ὡς δεῖ γεωργεῖν. Ἐκεῖνό μοι
δοκῶ, ἔφην ἐγώ, ὦ Ἰσχόμαχε, πρῶτον ἂν ἡδέως μανθάνειν 20
(φιλοσόφου γὰρ μάλιστά ἐστιν ἀνδρός) ὅπως ἂν ἐγώ, εἰ βουλοίμην,
γῆν ἐργαζόμενος πλείστας κριθὰς καὶ πλείστους πυροὺς
10 λαμβάνοιμι. Οὐκοῦν τοῦτο μὲν οἶσθα, ὅτι τῷ σπόρῳ νεὸν δεῖ
11 ὑπεργάζεσθαι; Οἶδα γάρ, ἔφην ἐγώ. Εἰ οὖν ἀρχοίμεθα, ἔφη, ἀροῦν
τὴν γῆν χειμῶνος; Ἀλλὰ πηλὸς ἂν εἴη, ἐγὼ ἔφην. Ἀλλὰ τοῦ θέρους 25
σοι δοκεῖ; Σκληρά, ἔφην ἐγώ, ἡ γῆ ἔσται κινεῖν τῷ ζεύγει.
12 Κινδυνεύει ἔαρος, ἔφη, εἶναι τούτου τοῦ ἔργου ἀρκτέον. Εἰκὸς γάρ,
ἔφην ἐγώ, ἐστι μάλιστα χεῖσθαι τὴν γῆν τηνικαῦτα κινουμένην.
Καὶ τὴν πόαν γε ἀναστρεφομένην, ἔφη, ὦ Σώκρατες, τηνικαῦτα
κόπρον μὲν τῇ γῇ ἤδη παρέχειν, καρπὸν δ᾿ οὔπω καταβαλεῖν ὥστε 30
13 φύεσθαι. οἶμαι γὰρ δὴ καὶ τοῦτό σ᾿ ἔτι γιγνώσκειν, ὅτι εἰ μέλλει
ἀγαθὴ ἡ νεὸς ἔσεσθαι, ὕλης τε καθαρὰν αὐτὴν εἶναι δεῖ καὶ ὀπτὴν
ὅτι μάλιστα πρὸς τὸν ἥλιον. Πάνυ γε, ἔφην ἐγώ, καὶ ταῦτα οὕτως

2 αὐτὴ Hartman   11 τὸ τοὺς ἁλιέας D al. G J O Hᵃ, unde τοὺς ἁλιέας
Cobet cum Vill. marg.   12 ἡσυχῇ K L   14 τῆς γῆς] αὐτῆς N in ras. R
Ven. 513   16 κατὰ ταῦτα J K L: κατὰ ταῦτα vel κατ᾿ αὐτὰ cet.   17 ἔφη
om. K L Q R *Ven.* 513: σώκρατες ἔφη F H   18 ἄρξωμαί F A (ω s.v.): ἄρξομαί cet.
27 ante ἔαρος add. ἄρα Schneider   30 καταβαλεῖ Richards   31 σ᾿ ἔτι
Haupt: ἔστι codd.   32 δεῖ post εἶναι add. Q: post τε Stephanus: om. cet.
33 τοῦ ἡλίου Hertlein

184

produce and nurture. But if, because of the laziness of its owners, the soil 4
is unable to display its distinctive capability, it is often possible to learn
more about it from the neighbouring farm than from the neighbouring
farmer. Even when the earth lies waste, it still shows its distinctive nature. 5
The soil that produces excellent wild plants, can also, when properly
tended, bear excellent cultivated crops. In that way, even people without
much experience in farming are nevertheless able to recognize the nature
of the soil.'

'Ischomachus,' I said, 'I feel so confident now about this point that there 6
is no need for me to keep away from farming through fear of not understanding the nature of the soil. For,' I went on, 'I am reminded of what fishermen 7
do. Their business is on the sea, and they don't stop to take a look or slow
down; nevertheless, when they see crops on the soil as they pass rapidly
alongside farms, they do not hesitate to express an opinion about which
parts of the soil are good and which are poor, disparaging this part and
praising that part. And I notice that generally they hold precisely the same
opinion about good soil as do those who are experienced in farming.'

'Well then, Socrates,' he asked, 'where would you like me to begin to 8
refresh your memory about farming? For I know that when I am telling
you how farming must be done, I shall be speaking to someone who already
knows a great deal about the subject.'

'Ischomachus,' I said, 'first I think I should like to learn (for it is very 9
characteristic of a philosopher to want to learn) how I should cultivate soil
if I want to get the largest yield of barley and wheat.'

'Well, I suppose you know that you must plough up fallow ground in 10
preparation for sowing?'

'Yes, I know,' I answered.   11

'Then suppose we begin to plough the soil in winter?', he asked.

'But it would be muddy then,' I replied.

'Do you think we should start in the summer?'

'No, the ground will be hard for the oxen to plough,' I answered.

'It looks as if we should begin the job in springtime, then,' he said.   12

'Yes,' I said, 'for the soil is most likely to crumble if it is turned at
that season.'

'And when the grass is ploughed up at that season, Socrates,' he continued, 'it then serves as fertilizer for the soil, but because it has not yet
scattered its seeds, it will not grow again. For I think you know this too, 13
that if the fallow is going to be good, it must be clear of weeds and baked
as much as possible in the sun.'

'Certainly,' I said, 'I realize it must be in that condition.'

14 ἡγοῦμαι χρῆναι ἔχειν. Ταῦτ' οὖν, ἔφη, σὺ ἄλλως πως νομίζεις μᾶλλον ἂν γίγνεσθαι ἢ εἰ ἐν τῷ θέρει ὅτι πλειστάκις μεταβάλοι τις τὴν γῆν; Οἶδα μὲν οὖν, ἔφην, ἀκριβῶς ὅτι οὐδαμῶς ἂν μᾶλλον ἡ μὲν ὕλη ἐπιπολάζοι καὶ αὐαίνοιτο ὑπὸ τοῦ καύματος, ἡ δὲ γῆ ὀπτῷτο ὑπὸ τοῦ ἡλίου, ἢ εἴ τις αὐτὴν ἐν μέσῳ τῷ θέρει καὶ ἐν 5
15 μέσῃ τῇ ἡμέρᾳ κινοίη τῷ ζεύγει. Εἰ δὲ ἄνθρωποι σκάπτοντες τὴν νεὸν ποιοῖεν, ἔφη, οὐκ εὔδηλον ὅτι καὶ τούτους δίχα δεῖ ποιεῖν τὴν γῆν καὶ τὴν ὕλην; Καὶ τὴν μέν γε ὕλην, ἔφην ἐγώ, καταβάλλειν, ὡς αὐαίνηται, ἐπιπολῆς, τὴν δὲ γῆν στρέφειν, ὡς ἡ ὠμὴ αὐτῆς ὀπτᾶται. 10

XVII Περὶ μὲν τῆς νεοῦ ὁρᾷς, ἔφη, ὦ Σώκρατες, ὡς ἀμφοτέροις ἡμῖν ταὐτὰ δοκεῖ. Δοκεῖ γὰρ οὖν, ἔφην ἐγώ. Περί γε μέντοι τοῦ σπόρου ὥρας ἄλλο τι, ἔφη, ὦ Σώκρατες, γιγνώσκεις ἢ τὴν ὥραν σπείρειν ἧς πάντες μὲν οἱ πρόσθεν ἄνθρωποι πεῖραν λαβόντες, πάντες δὲ οἱ
2 νῦν λαμβάνοντες, ἐγνώκασι κρατίστην εἶναι; ἐπειδὰν γὰρ ὁ 15 μετοπωρινὸς χρόνος ἔλθῃ, πάντες που οἱ ἄνθρωποι πρὸς τὸν θεὸν ἀποβλέπουσιν, ὁπότε βρέξας τὴν γῆν ἀφήσει αὐτοὺς σπείρειν. Ἐγνώκασι δή γ', ἔφην ἐγώ, ὦ Ἰσχόμαχε, καὶ τὸ μὴ ἐν ξηρᾷ σπείρειν ἑκόντες εἶναι πάντες ἄνθρωποι, δῆλον ὅτι πολλαῖς ζημίαις
3 παλαίσαντες οἱ πρὶν κελευσθῆναι ὑπὸ τοῦ θεοῦ σπείροντες. Οὐκοῦν 20 ταῦτα μέν, ἔφη ὁ Ἰσχόμαχος, ὁμογνωμονοῦμεν πάντες οἱ ἄνθρωποι. Ἃ γὰρ ὁ θεὸς διδάσκει, ἔφην ἐγώ, οὕτω γίγνεται ὁμονοεῖν· οἷον ἅμα πᾶσι δοκεῖ βέλτιον εἶναι ἐν τῷ χειμῶνι παχέα ἱμάτια φορεῖν, ἂν δύνωνται, καὶ πῦρ κάειν ἅμα πᾶσι δοκεῖ, ἂν ξύλα
4 ἔχωσιν. Ἀλλ' ἐν τῷδε, ἔφη ὁ Ἰσχόμαχος, πολλοὶ ἤδη διαφέρονται, 25 ὦ Σώκρατες, περὶ τοῦ σπόρου, πότερον ὁ πρώιμος κράτιστος ἢ ὁ μέσος ἢ ὁ ὀψιμώτατος. Καὶ ὁ θεός, ἔφην ἐγώ, οὐ τεταγμένως τὸ ἔτος ἄγει, ἀλλὰ τὸ μὲν τῷ πρωίμῳ κάλλιστα, τὸ δὲ τῷ μέσῳ, τὸ
5 δὲ τῷ ὀψιμωτάτῳ. Σὺ οὖν, ἔφη, ὦ Σώκρατες, πότερον ἡγῇ κρεῖττον εἶναι ἑνὶ τούτων τῶν σπόρων χρῆσθαι ἐκλεξάμενον, ἐάν 30 τε πολὺ ἐάν τε ὀλίγον σπέρμα σπείρῃ τις, ἢ ἀρξάμενον ἀπὸ τοῦ πρωιμωτάτου μέχρι τοῦ ὀψιμωτάτου σπείρειν; καὶ ἐγὼ εἶπον·
6 Ἐμοὶ μέν, ὦ Ἰσχόμαχε, δοκεῖ κράτιστον εἶναι παντὸς μετέχειν τοῦ σπόρου. πολὺ γὰρ νομίζω κρεῖττον εἶναι ἀεὶ ἀρκοῦντα σῖτον λαμβάνειν ἢ ποτὲ μὲν πάνυ πολὺν ποτὲ δὲ μηδ' ἱκανόν. Καὶ τοῦτο 35

7 τούτους ὅτι καὶ Ηᵃ   10 ὀπτᾶται Dind.: ὀπτῷτο vel ὀπτοῖτο codd.
12 οὖν L Q et O s.v.: αὖ cet.: om. G   13 ὥρας Castalio: ὁρᾷ(ᾷ)ς codd.
18 δή Reisig: δέ codd. (om. N)   20 σπείραντες G L   27 καί] ἀλλ' Weiske
34 τοῦ del. Dind.

'Do you think, then, that there is any better way to bring this about 14 than by turning the soil as often as possible in the summer?', he asked.

'I know for certain', I replied, 'that there is no better way to make the weeds lie on the surface and wither in the heat, and to bake the soil in the sun, than by ploughing in the middle of the day in mid-summer.'

'If the workers prepare the fallow by digging,' he asked, 'isn't it obvious 15 that they must also separate the weeds from the soil?'

'Yes,' I answered, 'and they must throw the weeds on the surface, too, so that they wither, and they must turn up the soil so that the underside of it may be baked.'

'You see, Socrates,' he remarked, 'how we are both in agreement about the fallow.'

'Yes, we certainly seem to agree,' I said.

'Concerning the proper season of sowing, Socrates,' he asked, 'do you XVII believe that it's necessary to sow in the season that all previous generations and all contemporary farmers too have determined is the best after experimenting? When autumn comes, all men, I suppose, look to the god to see 2 when he will send the rain upon the earth that will allow them to sow.'

'Well, certainly, Ischomachus,' I replied, 'all men have recognized that they should not sow in dry soil if they can help it, presumably because those who sowed before being commanded by the god had to contend with many losses.'

'So everyone agrees about this,' said Ischomachus. 3

'Yes, for in this way it turns out that all men think alike about what the divinity teaches,' I said. 'For example, all think it is better to wear thick clothes in winter, if they can, and all prefer to burn a fire if they have wood.'

'Yet, Socrates,' Ischomachus continued, 'many still disagree about one 4 point concerning the sowing: whether the beginning or middle or end of the rainy season is best.'

'The divinity', I commented, 'does not bring round each year regularly according to a fixed pattern, but he brings on one year in a manner in which early sowing is best, another in which mid-season, and another in which the end of the season.'

He asked, 'What about you, Socrates? Do you think it's better for a man 5 to select and use one of these sowing-times, whether he sows a lot of seed or just a little, or to start from the beginning of the season and continue through to the end?'

I replied, 'Ischomachus, I think it is best to share the sowing out over 6 the entire sowing season. For I believe it's much better to have enough grain all the time, rather than an abundance at one time and not enough at another.'

'On that point, Socrates,' he said, 'you, the pupil, agree with me, the

τοίνυν σύγε, ἔφη, ὦ Σώκρατες, ὁμογνωμονεῖς ἐμοὶ ὁ μανθάνων τῷ
διδάσκοντι, καὶ ταῦτα πρόσθεν ἐμοῦ τὴν γνώμην ἀποφαινόμενος.
7 Τί γάρ, ἔφην ἐγώ, ἐν τῷ ῥίπτειν τὸ σπέρμα ποικίλη τέχνη ἔνεστι;
Πάντως, ἔφη, ὦ Σώκρατες, ἐπισκεψώμεθα καὶ τοῦτο. ὅτι μὲν γὰρ
ἐκ τῆς χειρὸς δεῖ ῥίπτεσθαι τὸ σπέρμα καὶ σύ που οἶσθα, ἔφη. Καὶ 5
γὰρ ἑώρακα, ἔφην ἐγώ. 'Ρίπτειν δέ γε, ἔφη, οἱ μὲν ὁμαλῶς
δύνανται, οἱ δ' οὔ. Οὐκοῦν τοῦτο μέν, ἔφην ἐγώ, ἤδη μελέτης
δεῖται ὥσπερ τοῖς κιθαρισταῖς ἡ χείρ, ὅπως δύνηται ὑπηρετεῖν τῇ
8 γνώμῃ. Πάνυ μὲν οὖν, ἔφη· ἂν δέ γε ᾖ, ἔφη, ἡ γῆ ἡ μὲν λεπτοτέρα,
ἡ δὲ παχυτέρα; Τί τοῦτο, ἐγὼ ἔφην, λέγεις; ἆρά γε τὴν μὲν 10
λεπτοτέραν ὅπερ ἀσθενεστέραν, τὴν δὲ παχυτέραν ὅπερ
ἰσχυροτέραν; Τοῦτ', ἔφη, λέγω, καὶ ἐρωτῶ γέ σε πότερον ἴσον ἂν
9 ἑκατέρᾳ τῇ γῇ σπέρμα διδοίης ἢ ποτέρᾳ ἂν πλέον. Τῷ μὲν οἴνῳ,
ἔφην, ἔγωγε νομίζω τῷ ἰσχυροτέρῳ πλέον ἐπιχεῖν ὕδωρ, καὶ
ἀνθρώπῳ τῷ ἰσχυροτέρῳ πλέον βάρος, ἐὰν δέῃ τι φέρειν, 15
ἐπιτιθέναι, κἂν δέῃ τρέφεσθαί τινας, τοῖς δυνατωτέροις τρέφειν ἂν
τοὺς πλείους προστάξαιμι. εἰ δὲ ἡ ἀσθενὴς γῆ ἰσχυροτέρα, ἔφην
ἐγώ, γίγνεται, ἄν τις πλείονα καρπὸν αὐτῇ ἐμβάλῃ, ὥσπερ τὰ
10 ὑποζύγια, τοῦτο σύ με δίδασκε. Καὶ ὁ Ἰσχόμαχος γελάσας εἶπεν·
Ἀλλὰ παίζεις μὲν σύγε, ἔφη, ὦ Σώκρατες. εὖ γε μέντοι, ἔφη, ἴσθι, 20
ἂν μὲν ἐμβαλὼν τὸ σπέρμα τῇ γῇ ἔπειτα ἐν ᾧ πολλὴν ἔχει τροφὴν
ἡ γῆ ἀπὸ τοῦ οὐρανοῦ χλόης γενομένης ἀπὸ τοῦ σπέρματος
καταστρέψῃς αὐτὸ πάλιν, τοῦτο γίγνεται σῖτος τῇ γῇ, καὶ ὥσπερ
ὑπὸ κόπρου ἰσχὺς αὐτῇ ἐγγίγνεται· ἂν μέντοι ἐκτρέφειν ἐᾷς τὴν
γῆν διὰ τέλους τὸ σπέρμα εἰς καρπόν, χαλεπὸν τῇ ἀσθενεῖ γῇ ἐς 25
τέλος πολὺν καρπὸν ἐκφέρειν. καὶ συὶ δὲ ἀσθενεῖ χαλεπὸν πολλοὺς
11 ἁδροὺς χοίρους ἐκτρέφειν. Λέγεις σύ, ἔφην ἐγώ, ὦ Ἰσχόμαχε, τῇ
ἀσθενεστέρᾳ γῇ μεῖον δεῖν τὸ σπέρμα ἐμβαλεῖν; Ναὶ μὰ Δί', ἔφη,
ὦ Σώκρατες, καὶ σύ γε συνομολογεῖς, λέγων ὅτι νομίζεις τοῖς
12 ἀσθενεστέροις πᾶσι μείω προστάττειν πράγματα. Τοὺς δὲ δὴ 30
σκαλέας, ἔφην ἐγώ, ὦ Ἰσχόμαχε, τίνος ἕνεκα ἐμβάλλετε τῷ σίτῳ;
Οἶσθα δήπου, ἔφη, ὅτι ἐν τῷ χειμῶνι πολλὰ ὕδατα γίγνεται. Τί
γὰρ οὔ; ἔφην ἐγώ. Οὐκοῦν θῶμεν τοῦ σίτου καὶ κατακρυφθῆναί
τινα ὑπ' αὐτῶν ἰλύος ἐπιχυθείσης καὶ ψιλωθῆναί τινας ῥίζας ὑπὸ

3 ῥιπτεῖν D al. O Q R Ven. 513   6 ῥιπτεῖν H G N C   19 εἶπεν] ἔφη
F (omisso alt. ἔφη) K L   25 γῇ] γε Jacob: τῇ γῇ τῇ ἀσθενεῖ Hª   εἰς G N D
C   28 δεῖν Ven. 511₂: δεῖ Cet. (δὴ N)   30 προστάττειν H al. Q R Ven.
513 A in marg.: προστατεῖν cet. πράγματα] προστάγματα Markland

teacher, and, moreover, you stated your opinion before I did.'

'Well, then,' I asked, 'is a complicated skill involved in scattering the 7 seed?'

'We certainly ought to examine that as well, Socrates,' he answered. 'Even you, I suppose,' he said, 'know that the seed must be scattered from the hand?'

'Yes, I've seen it,' I replied.

'And some people can scatter it evenly, and others can't.'

'Then doesn't this need practice just as lyre-players need practice with their hand, so that it will carry out their intentions?', I asked.

'Certainly, but suppose part of the soil is relatively light and part heavier?' 8

'What do you mean by that?' I asked. 'By "relatively light" do you mean "rather poor", and by "heavier" do you mean "more fertile"?'

'Yes, I do,' he answered. 'And I'm asking you whether you should give the same amount of seed to both, or to which of them you would give more?'

I replied, 'I believe that one should add more water to a stronger wine, 9 and put a heavier burden on a stronger man, if something has to be carried. And if people have to be fed, I should instruct the richest men to feed the greatest number. But you must teach me', I said, 'whether weak soil becomes stronger when you put more produce in it just as beasts of burden do.'

Ischomachus laughed and said, 'You're joking, Socrates. But make sure', 10 he went on, 'you understand that after you have scattered the seed on the soil, that you plough it in again as soon as the first green shoot has sprouted from the seed, while the earth is receiving abundant nourishment from the sky. This serves as food for the soil and it gains strength from it as it would from manure. Otherwise if you allow the soil to complete its process of nourishing the seed until it matures, it is difficult for weak soil to produce a large crop in the end. Similarly, it is difficult for a weak sow to rear a big litter of strong pigs.'

'Do you mean, Ischomachus,' I asked, 'that a smaller amount of seed 11 should be scattered into weaker soil?'

'Certainly, Socrates,' he replied, 'and you agree, because you were saying just now that you think less work should be assigned to the weaker.'

'What about the men who do the hoeing, Ischomachus?', I asked. 'Why 12 do you put them to work on the grain?'

'I'm sure you know,' he replied, 'that it rains heavily in winter.'

'Of course,' I answered.

'Then let's suppose that some part of the grain is covered by the rain and smothered by mud and that some of the roots are uncovered by a

ρεύματος. καὶ ὕλη δὲ πολλάκις ὑπὸ τῶν ὑδάτων δήπου συνεξορμᾷ
τῷ σίτῳ καὶ παρέχει πνιγμὸν αὐτῷ. Πάντα, ἔφην ἐγώ, εἰκὸς ταῦτα
13 γίγνεσθαι. Οὐκοῦν δοκεῖ σοι, ἔφη, ἐνταῦθα ἤδη ἐπικουρίας τινὸς
δεῖσθαι ὁ σῖτος; Πάνυ μὲν οὖν, ἔφην ἐγώ. Τῷ οὖν κατιλυθέντι
τί ἂν ποιοῦντες δοκοῦσιν ἄν σοι ἐπικουρῆσαι; Ἐπικουφίσαντες, 5
ἔφην ἐγώ, τὴν γῆν. Τί δέ, ἔφη, τῷ ἐψιλωμένῳ τὰς ῥίζας;
14 Ἀντιπροσαμησάμενοι τὴν γῆν ἄν, ἔφην ἐγώ. Τί γάρ, ἔφη, ἂν ὕλη
πνίγῃ συνεξορμῶσα τῷ σίτῳ καὶ διαρπάζουσα τοῦ σίτου τὴν
τροφὴν ὥσπερ οἱ κηφῆνες διαρπάζουσιν ἄχρηστοι ὄντες τῶν
μελιττῶν ἃ ἂν ἐκεῖναι ἐργασάμεναι τροφὴν καταθῶνται; 10
15 Ἐκκόπτειν ἂν νὴ Δία [τὴν τροφὴν] δέοι τὴν ὕλην, ἔφην ἐγώ,
ὥσπερ τοὺς κηφῆνας ἐκ τῶν σμηνῶν ἀφαιρεῖν. Οὐκοῦν, ἔφη,
εἰκότως σοι δοκοῦμεν ἐμβαλεῖν τοὺς σκαλέας; Πάνυ γε. ἀτὰρ
ἐνθυμοῦμαι, ἔφην ἐγώ, ὦ Ἰσχόμαχε, οἷόν ἐστι τὸ εὖ τὰς εἰκόνας
ἐπάγεσθαι. πάνυ γὰρ σύ με ἐξώργισας πρὸς τὴν ὕλην τοὺς κηφῆνας 15
εἰπών, πολὺ μᾶλλον ἢ ὅτε περὶ αὐτῆς τῆς ὕλης ἔλεγες.

XVIII Ἀτὰρ οὖν, ἔφην ἐγώ, ἐκ τούτου ἄρα θερίζειν εἰκός. δίδασκε οὖν
εἴ τι ἔχεις με καὶ εἰς τοῦτο. Ἂν μή γε φανῇς, ἔφη, καὶ εἰς τοῦτο
ταὐτὰ ἐμοὶ ἐπιστάμενος. ὅτι μὲν οὖν τέμνειν τὸν σῖτον δεῖ οἶσθα.
Τί δ᾽ οὐ μέλλω; ἔφην ἐγώ. Πότερ᾽ ⟨ἂν⟩ οὖν τέμνοις, ἔφη, στὰς 20
ἔνθα πνεῖ ἄνεμος ἢ ἀντίος; Οὐκ ἀντίος, ἔφην, ἔγωγε· χαλεπὸν γὰρ
οἶμαι καὶ τοῖς ὄμμασι καὶ ταῖς χερσὶ γίγνεται ἀντίον ἀχύρων καὶ
2 ἀθέρων θερίζειν. Καὶ ἀκροτομοίης δ᾽ ἄν, ἔφη, ἢ παρὰ γῆν τέμνοις;
Ἂν μὲν βραχὺς ᾖ ὁ κάλαμος τοῦ σίτου, ἔγωγ᾽, ἔφην, κάτωθεν ἂν
τέμνοιμι, ἵνα ἱκανὰ τὰ ἄχυρα μᾶλλον γίγνηται· ἐὰν δὲ ὑψηλὸς ᾖ, 25
νομίζω ὀρθῶς ἂν ποιεῖν μεσοτομῶν, ἵνα μήτε οἱ ἁλῶντες μοχθῶσι
περιττὸν πόνον μήτε οἱ λικμῶντες ὧν οὐδὲν προσδέονται. τὸ δὲ ἐν
τῇ γῇ λειφθὲν ἡγοῦμαι καὶ κατακαυθὲν συνωφελεῖν ἂν τὴν γῆν καὶ
3 εἰς κόπρον ἐμβληθὲν τὴν κόπρον συμπληθύνειν. Ὁρᾷς, ἔφη, ὦ
Σώκρατες, ὡς ἁλίσκει ἐπ᾽ αὐτοφώρῳ καὶ περὶ θερισμοῦ εἰδὼς 30
ἅπερ ἐγώ; Κινδυνεύω, ἔφην ἐγώ, καὶ βούλομαί γε σκέψασθαι εἰ
καὶ ἁλοᾶν ἐπίσταμαι. Οὐκοῦν, ἔφη, τοῦτο μὲν οἶσθα, ὅτι ὑποζυγίῳ
4 ἁλῶσι τὸν σῖτον. Τί δ᾽ οὐκ, ἔφην ἐγώ, οἶδα; καὶ ὑποζύγιά γε
καλούμενα πάντα ὁμοίως, βοῦς, ἡμιόνους, ἵππους. Οὐκοῦν, ἔφη,
ταῦτα μὲν ἡγῇ τοσοῦτον μόνον εἰδέναι, πατεῖν τὸν σῖτον 35

---

1 τοῦ ῥεύματος D   5 δοκοῦμεν Jacob   11 τὴν τροφὴν de. Victorius
19 δεῖ Q: ἀεὶ cet.   20 πότερ᾽ ἂν Reisig: πότερα codd.   τέμνεις H al. Q R O
21 ἔνθεν Jacob   27 τὸ δὲ Weiske: τότε codd.   32 ὑποζυγίῳ H N:
ὑποζύγια cet.   33 γε Stephanus: τε codd.   35 τοσοῦτον H Q: τοσοῦτο cet.

stream of water. Then, because of flood-water weeds often spring up among the grain and cause it to be choked.'

'All these things are likely to happen,' I agreed.

'Don't you think that in such circumstances the grain needs some help?', 13 he asked.

'I certainly do,' I answered.

'What do you think people do to help the part that has been deluged with mud?'

'They remove the earth,' I answered.

'And how can they assist the part that has had its roots exposed?', he asked.

'By heaping up new earth on it,' I answered. 14

'What if weeds spring up with the grain and choke it by robbing it of its nourishment, in the way that useless drones rob the bees of the nourishment that they have worked to store up?'

'By Zeus,' I said, 'I suppose we should cut the weeds, just as we must remove the drones from the hives.'

'Then isn't it reasonable for us to send in men to hoe the soil?', he asked. 15

'Yes, certainly. But I am thinking, Ischomachus,' I said, 'what a splendid thing it is to introduce apt comparisons. You made me feel much angrier with the weeds by mentioning the drones, than when you were simply talking about weeds.

'Reaping comes after that, I suppose,' I said. 'Please teach me whatever XVIII you can that's relevant to this subject too.'

He replied, 'Yes, I will—unless it becomes obvious that you know just as much as I do about that as well. You know that the grain must be cut.'

'Of course I do,' I answered.

'Well, would you cut it standing with your back to the wind, or facing it?', he asked.

'I certainly shouldn't face it,' I replied. 'For I think it's hard on the eyes and hands to reap while facing the chaff and stalks.'

'And would you cut the ears near the top or close to the soil?', he asked. 2

'If the stalk of grain were short,' I replied, 'I think I should cut it at the bottom, so that the straw would be more useful. But if it were tall, I think I should be doing the right thing if I cut it in the middle, so that the reapers and the winnowers would not have to work too much over something that they do not need in the least. I think it would help the soil to burn the stubble that is left in the soil and to throw it into the soil as fertilizer so as to increase the amount of fertilizer.'

'Don't you see, Socrates, 'he retorted, 'that I'm catching you red-handed? 3 You know just what I do about reaping.'

'Yes, I suppose I do,' I said. 'But at least I'd like to discover whether I understand threshing too.'

'Well, you know one fact, that they use a beast of burden to thresh the 4 grain,' he went on.

'Of course, I do,' I said, 'and that the term "beasts of burden" includes oxen, mules, and horses.'

5 ἐλαυνόμενα; Τί γὰρ ἂν ἄλλο, ἔφην ἐγώ, ὑποζύγια εἰδείη; Ὅπως
δὲ τὸ δεόμενον κόψουσι καὶ ὁμαλιεῖται ὁ ἀλοατός, τίνι τοῦτο.., ὦ
Σώκρατες; ἔφη. Δῆλον ὅτι, ἔφην ἐγώ, τοῖς ἐπαλωσταῖς. στρέφοντες
γὰρ καὶ ὑπὸ τοὺς πόδας ὑποβάλλοντες τὰ ἄτριπτα ἀεὶ δῆλον ὅτι
μάλιστα ὁμαλίζοιεν ἂν τὸν δῖνον καὶ τάχιστα ἀνύτοιεν. Ταῦτα μὲν 5
6 τοίνυν, ἔφη, οὐδὲν ἐμοῦ λείπει γιγνώσκων. Οὐκοῦν, ἔφην ἐγώ, ὦ
Ἰσχόμαχε, ἐκ τούτου δὴ καθαροῦμεν τὸν σῖτον λικμῶντες. Καὶ
λέξον γέ μοι, ὦ Σώκρατες, ἔφη ὁ Ἰσχόμαχος, ἢ οἶσθα ὅτι ἂν ἐκ
τοῦ προσηνέμου μέρους τῆς ἅλω ἄρχῃ, δι' ὅλης τῆς ἅλω οἴσεταί
7 σοι τὰ ἄχυρα; Ἀνάγκη γάρ, ἔφην ἐγώ. Οὐκοῦν εἰκὸς καὶ ἐπιπίπτειν, 10
ἔφη, αὐτὰ ἐπὶ τὸν σῖτον. Πολὺ γάρ ἐστιν, ἔφην ἐγώ, τὸ
ὑπερενεχθῆναι τὰ ἄχυρα ὑπὲρ τὸν σῖτον εἰς τὸ κενὸν τῆς ἅλω. Ἂν
δέ τις, ἔφη, λικμᾷ ἐκ τοῦ ὑπηνέμου ἀρχόμενος; Δῆλον, ἔφην ἐγώ,
8 ὅτι εὐθὺς ἐν τῇ ἀχυροδόκῃ ἔσται τὰ ἄχυρα. Ἐπειδὰν δὲ καθάρῃς,
ἔφη, τὸν σῖτον μέχρι τοῦ ἡμίσεος τῆς ἅλω, πότερον εὐθὺς οὕτω 15
κεχυμένου τοῦ σίτου λικμήσεις τὰ ἄχυρα τὰ λοιπὰ ἢ συνώσας τὸν
καθαρὸν πρὸς τὸν πόλον ὡς εἰς στενότατον; Συνώσας νὴ Δί', ἔφην
ἐγώ, τὸν καθαρὸν σῖτον, ἵν' ὑπερφέρηταί μοι τὰ ἄχυρα εἰς τὸ κενὸν
9 τῆς ἅλω, καὶ μὴ δὶς ταὐτὰ ἄχυρα δέῃ λικμᾶν. Σὺ μὲν δὴ ἄρα, ἔφη,
ὦ Σώκρατες, σῖτόν γε ὡς ἂν τάχιστα καθαρὸς γένοιτο κἂν ἄλλον 20
δύναιο διδάσκειν. Ταῦτα τοίνυν, ἔφην ἐγώ, ἐλελήθη ἐμαυτὸν
ἐπιστάμενος. καὶ πάλαι ἐννοῶ ἄρα εἰ λέληθα καὶ χρυσοχοεῖν καὶ
αὐλεῖν καὶ ζωγραφεῖν ἐπιστάμενος. ἐδίδαξε γὰρ οὔτε ταῦτά με
οὐδεὶς οὔτε γεωργεῖν· ὁρῶ δ' ὥσπερ γεωργοῦντας καὶ τὰς ἄλλας
10 τέχνας ἐργαζομένους ἀνθρώπους. Οὐκοῦν, ἔφη ὁ Ἰσχόμαχος, 25
ἔλεγον ἐγώ σοι πάλαι ὅτι καὶ ταύτῃ εἴη γενναιοτάτη ἡ γεωργικὴ
τέχνη, ὅτι καὶ ῥᾴστη ἐστὶ μαθεῖν. Ἄγε δή, ἔφην ἐγώ, οἶδα, ὦ
Ἰσχόμαχε· τὰ μὲν δὴ ἀμφὶ σπόρον ἐπιστάμενος ἄρα ἐλελήθειν
ἐμαυτὸν ἐπιστάμενος.

XIX   Ἔστι δ' οὖν, ἔφην ἐγώ, τῆς γεωργικῆς τέχνης καὶ ἡ τῶν δένδρων 30
φυτεία; Ἔστι γὰρ οὖν, ἔφη ὁ Ἰσχόμαχος. Πῶς ἂν οὖν, ἔφην ἐγώ,
τὰ μὲν ἀμφὶ τὸν σπόρον ἐπισταίμην, τὰ δ' ἀμφὶ τὴν φυτείαν οὐκ

2 ἀλοητός H al.: ἀ(ἀ)λο(ω)ατός cet.   τούτω(ι) D al. G   aliquid excidisse videtur:
προστάξεις Hartman: ἐπιμελητέον Richards   5 τὸ δεινὸν codd.: corr.
Ruhnken   τάχιστ' ἂν Cobet   14 καθήρῃς Heindorf   15 τοῦ] τῆς G K
Hᵃ: del. Dind.   17 στενώτατον F G K L   21 ἐλελήθην A G: ἐλελήθειν cet.
22]νοων incipit Π²   εἰ ἄρα Cobet   23 εμε [ουτε τα]υτα Π²   24 γε]ωργειν
desinit Π²   27 ἄγε ... ἐπιστάμενος damnavit Leonclavius   ὦ om. Z O
28 ἐπιστάμενος del. Schneider   29 ἐπιστάμενος del. Dind.   30 ἔστι
δ'] ἔστιν A K L

'Do you think the beasts know one thing: how to tread the grain when they are driven?', he asked.

'What else should beasts of burden know?', I replied. 5

'And how do they make certain that they tread the right amount and that the threshing is uniform, Socrates?', he asked. 'Who is responsible for that?'

'It is obviously the duty of the threshers,' I replied. 'For by turning the untrodden grain at regular intervals and throwing it under the animals' hooves, they would obviously keep the threshing-floor level and complete the job very quickly.'

'Well then, you know as much as I do about these things,' he commented.

'Next, I suppose, Ischomachus,' I said, 'we will remove the impurities 6 from the grain by winnowing.'

'Yes, and tell me, Socrates,' asked Ischomachus, 'whether you know that if you begin the winnowing on the windward side of the floor, your chaff will be carried over the entire floor?'

'That's bound to happen,' I replied. 7

'Then probably some of it will fall on the grain,' he said.

'Yes, probably,' I agreed, 'because it is a long distance for chaff to be carried over the grain so that it lands in the empty part of the threshing-floor.'

'But what if the winnowing is started on the leeward side?', he asked.

'Obviously the chaff will instantly be in its proper place,' I replied.

'And when you have cleaned the grain as far as half-way across the 8 threshing-floor, will you immediately go on to winnow the rest of the chaff while the grain is scattered about, just as it is, or will you sweep the part of it that has had its impurities removed into a very small area towards the centre?', he asked.

'By Zeus,' I replied, 'I'll only do that after I've swept the clean grain into a heap, so that my chaff will be carried to the empty part of the threshing-floor, and so that I don't have to winnow the same grain twice.'

'Well, Socrates,' he said, 'it's you after all who could even teach someone 9 else about the quickest method of removing impurities from grain.'

'I didn't realize that I knew all that,' I said. 'And this has made me wonder for some time now whether I also know without realizing it how to smelt gold, and to play the flute, and to paint. For no one taught me these subjects, nor did anyone teach me farming, and I watch men employed in these other occupations, just as I watch men farming.'

'Well,' Ischomachus said, 'didn't I tell you just now that farming is a 10 most noble occupation, because it is easiest to learn?'

'Come on, Ischomachus, I know that,' I said. 'And I didn't realize that I knew the facts about sowing, even though I knew them.'

'Is planting trees part of the occupation of farming?', I asked. XIX

'Yes, it is,' replied Ischomachus.

'Then how is it that I knew about the techniques involved in sowing, when I don't know anything at all about those involved in planting?', I asked.

2 ἐπίσταμαι; Οὐ γὰρ σύ, ἔφη ὁ Ἰσχόμαχος, ἐπίστασαι· Πῶς; ἐγὼ
ἔφην, ὅστις μήτ᾽ ἐν ὁποίᾳ τῇ γῇ δεῖ φυτεύειν οἶδα μήτε ὁπόσον
βάθος ὀρύττειν †τὸ φυτὸν† μήτε ὁπόσον πλάτος μήτε ὁπόσον μῆκος
τὸ φυτὸν ἐμβάλλειν μήτε ὅπως ἂν ἐν τῇ γῇ κείμενον τὸ φυτὸν
3 μάλιστ᾽ ἂν βλαστάνοι. Ἴθι δή, ἔφη ὁ Ἰσχόμαχος, μάνθανε ὅ τι μὴ 5
ἐπίστασαι. βοθύνους μὲν γὰρ οἵους ὀρύττουσι τοῖς φυτοῖς οἶδ᾽ ὅτι
ἑώρακας, ἔφη. Καὶ πολλάκις ἔγωγ᾽, ἔφην. Ἤδη τινὰ οὖν αὐτῶν
εἶδες βαθύτερον τριπόδου; Οὐδὲ μὰ Δί᾽ ἔγωγ᾽, ἔφην,
πενθημιποδίου. Τί δέ, τὸ πλάτος ἤδη τινὰ τριπόδου πλέον εἶδες;
4 Οὐδὲ μὰ Δί᾽, ἔφην ἐγώ, διπόδου. Ἴθι δή, ἔφη, καὶ τόδε ἀπόκριναί 10
μοι· ἤδη τινὰ εἶδες τὸ βάθος ἐλάττονα ποδιαίου; Οὐδὲ μὰ Δί᾽,
ἔφην, ἔγωγε τριημιποδίου. καὶ γὰρ ἐξορύττοιτο ἂν σκαπτόμενα,
ἔφην ἐγώ, τὰ φυτά, εἰ λίαν γε οὕτως ἐπιπολῆς πεφυτευμένα εἴη.
5 Οὐκοῦν τοῦτο μέν, ἔφη, ὦ Σώκρατες, ἱκανῶς οἶσθα, ὅτι οὔτε
βαθύτερον πενθημιποδίου ὀρύττουσιν οὔτε βραχύτερον 15
τριημιποδίου. Ἀνάγκη γάρ, ἔφην ἐγώ, τοῦτο ὁρᾶσθαί γε οὕτω
6 καταφανὲς ὄν. Τί δέ, ἔφη, ξηροτέραν καὶ ὑγροτέραν γῆν γιγνώσκεις
ὁρῶν; Ξηρὰ μὲν γοῦν μοι δοκεῖ, ἔφην ἐγώ, εἶναι ἡ περὶ τὸν
Λυκαβηττὸν καὶ ἡ ταύτῃ ὁμοία, ὑγρὰ δὲ ἡ ἐν τῷ Φαληρικῷ ἕλει
7 καὶ ἡ ταύτῃ ὁμοία. Πότερα οὖν, ἔφη, ἐν τῇ ξηρᾷ ἂν βαθὺν ὀρύττοις 20
βόθρον τῷ φυτῷ ἢ ἐν τῇ ὑγρᾷ; Ἐν τῇ ξηρᾷ νὴ Δί᾽, ἔφην ἐγώ· ἐπεὶ
ἔν γε τῇ ὑγρᾷ ὀρύττων βαθύν, ὕδωρ ἂν εὑρίσκοις καὶ οὐκ ἂν δύναιο
ἔτι ἐν ὕδατι φυτεύειν. Καλῶς μοι δοκεῖς, ἔφη, λέγειν. οὐκοῦν
ἐπειδὰν ὀρωρυγμένοι ὦσιν οἱ βόθροι, ὁπηνίκα δεῖ τιθέναι ἑκάτερα
8 τὰ φυτὰ ἤδη εἶδες; Μάλιστα, ἔφην ἐγώ. Σὺ οὖν βουλόμενος ὡς 25
τάχιστα φῦναι αὐτὰ πότερον ὑποβαλὼν ἂν τῆς γῆς τῆς εἰργασμένης
οἴει τὸν βλαστὸν τοῦ κλήματος θᾶττον χωρεῖν διὰ τῆς μαλακῆς ἢ
διὰ τῆς ἀργοῦ εἰς τὸ σκληρόν; Δῆλον, ἔφην ἐγώ, ὅτι διὰ τῆς
εἰργασμένης θᾶττον ἂν ἢ διὰ τῆς ἀργοῦ βλαστάνοι. Οὐκοῦν
9 ὑποβλητέα ἂν εἴη τῷ φυτῷ γῆ. Τί δ᾽ οὐ μέλλει; ἔφην ἐγώ. Πότερα 30
δὲ ὅλον τὸ κλῆμα ὀρθὸν τιθεὶς πρὸς τὸν οὐρανὸν βλέπον ἡγῇ μᾶλλον
ἂν ῥιζοῦσθαι αὐτὸ ἢ καὶ πλάγιόν τι ὑπὸ τῇ ὑποβεβλημένῃ γῇ θείης
10 ἄν, ὥστε κεῖσθαι ὥσπερ γάμμα ὕπτιον; Οὕτω νὴ Δία· πλείους γὰρ
ἂν οἱ ὀφθαλμοὶ κατὰ τῆς γῆς εἶεν· ἐκ δὲ τῶν ὀφθαλμῶν καὶ ἄνω

2 τῇ del. Richards   3 βάθος βόθρον Schneider deletis τὸ φυτὸν
τῷ φυτῷ Reisig   4 ἐμβάλλειν Dind.: ἐμβαλεῖν codd.   6 βοθύνους]
βόθρους W. Dind.   16 γε οὕτω om. G K L: οὕτω γε Dind.   17 γῆν οὐ
Ven. 513   24 ἑκατέρα G K L: ἐν ἑκατέρα Weiske   32 γῇ om. K L N
34 τῆς Q R Y Hᵃ: om. cet.

'What? Don't you know about them?', Ischomachus said.

'How could I,' I answered, 'since I don't know what kind of earth to plant in, or how deep a hole to dig, or how wide, or what the length of the cutting should be when it's put in, or what position in the earth would cause it to grow best?'

'Come then,' continued Ischomachus, 'you must learn what you don't 3 know. I'm sure you've seen the type of trenches they dig for plants,' he said.

'Yes, I have, frequently,' I agreed.

'And have you ever seen any that are more than three feet deep?'

'No, by Zeus, not even two and a half,' I replied.

'Well then, did you ever see any more than three feet wide?'

'No, by Zeus, not even more than two,' I responded. 4

'Come then,' Ischomachus asked, 'answer this question for me too. Have you ever seen one less than a foot deep?'

'No, by Zeus, I haven't even seen one less than a foot and a half. For the plants would be uprooted when the earth is loosened around them, if they were put in like that too close to the surface,' I answered.

'In that case, Socrates, you already know this well enough,' he said, 'that 5 people dig the trenches neither deeper than two and a half feet nor shallower than one and a half feet.'

'I must have seen that, since it's so obvious,' I agreed.

'Well then, what about this? Can you distinguish between drier and 6 moister soil when you see it?', Ischomachus asked.

'I think that the soil around Lycabettus and any soil that's like it is dry, whereas the soil in the low ground at Phalerum and any soil that's like it is moist,' I replied.

'Would you dig a deep hole for your plant in the dry soil or in the moist? 7 How should you plant it in each kind?', he asked.

'In the dry, by Zeus,' I answered, 'because if you dig deep in moist soil you would find water, and you couldn't plant in water.'

'Good answer!', he exclaimed. 'And once the holes are dug, have you noticed when each variety of plant should be put in them?'

'Yes, of course,' I replied. 8

'Well, you want them to grow as quickly as possible; so do you think if you put some well-worked soil under them, the shoot from the cutting would come up more rapidly through soft soil or through unbroken soil into the hard ground?'

'Obviously it would grow more quickly through well-worked soil than through uncultivated ground,' I answered.

'Then earth should be placed beneath the plant.'

'Certainly it should,' I agreed.

'And do you think that if you put the whole cutting in upright, pointing 9 towards the sky, it would take root better? Or would you put part of it sideways beneath the earth that has been put in the hole, so that it rests like an L?'[6]

'The latter way, by Zeus, for then there would be more buds under- 10 ground; for I see that plants shoot up above ground from buds, and I

---

[6] Literally 'a gamma on its back'.

ὁρῶ βλαστάνοντα τὰ φυτά. καὶ τοὺς κατὰ τῆς γῆς οὖν ὀφθαλμοὺς
ἡγοῦμαι τὸ αὐτὸ τοῦτο ποιεῖν. πολλῶν δὲ φυομένων βλαστῶν
⟨κατὰ⟩ τῆς γῆς ταχὺ ἂν καὶ ἰσχυρὸν τὸ φυτὸν ἡγοῦμαι βλαστάνειν.

11 Κατὰ ταὐτὰ τοίνυν, ἔφη, καὶ περὶ τούτων γιγνώσκων ἐμοὶ
τυγχάνεις. ἐπαμήσαιο δ' ἂν μόνον, ἔφη, τὴν γῆν, ἢ καὶ σάξαις ἂν 5
εὖ μάλα περὶ τὸ φυτόν; Σάττοιμ' ἄν, ἔφην, νὴ Δί' ἐγώ. εἰ μὲν γὰρ
μὴ σεσαγμένον εἴη, ὑπὸ μὲν τοῦ ὕδατος εὖ οἶδ' ὅτι πηλὸς ἂν
γίγνοιτο ἡ ἄσακτος γῆ, ὑπὸ δὲ τοῦ ἡλίου ξηρὰ μέχρι βυθοῦ, ὥστε
τὰ φυτὰ κίνδυνος [ὑπὸ μὲν τοῦ ὕδατος] σήπεσθαι μὲν δι' ὑγρότητα,
αὐαίνεσθαι δὲ διὰ ξηρότητα, [ἤγουν χαυνότητα τῆς γῆς,] 10
12 θερμαινομένων τῶν ῥιζῶν. Καὶ περὶ ἀμπέλων ἄρα σύγε, ἔφη,
φυτείας, ὦ Σώκρατες, τὰ αὐτὰ ἐμοὶ πάντα γιγνώσκων τυγχάνεις.
Ἦ καὶ συκῆν, ἔφην ἐγώ, οὕτω δεῖ φυτεύειν; Οἶμαι δ', ἔφη ὁ
Ἰσχόμαχος, καὶ τἆλλα ἀκρόδρυα πάντα. τῶν γὰρ ἐν τῇ τῆς
ἀμπέλου φυτείᾳ καλῶς ἐχόντων τί ἂν ἀποδοκιμάσαις εἰς τὰς ἄλλας 15
13 φυτείας; Ἐλαίαν δὲ πῶς, ἔφην ἐγώ, φυτεύσομεν, ὦ Ἰσχόμαχε;
Ἀποπειρᾷ μου καὶ τοῦτο, ἔφη, μάλιστα πάντων ἐπιστάμενος. ὁρᾷς
μὲν γὰρ δὴ ὅτι βαθύτερος ὀρύττεται τῇ ἐλαίᾳ βόθρος· καὶ γὰρ
παρὰ τὰς ὁδοὺς μάλιστα ὀρύττεται· ὁρᾷς δ' ὅτι πρέμνα πᾶσι τοῖς
φυτευτηρίοις πρόσεστιν· ὁρᾷς δ', ἔφη, τῶν φυτῶν πηλὸν ταῖς 20
κεφαλαῖς πάσαις ἐπικείμενον καὶ πάντων τῶν φυτῶν ἐστεγασμένον
14 τὸ ἄνω. Ὁρῶ, ἔφην ἐγώ, ταῦτα πάντα. Καὶ ὁρῶν δή, ἔφη, τί
αὐτῶν οὐ γιγνώσκεις; ἢ τὸ ὄστρακον ἀγνοεῖς, ἔφη, ὦ Σώκρατες,
πῶς ἂν ἐπὶ τοῦ πηλοῦ ἄνω καταθείης; Μὰ τὸν Δί', ἔφην ἐγώ,
οὐδὲν ὧν εἶπας, ὦ Ἰσχόμαχε, ἀγνοῶ, ἀλλὰ πάλιν ἐννοῶ τί ποτε, 25
ὅτε πάλαι ἤρου με συλλήβδην εἰ ἐπίσταμαι φυτεύειν, οὐκ ἔφην. οὐ
γὰρ ἐδόκουν ἔχειν ἂν εἰπεῖν οὐδὲν ᾗ δεῖ φυτεύειν· ἐπεὶ δέ με καθ'
ἓν ἕκαστον ἐπεχείρησας ἐρωτᾶν, ἀποκρίνομαί σοι, ὡς σὺ φής, ἅπερ
15 σὺ γιγνώσκεις ὁ δεινὸς λεγόμενος γεωργός. Ἆρα, ἔφην, ὦ
Ἰσχόμαχε, ἡ ἐρώτησις διδασκαλία ἐστίν; ἄρτι γὰρ δή, ἔφη ἐγώ, 30
καταμανθάνω ᾗ με ἐπηρώτησας ἕκαστα· ἄγων γάρ με δι' ὧν ἐγὼ
ἐπίσταμαι, ὅμοια τούτοις ἐπιδεικνὺς ἃ οὐκ ἐνόμιζον ἐπίστασθαι
16 ἀναπείθεις, οἶμαι, ὡς καὶ ταῦτα ἐπίσταμαι. Ἆρ' οὖν, ἔφη ὁ
Ἰσχόμαχος, καὶ περὶ ἀργυρίου ἐρωτῶν ἄν σε, πότερον καλὸν ἢ

2 δὲ Q: γε vel γὰρ cet.   3 κατὰ add. Schneider   4 κατὰ del.
Schneider   ταὐτὰ L Q: ταῦτα cet.   6 μὲν del. Dind.   9 ὑπὸ
... ὕδατος del. Schneider   10 ἤγουν ... γῆς del. Kerst   13 οὕτως D al. O
18 δὴ Stephanus: ἂν codd.   26 πάλαι Hindenburg: πάλιν codd.   29 σὺ] δὴ
H N: δὴ σὺ cit. Nitsche   33 ἀναπείθεις Castalio: ἀναπεισθεὶς
codd. (ἀναπισθεὶς A, ἀναπείσθην Q)

deduce that buds below ground function in the same way. When it had many shoots sprouting below ground, I think the plant would grow quickly and vigorously.'

'Then it turns out that you agree with me about these matters too,' he 11 said. 'And would you merely heap up the earth, or would you pack it firmly around the plant?', he asked.

'I would pack it firmly, by Zeus,' I replied. 'Because I'm sure that if it weren't packed firmly, the loose earth would turn into mud because of the rain, and it would be dried by the sun to a considerable depth, so that plants would risk rotting because of the water and withering because of the heat when the roots became warm.'

'Well, Socrates, it turns out after all that you agree with me about the 12 planting of vines as well,' he declared.

'And should the fig be planted the same way?', I asked.

Ischomachus replied, 'Yes, I think so, and all the other fruit trees, too. And when you are planting other trees, why should you reject any of the methods that were successful with the vine?'

'But how shall we plant the olive, Ischomachus?', I asked. 13

'You know that best of all,' he said, 'and you're only testing me. For you certainly have observed that they dig a deeper hole to plant the olive, since it is very frequently planted by roadsides. And you've observed that stems are attached to all the shoots. And you've observed,' he continued, 'that clay is smeared on the tips of all the plants, and the tip of every plant above ground is protected,' he said.

'I've seen all that,' I answered. 14

'And when you see these things which of them do you fail to understand?', he asked. 'Or don't you know how to put the piece of pottery on top of the clay, Socrates?', he asked.

'Yes, of course, by Zeus, Ischomachus,' I replied. 'I'm not ignorant about any of the things you've mentioned. But now I'm wondering again why I ever said "no" a little while ago when you asked me in general terms if I understood planting. For I didn't think I would be able to say anything about how planting should be done. But now that you've undertaken to question me on individual topics, my answers, as you say, agree with those of an expert farmer such as yourself.

'Is questioning then a method of teaching, Ischomachus?' I asked. 'I 15 have just realized,' I said, 'what method you were using when you questioned me about individual topics: you lead me through the things I know and you show me that they are similar to the things I thought I did not know, in order to persuade me, I believe, that I really know those things as well.'

'Well,' said Ischomachus, 'if I asked you whether money was good or 16

οὔ, δυναίμην ἄν σε πεῖσαι ὡς ἐπίστασαι διαδοκιμάζειν τὰ καλὰ
καὶ τὰ κίβδηλα ἀργύρια; καὶ περὶ αὐλητῶν ἂν δυναίμην ἀναπεῖσαι
ὡς ἐπίστασαι αὐλεῖν, καὶ περὶ ζωγράφων καὶ περὶ τῶν ἄλλων τῶν
τοιούτων; Ἴσως ἄν, ἔφην ἐγώ, ἐπειδὴ καὶ γεωργεῖν ἀνέπεισάς με
ὡς ἐπιστήμων εἴην, καίπερ εἰδότα ὅτι οὐδεὶς πώποτε ἐδίδαξέ με 5
17 ταύτην τὴν τέχνην. Οὐκ ἔστι ταῦτ', ἔφη, ὦ Σώκρατες· ἀλλ' ἐγὼ
καὶ πάλαι σοι ἔλεγον ὅτι ἡ γεωργία οὕτω φιλάνθρωπός ἐστι καὶ
πραεῖα τέχνη ὥστε καὶ ὁρῶντας καὶ ἀκούοντας ἐπιστήμονας εὐθὺς
18 ἑαυτῆς ποιεῖν. πολλὰ δ', ἔφη, καὶ αὐτὴ διδάσκει ὡς ἂν κάλλιστά
τις αὐτῇ χρῷτο. αὐτίκα ἄμπελος ἀναβαίνουσα μὲν ἐπὶ τὰ δένδρα, 10
ὅταν ἔχῃ τι πλησίον δένδρον, διδάσκει ἱστάναι αὑτήν·
περιπεταννύουσα δὲ τὰ οἴναρα, ὅταν ἔτι αὐτῇ ἁπαλοὶ οἱ βότρυες
19 ὦσι, διδάσκει σκιάζειν τὰ ἡλιούμενα ταύτην τὴν ὥραν· ὅταν δὲ
καιρὸς ᾖ ὑπὸ τοῦ ἡλίου ἤδη γλυκαίνεσθαι τὰς σταφυλάς,
φυλλορροοῦσα διδάσκει ἑαυτὴν ψιλοῦν καὶ πεπαίνειν τὴν ὀπώραν, 15
διὰ πολυφορίαν δὲ τοὺς μὲν πέπονας δεικνύουσα βότρυς, τοὺς δὲ
ἔτι ὠμοτέρους φέρουσα, διδάσκει τρυγᾶν ἑαυτήν, ὥσπερ τὰ σῦκα
συκάζουσι, τὸ ὀργῶν ἀεί.

XX   Ἐνταῦθα δὴ ἐγὼ εἶπον· Πῶς οὖν, ὦ Ἰσχόμαχε, εἰ οὕτω γε καὶ
ῥᾴδιά ἐστι μαθεῖν τὰ περὶ τὴν γεωργίαν καὶ πάντες ὁμοίως ἴσασιν 20
ἃ δεῖ ποιεῖν, οὐχὶ καὶ πάντες πράττουσιν ὁμοίως, ἀλλ' οἱ μὲν
αὐτῶν ἀφθόνως τε ζῶσι καὶ περιττὰ ἔχουσιν, οἱ δ' οὐδὲ τὰ
2 ἀναγκαῖα δύνανται πορίζεσθαι, ἀλλὰ καὶ προσοφείλουσιν; Ἐγὼ δή
σοι λέξω, ὦ Σώκρατες, ἔφη ὁ Ἰσχόμαχος. οὐ γὰρ ἡ ἐπιστήμη
οὐδ' ἡ ἀνεπιστημοσύνη τῶν γεωργῶν ἐστιν ἡ ποιοῦσα τοὺς μὲν 25
3 εὐπορεῖν, τοὺς δὲ ἀπόρους εἶναι· οὐδ' ἂν ἀκούσαις, ἔφη, λόγου
οὕτω διαθέοντος ὅτι διέφθαρται ὁ οἶκος, διότι οὐχ ὁμαλῶς ὁ
σπορεὺς ἔσπειρεν, οὐδ' ὅτι οὐκ ὀρθῶς τοὺς ὄρχους ἐφύτευσεν, οὐδ'
ὅτι ἀγνοήσας τις τὴν [γῆν] φέρουσαν ἀμπέλους ἐν ἀφόρῳ
ἐφύτευσεν, οὐδ' ὅτι ἠγνόησέ τις ὅτι ἀγαθόν ἐστι τῷ σπόρῳ νεὸν 30
προεργάζεσθαι, οὐδ' ὅτι ἠγνόησέ τις ὡς ἀγαθόν ἐστι τῇ γῇ κόπρον
4 μιγνύναι· ἀλλὰ πολὺ μᾶλλον ἔστιν ἀκοῦσαι, ἀνὴρ οὐ λαμβάνει σῖτον
ἐκ τοῦ ἀγροῦ· οὐ γὰρ ἐπιμελεῖται ὡς αὐτῷ σπείρηται ἢ ὡς κόπρος
γίγνηται. οὐδ' οἶνον ἔχει ἀνήρ· οὐ γὰρ ἐπιμελεῖται ὡς φυτεύσῃ

2 ἄν Dind.: μὴ codd.   3 posterius περὶ om. Z F   posterius τῶν om.
K L N R Ven. 513   9 αὐτὴ φύσις Jacob   11 τι om. Z   αὐτήν L Q: αὑτὴν
cet.   16 διὰ πολυφορίαν δὲ om. Z   17 ἑαυτῆς Richards   24 σοί
γε D al. Hᵃ   27 ὁ σπορεὺς susp. Schneidero   29 γῆν del. Jacob: τὴν
φέρουσαν ἀμπέλους γῆν F   32 ἀνὴρ Dind.: ἀνὴρ codd.   34 et p. 200 2 ἀνὴρ
Dind.: ἀνὴρ codd.

not, could I persuade you that you know how to distinguish good money from counterfeit? And if I asked you about flautists, could I persuade you that you know how to play the flute; or about painters, or other artists of that kind?'

'Perhaps you could,' I replied, 'for you've persuaded me that I have the knowledge required to farm, although I know that no one ever taught me that occupation.'

'That's not possible, Socrates,' he said. 'But I said to you just now that 17 farming is such a humane and gentle occupation that she makes those who see her and hear her immediately knowledgeable about her. And she 18 herself,' he continued, 'also gives many lessons about how one might treat her best. For example, the vine, by climbing up the trees, when it has a tree nearby, teaches us to prop it up. By spreading its leaves around, when its bunches of grapes are still tender, it teaches us to provide shade for the parts exposed to the sun at that season. But when it is time for the clusters 19 to be sweetened by the sun, it sheds its leaves, and so it teaches us to strip it and allow the fruit to ripen. And by showing through its productiveness that some bunches are ripe, but others still sour, it teaches us to gather the fruit just as people pluck figs as each of them becomes plump.'

Then I asked, 'How is it, Ischomachus, if it's so easy, as you say, to learn XX the principles relevant to farming, and everyone has an equal amount of knowledge about what should be done, not everyone does equally well, but some live in plenty and have a surplus, whereas others cannot provide themselves with the necessities, but even get into debt as well?'

'I shall tell you, Socrates,' replied Ischomachus. 'It is not knowledge, or 2 lack of knowledge, on the part of the farmers that causes some to prosper and others to be poor. You are not likely,' he said, 'to hear a rumour 3 circulating that an estate has been ruined because the sower did not sow evenly, or because he failed to plant in straight rows, or that someone planted vines in unsuitable soil, because he did not know what kind of soil is suitable for vines, or because someone did not know that it is good to prepare the fallow for sowing, or because someone did not know that it is good to mix fertilizer with the soil. But you are much more likely to hear 4 people say "The fellow gets no grain from his earth because he isn't concerned that it's sown or fertilized." Or, "The fellow has no wine, because he isn't concerned to plant vines or to see that the vines that he has are

ἀμπέλους οὐδὲ αἱ οὖσαι ὅπως φέρωσιν αὐτῷ. οὐδὲ ἔλαιον οὐδὲ
σῦκα ἔχει ἀνήρ· οὐ γὰρ ἐπιμελεῖται οὐδὲ ποιεῖ ὅπως ταῦτα ἔχῃ.
5 τοιαῦτ᾽, ἔφη, ἐστίν, ὦ Σώκρατες, ἃ διαφέροντες ἀλλήλων οἱ
γεωργοὶ διαφερόντως καὶ πράττουσι πολὺ μᾶλλον ἢ [οἱ] δοκοῦντες
6 σοφόν τι ηὑρηκέναι εἰς τὰ ἔργα. καὶ οἱ στρατηγοὶ ἔστιν ἐν οἷς τῶν 5
στρατηγικῶν ἔργων οὐ γνώμῃ διαφέροντες ἀλλήλων οἱ μὲν
βελτίονες οἱ δὲ χείρονές εἰσιν, ἀλλὰ σαφῶς ἐπιμελείᾳ. ἃ γὰρ καὶ
οἱ στρατηγοὶ γιγνώσκουσι πάντες καὶ τῶν ἰδιωτῶν οἱ πλεῖστοι,
7 ταῦτα οἱ μὲν ποιοῦσι τῶν ἀρχόντων οἱ δ᾽ οὔ. οἷον καὶ τόδε
γιγνώσκουσιν ἅπαντες ὅτι διὰ πολεμίας πορευομένους βέλτιόν ἐστι 10
τεταγμένους πορεύεσθαι οὕτως ὡς ἂν ἄριστα μάχοιντο, εἰ δέοι.
τοῦτο τοίνυν γιγνώσκοντες οἱ μὲν ποιοῦσιν οὕτως οἱ δ᾽ οὐ ποιοῦσι.
8 φυλακὰς ἅπαντες ἴσασιν ὅτι βέλτιόν ἐστι καθιστάναι καὶ ἡμερινὰς
καὶ νυκτερινὰς πρὸ τοῦ στρατοπέδου. ἀλλὰ καὶ τούτου οἱ μὲν
9 ἐπιμελοῦνται ὡς ἔχῃ οὕτως, οἱ δ᾽ οὐκ ἐπιμελοῦνται. ὅταν τε αὖ 15
διὰ στενοπόρων ἴωσιν, οὐ πάνυ χαλεπὸν εὑρεῖν ὅστις οὐ γιγνώσκει
ὅτι προκαταλαμβάνειν τὰ ἐπίκαιρα κρεῖττον ἢ μή; ἀλλὰ καὶ τούτου
10 οἱ μὲν ἐπιμελοῦνται οὕτω ποιεῖν, οἱ δ᾽ οὔ. ἀλλὰ καὶ κόπρον λέγουσι
μὲν πάντες ὅτι ἄριστον εἰς γεωργίαν ἐστὶ καὶ ὁρῶσι δὲ αὐτομάτην
γιγνομένην· ὅμως δὲ καὶ ἀκριβοῦντες ὡς γίγνεται, καὶ ῥᾴδιον ὂν 20
πολλὴν ποιεῖν, οἱ μὲν καὶ τούτου ἐπιμελοῦνται ὅπως ἀθροίζηται,
11 οἱ δὲ παραμελοῦσι. καίτοι ὕδωρ μὲν ὁ ἄνω θεὸς παρέχει, τὰ δὲ
κοῖλα πάντα τέλματα γίγνεται, ἡ γῆ δὲ ὕλην παντοίαν παρέχει,
καθαίρειν δὲ δεῖ τὴν γῆν τὸν μέλλοντα σπείρειν· ἃ δ᾽ ἐκποδὼν
ἀναιρεῖται, ταῦτα εἴ τις ἐμβάλλοι εἰς τὸ ὕδωρ, ὁ χρόνος ἤδη αὐτὸς 25
ἂν ποιοίη οἷς ἡ γῆ ἥδεται. ποία μὲν γὰρ ὕλη, ποία δὲ γῆ ἐν ὕδατι
12 στασίμῳ οὐ κόπρος γίγνεται; καὶ ὁπόσα δὲ θεραπείας δεῖται ἡ γῆ,
ὑγροτέρα γε οὖσα πρὸς τὸν σπόρον ἢ ἁλμωδεστέρα πρὸς φυτείαν,
καὶ ταῦτα γιγνώσκουσι μὲν πάντες καὶ ὡς τὸ ὕδωρ ἐξάγεται
τάφροις καὶ ὡς ἡ ἅλμη κολάζεται μιγνυμένη πᾶσι τοῖς ἀνάλμοις, 30
καὶ ὑγροῖς [τε] καὶ ξηροῖς· ἀλλὰ καὶ τούτων ἐπιμελοῦνται οἱ μὲν
13 οἱ δ᾽ οὔ. εἰ δέ τις παντάπασιν ἀγνὼς εἴη τί δύναται φέρειν ἡ γῆ,
καὶ μήτε ἰδεῖν ἔχοι καρπὸν μηδὲ φυτὸν αὐτῆς, μήτε ὅτου ἀκοῦσαι
τὴν ἀλήθειαν περὶ αὐτῆς ἔχοι, οὐ πολὺ μὲν ῥᾷον γῆς πεῖρα

3 ἀλλήλων] ἄλλων Cobet: ἄλλοι ἄλλων Hartman   5 οἱ del. Schneider
7 χείρους D al. Hᵃ: cf. *Anab*. I. vii. 3, *Ages*. ii. 7   13 φυλακάς θ᾽ cit. Schenkl
14 πρὸ F L M₂ O Q R *Ven*. 513: πρὸς cet.   15 ἔχῃ M: ἔχει cet.   16 οὐ prius
del. Stephanus: ἴωσί που, χαλεπὸν Jacobs   19 αὐτομάτως H: αὐτομάτα (sic) N
22 ἄνωθεν ὁ Schneider   27 ὁπόσης Stephanus   28 γε Stephanus: τε
codd.   31 τε om. H N Q R *Ven*. 513

productive for him." Or, "The fellow has neither olive nor fig, because he isn't concerned, and he doesn't do anything in order to get them." It is in 5 ways like that, Socrates,' he continued, 'that farmers differ from each other, and that is why they achieve different degrees of success, much more so than the people who are believed to have discovered some clever device for doing their work. So too with generals: it is not because they differ from 6 one another in the amount of knowledge they possess about military matters that some do better and others worse, but clearly, because they differ in the amount of concern they show. For some of those in command put into practice what all generals and most private citizens know, while others do not. For example, they all know that when proceeding through enemy 7 territory, it is better to march in the formation in which they could fight to the greatest advantage, if necessary. Yet although they know it, some do it, but others do not. They all know that it is better to post guards day 8 and night before the camp, but some are concerned that this should be done, whereas others are not concerned. And again, when they march 9 through narrow passes, isn't it hard to find someone who doesn't know that it's better to seize the advantageous positions in advance, rather than otherwise? Yet some are concerned about doing this, while others are not. Everyone says that fertilizer is excellent for farming and observes that it is 10 created through natural processes. Yet although they know exactly how it is created, and although it is easy to produce a large supply, some are concerned to have it collected, whereas others are not concerned. Again, 11 the god above provides water, and all the hollows become standing pools, and the earth provides all kinds of weeds which the man who intends to sow must clear away. If he threw into the water what he pulls up and clears away, time alone would produce what the earth delights in. For what kind of weed is there, what kind of soil, that does not turn into fertilizer in stagnant water? Everyone knows how much attention the earth 12 requires when it is too wet for sowing or too salty for planting, and how the water is carried off by ditches, and how the salinity is corrected by mixing in salt-free substances, both wet and dry. Yet some are concerned about these matters, whereas others are not. If a man is totally ignorant 13 about what the earth can produce, and is unable to see a crop or a plant on it, and does not know anyone who will tell him the truth about it, isn't it much easier for anyone to make trial of soil, rather than of a horse, and

λαμβάνειν παντὶ ἀνθρώπῳ ἢ ἵππου, πολὺ δὲ ῥᾷον ἢ ἀνθρώπου; οὐ
γὰρ ἔστιν ὅ τι ἐπὶ ἀπάτῃ δείκνυσιν, ἀλλ' ἁπλῶς ἅ τε δύναται καὶ
14 ἃ μὴ σαφηνίζει τε καὶ ἀληθεύει. δοκεῖ δέ μοι ἡ γῆ καὶ τοὺς κακούς
τε καὶ ἀργοὺς τῷ εὔγνωστα καὶ εὐμαθῆ πάντα παρέχειν ἄριστα
ἐξετάζειν. οὐ γὰρ ὥσπερ τὰς ἄλλας τέχνας τοῖς μὴ ἐργαζομένοις 5
ἔστι προφασίζεσθαι ὅτι οὐκ ἐπίστανται, γῆν δὲ πάντες οἴδασιν ὅτι
15 εὖ πάσχουσα εὖ ποιεῖ· ἀλλ' ἡ ἐν γῇ ἀργία ἐστὶ σαφὴς ψυχῆς
κατήγορος κακῆς. ὡς μὲν γὰρ ἂν δύναιτο ἄνθρωπος ζῆν ἄνευ τῶν
ἐπιτηδείων, οὐδεὶς τοῦτο αὐτὸς αὑτὸν πείθει· ὁ δὲ μήτε ἄλλην
τέχνην χρηματοποιὸν ἐπιστάμενος μήτε γεωργεῖν ἐθέλων φανερὸν 10
ὅτι κλέπτων ἢ ἁρπάζων ἢ προσαιτῶν διανοεῖται βιοτεύειν, ἢ
16 παντάπασιν ἀλόγιστός ἐστι. μέγα δὲ ἔφη διαφέρειν εἰς τὸ λυσιτελεῖν
γεωργίαν καὶ μὴ λυσιτελεῖν, ὅταν ὄντων ἐργαστήρων καὶ πλεόνων
ὁ μὲν ἔχῃ τινὰ ἐπιμέλειαν ὡς τὴν ὥραν αὐτῷ ἐν τῷ ἔργῳ οἱ ἐργάται
ὦσιν, ὁ δὲ μὴ ἐπιμελῆται τούτου. ῥᾳδίως γὰρ ἀνὴρ εἷς παρὰ τοὺς 15
δέκα διαφέρει τῷ ἐν ὥρᾳ ἐργάζεσθαι, καὶ ἄλλος γε ἀνὴρ διαφέρει
17 τῷ πρὸ τῆς ὥρας ἀπιέναι. τὸ δὲ δὴ ἐὰν ῥᾳδιουργεῖν δι' ὅλης τῆς
ἡμέρας τοὺς ἀνθρώπους ῥᾳδίως τὸ ἥμισυ διαφέρει τοῦ ἔργου
18 παντός. ὥσπερ καὶ ἐν ταῖς ὁδοιπορίαις παρὰ στάδια διακόσια ἔστιν
ὅτε τοῖς ἑκατὸν σταδίοις διήνεγκαν ἀλλήλων ἄνθρωποι τῷ τάχει, 20
ἀμφότεροι καὶ νέοι ὄντες καὶ ὑγιαίνοντες, ὅταν ὁ μὲν πράττῃ ἐφ'
ᾧπερ ὥρμηται, βαδίζων, ὁ δὲ ῥᾳστωνεύῃ τῇ ψυχῇ καὶ παρὰ κρήναις
καὶ ὑπὸ σκιαῖς ἀναπαυόμενός τε καὶ θεώμενος καὶ αὔρας θηρεύων
19 μαλακάς. οὕτω δὲ καὶ ἐν τοῖς ἔργοις πολὺ διαφέρουσιν εἰς τὸ
ἀνύτειν οἱ πράττοντες ἐφ' ᾧπερ τεταγμένοι εἰσί, καὶ οἱ μὴ 25
πράττοντες ἀλλ' εὑρίσκοντες προφάσεις τοῦ μὴ ἐργάζεσθαι καὶ
20 ἐώμενοι ῥᾳδιουργεῖν. τὸ δὲ δὴ †καὶ τὸ καλῶς ἐργάζεσθαι ἢ κακῶς†
ἐπιμελεῖσθαι, τοῦτο δὴ τοσοῦτον διαφέρει ὅσον ἢ ὅλως ἐργάζεσθαι
ἢ ὅλως ἀργὸν εἶναι. ὅταν σκαπτόντων, ἵνα ὕλης καθαραὶ αἱ ἄμπελοι
γένωνται, οὕτω σκάπτωσιν ὥστε πλείω καὶ καλλίω τὴν ὕλην 30
21 γίγνεσθαι, πῶς τοῦτο οὐκ ἀργὸν ἂν φήσαις εἶναι; τὰ οὖν

3 post κακοὺς add. καὶ τοὺς καλούς Jacob   5 post τέχνας lac. stat.
Schenkl   6 προφασίσασθαι codd. multi post προφασίζεσθαι lac. stat. Heindorf
οἴδασιν codd. praeter Q   7 ἀντευποιεῖ Cobet   ἐν γεωργίᾳ ἀμέλεια Ven. 513:
γεωργία D C: ἐν γεωργίᾳ cet.: post γεωργίᾳ A in marg. add. ἐνέργεια   12 ἔφη,
διαφέρει Richards   13 λυσιτελεῖν om. Q   ἐργαστήρων F Q Ven. 511: ἐργαστηρίων
cet.   post πλεόνων add. καὶ μειόνων Hertlein   17 τῷ μὴ Leonclavius   20 τῷ
τάχει om. H N   21 ἐφ' ὅπερ Stephanus   27 καὶ τὸ del.
Schneider: δὴ καλῶς καὶ τὸ κακῶς ἐργάζεσθαι ἢ ἐπιμελεῖσθαι Holden   28 τοσοῦτο
D al.   29 οἷον ὅταν Zeune   σκαλλόντων et 30 σκάλλωσιν Hartman   30 καλλίω]
κακίω Richards   31 πῶς: οὕτως susp.: τοῦτο Schneider: οὕτω D al.

isn't it much easier than testing another man? For she[7] doesn't make a display in order to deceive, but speaks the truth and reveals clearly what she can do and what she can't. By providing all that she has in a form that is easy to learn and understand, I think the earth constitutes the best test 14 of evil and lazy men. For in other occupations, those who avoid working offer ignorance as an excuse, but that is not possible in the case of farming; because everyone knows that earth responds well to good treatment. But 15 laziness in farming is a clear indictment of an evil soul. For no one can persuade himself that a man could live without necessities. The man who understands no other money-making occupation, and refuses to farm, must obviously be determined to live by stealing, or robbery, or begging, or else be totally irrational.' He continued, 'It makes a great difference to the 16 profitability or unprofitability of agriculture, when labourers are available, and plenty of them too, that one man is concerned about whether the labourers are working during the working hours, whereas another is not concerned about this. For one man in a group of ten can easily make a difference by working at the proper time, whereas another makes a difference by leaving before the proper time. And to allow the workmen to work 17 slowly all day long may easily make a difference of half the total amount of work. Just as in walking two men, both young and in good health, may 18 differ in speed by as much as a hundred stades over a distance of two hundred, when the one, going along steadily, accomplishes the objective for which he started, while the other proceeds in an easy-going frame of mind, stopping at springs and in shady places looking around and searching for gentle breezes. So too in working, there is a great difference in achieve 19 ment between those who work at their assignments and those who do not work, but find excuses for not working and are allowed to work slowly. Performing work well or performing it badly are as different from each 20 other as total devotion to work and total idleness. When hoeing is done in order that the vines may be clear of weeds, if men hoe in such a way that the weeds become more plentiful and luxuriant, how could you deny that this is idleness? It is these things then that wear away estates more often 21

---

[7] The Earth is personified as female.

συντρίβοντα τοὺς οἴκους πολὺ μᾶλλον ταῦτά ἐστιν ἢ αἱ λίαν
ἀνεπιστημοσύναι. τὸ γὰρ τὰς μὲν δαπάνας χωρεῖν ἐντελεῖς ἐκ τῶν
οἴκων, τὰ δὲ ἔργα μὴ τελεῖσθαι λυσιτελούντως πρὸς τὴν δαπάνην,
ταῦτα οὐκέτι δεῖ θαυμάζειν ἐὰν ἀντὶ τῆς περιουσίας ἔνδειαν
22 παρέχηται. τοῖς γε μέντοι ἐπιμελεῖσθαι δυναμένοις καὶ 5
συντεταμένως γεωργοῦσιν ἀνυτικωτάτην χρημάτισιν ἀπὸ γεωργίας
καὶ αὐτὸς ἐπετήδευσε καὶ ἐμὲ ἐδίδαξεν ὁ πατήρ. οὐδέποτε γὰρ εἴα
χῶρον ἐξειργασμένον ὠνεῖσθαι, ἀλλ᾽ ὅστις ἢ δι᾽ ἀμέλειαν ἢ δι᾽
ἀδυναμίαν τῶν κεκτημένων καὶ ἀργὸς καὶ ἀφύτευτος εἴη, τοῦτον
23 ὠνεῖσθαι παρῄνει. τοὺς μὲν γὰρ ἐξειργασμένους ἔφη καὶ πολλοῦ 10
ἀργυρίου γίγνεσθαι καὶ ἐπίδοσιν οὐκ ἔχειν· τοὺς δὲ μὴ ἔχοντας
ἐπίδοσιν οὐδὲ ἡδονὰς ὁμοίας ἐνόμιζε παρέχειν, ἀλλὰ πᾶν κτῆμα
καὶ θρέμμα τὸ ἐπὶ τὸ βέλτιον ἰόν, τοῦτο καὶ εὐφραίνειν μάλιστα
ᾤετο. οὐδὲν οὖν ἔχει πλείονα ἐπίδοσιν ἢ χῶρος ἐξ ἀργοῦ πάμφορος
24 γιγνόμενος. εὖ γὰρ ἴσθι, ἔφη, ὦ Σώκρατες, ὅτι τῆς ἀρχαίας τιμῆς 15
πολλοὺς πολλαπλασίου χώρους ἀξίους ἡμεῖς ἤδη ἐποιήσαμεν. καὶ
τοῦτο, ὦ Σώκρατες, ἔφη, οὕτω μὲν πολλοῦ ἄξιον τὸ ἐνθύμημα,
οὕτω δὲ καὶ μαθεῖν ῥάδιον, ὥστε νυνὶ ἀκούσας σὺ τοῦτο ἐμοὶ
25 ὁμοίως ἐπιστάμενος ἄπει, καὶ ἄλλον διδάξεις, ἐὰν βούλῃ. καὶ ὁ
ἐμὸς δὲ πατὴρ οὔτε ἔμαθε παρ᾽ ἄλλου τοῦτο οὔτε μεριμνῶν ηὗρεν, 20
ἀλλὰ διὰ τὴν φιλογεωργίαν καὶ φιλοπονίαν ἐπιθυμῆσαι ἔφη
τοιούτου χώρου ὅπως ἔχοι ὅ τι ποιοίη ἅμα καὶ ὠφελούμενος
26 ἥδοιτο. ἦν γάρ τοι, ἔφη, ὦ Σώκρατες, φύσει, ὡς ἐμοὶ δοκεῖ,
φιλογεωργότατος Ἀθηναίων ὁ ἐμὸς πατήρ. Καὶ ἐγὼ μέντοι
ἀκούσας τοῦτο ἠρόμην αὐτόν· Πότερα δέ, ὦ Ἰσχόμαχε, ὁπόσους 25
ἐξειργάσατο χώρους ὁ πατὴρ πάντας ἐκέκτητο ἢ καὶ ἀπεδίδοτο,
εἰ πολὺ ἀργύριον εὑρίσκοι; Καὶ ἀπεδίδοτο νὴ Δί᾽, ἔφη ὁ
Ἰσχόμαχος· ἀλλὰ ἄλλον τοι εὐθὺς ἀντεωνεῖτο, ἀργὸν δέ, διὰ τὴν
27 φιλεργίαν. Λέγεις, ἔφην ἐγώ, ὦ Ἰσχόμαχε, τῷ ὄντι φύσει τὸν
πατέρα φιλογέωργον εἶναι οὐδὲν ἧττον ἢ οἱ ἔμποροι φιλόσιτοί εἰσι. 30
καὶ γὰρ οἱ ἔμποροι διὰ τὸ σφόδρα φιλεῖν τὸν σῖτον, ὅπου ἂν
ἀκούσωσι πλεῖστον εἶναι, ἐκεῖσε πλέουσιν ἐπ᾽ αὐτὸν καὶ Αἰγαῖον
28 καὶ Εὔξεινον καὶ Σικελικὸν πόντον περῶντες· ἔπειτα δὲ λαβόντες
ὁπόσον δύνανται πλεῖστον ἄγουσιν αὐτὸν διὰ τῆς θαλάττης, καὶ
ταῦτα εἰς τὸ πλοῖον ἐνθέμενοι ἐν ᾧπερ αὐτοὶ πλέουσι. καὶ ὅταν 35

---

6 συντεταμένοις vel συντεταγμένοις codd.: corr. Stephanus   13 posterius τὸ
om. Υ Hᵃ   18 καὶ μαθεῖν ῥάδιον H al.: καὶ ῥάδιον μαθεῖν F: ῥάδιον καὶ μαθεῖν cet.
22 χωρίου Κ L   ποιοίη Cobet: ποιῇ vel ποιεῖ (ποιοῖ Α s.v.) codd.   27 post
εἰ add. τις Jacob   28 δέ Κ Ν: om. cet.

than sheer lack of knowledge. For the expenses that have to be paid out from the estate remain undiminished, while the work done does not bring in enough profit to defray the expenditures. So no wonder these practices produce a loss instead of a surplus. However, for those who are capable of 22 paying attention to it, and who farm energetically, it provides a most effective way of making money. That was my father's own practice and that is what he taught to me. For he never allowed me to buy a well-cultivated plot of land, but encouraged me to buy any that was uncultivated and unproductive because of the lack of concern or the inability of its owners. For he said that plots of land that are well cultivated cost a lot of 23 money and provided no opportunity for improvement, and he believed that plots that are incapable of improvement did not provide as much pleasure, whereas he regarded every possession or living creature that was constantly improving as particularly delightful. And there is nothing that is capable of showing greater improvement than land that becomes fully productive after being uncultivated. Believe me, Socrates,' he said, 'we 24 have already increased the original price of numerous plots of land many times over. And, Socrates,' he went on, 'this concept is so valuable and so easy to learn, that just because you have been listening now you will go away with as much knowledge as I have, and you can teach someone else, if you like. And my father didn't learn this from anyone else or find it out 25 by concentrated study, but because of his love of farming and love of work he said he wanted a plot of land that would at the same time be an activity and a pleasurable means of making a profit. For, you know, Socrates,' he 26 said, 'I think, of all Athenians, my father was, by nature, the most devoted to farming.'

When I heard this, I asked him, 'Ischomachus, did your father keep all the plots of land he cultivated, or did he sell them if he could get a good price?'

'He would sell them, by Zeus,' replied Ischomachus, 'and he would buy another uncultivated plot immediately to replace it, because he loved working.'

'You are telling me, Ischomachus,' I said, 'that your father naturally 27 loved farming as much as merchants love grain? For because of their great love of grain, merchants sail wherever they hear there is an abundance of it, so as to get it, across the Aegean, the Euxine, and the Sicilian Sea. And 28 when they have taken as much as they can on board, they carry it across the sea, even storing it in the same ship in which they themselves sail. And when they need money, they don't unload the grain anywhere they happen

δεηθῶσιν ἀργυρίου, οὐκ εἰκῇ αὐτὸν ὅπου ἂν τύχωσιν ἀπέβαλον,
ἀλλ' ὅπου ἂν ἀκούσωσι τιμᾶσθαί τε μάλιστα τὸν σῖτον καὶ περὶ
πλείστου αὐτὸν ποιῶνται οἱ ἄνθρωποι, τούτοις αὐτὸν ἄγοντες
παραδιδόασι. καὶ ὁ σὸς δὲ πατὴρ οὕτω πως ἔοικε φιλογέωργος
29 εἶναι. Πρὸς ταῦτα δὲ εἶπεν ὁ Ἰσχόμαχος· Σὺ μὲν παίζεις, ἔφη, ὦ 5
Σώκρατες· ἐγὼ δὲ καὶ φιλοικοδόμους νομίζω οὐδὲν ἧττον οἵτινες
ἂν ἀποδιδῶνται ἐξοικοδομοῦντες τὰς οἰκίας, εἶτ' ἄλλας
οἰκοδομῶσι. Νὴ Δία, ἐγὼ δέ γέ σοι, ἔφην, ὦ Ἰσχόμαχε, ἐπομόσας
λέγω ἦ μὴν πιστεύειν σοι φύσει [νομίζειν] φιλεῖν ταῦτα πάντας
ἀφ' ὧν ἂν ὠφελεῖσθαι νομίζωσιν.   10

ΧΧΙ   Ἀτὰρ ἐννοῶ γε, ἔφην, ὦ Ἰσχόμαχε, ὡς εὖ τῇ ὑποθέσει ὅλον τὸν
λόγον βοηθοῦντα παρέσχησαι· ὑπέθου γὰρ τὴν γεωργικὴν τέχνην
πασῶν εἶναι εὐμαθεστάτην, καὶ νῦν ἐγὼ ἐκ πάντων ὧν εἴρηκας
2 τοῦθ' οὕτως ἔχειν παντάπασιν ὑπὸ σοῦ ἀναπέπεισμαι. Νὴ Δί', ἔφη
ὁ Ἰσχόμαχος, ἀλλὰ τόδε τοι, ὦ Σώκρατες, τὸ πάσαις κοινὸν ταῖς 15
πράξεσι καὶ γεωργικῇ καὶ πολιτικῇ καὶ οἰκονομικῇ καὶ πολεμικῇ
τὸ ἀρχικὸν εἶναι, τοῦτο δὴ συνομολογῶ σοι ἐγὼ πολὺ διαφέρειν
3 γνώμῃ τοὺς ἑτέρους τῶν ἑτέρων· οἷον καὶ ἐν τριήρει, ἔφη, ὅταν
πελαγίζωσι, καὶ δέῃ περᾶν ἡμερινοὺς πλοῦς ἐλαύνοντας, οἱ μὲν
τῶν κελευστῶν δύνανται τοιαῦτα λέγειν καὶ ποιεῖν ὥστε ἀκονᾶν 20
τὰς ψυχὰς τῶν ἀνθρώπων ἐπὶ τὸ ἐθελοντὰς πονεῖν, οἱ δὲ οὕτως
ἀγνώμονές εἰσιν ὥστε πλέον ἢ ἐν διπλασίῳ χρόνῳ τὸν αὐτὸν
ἀνύτουσι πλοῦν. καὶ οἱ μὲν ἱδροῦντες καὶ ἐπαινοῦντες ἀλλήλους, ὅ
τε κελεύων καὶ οἱ πειθόμενοι, ἐκβαίνουσιν, οἱ δὲ ἀνιδρωτὶ ἥκουσι,
4 μισοῦντες τὸν ἐπιστάτην καὶ μισούμενοι. καὶ τῶν στρατηγῶν ταύτῃ 25
διαφέρουσιν, ἔφη, οἱ ἕτεροι τῶν ἑτέρων· οἱ μὲν γὰρ οὔτε πονεῖν
ἐθέλοντας οὔτε κινδυνεύειν παρέχονται, πείθεσθαί τε οὐκ ἀξιοῦντας
οὐδ' ἐθέλοντας ὅσον ἂν μὴ ἀνάγκη ᾖ, ἀλλὰ καὶ μεγαλυνομένους
ἐπὶ τῷ ἐναντιοῦσθαι τῷ ἄρχοντι· οἱ δὲ αὐτοὶ οὗτοι οὐδ' αἰσχύνεσθαι
5 ἐπισταμένους παρέχουσιν, ἄν τι τῶν αἰσχρῶν συμβαίνῃ. οἱ δ' αὖ 30
θεῖοι καὶ ἀγαθοὶ καὶ ἐπιστήμονες ἄρχοντες τοὺς αὐτοὺς τούτους,
πολλάκις δὲ καὶ ἄλλους παραλαμβάνοντες, αἰσχυνομένους τε
ἔχουσιν αἰσχρόν τι ποιεῖν καὶ πείθεσθαι οἰομένους βέλτιον εἶναι,
καὶ ἀγαλλομένους τῷ πείθεσθαι ἕνα ἕκαστον καὶ σύμπαντας, πονεῖν
6 ὅταν δέῃ, οὐκ ἀθύμως πονοῦντας. ἀλλ' ὥσπερ ἰδιώταις ἔστιν οἷς 35

2 ὅπου] ὅποι W. Dind.   8 οἰκοδομοῦσι codd.: corr. Voigtländer   9 νομίζειν
del Bremi: O s.v.   πάντας G: πάντα cet.   10 ἀφ' Κ: ὑφ' vel ἐφ' cet.   17 ἐγὼ
om. D O   19 ἡμερινοὺς Stephanus: ἡμερίους codd.   21 τὸ H N Q: τῶ cet.
28 ἂν om. Z   34 πονεῖν del. Cobet   35 πονοῦντας H N: ποι(vel ν)οῦντες cet.

to be, but rather they take it and sell it wherever they hear that grain sells for the highest price and where men place the highest value on it. And your father appears to have loved farming in much the same way.'

Ischomachus replied to this, 'You may be joking, Socrates, but I genu- 29 inely believe that men who sell houses as soon as they have built them, and then build others, are lovers of building to just the same degree.'

'By Zeus, Ischomachus,' I said, 'I declare to you on oath that I accept your view that all men naturally love those things which they think will bring them profit.

'But I'm considering, Ischomachus,' I said, 'how well you have presented XXI the whole argument in favour of your proposition. Your proposition was, you recall, that farming was the easiest of all occupations to learn, and now, on the basis of all that you said, I am totally convinced that this is so.'

'By Zeus,' said Ischomachus, 'I agree, Socrates, that men differ very 2 much from each other in intelligence when it comes to the skills of governing that are common to all skilled activities, to farming, politics, estate manage- ment, and warfare. For example,' he said, 'when men are crossing the open 3 sea in a trireme, and they have to row all day long to complete their journey, some of the coxswains have the ability to speak and act in such a way that they rouse the morale of their men so that they are keen to work hard, but others are so unintelligent that it takes their crews more than twice the time to complete the voyage. The former disembark dripping with sweat, with the coxswain and his crew exchanging congratulations, while the latter arrive without a drop of sweat, but they hate their com- mander and he hates them.' He continued, 'Some generals, too, differ from 4 others in this respect: some of them make their men unwilling to work hard or to run any risks, not bothering to obey, nor even willing to do so unless it is absolutely necessary, and even going so far as to take pride in opposing their commander. It is these generals who produce men who have no sense of dishonour if something disgraceful happens. But when divine, brave, and 5 knowledgeable generals command these same troops, and often others as well, the troops that they have are ashamed to do anything disgraceful because they are convinced that obedience is better, and, since they take delight in being obedient individually and as a group, they work hard when necessary, and they do so enthusiastically. Just as a kind of love of 6 work can arise in individuals, so too there can arise in an entire army

ἐγγίγνεται φιλοπονία τις, οὕτω καὶ ὅλῳ τῷ στρατεύματι ὑπὸ τῶν
ἀγαθῶν ἀρχόντων ἐγγίγνεται καὶ τὸ φιλοπονεῖν καὶ τὸ
7 φιλοτιμεῖσθαι ὀφθῆναι καλόν τι ποιοῦντας ὑπὸ τοῦ ἄρχοντος. πρὸς
ὅντινα δ' ἂν ἄρχοντα διατεθῶσιν οὕτως οἱ ἑπόμενοι, οὗτοι δὴ
ἐρρωμένοι γε ἄρχοντες γίγνονται, οὐ μὰ Δί' οὐχ οἳ ἂν αὐτῶν 5
ἄριστα τὸ σῶμα τῶν στρατιωτῶν ἔχωσι καὶ ἀκοντίζωσι καὶ
τοξεύωσιν ἄριστα καὶ ἵππον ἄριστον ἔχοντες ὡς ἱππικώτατα ἢ
πελταστικώτατα προκινδυνεύωσιν, ἀλλ' οἳ ἂν δύνωνται ἐμποιῆσαι
τοῖς στρατιώταις ἀκολουθητέον εἶναι καὶ διὰ πυρὸς καὶ διὰ παντὸς
8 κινδύνου. τούτους δὴ δικαίως ἄν τις καλοίη μεγαλογνώμονας, ᾧ 10
ἂν ταῦτα γιγνώσκοντες πολλοὶ ἕπωνται, καὶ μεγάλῃ χειρὶ εἰκότως
οὗτος λέγοιτο πορεύεσθαι οὗ ἂν τῇ γνώμῃ πολλαὶ χεῖρες ὑπηρετεῖν
ἐθέλωσι, καὶ μέγας τῷ ὄντι οὗτος ἀνὴρ ὃς ἂν μεγάλα δύνηται
9 γνώμῃ διαπράξασθαι μᾶλλον ἢ ῥώμῃ. οὕτω δὲ καὶ ἐν τοῖς ἰδίοις
ἔργοις, ἄν τε ἐπίτροπος ᾖ ὁ ἐφεστηκὼς ἄν τε καὶ ἐπιστάτης, ὃς 15
ἂν δύνηται προθύμους καὶ ἐντεταμένους παρέχεσθαι εἰς τὸ ἔργον
καὶ συνεχεῖς, οὗτοι δὴ οἱ ἀνύτοντές εἰσιν ἐπὶ τἀγαθὰ καὶ πολλὴν
10 τὴν περιουσίαν ποιοῦντες. τοῦ δὲ δεσπότου ἐπιφανέντος, ὦ
Σώκρατες, ἔφη, ἐπὶ τὸ ἔργον, ὅστις δύναται καὶ μέγιστα βλάψαι
τὸν κακὸν τῶν ἐργατῶν καὶ μέγιστα τιμῆσαι τὸν πρόθυμον, εἰ 20
μηδὲν ἐπίδηλον ποιήσουσιν οἱ ἐργάται, ἐγὼ μὲν αὐτὸν οὐκ ἂν
ἀγαίμην, ἀλλ' ὃν ἂν ἰδόντες κινηθῶσι καὶ μένος ἑκάστῳ ἐμπέσῃ
τῶν ἐργατῶν καὶ φιλονικία πρὸς ἀλλήλους καὶ φιλοτιμία
κρατιστεῦσαι ἑκάστῳ, τοῦτον ἐγὼ φαίην ἂν ἔχειν τι ἤθους
11 βασιλικοῦ. καὶ ἔστι τοῦτο μέγιστον, ὡς ἐμοὶ δοκεῖ, ἐν παντὶ ἔργῳ 25
ὅπου τι δι' ἀνθρώπων πράττεται, καὶ ἐν γεωργίᾳ δέ. οὐ μέντοι μὰ
Δία τοῦτό γε ἔτι ἐγὼ λέγω ἰδόντα μαθεῖν εἶναι, οὐδ' ἅπαξ
ἀκούσαντα, ἀλλὰ καὶ παιδείας δεῖν φημι τῷ ταῦτα μέλλοντι
δυνήσεσθαι καὶ φύσεως ἀγαθῆς ὑπάρξαι, καὶ τὸ μέγιστον δὴ θεῖον
12 γενέσθαι. οὐ γὰρ πάνυ μοι δοκεῖ ὅλον τουτὶ τὸ ἀγαθὸν ἀνθρώπινον 30
εἶναι ἀλλὰ θεῖον, τὸ ἐθελόντων ἄρχειν· ⟨ὃ⟩ σαφῶς δίδοται τοῖς

1 ἐθελοπονία Stephanus   4 οὗτοι Stephanus: οὕτω codd.   6 τῶν στρατιωτῶν
susp. Schenkelio   9 καὶ διὰ παντὸς κινδύνου del. Cobet   11 ταῦτα codd:
ταὐτὰ Stephanus: ἔπωνται A s.v.: ἔπονται cet. εἰκότως ἂν Cobet   12 οὗτος F
M cor. Ven. 368 et 511: οὕτως cet.: om. O   13 ἀνὴρ Mehler: ἀνὴρ codd.   18 δὲ
Castalio: τε vel γε codd. (om. R Ven. 513)   post ἐπιφανέντος Y Hᵃ N O add. αὐτῶν
19 μέγιστα H al. Hᵃ: μεγίστως cet.   20 τὸν κακὸν Q: τῶν κακῶν cet.   24 κρατιστεῦσαι Heindorf: κρατιστοῦσαι vel κρατίστη οὖσα codd.   27 ἔτι H: ὅτι cet.   31 ὃ
add. Marchant   δίδοται R Ven. 513: φείδονται cet.: δὲ δίδοται Stephanus: τοῦτο μὲν
γὰρ ὑπὸ τῶν θεῶν σαφῶς δίδοται cit. Schenkl

under the influence of good commanders both a love of work and an
ambition to be seen by their commander when they are doing something
good. When a commander's followers have a relationship of that kind with 7
him, it's these men, I assure you, who become the strongest commanders—
not, by Zeus, those whose soldiers have the best physiques or are the best
with javelin and bow and have the most skilled cavalry so that they are in
the forefront of danger because they are the best possible cavalry or peltasts,
but those who can inspire in their soldiers the notion that they must follow
them through every danger and even through fire. It would be quite right 8
to call men who have many followers who agree with them "high-minded".
Indeed it would be reasonable to describe a man as "advancing with a
mighty army" when there are many arms prepared to do what he has in
mind. And truly great is the man who can accomplish great deeds by the
strength of his mind rather than by muscle. The same is true in private 9
enterprises. The man in charge—whether he is a foreman or a supervisor—
who can produce workers who are enthusiastic, eager for work, and perse-
vering, these are the ones who manage to prosper and to make their surplus
a large one. Socrates,' he said, 'if the master turns up at the scene of the 10
work (a man who can punish the lazy worker very severely and reward
the eager one most generously), and the workmen do not make a conspicuous effort, then I for one should not envy him. But if they are stimulated
when the master appears and a new vigour descends on each of the workers,
and mutual rivalry and an ambition in each worker to be the best, I would
say that this master possesses a portion of the nature of a king. And this is 11
of utmost importance, I think, in every activity that is performed by human
beings, including farming. However, by Zeus, I am still not saying that it
is possible to learn this by seeing it, or by hearing it only once; but I am
saying that the person who intends to possess these abilities needs education,
and must possess the right kind of nature, and most important of all, he
must be divine. For ruling over willing subjects, in my view, is a gift not 12
wholly human but divine, because it is a gift of the gods: and one that is
obviously bestowed on those who have been initiated into self-control. The

ἀληθινῶς σωφροσύνη τετελεσμένοις· τὸ δὲ ἀκόντων τυραννεῖν διδόασιν, ὡς ἐμοὶ δοκεῖ, οὓς ἂν ἡγῶνται ἀξίους εἶναι βιοτεύειν ὥσπερ ὁ Τάνταλος ἐν Ἅιδου λέγεται τὸν ἀεὶ χρόνον διατρίβειν φοβούμενος μὴ δὶς ἀποθάνῃ.

gods give tyranny over unwilling subjects, I think, to those who they believe deserve to live a life in Hades like Tantalus, who is said to spend the whole of eternity in fear of a second death.'

COMMENTARY

Title. Οἰκονομικός. D.L. 2. 57, Athen. 1. 23 B, Col. *RR* 11. 1. 5,
12 pr. 1, 2, 12. 2. 6, and the manuscripts give the title *Oikonomikos*.
This adjective implies a masculine noun, perhaps ἀνήρ 'man', as
reflected in the title of Wedderburn's and Collingwood's translation *The Economist of Xenophon* and of Waterfield's *The Estate
Manager*, or, as I understand it, λόγος 'discourse'.[1] Cic. *De Sen.* 59,
is in agreement, for he also gives the masculine singular nominative
Oeconomicus. Philodemus and Galen give as the title the abstract
plural Οἰκονομικά, perhaps by analogy with Ἑλληνικά, but more
probably they confused the title of Xenophon's treatise with that
of the *Oeconomica* attributed to Aristotle. D.L. 6.16 lists Περὶ νίκης·
οἰκονομικός (*On Victory: A Work on Estate Management*) as a title in
the third volume of Antisthenes (see Ch. 3, sect. B). It is difficult
to speculate about the contents of this work. Probably the text is
corrupt, and two distinct works have been listed as one. As is the
case for many classical texts, there is no evidence that the author
gave his book the title which has come down to us, or that he
gave it any name at all. Indeed, some scholars consider the
Oeconomicus as part of the *Memorabilia* and not an independent
work needing a title. (See on i. 1 δέ ... αὐτοῦ, and Ch. 7, sect. C.)
Thus it is possible that the title was invented by librarians in the
Hellenistic period.

Οἰκονομικός is derived from οἰκονόμος and the suffix -ικός. -νόμος
is related to νέμω ('to regulate' or 'to manage'). The meaning of
οἶκος is broad; there is no single precise English equivalent that
would be appropriate in all contexts.[2] In the twentieth century,

---

[1] See also Marchant, *Xenophon*, iv (1923), pp. vii–viii, in favour of the latter. The
same ambiguity occurs in the titles of Xenophon's Ἱππαρχικός (the *Cavalry Commander*
or *Discourse on Commanding Cavalry*), Κυνηγετικός (the *Hunter* or *Discourse on Hunting*),
and Τυραννικός (the *Tyrant* or *Discourse on Tyranny*, an alternative title for *Hiero*).

[2] Douglas M. MacDowell, 'The *Oikos* in Athenian Law', *CQ*, NS 39 (1989), 10–21,
argues that the meaning of οἶκος changed over time. In legal texts it probably at first
denoted only house or property. Not until the forensic orations of the late 5th and
4th cc. did it begin to refer to people as well, i.e. 'family'. But MacDowell is not
convincing, for his view is based in part on a controversial interpretation of a law
quoted in Ps.-Dem. 43. 75. In any case, he does not comment on the meaning of
οἶκος in derivates such as οἰκονομικός. Lin Foxhall, 'Household, Gender, and Property
in Classical Athens', ibid. 22–44, offers a more fruitful analysis of a complex but

213

the English derivative 'economy' refers more to property than people. The *Oxford English Dictionary* gives the following definition: 'the art or science of managing a household, esp. with regard to household expenses'.

In the first chapter of the *Oeconomicus* (i. 5), Socrates attempts to define οἶκος by distinguishing it from οἰκία ('house'). His definition includes movable and immovable property, but it appears incomplete to a modern scholar. W. K. Lacey defines οἶκος as 'a family, including its property as well as its human members ...',[3] a definition applicable to the range of meanings with which Xenophon uses the word in the *Oeconomicus*. However, it is important to note that slaves would normally be classified as part of the family's property rather than among its human members. Slaves were not ordinarily considered members of the Greek family (see Ch. 5, sect. I).

Owing to the multiple connotations of οἶκος, subsequent authors and translators have devised solutions to translating the compound οἰκονομικός. At *De Sen.* 59 Cicero refers to his Latin translation as 'de tuenda re familiari' ('On looking after one's possessions').[4] Cicero translates οἶκος as *res familiaris* and with this title he manages to convey both the notions of household and of property. Vives discussed οἰκονομική and Xenophon's treatise under the rubric of moral philosophy, for he concentrated on the first ten chapters of the book (see Ch. 6, sect. E). His interpretation accentuates the ethical aspect of the word, also emphasized by LSJ s.v., who translate Xenophon's title as 'On the duties of domestic life'. This translation, however, is not literal: the idea of obligation is not implied by the Greek.

The first English translation was made by Gentian Hervet for a woman, perhaps for this reason his title *Xenophon's Treatise of Householde* (1532) draws attention to people and property connected with the interior of the house rather than with the estate. The title of R. Bradley's translation *The Science of Good Husbandry* (1727), ignores the contribution of housewifery (see Ch. 5, sect. E). In his Loeb edition E. C. Marchant gives the most inclusive title: 'A Discussion on Estate Management'. However, this translation fails to render the technical quality of the suffix -ικός.

---

unitary concept of the household in terms of use and function rather than legal concepts of ownership.

[3] *The Family in Classical Greece* (Ithaca, NY, 1968), 13.
[4] Petrarch refers to it by this title (see Ch. 6, sect. C).

Words in -ικός ('skilled in', 'working in')[5] began to be current
at the end of the fifth century and are common in philosophical
works of the fourth. Aristophanes (*Knights* 1378–81), ridicules the
use of adjectives in -ικός as an affectation of conceited young
Athenians. Charles W. Peppler counted approximately 38 such
words in Thucydides, 347 in the genuine dialogues of Plato, and
136 in Xenophon, of which 35 per cent are used by him only once
or are rare or hapax legomena.[6] Consequently, defining such words
was not a mere academic exercise but a necessity (see on i. 1–2
ὄνομα ... ἔργον). The same suffix appears in the titles of Xenophon's
Ἱππαρχικός, Κυνηγετικός, and Τυραννικός.

i. 1. Ἤκουσα. For the time-frame see Ch. 2, sects. E–F. In the
Symposium Plato employs a similar, though less elaborate narrative
technique: the narrator Apollodorus reports an event which had
taken place when he was a child and which he heard about many
years later from Socrates' friend Phoenix and from Socrates himself. It should also be noted that Socrates is never described as
writing, that literacy was not widespread in Athens in the fifth
century, and that oral tradition was regarded as trustworthy.[7]
Thus the series of narrations makes conversations that are remote
in time seem to be trustworthy historical reports, although in fact
they are not (see further Ch. 3).

Xenophon himself must have owned a collection of books, for
there are several references to book-rolls in his works.[8] He may
have read about the events at which he alleges he was present, or
he may have heard about them from older associates of Socrates,
or he may have invented them. On the unlikelihood of Xenophon's
presence at a conversation between Socrates and Critobulus after
the battle of Cunaxa see on iv. 18 μαχούμενος. Similarly, in the
opening of Xenophon's *Symposium*, the author claims to have been
present at a banquet in 422, when his youth would surely have
precluded his attendence. Athen. 5. 216 D objects to the anachron-
ism. Xenophon does not portray himself as actually participating
in the discussions in either the *Oeconomicus* or the *Symposium*, though
he does in *Mem.* 1. 3. 8. In *Mem.* 1. 4. 2, 1. 6. 14, 2. 4. 1, 2. 5. 1,

---

[5] For these and other translations see Carl Darling Buck and Walter Peterson, *A
Reverse Index of Greek Nouns and Adjectives* (Chicago, 1944), 636–7.

[6] 'The Termination -κός, as Used by Aristophanes for Comic Effect', *AJP* 31
(1910), 428–44.

[7] On Socrates' hostility to writing and on oral tradition in general see W. V.
Harris, *Ancient Literacy* (Cambridge, Mass., 1989), esp. 80–1, 91–2.

[8] According to Delebecque, *Essai*, 241, Xenophon had a library.

and 4. 3. 2, he claims to have been present himself at the conversation of Socrates which he reports. He also inserts himself into the opening sentences of the *Apology*, the *Memorabilia*, the *Spartan Constitution*, *Revenues*, *Agesilaus* and *On Horsemanship*. Herodotus had used the same device to establish the veracity of his report, asserting 'I asked', 'I saw', etc.

δέ ... αὐτοῦ. Since δέ commonly implies continuation or difference from what precedes, and pronouns usually have antecedents K. Schenkl,[9] H. A. Holden,[10] J. Luccioni,[11] and others suggest that the *Oeconomicus* was preceded by the *Memorabilia* (see also Ch. 7, sect. E). However, αὐτός does not need a stated antecedent, for it commonly refers to 'the master'.[12] Moreover, Xenophon is fond of beginning in *mediis rebus*. He also uses δέ as the second word in the *Apology* and he begins both the *Symposium* and *Spartan Constitution* with the conjunction ἀλλά. The *Hellenica* begins with μετὰ δὲ ταῦτα, but this is different: it indicates that Xenophon is writing a continuation of Thucydides. Interestingly enough, δέ is also the second word in Pseudo-Xenophon, *Athenaion Politeia*.

οἰκονομίας. Practical concerns are not uncommon in the Socratic dialogues. For example, in *Memorabilia* 2. 7 Xenophon discusses weaving and there are brief mentions of household management in Pl. *Prot.* 318 E, *Lysis* 209 D, and *Pol.* 259 C. In *Rep.* 369 D Socrates asserts that procuring food is a basic necessity of life. But in Plato, practical concerns are mentioned in passing: they do not constitute the chief subject of any dialogue (see further Ch. 3).

Κριτόβουλε. Critobulus, son of Crito from Alopeke, of the tribe of Antiochis, is well attested in Plato and Xenophon. He was a fellow demesman of Socrates and characterized as being on familiar terms with him. Plato (*Euthyd.* 306 D 5) represents Crito as consulting Socrates about his son's education. The *Oeconomicus*, too, shows Socrates as Critobulus' teacher. In *Mem.* 1. 3. 8–10, and 2. 6. 15 Xenophon depicts Critobulus as one of his own associates. In Xen. *Symp.* 2. 3 he is portrayed as newly married in 422. The identity of his wife, who is said to be young (iii. 13), is not known. Since Crito was born *c.*469, the men in this family apparently married before 25—an age younger than average for upper-class

[9] 'Xenophontische Studien, 2: Beiträge zur Kritik der Apomnemoneumata', *SB k. Akad. Wiss.* (Vienna), 80 (1875), 147.
[10] *The Oeconomicus of Xenophon* (London, 1884), 96.
[11] *Xénophon et le socratisme* (Paris, 1953), 112.
[12] See H. W. Smyth, *Greek Grammar* (Cambridge, Mass., 1920), 303, para. 1209d.

males.[13] Thus, although Critobulus was married, he was still young enough for παιδικά (see on ii. 7). According to ii. 3 his property was worth over 8 tal. 2,000 dr. Thus he was one of the wealthiest men at Athens, and a member of the liturgical class obligated to pay for various public expenses (see ii. 5–6). Critobulus is one of many upper-class young men with whom Socrates converses in various dialogues by Xenophon and Plato. From iii. 1 it appears that other friends are also assumed to be present, but they do not speak. However, from time to time Critobulus refers to them (see on ii. 1 δοκοῦμεν). In Xenophon Critobulus has a distinctive personality. His speech is liberally laced with expletives, especially 'By Zeus!'—which he uses for the first time at i. 4. He is capable of responses which are so original and imaginative that they almost seem to be non-sequiturs (for example, his humorous reference to the deadly henbane in i. 13). When Socrates is criticizing him, he tries to insert some humour into the situation, with a pun (iii. 10 πώλησιν . . . Πωλοδαμνεῖν).

ἐπιστήμης. The prestige awarded to the management of the oikos in classical Greece may come as a surprise to the modern reader who may be familiar with the activities of the Greeks in the public sphere and who may also despise 'housework'. However, the oikos was fundamental to the welfare of human beings and their cities (see further Ch. 3, sect. D, and Ch. 5). Therefore it should come as no surprise that in *Mem.* 4. 1. 2 οἶκον καλῶς οἰκεῖν is a μάθημα. Plato also refers to οἰκονομία as a field of knowledge. In *Prot.* 318 E managing a household is called a μάθημα, and in *Lysis* 209 D περὶ οἰκονομίας is used with φρονεῖν.

1–2 ὄνομα . . . ἔργον. In *Mem.* 1. 1. 16 and elsewhere Xenophon refers to Socrates' search for definitions. Plato too gives many illustrations, and Aristophanes, in the *Clouds*, portrays this quest as mere quibbling about words. Aristotle (*Metaph.* 1078ᵇ27) considered both this search for definitions and inductive reasoning as Socrates' principal contribution to the development of scientific thought. Socrates frequently buttresses his arguments with examples from the crafts (e.g. vi. 13–16, *Mem.* 3. 10, Pl. *Rep.* 1, *Apol.* 22 c–d). His definitions of crafts such as medicine, smithing, and carpentry, did not merely describe, but gave the ἔργον or function of the field of knowledge.[14] In Xenophon and Plato Socrates is portrayed searching for definitions by means of an elenchus, which as illustrated in i. 6–15 consists of a series of

---

[13] See Davies, *Athenian Propertied Families*, 336, nos. 8802 and 8823.
[14] See further W. K. C. Guthrie, *A History of Greek Philosophy*, iii. chs. 12–14.

questions and answers. Often, as in the *Oeconomicus*, his partner in the dialogue is a younger man who is a friend or disciple. The interlocutor usually gives an initial response which the elenchus demonstrates is incorrect. As Socrates does frequently elsewhere (especially in Plato), here he leads the argument to a *reductio ad absurdum* before finding a satisfactory definition. Often the deduction from the first attempt at definition is said to be 'ridiculous' (e.g. i. 6 γέλοῖον). Socrates appears less aggressive here, and permits Critobulus and to a greater extent Ischomachus (cc. vii–xxi) to play a larger role in directing the investigation than was usual for Socrates' companions in the dialogues. Plato's Socrates usually rejects responses offered by interlocutors, as in i. 6.

3–4. τὸν ἀλλοῦ δὲ οἶκον . . . μισθοφορεῖν. According to Plut. *Per.* 16. 5 Evangelus, a slave who displayed unique expertise in oikonomia, managed Pericles' household. Plutarch suggests that he either was naturally gifted or had been trained by Pericles for this work. Supervisory positions in households and on farms were generally held by slaves (see on xii. 3 ἐπιτρόπους . . . ὠνεῖσθαι). Thus it is of some significance that Xenophon is here allowing the possibility of a free manager or perhaps a freedman, who will earn money for managing the estate. If he is thinking also of a tenant farmer, then τελεῖν just below would include rent payments. Considering that the wealthy usually delegated supervision of their estates, it is interesting that Socrates assumes that Critobulus should take personal responsibility for his.

4. τελεῖν. Critobulus is referring to payments, presumably for equipment and other operating expenses. See on ii. 2–4.

5–6. Οἶκος . . . οἰκία . . . οἴκου. See on title Οἰκονομικός.

7–8. κτήματα . . . χρήματα. Socrates plays with the ambiguity in the words κτήματα and χρήματα. That the two words are metrical equivalents and rhyme suggests that their connotations are linked. (On Socrates' interest in the sounds of words see on i. 22.) After the introduction of coinage χρήματα frequently meant 'money', but also retained its more general sense of 'property', or 'wealth' as here, where it refers to property which one possesses (κτῶμαι) and may use (χρῶμαι). κτήματα means simply 'possessions'. Greek economic terminology was vague (see on title Οἰκονομικός). Xenophon was the first to attempt some clarification: in fact, he wrote an entire treatise on *Revenues* (see further on Ch. 5, sect. B). In the present chapter, Socrates adds the important prerequisite that one must know how to use something for it to be χρήματα (10 ἐπισταμένῳ, 11 ἐπισταμένοις, 12, 14 ἐπίσταιτο, ἐπίστηται, 15 ἐπίστασθαι). Most Greeks probably would not have agreed. According to Arist. *Rhet.* 1367ᵃ23–4, χρήματα rather than κτήματα, are the basis of getting wealth.

8. ἵππον. Horse-ownership was a mark of great wealth.[15] At Athens the cavalry (or knights) and the liturgical class owned horses. In the fourth century the average price of a cavalryman's horse, as listed on tablets found in the agora, was 408 dr. But expensive horses might cost 1,200 dr. or more: see Xen. *Anab.* 7. 8. 6 (50 darics = 1,250 dr.), Ar. *Clouds* 21–3, 1224–5, Lys. 8. 10. In addition, the cavalryman had to maintain his horse and gear as well as the animal on which his groom rode.[16] In the *Oeconomicus* remarks about horses indicate that their owners are wealthy: like Ischomachus they are likely to own land on which to graze the horse and ride and a groom who is a slave (xi. 15–18). The work is studded with allusions to horses, since a principal participant is Critobulus, a wealthy young man who must maintain horses as a public service (ii. 6), who potentially could make a profit from keeping them (iii. 8, 9), and who evidently is quite familiar with them. The repeated references to breeding and riding horses (v. 5, 6, ix. 15, xi. 4, 17) also suggest that Xenophon's readers were wealthy men like himself, members of the cavalry. He assumes that a wealthy man would know how to keep his seat on a horse. He himself wrote two treatises on equitation: *On Horsemanship* and the *Cavalry Commander*. The man who continually falls off his horse, is, in Xenophon's view, not a gentleman: therefore it is appropriate to blame the owner for neglecting to train the animal properly. The other examples apply not only to gentlemen but to all those who own land, sheep, or anything else, but cannot use them properly.

ἐπίστηται ... χρῆσθαι. Proper usage of material goods is a common theme in Xenophon as well as in the other Socratics: see e.g. *Mem.* 3. 8. 6–7, 10, Pl. *Euthyd.* 280 B, Ps.-Pl. *Eryxias* 399 E–403 D.[17] W. Nestle draws attention to similarities in thought and language between the *Oeconomicus* and the *Eryxias* in the discussions of ὀρθὴ χρῆσις where things are said to be good or bad

---

[15] See e.g. Xen. *Hiero* 11. 5, *Ages.* 9. 6, *Cav. Comm.* 1. 11–12, Thuc. 6. 15. 3, Isoc. 16. 33, Pl. *Lys.* 205 C, Lyc. 139, Arist. *Pol.* 1289ᵇ33–5, 1321ᵃ11, Ps.-Dem. 42. 24, J. K. Anderson, *Ancient Greek Horsemanship* (Berkeley and Los Angeles, 1961), esp. ch. 11, Davies, *Athenian Propertied Families*, p. xxv n. 7, and on ii. 6 ἱπποτροφίας.

[16] I am grateful to I. G. Spence for information on the cost of cavalry service in classical Athens; see app. 4 of id., *The Cavalry of Classical Greece* (Oxford, 1993).

[17] Joseph Souilhé, *Platon: Œuvres complètes* (Paris, 1930), xiii/3. 88, dates the *Eryxias* to the 3rd c. BC.

according to their use, and suggests Prodicus as the source.[18] In his dialogue *Callias* (fr. 17 = Plut. *Arist.* 25. 5–6) Aeschines Socraticus discusses the ὀρθὴ χρῆσις of wealth, and makes the paradoxical point that it is more admirable, as being rarer, to bear poverty nobly, than to use wealth well or badly. See further on ii. 4.

10. αὐλοὶ ... λίθοι. αὐλοί may be plural, or it may refer to a single instrument. The conventional translation is 'flute', though the aulos is not the same as a modern flute. Flutes were common instruments and were played at many occasions, ranging from religious celebrations to private entertainments where they might be played by prostitutes or 'flute-girls'; perhaps it is the reference to a hetaira in i. 13 that leads Xenophon to mention them. In the classical period they were usually made from reeds, though some were of ivory, precious woods, or metal, with finely calibrated holes. Primitive flutes were made from hard materials such as horn or stone, pierced by one or more holes. Inasmuch as it was more difficult to produce pleasing music on a stone flute than on a reed, Xenophon may have had a stone flute in mind here, or he may merely be thinking of those proverbially useless things: stones.

13. ἑταίραν. In classical Athens, this word meant 'companion' [to a man]. Both hetairai who appear in Xenophon's work, Aspasia (iii. 14) and Theodote (*Mem.* 3. 11), made their living by providing emotional and intellectual companionship as well as sexual favours in return for payment; Xenophon draws attention to Theodote's beauty and wit, and to the fortune she amassed by practising her profession. The hetaira should be distinguished from a πόρνη, who is a woman on the lowest level of the scale of prostitution where there is no pretence of anything other than quick sex for money. A hetaira, unlike a wife who has a dowry and is productive (see on vii. 13), brings nothing material to a relationship. Rather, a man must continually deplete his resources in order to maintain her and retain her exclusive or near-exclusive services, as envisaged here. According to Ps.-Dem. 59. 29, the purchase price of a young but experienced slave hetaira was 3,000 dr.[19] Unlike a wife who is

[18] 'Die Horen des Prodikos', *Hermes*, 71 (1936), 158–60.

[19] Prices of hetairai in other classical sources are inflated or otherwise unreliable. See Hans Herter, 'Soziologie der antiken Prostitution im Lichte des heidnischen und christlichen Schrifttums', *Jahrbuch für Antike und Christentum*, 3 (1960), 83. The average price of a slave of the Hermocopidae was 174 dr.: see W. K. Pritchett, 'The Attic Stelai, Part II', *Hesperia*, 25 (1956), 255–8, 276–9, and on vii. 41. Cf. ii. 2 for other prices, and see further on iii. 14 Ἀσπασίαν, and Sarah B. Pomeroy, *Goddesses, Whores, Wives, and Slaves*, 89–92.

'given' in marriage by her parents and 'taken' by her husband (see on vii. 4), a successful free hetaira like Theodote could choose to be with whoever pleased her (*Mem.* 3. 11. 1).

ὑοσκύαμον. Henbane belongs to the family Solanaceae. It is a poisonous hallucinogenic, sometimes used for medicinal purposes.[20]

15. ἀπὸ τῶν ἐχθρῶν ὠφελεῖσθαι. There is no need to agree with Schenkl that a section is missing in which Socrates explained how enemies might be beneficial. Inasmuch as it was a traditional Greek idea that it was right to harm enemies (see e.g. Pl. *Rep.* 1) one way of harming them was to make a profit at their expense. The competition for honour is a 'zero-sum' game: the enemy's loss is his opponent's gain. A further explanation is forthcoming in i. 23. Plutarch refers to Xenophon's phrase twice as his inspiration for *How to Profit by One's Enemies* (1–2 = *Mor.* 86 c–e) explaining that enemies make one more careful, stimulate one to greater virtue, and force one to examine one's actions and to become superior to them. The present passage refers to personal enemies; in i. 23 Xenophon sets forth benefits conferred by enemies who make war against one's country, but who are gentlemen.

17. δούλων. The implication is that, like free people, slaves may have the talent and ability required for work, but because they may be lazy the authority of a good supervisor is necessary to make them perform profitably. The notion of enslavement is resumed in i. 22 (see further Ch. 5).

εὐπατριδῶν. Literally 'those descended from noble fathers'. At Athens Eupatrids were at the top of the social scale, in contrast to the slaves whom Socrates mentioned in the previous sentence. In Xen. *Symp.* 8. 39–40, Socrates refers to Callias as a Eupatrid, descended from Erechtheus, and reminds him that he is a priest, proxenus of the Spartans, and well qualified for political leadership. Callias, however, is enamoured of the boy Autolycus; Socrates attempts to persuade him to elevate his feelings from the base physical level to a spiritual plane. Eupolis portrayed this affair in his comedy, *Autolycus* (testimonia in Kassal–Austin 5 s.v. v. *Autolycus* and *Kolakes*), and other contemporary sources also show Callias as thoroughly dissolute (see Davies, *APF* 7826, and on vi. 17 Ἰσχόμαχον). Therefore, we, or for that matter Critobulus, need look no further than Socrates' and his own companions for an example of degeneracy among those of the highest birth. Other notorious profligates of the day who are identified as Eupatrids

---

[20] See further Dioscurides 1. 35, 4. 68 and Hellmut Baumann, *Die griechische Pflanzenwelt* (Munich, 1982), 104 and pl. 174.

included Alcibiades (Isocr. 16. 25, and see Davies, *APF* 600) and
Andocides (Ps.-Plut. *Mor.* 834 B–E, and see Davies, *APF* 828).

The origins of the Eupatrids are difficult to determine.
According to Plutarch (*Thes.* 25), who gives the fullest account
and draws to some extent on a now-lost section of Arist. *Ath. Pol.*,
Theseus separated the Athenians into three groups: Eupatrids,
farmers, and craftsmen. To the Eupatrids he allocated the right
to hold certain priestly and political offices, and to serve as teachers
of the law. Even after the reforms of Solon made wealth, rather
than birth, a qualification for holding political office, some priest-
hoods continued to be restricted to Eupatrids. Thus, for example,
Callias was a torchbearer at the Eleusinian Mysteries.

We lack sufficient information about Critobulus' ancestors to be
able to verify that he himself was qualified to be called 'Eupatrid'
in terms of lineage, though he surely was upper-class in terms of
wealth. If, as he does in the passage in the *Symp.*, Socrates is using
the word here in a technical sense, to refer to a degenerate nobility,
Critobulus could nevertheless have understood Socrates' subsequent remarks about the degenerate upperclass as alluding to
him personally: he was a member of the élite, whether or not he
was actually a Eupatrid.[21] See further Ch. 5, sect. D.

18. δεσπότας. On Xenophon's view of moral servitude as voluntary
see Ch. 5, sect. I, and v. 18.

19. ἀργίαν. On idleness see on vii. 33.

20. δέσποιναι. In i. 17–19 the baneful influences are described as
masculine, but in i. 20 they become feminine.[22] Xenophon ends
the discussion by referring to them as female 'mistresses' who, like
the hetaira described in i. 13, weaken men's bodies, souls, and
estates. The word δέσποινα indicates dominance: it has not the
sexual connotation of ἑταίρα (for which see i. 13). In *Mem.*
2. 1. 29–31 vice is also personified as a woman. These personifica-
tions correspond to the grammatical fact that most abstract nouns
denoting good and bad qualities are feminine. See also on v. 18
ἀδύνατα.

---

[21] R. Sealey, 'Eupatridai', *Historia*, 10 (1961), 512–14, asserts that in the late 5th
c. 'Eupatrid' became a legal word for a class, but he does not persuade us that the
obvious conclusion that Eupatrids of the classical period were simply descendants of
the aristocrats of the Archaic period is not correct. See also H. T. Wade-Gery,
'Eupatridai, Archons, and Areopagus', *CQ* 4 (1931), 1–11, 77–89.

[22] Hence Marchant, in his Loeb text, iv. 373, prefers the emendation δεσποινῶν in
i. 22, although he does not adopt it for his Oxford Classical Text edition. However,
the masculine δεσποτῶν is satisfactory, inasmuch as Xenophon returns to universal
truths.

22. λιχνειῶν ... λαγνειῶν. As is especially appropriate for a person whose words were spoken rather than written (to be read silently), Socrates is characterized as delighting in alliteration, rhyme, and other forms of word-play: see e.g. i. 7–8 κτήματα ... χρήματα. In his discussion of vices here he may be alluding to Critobulus' predilections, which he finally mentions directly in ii. 7.

ἀδυνάτους ... ἐργάζεσθαι διὰ τὸ γῆρας. That gluttony and sex could destroy wealth was a topos: cf. Aesch. 1.42 for similar language asserting that a man dissipated an estate as a slave to vicious pleasures, including gluttony and hetairai. (For accusations of shameful indulgences see also Aesch. 1. 75, Dem. 18. 296, 19. 229, Lys. 19. 9–10.) There is no evidence for the abandonment of aged slaves in classical Greece (but see on ix. 14–15). Perhaps abandonment occurred, but was considered too repugnant, or too unremarkable, to record.[23] Cf. vii. 42 for the possibility that a wife and mother may be dishonoured when old age has rendered her unproductive.

23. πολέμιοι. See on i. 15.

καλοὶ κἀγαθοί. This passage has an oligarchic tone. A gentlemanly political 'enslavement' makes the vanquished demos, which usually lacks σωφροσύνη, better and more sensible. For a similar tone see ii. 6–7. For the oligarchic use of σωφροσύνη see, e.g. Thuc. 8. 64. 5 and the comments of K. J. Dover.[24] On sophrosyne as a personal virtue see on vii. 14. On καλοὶ κἀγαθοί see on vi. 12.

ii. 1. ἐξετάζων ... κατέγνωκας. The metaphor comes from the lawcourt (lit. 'examining' and 'reaching a verdict against').

2. δοκοῦμεν. Here and again in vi. 1 Critobulus moves from the first person singular to the plural. If this is not merely the deprecatory use of 'we' for 'I', presumably he is thinking either of his family or of the friends who are present and actually mentioned in iii. 1. Socrates deliberately misunderstands.

2–4. ἱκανῶς πλουτεῖν ... πόσον ... πέντε μνᾶς ... ἑκατονταπλασίονα ... ἱκανά. With five minae, or 500 dr., Socrates would belong to the class of thetes. Socrates' poverty is attested by Plato, Xenophon, Aristophanes, and Diogenes Laertius. But see Ch. 3, sect. C, for the deterioration in Socrates' finances so that he fell

[23] For speculation, see G. E. M. de Ste. Croix, 'Slavery and Other Forms of Unfree Labour', in L. J. Archer (ed.), *Slavery and Other Forms of Unfree Labour* (London, 1988), 25–6.

[24] A. W. Gomme, A. Andrewes, and K. J. Dover, *A Historical Commentary on Thucydides* (Oxford, 1945–1981), ad loc.

from hoplite status to thete. The evidence for the qualifications of thetes and their numbers in the fifth century is hazy. The thete was too poor to afford the armour needed for hoplite service: the probable cut-off point in the fourth century was 2,000 dr. (Diod. 18. 18. 4–5, Plut. *Phoc.* 27–8).[25] With more than 8 tal. 2,000 dr. Critobulus is a member of the liturgical class. For some expenditures and obligations of a young man in the liturgical class see i. 8 (1,200 dr. for a horse); i. 13 (3,000 dr. for a hetaira); ii. 5–6 (300 to 6,000 dr. for a liturgy).

That the poor may, relatively speaking, be better off than the wealthy is an example of Socrates' use of paradox. Such usage is characteristic of Socrates as portrayed by Xenophon and Plato. For an extended encomium of poverty see also Xen. *Symp.* 4. 29–45 and ii. 3–4. In *Mem.* 4. 2. 37 Socrates also defines the rich as those who have what is sufficient, and the poor as those who lack it. In *Hiero* 4. 8–9 possessions are said to be numerous or few in relation to the owner's needs. Therefore the despot has more difficulty in satisfying his needs. See further on i. 8 ἐπίστηται ... χρῆσθαι.

5. θύειν πολλά. This phrase covers various private and public obligations ranging from those required at family rituals on occasions such as births, marriages, and deaths to public sacrifices at deme (i.e. local) and polis level. Almost half the days in the Athenian calendar were festival days.[26] For the sacrificial calendar at Erchia see on ii. 5–6.

ξένους. Ξένοι or 'guest-friends' were persons linked to oikoi or social groups other than their own by reciprocal, hereditary, friendship relationships. They were accepted into the oikos as temporary members. See vii. 2 for an example of Ischomachus' obligations toward them. The host was obliged to furnish hospitality, protection, services, and provisions to the guest and would receive these, in turn, when the roles of guest and host were reversed. Like Ischomachus, Critobulus had a duty to receive friends from abroad. Because of his peripatetic life as well as his

---

[25] Most recently Barry Strauss, *Athens After the Peloponnesian War*, 80–1, 177, argued persuasively that the number of thetes was equal to the number of hoplites in 431, but the thetes suffered disproportionately in the course of the war so that they were outnumbered by the hoplites by at least 20 per cent at the end of the 5th c. M. A. Levi, 'Il dialogo di Critobulo', *Quattro studi spartani e altri scritti di storia greca* (Milan, 1967), 153, and A. H. M. Jones, *Athenian Democracy* (Oxford, 1957), 79–81, had estimated that 60 per cent of Athenians were thetes, but Strauss's figures are more nuanced and are based on a more thorough consideration of such evidence as there is.

[26] See Jon D. Mikalson, *The Sacred and Civil Calendar of the Athenian Year* (Princeton, NJ, 1975), 201–3.

upper-class origin, Xenophon had personal experience of ξενία. He refers to his own ties with Proxenos of Boeotia (*Anab.* 3. 1. 4, 5. 3. 5) and with Cleander of Sparta (*Anab.* 6. 6. 35, 7. 1. 8) as well as to ξενία relationships between others (e.g. *Anab.* 1. 3. 2, 3. 2. 4, and *Hell.* 4. 1. 39, 6. 5. 4). The historical sources are rich in references to guest-friend relationships that were actively employed during the Peloponnesian War.[27]

5–6. εὖ ποιεῖν . . . οὐ ῥᾳδίως ὑποίσεις. A wealthy man was obliged to discharge specific liturgies ('public services') and pay other expenses imposed by the state, and to do so with enthusiasm and generosity, even beyond what his resources permitted (Thuc. 6. 15. 3, Lys. 21. 16). The prices of liturgies that occurred regularly ranged from 300 dr. for a chorus at the Lesser Panathenaea (Lys. 21. 2) to one talent for a trierarchy.[28] In a show of public-spiritedness, some men did not await the imposition of liturgies, but volunteered to serve as trierarchs or made contributions of items as costly as ships and gear (Xen. *Hell.* 2. 3. 40, Lys. 29. 7). The sacrificial calendar of Erchia lists 59 different sacrifices that occurred during the year.[29] Wealthier members of the deme probably paid for the animals, either as a liturgy or a voluntary contribution. A prosperous man (like Ischomachus, xi. 9–10) was also expected to confer private benefactions voluntarily. Thus friends and associates might turn to him for help in providing dowries, or for a loan of money, or would expect to be invited when a large sacrifice produced a good dinner (e.g. Dem. 21. 13, 159, 189, 23. 112, 38. 26, 49. 46, Isaeus 6. 60, Lys. 21. 1–11, 15, 16).

6. ἔρημον συμμάχων. In §§ 6–8 Socrates abandons the good-humoured tone of the preceding part of the conversation and says some harsh words to Critobulus, intimating that his friends do not care for him but for his money, that he might be bereft of personal allies (whom, presumably, he would need in legal and political contexts), and that he is a pitiful creature.

μεγάλα τελεῖν. The obligations mentioned in the preceding paragraph fall roughly into the realm of voluntary benefactions conferred by wealthy men like Critobulus or Ischomachus in order to cultivate the good will of friends, allies, and fellow citizens. The

---

[27] See further Gabriel Herman, *Ritualised Friendship and the Greek City* (Cambridge, 1987), 130–42, 179–84.

[28] See notes on ii. 6 on specific liturgies and expenses and Davies, *APF*, pp. xxi f.

[29] *SEG* 21. 541, see 'Xenophon's Life: Youth'. There is little evidence for the funding of cults on the deme level; however, the hypothesis of David Whitehead, *The Demes of Attica 508/7–ca.250 B.C.* (Princeton, NJ, 1986), 173–5, that they were financed in the 4th c. by individual wealthy demesmen is reasonable.

liturgies that are mentioned in the present paragraph were imposed
by the state and could not be avoided without a legal proceding
for ἀντίδοσις (challenging another, supposedly wealthier man to
undertake the liturgy or to exchange property: see on vii. 3 εἰς
ἀντίδοσιν καλῶνται). Some of these liturgies, especially those connected with religious rituals, recurred annually or at fixed times;
others were imposed in the extraordinary circumstances of war
(see below on εἰσφοράς). For references to heavy taxes roughly
contemporaneous with the writing of the *Oeconomicus* see Ar. *Eccles.*
197–8, and Lys. 18. 21, 28. 3–4, 29. 4. G. E. M. de Ste. Croix[30]
suggests that, despite the complaints of upper-class Athenians, the
rate of taxes in classical Athens (0.25% per annum) was not
excessively heavy. However, Davies argues persuasively that taxation abetted by other factors such as imprudence or misfortune
might well cause an Athenian to fall from the liturgical class.[31] On
links between the public and private economy see Ch. 5.

ἱπποτροφίας. Horse-ownership was not only a sign of wealth
(see on i. 8), but a conspicuous indication that a man possessed
the resources necessary for service in the cavalry (see further Xen.
On Horsemanship, esp. 2. 1, 11. 1, *Cav.* 1. 11). Horses were employed
for purposes other than purely military, but in the present context
Socrates is referring to Critobulus' perennial obligation to provide
his own horse for his military service. As Ischomachus makes clear,
there was a direct connection between military preparedness and
riding for pleasure and exercise (xi. 17, sim. *On Horsemanship* 3. 7).
Breeding horses for the cavalry was essential for the security of the
state. The wealthy Lycophron claimed that he raised horses not
as a rich man's hobby, but as a public service (Hyperides 1. 16,
sim. Alcibiades in Thuc. 6. 16. 1–2).

χορηγίας. The choregia was an annual liturgy imposed on the
wealthiest citizens (Ps.-Xen. *Const. of Ath.* 56. 3). Choregoi were
responsible for the selection, training, and costuming of choruses,
dancers, actors, and musicians who performed at various religious
festivals including the City Dionysia, Lenaea, Panathenaea,
Thargelia, Hephaesteia, and Prometheia. The amount expended
might be decisive in winning a victory. The victorious choregos
also paid to erect a commemorative tripod. One choregos claims
to have spent 5,000 dr. in 409 for a men's dithyrambic chorus and
for the tripod and 3,000 for a tragic chorus (Lys. 21. 1–2, 4). But
these figures are high. At the other extreme is the 300 for a cyclic

---

[30] 'Demosthenes' *Τίμημα* and the Athenian Eisphora in the Fourth Century BC'.
[31] *Wealth*, 82–7.

chorus at the Lesser Panathenaea mentioned by the same source. The choregos for the cyclic or dithyrambic chorus (such as the one mentioned in viii. 20) was nominated by his tribe. Other choregoi, e.g. those for tragedy and comedy, were appointed by the magistrate in charge of the festival.[32] As choregos for Antiochis in the men's dithyramb at a Dionysia, Critobulus won a victory perhaps early in the fourth century (*IG* ii². 3036, Davies, *APF* 337).

γυμνασιαρχίας. The archon basileus selected gymnasiarchs from lists submitted by their tribes. The gymnasiarchy was an annual liturgy and it was one of the most costly (Isaeus 6. 60, Ps.-Xen. *Const. of Ath.* 1. 13). The gymnasiarch was responsible for presenting a team of runners for a torch-race at a festival, such as the Panathenaea (e.g. *IG* ii². 2371), and festivals of Prometheus (Isaeus 7. 36) and Hephaestus (e.g. And. 1. 132).[33] The gymnasiarch paid for selecting and training the team, for their instructor, and for their torches, oil, and other expenses. If his team was victorious he also paid for a commemorative monument. In the fifth century the wealthiest men including Nicias (Plut. *Nic.* 3, *Comp. Nic. and Crass.* 4) and Alcibiades (Isocr. 16. 35) were gymnasiarchs.[34] In 405 a gymnasiarch spent 12 minae at the Prometheia (Lys. 21. 3).

προστατείας. Two meanings are possible here: (i) holding presidencies (acting as patron or taking chief responsibility especially for religious and civic associations or enterprises) and (ii) patronage of metics. Since προστατείας is listed along with obligations in the public sphere and was likely to be more expensive than patronage of metics, the first interpretation is preferable. Xenophon uses the related words προστατεύειν, προΐστασθαι, and προστάτης to convey the notion of leadership fraught with responsibilities and obligations which varied according to circumstances (e.g. ii. 9 *bis*, xii. 4, *Hell.* 3. 5. 14, 4. 8. 28).

τριηραρχίας. Trierarchs were appointed annually to pay for the maintenance of a warship. There is little specific evidence concerning the trierarchy before the Sicilian Expedition (415), but

---

[32] See further Antiphon 6. 11–12, Ps.-Xen. *Const. of Ath.* 1. 13, 3. 4, Arist. *Ath. Pol.* 56. 3, *Pol.* 1309ᵃ19, *IG* ii². 1138, and A. W. Pickard-Cambridge, *The Dramatic Festivals of Athens*, 2nd edn., rev. J. Gould and D. M. Lewis, with supplement (Oxford, 1988), 75–8, 86–93.

[33] J. K. Davies, 'Demosthenes on Liturgies: A Note', *JHS* 87 (1967), 40, is uncertain whether the torch race in honour of Pan was liturgical. It does not appear to be qualitatively different from races that were financed by liturgies, but there is no evidence that it was so financed.

[34] For other gymnasiarchs see Davies, *APF*, nos. 2760, 7336, 9207, 14274, 15164, 15446, A27, B25, D7–10.

Ps.-Xen. *Const. of Ath.* 1. 13 mentions that the wealthy were responsible for χορηγία, γυμνασιαρχία, and τριηραρχία. It appears that one of the strategoi appointed the trierarchs and that the trierarchs may, at times, have personally commanded their ships.[35] Trierarchies were frequent during the Peloponnesian War and the expenses were heavy. Defendants, who of course want to demonstrate their public-spiritedness, declare that the trierarchy has cost them as much as 1 tal. (Dem. 21. 155), 2,400 dr. from one of two syntrierarchs (Lys. 32. 24, 27), 6 tal. in seven years (Lys. 21. 2), and 1⅓ tal. in three years (perhaps a syntrierarchy shared with one other man: Lys. 19. 29, 42).

εἰσφοράς. Special assessments were sometimes levied on taxable property in times of war. Thuc. 3. 19. 1 mentions the εἰσφορά of 428/427 that produced 200 tal. *IG* i². 92 (= Tod 51B), ll. 17–20, is also evidence for fifth-century eisphorai. Such levies were repeated. Lys. 21. 3 provides evidence for two εἰσφορά payments of 3,000 and 4,000 dr. between 411 and 404 and alludes to others (12. 20, 25. 12, 30. 26). Past the dramatic date of the *Oeconomicus*, but known to Xenophon, would have been the εἰσφοραί imposed during the fourth century.[36] Although the details of the system are debatable, it is clear that men who possessed over a certain amount of property were divided into συμμορίαι which were obliged to pay their share of the tax as a group. In *Revenues* 3. 7–11, 4. 40, Xenophon refers to the levies of 364/3 and 362 and sets forth his own proposals for εἰσφορά. However, there is no indication that Xenophon is being anachronistic here: he is merely referring to the payment of εἰσφορά as it existed during Socrates' lifetime.

6–7. τιμωρήσονται . . . κλέπτοντα. Wealthy, politically prominent men were a natural target for the charge of embezzlement, for it could be asserted that they had increased their personal fortune at the expense of the state (as in Lys. 27. 9, 28. 13, Dem. 21. 189, 24. 124). For example, Pericles was tried on a charge of κλοπή ('theft of public money'), found guilty, and fined (Thuc. 2. 65. 3, Plut. *Per.* 35. 4, Pl. *Gorg.* 516 A, Diod. 12. 45. 4). The death penalty

---

[35] Ar. *Knights* 912–18, Lys. 21. 9, Arist. *Ath. Pol.* 61. 1, and see B. Jordan, *The Athenian Navy in the Classical Period* (Berkeley, 1975), 70.

[36] See Lys. 19. 29, 43, 57 (two men paid a total of 4,000 dr.), 27. 10, 28. 3, 29. 9, Isaeus 5. 37, 45, Dem. 27. 37 (1,800 dr for ten years), Isoc. 17. 41 (metics). The tax was reorganized in 378/7 (Polyb. 2. 62. 7, Harpocration, *Lex.*, s.v. συμμορία (= Philochorus, *FGrH* 328 F 45), Dem. 27. 7, Photius, *Lex.* s.v. ναυκραρία (= Cleidemus, *FGrH* 323 F 8), Isoc. 15. 145, Dem. 14. 27, 20. 28, 21. 157, etc., and see de Ste. Croix, 'Demosthenes' Τίμημα', and E. Ruschenbusch, 'Die athenischen Symmorien des 4. Jh. v. Chr', *ZPE* 31 (1978), 275–84.

could also be imposed on an embezzler.[37] For thefts committed against private property see on xiv. 4. The tone of this passage is oligarchic, stressing the unfairness of burdens, and asserting that the demos, in effect, regarded the wealth of the rich as 'their property'. For a similar tone see i. 23, but compare xi. 9 for Ischomachus' more generous attitude toward the city.

7. παιδικοῖς δὲ πράγμασι. These words are ambivalent. Critobulus was young when he married (see on i. 1 Κριτόβουλε) and thus the statement may refer to childish behaviour, but more probably it alludes to his deep involvement in an amorous affair with another young man. Xenophon also uses παιδικός with homosexual implications to describe a subject of conversation between Agesipolis and Agesilaus (*Hell.* 5. 3. 20, see on xii. 13–14). Critobulus was the lover of Cleinias and continued to praise him extravagantly even after marrying (Xen. *Mem.* 1. 3. 8–10, *Symp.* 4. 12–16, 23; Pl. *Euthyd.* 271 B, 275 A–B). Serious erotic liaisons might prove not only distracting, but costly, for the lover bestowed gifts on his beloved. Hence such relationships were usually terminated upon marriage.[38] According to Athen. 5. 220 A, Aeschines Socraticus in *Telauges* mocked Critobulus for ignorance and sordid behaviour. H. Dittmar, for whom Critobulus was profligate, suggests that Xenophon found the model there for the present dialogue between him and Socrates.[39] However, only nine brief fragments of the dialogue are extant (Dittmar 290–2, nos. 40–8) and only the excerpt from Athenaeus seems to support his hypothesis at all. Critobulus' wealth and flamboyance surely made him a topic of gossip. Thus Xenophon not only had heard about Critobulus from others, but doubtless knew him personally (see on i. 1 Κριτόβουλε). He did not need to base his characterization primarily upon an earlier written description, though he probably did know Aeschines' work. Perhaps one of Xenophon's motives for writing the present section of the dialogue was to respond to the charge of corrupting youth that had been levelled against Socrates at his trial (Xen. *Apol.* 19).

Diogenes Laertius (ii. 49) reports that in his youth Xenophon too was in love with Cleinias. If this report is true, Xenophon may have been in competition with Critobulus and others for the

[37] Lys. 30. 26, 27. 7, 29. 11, and see further David Cohen, *Theft in Athenian Law* (Munich, 1983), 10–13, 30–3, 49–51, 121–4.

[38] See Isaeus 10. 25 for a man who dissipated the wealth of an oikos by such activities, and K. J. Dover, *Greek Homosexuality* (London, 1978), for general discussion.

[39] *Aischines von Sphettos*, 231–7.

affections of Cleinias. Such rivalries and attachments were common among aristocratic young men before marriage. But in his own writings Xenophon was not so tolerant of homosexuality as Plato was, at least before he reached old age and wrote the *Laws*. In xii. 13–14 pederasty disqualifies a slave from becoming an overseer and in *Mem.* 2. 1. 30 he condemns using men as women.

8. φίλοι. At Socrates' trial, friends offer to pay the fine (Pl. *Apol.* 38 b; cf. *Crito* 45 b, cf. Xen. *Apol.* 23).⁴⁰

15. μαθεῖν. This is the first example in the *Oeconomicus* of Socrates' well-known respect for expertise and for his denial that he himself possesses knowledge. For other descriptions of his search for ἐπιστήμη see e.g. Xen. *Mem.* 4. 4–5, Pl. *Apol.* 21 c–22 e, *Rep.* 536 e –537 e, *Theaet.* 150 c.

16–18. ὁμολογῶ . . . πράττοντας. Cf. similar investigations reported by Socrates in Pl. *Apol.* 30 e–33 b, etc. See Ch. 3, sect. C.

18. ὁ θεός. Socrates is referring to some unnamed divinity. He is not a monotheist, though in Marchant's and Waterfield's translations 'God' with a capital letter implies as much.

iii. This chapter is a kind of survey of the contents of the *Oeconomicus*, mentioning the house and the need for orderliness, the training of slaves and administrators, agriculture, horses, and husband and wife. All these subjects are discussed at length in the remainder of the treatise, though in cc. vi–ix οἰκονομία is not so much a theoretical as a practical and profitable kind of knowledge.

1. τῶν φίλων τουτωνί. This is the first time the reader is explicitly told that others are present at the dialogue between Socrates and Critobulus. But see on ii. 1 δοκοῦμεν.

οἰκίας. Because the word οἶκος includes the structure, building a house is part of οἰκονομία. The architecture of Ischomachus' and his wife's house is described in c. ix.

2. ἔπιπλα. On the furnishings of such a household see on viii. 19–20. According to Xen. *Revenues* 4. 7, the furnishings should be limited to what is sufficient for the oikos. As vase-paintings indicate, the Athenians used less furniture than we in the modern Western world do. The importance of orderly storage of household goods is elaborated in cc. viii and ix.

οἰκέτας. This term evokes the close connection between the slaves and the oikos (but see on iii. 10). Philippe Gauthier observes

---

⁴⁰ On the Greek tradition of borrowing and lending among friends, relatives, and neighbours see Osborne, *Classical Landscape*, 93–4.

that in the *Oeconomicus* rural slaves are always called οἰκέται.[41]
However, slaves so described in c. vii–ix live in Ischomachus'
house, which is probably in the city (see on xi. 14–15 κατὰ πόλιν
... εἰς ἀγρόν) and there is no indication of location for the οἰκέται
mentioned here and in iii. 4. For the treatment of slaves see also
v. 16, ix. 11, xiii, and Ch. 5, sect. I. On the employment of slaves
in agriculture see on xii. 3.

3. ἐν χώρᾳ ἕκαστα τεταγμένα. In c. viii Xenophon develops the
concept of order as basic not only to estate management but to
human welfare in general.

7. κωμῳδῶν θέαν ... μακρὰν ὁδὸν βαδίζοντα. Inasmuch as
Critobulus is said to walk a great distance, Socrates must be
thinking of comedies performed outside the city walls at festivals
such as the Rural Dionysia. In the early fourth century Rural
Dionysia were arranged by the demes and though they occurred
during the month of Posideon, they were not held everywhere
simultaneously. Critobulus could have attended quite a few festivals in widespread areas of Attica in one month.[42]

8. ἱππικῆς. On financial ruin from keeping horses see Strepsiades
and his extravagant son Pheidippides ('Horse-sparer') in
Aristophanes' *Clouds*. See further on i. 8 ἵππον.

10. Πωλοδαμνεῖν ... ἡλικίαι ... ἵππων. According to Xen. *On
Horsemanship* 2–3 owners turned over their horses to experts who
would break them in. Xenophon advises those who would purchase
a horse that is already broken to buy one not more than 5 years old.

    γεωργοὺς ... ὠνούμενον. In the *Oeconomicus* Xenophon uses
γεωργός to refer to a farmer who, as the context indicates, is free
(as in vi. 6 and xix. 15), or whose status is not specified (as in
xv. 11). The term was also used of metics: see *IG* ii². 10 (Athens,
401/0 BC). Therefore the participle is required here. See further
on xii. 3.

11. αἰτιᾶσθαι ... Πρόβατον ... νομέα. In the Mediterranean world
of 'honour–shame' societies, a wife's virtues and vices reflect directly upon the man who exercises patriarchal authority over her.
See xii. 5–9 and *Mem.* 3. 13. 4 for the owner's responsibility for
training slaves and vii. 10 for training a wife. In the preface to
the *Cyropaedia* (1. 1. 2–3), Xenophon also compares men in positions of authority over others with herdsmen. Analogies between

---

[41] *Un commentaire historique des Poroi de Xénophon* (Paris, 1976), 151, citing vii. 35,
37, viii. 22, ix. 5, 9, 16, etc.
[42] On comic performances in rural settings see David Whitehead, *The Demes of
Attica 508/7-ca.250 B.C.*, 215–22.

animals and human beings are common in the works of the
Socratics. See e.g. the analogies between horses and men in iii. 10,
ix. 15, and xi. 4 and in Pl. *Apol.* 20 A–B. See also iv. 24 ἱδρῶσαι,
vii. 10 χειροήθης ... ἐτετιθάσευτο, vii. 32 ἡ τῶν μελιττῶν ἡγεμών,
and xiii. 6–9.[43] Comparisons with animals are often
complimentary.

12. σπουδαίων. Managing a household in the liturgical class, including supervising slaves and caring for children, were very serious
concerns. See further on cc. vii–x.

12–13. πλείω ἐπιτρέπεις ... ἐλάττονα διάλεγῃ. 'Entrust a greater
number ... have fewer conversations' is an example of Socrates'
use of paradox. For others see on iii. 3, vii. 5–6, and vii. 10.

13. παῖδα νέαν. Upper-class girls married at about 14 years of age.
See on vii. 5.

    ἐλάχιστα ἑωρακυῖαν καὶ ἀκηκουῖαν. See on vii. 5–6 ὑπὸ πολλῆς
ἐπιμελείας ... ἐλάχιστα μὲν ὄψοιτο, ἐλάχιστα δ' ἀκούσοιτο, ἐλάχιστα
δ' ἔροιτο. The passages are linguistically very similar. Ischomachus'
wife had also seen and heard very little. Here the ignorance of
Critobulus' wife is seen as a defect in the customary system of
women's education, which the husband ought to remedy.

14. γυναῖκας ... ἐπαίδευσαν. In Xen. *Symp.* 2. 9, Socrates recommends that each man teach his own wife, and in *Oec.* vii–x
Xenophon gives a detailed example of such teaching.

    Ἀσπασίαν. It is quite remarkable that Socrates (or Xenophon),
should choose the hetaira Aspasia as an example, inasmuch as he
is discussing wives and has previously warned Critobulus about
hetairai (i. 3). In fact, in vi. 6 Ischomachus is brought in to serve
as the authority on household management. Socrates mentions
Aspasia here only to cast doubt on Critobulus' remark: she is an
effective argument against his assumption, for she had neither a
husband nor, consequently, her own full-fledged oikos. As in i. 3,
the conclusion is that even a person like Aspasia can understand
οἰκονομία without actually owning an oikos.

    That the promise to bring in Aspasia is never fulfilled may be
due to Xenophon's stitching together at this point two literary
sources—a dialogue between Socrates and Critobulus and another
between Socrates and Ischomachus—and failing to eliminate what
some scholars view as an inconsistency that resulted. (On the unity
of the *Oeconomicus* see Ch. 1, sect. D.) Or the promise may be an
example of Xenophon's humour, a teasing and surprising idea
that he never intended to develop. Or perhaps the explanation is

---

[43] For other examples see P. Louis, *Les Métaphores de Platon* (Paris, 1945), 185–8.

that actually Socrates promises he will bring Critobulus and
Aspasia together at some time in the future, not necessarily in this
dialogue, although the reader would expect ποτέ ('one day') or
the like. Of course, Aspasia is not standing around with Socrates
and the young men at the dramatic time of the dialogue.
Meanwhile Socrates tells Critobulus what he knows about
οἰκονομία.

Aspasia of Miletus appears frequently in the works of the
Socratics.[44] Aischines and Antisthenes both wrote dialogues titled
Ἀσπασία; though these works are no longer extant they were
consulted by later authors, probably including Xenophon.[45]
Ischomachus, like Critobulus, never gives us his wife's name.
Inasmuch as referring to a respectable living woman by name,
unless absolutely necessary, was a breach of etiquette,[46] Aspasia is
the only women mentioned directly by name in the *Oeconomicus*.
Because Aspasia's name was already well known in her own lifetime, and because she was by Xenophon's time a traditional figure
in the works in the Socratics, and because she was no longer alive
when Xenophon wrote the *Oeconomicus*, his mentioning her by
name was not necessarily intended as an insult.[47] However, in his
youth Xenophon would have heard Aspasia's name bandied about
and he is usually reticent about giving the names of respectable
Greek women. Plut. *Ages.* 19. 6, points out that Xenophon did
not state the name of Agesilaus' daughter.

Because Aspasia was reputed to be wise and spent her days in
the company of men it is not surprising that she is portrayed in
Pl. *Menex.* 235 E–236 C and Lucian, *Salt.* 25, as knowledgeable
in fields such as rhetoric and politics, and conversant with serious
matters which are of concern to men. It is, however, of some
interest to find her cited as an authority on domestic matters
(which are usually associated with respectable women) and using
metaphorical language drawn from female experience. For
example, in Xen. *Mem.* 2. 6. 36, she comments on matchmakers
and marriage and in Pl. *Menex.* 237 E–238 A, she draws analogies
from pregnancy and breastfeeding. Perhaps this interest in domest-

---

[44] e.g. Xen. *Mem.* 2. 6. 36 and see further W. Judeich, 'Aspasia', *RE* ii (Stuttgart,
1895) cols. 1716–21.

[45] See Ch. 3, Dittmar, *Aischines*, 31–41, 61–2, and for a reconstruction of Aeschines'
dialogue Barbara Ehlers, *Eine vorplatonische Deutung des sokratischen Eros*.

[46] See David Schaps, 'The Woman Least Mentioned: Etiquette and Women's
Names', *CQ,* NS 27 (1977), 323–30.

[47] On the post-classical tradition of an erotic relationship between Socrates and
Aspasia see Ch. 6, sect. E.

icity can be attributed to Aspasia's transformation from a hetaira to a closer approximation to a respectable woman. Her status was elevated when she became involved in a monogamous relationship with Pericles, and when her sons were granted citizenship.[48] Plut. *Per.* 24. 3 reports that Socrates and his associates and their wives went to listen to her. According to Cic. *De Inv.* 1. 51–2, Aeschines portrayed her conversing with Xenophon and his wife. But such a meeting was improbable (see Ch. 6, sect. B). Perhaps it is actually due to the seclusion of respectable women that Aspasia must serve as the female authority on domestic economy and the proper relationship between husband and wife. Of course, married life does include sexual relations—a subject about which Aspasia would be expected to have adequate knowledge and Socrates might be coy. (Socrates changes the subject in c. xi as soon as Ischomachus begins to talk about sexual arousal.) Moreover, as the controversy on the hetairai who are depicted on Athenian vases in the act of spinning indicates,[49] such women might have their own homes and do housework; but Socrates, who was depicted by both Plato and Xenophon as uncompromising in his search for expertise, certainly knew that their major talents were in other areas (see further on vii. 32).

Socrates' relationship with his own wife Xanthippe and the poverty of his household were so notorious that he could scarcely claim expertise in the domestic realm. Therefore, he promises to introduce Aspasia to discuss these matters. That, at least in his own opinion, Socrates' household was well managed (ii. 4) may be to Xanthippe's credit. But Socrates could not promise to bring in his own wife to discuss household economy with Critobulus because she was a respectable woman and Critobulus was a stranger to her and a *bon vivant* as well. Besides, his oikos was not of the same economic status as Critobulus'. Because a slave steward managed Pericles' oikos, whatever Aspasia knew about such management she had not learnt by practical experience in Pericles' household (see on i. 3–4 and vii. 36).

---

[48] P. J. Bicknell, 'Axiochos Alkibiadou, Aspasia and Aspasios', *AC* 51 (1982), 240–50, argues that Aspasia was freeborn, that her father was an aristocrat, that she came to Athens with her married sister and brother-in-law, and that she had begun living with Pericles as his 'de facto wife' by 441/0. But if this scenario is true, why did her brother-in-law not make certain that the liaison did not become a source of notoriety?

[49] See e.g. Sutton, *The Interaction between Men and Women on Athenian Vases*, 347–64, and Eva C. Keuls, 'Attic Vase-Painting and the Home Textile Industry', in W. G. Moon (ed.), *Ancient Greek Art and Iconography* (Madison, Wis., 1983), 209–30.

15. γυναῖκα ... οἴκου. On the relationship between spouses see Chs. 4–5 and notes on cc. vii–x.

iv. 2–3. βαναυσικαὶ ... πόλεων ... βαναυσικὰς τέχνας. According to *Etym. Magn.* 187–40, βάναυσος derives from βαῦνος ('furnace') and αὕειν ('light a fire') meaning workers who perform their work with fire (cf. iv. 2 πῦρ); it is also used of mechanical artisans (χειροτέχναι) in general. Clearly, Xenophon uses the word in this sense. However, H. Frisk, *Griechisches etymologisches Wörterbuch*, I. 218, s.v. βάναυσος considers the former interpretation to be a folk etymology, and derives the word from *μάναυσος < μανός ('spreading apart').

Although Socrates himself was a stonemason (D.L. 2. 19, Luc. *Somn.* 12) the texts of the Socratics do not indicate that he spent much time working for a livelihood. (For Socrates' financial status, see on ii. 2–4.) For those who did not farm exclusively by supervising, farming was, of course, a form of manual labour, but it was performed out of doors, not seated before a fire. In this passage Socrates displays the conventional aristocratic scorn for handiwork that was performed indoors.

Such work was deemed appropriate for women and slaves, but not for free men, whose proper spheres were politics, the military, and, as Ischomachus asserts, agriculture (vii. 22). The rejection of banausic trades stemmed, in part, from an idea that they left a man no time to participate in the running of the state. So Arist. *Pol.* 1278ᵃ8, declares that the best state will not make a craftsman (βάναυσος) a citizen. Some accusations of servile or foreign origin were linked to the assertion that a man, or one of his parents had worked at a menial, though not morally disreputable, job.[50] Xenophon's Socrates (vi. 5), like Plato's, expresses an unqualified disdain for vulgar occupations, declaring that they are injurious to both body and soul (Pl. *Rep.* 495 D–E, 522 B, 590 C, *Laws* 848 A, 919 C). In addition to concurring with normal upper-class Athenian sentiment, Xenophon's reference to states eminent in war suggests that he was thinking of Spartans, and perhaps Thebans (Plut. *Pel.* 19), Cretans (Arist. *Pol.* 1272ᵃ24), Chalcidians (Arist. fr. 93 1492ᵇ22), and of course Persia, the subject of the chapter. For Persian military prowess see on c. iv below and Herod. 2. 167, Pl. *Laws* 637 D, Isocr. *Panegyr.* 67. For the same attitude among the Egyptians, from whom the Greeks may have

---

[50] For example, Dem. 57. 34–5, 45, Cleon 'the Paphlagonian' and 'tanner' in Ar. *Clouds*, 581, *Knights*, 2, 6, 136, and see further K. J. Dover, *Greek Popular Morality*, 32–3.

learnt it, and for Corinth (a commercial city) being less hostile see Herod. 2. 167. In Sparta banausic work was delegated to helots and perioikoi (i.e. 'free non-citizens'). Spartan men were engaged in military and civil occupations, and Spartan women were devoted to motherhood.[51] Some significant differences, however, are that in Sparta helots made the clothing and performed agricultural work (Xen. *Sp. Const.* 1. 4), whereas Xenophon finds such work appropriate for free women and men, even those of the highest class, including the Persian king himself. Furthermore, Spartans were forbidden to handle silver and gold coins or to engage in any kind of business (Xen. *Sp. Const.* 7. 2–6), whereas Xenophon approves of making money in socially acceptable ways. The blatant commercialism of manufacturing products for sale in the market in order to earn a living that characterized banausic work was not acceptable.[52] Following Xenophon, Ps.-Arist. *Oec.* 1343[b]4–6, praises agriculture for rendering men courageous as soldiers. In contrast, Arist. *Pol.* 1328[b]41–1329[a]2 specifically distinguishes the farmer from the good citizen.

In the *Oeconomicus* we detect the aristocratic ideal found also in Homer: integral to such a society are kings such as Odysseus who plough their lands and royal women who weave and launder (see further Ch. 5, sect. C, and on vii. 32). However, Ischomachus, unlike Cyrus, does not actually engage in agricultural labour. Instead, he supervises the workers, and he himself gets his exercise by walking and riding. Chantraine, *Xénophon, Économique*, 9, mistakenly comments that in c. iv Socrates expresses the prejudices of the Athenian *bonne bourgeoisie*. Socrates' attitudes remain those of the élite. However, in cc. i–iii he is more theoretical, while beginning with c. iv, he is more directly concerned with material matters.

Stobaeus (4. 18. 16) quotes from iv. 2 καὶ γάρ to iv. 3 τέχνας ἐργάζεσθαι. Marchant gives the variants in the apparatus criticus. Phrynichus (fr. 83 de Borries) gives the first sentence. Stobaeus and Phrynichus offer different texts, which, in turn vary to some extent from the manuscripts. Phrynichus, who is not cited by Marchant, gives: καὶ γὰρ οἵ γε βάναυσοι καλούμενοι ἐπίρρητοί τέ εἰσι, καὶ εἰκότως ἀδοξοῦνται πρὸς τῶν πόλεων. Since Phrynichus is interested in the use of ἀδοξοῦνται with πρός, his variants in the

---

[51] See Xen. *Sp. Const.* 1. 4, Plut. *Comp. Lyc. and Numa* 2. 3–4, and Olaf Gigon, *Sokrates: Sein Bild in Dichtung und Geschichte*, 139–40.

[52] See further on xx. 27 ἔμποροι, André Aymard, *Études d'histoire ancienne* (Paris, 1967), 317, and Jean-Pierre Vernant, *Mythe et pensée chez les Grecs* (Paris, 1985), 243.

first part of the sentence are not significant. On the indirect tradition, see further Ch. 7.

2. ἔνιαι ... θηλυνομένων. Sedentariness is also associated with slavishness and womanishness in x. 10, 13. But, as the present passage demonstrates, these qualities are not biologically determined. Men who engage in banausic occupations may become slavish and womanish, whereas, according to cc. vii–x, women can avoid slavish and womanish behaviour. See Ch. 5, sect. I, and on vii. 30.

3. ἀλεξητῆρες. In v. 7, 13 Xenophon expands on the idea that farming prepares men to defend their country. This notion corresponds to the Roman ideal of the citizen soldier (see e.g. Cato, *RR* pr. 4 and Col. *RR*, 1 pr. 17). ἀλεξητήρ is poetic and rare in prose. The word was first used in *Il.* 20. 396 of Demoleon, son of Antenor. Such a hero was the antithesis of a man engaged in banausic arts. See Ch. 2, sect. B.

4. Περσῶν. That Xenophon's view of the Persians was idealistic rather than realistic was recognized by his contemporary Plato (see on iv. 5 γεωργίας).[53] Nevertheless, it does not necessarily follow that all Xenophon's statements about Persia are lies. Historians nowadays vary in their estimate of the veracity of Xenophon's testimony. For example, Chester G. Starr declares that Xenophon 'does not significantly advance our knowledge of the real nature of the Persians in the fourth century'.[54] Christopher Tuplin scrutinizes details supplied by Xenophon and concludes that he can find little corroboration for Xenophon's reports.[55] In contrast, Pierre Briant[56] and Steven W. Hirsch[57] accept the *Oeconomicus, Cyropaedia,* and *Anabasis* as valid sources of information, although they are both also aware of Xenophon's idealization of the 'mirage perse'.

---

[53] Some of the material in the remainder of this chapter has been published in Sarah B. Pomeroy, 'The Persian King and the Queen Bee', *AJAH* 9 (1984), 98–108.

[54] 'Greeks and Persians in the Fourth Century B.C.', *IA* 11 (1975), 39–99.

[55] e.g. 'Persian Garrisons in Xenophon and Other Sources', in Amélie Kuhrt and Heleen Sancisi-Weerdenburg (eds.), *Achaemenid History,* iii: *Method and Theory* (Leiden, 1988), 67–70, and 'The Administration of the Achaemenid Empire', in *Coinage and Administration in the Athenian and Persian Empires: The Ninth Oxford Symposium on Coinage and Monetary History (BAR* Int. Ser. 343; Oxford, 1987), 109–66; but see on iv. 9–12 below for Tuplin's most recent views vindicating Xenophon's testimony.

[56] e.g. 'Contrainte militaire, dépendance rurale et exploitation des territoires en Asie achéménide', *Rois, tributs et paysans* (Paris, 1982), 185, 'Sources grecques et histoire achéménide', ibid. 491–538, and *État et pasteurs au Moyen-Orient ancien* (Cambridge, 1982), 34 n. 6.

[57] *The Friendship of the Barbarians: Xenophon and the Persian Empire* (Hanover, NH, and London, 1985), 62.

Despite Xenophon's errors in some details, because inscriptions and the visual arts of the Achaemenids corroborate Xenophon's reports about Persian culture in general, Iranologists have long accepted this testimony and pay as much attention to the *Cyropaedia* and *Oeconomicus* as they do to the *Anabasis*;[58] they understand that Xenophon provides valid background material on Persia. For example, Wolfgang Fauth opens an exhaustive investigation of the gardener-king with the evidence of *Oeconomicus* iv.[59] Similarly, Gerold Walser finds that Xenophon relates some authentic Persian traditions.[60] W. Knauth uses Xenophon along with Iranian sources.[61] Dandamaev relies on *Oec.* iv for his interpretation of Persian administration.[62]

φασιν. Similarly iv. 15 *Φασὶ δέ τινες* and iv. 16 *λέγεται*. According to H. R. Breitenbach these words indicate that Xenophon is drawing on a literary source for information about Persia.[63] However, Xenophon did have first-hand contact with Cyrus (who knew Greek). Furthermore, he might have heard these stories during his travels in Asia Minor. He might have heard the story about Lysander and Cyrus (iv. 20–5) from Cyrus himself, or from a Spartan source (i.e. someone who knew Lysander, if not Lysander himself). All that *φασιν* really does is to make Socrates disclaim responsibility for the statement, inasmuch as he himself did not know Cyrus.

5. γεωργίας. The tradition of the gardener-king can be traced back to Mesopotamian and Chaldaean sources.[64] The picture of God as a gardener comes across vividly in Gen. 2: 8–9: 'And the Lord God planted a garden. . . . And out of the ground made the Lord God to grow every tree that is pleasant to the sight, and good for food.' The visual arts depict the king engaged in agriculture. For the king driving a plough see Pl. 1.

The interest of the Persian king in agriculture was noted by

[58] Most recently, Heleen Sancisi-Weerdenburg has expressed scepticism about the veracity of the *Cyropaedia* and questioned whether Xenophon could have had reliable knowledge of the period of Cyrus the Great. See e.g. 'The Death of Cyrus: Xenophon's *Cyropaedia* as a Source for Iranian History', in H. Bailey *et al.* (eds.), *Papers in Honour of Professor Mary Boyce* (Leiden, 1985), 459–71.

[59] 'Der königliche Gärtner und Jäger im Paradeisos', *Persica*, 8 (1979), 1–53.

[60] *Hellas und Iran* (Darmstadt, 1984), 114.

[61] *Das altiranische Fürstenideal von Xenophon bis Ferdousi* (Wiesbaden, 1975).

[62] Muhammad A. Dandamaev and Vladimir G. Lukonin, *The Culture and Social Institutions of Ancient Iran* (Cambridge, 1989), esp. 102–3, 111, 222–3, 395.

[63] *Xenophon von Athen*, col. 1843.

[64] See Fauth, 'Der königliche Gärtner und Jäger im Paradeisos', and Robert Drews, 'Sargon, Cyrus and Mesopotamian Folk History', *JNES* 33 (1974), 389–90.

Pl. 1. Stater, Tarsos, 420–380 BC, showing Persian king ploughing. Reproduced from
P. R. Franke and M. Hirmer, *Die griechische Münze* (Munich, 1964), 141, pl. 194,
no. 673.

Greek historical sources, especially in the Hellenistic period. For
example, according to Athen. 1. 28 D (= Posidonius, *FGrH* 87
F 68), the Persians introduced viticulture into Syria. The 'Letter
of Darius', regardless of its authenticity, is true to the spirit of
the tradition.[65] In part of the letter Darius thanks his satrap
Gadates for his good cultivation of land in Asia Minor.

Not only was the Great King interested in agriculture, but as
R. T. Hallock points out 'the Achaemenid Elamite texts ... inform
us about the far-reaching organization of men and materials for
economic purposes'.[66] The king was not merely the recipient of

[65] For the text see R. Meiggs and D. M. Lewis, *A Selection of Greek Historical
Inscriptions*, 2nd edn. (Oxford, 1988), no. 12. At p. 21 they support the authenticity
of the inscription, noting that the Greek is a translation and the content credible.
Most recently Ove Hansen, 'The Purported Letter of Darius to Gadates', *RhM* 129
(1986), 95–6, argued that the original text was a forgery that should be dated to
494–491 BC and that the existing copy is a republication of the text in the 2nd c. AD.
[66] 'The Evidence of the Persepolis Tablets', in *The Cambridge History of Iran*, ii, ed.
Ilya Gershevitch (Cambridge, 1985), 588.

income. As Xenophon recognized (iv. 5, 16) the maintenance of peace was directly connected to agricultural prosperity. In Persian ideology the king protected and maintained fertility. Briant argues that religion reinforced the subjects' obligation to pay the tribute that, in turn, allowed the king to maintain the military force that not only protected them from external enemies but served as the principal instrument by which the king exploited them internally.[67] But the economic administration of the Persian Empire is not yet thoroughly understood.[68]

Perhaps it is because Plato uses οἰκονομία in the narrowest sense, as referring strictly to the management of a household, that he asserts that Cyrus did not care for oikonomia (*Laws* 694 c, quoted by Athen. 11. 505 A). Such indifference would have made Cyrus exceptionally unsuccessful among Achaemenid rulers.[69] Xenophon (*Cyrop.* 8. 1. 14) and other 4th c. Greek authors (e.g. Arist. *Pol.* 1288ª34, Deinarchus 1. 97) extend the meaning of οἰκονομία, and words related to it, to refer to the administration of states. Ps.-Arist. *Oec.* 1345ᵇ7–1346ª25, distinguishes four types of economy: royal, satrapic, polis, and private.[70]

Xenophon structures the *Oeconomicus* by a series of repetitions and variations on themes (see Ch. 2, sect. E). The administration of the Persian Empire serves as a paradigm for the management of Ischomachus' oikos (cc. vii–x). Socrates presents two examples of successful administration to Critobulus: first the Persian Empire, and secondly the household of Ischomachus and his wife. The orderly park (παράδεισος) provides a model for the orderly household that will be described in cc. vii–x, and the king serves as a model for Ischomachus' wife, who is compared to a queen bee. As the park is a walled space containing trees planted in straight lines, so within the walls of the house of Ischomachus and his wife utensils are laid out in rows (viii. 19–20). The park contains fine food within it, plants, fruit, and game; the storerooms

[67] 'Forces productives, dépendance rurale et idéologies religieuses dans l'Empire achéménide'; id., 'Appareils d'État et développement des forces productives au Moyen-Orient ancien: le cas de l'Empire achéménide', *Rois, tributs, et paysans*, 431–74.

[68] See e.g. W. M. Sumner, 'Achaemenid Settlement in the Persepolis Plain', *AJA* 90 (1986), 3–31. Tuplin, 'The Administration of the Achaemenid Empire', has designed a framework for future investigations.

[69] Interestingly, Dandamaev, *The Culture and Social Institutions of Ancient Iran*, 145, refers to 'a huge royal household which embraced Persia and Elam'.

[70] C. Ampolo, 'Οἰκονομία: Tre osservazioni sui rapporti tra la finanza e l'economia greca', *AIΩN (archeol.)*, 1 (1979), 124, ignores Xenophon's use of οἰκονομία in the present passage and argues that the earliest use of the word in the sense of 'public finance' occurs in the Deinarchus passage, which may be dated to 324 BC.

of the house are also stocked with provisions. The house is a peaceful fertile paradise. As the king is fond of spending his time in his parks surrounded by all manner of lovely fragrant plants, so would bees spend their days among the flowers. Aelian (*NA* 1. 59–60), must have been thinking of the *Oeconomicus* when he mentioned the palaces of the Persian kings and the visit of Lysander, and in the paragraph immediately following discussed the architecture of beehives. An encyclopaedist, Aelian may have picked up the notion of palaces for king bees from Pliny, *NH* 11. 29, or he may have used the same source as Pliny. In both the description of the garden of Cyrus and that of the household of Ischomachus and his wife, we sense Xenophon's nostalgia for times gone by when Persia was well governed, and Athens was prosperous.

Empire and oikos, public and private, are organized according to the same principles. The king rewards governors whose land is well cultivated and densely populated (iv. 7), just as Ischomachus and his wife in their efforts to increase their estate give a share of the profits of the oikos to the housekeeper and the foreman (ix. 12–13, 15, xii. 6). The emphasis on rewarding, not merely punishing, their subordinates is a feature of Persian administration[71] that is also practiced by Ischomachus and his wife. It is also fundamental to Xenophon's systems of horsemanship and military discipline (see *Anab.*, *On Horsemanship, passim*). The emphasis on rewards, rather than punishments, is one of the features, in fact, that distinguishes the treatment of slaves in the *Oeconomicus* from that recommended in Ps.-Arist. *Oec.* 1344^a–45^{b}9—a work which, though derivative of Xenophon's *Oeconomicus*, eschews any mention of the Persian king.

Like the king (iv. 8), Ischomachus and his wife inspect their domains personally and act as magistrates and judges, upholding the laws of the community, and settling disputes among their subordinates (ix. 15). Ischomachus and his wife rule slaves; the subjects of the Persian king are the equivalent of slaves.[72]

---

[71] Cf. R. G. Kent, *Old Persian: Grammar, Texts, Lexicon*, 2nd edn. (New Haven, Conn., 1950), 140, DNb § 8c. 16–21 of Darius: 'The man who cooperates, him according to his cooperative action, him thus do I reward. Who does harm, him according to the damage thus I punish. It is not my desire that a man should do harm; nor indeed is that my desire, if he should do harm, he should not be punished.'

[72] The Persian king treated his subjects, even those in positions of authority, as his slaves. In line 4 of the Gadates inscription Gadates is called δοῦλος ('slave') and despotic language recurs in the inscription of Darius at Behistun. See Kent, *Old Persian*, 117 DB i. 19. This idea appears in Greek literature: e.g. Aes. *Pers.* 241–2, 584–90, 762–4, Xen. *Anab.* 2. 5. 38, 3. 2. 13, *Hell.* 6. 1. 12, Nic. Dam. *FGrH* 90 F 66 (22) and see further Richard N. Frye, *The History of Ancient Iran* (Munich, 1983), 109.

According to Frye, there is no evidence of any rebellion against
the elder Cyrus (see iv. 18 αὐτομολῆσαι). Xenophon reports that
not one soldier deserted from Cyrus the younger (iv. 18–19), nor
would the worker bees, that is to say the slaves, desert
Ischomachus' wife, who is their queen (vii. 38). Achaemenid art
portrays the subjects rendering gifts and tribute voluntarily.[73] To
both Cyrus the Younger and the wife of Ischomachus lucre and
loyalty are freely given. Thus Persian king and 'queen bee' are to
be distinguished from the tyrant who lives in fear of assassination
(xxi. 12).

Both the description of the Persian king and that of
Ischomachus' and his wife's household are idealized, and both also
anticipate developments in Hellenistic thought. The Persian king
mediates between his subjects and the gods (see below on iv. 21).
In ancient thought, bees were also associated with the divine.[74]
Xenophon's description of the Persian king foreshadows the view
of the divine Hellenistic prince that blossomed especially in some
artistic portrayals of Alexander the Great. His view of marriage
also contains many elements which appear later in Hellenistic
philosophy as well as in actual marriage-contracts.[75]

6. τροφήν. Xenophon's description confirms the statement in Herod.
1. 192 that the land of the Persian Empire was distributed to
provincial governors who should maintain the king and the army
and also pay tribute.

πάντας ... συνάγων. On the mobilization of local troops in
various centers see also *Anab.* 1. 1. 2, 1. 9. 7, and *Hellenica* 1. 4. 3.

6–7. πιστοὺς πέμπει ἐπισκοπεῖν. Sim. iv. 8. The 'eyes' and 'ears'
of the Persian kings were well known to the Greeks (see e.g. *Cyrop.*
8. 2. 10–12, Herod. 1. 114, Ar. *Ach.* 91–2, Plut. *Artax.* 12. 1, Aes.

[73] Gerold Walser, *Audienz beim persischen Großkönig* (Zurich, 1966), 5, and 'Die
Bedeutung des "Tributzuges" von Persepolis', *AA* 81 (1966), 546, observes that the
king is not shown as the recipient of tribute but rather of gifts of honour; however,
in *Die Völkerschaften auf den Reliefs von Persepolis* (Berlin, 1966), 23, he puts 'freiwillig'
in quotation marks, suggesting some ambivalence. Oscar White Muscarella, reviewing
this work in *JNES* 28 (1969), 280–5, points out that because the king commissioned
and paid for the monuments, they depict his reign as benevolent and his subjects as
willing donors. Margaret Cool Root, *The King and Kingship in Achaemenid Art* (Leiden,
1969), 228–9, 262, also discusses the subtle reality of the apparently voluntary
donations.

[74] See on vii. 32 ἡ τῶν μελιττῶν ἡγεμών ... ὑπὸ τοῦ θεοῦ, and Arthur B. Cook, 'The
Bee in Greek Mythology', *JHS* 15 (1985), 1–24.

[75] See Ch. 4 and Pomeroy, *Women in Hellenistic Egypt*, 67–71, 83–124.

Pers. 979, and iv. 8). The 'eye' was the chief overseer, while the 'ears' were the many spies who relayed to the king information about the Empire, especially the provinces, and who acted independently of the military commanders and civilian governors.[76] Persian sources do not confirm the existence of the 'eyes' and 'ears'.[77] Inasmuch as the Persian sources are official, it is not surprising that they do not mention their intelligence service. In any case, even lacking an official secret service, the king would be kept well informed by the mutual accusations that he encouraged between civilian and military commanders iv. 10; (cf. xi. 24 for the practice of accusation and defence in Ischomachus' household).

7. **χιλιάρχων.** χιλίαρχος, 'Commander of a thousand', is the Greek word for *hazārapatiš*. Here and in *Cyropaedia* 8. 6. 1, 9, the chiliarch is a military official directly under the king's (not a satrap's) control. According to late sources (Nepos, *Con.* 3, Diod. 18. 48. 5) the word may also designate a high court official. However, M. L. Chaumont, citing the *Cyropaedia* but not the *Oeconomicus*, has argued convincingly that a chiliarch did not function as something of a 'grand vizier' under the Achaemenids.[78]

δοκίμοις ἵπποις. The appearance of the horses was evaluated, for horses were an essential part of the military apparatus. The Persian king's interest in horses is well attested. Indeed, some inscriptions indicate that the king considered horses as important as people. Thus Arsames at Hamadan: Ahuramazda, great god, the greatest of gods, made me king. He bestowed on me the land Persia, with good people, with good horses.... Darius at Susa: 'Great Ahuramazda, the greatest of the gods—he created Darius the king, he bestowed upon him the kingdom, good, possessed of good charioteers, of good horses, of good men', at Naqsi-Rustam: 'As a horseman I am a good horseman.... As a spearman I am a good spearman both afoot and on horseback', and at Persepolis: 'This country Persia which Ahuramazda bestowed upon me, good, possessed of good horses, possessed of good men ...'.[79] Horses are the animals mentioned most frequently in Persepolis texts record-

---

[76] Thus Frye, *The History of Ancient Iran*, 108–9, and D. M. Lewis, *Sparta and Persia* (Leiden, 1977), 19–20.

[77] Hirsch, *Friendship*, 130, does not believe in the existence of the 'eyes'. Tuplin, 'The Administration of the Achaemenid Empire', 120, argues that there was only one 'eye' and no 'ears'.

[78] Chiliarque et curopalate à la cour des Sassanides', *IA* 10 (1973), 139, 142.

[79] Kent, *Old Persian*, 116, AsH, § 2; 146, DSp, sim. 146 DSs; 140, DNb § 8h; 136 DPd, § 2.

Pl. 2. Achaemenid cylinder-seal showing King Darius I (521–485 BC) hunting lions from a chariot. Hovering above is the disc of Ahuramazda. Palm-trees flank the scene. British Museum 89132, agate. By permission of the Trustees of the British Museum.

ing rations for animals.[80] For a portrayal of the king riding in a chariot see Pl. 2.

τιμαῖς . . . δώροις . . . κολάζει. Competition produced jealousy among the Persians, but promoted the king's interests (*Cyrop.* 8. 2. 26–8). Cyrus' system of rewards and punishments is also described in *Anab.* 1. 9. 19 and *Cyrop.* 8. 1. 39, 8. 6. 11. Ischomachus and his wife employ a similar system of incentives with their slaves (see Ch. 5, sect. I, and iv. 5).

8. συνοικουμένην . . . ὀλιγάνθρωπον. Increased rations allocated to nursing mothers which are recorded in the Persepolis tablets indicates that the authorities encouraged human reproduction.[81] W. M. Sumner suggests that low population density in some regions of the Persian Empire was the result of pastoralism.[82] Warlike peoples commonly believe that they have not enough men. Thus Xenophon opens the *Spartan Constitution* with a statement about the paradox that Sparta, the most sparsely populated state, was the most powerful and glorious. In *Hell.* 5. 2. 16 he

[80] R. T. Hallock, 'The Evidence of the Persepolis Tablets', 607.
[81] R. T. Hallock, 'The Evidence of the Persepolis Tablets', 607.
[82] 'Achaemenid Settlement in the Persepolis Plain'.

reports that plentiful food and an abundant population contributed to the strength of Olynthus.[83]

δένδρων. The Persian appreciation of trees is well documented in Greek literature and can also be perceived in Persian art. For example, young pine or cypress trees are depicted on the Apadama reliefs at Persepolis, and two palms appear on a royal cylinder-seal (see Pl. 2). Literary testimony indicates that groves were planted around royal tombs. Trees were planted around the tomb of Cyrus, which was built in a park (Arrian, *Anab.* 6. 29. 4, Quintus Curtius 10. 1, Strabo 15. 3. 7, 730 C). Archaeological sources indicate that not only Cyrus the Great's palace but also his grave at Pasargadae was planted with a park complete with canals, pools, pavilions, and avenues of trees.[84] See further on iv. 5 γεωργίας and on iv. 13 παράδεισοι.

ἕδραις ἐντίμοις. προεδρία refers to seats in the front row at gatherings such as public assemblies and dramatic and athletic festivals. The honours bestowed are thus publicized. Similarly, virtuous slaves in the household of Ischomachus can be recognized by their superior clothing (xiii. 10).

9–12. ἑκάτερον . . . ἐπιμελεῖται. That is, the separation of civilian from military power was undermined in some parts of the Empire by the appointment of a satrap who controlled both.

Analogies between the Persian Empire and the household of Ischomachus and his wife render Xenophon's controversial report of the division of civilian and military power and its unification under a satrap more intelligible. He states that one class of officers governed the inhabitants and another group commanded the troops, but in some parts of the Empire a satrap held both military and civilian power. Modern historians differ in their acceptance of Xenophon's account of Persian government: attitudes range from total rejection to acceptance for particular time-periods or geographical areas to total belief in all the information. For example, J. M. Cook asserts that even the *Cyropaedia* has been overestimated as a historical source.[85] Regarding Xenophon's reports in the *Oeconomicus* and the *Cyropaedia* of the division of

---

[83] For similar statements in other authors see Luigi Gallo, 'Popolosità e scarsità di popolazione', *ASNP*, 3rd ser., 10 (1980), 1233–70.

[84] See David Stronach, 'The Royal Garden at Pasargadae', in L. De Meyer and E. Haerinck (eds.), *Archaeologia Iranica et Orientalis: Miscellanea in honorem Louis Vanden Berghe* (Ghent, 1989), 475–502, and Fauth, 'Der königliche Gärtner und Jäger im Paradeisos', 6.

[85] 'The Rise of the Achaemenids and the Establishment of their Empire', in *The Cambridge History of Iran*, ii. 200–91.

power in the provincial governments as inconsistent, he rejects them both, hypothesizing that Xenophon's idealization of Cyrus will have led him to credit the first Achaemenid with much that he regarded as praiseworthy in the Persian Empire. Mortéza Ehtécham cites *Oec.* iv. 9 and argues that the separation of military and civilian power existed only in the time of Xerxes and of Xenophon himself, but not in the days of Cyrus.[86]

In contrast, Richard N. Frye uses the *Cyropaedia* and *Anabasis* as historical sources, but ignores the *Oeconomicus*, although sometimes the testimony of the latter differs from that of the other two works. He agrees with Xenophon's positive view of the elder Cyrus, and, moreover, suggests that there was a distribution of power among the court, the bureaucracy (perhaps including priests), and the military, as well as a variety of governmental structures throughout the Empire.[87] Pierre Briant accepts Xenophon's description of the administrative hierarchy and explains that there were several phrourarchs or garrison commanders in each satrapy.[88] Military powers were exercised by phrourarchs, civilian powers by tax officials. In addition, a satrap united both military and civilian authority. The system varied throughout the Empire in response to military necessities. Amélie Kuhrt[89] and Dandamaev[90] draw attention to the division of power and to the absence of any administrative reorganization of conquered peoples and question whether a monolithic system of government was ever imposed. No scholar has ever found evidence for a division between civil and military power in Asia Minor at any time we know about. Yet it is true that the king (when he had the power) appointed phrourarchs and tax-collectors who served under the satrap and acted as checks and spies on him. Weak kings, of course, probably could not make such appointments everywhere: one cannot imagine the Persian king doing this to any satrap who was as independent a ruler as the subject-king Mausolus. It seems reasonable to assume that Xenophon is telling the truth for the most part, and that the vastness of the Empire, the variety of the territories and peoples ruled, and the fact that not all parts of the Empire had been conquered at the same time resulted in a system of administration that was

---

[86] *L'Iran sous les Achéménides* (Fribourg, 1946), 113 n. 3, and 114.

[87] *The History of Ancient Iran*, 95, 112–14.

[88] *Rois, tributs et paysans*, 190, 210–11.

[89] 'A Brief Guide to Some Recent Work on the Achaemenid Empire', *LCM* 8 (1983), 148, 150.

[90] *The Culture and Social Institutions of Ancient Iran, passim.*

not uniform throughout.[91] However, Xenophon has probably exaggerated the division of power for didactic and literary purposes.

The division of labour between the civil and military commands and their interdependence are paralleled by the reciprocal relationship of the domestic sphere, which is supervised by the wife, and of the husband's realm, which lies beyond the house. The spheres of husband and wife are complementary and mutually dependent, paralleling the military and civilian spheres in the Empire. Normally, the powers of husband and wife are divided between them. The household is both monarchy and meritocracy. If the wife proves to be more competent than her husband, she may also exercise supreme authority and rule over him (vii. 27, 42, xi. 25). Ischomachus' wife eventually even sits in judgement on him, sentencing him to endure punishments or to pay fines (xi. 25). Thus, like a satrap, she unites, as it were, the two kinds of power in the oikos. In both household and Empire, authority to govern is awarded to those who deserve it, and the extent of the authority varies according to the merits of those to whom it is delegated.

13. παράδεισοι. *Pairidaēza* in Avestan is constructed of *pairi* ('around') and *daēza* ('wall') and means 'walled garden'.[92] So Xen. *Hell.* 4. 1. 15, writes περιειργμένοις παραδείσοις. He was the first to use the term παράδεισος in a Greek text to refer to a Persian garden. He saw many parks on his travels in Asia. These were not merely places for recreation; the fruit trees and other plants provided food, and the animals were hunted for both sport and meat,[93] see on iv. 25 φιλοτιμούμενος.

The gardens of earlier Greek literature, such as the garden of Alcinous described in Hom. *Od.* 7. 114–31, seem to have been less formal and to have contained no fauna, but only flora, including fruit, vines, and herbs. The Persian παράδεισοι must have provided the model for the park that Xenophon created at his estate in Scillus (*Anab.* 5. 3. 7–11). Xenophon not only created the first park on the Greek mainland, but through his descriptions he also

[91] Thus Christopher Tuplin, 'Xenophon and the Garrisons of the Achaemenid Empire', *AMI* 20 (1987), 232–4, argues that the information about garrisons in iv. 5–11 and *Cyr.* 8. 6 indicates that Xenophon is generalizing from the satrapy of Lydia to the rest of the Empire.

[92] The Old Persian *paradayadam* ('pleasant retreat') may have been incorrectly written for **paridaidam* ('that which is walled around'). See Kent, *Old Persian Grammar, Texts, Lexicon*, 195, and W. Hirz, *Altiranisches Sprachgut der Nebenüberlieferungen* (Wiesbaden, 1975), 179.

[93] See further Marie Luise Gothein, *A History of Garden Art* trans. [Laura] Archer-Hind (1928, repr. New York, 1979), 39–43, and Tuplin 'The Administration of the Achaemenid Empire', 144 n. 130.

contributed to the creation of parks in the Hellenistic and Roman worlds.[94] In these parks the plantings were often in rows as straight as military formations (see below on iv. 21 ἴσου ... ὀρθοὶ ... εὐγώνια).

16. ἄριστος. Greek readers would not have found this boast offensive; modesty was not among the repertoire of qualities which they regarded as virtues. In *Cyrop.* 8. 1. 40 Cyrus is reported to have believed that a ruler should be better than his subjects.

18. Κῦρός γε, εἰ ἐβίωσεν. Xenophon moves from Cyrus the Great (who is designated βασιλεύς in § 16) to Cyrus the Younger (who had never reigned as king) without signalling the transition.

A. Pelletier reviews and rejects attempts of previous scholars to attribute this anomaly to a textual problem, such as an interpolation or lacuna. He suggests that to Xenophon's contemporaries εἰ ἐβίωσεν would have been the equivalent of ὁ νεώτερος as a distinctive epithet that would have clarified the change of subject.[95] Moreover, γε can serve to delimit a new idea.[96] But apologies for the text are unconvincing. If Xenophon had wanted to distinguish between the two Cyruses he would have added a phrase here: e.g. Κῦρός γ' ὁ καθ' ἡμᾶς.

The confusion between the two Cyruses is deliberate. Georges Cousin notes that in the *Cyropaedia* Xenophon describes Cyrus as an amalgam of two people: the childhood is a legend attributed to the elder Cyrus, the maturity belongs to the younger Cyrus.[97] The two resemble one another like brothers. Cousin gives a partial list of similar phrases that Xenophon applies to both Cyruses. A comparison between the *Cyropaedia* and the *Anabasis* shows that Xenophon has portrayed both the elder and the younger Cyrus as the same in an attempt to transfer the acknowledged virtues of Cyrus the Great to the ill-fated pretender.[98] Delebecque notes that Xenophon emphasizes parallels between past and present, especially in the *Cyropaedia*, by using expressions such as ἔτι καὶ νῦν and ἔτι νῦν.[99] Xenophon expects his readers to make the switch from the elder to the younger Cyrus through his comment 'if he had lived', but by avoiding doing so more explicitly is suggesting that the younger would have been like the elder in all relevant respects, especially as concerns attention to οἰκονομία.

---

[94] See further Elizabeth B. Moynihan, *Paradise as a Garden: In Persia and Mughal India* (New York, 1979), 2.

[95] 'Les deux Cyrus dans l'Économique de Xénophon', *RPh*, NS 18 (1944), 91–2.

[96] See J. D. Denniston, *The Greek Particles*, rev. edn. (Oxford, 1954), 122–3.

[97] *Kyros le jeune en Asie mineure* (Paris and Nancy, 1905), pp. xli–xliii.

[98] See Pelletier, 'Les deux Cyrus', 87–8.

[99] *Essai*, 395–6, 422 n. 36.

Steven W. Hirsch suggests that the younger Cyrus himself exploited his homonymous ancestor and issued propaganda claiming that his own reign would bring about a reincarnation of Persia as it had been under the reign of Cyrus the Great; he suggests, less persuasively, that Xenophon used the younger Cyrus as a model for his portrayal of Cyrus the Great.[100] It appears to me that the opposite was more likely, inasmuch as Cyrus was already glorified in Oriental and Greek tradition so that later kings wanted to be associated with him.[101] For example, Jewish tradition recorded in Isa. 45: 1 refers to Cyrus as the Lord's anointed; Ezra 1 shows the reason for his enjoyment of divine favour: he granted permission to the Jews to rebuild their temple. In Mesopotamian oral tradition by the late fifth century, the exploits of the hero Sargon as well as the tradition that he was a gardener were attributed to Cyrus.[102] Herodotus (1. 86–90, 130, 155, 3. 89, 159–60), presents Cyrus as honoured and fatherly to his subjects, though he does have some character faults (1. 114–15). Arrian, *Anab.* 6. 29, reports that the tomb of Cyrus was a shrine throughout the Achaemenid period until it was plundered before the visit of Alexander.[103] The reputation of the elder Cyrus survives to this day, for example, in the eulogy in the *OCD*: 'This vast Empire he administered with wisdom and tolerance. In the conquered territories he was welcomed as a liberator; he respected their customs and religion, honouring Marduk at Babylon and freeing the captive Jews to build their temple in Jersualem. To the Greeks he became a model of the upright ruler.'[104]

Athenaeus (11. 504 F–505 A), Diogenes Laertius (6. 84), and Sir

[100] '1001 Iranian Nights: History and Fiction in Xenophon's *Cyropaedia*', in M. Jameson (ed.), *The Greek Historians, Literature and History: Papers Presented to A. E. Raubitschek* (Stanford, 1985), 76–9.

[101] Amélie Kuhrt, 'The Achaemenid Empire: A Babylonian Perspective', has demonstrated that the favourable view of Cyrus the Great emanated originally from the ruler's own propaganda.

[102] See Robert Drews, 'Sargon, Cyrus and Mesopotamian Folk History'. Heleen Sancisi-Weerdenburg, 'The Death of Cyrus', argues that Xenophon drew upon Iranian oral tradition and presented a more favourable view of Cyrus than appears in earlier Greek authors.

[103] On Xenophon's sources for his favourable portrait of the elder Cyrus, see most recently Hirsch, *Friendship*, 68–71. Hirsch, however, does not do justice to the visual arts, for which see Margaret Cool Root, *The King and Kingship in Achaemenid Art*, 38–40, 298–9.

[104] 2nd edn., 308. For another expression of the praise of Cyrus, in a standard reference book see Max Mallowan, 'Cyrus the Great (558–529 B.C.)', in *The Cambridge History of Iran*, ii. 412–15.

Thomas Browne[105] also follow Xenophon's precedent and discuss
the elder Cyrus in tandem with the younger Cyrus without signalling the transition. Their readers, like Xenophon's, were probably
familiar enough with Greek history to have understood the distinction. Nevertheless, the juxtaposition of the two Cyruses and the
consequent telescoping of some 150 years of Persian history are
noteworthy. Xenophon apparently followed the principles of
Achaemenid art (which he surely knew) in portraying the kings
in an archetypal rather than an idiosyncratic or personal
manner.[106] The result of this iconographic device is an emphasis
on dynastic concerns, on permanence, hierarchy and order, and
on the concept of kingship itself, rather than upon any individual
king. In short, Xenophon intended the reader to understand that
both the elder and younger Cyrus were indistinguishable in their
interest in οἰκονομία.

μαχούμενος. Socrates is referring to the battle of Cunaxa of
401 BC. Xenophon was present at the battle and describes it in
Anab. 1. 8. It is doubtful that Socrates really could have had such
detailed knowledge of what transpired. Moreover, because
Xenophon was still in Asia Minor at the time of Socrates' execution, it is impossible that he could have been present at a conversation when Socrates discussed Cunaxa. On anachronisms in the
Oeconomicus see on i. 1 ἤκουσα.

αὐτομολῆσαι. Xenophon states that not one soldier deserted
from Cyrus the Younger, with the exception of an attempt
by Orontas (*Anab.* 1. 9. 2–3), he reports an incident when 400
hoplite mercenaries changed sides to join Cyrus (*Anab.* 1. 4. 3).
There is also no evidence of any rebellion against the elder Cyrus.
Similarly, in xxi. 7 soldiers do not desert strong commanders, nor
do the worker bees desert their queen (vii. 38 and see above
on iv. 5).

Münscher's conjecture at *Suda*, s.v. Ξενοφῶν (iii. 495) is consistent with Xenophon's statements:[107] υ′ δὲ κατέλιπον ⟨βασιλέα καὶ
ἦλθον παρὰ⟩ τὸν Κῦρον καὶ ἔφυγον ἐκ τῶν συστρατευσάντων ὁπλῖται

[105] *The Garden of Cyrus* (1658), repr. *Urne Buriall and The Garden of Cyrus*, ed. John
Carter (Cambridge, 1967), 58–60.
[106] On conventions in Achaemenid art see Margaret Cool Root, *The King and
Kingship in Achaemenid Art*, 310.
[107] *Xenophon in der griechisch-römischen Literatur*, 221–2, rejected by Adler following
Sigfrid Lindstam, 'Xenofoncitaten hos Lakapenos', *Eranos*, 24 (1926), 121–2, who
argued that the *Suda* might include data in conflict with Xenophon. Though
Xenophon was motivated to portray Cyrus in a favourable light, there is no evidence
that the general course of events turned out otherwise than as he narrates.

καὶ πελτασταὶ, γφ'. It is more likely that the 400 mercenaries and 3,500 hoplites and peltasts deserted the king in favour of Cyrus. Although Xenophon evidently was the source for the exact figure of 400, he was not for the figure of 3,500. The latter total may have been compiled from various numbers in the *Anabasis*, Diod. 14. 19. 7 (from Ephorus), D.L. 8. 54, Plut. *Artax*. 6. 5, and other authors who are no longer extant, for according to Plut. *Artax*. 8, many writers, in addition to Xenophon, described the battle of Cunaxa.

19. Ἀριαίου. Ariaeus commanded the left wing of cavalry at Cunaxa. He fled with his troops when he discovered that Cyrus had been killed (*Anab*. 1. 9. 31). His treacherous character was revealed once again when he marched with the Greeks and later betrayed them (*Anab*. 2. 5. 39–40, 3. 2. 2). Xenophon reports his own conversation with Ariaeus (*Anab*. 2. 5. 41).

20. Λυσάνδρῳ. The meeting between Lysander and Cyrus took place in 407 BC (Xen. *Hell*. 1. 5. 1–7; for Aelian's version of their meeting see on iv. 5; for meetings between Lysander and Cyrus see Plut. *Lys*. 4. 1, 9. 1; and for an alliance of Spartans and Cyrus against Artaxerxes see Diod. 14. 11). Xenophon might have heard the story of Lysander's meeting with Cyrus from senior Spartan officers who had heard the story from Lysander himself.[108] However he also may have read it in Ctesias. The Spartan general provides a contrast to the faithless Persian Ariaeus. Despite Lysander's many faults, he was never corrupted by wealth. Cyrus trusted him so much that when he went to visit his sick father he left his province in the Spartan's charge, rather than turning it over to a Persian (Xen. *Hell*. 2. 1. 13–15). At their best, Spartans and Persians in Xenophon have in common a tightly organized hierarchical government, a willingness to obey orders, and a static society which provides a contrast to turbulent Athens. Plutarch (*Lys*. 2. 3, 4. 2) observes that Lysander cultivated those in power beyond what was natural for a Spartan. The present passage may be viewed as an example of his sycophantic behaviour toward Cyrus. But it is difficult to be certain about Xenophon's tone. The passage may also illustrate Greek disparagement of the Persians' effeminate dress.

Cicero (*De Sen*. 59) paraphrases the anecdote about Lysander and Cyrus the Younger, in the course of a discussion of agriculture as a pursuit appropriate to an older man (see Ch. 6, sect. B).

For the narrative technique employed here of nesting a story

---

[108] So J. K. Anderson, *Hunting in the Ancient World*, 60.

within a story see Ch. 2, sect. E. The tale of Cyrus and Lysander is relayed by more speakers than any other such story in the *Oeconomicus*.

21. ἴσου ... ὀρθοὶ ... εὐγώνια. Visual depictions indicate that Assyrio-Babylonian parks—which came into Persian possession— had been characterized by rows of trees.[109] The garden of the elder Cyrus at Pasargadae was planted according to a geometrical, rectilinear plan.[110] Later gardens, including that of the younger Cyrus, followed the same pattern. Werner Müller elucidates the relationship between Persian cosmology and geometric patterns; in his view the park is a sanctuary for a king who mediates between gods and men.[111] Sir Thomas Browne also described the quincuncial rows of the orchards with admiration as a manifestation of divine order in nature.[112] The orderly park provides a model for the orderly household which will be described in cc. vii–x (see above on iv. 5 γεωργίας). The arrangement of this household has also been divinely ordained (vii. 8, 12, 18, 22–31, etc).

It is not uncommon to plant trees in a geometrical arrangement. Not only is such an arrangement aesthetically pleasing, but it facilitates agricultural work. In fact, the quincuncial pattern is still used in modern orchards and vineyards and was normal in Rome (Verg. *Georg.* 2. 278, Colum. *RR*, 3. 14. 4, 3. 15. 1–2, Quint. 8. 3. 9, Pliny, *NH* 17. 78). In Cic. *Sen.* 59, the arrangement of trees in Cyrus' garden is described as a quincunx, i.e. groups of five arranged in alternate rows or diagonally:

23. κάλλος. According to *Cyrop.* 8. 1. 41, the elder Cyrus encouraged the wearing of cosmetics and platform shoes to hide bodily defects. Ischomachus criticizes his wife for employing such means of deception (c. x).

24. Μίθρην. Mithra was an old Persian god of light and truth. Although he does not occur among the gods mentioned in the

---

[109] Gothein, *Garden Art*, 39.

[110] For the plans see Stronach, 'The Royal Garden at Pasargadae'.

[111] *Die heilige Stadt* (Stuttgart, 1961), ch. 8.

[112] *The Garden of Cyrus*, 59–60. Guy Davenport, *The Geography of the Imagination* (San Francisco, 1981), 14, observes that this design is used with the same symbolism in 18th c. American painting.

Persepolis Fortification Tablets as published thus far,[113] there are theophoric names compounded with *Mithra-*.[114] Some classical Greek sources ascribe the worship of Mithra to the early Achaemenids. Herod. 1. 131 correctly reports that the Persians worshipped Mithra (although he mistakenly identifies him with Aphrodite). Strabo 11. 14. 9, 530 C, mentions the Μιθράκανα, an annual festival of Mithra celebrated in the Achaemenid period, but does not indicate when these celebrations were instituted. Xen. *Cyrop.* 7. 5. 53, represents an associate of Cyrus the Great swearing an oath by Mithra. The god gains in importance and does appear in inscriptions from the reign of Artaxerxes II (404–358 BC).[115] Plutarch (*Moralia* 174 A, *Artax.* 4) depicts Artaxerxes swearing by Mithra, as Cyrus the Younger does in the present passage.

ὑγιαίνω . . . ἰδρῶσαι. This statement reflects Zoroastrian emphasis on physical discipline.[116] According to Xen. *Cyrop.* 2. 1. 29, 8. 6. 12, Cyrus the Great also exercised before eating. In Xenophon's works human beings and animals are often treated according to analogous principles. Thus Cyrus never fed his horses before exercising them (*Cyr.* 8. 1. 38, *Eq.* 4. 3). Xenophon offers different views of the Persians in his various works, tailoring his presentation to his themes and purposes.[117] In the *Oeconomicus*, Xenophon's portrayal of the younger Cyrus is quite complex. Although his costume may appear effeminate and seems to render the wearer incapable of physical activity,[118] his actual accomplishments in peacetime earn the admiration of a Spartan, a member of a people with a reputation for physical fitness. Indeed, the wearing of gorgeous, expensive garments does not inhibit the Persian staff officers from heaving wagons out of the mud (*Anab.* 1. 5. 8). This description of Cyrus prefigures Ischomachus' advice to his wife in cc. vii–x: she is to engage in physical activity and eventually show that she has a masculine mind. Xenophon con-

---

[113] See Hallock, 'The Evidence of the Persepolis Tablets'. According to Heidemarie Koch, 'Götter und ihre Verehrung im achämenidischen Persien', *Zeitschrift für Assyriologie*, 77 (1987), 255–6 with n. 93, the former identification of Mithra in the Tablets was incorrect.

[114] See M. Mayrhofer, *Onomastica Persepolitana* (SBÖAW 286; Vienna, 1973), 314, no. 11. 6. 3.

[115] For these, see Kent, *Old Persian Grammar*, 154–5, A²Sa, A²Sd, A²Hb.

[116] Cyrus' reply is quoted in C. Clemen, *Fontes Historiae Religionis Persicae* (Bonn, 1920), 16.

[117] See further Hirsch *Friendship*, 4–5.

[118] Chester Starr, 'Greeks and Persians in the Fourth Century B.C.', 41, 51–2, refers to the 'effeminate rule of the Persians in the fourth century' as they are described by Xenophon, Isocrates, Plato, and Aristotle.

tinues the discussion of exercise in v. 1 where he states that farming
is σωμάτων ἄσκησις.

25. φιλοτιμούμενος. Cylinder seals of the Achaemenids depict the
king engaging in games of contest.[119] See Pl. 2 for a seal depicting
Darius standing in a chariot with drawn bow, hunting a lion.

v. 1. γεωργίας ... μακάριοι. Because agriculture was fundamental
to Greek life, it is often mentioned in poetry and is the focus of
Hesiod's *Works and Days*. However, it appears that c. v is the
earliest extensive eulogy of rural life in Greek prose. Xenophon's
perspective on farming differs from Hesiod's pessimistic view: in
the *Works and Days* the earth does not easily relinquish her produce
and the farmer must warily watch the celestial signs lest all his
work be destroyed. Furthermore, human justice does not flourish
in the country any more than it does in an urban environment.
Only in the Golden Age (*WD* 116–20) before the introduction of
agricultural labour was the earth generous with her gifts. In contrast, Xenophon's view is that of an aristocrat who, like the Persian
king in c. iv, works only when he so chooses, and who expects to
reap a reward from the land and to enjoy himself while doing so.
Xenophon was not alone in considering farming as the basis of
the economy and the source of virtue for men.[120] In c. v agriculture
is praised for providing pleasure, profit, opportunities for piety,
and a proper training for free men. The images of domestic comfort
and happiness in c. v prefigure the description of the household
of Ischomachus and his wife in cc. vii–x.

The abundance and generosity of nature is reflected in the
richness of Xenophon's prose. The rhetorical structure is
Gorgianic, employed so lavishly as to create a 'purple patch'. (For
another see on viii. 8 and see further Ch. 2.) For example, note
the parallel arrangement and rhyme in § 1 αὔξησις ... ἄσκησις;
isocola in § 6; personification of Earth, and the series of rhetorical
questions, in §§ 8–11. Many of Xenophon's statements became
topoi in later adaptations of the theme.[121] Xenophon sets forth the
subjects of the eulogy principally in dualities that are sometimes
repeated:

---

[119] See Dominique Collon, *First Impressions: Cylinder Seals in the Ancient Near East*
(London, 1987), 129. I am grateful to Heleen Sancisi-Weerdenburg for the references
to seals.

[120] See further Ch. 5 and K. J. Dover, *Greek Popular Morality*, 114.

[121] For rural encomia, most of which were written in Latin, see H. Kier, *De
Laudibus Vitae Rusticae* (diss. Marburg, 1933).

pleasure and utility (1, 2, 11)
sight and smell (3)
gods and men (3, 10)
nature and nurture (4)
animal husbandry and agriculture (3, 6)
winter and summer (4, 9)
country and city (4)
war and peace (5).

Within this conventional thought-pattern expressed in traditional rhetorical language reiterating the pleasures of country life,
Xenophon intrudes references to war (5, 7, 13–16) that shatter
the idyll. The family farm must be defended: the value of the land
and its products makes it attractive to the enemy.

5. ἐπικαιριώταται πράξεις. For the timing of the most urgent agricultural operations see on xvii. 2 βρέξας.

10. ἀπαρχάς. By offering first-fruits at harvest time, the farmer
shared with the gods the produce he believed he had gained
through divine favour. For this concept see Xen. *Symp.* 4. 47–9,
Oec. v. 20 σώφρονες ... τοὺς θεούς, and Isoc. 7. 30. Ἀπαρχαί were
donated by the community as well as by individuals. For example,
first-fruits were offered at the Thalysia after the grain harvest and
at the Pyanopsia after the fruit harvest. The εἰρεσιώνη, a first-fruit
offering to Apollo at the Pyanopsia, was a branch wreathed with
wool to which figs, loaves of bread, and vessels of wine, oil, and
honey were attached. A boy whose parents were both alive was
chosen to carry the branch. It was then placed before the door of
the house to remain there until it was replaced by another εἰρεσιώνη
the following year (Plut. *Thes.* 22, Lyc. fr. 82 Blass, Ar. *Knights*
729 and schol., *Pl.* 1054 and schol., Porph. *Abst.* 4. 22). In 329/8
as ἀπαρχή to Demeter and Kore each tribe gave 1/1,200 of its
wheat crop and 1/600 of its barley (see *IG* ii². 1672, cf. i³. 78).
The term ἀπαρχή occurs frequently in votive inscriptions from
classical Athens.[122]

13. ἔργων στερηθῶσιν ... θρέψονται. Plundering the land of the
enemy was a normal means of obtaining provisions and causing
distress (e.g. in Thuc. 2. 27. 2, 2. 57. 2, 3. 1. 1, 3. 26. 3, 4. 84. 1–2,
4. 88. 1–2, 7. 19. 1–2, 7. 27. 3–5). The threat of seizure or
destruction of crops was a customary strategy designed to bring
the owners out to do battle or to cause them to capitulate.

In contrast to the Persians described in c. iv, who—with the

---

[122] See e.g. Antony E. Raubitschek, *Dedications from the Athenian Akropolis*
(Cambridge, Mass., 1949), *passim*.

exception of the king and the highest administrators—were engaged in either civilian or military pursuits, Greek citizens might both farm and defend the land. In Athens ownership of land was restricted to male citizens. In the archaic period, qualifications for holding archonships and exercising other rights of citizens were based on agricultural wealth, and criteria of wealth in turn affected a man's military status. Thus citizenship, farming, and defence were intimately connected.

14–15. συμπαιδεύει ... ἡ ἐργασία. Farming together serves as training for fighting together when necessary. Able supervision is required for both activities. The tasks of the farm supervisor and the general are similar; but the analogy is less apt when the farm workers and their supervisor are slaves. War and farming alike pose obligations in the religious sphere.[123] In modern Greece agriculture is a social activity. Relatives or neighbours help one another on their farms.[124]

16. ἐλπίδων ... δοῦλοι. On the employment of slaves in agriculture see xii. 3 and Ch. 5, sect. I. Xenophon mentions a variety of rewards that slaves might hope for, including a share in the profits of the oikos (ix. 11–13, xii. 9, 15), good clothing (xiii. 10), abundant food (xiii. 9), and permission to produce children (ix. 5). Ps.-Arist. *Oec.* 1344^{b}15–18 mentions manumission, but Xenophon never does.

17. ἔφη. The source of the saying has not been identified.

18. ὅτι. Rather than postulate a lacuna and the actual loss of a phrase such as οὔπω εἶπας, I prefer to adopt the explanation of L. Breitenbach: the introductory phrase is to be added mentally.[125] Such ellipses appear in *Anab.* 7. 5. 15 and *Cyrop.* 5. 2. 17.

ἀδύνατα προνοῆσαι. In i. 21 Critobulus had raised a similar objection, that although men may be virtuous and have the best intentions, they may nevertheless be engulfed by misfortune. He was probably referring to himself, attempting to exonerate himself from the implications of the preceding conversation, but Socrates rejected the view that virtuous men may be so afflicted and asserted that such misfortune indicated that its victims were enslaved by evil influences. Here he states that misfortune results from a lack of piety.

[123] See on v. 20 and xvii. 2–4, but for differences between training for military action through farmwork and through practice with other hoplites see Osborne, *Demos*, 146.

[124] See on xii. 3 and see further Stanley Aschenbrenner, *Life in a Changing Greek Village: Karpofora and its Reluctant Farmers* (Dubuque, Iowa, 1986), 11, 18.

[125] *Xenophontis Oeconomicus* (Gotha, 1842), 50, ad loc.

18–19. χάλαζαι . . . ἀπώλεσεν. Although in *Revenues* i. 3 Xenophon states that owing to the mildness of the climate Attica was suitable for growing many crops, Plut. *Demet.* 12 mentions a late frost that destroyed the crops there. Theophrastus describes the disastrous effects of a late frost in Euboea (*HP* 4. 14. 11), and discusses the effects of excessive heat and chill (*CP* 5). References to the weather are scattered throughout the *Oeconomicus*. All farmers wait to see when the god will send rain (xvii. 2), but the rains can be torrential. In xvii. 12–13, xix. 11, and xx. 12, Xenophon mentions problems encountered when trying to plant in mud and in xi. 17 the effects of run-off water. Each year is different (xvii. 4). Modern observations of the Greek climate are consistent with those of antiquity.[126] The climate and amount of rainfall fluctuate widely. Rain can vary from double the normal maximum to one-third of it; four to six dry years may be followed by one to ten rainy ones. Regional variation is enormous. In one year there were forty-four days of hail at Decelea and fifteen at Chalkis. Farmers in Greece nowadays still rely on cultivating a variety of crops on scattered plots of land as insurance against total loss due to weather conditions.[127]

20. σώφρονες . . . τοὺς θεούς. Socrates is referring to observing the cults of the oikos, especially those of Hestia, Hecate, Apollo Agyieus, Zeus Herkeios, and Zeus Ktesios. He is also, no doubt, thinking of the obligation to celebrate the agricultural rituals which arose throughout the year such as the Haloa, a festival of gardens in honour of Demeter, Persephone, and Dionysus, the Anthesteria, a festival of spring flowers and wine, the Oschophoria, a vintage festival, and other cult activities. Individuals also chose to communicate with their favourite gods. For example, two inscriptions reveal that the owner of a farm invoked Artemis and his supervisor dedicated a calendar to Hermes Agathos.[128]

In view of the capriciousness of climatic factors in Greece,

---

[126] E. G. Mariolopoulos, *Étude sur le climat de la Grèce* (Paris, 1925), argued persuasively that the climate of Greece was the same as in classical antiquity; his study is especially valuable, for he observed the climate before the ecological problems caused by human ingenuity in the latter part of the 20th c. Peter Garnsey, *Famine and Food Supply in the Graeco-Roman World* (Cambridge, 1988), esp. 11, 105, using contemporary data, observes that owing to inadequate rainfall in Attica the wheat crop will fail more than one year out of four and the barley crop one year out of twenty.

[127] See further on v. 20, Aschenbrenner, *Life in a Changing Greek Village*, 2, Hamish A. Forbes, '"We Have a Little of Everything"', 244, and Thomas Gallant, *Risk and Survival in Ancient Greece* (Stanford, 1991), 41–5.

[128] See on ii. 5 θύειν πολλά, v. 10 ἀπαρχάς, xvii. 2–4 πρός τὸν θεόν, and Merle K. Langdon and L. Vance Watrous, 'The Farm of Timesios: Rock-Cut Inscriptions in South Attica', *Hesperia*, 46 (1977), 162–77.

prayers and prudent agricultural practices were seen to be bulwarks against disaster (xvii. 2–4). Because some calamities such as hailstorms can devastate a plot of land and leave a neighbouring plot unscathed, a Greek farmer might well have thought the gods were intimately involved in rewarding the pious farmer and punishing the evildoer. Plut. *Moralia* 700 E and Sen. *Q.N* 4b. 6. 2 mention χαλαζοφύλακες ('hail-wardens') who predict and avert hail. Of course Zeus, as weather-god, was often the recipient of offerings and prayers, and rain magic was practised as well.[129]

Here Socrates states for the first time that human success is to be attributed to a combination of the favour of the gods and human virtue and diligence (ἐπιμέλεια). This view recurs in vii. 22, xi. 7–8, and xx. 14. Xenophon's attitudes toward the divine were typical of the late fifth and the fourth centuries. Thus in his theology Xenophon is neither archaizing nor attempting to exonerate Socrates from the charge of impiety, but rather expressing conventional beliefs.[130]

vi. 1. σὺν τοῖς θεοῖς ἄρχεσθαι παντὸς ἔργου. Conventional piety demanded that all undertakings, public and private, begin with the gods, and that the gods be continually taken into account. Xenophon follows this principle throughout the *Oeconomicus*. See ii. 18, v. 20, vii. 8, xi. 8. For examples of Xenophon's own piety see *Anab.* 4. 3. 13, 5. 2. 9, 24–5, 6. 1. 24, and 7. 10. 20.

2. ἐπανέλθοιμεν. A superb teacher, Socrates gives a summary review of the discussion, which has included definitions and generalizations, before proceeding to the specific example which constitutes the next part of the lesson. The points are reviewed, by and large, in the same order as their original statement (but see further Ch. 1, sect. D). A list of the major points with a reference of their original statement follows:

(4) Definition of οἰκονομία as a branch of knowledge	i. 1
by which estates can be increased	i. 4
Definition of oikos as all the property a person possesses	i. 5

---

[129] See further Merle K. Langdon, *A Sanctuary of Zeus on Mount Hymettos* (Princeton, NJ, 1976), esp. 80–6.

[130] See further on xi. 18 and Jon D. Mikalson, *Athenian Popular Religion* (Chapel Hill, NC, and London, 1983), 22, 25, *et passim*.

Definition of property as whatever is
beneficial for a livelihood   i. 7
(5) Definition of beneficial as what one
knows how to use   i. 13
It is not possible to learn all the branches
of knowledge   iv. 1
States exclude the banausic arts   cf. iv. 2
(6–7) Farmers are superior citizen-soldiers   iv. 2–3, 16
(not explicitly stated but implied in   v. 5, 7, 13, 14)
(9) Farming is easy to learn
(has not yet been explicitly stated,
but implied in   xv. 10, xxi. 1, v. 8)
Farming is pleasant   v. 9
and beneficial to the body   v. 4, 5, 8, iv. 2
and leaves time for friends and affairs
of state   iv. 3
(10) Farming produces the best citizens   v. 7–8

12. καλός τε κἀγαθός. 'A decent gentleman' (lit. 'beautiful and
good'). The phrase recurs in connection with Ischomachus in vi. 8,
12, 14, 16, 17, vii. 2, 3, 43, xi. 1, 3, 22, xii. 2, and xiv. 9. This
common description of moral qualities connotes, as well, magnan-
imous, honourable, courageous, and fine.[131] Xenophon ordinarily
uses the phrase of men whose observable behaviour earns his
approval, for example a person who teaches virtue (*Mem.* 1. 6. 14),
two brave soldiers who died in battle (*Anab.* 4. 1. 9), an army
(*Mem.* 2. 6. 27, cf. 3. 5. 19), and well-born Perioeci who followed
a Spartan king on a campaign (*Hell.* 5. 3. 9). The expression is
normally applied only to members of the upper class: for its
oligarchic connotations see i. 23. Thus Ischomachus' statement
that he treats virtuous slaves as καλοί τε κἀγαθοί is striking.[132]

13–17. ἦλθον ... ἐλθεῖν. This 'autobiographical' description of
Socrates' personal interviews with persons reputed to have specialized knowledge is similar to several in Plato. See Ch. 3, sect. B.

17. Ἰσχόμαχον. Ischomachus may be a totally fictional person or he
may be a thinly disguised *alter ego* for Xenophon himself (see
Ch. 1). A third possibility is that he is a literary representation of

---

[131] See the exhaustive survey in H. Wankel, *Kalos kai Agathos* (diss. Würzburg,
1961), esp. 55–8, on the *Oeconomicus*. See also. J. Jüthner, 'Kalokagathia', in *Charisteria
Alois Rzach zum achtzigsten Geburtstag dargebracht* (Reichenberg, 1930), 99–119, who
notes (99–100), that Xenophon was the first to use the abstract noun καλοκἀγαθία,
e.g. in *Mem.* 1. 6. 14.

[132] See Ch. 5, sect. I, on xiv. 9–10, and de Ste. Croix, *The Origins of the Peloponnesian
War* (London, 1972), 371–6.

a historical person. The name Ischomachus appears in the following historical sources, in addition to the *Oeconomicus*.[133]

1. Cratinus fr. 365 Kassel–Austin = Athen. 1. 8 A, a remark
addressed to Ischomachus' son: 'How could you, the son of
Ischomachus the Myconian, be generous?'

   'Myconian' means stingy. The remark, out of context, is ambiguous: of course, how could the son of a stingy man not be stingy?
or, with amazement, how could he be generous? Cratinus seems
to have died by 421. Therefore, even if 'the Myconian' had been
Xenophon's Ischomachus, the son could not have been either of
the two orphans who became wards of Callias III. The miser,
more likely, was our Ischomachus' father (cf. xx. 26); our
Ischomachus was generous (xi. 9).

2. Plut. *Mor.* 516 c = Aeschines Socraticus fr. 49 Dittmar: an
Ischomachus was questioned at Olympia about Socrates by
Aristippus.

   Dittmar conjectures that the passage derives from an unknown
dialogue of Aeschines.

3. And. 1. 124, in 399, in the course of relating the vicissitudes of
Ischomachus' daughter, her two daughters, and her mother
Chrysilla (see below).

4. Lys. 19. 46, *c*.387; when Ischomachus was alive, everyone
thought he had more than 70 tal., but when he died, he left barely
10 tal. to each of his two sons.

   This legacy was by no means negligible (cf. the 14 tal. inherited
by Demosthenes who was an only son); 10 tal. would have been
sufficient to place the sons in the liturgical class. Ischomachus'
property had probably been damaged by the Deceleian War.[134]

5. Lys. 'Pros Diogenen', fragments in *P. Oxy.* XXXI. 2537, verso,
8–11, and F 32 (Thalheim) *c*.388/7, referring to Callias, who as
the guardian of Ischomachus' sons, had leased their estate to a
certain Diogenes (and Archestratus?) for less than its assessed
value.

6. Heracleides Ponticus fr. 58 Wehrli = Athen. 12.537 C, asking
who squandered the fortune of Ischomachus, and responding
Autocles ('Self-Invited') and Epicles ('Invited Too').

   In other words, his property was devoured by parasites. These
parasites were not necessarily Ischomachus' contemporaries;

---

[133] For the name of Ischomachus' father see on vii. 3 πατρόθεν.
[134] See Davies, *Wealth*, 28, and *APF* 261, 268.

rather, they may have dissipated the property left to his heirs. The names indicate that they were characters in comedy.

7. Araros, the comic poet, Aristophanes' son (fr. 16=Athen. 6. 237 A), mentioning an Ischomachos who supported parasites.

This Ischomachus was probably identical with the one mentioned by Heracleides Ponticus, above. But he need not have been a contemporary of the poet (who began to write in the mid-380s) to have been pilloried by him.

8. Isaeus fr. 19=Harpocration, s.v. χίλιοι διακόσιοι, a prosecution of an Ischomachus, *c*.357–350.

Inasmuch as Isaeus was a specialist in speeches dealing with property, presumably the speech was about an inheritance. This Ischomachus may be identical with the one in

9. Ps.-Dem. 58. 30, a wealthy Ischomachus (Davies, *Athenian Propertied Families*, 6, no. 436) who died in the late 340s leaving a young son Charidemus and a widow.

10. SEG 36 (1986), no. 155. 112–13, a list of ephebes from Xypete *c*.332/1, in which the name appears twice: Ischomachus father of Asopodorus and Ischomachus son of Aristomachus.

Unless the occurrences of the name Ischomachus are merely fortuitous, Asopodorus and Ischomachus may be cousins, descended from the two sons of Ischomachus. The father of Asopodorus would be the right age to be identical with the Ischomachus mentioned by Isaeus above, but if this is true, he is not the same as the father of Charidemus.

According to a plausible, though incomplete and necessarily conjectural, reconstruction by J. K. Davies, the description in the *Oeconomicus* is consistent with that of an Ischomachus who was born at the latest by 460, married Chrysilla, and by her became the father of a daughter (*c*.435–30) and of two sons who were minors when their father died, probably by 404.[135]

The daughter of Ischomachus and Chrysilla married Epilycus (*c*.420–15) and then Callias. The economic status of Epilycus is not known, but he is likely to have been wealthy too at the time of his marriage, since the wealthy in Athens were endogamous. However, he died in debt (And. 1. 118). The two daughters born of this marriage were sufficiently desirable ἐπίκληροι ('heiresses') to have been the subject of litigation by male relatives who wanted to claim them in marriage, despite Andocides' allegations (1. 119)

---

[135] *Athenian Propertied Families*, 248, 265–8, no. 7728.

that they were the objects of their relatives' charity (Andocides is not an impartial source in the case). The daughters were destined to inherit their mother's dowry. The daughter of Ischomachus and Chrysilla probably had a substantial dowry appropriate to Callias' economic status. On Callias' finances see on i. 17 εὐπατριδῶν; his expectations may be deduced from his sister's dowry. The largest dowry known from classical Athens was the 20 tal. of Hipparete, sister of Callias (Plut. *Alc.* 8. 2). According to Andocides (1. 124–7), Callias repudiated his wife and began to live with her mother Chrysilla. The younger woman tried to hang herself and then left home. Callias grew tired of the mother and drove her out as well. Although Chrysilla was already a grandmother, probably in her forties, and Andocides refers to her as γραῦς ('old woman', 1. 127), she was still fertile. When she bore a son her relatives asked Callias to acknowledge him as his own, but he denied that he was the father. Years later, Callias received Chrysilla back into his house and acknowledged the boy as his son (ibid.).

It is interesting to observe that the *ménage à trois* had come into being despite the existence of Chrysilla's male relatives. Such a situation could have developed in the confusion reigning in Athens at the end of the Peloponnesian War. As a widow with sons, Chrysilla could have continued to live in Ischomachus' house, rather than with Callias and her daughter. But during the war and its turbulent aftermath, women were moving in with relatives living in safer areas (Xen. *Mem.* 2. 7. 2; for the location of Ischomachus' house, see on xi. 14–15) and Chrysilla might have consolidated her household with that of her son-in-law. Intimacy between them could readily develop since Callias was her sons' guardian: he will have spent time discussing the boys' finances and the management of their household with Chrysilla. As we shall see in cc. vii–x, owing to Ischomachus' tutelage she was accustomed to conversing with a man and was more knowledgeable than most respectable women about economic matters. The control of widows and other unmarried women may have been one of the purposes of the law the Athenians are said to have passed which permitted a man to marry one Athenian woman and have children by another.[136] In the Funeral Oration delivered at the end of the first year of the Peloponnesian War, Pericles had perhaps anticipated a problem when he warned widows that the

---

[136] See D.L. 2. 26, Athen. 13. 555 d–556, Gell. 15. 20. 6, and Pomeroy, *Goddesses, Whores, Wives, and Slaves*, 66–7.

best women were those who had no reputation, whether good or bad (Thuc. 2. 46).

If the paradigmatic married couple in the *Oeconomicus* is based on the historical Ischomachus and Chrysilla, an explanation is in order. F. D. Harvey is certain that they are identical, and suggests that Xenophon was attempting to remove the scandal attached to a woman he had 'known and respected'.[137] However, if Xenophon, as a young unmarried man who was not a close relative, had actually known Chrysilla well enough to care about her reputation (in Athenian society, where respectable women did not mingle with men who were not close relatives), their acquaintance, *ipso facto*, would be evidence of her lack of proper deportment. Debra Nails rejects Harvey's suggestion and proposes instead that Xenophon is simply being ironic and misogynistic by demonstrating that any woman, despite her education, will misbehave if given an opportunity to do so.[138] But if Xenophon intended to undermine his entire treatise by introducing as a successful businessman an Ischomachus who later lost the bulk of his property and as Ischomachus' wife an unnamed woman who became depraved and notorious when widowed, there would have been little point in his writing the *Oeconomicus*. Moreover, Xenophon shows less misogyny than his contemporaries (see further Ch. 4 and on cc. vii-–viii). The theory that the character of Ischomachus is based— even to a limited extent—on that of Xenophon himself (see Ch. 1) would be untenable if the author had been aware of Ischomachus' drastic fall from fortune and of the humiliation of his wife and daughter. In that case, Xenophon would have displayed a self-critical attitude unique in the literature of the period. Ischomachus would be elevated to the status of a tragic protagonist, a moderately good man who falls into misfortune through no deliberately evil deed (Arist. *Poet.* 1453^{a}11–17) and whose history thus provides an ironic demonstration of the limits of reason, the powerlessness of man, and the inexorability of fate. Such a characterization seems inappropriate for a work which combines features of a philosophical dialogue with those of an agricultural treatise. Therefore it seems best to seek elsewhere for the reasons for the introduction of Ischomachus and his wife as a model couple.

Because Xenophon had departed from Athens before Andocides' trial in 399, and remained away from the Greek mainland for seven continuous years, he may not have been aware of the scandal

[137] 'The Wicked Wife of Ischomachos', *EMC* 28 = NS 3 (1984), 68–70.
[138] 'The Shrewish Wife of Socrates', *EMC* 29 = NS 4 (1985), 97–9.

at its height (see Ch. 1). On the other hand, Plato did not hesitate
to include in his casts of characters people who, after the dramatic
date of the dialogue in which they appear, are known to have
experienced adverse changes in fortune. Of course, as is the case
for all Socratic dialogues, we do not know whether the characters
actually met as described or whether they ever propounded the
philosophy attributed to them. The historical Ischomachus' reputation as an ἀνὴρ χρηματιστικός (i.e. 'businessman') was probably
most important to Xenophon. Xenophon may have chosen to
portray him at a time in his life when his marriage and his financial
situation were exemplary. (On the dramatic date of the dialogue
see Ch. 2, sect. F.) Later, like so much else in Athens, this good
marriage and well-run oikos deteriorated. Thus the *Oeconomicus* is
a dialogue between past and present. Xenophon expresses nostalgia
for the days when Athens was prosperous as he did in c. iv for the
time when Persia was well governed.

vii. 1. στοᾷ. The stoa of Zeus Eleutherios was a popular meeting
place. Socrates' dialogue with his pupil Theages took place there
(Pl. *Theages*, 121 A, also Ps.-Pl. *Eyrx.* 392 A). In Aeschines
Socraticus' dialogue *Miltiades*, Socrates, Hagnon (father of
Theramenes), and Euripides are sitting in the stoa when Miltiades
appears (*P. Oxy.* XXXIX 2888, 2889). The dramatic date of the
Theages cannot be fixed precisely, but the *Miltiades* probably precedes Euripides' move to Macedonia in 408 and certainly antedates
his death in 406. Such colonnades, protected from rain, wind, and
sun, provided a comfortable, though not private, place for conversations such as the one about to be narrated. Harpocration (ed.
Dindorf 1853 [1969]), Hesychius, and the *Suda*, s.v. Ἐλευθέριος
Ζεύς, refer to Hypereides' statement (fr. 197) that the stoa was
constructed by freedmen. But these three sources, in addition to
Etym. Magn., s.v. Ἐλευθέριος, and a scholion on Ps.-Pl. *Eyrx.* 392 A,
prefer the aetiology of Didymus, according to which Zeus acquired
the title 'Giver of Freedom' when Athens was freed from the
Persian threat.

The stoa was built in the last third of the fifth century.[139] On
stylistic grounds, and on examination of the pottery fill beneath

[139] For the date, architecture, and location see R. E. Wycherley, *The Athenian
Agora*, iii: *Literary and Epigraphical Testimonia* (Princeton, NJ, 1957), 25–31, and Homer
A. Thompson and R. E. Wycherley, *The Athenian Agora*, xiv: *The Agora of Athens*
(Princeton, NJ, 1972), 96–103. This dating is still accepted. The Nike acroteria are
dated about the turn of the century, but these were probably added to a completed
building. I am grateful to Homer A. Thompson for this information.

the floor, archaeologists date the beginning of construction to
429. It was located in the north-west corner of the Agora, just
north of the Temple of Apollo Patroos. The location of the stoa
may have inspired some of the material of the dialogue. Statues
of great generals such as Conon, Timotheus, and Evagoras of
Cyprus stood outside it (Paus. 1. 3. 2, Isoc. 9. 57, Dem. 20. 70,
Schol. Dem. 21. 62, and Nepos, *Timotheus* 2. 3): Ischomachus often
refers to generals and armies. It faced the agora: Ischomachus
mentions sending a slave on an errand in the agora (viii. 22).
Athenian courts and perhaps inscriptions of laws were to be found
in the vicinity of the stoa:[140] Ischomachus makes several references
to legal matters (xi. 25, xiv. 4). In it, Ischomachus was in the
centre of Athenian political life; he could look out on the city
which his contributions had helped to support and to adorn
(xi. 9–10).

The stoa was originally designed as a picture gallery.[141]
Pausanias (1. 3. 1–4, 9. 15. 5) reports that Euphranor had depicted
the battle of Mantinea in it. He adds that Xenophon had written
the history of the whole war, and that in the picture, which showed
a cavalry battle, the best-known Athenian was Gryllus, son of
Xenophon, depicted in the act of killing Epaminondas. (See also
Plut. *De Gloria Athen.* 2 = *Mor.* 34 B–F.) The floruit of Euphranor
(364–361) in Pliny, *NH* 35. 128–9, is based largely on the paintings
in this stoa. Xenophon, then, chose to set the *Oeconomicus* in a
building which paid him great honour. See further Ch. 1, sect. D.

2. ξένους. On ξενία ('guest-friend relationships') see ii. 5. Judging
from the dramatic date of the *Oeconomicus*, Ischomachus could well
have been waiting for ξένοι who were on some diplomatic mission
(see Ch. 2, sect. F). Loyalty to one's ξένοι was of the same quality
as loyalty to the permanent members of the oikos. Thus
Ischomachus does not complain about giving up a morning to
wait for some ξένοι, although in the course of the dialogue they
fail to arrive.

καλὸς κἀγαθός. See on vi. 12. In his response to Socrates,
Ischomachus eschews the moral or abstract connotations of the
expression and answers in terms of his wealth alone. Thus he is
characterized at the outset as a realist with a particular interest
in material goods.

3. εἰς ἀντίδοσιν καλῶνται. 'Challenge to an exchange of property'.
Ischomachus, like Critobulus, is wealthy enough to be liable for
liturgies (see on ii. 5–6). When a liturgy was imposed on a man

---

[140] Thompson–Wycherley, *The Athenian Agora*, xiv. 102.   [141] Ibid. 101–2.

he had the right to challenge another whom he judged better able to bear the burden and ask him either to assume responsibility for the liturgy or to submit to a mutual exchange of property (ἀντίδο-σις). After such an exchange, the original challenger would, theoretically, be able to perform the liturgy. No actual exchanges are recorded. The language in this sentence is technical: the challenger had to summon (καλέω) the challengee.[142] Davies estimates that there were probably 400 men in the liturgical class at any given time in the 5th c. and identifies seventy-one men liable for liturgies in the last third of the century.[143]

It was important that the man who was challenged appear to be wealthy, for the decision was not based on a census or any objective accounting.[144] Thus it was possible to assert that a challengee had hidden his assets (as in Ps.-Dem. 42. 20–4). As I have mentioned above, a historical Ischomachus was reputed to have had more than 70 tal. during this lifetime but to have left less than 10 tal. to each of his sons when he died (see on vi. 17). If the attribution of 70 tal. to Ischomachus is correct, then he was one of the wealthiest Athenians we know of, surpassing Pasion, who left an estate worth approximately 66 tal.[145] Isaeus 8. 35 defines visible property as land, buildings, slaves, animals, and household property. In contrast, cash and movables could be concealed. If Xenophon's portrait is based on the historical Ischomachus, then it contributes additional information about this man. Ischomachus' conspicuous interest in visible property may have persuaded his peers that he was even wealthier than he actually was, and thus he may have been subject to challenges more frequently than his fortune actually warranted.

πατρόθεν. According to Arist. *Ath. Pol.* 21. 4, Cleisthenes prohibited the identification of a man πατρόθεν. This regulation is probably a fourth-century invention rather than a law which fell out of use. At any rate it was not observed. By Xenophon's time it was customary to identify a man by both his patronymic and deme, but sometimes only one was used.[146] The name of the father

[142] For this terminology see Ps.-Dem. 42. 5, 19, 23, Dem. 21. 78, Lys. 24. 9, Isoc. 15. 4, and in general A. R. W. Harrison, *The Law of Athens*, ii. 236–8.

[143] *Wealth*, 33; *APF*, p. xxvii.

[144] Vincent Gabrielsen, 'The Antidosis Procedure in Classical Athens', *C&M*, 38 (1987), 12.

[145] Dem. 36 and Davies, *APF* 431–5.

[146] Although it has been argued that a member of the upper class with aristocratic sympathies was often identified by his patronymic while a common citizen with democratic tendencies would usually be known by his demotic, this hypothesis has not yet been corroborated by statistical evidence. See further P. J. Rhodes, *Commentary*

of the historical Ischomachus is not known (see on vi. 17). πατρόθεν here without further clarification may indicate that the father was also named Ischomachus. While it was more common to use a name in alternate generations, sometimes a son was given the same name as his father. This pattern may well have prevailed in Ischomachus' family. One of his sons seems to have been named after him, and the name reappears in successive generations (see on vi. 17).

4. ἡ γυνή. Ischomachus, like Critobulus, abides by Athenian etiquette and never gives us his wife's name (see on iii. 14 Ἀσπασίαν). In slander, Andocides supplies the name Chrysilla (see on vi. 17).

ἐπαίδευσας ... ἐπισταμένην. Socrates assumes that, like most girls, Ischomachus' wife had no formal education. However, as indicated below (vii. 6), she is not totally ignorant.

Education is a central concern in all Xenophon's books. Some of his works, such as *On Hunting*, *On Horsemanship*, and the *Cavalry Commander*, are didactic; in other works, such as the *Cyropaedia*, the *Anabasis*, and the *Hellenica*, Xenophon presents personages and situations as paradigms; in still other works, including the *Spartan Constitution* and the *Oeconomicus*, education is shown to be the foundation of social institutions. Thus in the *Oeconomicus* all members of the household ranging from the wife and the children-to-be to the slaves, the housekeeper, and the farm foreman are subject to education. Ischomachus was a success as his wife's teacher. He easily steps into a pedagogical role in his relationship with Socrates. Then the entire system is presented by Socrates to Critobulus as a model.

In the last quarter of the fifth and in the fourth century the education of men was transformed. Previously the élite had been educated privately under the supervision of the oikos by relatives and family friends. The Sophists professionalized higher education, took pay for instruction, and established schools. With the exception of women who were related to philosophers and Lastheneia of Mantinea, Axiothea of Phlius (D.L. 3. 46, 4. 2), and another woman (*P. Oxy.* LII. 3656), who were enrolled at Plato's Academy, women at Athens did not have access to such education. For presenting a systematic programme for the education of Athenian women, regardless of its content, Xenophon must be viewed as a radical thinker. Although some modern readers may disdain the subject-matter, for most of the world's women, past and present,

on the Aristotelian Athenaion Politeia, 254, P. J. Bicknell, *Studies in Athenian Politics and Genealogy* (Wiesbaden, 1972), 43–4, and Whitehead, *The Demes of Attica*, 69–72.

managing the domestic economy is of primary importance, so they
may as well do it with knowledge and efficiency (see Ch. 6, and
on i. 1 ἐπιστήμης). In proposing that a woman's education was to
take place in the home and that her husband was to be her teacher,
Xenophon is adopting and transforming a traditional practice.
For the husband as teacher, compare the advice of Hesiod to
marry a young woman and teach her careful ways (*WD* 699).
Ischomachus is also imposing on his wife a system that had prevailed for the education of aristocratic males in a slightly earlier
time. The erotic feeling that might be present between the older
male and the younger in the private form of education was likewise
found between husband and wife.[147]

ἔλαβες παρὰ τοῦ πατρὸς καὶ τῆς μητρός. Sim. vii. 5 παρέλαβον.
In ordinary and legal Athenian usage, the groom regularly takes
(λαμβάνει) the bride, and the father or κύριος alone gives her in
marriage (Men. *Peric.* 436–7 and LSJ s.v. λαμβάνω ii. 1c and s.v.
δίδωμι ii. 2). In this passage and in vii. 10 and 11 (οἱ σοὶ γονεῖς,
bis) Xenophon has enhanced the mother's role in giving away the
bride. In the earliest extant Greek marriage contract, *P. Elephantine*
I (311 BC), the mother also joins the father in giving away the
bride. Further evidence of women's expanding social role appears
in some documents of the third century BC (*P. Tebtunis* III. 815
and *P. Petrie* III. 19c), where mothers alone, acting with the
approval of male κύριοι, give daughters in marriage.[148] See on
vii. 13 for the age difference between the spouses which results in
the fact that the groom is his own κύριος and he himself, rather
than his father, takes the bride in marriage.

5. **οὔπω πεντεκαίδεκα.** Ischomachus' bride is old enough for him to
marry but still young enough for him to educate. Information
about the upper classes indicates that men tended to marry at
about 30, but 14 was a normal age for the first marriage of an
Athenian girl. The age of marriage for girls in the Greek world
varied from place to place, and over time. No doubt class also
played an important role, at least because a girl's nurture and
activities affect the age of menarche, which in turn tended to
coincide with the age of marriage. Ischomachus' bride was surely
upper-class and probably reached puberty earlier than her harder-

[147] For a comparison of Xenophon's views on education with those of other authors
see e.g. Wener Jaeger, *Paideia*, 2nd edn. (Leipzig, 1944), iii, and H. I. Marrou, *Histoire
de l'éducation dans l'Antiquité*, 6th edn. (Paris, 1965). For women's education outside
the home see Sarah B. Pomeroy, 'Technikai kai Mousikai'.
[148] See further Pomeroy, *Women in Hellenistic Egypt*, 90.

working and less well nourished contemporaries. The recommendations of philosophers such as Plato (*Laws* 785 B) or didactic
poets such as Hesiod (*WD* 698–9) do not necessarily correspond
to reality.[149] Demosthenes (27. 4, 65) pleads that Demophon had
been negligent in carrying out his obligation to marry his sister,
who was about 15 years old. Xenophon refers to Critobulus' wife
as a παῖς ('mere child', iii. 13), and also uses the word to connote
the immaturity of a woman who has not made the transition from
daughter to wife: the daughter of Cyaxares, who must be at least
18, is called 'παῖς' (*Cyr.* 8. 5. 19).

Girls performed rites in honour of Artemis at Brauron before
marriage. The celebrations were quinquennial and the participants
were 5 to 10 years old.[150] See also the story of Atalanta in Ael. *VH*
13. 1 and on vii. 10 χειροήθης ... ἐτετιθάσευτο. The average age of
menarche was 14.[151] Thus the young bride might well be a mother
within a year or two of marriage. The reconstruction of the life of
Chrysilla requires that she gave birth to her daughter soon after
her marriage to Ischomachus (see on vi. 17).

That brides depicted on Attic vases appear mature to the
modern viewer[152] is due to the painters' intention to show them as
ripe and blooming, and to the modern notion that associates
slenderness with youth and plumpness with age. The portrayal of
Demeter and Persephone on the 'Triptolemus relief' in the
National Museum at Athens (no. 126 and the copy in the
Metropolitan Museum of Art in New York, no. 14. 130. 9) in
which the mother is thinner than the daughter indicates that ways
of representing the ages of women were different in classical Greece
from modern artistic conventions.

5–6. ὑπὸ πολλῆς ἐπιμελείας ὅπως ὡς ἐλάχιστα μὲν ὄψοιτο, ἐλάχιστα δ' ἀκούσοιτο, ἐλάχιστα δ' ἔροιτο. Critobulus' wife had also
seen and heard almost nothing (iii. 13). Upper-class girls and
women were usually protected and secluded, leaving the environs
of their house only to attend funerals or festivals. Although there

---

[149] See further, ibid. 14, 89, 106–8, 175–6 n. 14.

[150] On the Arcteia see e.g. Harpocration, *Lex.*, s.v. ἀρκτεῦσαι; *Suda.* s.vv. ἄρκτος ἢ
Βραυρωνίοις and ἀρκτεῦσαι; *Anec. Graec.* i. 206 Bekker, s.v. ἀρκτεῦσαι; and e.g. Lilly
G. Kahil, 'Artémis de Brauron: Rites et Mystère', *AK* 8 (1965), 20–33.

[151] Soranus, *Gynaecology*, 1. 4. 20, and see D. W. Amundsen and C. J. Diers, 'The
Age of Menarche in Classical Greece and Rome', *Human Biology*, 41 (1969), 125–32.

[152] W. K. Lacey, *The Family in Classical Greece*, caption to pl. 24, observes that the
bride is 'fully mature'. On Attic iconographic conventions governing the representation of prepubertal and fully mature females see Christiane Sourvinou-Inwood, *Studies
in Girls' Transitions* (Athens, 1988).

were many festivals, both local and city-wide (see on ii. 5 θύειν πολλά), as the remarks of Critobulus and Ischomachus indicate, attendance did not provide a significant educational opportunity for girls. Plutarch (*Isis and Osiris* 381 E–F, *Conj. Prec.* 142 D) gives the conventional view when he declares that for unmarried girls surveillance is required and for married women staying at home and silence are suitable. He refers to this passage when he states in *De Pyth. Orac.* 450 C that like the bride in Xenophon, a girl who is chosen as Pythia should have seen and heard as little as possible.[153]

6. ἔρια ... ταλάσια. Wool-working was characteristically women's work, and it would have been surprising if a well-brought-up woman did not know how to spin and weave and to supervise the manufacture of textiles by domestics (see Ch. 5). At Athens girls as young as 10 years of age who were selected to serve as ἀρρηφόροι were able to begin weaving the peplos of Athena. In Ischomachus' opinion making a cloak and supervising the wool-work of slaves is not enough. He believes his wife has potential capabilities in other areas and cherishes greater expectations for her.

Ischomachus' wife must have learnt more than he gives her credit for from other women in the women's quarters, though perhaps she would not have learnt about estate management if the women there had been as lazy and unproductive as those described in x. 13. At least her mother imparted moral values such as self-control (vii. 14). In any event, a didactic work like the *Oeconomicus* must imply the need for a lesson, regardless of reality. Furthermore, Xenophon's intended audience was male, including men like Critobulus who needed elementary lessons in estate management. (See also the discussion of Renaissance treatises on household management in Ch. 6, sect. E.) Most upper-class women could probably sing and dance as required at religious ceremonies, but Ischomachus does not attribute such accomplishments to his wife. However, she does know how to read, for she and her husband make a list of the utensils in the house (ix. 10). Ischomachus also assumes that she knows something about nursing and pharmacology, since he tells her that one of her responsibilities is the care of the slaves when they are ill (vii. 37).

θεραπαίναις δίδοται. In order to prevent theft, the mistress of the house not only supervised the work but weighed out wool for spinning. Erinna, *Distaff* 23, relates that her mother distributed

---

[153] On the seclusion of women see Pomeroy, *Goddesses, Whores, Wives, and Slaves*, 79–84, 111, 131.

wool. See also vii. 36 διανεμητέον for the wife as distributor of commodities.

τὰ . . . γαστέρα. Women spent much of their time preparing food, and men could not control their access to it. Hence a common misogynistic complaint was that women were insatiable (e.g. Semonides, fr. 7. 24, 46–7, Ar. *Lys.* 36, 537). Mistaken notions about women's anatomy doubtless fostered the idea of woman as vessel. The abdominal cavity of the female body was thought to be vast and empty so that the uterus could wander through it. ἐν γαστρὶ ἔχειν is a colloquial expression for to be pregnant already in Herodotus (LSJ, s.v. γαστήρ). Gluttony was simply one facet of a view of woman as non-productive, a parasite, a consumer, like the first human bride Pandora (Hesiod, *WD* 80–2, *Theog.* 574–99). Ischomachus, in contrast, educates his wife to make an economic contribution to the household.

γαστήρ is not confined to food. It is also used by Xenophon with a more general connotation of physical appetites. This connotation is certainly not to be excluded here. See xiii. 9, *Mem.* 1. 6. 8, 2. 6. 1, and *Sp. Const.* 2. 1.

7. ἀνδρὶ καὶ γυναικί. The virtue of control over one's bodily appetites, like that of σωφρονεῖν (vii. 14–15), is the same for men and women. Socrates, in Xen. *Symp.* 2. 9, in conversation with the philosopher Antisthenes, asserts that women's nature is in no way inferior to men's except in its lack of judgement and physical strength. In vii. 23–6 Xenophon elaborates on the difference in physical strength. In that passage he also insists that some values traditionally rated very highly by the Greeks are found in men, others in women. According to D.L. 6. 10 Antisthenes himself stated simply that the virtue of man and woman is identical. The Stoic Cleanthes wrote a book *Concerning the Proposition that the Virtue of Man and Woman is the Same* (D.L. 7. 175). Views attributed to Socrates on the virtue of men and women are also developed at far greater length in Pl. *Rep.* 5 and *Meno* 71 E–73 B.[154] In *Meno* 73 A 6–7 Socrates implies that the virtue of all human beings is basically the same. Perhaps it is superfluous to point out that the ideas on the equality of women and men were held by a small number of philosophers, not by the majority of Greeks. See further on vii. 15 and x. 1.

8. ἔθυσα καὶ ηὐξάμην. Ischomachus begins every important undertaking by cultivating the good will of the gods (see on vi. 1).

---

[154] See Ch. 4, on vii. 23, and Sarah B. Pomeroy, 'Plato and the Female Physician', *AJP* 90 (1978), 496–500.

Ischomachus initiates the prayers and sacrifices, and determines
that his wife should participate too. In patriarchal societies, the
family religion, like the family itself, is controlled by men.[155]

10. χειροήθης . . . ἐτετιθάσευτο. The same words often connoted
the domestication of animals. (On analogies between people and
animals see on iii. 11, iv. 24; on civilizing women see on vii. 5–6.)
It was traditional for the husband to be the wife's teacher, and a
natural result of the difference in their ages (see on vii. 4–5 and
Xen. *Symp.* 2. 7). References to the education of the nubile woman
as 'taming' were common in Greek literature. For example Medea,
who complains that a new bride is like a resident in a foreign land
who must learn the νόμοι of the place, uses the word νεοδμής 'newly
tamed' when she refers to Jason's relationship with his young
second wife (Eur. *Med.* 623). Creon (Soph., *Ant.* 477–8, 579)
declares that Ismene and Antigone must no longer run free, but
should be bridled.[156] Before they married, young Athenian girls
participated in the cult of Artemis at Brauron. The girls dressed
as bears. This costume symbolized, *inter alia*, their primitive state
before they were domesticated by marriage (see on vii. 5 οὔπω
πεντεκαίδεκα).

Of course, the Athenian wife actually is a stranger in a new
domestic situation. Thus the mythical marriage of Procne to the
savage Thracian Tereus, depicted by Sophocles in *Tereus* (fr. 583
Radt), was a paradigmatic marriage to a stranger: she laments
the fate of young women who are given in marriage to strangers
and to barbarians and who must move to uncongenial and conten-
tious houses. In contrast, Ischomachus is concerned to transform
the wife, who was an outsider to his oikos, to an insider by means
of education.

Dem. 3. 31, couples τιθασεύω and χειροήθης to describe the
humiliation of the Athenian citizenry by rival politicians. Plut.
Dem. 5. 3 employs the two words to characterize the power of
Demosthenes' oratory over his opposition.

διαλέγεσθαι. Women were expected to be silent. Ischomachus'
wife had been brought up properly by conventional standards so
that she spoke as little as possible (vii. 6). See also iii. 12 for
Critobulus' admission that there are few people with whom he
converses less than with his wife. According to Aristotle (*Pol.*

[155] H. J. Rose, 'The Religion of a Greek Household', *Euphrosyne*, 1 (1957), 97–8,
unduly emphasizes women's role in family religion.
[156] For other examples, see Claude Calame, *Les Chœurs de jeunes filles en Grèce archaïque*
(Rome, 1977), ii. 411–20.

1253ᵃ9–18) the ability to speak distinguishes men from other animals. Therefore women's deficiency in this sphere would seem to render them less than fully human. Initiation into the arts of speaking continues the idea expressed in the preceding phrase of transforming the wife into a fully civilized human being. Ischomachus must teach his wife to think and to represent her thoughts in speech. This lesson is the preliminary step in educating her to be his peer. διαλέγεσθαι has many meanings, ranging from conversation to the formal philosophical discussion called dialectic (see LSJ s.v. διαλέγω). In *Mem.* 4. 5. 12, Socrates was reported to have defined διαλέγεσθαι as 'to deliberate in common by meeting together, classifying (διαλέγοντας) things by categories.... From this men become excellent, show leadership, and become skilled in dialectic.' Dialectic consists of question and answer (see Ch. 2, sect. G).

In the present chapter the wife gradually assumes more prominence in the conversation, beginning with brief and simple questions (14, 16, 32, 35), progressing to a clever response (37), and finally expressing an original thought (39). In xi. 25 she is capable of conducting a mock trial.

11. ἐκαθεύδομεν ... κοινωνόν. Ischomachus begins to reveal his idea of marriage as a partnership. This view was radical (see Ch. 4, and on vii. 23–9).

Partnership in marriage is also discussed in vii. 30 and x. 4. Citing these passages, G. Raepsaet contrasts Ischomachus' 'système familial utilitariste' with the conception of marriage found in Plato and Aristotle, where the emphasis is on the unity created by sentiment, in particular by φιλία.[157] He fails to realize that Ischomachus is describing his marriage in its early days. Because the marriage was arranged, rather than the result of romantic attachment, time was needed for the development of sentiment.

For the administration of the Persian Empire as a model for the household of Ischomachus and his wife, see notes to c. iv.

11–12. τέκνων ... τέκνα. Ischomachus quite naturally expects that his children will support their parents when they are old. τέκνα here, as in a similar, and probably derivative, passage in Ps.-Arist. *Oec.* 1343ᵇ21–3, must refer to male children only. At Athens the obligation to maintain parents was endorsed not only by custom but also by law. Penalties for maltreatment of parents apparently included payment of a fine, disenfranchisement, and death (Xen.

---

[157] 'Sentiments conjugaux à Athènes aux vᵉ et ivᵉ siècles avant notre ère', *AC* 50 (1981), 682.

Mem. 2. 2. 13, Dem. 24. 103–7, Lys. 13. 91, Aesch. 1. 28). Sons who had themselves been mistreated by their fathers or not taught a trade were relieved of the obligation to care for them when they were old (Plut. *Sol.* 20, 22, Aesch. 1. 13). For the possibility that an older woman might be mistreated by her husband and children, see vii. 42.

13. ἀποφαίνω . . . κοινὸν κατέθηκας. The present tense of ἀποφαίνω indicates that Ischomachus makes payments, from time to time, into the common resources; in contrast, the aorist of κατατίθημι indicates that his wife contributed her dowry all at once (See Ch. 5, sect. G). Even if Ischomachus and his bride's father were members of the same economic class, it is likely that the dowry did not equal the bridegroom's initial contribution to the marriage. Among wealthy Athenians, a son's inheritance of parental property was many times larger than the amount taken as dowry by a daughter. For example in Isaeus 5. 27 four sisters share two-thirds of an estate, while an adopted son receives one-third.[158] On Chrysilla's dowry, see on vi. 17.

Marriage was the foundation of the oikos. For didactic purposes, Xenophon begins the story of the life-cycle of Ischomachus's oikos with marriage. Since the bride is barely 15 her parents are still living (§ 4 ἔλαβες παρὰ τοῦ πατρὸς καὶ τῆς μητρός). Ischomachus is much older than his wife: his mother is probably dead, for otherwise she would be living in his house and probably telling her son's bride how to manage the oikos. Evidently Ischomachus has been without a woman to run the house for quite some time: his possessions are in a mess (viii. 10). However, the disorder may be a didactic device. Ischomachus' father is also dead (xx. 25) and he has come into possession of his patrimony. Ischomachus represents the property as held in common, or merged. As was natural at the beginning of marriage, the relationship was expected to be permanent. In case of divorce, however, the husband was obliged to return the dowry.

13–14. ὁπότερος . . . συμβάλλεται. Normally weaving was women's only productive activity that was accorded some recognition (see on vii. 6 ἔρια . . . ταλάσια). On Ischomachus' methods of reckoning whether his wife or he had made a greater contribution to the estate, see Ch. 5, sect. E, and on xx. 16 λυσιτελεῖν.

14. τίς . . . δύναμις. Ischomachus' wife is herself unaware of her

---

[158] See further David M. Schaps, *Economic Rights of Women in Ancient Greece* (Edinburgh, 1979), and Lin Foxhall, 'Household, Gender, and Property in Classical Athens'.

future contribution to the household (see on vii. 5–6). Or she may be displaying the diffidence usually appropriate to a Greek wife, and especially to a young girl, though not acceptable to Ischomachus.

15. σωφρονεῖν . . . ἀνδρὸς καὶ γυναικός. σωφροσύνη was the most characteristic virtue attributed to women. As a traditional female quality it bore the connotations of inhibition, self-restraint, and chastity. In this conventional sense it was akin to a woman's control over her γαστήρ (see on vii. 6). In the fourth century the Socratics defined σωφροσύνη more broadly. According to Pl. *Meno* 71 E–73 B, both men and women may exhibit the same qualities of δικαιοσύνη and σωφροσύνη, but the man's ἀρετή is displayed in managing the polis, the woman's in managing the household. (On male and female virtue see further Ch. 4 and on ix. 14–15, x. 1.)

In his various works, Xenophon mentions σωφροσύνη often and with a wide range of connotations. He is the first to connect the σωφροσύνη of both men and women with good administration of the household and with the military virtues of obedience, discipline, orderliness, and practical knowledge.[159] For σωφροσύνη as a virtue of a person in authority, see its attribution to Cyrus (*Cyrop.* 8. 1. 30), xii. 11–13, and xxi. 12.

16. οἱ θεοὶ ἔφυσάν σε . . . ὁ νόμος. οἱ θεοί and ὁ θεός are used without distinction in the *Oeconomicus*. See vii. 23, 30 where φύσις (the physical nature of human beings) is also under the direction of the divine. In vii. 30 divine law is again paired with νόμος (man-made law). F. Heinimann cites *Oec.* vii. 16 as an illustration of the notion that νόμος and φύσις are to be considered as influences, but not as opposing forces, in the formation of human beings.[160] By the end of the fifth century in Athens νόμος meant 'statute' or 'written law', rather than custom, and implied obligation.[161]

17–18. ἡ ἐν τῷ σμήνει ἡγεμὼν μέλιττα. The activities of the bee-wife are also referred to in §§ 32, 33, and 38. On the wife as queen bee see on vii. 32.

---

[159] See further Helen F. North, *Sophrosyne* (Ithaca, NY, 1966), 121–32, and 'The Mare, the Vixen, and the Bee: Sophrosyne as the Virtue of Women in Antiquity', *ICS* 2 (1977), 35–48. M. Untersteiner, 'Prodico e Xenoph. *Oec.* vii', in A. Rostagni *et al.* (eds.), *Studi in onore di Luigi Castiglioni* (Florence, 1961), ii. 1059–70, draws attention to parallels between the discussions of σωφροσύνη and of νόμος and φύσις in Prodicus' *Horai* and *Arete*, and Xenophon's views on these subjects.

[160] *Nomos und Physis* (Basle, 1965), 168 n. 8.

[161] M. Ostwald, *Nomos and the Beginnings of Athenian Democracy* (Oxford, 1969), 7, 55, 57, *et passim*.

18. ἔφη φάναι. Reminders of the time-frame of the dialogue recur (cf. vii. 23); see Ch. 2, sect. E.

19. τὸ ζεῦγος. The basic necessities of life referred to in this passage are: children, who will care for their parents when they are old; shelter; and provisions, including food and clothing. It is illuminating to compare this passage with Pl. *Rep.* 369 D, where the necessities of life can be provided by a farmer, a builder, and a weaver, and perhaps a cobbler and someone else who serves physical needs. No one in Plato's primitive city is female, not even the weaver or the person who provides for the needs of the body.

23–9. ῥίγη . . . διαπράττεσθαι. Although the conjugal relationship of Ischomachus and his wife is based on a division of labour, they are mutually dependent and their marriage is thus a partnership. Greek marriage contracts from Roman Egypt also stipulate a division of labour. For example, in *P. Ryl.* II. 154 (66 AD) a husband agrees to perform all the agricultural labour and pay taxes, bringing the harvest into the couple's common abode, and in *CPR* 24 (= *Chrest. Mitt.* 288, 136 AD), a husband is responsible for ἔργα and τελέσματα (see Ch. 5 and vii. 11 ἐκαθεύδομεν ... κοινωνόν).

30–1. ἀνδρὶ αἴσχιον ἔνδον μένειν. Banausic work, by forcing men to remain sitting indoors by a fire, renders their bodies womanish (iv. 2) whereas farming creates men capable of undertaking military endeavours (vi. 7).

Ps.-Dem. 59. 122 distinguishes a wife from other women by her role as bearer of legitimate children and as guardian of the property that is indoors (τῶν ἔνδον φύλακα). Shame accrues to the man who remains indoors, for such behaviour is womanish and cowardly (see e.g. Aes. *Agam.* 1625–6). The same attitude prevails in some contemporary Mediterranean societies.[162]

32. ἡ τῶν μελιττῶν ἡγεμών. For additional references to the queen bee see §§ 17, 33, 38, and ix. 15. For the Persian king as a model for Ischomachus' wife as queen bee and for the extensive parallels between cc. iv and vii see notes in c. iv. The concept of queens and influential royal women was, of course, not new to Xenophon. In the *Anabasis* (e.g. 1. 1. 4, 2. 4. 27) he refers repeatedly to Parysatis, who favoured Cyrus over her elder son Artaxerxes, and in the *Cyropaedia* (5–7 *passim*) he tells the story of Panthea, wife of Abradatas king of Susa, whose actions helped determine the outcome of political events. Rule by a woman was repugnant to the

---

[162] See e.g. P. Bourdieu, 'The Berber House', in M. Douglass (ed.), *Rules and Meanings*, (Harmondsworth, 1977) 98–110.

usual Greek view of gender hierarchy; the barbarian world, however, produced some illustrious queens who, to varying degrees,
exercised power in their own right, and not merely as consorts of
kings. For example, Herodotus uses the word βασίλεια not only of
the wife of Candaules of Lydia (1. 11. 1), but of Nitocris, queen
of the Babylonians (1. 185. 1, 187. 1, 5, 191. 3) and Tomyris,
queen of the Massagetae (1. 205. 1, 211. 3, 213). The most famous
female ruler of all was Artemisia of Halicarnassus, who accompan-
ied Xerxes' fleet on his expedition against Athens (Her. 7. 99,
8. 87–8, 101–3). Furthermore, like any other Athenian, Xenophon
knew that in the Homeric epics queens such as Penelope, Arete,
and Helen personally supervised their households and actually did
some work themselves. But none of these queens of epic were as
busy as the 'queen bee' described here.

The analogy between the good housekeeper and the bee can be
traced in Greek literature as far back as Semonides (fr. 7. 83–93).[163]
As Semonides, and then Phocylides (fr. 2 Diehl) had envisaged
her, the bee-wife makes her husband's property increase. The
industriousness of the good wife was a common theme in Greek
epitaphs;[164] see further Ch. 5. But, in addition, the good wife serves
as a catalyst for general prosperity. Similarly, not only does the
activity of worker bees produce honey, but by pollination bees
enhance the fertility of plants and crops.

The hive is an appropriate metaphor for many reasons, including the fact that it is a neat and orderly edifice housing a social
organization with a class structure. (Plato uses the same metaphor
in *Rep.* 522 c). Like wives, bees must be domesticated in order to
produce sustenance for the oikos. For example, Pliny, *NH* 11. 59,
distinguishes between wild and domesticated bees. Bees should not
be left to behave 'naturally', but trained by the beekeeper, who
must lure them to new hives by offering pleasant tastes and fragrances. The bees are willing to stay because they love the flowers
the keeper offers (Pliny, *NH* 21. 71, and see on vii. 35 ἀποικίζει
and 38–9 τῷ σμήνει ... ἀπολειπτέον). The division of labour appropriate to husband, wife (see vii. 23–9 ῥίγη ... διαπράττεσθαι), and
other members of the oikos has its counterpart among bees.

[163] As early as the 9th c. pottery vessels shaped like beehives were placed in a
woman's grave in the Athenian agora. See Armando Cherici, 'Granai o arnie?
Considerazioni su una classe fittile attica tra IX e VIII sec. a.C.', *RAL* 44 (1989),
218–21. I am grateful to Michael Vickers for this reference.
[164] Anne-Marie Vérilhac, 'L'image de la femme dans les épigrammes funéraires
grecques', in ead. (ed.), *La Femme dans le monde méditerranéen* (Lyon, 1985), iii. 85–112,
discusses the recurrent use of φιλεργία and synonyms in praise of women.

Ischomachus tells his wife she is like a queen bee because she is to stay indoors, care for the young, supervise the workers, and oversee the transformation of raw material into manufactured products. The hive also houses ordinary workers, including the guardian bees, who defend the queen and larvae against predators who would invade the hive. Although the hive contains drones, Ischomachus and his wife endeavour to eliminate unproductive elements from their oikos (see vii. 33 ἀργούς). On the relationship between the hive and the bridal chamber see ix. 3 θάλαμος ἐν ὀχυρῷ. Analogies between bees and human beings are abundant in c. vii.

Honey was a staple of the Greek diet, and beekeeping was very common. Legislation attributed to Solon prescribed the distance between hives (Plut. *Sol.* 23). Arist. *HA* 553ᵃ17ᵇ2 reports that there was considerable discussion about the habits of bees. The construction of wooden or pottery beehives permitted beekeepers to observe the interior of the hive.[165] Thus Xenophon's readers, and probably Ischomachus' wife as well, would have readily understood the metaphor, including the details of its implications.

Xenophon adopts practices from civic management, but the household is not a democracy. Rather it is governed on monarchical and meritocratic principles. The wife may be the supreme ruler, and may even be compared to the Persian king. Semonides does not refer to the bee-wife as a 'queen' (see on vii. 6 τά ... γαστέρα). Ischomachus, in contrast, tells his wife 'the greatest happiness of all will result from showing yourself better than I am and making me your servant' (vii. 42). Ischomachus' wife eventually even sits in judgement on him, sentencing her husband to endure punishments or to pay fines (xi. 25 and see Ch. 4).

In these passages, as in vii. 39, where Ischomachus' wife uses the masculine article to describe her husband as the leader of the bees, Xenophon's identification of the leader of the hive as female is deliberate: it results from the metaphor he is constructing rather than from scientific knowledge. In the *Cyropaedia* (5. 1. 24), the ruler of the hive is male; the Persian king is compared to the leader (masculine) of bees (feminine) in the hive. At *Hell.* 3. 2. 28 the leader is also male. Plato (*Rep.* 520 B and *Pol.* 310 E) and Aelian

---

[165] See e.g. J. E. Jones, A. J. Graham, and L. H. Sackett, 'An Attic Country House below the Cave of Pan at Vari', *ABSA* 68 (1973), 397–412. For beehives at an isolated country villa at Pasha Limani in Attica see H. W. Catling 'Archaeology in Greece, 1988–89', *AR* 35 (1989), 17–18, and in general see E. Crane and A. J. Graham, 'Beehives of the Ancient World', *Bee World*, 66 (1985), 23–41, 148–70.

(*NA* 5. 10–11) speak of king bees. Aristotle (*HA* 553ᵃ26ᵇ1) reports that Greek entomologists were uncertain about both the sex of the leader of the bees and of the drones, although there was general agreement that the workers were female.[166] Despite the controversy, Aristotle, unlike Xenophon, consistently refers to the leaders as male. Misogyny coupled with the Greek tradition of seeing analogies between human society and the hive affected Aristotle's view of the sex of the bees.[167] Arrian (*Indica* 8. 11 and *Epict.* 3. 22. 99) revives the idea that the leader may be female.

The bee was famous for purity and abstinence. Ancient entomologists did not understand the sexual reproduction of bees; therefore they associated this insect with chastity. Pliny, *NH* 11. 46, notes that no one has ever observed the coitus of bees. Ael. *NA* 5. 11, remarks on this creature's σωφροσύνη. According to Semonides (fr. 7. 90–2), the wife who is like a bee is so uninterested in sex that she does not even like to sit and listen to other women when they gossip about it. Various priestesses were called μέλισσα (LSJ, s.v. μέλισσα). These included virgin priestesses of Apollo at Delphi and some who served Demeter and Persephone at Eleusis (Schol. Pi. *Pyth.* 4. 60 = ii. 112–13 Drachmann, Call. *Hymn to Ap.* 110–11, and Schol. Theoc. 15. 94). Married women who participated in the Thesmophoria were also referred to by this term (Apollodorus of Athens, *FGrH* 244 F 89). Bees were said to be censorious about human beings. Plutarch (*Conj. Prec.* 44 = *Moralia* 144 D–E), stating that bees behave in a hostile manner towards men who have been with women, and wives do likewise, urges husbands not to have had intercourse with other women when they approach their wives. He also (*Natural Phenomena* 36 = Loeb xi. 218–19) cites incidents of bees stinging adulterous or perfidious lovers in Theoc. 1. 105, and in Pind. fr. 252 Snell–Maehler. Charon of Lampsacus, giving a different version of the myth told by Pindar, states that a nymph who had promised to sleep with Rhoecus on condition that he remain chaste until she summoned him punished him for insulting the bee that she had sent as a messenger (see *FGrH* 262 F 12 and comments by Jacoby ad loc.). According to the *Geoponica* (15. 2. 19) bees hate men who reek of wine and myrrh, and attack women who have had sexual intercourse. Col. *RR* 9. 14. 3 advises the man who intends to handle

---

[166] For citations in Greek and Roman authors, see T. Hudson-Williams, 'King Bees and Queen Bees', *CR* 49 (1935), 2–4.

[167] See further Malcolm Davies and Jeyaraney Kathirithamby, *Greek Insects* (London, 1986), 63.

bees to abstain from sexual relations for a day. Similarly, Pall. I. 37. 4 advises the guardian of the hive to be pure and chaste. Among the tasks that Columella assigns to the *vilica* or bailiff's wife is collecting honey; so that her husband will be sexually faithful but not lascivious, Columella recommends that she be neither too pretty nor too ugly (*RR* 12. 1. 1–2).

ὑπὸ τοῦ θεοῦ. The association of bees with divinity and immortality was traditional in Greek and Roman literature.[168] For parallels with the Persian king, who was associated with Ahuramazda, see on iv. 21 and xxi. 12.

33. ἀργούς. Sim. i. 19 and *Cyrop.* 1. 6. 17, 2. 2. 25 for criticism of idle households. In vii. 1–2 we observe Socrates' surprise at finding Ischomachus at leisure. Condemnation of idleness was traditional in Greek thought. Hes. *WD* 303–7 compares the idle man to a drone. In Athens laws punishing idleness were attributed to Draco, Solon, and Peisistratus (Plut. *Sol.* 17. 2, 22. 3, 31. 5, Herod. 2. 177, D.L. 1. 55, Pollux 8. 42). In *Mem.* 2. 7. 8 work is praised. But the work must be appropriate to a free person: see on iv. 2–3.

35. ἀποικίζει. On the reproduction of slaves see on ix. 5.

The metaphor of swarming is employed here. Varro, *RR* 3. 16. 29 and Ael. *NA* 5. 13 follow Xenophon in applying the image of swarming to human colonization. Modern hives often house some 60,000 bees. Swarming commences when the bees need more room.[169] Ancient beekeepers encouraged and controlled the swarming of their bees.[170] The new swarm needed a queen (or 'king'), who is referred to here as τινὶ ἡγεμόνι. The swarming metaphor continues in vii. 38.

The Greeks often dealt with the potential problem of population increase by sending citizens to form colonies. In the present context, perhaps excess slaves are to be sent from the main house to rural dwellings. In Attica, though settlements in towns or villages were more common than nucleated farm dwellings, permanent rural buildings, often belonging to wealthy men, were also found.[171]

---

[168] See, e.g. Pind. fr. 123. 11 Snell–Maehler, Cic., *Tusc.* 1. 108, Verg. *Georg.* 4. 219–20, Petr. *Sat.* 56. 6 and see further A. B. Cook, 'The Bee in Greek Mythology', *JHS* 15 (1985), 1–24, and Davies–Kathirithamby, *Greek Insects*, 69–70.

[169] See Sue Hubbell, *A Book of Bees* (New York, 1988), 18–19.

[170] Arist. *HA* 624ᵃ26, Col. *RR* 9, Pliny, *NH* 11. 53–4, *Geoponica* 15. 3, H. Malcolm Fraser, *Beekeeping in Antiquity*, 2nd edn. (London, 1951), 26–7, 46–7, and see on vii. 38.

[171] For examples see J. Pečírka, 'Homestead Farms in Classical and Hellenistic Hellas', in M. I. Finley (ed.), *Problèmes de la terre en Grèce ancienne* (Paris, 1973), 113–47, D. R. Keller and D. W. Rupp (eds.) *Archaeological Survey in the Mediterranean Area* (*BAR* Int. Ser. 155; Oxford, 1983), 392 *et passim*, and J. L. Bintliff and A. M. Snodgrass, 'The Cambridge/Bradford Boeotian Expedition: The First Four Years', *JFA* 12 (1985), 139.

Archaeologists are just beginning to pay serious attention to smaller sites. In the absence of conclusive evidence scholars are divided in their views concerning whether rural settlements were inhabited permanently or only for part of the year. The function of rural buildings is unclear: they are not necessarily residences, but they may have been used to house workers temporarily.[172] However, it appears likely that workers of lower status did dwell on farm properties.[173] A calendar dedicated to Hermes by the ἐπίτροπος χωρίου and a small farmhouse found on a farm in Agrileza north of Sounion indicate that the foreman lived on the premises.[174] The present passage as well as the implications of xii. 3 give some support to the view that those who worked on the farm might be housed permanently there.

35–7. οἷς μὲν ἂν ἔξω ... ὃς ἂν κάμνῃ. Ischomachus' wife is to supervise not only female slaves but also males who live in the house. She will probably be required to enter the men's quarters to minister to male slaves who are ill. Ischomachus evidently considers the slaves as property whose value warrants the mistress's personal attention rather than as strange men whose bodies are taboo to a respectable woman.[175]

36. δαπανᾶν. What is most interesting about the description of the wife's activities here, as in iii. 15, is that she alone is in charge of the expenditures. (In ix. 8 decision-making is shared by husband and wife.) When Socrates first mentioned the serious matters that Critobulus entrusted to his wife (iii. 12), one subject which he had in mind must have been her role as financial manager. Managing the finances of a household in the liturgical class was indeed a great responsibility and did require training

---

[172] So Robin Osborne, 'Buildings and Residence on the Land in Classical and Hellenistic Greece: The Contribution of Epigraphy', *ABSA* 80 (1985), 127.

[173] So Pečírka, 'Homestead Farms in Classical and Hellenistic Hellas', 118–19.

[174] See Langdon–Watrous, 'The Farm of Timesios'. 162–7.

[175] Pauli Murray gives the following description of Mary Ruffin Smith, a slave-owner in North Carolina to whom her grandmother had belonged: 'Sooner or later, everything which happened in the slave quarters had to be resolved by "Miss Mary".... she had to look after the old folks, give medicine to the sick, bandage the sores and cuts of slave children, run down to the cabins when a mother was in childbirth. She must order food and clothing and parcel it out among them, find clothes and refreshments for slave marriages, approve husbands for the women and wives for the men, arbitrate in their family squabbles, supervise the training of growing girls, be present at all their prayer meetings, bury them when they died and keep the whole kit and caboodle in smooth working order. She seldom had a minute to herself day or night, since she was "on call" at all times for any emergency ...'. *Proud Shoes* (1956, repr. New York, 1987), 160.

and knowledge beyond what a 14-year-old girl would possess. It was by no means the usual situation for an Athenian housewife to be in charge of managing a household, even one of modest size. But some women did acquire expertise. Scattered references in comedy and in orations dealing with family matters indicate that women were conversant with their household finances, although their formal legal capacity to manage money was severely restricted.[176] For example, in Lys. 32. 14–15 a widow can list the property left by her husband, and in Isaeus 11. 43 a widow can recount loans made by her husband. Demosthenes' father entrusted his wife with knowledge of hidden property (Dem. 27. 55). In Ps.-Dem. 47. 57 a wife knows her husband's financial dispositions in detail. In Lys. 1. 6 a husband relates that he delegated the management of his household to his young wife after apparently a year or two of marriage. But the speaker was a man of modest means. In Ar. *Clouds* 19–22 Strepsiades, who is managing a household in the style of the rich, goes over his accounts himself. Pericles, who was quite wealthy, and who had his sons and daughters-in-law living with him, managed his household finances quite differently from the way Ischomachus recommends. Plutarch (*Per.* 16. 5) reports that Pericles turned his finances over to a male slave who was either naturally talented or trained by Pericles himself. In any event, in Athens independent women such as Aspasia were the only ones who regularly got to manage large amounts of money (see on iii. 14 Ἀσπασίαν). However, Xenophon knew that women were capable of managing oikoi, for he reports that Spartan women controlled their oikos and that some controlled more than one (*Sp. Const.* 1. 9).

διανεμητέον. According to Ps.-Arist., *Oec.* 1344^{b}30–1, the Persians and the Spartans administer their households in the same fashion, by dividing and storing their supplies. In contrast, Athenians with smaller households immediately spend whatever cash their produce has yielded and do not store supplies.[177] On budgeting, see also ix. 8.

As honey is stored in the hive, so supplies are stored in the house (see on ix. 4). The beekeeper must determine how much honey may be taken and how much should be left for the bees (Pliny, *NH* 11. 33–5, 40, 42, Pall. 11. 13, 12. 8, *Geoponica* 15. 5). Hes. *WD*

---

[176] See further G. E. M. de Ste. Croix, 'Some Observations on the Property Rights of Athenian Women', *CR*, NS 20 (1970), 273–8, and Schaps, *Economic Rights of Women*.
[177] Philodemus, Περὶ οἰκονομίας 11. 22–5 does not consider the latter system practical.

298–302, 361–3 draws attention to the importance of storing adequate supplies of food. Looking after stored food is a major responsibility of Ischomachus' wife.

Subsistence farmers in Greece nowadays calculate their future needs generously, and thus retain a surplus as insurance against a poor yield in the following year.[178] In antiquity the standard ration of one choinix of wheat per man per day not only provided sufficient calories for a man performing heavy labour, but was more than enough for a person engaged in less strenuous activities. A slave might be given half the allocation of a free man without danger of starvation.

In the classical period accounts consisted of entries for receipts and expenditures entered in narrative form.[179] As Aristotle (*Pol.* 1338ᵃ15–17) and Theophrastus (fr. 662 Fortenbaugh *et al.*) point out, literacy is useful for οἰκονομία. Thus the ability to write is particularly advantageous to Ischomachus' wife in managing finances. (For her literacy, see ix. 10.) Literacy is also symptomatic and predictive of the wife's independence and high status, for in classical Greece, as elsewhere, women's illiteracy is linked to gender inequality.

προνοητέον. Also in vii. 38 and again of the housekeeper in ix. 11.

37. ἐπιχαριτώτατον. That slaves, especially male slaves, be well disposed was essential for the slave-owner's peace of mind. In *Hiero* 4. 3 Xenophon remarks that citizens served as guards for one another against their slaves. (See also on xii. 6 and xxi. 12 τὸ ἐθελόντων ἄρχειν.) Ps.-Xen. *Const. of. Ath.* 1. 10–11 complains about the fearlessness and presumptuousness of slaves at Athens.

38–9. τῷ σμήνει ... ἀπολειπτέον. The swarm follows its leader; analogously, slaves will not desert their mistress. Thus this thought is connected to the mention of slaves in the preceding paragraph. See on vii. 34 ἀποικίζει and iv. 18–19 for the statement that Cyrus' followers did not desert him. Here the emphasis is on the loyalty of slaves to the mistress; of course Ischomachus' wife will not be the queen bee who leads the swarm from the house.

40. τὸν τετρημένον πίθον. Drawing water in a leaky vessel was proverbial for wasted labour. The expression appears also in Arist.

---

[178] See further L. Foxhall and H. A. Forbes, 'Σιτομετρεία: The Role of Grain as a Staple Food in Classical Antiquity,' *Chiron,* 12 (1982), 54, 57, 74. Foxhall–Forbes adopt wheat as their standard, though they recognize that barley and other grains were consumed.

[179] See de Ste. Croix, 'Greek and Roman Accounting', 26.

Pol. 1320ᵃ31–2 and Ps.-Arist. *Oec.* 1344ᵇ26. Judging from the
countless potsherds found in Greek sites, broken pots were not
uncommon. Drawing water, carrying it, and then discovering it
had leaked out must have been a frequent occurrence producing
intense despair and vexation. Carrying water was usually a
woman's chore.¹⁸⁰ Although female slaves would have performed
this chore in wealthy homes, Ischomachus' wife will have been
aware of the labour involved. Therefore she expresses sympathy
with those who must draw water to no avail.

The most wretched souls in the underworld carry water in leaky
vessels (see e.g. Pla. *Gorg.* 493 B, *Rep.* 363 D5–E). These include
souls of those who failed to be initiated into the Mysteries and the
Danaides, who murdered their bridegrooms. The water-carriers
in the *Oeconomicus* may be ordinary people and not necessarily
those in Hades. If Xenophon does have the Danaides in mind,
then his reference to those who draw water as masculine must be
due to the analogy with husbands who bring in produce.¹⁸¹

41. ἀνεπιστήμονα ταλασίας ... διπλασίου. On weaving see above
on vii. 6 ἔρια ... ταλάσια, θεραπαίναις δίδοται, and Ch. 5. Wool-
working is the most frequently attested occupation of Athenian
freedwomen. It is also the job most frequently attested for female
slave apprentices in Graeco-Roman Egypt.¹⁸² Slave women whose
primary task was not wool-working were expected to spin if they
had any spare time. Xenophon may be referring to such activities
when he mentions doubling a slave's value to her mistress. So few
sale-prices of female slaves are known for this period that it is not
demonstrable that a skilled wool-worker actually cost twice as
much as an unskilled labourer. In his first speech against his
guardians, Demosthenes reckons the value of his property, including his male slaves, in excruciating detail, but he never places a

¹⁸⁰ Pomeroy, *Goddesses, Whores, Wives, and Slaves*, 72; Eur. *El.* 55–6, 64–5, for water-
carrying as hard labour; Ar. *Lys.* 319–83, for water as the women's weapon; and
Sutton, *The Interaction between Men and Women Portrayed on Attic Red-Figure Pottery*,
161–2, for hydriae being frequently painted with wedding scenes as women's vases.
¹⁸¹ See further Erwin Rohde, *Psyche*, trans. W. B. Hillis (London, 1925),
588. According to Eva Keuls, *The Water Carriers in Hades: A Study of Catharsis through
Toil in Classical Antiquity* (Amsterdam, 1974), 25, 45, in the visual arts the water-
carriers in the underworld were first represented without clear designation of sex or
age. On Italiote vases from *c.*350–300 BC they are always shown as women in the
prime of life. For these see H. R. W. Smith, *Funerary Symbolism in Apulian Vase-Painting*
(Berkeley, 1976), 88–92, 176–85. Ps.-Plato, *Axiochus* 371 E (1st c. BC) and Plut. *Sept.
Sap.* 160 *b*, assume that the water-carriers in Hades are the Danaides.
¹⁸² Clarence A. Forbes, 'The Education and Training of Slaves in Antiquity',
TAPhA 86 (1955), 330–1.

specific value on his female slaves although he alleges that they had been sold (27. 46). However, the few extant prices from the classical period show that female and male slaves were of equal value: about 200 dr. for skilled workers, and less for unskilled.[183] Men and women paid the same price (100 dr.) for the phiale that they dedicated to Athena at manumission. Study of contracts from Graeco-Roman Egypt show that specialized training affected a slave's earning ability.[184] *P. Oxy.* XIV 1647, stipulates that a slave (described as under-age) apprenticed to a master weaver for four years is to earn 8 dr. monthly the first year, 12 dr. the second, 16 dr. the third, and 20 dr. during the final year. The same principle of increasing the value of movable property through training is applicable to animals. In *On Horsemanship* 11. 13 Xenophon talks of training horses well so that they become more valuable.

42. κολάσαι. See on iv. 5, 7 for Cyrus' system of rewards and punishments and ix. 5, 11–15 for the rewards and punishments of slaves.

ἐμὲ σὸν θεράποντα. See above on vii. 32, 33, 38–9, and Ch. 4. In *Mem.* 3. 9. 11 women are said to govern (ἀρχούσας) men in spinning because they know how to do it.

προϊούσης τῆς ἡλικίας ἀτιμοτέρα. Aristophanic comedy, especially *Ecclesiazusae* and *Lysistrata*, shows old women being treated with disrespect. Despite allusions in vii. 12–13, 19, to honour due to parents this passage raises the possibility that a wife will be rejected once she has lost her youthful beauty. This attitude toward older women was common.[185]

43. καλά τε κἀγαθά. This phrase refers here to both spiritual and material goods. See on vi. 12 καλός τε κἀγαθός and vii. 2 καλὸς κἀγαθός.

viii. In this chapter the concept of order first proposed in iii. 3 is developed as fundamental to successful estate management. This chapter contains some of the most elaborate prose in the entire work. Xenophon's admiration for order was apparent in the description of the straight rows of trees that Cyrus had planted at Sardis. (See on iv. 21 for the cosmic connotations of the orderly garden.) Orderliness as a principle of organization appears here

---

[183] See William L. Westermann, *The Slave Systems of Greek and Roman Antiquity* (Philadelphia, 1955), 14–15, and W. K. Pritchett, 'The Attic Stelai: Part II', 276.

[184] Clarence A. Forbes, 'The Education and Training of Slaves in Antiquity'.

[185] See Jan N. Bremmer, 'The Old Women of Ancient Greece', in Josine Blok and Peter Mason (eds.), *Sexual Asymmetry* (Amsterdam, 1987), 191–215.

in Ischomachus' concern with the proper disposition of household possessions, and again in c. ix in the description of the arrangement of rooms. Interest in orderliness may be attributable, in part, to Xenophon's military background.[186] In the context of the education of a wife, the ability to separate items into appropriate categories and to bring order out of chaos distinguishes her as a civilized person.

1. Ἦ ... ἐπιμέλειαν. At the opening of c. ix and in ix. 18 Socrates makes similar queries about the efficacy of the teaching Ischomachus imparted to his wife.

3. καλὸν ἀνθρώποις ὡς τάξις. Order is nothing less than a part of a cosmological system. Good housekeeping has an ethical basis. In traditional Greek thought, the appearance of the house was a direct reflection of the wife's sexual probity.[187] Xenophon expands this notion so that a successful household economy is the result of the virtue of all its administrators. Cyrus the Great, one of the wealthiest men, is also one of the most virtuous. Because Critobulus is an aristocrat he is likely not only to be impressed by the success of the world's most powerful and wealthiest men, but to find it personally relevant to him.

In Pl. *Gorg.* 504 A, Socrates praises the order produced by craftsmen and discusses the effect of regularity and order (τάξις and κόσμος) on the body and soul.

χορός. The example of a chorus is used again in viii. 20. Choral performances were common at festivals. Therefore, like the beehive that was used as a metaphor in c. vii, the chorus would be known to all Xenophon's readers as well as to Ischomachus' wife.

4. στρατιά. Ischomachus lists the regular components of a Greek army, including both warriors and the support system that conveyed supplies and equipment. In *Mem.* 3. 1. 6–7 Xenophon points out that a skilled general was needed to co-ordinate the variety of troops that constituted a Greek army.[188] In *Cyrop.* 8. 5. 2–16 Xenophon describes the orderly army camp where each soldier knows his place, and in 8. 5. 7 he remarks that Cyrus practised orderliness in household management. Choruses, armies, ships, and beehives are clearly delimited, hierarchical social organizations in which all participants must know their specific duties and

---

[186] So Anderson, *Xenophon*, 14.

[187] See vii. 32 ἡ τῶν μελιττῶν ἡγεμών and Pomeroy, *Women in Hellenistic Egypt*, 97–8.

[188] On the composition of the Greek army of the classical period see F. E. Adcock, *The Greek and Macedonian Art of War* (Berkeley and Los Angeles, 1967).

all work together for the good of the entire group. The analogies from the public world of ships, cavalry, and men's choruses, rather than being ill chosen, serve to enhance the private sphere and imply that both spheres are equal (sim. iii. 15). Inasmuch as the private sphere is associated with the woman and the public sphere with the man, equality of the sexes is also implied. The education of Ischomachus' wife is not to be limited to what convention prescribed for women: eventually she is said to have a masculine mind (x. 1). But because of the innate differences between male and female described in vii. 22–5, women are not given roles in the public sphere and vice versa. Although it is unlikely that Ischomachus' wife will have been familiar with the sight of a real army or a Phoenician ship, she may have seen artistic representations or heard descriptions of them. She certainly will have had personal experience of synchronized choruses. In any case, it is necessary to remember that Xenophon did not write the *Oeconomicus* for women like her but rather for male readers. Like Xenophon himself, this audience will have had first-hand knowledge of armies and ships. Metaphors of army and ship recur in the final chapter.

8. τριήρης. Because of the importance of navies and overseas trade, and their use for general travel, Xenophon's readers would have been familiar with the trireme and other ships. A ship was not simply utilitarian, but could be emblematic of its owners. The metaphor of the ship of state was common in Greek literature (e.g. Alcaeus fr. 18, Aes. *Sept.* 2, 62, 208, Soph. *Ant.* 162–3), for, as Xenophon suggests here, the well-organized work of the men on board is indicative of the favour of the gods (viii. 16) and predictive of wide-spread harmony and prosperity.

A trireme of the classical period measured about 36 m × 6 m and carried about 200 men. Even in a large country house most rooms—with the exception of the andron, which was used for entertaining—were quite small by modern upper-class Western standards[189] (but see viii. 13 ἐν ⟨ἐν⟩δεκακλίνῳ). Furthermore, there were no closets or cupboards. Thus there were advantages in storing possessions at home as neatly as they would be on a ship.[190]

---

[189] e.g. the house described by J. E. Jones, L. H. Sackett, and A. J. Graham, 'The Dema House in Attica', *ABSA* 57 (1962), 75–114.

[190] On the trireme see e.g. J. S. Morrison and J. F. Coates, *The Ancient Trireme: The History and Reconstruction of an Ancient Greek Warship* (New York, 1986), and Lionel Casson, *Ships and Seamanship in the Ancient World* (Princeton, NJ, 1971), 77–96.

διὰ τί δὲ ἄλλο. The ecphrasis of the trireme contains a liberal sample of obvious rhetorical devices. (See Ch. 2, sect. D.) For example, in § 8 note the repetitions of διὰ τί ἄλλο and of ἐν τάξει (anaphora), the rhetorical questions, the alliteration of ἄλλο ἄλυποι ἀλλήλοις, and the rhymes in προνεύουσιν ... ἀναπίπτουσιν ἐμβαίνουσι ... ἐκβαίνουσιν. Like the eulogy on agriculture (v. 1) the present passage is fulsome, reflecting in its overblown style the size of the ship and the quantity and variety of its contents. At the same time, balance and repetition of words and rhetorical figures serve to emphasize the importance of order. Athen. 1. 23 B paraphrases the second question and answer.

11. τὸ μέγα πλοῖον τὸ Φοινικικόν. Unlike the trireme, which was narrow and streamlined, the cargo-ship was so round and capacious that it was called γαῦλος ('bowl').[191] The only other extensive ancient literary reference to a merchantman is in Lucian, *Ship*, 1–5: Lucian emphasizes the enormous size of a Roman cargo-vessel named *Isis*. In the present passage Ischomachus must be referring to a particular well-known Phoenician cargo-ship. He moves from the trireme (which was built for speed rather than storage) to the cargo-ship in order to make his point about stowing a variety of material objects (see on xxi. 3). That he compares his house to a cargo-ship suggests that it too is large and packed with goods.

11–12. σκεύη ... ξυλίνων ... πλεκτῶν. Xenophon divides the ship's gear into two types: wooden and woven. These categories correspond to the ξύλινα and κρεμαστά ('hanging') mentioned in Athenian naval lists of the fourth century (*IG* ii². 1604–32). Included in the wooden gear are oars of various sizes and shapes, poles, ladders, shores, sailyards, and masts. Hanging gear encompasses woven materials such as ropes and sails.[192]

13. ἐν ⟨ἐν⟩δεκακλίνῳ ... συμμέτρῳ. LSJ s.v. cite this passage (sc, without emendation) and translate literally a room 'holding ten dinner-couches'. But Chantraine, *Xénophon: Économique*, 20–1, argues that Xenophon uses this word as an approximate, or figurative measure. The use of the word συμμέτρῳ in the present context undermines his suggestion here, although in other contexts couches could be used figuratively as a standard of measure.[193] The capacity

---

[191] See LSJ s.v. and Casson, *Ships and Seamanship in the Ancient World*, 66.

[192] For detailed descriptions of these items see J. S. Morrison and R. T. Williams, *Greek Oared Ships: 900–322 B.C.* (Cambridge, 1968), 289–307.

[193] e.g. in Telecleides fr. 47 Kassel–Austin = Plut. *Per.* 3. 6, and see Eugene S. McCartney, 'The Couch as a Unit of Measurement', *CP* 29 (1934), 30–5.

of the standard square dining-room was eleven couches. Three couches were arranged on each of three walls; the fourth wall had only two couches in order to leave space for the entrance. Thus dining rooms are usually described in terms of an odd number of couches.[194] Athen. 2. 47 E–F, mentions that the ancients had rooms with five, seven, and more than nine couches. A house from the classical period at 9 Menander St. had a dining-room with a capacity of eleven, or perhaps fifteen, couches.[195] In private houses at Olynthus, the largest dining-room had a capacity of nine couches.[196] A dining-room with ten couches has the same capacity as one with eleven: the former is simply missing one couch.

It makes less sense to describe a space as a 'ten-couch' space rather than an 'eleven-couch' space. Therefore it is tempting to emend the text here to read ἐν ἑνδεκακλίνῳ, and to postulate that the second *EN* was omitted either because of the scribes' wish to avoid dittography, or because they missed the second *EN* by haplography.

In any case, Ischomachus is making the point that sailors can store all that is necessary for their lives in a space not much bigger than one large dining-room that was usually 6.30 m square.[197] If Ischomachus has his own dining-room in mind, then his house was grandiose by Greek standards, though not unique, and not inappropriate for a man of his wealth and generosity.

14. πρῳρεύς. The πρῳρεύς ('first-mate' or 'look-out') stands on the prow. In the hierarchy of leadership he is just below the captain and can substitute for him (Ar. *Knights* 541–4, Arist. *Pol.* 1253[b]29, Plut. *Agis*, 1. 2, Theodoret of Cyrrhus, *Epist.* 78 (ed. Y. Azéma [Sources chrétiennes, 98; Paris, 1964], 176).

19–20. ὑποδήματα . . . σκευῶν. The possessions of the household are further enumerated in ix. 6–7. They consist of bedding, clothing, furniture, and utensils for washing and spinning and for the preparation and serving of food. Although Ischomachus does

---

[194] See further Stephen G. Miller, *The Prytaneion* (Berkeley, Los Angeles, and London, 1978), 223 n. 9.

[195] See J. E. Jones, 'Town and Country Houses of Attica in Classical Times', in H. Mussche, P. Spitaels, and F. Goemaere-De Poerck (eds.), *Thorikos and the Laurion in Archaic and Classical Times* (MIGRA, 1; Ghent, 1975), 96.

[196] This room measured 8.70 m × 4.95 m. See D. M. Robinson and J. W. Graham, *Excavations at Olynthus*, viii: *The Hellenic House*, 173–4.

[197] R. A. Tomlinson, 'Ancient Macedonian Symposia', in B. Laourdas and C. Makaronas (eds.), *Ancient Macedonia* (Thessaloniki, 1970), 309, estimates this capacity on the basis of couches 1.85 m long. For variations see Birgitta Bergquist, 'Sympotic Space: A Functional Aspect of Greek Dining-Rooms', in Oswyn Murray (ed.), *Sympotica* (Oxford, 1990), 37–65.

not describe these items in detail, there would have been quite a variety in each category and, owing to the size of his establishment, a large number of each type of thing. For example, footwear in the classical period included a great variety of sandals, shoes, buskins, and boots. Within these categories there were numerous styles, some specific to men or women, others worn by both. The footwear also varied according to material, colour, and, of course, size. There were also several qualities (xiii. 10).[198] Consequently, the need for organization was great. Indeed it would be wrong to ascribe an obsessive concern with neatness to Ischomachus. Even nowadays, pots, dishes, silverware, and other household utensils are usually stored in groups organized according to function, shape, size, and frequency of use. But the rhapsodic and hyperbolic quality of the entire passage might make it seem funny to the reader. It was certainly memorable. Cicero (as quoted by Col. *RR* 12. 2) and Plut. *Mor.* 515 E refer to it.

A contemporary inventory of possessions from the households of Alcibiades and others which were confiscated and sold after the profanation of the Mysteries and mutilation of the Herms in 415/14 provides a more elaborate description of the contents of the house of a wealthy Athenian.[199] An impressive number of ceramic vessels, including glazed tableware, pottery for domestic use, and vessels for cooking and storage was found in houses in Attica.[200] The country house at Vari also contained ceramic beehives. Within these categories there is a wide variety of sizes, shapes, and manufacture. Owing to their variety, ancient pots and dishes, unlike modern ones, did not lend themselves to storage in neat stacks. In addition, many houses in town contained equipment used in agricultural activities and food-processing such as might be needed to make olive oil and wine.[201] The Attic stelai list large amounts of grain, and also mention olive oil, vinegar, wine, and barley among

---

[198] See further A. A. Bryant, 'Greek Shoes in the Classical Period', *HSCPh* 10 (1899), 57–102.

[199] See Pritchett, 'The Attic Stelai; Part II'. For the newest text of the stelai see *IG* i³. 421–30.

[200] See e.g. J. E. Jones, A. J. Graham, and L. H. Sackett, 'An Attic Country House below the Cave of Pan at Vari', 374–97; eidd., 'The Dema House in Attica', 88, 100; D. A. Amyx, 'The Attic Stelai; Part III', *Hesperia*, 27 (1958), 163–310, for the pottery of the Hermocopidae, and in general, B. A. Sparkes and L. Talcott, *Pots and Pans of Classical Greece* (Princeton, NJ, 1958).

[201] See e.g. Jones–Sackett–Graham, 'An Attic Country House below the cave of Pan at Vari', 418–19 n. 141.

the property of the Hermocopidae (*IG* i³. 421, col. iii). Storage-jars would have been essential for all these provisions.

20. κύκλιος χορός. To emphasize his point Ischomachus alludes to a dithyrambic chorus of fifty people who danced in a circle around an altar rather than of a smaller group such as performed in tragedy and comedy, which danced in patterns of right angles.[202]

ix. 2. τῆς γε οἰκίας τὴν δύναμιν. The design of a house is part of οἰκονομία (see above on iii. 1). The floor-plan of the Greek house permitted a greater degree of flexibility than we are familiar with nowadays in the West, for the use of space was not predetermined permanently by plumbing. Thus although rooms are differentiated by size and location, archaeologists are often unable to decide how a particular room was used; nevertheless excavations have revealed houses designed as Ischomachus describes (see further on ix. 4 μεσημβρίαν).[203]

οὐ γὰρ ποικίλμασι. In *Mem.* 3. 8. 10 Xenophon also eschews paintings and decorations in the home. It was fashionable for wealthy Athenians to decorate their houses with paint and stucco ornamentation. Although Alcibiades' furnishings were simple (see above on viii. 19–20), he kept the scene-painter Agatharchus captive painting murals on his walls (Plut. *Alc.* 16. 4). The Attic stelai list pictures of Axiochus among the property of the Hermocopidae (*IG* i³. 427. 59–62). The houses of Alcibiades and others condemned along with him were noteworthy for their lack of luxury: their tastes may have been influenced by Spartan ideas.[204] However, this phenomenon was even more widespread.[205] Houses of the classical period were furnished simply and looked rather bare by later standards. Ostentatious displays of wealth were also frowned upon at Athens: the sumptuary legislation of Solon was designed to reduce such displays since they created friction between citizens. Ischomachus preferred unadorned simplicity rather than artificial decoration in both his house and his wife (c. x).

---

[202] See LSJ s.v. κύκλιος, and T. B. L. Webster, *The Greek Chorus* (London, 1970), 68, 91.

[203] On private houses in general see Wolfram Hoepfner and Ernst-Ludwig Schwandner, *Haus und Stadt im klassischen Griechenland* (Munich, 1986).

[204] So Pritchett 'The Attic Stelai: Part II', 210.

[205] See further G. M. A. Richter, *The Furniture of the Greeks, Etruscans and Romans* (London, 1966), 3.

3. θάλαμος ἐν ὀχυρῷ. LSJ s.v. and Marchant, *Xenophon: Memorabilia
and Oeconomicus*, 439, render θάλαμος as 'store-room' and are followed by Anderson[206] and R. Laurenti,[207] but Carnes Lord[208]
translates 'bedroom'. Sturz renders 'interior aedium pars', though
for appearances of this word in other works of Xenophon he gives
'cubiculum virginum aut ... coniugum'.[209] Robin Osborne gives
the most flexible definition 'an internal room whether on an upper
or a lower storey'.[210] Here the room, which is supplied with the
best linens and furniture, is probably an internal room used as the
bridal chamber where the newly married couple sleep.[211] After the
night spent in the bridal chamber, sleeping arrangements seem to
have altered. Pl. *Laws* 808, implies that husband and wife sleep
apart, but within reach of their slaves of the same sex. Thus in
Lys. 1 the wife usually slept upstairs with a female slave before
the birth of a fretful child made such an arrangement inconvenient.
In the opening scene of Aristophanes' *Clouds*, father and son are
shown in the same bedroom.

Eva Keuls[212] argues that the narrowness of Greek beds indicates
that two people might have used them for intercourse, but would
not usually have spent the entire night together; however, this
argument is anachronistic. Ischomachus' domestic planning
reflects the congenial nature of his conjugal relationship. In x. 8
ἐξ εὐνῆς suggests that Ischomachus and his wife are often together
in bed. Furthermore, although his house is large enough to afford
separate quarters that would have been adequate for his wife, in
ix. 5, Ischomachus must show the women's quarters to his wife,
since she has not been there before (unless Xenophon is simply
using this tour of the house as a narrative device to motivate his
decription of the house). It is most significant that he shows his
wife the *gynaikonitis* not as her own quarters, but as the female
slaves'. According to D. M. Robinson θάλαμος is 'the bedroom of
the master and mistress of the family, where the available [*sic*]

---

[206] *Xenophon*, 12.   [207] *Le opere socratiche* (Padua, 1961), 192.

[208] In Leo Strauss, *Xenophon's Socratic Discourse*, 41.

[209] *Lexicon Xenophonteum*, s.v.

[210] 'Buildings and Residence on the Land in Classical and Hellenistic Greece: The
Contribution of Epigraphy', *ABSA* 80 (1985), 121–2.

[211] J.-P. Vernant, *Mythe et pensée chez les Grecs* (Paris, 1985), 183–5, notes that
θάλαμος and θόλος ('round building') are related words, and, reviewing some of the
connotations of θάλαμος from the *Odyssey* till the end of the classical period, finds that
the room is always, in some way, used by women. θάλαμος is also related to θαλάμη
for which LSJ s.v. give 'hive or nest of bees', but this is presumably a metaphor.

[212] *The Reign of the Phallus* (New York, 1985), 212.

were'.[213] Hoepfner–Schwandner also interpret θάλαμος as 'bed-room' and show it in their plans of private houses that were typical of the classical city as upstairs and adjacent to the *gynaikonitis* (see Fig. 1).[214] Vitr. *Arch* 6. 7. 2 states that one of the *cubicula* in a Greek house is called *thalamus* and the other *amphithalamus*, and that *gynaeconitis* refers to a complex of rooms including the *thalamus*, dining-rooms, bedrooms, and privies. However, in his day upper-class Greek women, especially in other parts of the Greek world, were no longer secluded as they had been in classical Athens.[215] Vitruvius' description does not suit Ischomachus' house for on the tour many rooms, including public rooms and storerooms, inter-vene between the θάλαμος and the *gynaikonitis*. That the word designates a room that could be used for storage or as a bridal chamber, and that the master of the house used a locked door to guard only the women's quarters and the storeroom suggests that he counted his women among his most valuable possessions.

τὸν σῖτον. σῖτος is a generic word for grain.[216] Barley and wheat were the grains most likely to have been stored in quantity.[217]

4. διαιτητήρια. The living-quarters included the andron (a dining-room for men).[218] The function of other rooms in the vicinity of the andron is not clear: they may have served as family rooms and have been used for dining. Because Robinson and Graham believed that houses at Olynthus did not have segregated quarters for women they suggested that when men were dining in the andron, women used the other rooms in the living quarters; but see below.

μεσημβρίαν. See on ix. 2 τῆς γε οἰκίας τὴν δύναμιν. Similar advice is given in Ps.-Arist. *Oec.* 1345[a]33, Col. *RR* 1. 6. 1–2, Varro, *RR* 1. 4. 4, 7, and *Geoponica* 6. 2. 1. In *Mem.* 3. 8. 8–9 Xenophon explains that if the south side of the house is built on a higher elevation, it will trap the winter sun, while the north side, being

---

[213] *Excavations at Olynthus*, xii: *Domestic and Public Architecture* (Baltimore, 1946), 197, and see 460, s.v.

[214] For the reproduction of one of their houseplans see *Haus und Stadt*, Pl. 7.

[215] Nepos, pr. 6–7, states that Greek women did not accompany their husbands at dinner-parties. However, from the 4th c. and the Hellenistic period, some respect-able (and royal) women had careers and roles that were not possible for women in seclusion: see further Pomeroy, 'Technikai kai Mousikai'.

[216] F. Heichelheim, 'Σῖτος' *RE*, suppl. vi (Stuttgart, 1935), cols. 819–92.

[217] See Pritchett, 'The Attic Stelai: Part II', 185–6, and notes on xvi. 9 κριθάς ... πυρούς, and xx. 27 σῖτον.

[218] See further Robinson–Graham, *Olynthus*, viii. 167–72, sim. Robinson *Olynthus*, xii, *passim*.

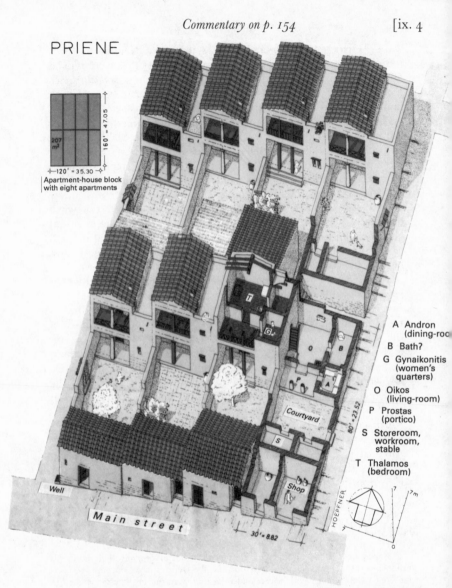

PRIENE

Apartment-house block
with eight apartments

207 m²

120' = 35.30

160' = 47.05

A Andron
   (dining-roo

B Bath?

G Gynaikonitis
   (women's
   quarters)

O Oikos
   (living-room)

P Prostas
   (portico)

S Storeroom,
   workroom,
   stable

T Thalamos
   (bedroom)

Courtyard

Shop

Well

Main street

30' = 8.82

80' = 23.52

HOEPFNER

Fig. 1. Reconstruction of houses at Priene showing women's quarters and thalamos
upstairs. After Wolfram Hoepfner and Ernst-Ludwig Schwander, *Haus und Stadt im
klassischen Griechenland* (Munich, 1986), 171

lower, will avoid winter winds. Houses conforming to this description have been excavated in Attica, Olynthus, Priene, Eretria,
Pella, Colophon, and Seuthopolis. For example, the Dema House
at Ano Liossia north of Athens, a large, free-standing, country
house of the late fifth century, faces south.[219]

The analogy between the hive and the house continues in this
chapter: storage is a major function of both types of domicile (see
vii. 36 διανεμητέον). Preventing pests and natural deterioration
from destroying food that has been stored for the winter may make
the difference between comfortable survival and virtual extinction
(see further on xx. 4 οὐδὲ οἶνον ἔχει). Classical treatises on beekeeping similarly advise that hives be situated so as to be warm in
winter and cool in summer. See Pall. 1. 37. 1, Col. *RR* 9. 5, Pliny,
NH 21. 80, and Verg. *Georg.* 4. 35–6.

5. ἔδειξα ... γυναικωνῖτιν. Evidently Ischomachus' wife has not
been secluded in the women's quarters, for she has the run of the
house, including the men's quarters (see on vii. 35–7). Ordinarily,
the women of an Athenian family occupied separate quarters in a
household that could afford their doing so. Such quarters were in
the most protected part of the house, remote from areas accessible
to male visitors who were not kin. For women's quarters at Athens
see, e.g. Ar. *Thesm.* 414–17, *Eccl.* 693, 961, Lys. 1. 9, 3. 6, and
Eur. *Phoen.* 89–100. In Dem. 47. 56 female slaves live in a tower.[220]

Separate quarters for women may have existed in the Greek
world beyond Athens, but the evidence is not absolutely reliable.
Plut. *Pelop.* 9. 5, mentions women's quarters at Thebes, Xen. *Cyr.*
5. 5. 2, in the tent of the Assyrian king, and Herod. 5. 18–20 in
the court of Amyntas at Macedonia. Literary allusions to women's

[219] See Jones–Sackett–Graham, 'The Dema House in Attica', 103, 105. See also
eidd. 'The Vari House', 419, and Borimir Jordan and John Perlin, 'Solar Energy Use
and Litigation in Ancient Times', *Solar Law Reporter*, 1 (1979), 583–94.

[220] Scholarly opinion is not unanimous on the subject of the *gynaikonitis* at Athens.
Gareth Morgan, 'Euphiletos' House: Lysias I', *TAPhA* 112 (1982), 115–23, suggests
that women spent most of their time upstairs in women's quarters. Susan Walker,
'Women and Housing in Classical Greece: The Archaeological Evidence', in Averil
Cameron and Amélie Kuhrt (eds.), *Images of Women in Antiquity* (London and
Canberra, 1983), 81–91, assumes that women's quarters in Athens existed and that
these were isolated from areas frequented by men. In direct contrast to Walker,
Michael Jameson, 'Private Space and the Greek City', in Oswyn Murray and Simon
Price (eds.), *The Greek City: From Homer to Alexander* (Oxford, 1990), 172, 186–92,
maintains that Greek domestic architecture does not reveal a distinction between
genders, but that the use of space by men and women was flexible though prescribed
by custom. I am grateful to Professor Jameson for showing me his paper before
publication.

quarters in the court of Amyntas and in the palace of Ptolemy IV
were not based on direct observation by the male authors who
mention them, and may simply be the result of analogy with the
Athenian practice. Certainly in the latter case they do not imply
that women who used them were permanently secluded.[221]

The textual evidence for the *gynaikonitis* is more persuasive than
the archaeological data. Because these quarters were often on a
second storey, some archaeologists have been unable to identify
them with certainty. Thus, although the excavators of late fifth-
century houses at Olynthus maintain that they found no trace of
women's quarters, they do report finding spindles and loomweights scattered about on the ground floor of the houses.[222] They
fail to entertain the possibility that this material dropped from the
upper storey when the houses collapsed, or that on very hot days
the women might have worked downstairs temporarily. The walls
of some of the houses in Attica of the classical period were thick
enough to have supported an upper storey, and the existence of
pyrgoi attached to houses has been confirmed.[223] Remains of a
fifth- or fourth-century stone house in Euboea reveal traces of a
second storey.[224] Loomweights have been found in excavated
pyrgoi in Athens and Siphnos and dyeing equipment in a tower
in Argolis.[225] The weight of such evidence has justifiably caused
the pendulum to shift away from the negative view of Robinson
and Graham. Hoepfner–Schwandner, *Haus und Stadt*, postulate the
existence of women's quarters in virtually every city they study,
including Olynthus, although they do not cite any evidence (such
as finds of spindles) which would corroborate this hypothesis.[226]

Seclusion of the free women of a household was a luxury and
could be practised only by a household with at least one slave. At
Athens lower-class women who were not secluded ran the risk of

[221] See Pomeroy, *Women in Hellenistic Egypt*, 4, 134. In some coeducational universit-
ies in the USA, in order to protect women students from intruders, they are not
assigned dormitory rooms on the ground floor.

[222] See Robinson–Graham *Olynthus*, viii. 167–9, sim. Robinson in *Olynthus*, xii. 57,
and Graham, 'Olynthiaka', *Hesperia*, 22 (1953), 200.

[223] For the tower of the Vari house, see Jones–Graham–Sackett, 'An Attic Country
House Below the Cave of Pan at Vari', 437–8, and see J. E. Jones, 'Town and Country
Houses of Attica in Classical Times'.

[224] See J. V. Luce, 'The Large House at Dystos in Euboea', *G&R*, 2nd ser., 18
(1971), 143–9.

[225] John Young, 'Studies in South Attica: Country Estates at Sounion', *Hesperia*,
25 (1956), 141.

[226] L. B. Holland, 'Colophon', *Hesperia*, 13 (1944), 130 assumes that women's
quarters existed in 4th-c. Colophon.

having their citizenship (and subsequently their children's citizenship) questioned. Female slaves would move about town shopping, carrying water, and doing whatever their jobs required, but they attended their mistresses and slept in the women's quarters. Vase-paintings and literary allusions indicate that women might spin, care for children, spend their leisure hours, and sleep in such segregated quarters. In traditional Mediterranean societies the allocation of space according to gender has the effect of perpetuating gender hierarchy and male dominance. However, Ischomachus revises the conventional Athenian role for his wife (x. 13 and *passim*).

θύρᾳ βαλανωτῇ. Rooms in a Greek house were usually closed off by curtains. Doors were considered to be movable furniture and thus are inventoried among the furnishings of the Hermocopidae.[227] It was necessary to prevent theft from the women's quarters, for the manufacture of textiles took place there. Wool, spinning and weaving equipment, and the textiles themselves were valuable (see vii. 6 and Ch. 5, sect. E). Doors with locks were rarely found except on storerooms and women's quarters.[228] The doors were locked from the outside (Lys. 1. 13, Ar. *Thesm.* 414–23). In the classical period the door was locked with a simple horizontal bolt (μοχλός) made of wood. From above, a vertical pin (βάλανος) slipped into the bolt. The bolt had one or more slots cut into it. A key (βαλανάγρα) had to be inserted to raise the pin before the bolt could be moved and the door opened. In vase-paintings, as in this passage, possession of a key is a symbol of power.[229]

τεκνοποιῶνται οἱ οἰκέται. The master of the house controlled sexual access to the slaves and even one with a young wife might take advantage of his privilege.[230] That Ischomachus' wife is to share control of sexual access to slaves indicates that she is a partner in the patriarchal powers usually exercised by the man of the house. It goes without saying, however, that the double standard continued to operate, so that the wife herself has not the same

---

[227] *IG* i³. 422, col. 1. 13, 15, 425 col. 1. 5, 8 and see Pritchett, 'The Attic Stelai: Part II', 233–4.

[228] Lys. 3. 6; Dem. 47. 56; Pritchett, 'The Attic Stelai: Part II', 236, Jones–Graham–Sackett, 'The Vari House', 427–8.

[229] For the lock see Ar. *Wasps* 155, 200, *Eccl.* 361, Aen. Tact. 18–20, R. Vallois, *Dar.-Sag.* s.v. sera, esp. 1244, and Robinson–Graham, *Olynthus*, viii. 259–63.

[230] The material on slave reproduction was previously published in greater detail in Sarah B. Pomeroy, 'Slavery in the Light of Xenophon's *Oeconomicus*', *Index*, 17 (1989), 11–18.

right that her husband has, to have sexual relations with slaves, although she will have personal contact with them (vii. 35–7). In contrast, the master of the house enjoyed sexual access to his slaves. In Lys. 1, a husband who is on trial for murdering his wife's seducer admits jovially that he dallied with his domestic slave and that his wife teased him about it. Ischomachus himself is explicit about the sexual availability of his slaves to himself as their master (see Ch. 4 and x. 12–13 ἑκοῦσαν ... ἀναγκαζομένην).

Inasmuch as slaves did not legally possess their own bodies, they were not supposed to have intercourse or raise children without their owner's permission. Here Ischomachus declares that selected slaves will be granted such permission if his wife and he agree that they should be so rewarded. Cf. Pl. *Rep.* 468 c, where the most valiant guardians are rewarded by the grant of more frequent opportunities to have sexual intercourse. Plato explicitly adds eugenics to the notion of reward. Perhaps this notion is implicit in the *Oeconomicus*. In Ps.-Arist. *Oec.* 1344^{b}17–18 the birth of slaves is encouraged, for the children will act as guarantees or hostages for their parents' good behaviour and will replace them when the older generation is given its freedom. In contrast, virtuous slaves will not want to leave the oikos of Ischomachus; hence there need be no mention of manumission as an incentive. It is interesting to note that in Ischomachus' view the slaves are not motivated by passion to engage in sexual intercourse but rather by the wish to have offspring. Yet he himself admits to finding his wife or a slave sexually stimulating (see on x. 12). Ischomachus makes lack of interest in sex a criterion for the choice of the housekeeper and overseer (ix. 11, xii. 13–14). In this sexually segregated society, Ischomachus is concerned only about the potential distractions of erotic liaisons between the men whom he selected to serve as overseers and boys (xii. 13–14).

How much can be gleaned from the present passage about sources of slave supply and slave reproduction in classical Athens? Reproductive rates depend, in large part, on the number of fertile females. Henri Wallon interpreted the present passage in the *Oeconomicus* as meaning that propagation at home was discouraged; he argued that male slaves far outnumbered females in the Athenian household of the classical period and that therefore the rate of slave reproduction was low.[231] He cited Demosthenes (27. 9), who lists only fifty-two male slaves in the property left to him by his father. But Demosthenes mentions these slaves specific-

---

[231] *Histoire de l'esclavage dans l'antiquité*, 2nd edn. (Paris, 1879), i. 5–6, 158.

ally only because their work produced cash income, and he is reckoning income lost to him. The fifty-two slaves were all craftsmen. Because his father's household was wealthy, at least when he was still alive and the oikos intact, there must have been female slaves to perform the domestic labour for the family and probably for the male slaves as well. Demosthenes may have included the value of his female slaves in the value of his house. Similarly David Hume cited the passage in Dem. 27. 9 and the foreign names of slaves in New Comedy as evidence that Greek masters preferred to purchase rather than to breed slaves.[232] But, as I have argued above, female slaves probably outnumbered male in classical Athens (see further Ch. 5, sect. H, and on vii. 41). Moreover, their sexual availability made them vulnerable to pregnancy. Certainly, the existence of slave wetnurses (e.g. Dem. 47. 56) indicates that some slaves gave birth.

Analyses of slavery in the United States prove that slave populations were able to reproduce themselves, particularly if they were encouraged to form quasi-families with sex ratios approaching equality. Ischomachus implicitly prefers such a system. Slaves born at home are the only acceptable source of slaves for him, although from remarks in the dialogue it is clear that less fastidious landowners purchased slaves and trained them as agricultural labourers or purchased men already trained as bailiffs (iii. 10, xii. 3). In *Mem.* 2. 7. 6 Xenophon implies that foreign slaves who are purchased can be exploited most intensively. In any case, Ischomachus' slaves evidently do more than reproduce their numbers, if their offspring must be sent away (vii. 34).

Modern historians writing about slavery in the United States have distinguished breeding from natural increase. Breeding is a deliberate effort to produce more babies than would be born without such interference. There is no evidence that Greek masters manipulated the reproductive lives of their slaves so as to increase the number of babies born, although, as the present passage indicates, they might curtail slave reproduction as an inevitable consequence of limiting sexual access to their female slaves. In this context it is relevant to observe that 70 per cent of the slaves of the Hermocopidae were non-Greek and only 7.5 per cent were homeborn.[233] An examination of the first thousand names listed in Linda Collins Reilly, *Slaves in Ancient Greece: Slaves from Greek*

---

[232] *Of the Populousness of Ancient Nations* (1742).
[233] W. Kendrick Pritchett, 'The Attic Stelai: Part II', 281.

Manumission Inscriptions,[234] indicates that 12 per cent of the slaves were born at home (οἰκογενής, or more rarely ἐνδογενής). Most of the slaves she lists were Hellenistic. Owing to sentiment, or to the fact that their masters were often their biological fathers, slaves born at home might have been manumitted at a higher rate than purchased slaves; therefore the actual percentage of slaves born at home among the slave population in Greece may have been somewhat less than 12 per cent.

Of course, some infants born to slaves may have been exposed, neglected, or sold so that they failed to be counted. Jacquelyn Jones has pointed out that in the United States in the nineteenth century malnutrition and excessively hard labour on the part of mothers meant that the mortality rate of children born to slave mothers was high.[235] In *Beloved*,[236] a fictional account of a North American slave, Toni Morrison depicts a woman who kills her daughter rather than see her raised as a slave. But Ischomachus avoids such a waste of human capital by permitting only virtuous slaves to reproduce, with the explicit intention of allowing them to rear a family. Having children is presented as a privilege. Because only selected slaves are permitted to reproduce, while the troublesome ones must remain childless, and because some of the male slaves have homosexual relationships (xii. 13–14), the result would have been a lower than natural rate of increase.

The attitude toward slave reproduction in antiquity must have varied according to need and to the external supply of slaves available through capture, exposure of infants, and the market. Hesiod had advised farmers to purchase a slave woman without children, for a slave with a child to nurse is troublesome (*WD* 602–3). But, in the fourth century, when the Athenians were no longer engaged in the wars of expansion in which they might enslave their enemies, and when large estates like that of Ischomachus employed substantial numbers of slaves, reproduction at home probably increased in importance, though no source was ever so prolific as totally to exclude the others.

χρηστοί. In xii. 19, Ischomachus observes that a good master may have bad slaves.

6. κατὰ φυλὰς διεκρίνομεν. φυλή can mean 'type', 'race', 'class', or 'tribe'. If the meaning here is 'type', then Ischomachus is simply

---

[234] (Chicago, 1978).
[235] *Labor of Love, Labor of Sorrow: Black Women, Work, and the Family from Slavery to the Present* (New York, 1985), 35, 123.
[236] (New York, 1987).

separating possessions by categories. However, it is possible that he is thinking of 'tribe', for Xenophon uses φῦλον much more frequently in the sense of 'type' (e.g. *Hiero* 9. 5, *Cyr.* 1. 2. 5, 1. 4. 17, *Revenues* 4. 30, etc.: and see Sturz, *Lexicon Xenophonteum*, s.v. φυλή). If this hypothesis is valid, analogies between the public and private spheres begin here and are continued in ix. 14–15. (See c. iv on the parallels between the Persian king and Ischomachus' wife). Athenian democracy was based on the distribution of the citizen body into ten tribes.[237] These tribes, in turn, were subdivided into demes (cf. ix. 7 διεχωρίσαμεν). Members were heterogeneous, drawn from three different geographical regions: Ischomachus' tribal division is based on distributing similar items into various groups according to function not nature. Thus sacrificial implements are separated from ordinary cooking utensils, rather than all pots in one group, and all knives in another as φῦλα would have suggested.

ἔπιπλα. As ix. 6–9 makes clear, this word refers to utensils, furnishings, and clothing needed for the use and maintenance of the household. Because of the great variety[238] the system would have required quite a bit of space.

Folk etymology associated ἔπιπλα with πλεῖν ('to sail'; Frisk, *Griechisches etymologisches Wörterbuch*, s.v. ἔπιπλα). Thus Herod. 1. 94. 6 uses πλοῖα, ἐπίπλοα, and ἀποπλέειν in one sentence. The verbal association may have suggested to Xenophon the analogy between house and ship (see on viii. 11 τὸ μέγα πλοῖον τὸ Φοινικικόν).

8. κατὰ μῆνα δαπανώμενα. On the allocation of supplies, see notes on vii. 36, δαπανᾶν and διανεμητέον.

Cic. (fr. 13 Garbarino = Col. *RR* 12) mistranslates the passage: 'Postea ex is quibus quotidie utimur, quod menstruum esse seposuimus, anuum quoque in duas partes diuisimus; nam sic minus fallit, qui exitus futurus sit.'

11. ταμίαν . . . προνοεῖν. The criteria for selecting the housekeeper are similar to those given in much greater detail in cc. xii–xiv for choosing the male overseer. πρόνοια is a virtue of the housekeeper as it is of the wife in vii. 36, 38.

13. δικαιοσύνην. Similarly, according to Xen. *Cyrop.* 8. 2. 27, a leader must display justice.

---

[237] See further Arist. *Ath. Pol.* 21. 6 and P. J. Rhodes, *A Commentary on the Aristotelian Athenaion Politeia*, ad loc.

[238] For which see on viii. 19–20, xiii. 10, xvii. 12, and R. J. Forbes, *Studies in Ancient Technology*, i–iii (Leiden, 1955–72), iv–ix, 2nd edn. (Leiden, 1964–72), *passim*.

14–15. νομοφύλακας . . . φρούραρχος . . . δοκιμάζειν. The execut-ive powers of the wife in the oikos are analogous to those exercised by male magistrates in the state. On parallels between the wife and the Persian king see on iv and vii. 32. In xi. 25 she serves as judge and jury in a mock domestic court.[239]

From the time of Draco and probably even earlier, until the democratic reforms of Ephialtes in 462/1 the Areopagus was assigned to watch over the city's laws. According to Philochorus, the νομοφύλακες were established at the time of Ephialtes' reforms (*FGrH* 328 F 64, IIIb Suppl. and Jacoby *ad loc.*). Philochorus is the only source for the office of νομοφύλαξ in classical Athens. Because there is no additional evidence about them, Rhodes main-tains that the office did not exist in the classical period, and Jacoby asserts that it was probably not important, or may have disap-peared completely until it was revived in the last quarter of the fourth century.[240] Neither Rhodes nor Jacoby uses the present passage as evidence for the magistracy, though it is doubtful that Xenophon would have invented it and included it in a list of offices which definitely did exist. The idea that existing laws should be enforced, preserved, and guarded (against new legislation of the democratic Assembly) is essentially aristocratic and conservat-ive and is pervasive in Plato's *Laws*.

Phrourarchs in the Persian Empire are mentioned in iv. 10, 11. Military officers bearing this title appear in Greek contexts as well, e.g. in the Athenian Empire: *IG* i³. 14 (mid 5th c.). δοκιμασία was a general term applied to official examinations, e.g. of magis-trates before taking office, of members of the Boule, of ephebes, and of invalids. As stated here and elsewhere (e.g. Xen. *Cav. Comm.* 1. 8. 13, 3. 9–14, Arist. *Ath. Pol.* 49. 1–2, and Hesychius, s.v. τρυσίππιον, cols. 1477–8 Schmidt), the Boule conducted the δοκιμ-ασία of cavalry and inspected the horses; it cancelled the sustenance allowance for horses that were poorly fed, branded and discharged those no longer capable of being ridden in battle, checked the lists,

[239] Sheila Murnaghan, 'How a Woman can be More Like a Man: The Dialogue between Ischomachus and his Wife in Xenophon's *Oeconomicus*', *Helios*, 15 (1988), 9–22, interprets the assimilation of the wife to a man as part of a degrading view of women. For a different interpretation see my comments on vii. 32, *et passim*.

[240] Arist. *Ath. Pol.* 3. 6, 4. 4, 8. 4, 25. 2, 52. 1, and P. J. Rhodes, *A Commentary on the Aristotelian Athenaion Politeia*, 315–17. According to And. 1. 84, in 403/2 (see also Lys. fr. 178 Sauppe) the Areopagus was again assigned to guard the laws. According to G. L. Cawkwell, 'ΝΟΜΟΦΓΛΑΚΙΑ and the Areopagus, *JHS* 108 (1988), 1–12 who cites *Ath. Pol.* 3. 6, it exercised a supervisory role over morals in the 4th c. There is no evidence that it did so, though such an activity would certainly be appropriate to Ischomachus' wife.

and required every cavalryman to make a personal appearance before it.[241] The analogy implies that Ischomachus' wife is to examine all the slaves and consider whether they are capable of carrying out their duties. If they can no longer perform their tasks they are probably given less arduous duties or dismissed. (On the treatment of older slaves see on i. 22.)

15. βασίλισσαν. This word appears here and in Xenophon's contemporary Alcaeus the comic poet, fr. 6, for the first time. βασίλισσα became normal for βασίλεια in the Hellenistic period. Xenophon may have coined the word.[242] On the wife as queen bee, see further vii. 32 ἡ τῶν μελιττῶν ἡγεμών.

16. πλείω αὐτῇ πράγματα. Those in charge bear the heaviest burdens as in *Cyrop.* 1. 6. 25 and Plato, *Republic*.

χρῆσθαι δὲ οὐδενί. On the relationship between possession and use see i. 7–8 κτήματα . . . χρήματα.

19. τῶν ἑαυτῆς. In vii. 13 Ischomachus represented the property of the married couple as held in common, or merged. His wife finally comes to agree with this vision.

x. 1. ἀνδρικήν . . . ἀκούσασα . . . ἐπείθετο. Ischomachus reminds Socrates that, despite the masculinity of his wife's mind, she continues to obey her husband, and to live in accordance with his teachings (x. 13). It is insulting to describe a man as 'womanish' (see LSJ, s.v. γυναικεῖος). Aristotle doubtless transmits the common view in stating that the virtues and aptitudes of men and women are different. But in some passages in more radical philosophical works, for example the *Oeconomicus* and Plato's *Republic*, it is a compliment to ascribe masculine traits and virtues to a woman.[243] In these works, despite Plato's and Xenophon's insistence that the soul has no sex, the patriarchal framework of Greek society is not totally eliminated.

On male and female virtue in the *Oeconomicus* see Ch. 4 and notes on vii. 7, 15, 23–9, ix. 14–15. See also Xen. *Symp.* 2. 12, where Socrates asserts that ἀνδρεία ('courage') can be taught, for even a woman can learn it.

Ζεῦξις. The painter from Heraclea in Lucania whom Xenophon

---

[241] See further G. R. Bugh, *The Horsemen of Athens* (Princeton, NJ, 1988), 15–19, 53–60, 133–4, and P. J. Rhodes, *The Athenian Boule* (Oxford, 1972), 174–5.

[242] So C. D. Buck, 'Is the Suffix of βασίλισσα, etc., of Macedonian Origin?', *CP* 9 (1914), 370–3.

[243] In the Neo-Pythagorean treatise of Perictione, the harmonious woman is manly (ἀνδρηίη). For the text see Holger Thesleff, *The Pythagorean Texts of the Hellenistic Period* (Åbo, 1965), 142–45 = Stob. 4. 28. 10. He dates the text to the 4th or 3rd c. BC (113).

also mentions in *Symp.* 4. 63 and *Mem.* 1. 4. 3. According to Pliny, *NH* 35. 61, his floruit was 397 BC. Pl. *Prot.* 318 B–C (dramatic date *c*.430) mentions his recent arrival in Athens. Socrates names him here not merely because he was the most famous painter of his day but because he was known for his realistic portrayals and for his paintings of beautiful women (Pliny, loc. cit., Cic. *De Inv.* 2. 1. 1). Ar. *Ach.* 991–2, refers to his painting of Eros (Schol. ad loc.). Because of Zeuxis' popularity it is quite possible that some of his work was also visible in the Stoa of Zeus Eleutherius, where the dialogue takes place, or in another nearby picture gallery (see on vii. 1 στοậ).

Socrates may be portrayed here as engaging in specific criticism of Zeuxis' innovative style as he is shown doing in Pl. *Phil.* 53 B, where he rejects mixed in favour of pure colour. Plato (*Rep.* 602 C–603 B), like Xenophon in the present chapter, criticizes human attempts to use paint for purposes of deception. The simple décor of Ischomachus' house (ix. 2 οὐ γὰρ ποικίλμασι) is consistent with the rejection of Zeuxis here.[244]

2. ἐντετριμμένην. Socrates' remark about a woman painted by Zeuxis and a living woman reminds Ischomachus of a time when his wife had painted her face. With the exception of Ovid, no Greek or Roman author approves of cosmetics. Rather, moralistic texts assert that make-up is worn to conceal blemishes and signs of age and that it is not appropriate for respectable women.[245] This attitude culminated in the misogynistic tirades of Christian authors such as Gregory of Nazianzus, κατὰ γυναικῶν καλλωπι-ζομένων ('Against Women who Use Cosmetics'). Andreas Knecht considers *Oec.* x as the indisputable model for such works, but perhaps exaggerates the influence of this passage.[246] In Greek tradition, cosmetics were linked with drugs and deception and were condemned as a needless expense. Of course, all these texts were written by men. The visual arts in the Greek world as far back as Bronze Age frescoes from Cnossus and Thera indicate that most women—even those of the highest rank, including priest-esses—used cosmetics liberally with no attempt to render their

[244] On Zeuxis see R. G. Steven, 'Plato and the Art of his Time', *CQ* 17 (1933), 149–55, and Vincent J. Bruno, *Form and Color in Greek Painting* (New York and London, 1977).

[245] See Bernard Grillet, *Les Femmes et les fards dans l'antiquité grecque* (Lyon, 1975), 97–100.

[246] Andreas Knecht, *Gregor von Nazianz: Gegen die Putzsucht der Frauen* (Wissenschaftliche Kommentare zu griechischen und lateinischen Schriftstellern; Heidelberg, 1972), 107.

appearance as natural. Athenian marriage-vases show that application of cosmetics was an important part of the bride's toilette and the cosmetic containers found among women's grave-goods reveal that cosmetics were considered essential for respectable women. Literary evidence such as the opening scenes of Aristophanes' *Lysistrata* and Lys. 1. 14 also implies that wives applied cosmetics in order to make themselves attractive to their husbands. Most husbands must have approved of the use of cosmetics or at least have tolerated it.

Xenophon's censorious attitude was perhaps shaped by his experience in Sparta or by the Spartan ideal, according to which cosmetics, perfumes, and other bodily adornments were banished and beauty was the natural result of good health and hard work (Xen. *Sp. Const.* 5. 8, Plut. *Lyc.* 1. 4. 4, Athen. 686–7). Xenophon portrays Socrates as concurring with Ischomachus. In x. 1 Socrates asserted a preference for reality over appearance. He voiced strictures on the use of perfume too (Xen. *Symp.* 2. 3 quoted by Athen. 612 A). In Socrates' description in *Mem.* 2. 1. 22, the woman who is called by some 'Good Fortune' and by others 'Vice' makes herself up so that she has a white and pink complexion and appears taller than she really is. Compare also the condemnation of female 'mistresses' in i. 20–3, and the praises of agriculture for her lack of artifice in xix.17–18, xx. 14.

ψιμυθίῳ. Despite its toxicity lead carbonate was used to whiten the complexion.[247] Respectable women ideally spent their time indoors, though some in unfortunate circumstances had to perform work out of doors. As Arist. *Pol.* 1323ᵃ5–6 pointed out, the poor must use their wives and children to perform the tasks of slaves. Therefore a fair skin marked a woman as a member of the leisured class. This idea of beauty can be traced as far back in the eastern Mediterranean world as the frescoes of Cnossus and Thera, where women are portrayed with white skin and men with suntanned flesh. The same conventions are followed in Egyptian painting. The fashion was long-lasting. Round tablets of lead carbonate have been found in third-century-BC tombs of women in Attica and Corinth.[248]

ἐγχούσῃ . . . ἐρυθροτέρα. A rouge made from the plant alkanet commonly used by women, see e.g. Ar. *Lys.* 48. See also on x. 5 μίλτῳ.

---

[247] See T. Leslie Shear, 'Psimythion', *Classical Studies Presented to E. Capps* (Princeton, NJ, 1937), 314–16.
[248] See Grillet, *Les Femmes*, 33.

ὑψηλά. Height was an attribute of beautiful women as well as an indication of superior social status. Thus Greek art portrays gods and heroes as taller than mortals. In Hom. *Od.* 6. 102–7 Nausicaa is compared to Artemis as she towers above her companions. Theocritus (18. 29–30) compares Helen, whom he calls a daughter of Zeus, to a tall cypress. Phya, whom Peisistratus chose to impersonate Athena, was very tall and good-looking (Herod. 1. 60). In Xen. *Anab.* 3. 2. 25, the women of the Medes and Persians are tall and beautiful. For high heels see also Alexis fr. 98. 7–8.

3. ἀξιοφίλητον. Chapter x touches delicately, though frankly enough, on the sexual aspect of marriage (4–5 τῶν σωμάτων κοινωνήσοντες ἀλλήλοις, 5 σώματος ... κοινωνός), the physical attractiveness of husband and wife (2–13), and their spending the night together (8). The wife is referred to as loving the husband (3, 5 ἀξιοφίλητος, 4 ἀσπάσασθαι ἐκ τῆς ψυχῆς) and willing to engage in intercourse (12 ἑκοῦσαν χαρίζεσθαι). However, she is more modest than her husband in speaking of these matters, for example, responding φασὶ γοῦν (5) to his forthright question about bodies. The husband expects to be sexually stimulated by his wife's appearance (12 κινητικόν), although he raises the possibility of having sexual relations with a slave (12 διακόνῳ; see also on vii. 42 προϊούσης τῆς ἡλικίας ἀτιμοτέρα). Socrates, not wanting to hear further confidences about this intimate subject, abruptly terminates the discussion of marriage here.

5. μίλτῳ. The rouge μίλτος ('red ochre' or 'ruddle') was probably more brownish-red in colour than the alkanet mentioned in x. 2 and thus approximated the sun-tanned skin appropriate for men. It was also used for other purposes, especially as a pigment and pharmaceutical, and was important enough for the Athenians to control its export.[249]

ἀνδρεικέλῳ. A natural-coloured foundation created by various tinted powders, used as eye make-up (Pl. *Crat.* 424 E, Arist. *GA* 725ᵃ27). The pigment was also used by artists.[250]

7. ἵπποις ... βουσί ... προβάτοις. Arguments employing examples from the animal world are common in the works of Xenophon and Plato, where they are typically attributed to Socrates (see e.g. on iii. 11).

8. τοὺς ... ἔξω. A respectable woman might be seen by strangers

[249] See M. N. Tod, *A Selection of Greek Historical Inscriptions*, ii (Oxford, 1948), no. 162.
[250] See Grillet, *Les Femmes*, 48, 79 n. 135.

Pl. 3. Left: woman spinning. Centre: women weaving at a vertical loom. Right: woman weighing wool. Attic, 6th-c. BC black-figure lekythos, attributed to the Amasis Painter. New York: Metropolitan Museum of Art, Fletcher Fund, 1931 (31.11.10).

at festivals or funerals. Cosmetics certainly constituted part of women's dressing-up for festivals although they were not deemed appropriate for periods of mourning (Lys. 1. 14).

10. ἱστὸν προσστᾶσαν. Weaving was done seated, using small hand-looms, or standing up at vertical looms. Some looms were so wide that two women worked together throwing the shuttle between them (as depicted, e.g. by the Amasis painter *ABV* 154, see Pl. 3). Otherwise a solitary weaver had to walk back and forth. Thus weaving could provide exercise for Ischomachus' wife.[251]

11. περίπατος. Ischomachus states in xi. 15, 18 that he himself walks every day for exercise. Aristotle (*Pol.* 1335[b]12–14) suggests that pregnant women should. Plato (*Rep.* 452 A–D, 460 E, *Laws* 833 C–D, cf. 785 B) recommends physical education for women. The Spartan educational system prescribed outdoor athletics for girls and women. In contrast, Athenian women had few opportunities to exercise. The only indications that girls did so are depictions of them running around an altar on vases from the sanctuary of Artemis at Brauron.[252] Of course dancing (which was an integral part of many religious ceremonies) involved some physical activity for women.

[251] For a description of the vertical loom see R. J. Forbes, *Studies in Ancient Technology*, 2nd edn., iv. 200–5.
[252] See Lilly G. Kahil, 'Auteur de l'Artémis attique', *AK* 8 (1965), 20–33, esp. Pl. 8.

δεῦσαι . . . μάξαι. Bread was the staple food of the Greeks. Supplying a large household with sufficient bread was a major chore, and doubtless the bread-makers could always do with additional help. Ischomachus recognizes that physical labour was expended in kneading, and recommends it as a form of exercise.

12. διακόνῳ . . . κινητικόν. This section is not set out as what Ischomachus said to his wife. Evidently he feels he can make observations to Socrates about sexual arousal and extra-marital intercourse that he would not make to his wife.

The comparison with the wife has induced translators to assume that the slave, whose sex is not specified, is female.[253] The context makes it likely that the slave is female. In the *Oeconomicus*, however, Xenophon uses διάκονος of both males (viii. 14) and females (viii. 10). Because bisexuality was not uncommon among upper-class Greeks, the sex of the slave who was the pathic partner probably made little difference to many men who, like Ischomachus, owned both male and female slaves. Intercourse with one's slaves need not cost anything; for expensive affairs with free youths see on ii. 7 παιδικοῖς δὲ πράγμασι.

12–13. ἑκοῦσαν . . . ἀναγκαζομένην. Euripides had portrayed Andromache, in his play of that name, as a female slave who resented being her master's concubine, although she hoped for his protection. But Andromache had special reasons to hate Neoptolemus, for the Greeks had killed her husband and son and had destroyed her homeland. Xenophon is the first Greek author to recognize that an ordinary slave without such a history may be reluctant to have sexual intercourse with a master. It is worth noting that Ischomachus is not excited by the idea of forcing himself on an unwilling partner, but prefers reciprocity in a sexual relationship. In Xen. *Hiero* 1 the despot's sexual pleasure is diminished by the ease with which he makes his conquests.

The bodies of slaves belonged to their master and he alone enjoyed sexual access to them, or might make them available to others. Thus Odysseus decrees a shameful death for his slavewomen who had slept with the suitors without his permission (Hom. *Od.* 22. 443–5). Not all masters took advantage of the vulnerability of slaves. Laertes, it is pointed out, abstained from a relationship with Eurycleia. Although he was attracted to Eurycleia, he respected his wife's feelings. Eurycleia must have had a baby and

---

[253] So C. Natali, *Senofonte: L'amministrazione della casa*, 137: 'ancella'; Marchant, *Xenophon*, iv. 451: 'she'; Waterfield, *Conversations*, 326: 'servant girl'; and Chantraine, *Xénophon: Économique*, 78: 'servante'.

remained in her master's good graces, for she served as wet-nurse
to Odysseus (*Od.* 1. 433, 19. 482–9). Similar situations occurred
in classical Athens. A husband who was considerate of his wife's
feelings did not necessarily abstain from sexual liaisons with others,
but he did not flaunt them in her presence. Thus Alcibiades'
notorious relationships with prostitutes were cause for censure
(Plut. *Alc.* 8. 3), while Lysias was more discreet in arranging for
his mistress to stay with one of his unmarried friends (Ps.-Dem.
59. 22). See further on ix. 5 τεκνοποιῶνται οἱ οἰκέται.

xi. In the remainder of the treatise Xenophon continues to discuss
wealth, piety, education, and human virtue, but he devotes special
attention to the subject of farming. Xenophon does not need to
give detailed instructions on it, for his audience lived in an agricultural society and must have had a general idea about how farms
were managed, even if they were not aware of details and contro-
versies. Ischomachus and his upper-class contemporaries employ
experienced labourers and foremen (see i. 3–4 τὸν ἄλλου δὲ οἶκον
and Ch. 2, sect. A). They must know how to supervise these
specialists and must understand enough about the agricultural
operations to enable them to make decisions and to suggest alternative methods of production. Like Cyrus (iv. 24), they may actually
perform some agricultural chores for the sake of exercise, but for
the most part they farm by supervising others.

1. καλοῦ κἀγαθοῦ. See on vi. 12.

3. ἀδολεσχεῖν. Aristophanes (*Clouds* 1485) and Eupolis (386 and 388
Kassel–Austin) use this verb and its noun form to describe
Socrates; sim. Lucian (*Ver. Hist.* 17). These words were commonly
used of Sophists (see LSJ, s.v.).

ἀερομετρεῖν. Sim. Aristophanes, *Clouds* 225, 1503 ἀεροβατῶ.

πένης. Eupolis (386 Kassel–Austin) describes Socrates as
πτωχόν. See ii. 2–3 for Socrates' own perspective on his material
resources.

4–5. Νικίου . . . χρήματα . . . πένητι ἵππῳ. Socrates humorously
transfers the wealth of the owner Nicias (not otherwise known) to
his horse. To argue by analogy from animals to human beings is
a standard feature of Socratic literature (see on iii. 11 αἰτιᾶσθαι . . .
Πρόβατον . . . νομέα). But the opposite, to impose human characteristics on animals, is bizarre and amusing. Anthropomorphization
of animals is the stuff of comedies: extant works in which such
transformations occur are Aristophanes, *Birds*, *Frogs*, and *Wasps*.
Another genre in which animals behave as though they were

human is the Aesopic fable. Horses are not infrequently found in
the fables (269, 269a, 318–20, 345 Perry) where they are typically
shown as exceptionally pampered. The present passage is closest
in characterization to fable 357 (Perry) in which a poor donkey
envies the luxurious existence of a horse. But when the horse is
mortally injured in battle the donkey realizes that one should not
envy those who have power and wealth, but rather, thinking about
the jealousy and dangers such status inevitably creates, one should
resign oneself to poverty. The present passage has the shape of the
Aesopic fable in that it ends with Socrates drawing a moralistic
conclusion and serves to make the point that horses are valued for
their inherent characteristics and so should people be. On horse
ownership as a mark of great wealth see on i. 8. The crowd gathers
around an expensive horse as they would nowadays gape at an
expensive sports car.

6. αὔριον. Diets and other projects for self-improvement begin tomorrow (cf. Sen. *Brev. Vit.* 9. 1, Persius 5. 66–9, Martial 5. 58).

8. ἄρχομαι μὲν τοὺς θεοὺς θεραπεύων. An act of cult inaugurates
all important activities (see on vi. 1). The pious person believes
that the gods intervene directly in daily life. Piety is especially
important for farmers, because their families and possessions are
vulnerable to the hazards and risks caused by natural phenomena
which were thought to be controlled by the gods.

9. θεοὺς ... φίλους ... πόλιν. The concerns that motivate
Ischomachus' quest for wealth are the same as those that ought
to motivate Critobulus in ii. 5–8. In neither case are any selfish
desires mentioned, such as a wish to enrich his family or himself.
Generosity towards friends and city are essential to a virtuous
man's φιλοτιμία ('sense of honour').[254]

10. καλά. Despite Ischomachus' avowed generosity and patriotism,
wealth does bring him increased prestige and material benefits for
his personal use. Although Ischomachus' lack of modesty is typical
and unreprehensible in his social context, Socrates' own predilec-
tion for humiliating the arrogant may motivate an element of
tongue-in-cheek humour in his reply. For Ischomachus' high self-
regard cf. his pleasure at Socrates' compliments (vii. 3).

12. ἐσθίειν ... ἱκανά. This statement implies awareness that it is
possible not to have enough to eat. References to the harsh realities
of the lives of the impoverished are relatively rare until the late
plays of Aristophanes (*Eccles.* 421–6, *Wealth* 219, 504, 543–6, 562,
594–7, 763). (On fear of famine see e.g. Thuc. 2. 54. 3 and on

---

[254] See further Ch. 5, note on vii. 3, and Dover, *Greek Popular Morality*, 175–7.

agricultural crises in the fourth century see on xx. 22, 27. On hungry animals see on xvii. 9–10.)

ἐκπονοῦντι. This statement and the repetition in xi. 13 imply that it is preferable to exercise after eating. In *Cyrop.* 1. 2. 16 Xenophon reports that the Persians exercised after eating to work off what they had consumed. But in iv. 24 Cyrus declared that he exercised before eating, and Ischomachus follows the same routine—one which nowadays is considered most healthy.

14. ἐξ εὐνῆς. Xenophon regards early rising as a virtue: in *Cyrop.* 1. 2. 10, he states that Persian boys get up early. In a Mediterranean country it makes sense for a person who spends his day outdoors to get up early. But Ischomachus arises even earlier than his neighbours so that he can catch them still at home.

15–16. κατὰ πόλιν . . . εἰς ἀγρόν. These phrases indicate two opposite locations: city and countryside.

According to Thuc. 2. 16. 1 the majority of Athenians lived in rural areas of Attica until the Peloponnesian War forced them to move within the city walls. In xi. 14, 15, and 18 (εἰς ἄστυ), where Ischomachus describes his daily trip to his farmland, he fails to give the exact location of the house and farm. The house must be in town for Ischomachus gets up before most people to make sure of finding them at home before he visits his farm. Ischomachus does not usually spend the morning in the Athenian agora, unless he has an appointment there (vii. 2). Furthermore, in xi. 18 the slave leads the horse back home from the country. The farmland must be in the immediate vicinity of Athens and not very far from his house for Ischomachus is able to walk from his house to downtown Athens then to his farm, spend some time there, and walk back home again before lunch. His plots of land may well be scattered over Attica (see Ch. 5). However, there was quite a bit of farmland even within the city walls. In Melos farmers walked from home to their farms a mean of two hours.[255] If Ischomachus needed to go such a distance, he would probably travel on horseback, although it is clear that he has plenty of energy and is an active man who regards walking as good exercise. For two other Athenian landowners who commute to their farms see Lysias 1. 11, 13, 20, 22.

Delebecque conjectures that Ischomachus' house is modelled after the villa Xenophon occupied during his exile.[256] He argues

---

[255] Reported by Malcolm Wagstaff and Siv Augustson, 'Traditional Land Use', in Colin Renfrew and Malcolm Wagstaff (eds.), *An Island Polity* (Cambridge, 1982), 110.
[256] 'Sur la date et l'objet de l'Économique', 34–5, *Essai*, 371, and see Ch. 1.

that owing to the necessities of the text, the house must be in Athens, but that since it is unbelievable that an urban dwelling would be large enough to have a stable, the house must really be in the country outside the city walls. However, Ischomachus is very wealthy. Like the trierarch in Dem. 47, he probably owns houses in both the city and the country. For this reason he does not supply specific details about his morning routine, for it would have varied according to the season and to his place of residence. His main house is large enough for him to consider that walking within its confines can constitute exercise for his wife (x. 10, and see viii. 11 and Pl. *Prot.* for the large house of Callias). Hoepfner–Schwander suggest that certain areas of houses were designated for slaves, workrooms, and stables, but only for Kassope have they archaeological evidence for the existence of a stable.[257] Robinson and Graham also postulate that horses were stabled in houses in Olynthus.[258] Ischomachus does not mention a separate stable building. In the Mediterranean, it is quite common to see farm animals in and around houses. Vitr. 6. 7. 1 reports that Greek houses had a stable next to the entrance. The floors of houses and courtyards in the classical period were made of stone and hard-packed earth. Therefore there is no reason why Ischomachus' horse could not have been stabled in a closed area on the ground floor or in the courtyard. A stable for one horse does not need to be very large. Because horses were valuable, Xenophon (*On Horsemanship* 4. 1) advises owners to keep them where they could be watched. For example, the country house at Vari had an outer enclosure which could have served as a pen for animals.[259]

15. παῖς. Also xi. 18: the groom rode too, perhaps not on a horse but on a less expensive animal, such as a donkey as Xanthias does in Ar. *Frogs*.

περιπάτῳ. See x. 11 for Ischomachus' advice to his wife to combine work with a walk for physical exercise.

16. ξυστῷ. LSJ, s.v., suggest that here ξυστός means walking-place in the grounds of a private residence. However, the word usually referred to a covered colonnade at the gymnasium. In any case, Ischomachus expresses a preference for exercising out of doors in the countryside.

εἰς ἀγρόν. For a contrast to the concern Ischomachus displays

---

[257] *Haus und Stadt*, 18, 57, 64, 117, 180, 274.
[258] *Olynthus*, viii. 210–11.
[259] See Jones–Graham–Sackett, 'The Vari House', 370–2.

for his farmland, cf. Soph. *Trach.* 32–3, where Deianeira compares Heracles to a farmer who visits his fields only for sowing and reaping, and Dem. 55. 11 where an owner neglects water damage to his property. See also xx. 4 οὐδὲ οἶνον ἔχει.

17. ἵππον . . . πολέμῳ. Ischomachus, as is expected of a wealthy man, is a member of the cavalry. See on i. 8.

τάφρου . . . ὀχετοῦ. The terrain will have presented natural obstacles, for example, natural water-courses, such as seasonal brooks, which become dry beds in summer. In addition, as a careful farmer, Ischomachus will have had trenches in vineyards and around or between trees as well as run-off ditches on his land. Controlling the water supply was a major concern of the Greek farmer (see on v. 18–20). When covered drains built according to Theophrastus' description (*CP* 3. 6. 3–4) deteriorated, they will also have caused a horse to stumble. See also xix. 11, xx. 11–12, Xenophon, *On Horsemanship* 8, *Cavalry Commander* 8. 3.

18–19. μήτε κενὸς μήτε ἄγαν πλήρης. Control over the appetite was mentioned as a virtue in vii. 6.

22. ἀπολογεῖσθαι . . . κατηγορεῖν. Rhetoric was fundamental to Athenian education.[260] But practice in verbal skills can take place not only in a formal educational context but also in private or public life. Professional rhetoricians are not necessary. κατηγοροῦντός τινος τῶν οἰκετῶν ἢ ἀπολογουμένου (xi. 23) implies that Ischomachus' slaves (like his wife, xi. 25) had some understanding of rhetoric. According to *Cyrop.* 1. 2. 6–7, a substantial part of the Persian boys' curriculum consisted of bringing one another to court on criminal charges. Their officers spent most of the day judging these charges.

25. ἐκρίθην . . . γυναικός. Here Ischomachus relates that he endowed his wife with judicial powers in the oikos just as in ix. 15 he told her to consider herself a νομοφύλαξ. These powers were, of course, exercised in the polis solely by men. Some women did understand legal matters (see on vii. 10, cf. xiv. 4–5 for slaves' knowledge of the law). Ps.-Dem. 59. 110–11 declares that wives ask their husbands how they voted when they served on juries. Ischomachus stated that he taught his wife διαλέγεσθαι, that is the formal method of discussion which enables philosophers to determine the truth.[261]

ἥττω λόγον . . . κρείττω. See Pl. *Apol.* 18 B, 19 B, where these

---

[260] See further H.-I. Marrou, *Histoire*, 95, 137–8, 292–307.
[261] See on vii. 10 and Donald L. Clark, *Rhetoric in Greco-Roman Education* (New York, 1957), 27.

expressions appear in the charges against Socrates, and 23 D, where
Socrates declares that all philosophers are said to make the worse
argument appear the better (see further Ch. 3). But Ischomachus,
a gentleman (καλὸς κἀγαθός) cannot successfully use rhetorical
skills devoid of an ethical component: xi. 23–5 contain an implicit
criticism of professional rhetoricians like Gorgias who are able to
divorce rhetoric from honourable purposes, and to teach others to
do so (cf. Gorg. *Helen* 6).

xii. 2. ἀγορὰ λυθῇ. Just after midday when the market emptied (see
LSJ s.v. *ἀγορά*).

Evidently the visitors with whom Ischomachus had made an
appointment (vii. 2) had not shown up. As Socrates' response
indicates, a polite gentleman would continue to wait.

3. ἐπιτρόπους . . . ὠνεῖσθαι. The landed property of Ischomachus,
like that of other wealthy Athenians, consisted of several non-
adjacent plots (see Ch. 5 and xx. 22). Fragmentation was no doubt
exacerbated in the case of Ischomachus because his father and he
made a practice of buying and selling land. Therefore he must
establish trustworthy slaves in positions of independence and
authority on his distant properties, as though they were colonies.
See on i. 3–4, iii. 10, iv. 5, and vii. 34.

The extent to which slaves were employed in Athenian agriculture has engendered much debate. Although agriculture was fundamental to the economy we have little information on the labour
supply, and the existing evidence is conflicting. The issue of the
employment of slaves is related to other controversial questions,
in particular the size and composition of the population, the
amount of land in the hands of large property-owners compared
to that cultivated by small farmers, and the proportions of domest-
ically produced and imported grain which were consumed (see on
c. xx). The picture of slave employment is complicated by the
likelihood that it changed over time (see on c. ix).[262] The agricultural labour force was affected not only by major historical events
such as the Peloponnesian War, but also by seasonal demands.
Doubtless at harvest or vintage or other critical periods in the
agricultural year nearly all able-bodied people including children,

---

[262] Regional variation must be taken into account as well. As H. Bolkestein,
Economic Life in Greece's Golden Age (1923), rev. E. J. Jonkers (Leiden, 1958), 81–2,
argued, the use of slaves may have been more common in Attica than in the interior
of the mainland. Gallant, *Risk and Survival in Ancient Greece*, 3–33, suggests flexibility
in the life-cycle of the individual peasant oikos, with ownership of slaves only at
certain periods.

the elderly, women whose economic position did not provide a
sufficient cushion from this necessity, and slave and free men and
women normally engaged in non-agricultural labour were pressed
into service (see xvii. 2 βρέξας and xviii. 1).[263] Thus in *Hiero* 6. 10
Xenophon mentions hiring harvesters.

Owing to the lack of much other reliable evidence, references
in the *Oeconomicus* are crucial to the arguments of scholars concerning the employment of slaves in agriculture. While there is
general agreement that the propertied classes used slaves, the
debate centres on whether slaves were employed by landowners
further down on the social scale. Opinion also varies on the extent
to which free workers were hired. Considerations of space allow
me to draw attention to only two recently published, but opposed
conclusions. G. E. M. de Ste. Croix relies upon the *Oeconomicus* in
his assertion that the propertied classes must have used slaves
rather than hired hands.[264] Though he believes slaves were numerous, he concedes that most agricultural production was performed
by small peasants. In partial support of his position, he cites M. I.
Rostovtzeff's view that agriculture in the Greek East was dependent on slave labour.[265] Rostovtzeff had argued that inasmuch as
Roman agricultural writings show that the bulk of labour was
performed by slaves and these writings are based on Greek sources,
the Greek originals must have contained the same information.
However, Roman and Hellenistic agricultural production was frequently on a much larger scale than anything we know of from
classical Athens. Furthermore, a close analysis of the differences
between the *Oeconomicus* and Columella's adaptation shows an
increase in the allocation of tasks to slaves in Rome (see Ch. 6,
sect. B). Ellen Meiksins Wood rejects de Ste. Croix's views and
takes the common-sense position that most families worked their
own farms, and that even owners of large holdings leased small

[263] After the Peloponnesian War, owing to poverty, freeborn women worked as
hired labourers in agriculture, a type of employment that was previously disdained
(Dem. 57. 45).

[264] *The Class Struggle in the Ancient Greek World*, 179–82, 505–9. In agreement with
de Ste. Croix, M. H. Jameson, 'Agriculture and Slavery in Classical Athens', *CJ* 73
(1977–8), 122–45, asserts that the use of slaves in agriculture was widespread. In
contrast, M. I. Finley, 'The Study of the Ancient Economy: Further Thoughts', and
The Ancient Economy, 70, argues that agricultural slavery was limited to large holdings
and that even owners of large holdings employed seasonal free workers in addition
to slaves.

[265] *The Social and Economic History of the Hellenistic World* (Oxford, 1941), 1196, cit.
de Ste. Croix. 508–9.

parcels to individuals who exploited them with free labour.[266] Wood bases some of her arguments on an alleged ambiguity in Greek words in the *Oeconomicus* used to designate workers. In her attempt to minimize the employment of slaves, Wood argues that words such as οἰκέτης and διάκονος do not inevitably indicate slave status.[267] However, the context in which these words appear in Xenophon's text leaves little doubt that the workers are slaves.[268] Surely the domestic in x. 12–13 who is not able to refuse her master's sexual advances is a slave. Furthermore, men who leased both public land and large private estates were wealthy.[269] Such men probably used slave labour to exploit their holdings. Fewer lessees of private land can be identified, but some who leased private estates on unfavourable terms appear to have been marginal (e.g. a freedman in Lys. 7), and not of an economic status that would allow them to own slaves. There is no basis for speculation that the Athenian peasant increased his holdings by leasing available land and working it with free labour.

There is no doubt that slavery as shown in the *Oeconomicus* is not a fiction. In the early fourth century men with large holdings used slaves to work them. But it may be wrong to generalize from the *Oeconomicus* as E. Grace does and to draw the conclusion that 'the farm worker at that time was typically a slave'.[270] Rather, as I have stated above, the labour force was flexible, subject to the forces of historical change, and varied according to the needs and circumstances of land-owners.

The question here is whether the foreman mentioned at this point in the text and in xii. 9, xiv. 1, xv. 1, 5 is a slave. Ischomachus does not say so explicitly, although ὠνεῖσθαι, of course, raises such a possibility. In iii. 10 Socrates mentions purchasing slaves and training them to be farmers. Socrates and Critobulus agree that a propertyless man can manage the estate of another and be paid a salary. Although he is a surrogate for the owner, he may be a slave (see on i. 3–4). In Xen. *Mem.* 2. 8. 3 Socrates advises an

---

[266] 'Agricultural Slavery in Classical Athens', *AJAH* 8 (1983), 1–47, and *Peasant-Citizen and Slave: The Foundations of Athenian Democracy* (London and New York, 1988), 64–80.

[267] *Peasant-Citizen and Slave: The Foundations of Athenian Democracy*, 49–50.

[268] Ischomachus certainly used slaves in the house (vii. 6, 35, 37, 41, viii. 22, ix. 5, 10, 16, x. 12, xi. 15, 18, 23, xii. 19–20), and some of them were sent to work out of doors, presumably performing agricultural labour (vii. 33, 35, xi. 15, 18).

[269] See Osborne, 'Buildings and Residence on the Land in Classical and Hellenistic Greece', 127.

[270] 'Athenian Views on What is a Slave and How to Manage People', *VDI* 111 (1970), 49–66.

impoverished free man to take a job as a foreman, but the man
rejects the idea for he considers it slavery (δουλεία), and his must
be the conventional view of the job of foreman, while Socrates' is
as radical as his notion in *Mem.* 2. 7 that freeborn women should
work to support themselves. In v. 14, Xenophon praises agriculture
as a preparation for military command. He is doubtless referring
to farming by supervision as well as to the physical exercise provided by farming (but see on v. 14–15 συμπαιδεύει ... ἡ ἐργασία).
Thus the praise of agriculture should not lead us to assume that
all who were involved in farming were free and eligible for military
service. Considering the efficiency with which he managed his
oikos, it seems unlikely that Ischomachus would expend as much
effort as is mentioned in this chapter on training men and women
who were free to sell their services elsewhere. Thus Ps.-Arist. *Oec.*
1344ᵃ27–9 is consistent with Xenophon's *Oeconomicus* in stating
that there are two kinds of slaves: the foreman or supervisor
(ἐπίτροπος) and the worker (ἐργάτης).

4. παιδεύεις. See also vii. 41. Ps.-Arist. *Oec.* is more explicit than
Xenophon on the training of slaves in general and in 1344ᵃ27–9
recommends careful education for slaves who are to engage in
tasks appropriate to the free.

6. εὔνοιαν ... Εὐεργετῶν. Through the same system of rewards
that was prescribed for the housekeeper (ix. 12) the farm foreman
is encouraged to be loyal and do good work. In the Oxford text
184 lines are devoted to the selection and training of the foreman
and 14 lines to the housekeeper.[271] On the importance of procuring
the good will of slaves, see vii. 37, xxi. 12 τὸ ἐθελόντων ἄρχειν, and
Ch. 5, sect. I.

11–13. οἴνου ἀκρατεῖς ... ἀφροδισίων. The foreman is to have the
same virtues as the housekeeper. The virtues of men and women
(among slaves as among their master and mistress) are the same.
Allusions to over-indulgence in wine and sex indicate that slaves
had such options available and could exercise some independent
choice. See Ch. 5, sect. I, and on iii. 10 γεωργούς.

13–14. δυσέρωτες ... παιδικῶν. ἀφροδίσια can refer to either homosexual or heterosexual intercourse. One result of the seclusion of
female slaves in the γυναικωνῖτις (ix. 5) is that homoerotic relationships between slaves were quite likely to occur. Although deserving
slaves are granted permission for heterosexual activities, such relationships exist not for the sake of sexual pleasure (ἀφροδισίων) but
rather for producing children (ix. 5 τεκνοποιῶνται). Columella's

---

[271] See Breitenbach, *Xenophon von Athen*, col. 1860.

discussion of the duties of the foreman (*RR* 12. 1) illustrates the difference between Greek and Roman sexual behaviour (See Ch. 6, sect. B).

When Xenophon refers to desperate sexual craving, he usually alludes to a relationship between two males. For example, Critobulus is so enamoured of Cleinias that he has lost his self control (*Symp.* 4. 15–26, and see on i. 1 Κριτόβουλε, and ii. 7 παιδικοῖς δὲ πράγμασι). A tyrant indulges in παιδικοῖς ἀφροδισίοις with unwilling youths (*Hiero* 1. 29, 36). Cyrus declares that he will avoid looking at a beautiful woman lest she distract him from his obligations and he become like men who are enslaved to their ἐρωμένοις (*Cyrop.* 5. 1. 12). Xenophon does not disapprove of erotic relationships between males as long as they are not overtly sexual. He reports that at Sparta, associations between men and boys were permitted for educational purposes only; physical relationships between them were considered just as shameless as if they were incestuous (*Sp. Const.* 2. 13–14, *Symp.* 8. 35).[272] He also relates that Agesilaus, whom he admired, declined to kiss a handsome Persian youth because he was in love with him and did not wish to be further inflamed (*Ages.* 5. 4–6). He ascribes such feelings to himself, writing that Socrates told Xenophon that he was tempted by handsome young men, but he said that he controlled his passion, and advised him to follow his example (*Mem.* 1. 3. 13, see also Xen. *Symp.* 8. 2).

15. ἐρωτικῶς . . . κερδαίνειν. The discussion of physical desire serves as a transition to the notion of desire for material gain.

17. τῶν παιδευομένων. Everyone in the household is subject to education (see on vii. 4).

19. χρηστοῦ . . . πονηρούς. As in ix. 5, a good master may have bad slaves.

20. δεσπότου ὀφθαλμός. Sim. Ps.-Arist. *Oec.* 1345[a]2–5. Likewise, Cyrus inspects his realm and sends trusty agents to look after the regions he does not visit personally (iv. 8). On the detrimental effects of absentee ownership see also on xi. 15–16 κατὰ πόλιν . . . εἰς ἀγρόν.

xiii. 4. Ἄρχειν . . . παιδεύεις. Like women, slaves in positions of authority can be taught the art of ruling (see Ch. 5, sect. I).

9. συμφέρει . . . πείθεσθαι. Ps.-Arist. *Oec.* 1344[b]15–18, and Arist.

---

[272] But the Spartan rule was complicated: see Pl. *Symp.* 182 A. on the existence of overtly sexual relationships between prominent Spartans see Paul Cartledge, 'The Politics of Spartan Pederasty', *PCPhS*, NS 27 (1981), 17–36.

Pol. 1330ᵃ32–3 mention the hope of freedom as an incentive for co-operative behaviour. Although Xenophon writes of treating slaves as though they were free, he does not mention manumission.

δούλοις . . . θηριώδης . . . γαστρί. Cf. vii. 10 for the training of the wife, who must first be tamed and domesticated. The wife, however, has already learned control over her appetites (vii. 6 γαστέρα).

In *Cyrop.* 8. 1. 43–4, Cyrus inculcates a slavish nature into those subjects designated to be subordinates by catering to their appetites for food and drink, for example, leading them to water 'like beasts of burden'. The gluttony of slaves, who can be controlled by satisfying their appetites for food and drink, was a topos in Greek literature: see e.g. Alexis fr. 25 Kassel–Austin and Men. *Perik.* 289–90.

10. ἱμάτιά. According to Ps.-Xen. *Const. of Ath.* 1. 10, in Athens it was impossible to distinguish slave from free by their apparel. Vase painting and funerary stelai rarely differentiate slave status from free by means of dress. Either the artist was loath to represent shabby dress, or, more likely, the slaves were allocated clothing commensurate with the economic means of their owners. The Athenian ideal of equality tended to eliminate invidious displays of wealth through clothing (Thuc. 1. 6. 3–5, see also Arist. *EN* 1127ᵇ27–9). However, the household of Ischomachus is a meritocracy operating on principles of hierarchy rather than equality. Clothing will not only serve to punish or reward slaves but will announce their ranking *vis-à-vis* one another so that those who have dealings with them will know how each is to be treated. Cf. on iv. 5 γεωργίας for the public nature of Cyrus' rewards and punishments. For the variety of clothing in Ischomachus' storerooms see viii. 19 and ix. 6.

xiv. 4. Δράκοντος νόμων . . . Σόλωνος. In the fourth century there was a tendency to attribute all early legislation to Draco and Solon. It was common in the fourth century to refer to Draco's laws as νόμοι, though earlier they were called θεσμοί.[273] According to Arist. *Ath. Pol.* 7. 1, Solon revised all Draco's legislation except the homicide laws. (For the antiquity of the laws on homicide see e.g. Dem. 23. 66, Plut. *Solon* 17. 1, Ael. *VH* 8. 10, Eusebius, *Chron.* 99 B Helm.) However, the present passage indicates that Ischomachus believed that some part of Draco's legislation on theft remained valid and that the laws on theft in force in the late

---

[273] See Ostwald, *Nomos,* 5.

fifth century derived from both Draco and Solon. It is likely that Solon did not present totally new laws on theft, but retained selected features of previous laws. The self-help and severity of the penalty mentioned by Ischomachus are characteristic of Draco's laws. The severity of Draco's laws was legendary, but not all crimes earned the death penalty.[274]

The clearest, but by no means unambiguous, statement of the Athenian law on theft is given in Dem. 24. 113, where it is attributed to Solon.[275] Plut. *Solon* 17 reports that Solon repealed Draco's death penalty for stealing fruit and vegetables (sim. Tzetzes, *Chil.* 5. 342–4). But the confusion between Draco and Solon persisted. Alciphron (*Ep.* 2. 38) states that according to the laws of both Draco and Solon all thefts were punishable by death. Some categories of thefts including those which were perpetrated at night, or in the harbour, or in a place of athletic activity, were punishable, according to the principle of self-help, by immediate death. Moreover, the Eleven (Police Commissioners) could summarily execute a thief caught in the act.

Ischomachus, not being in court, nor faced with an opponent who might test his veracity, is not motivated to quote the law precisely. Before the republication in 403 BC of Draco's laws on homicide (which may not have included the verbatim republication of his laws on theft), the archaic legislation would have been extremely difficult to read. At the time of the dramatic date of the *Oeconomicus* the laws of Draco were inscribed in archaic letters in boustrophedon style (written left to right and right to left in alternating lines) on ἄξονες (revolving slabs), and copied on other tablets, stelai, and altars scattered about the agora, Acropolis, and Areopagus.[276] Although Ischomachus' slaves were sufficiently familiar with the lawcourts to be able to present accusations and defences (xi. 23), it is hardly likely that they could have checked the wording of the law which their master claims to be quoting. In fact, quotations of laws in orations written by specialists are often inconsistent and incomplete. Though, of course, some slaves in Athens could read, doubtless very few of Ischomachus' slaves were literate. One of the qualifications of the housekeeper is that she has a good memory (ix. 10–11). Moreover, Ischomachus' abbreviated

---

[274] Sources in A. C. Schlesinger, 'Draco in the Hearts of his Countrymen', *CP* 19 (1924), 370–3.

[275] See also Dem. 22. 26–7, Philodemus, Περὶ οἰκονομίας, col. 7. 14–21, Gell. *NA* 11. 18. 3, and David Cohen, *Theft in Athenian Law* (Munich, 1983).

[276] Arist. *Ath. Pol.* 35. 2, Lys. 1. 30, R. Stroud, *Dracon's Law on Homicide* (Berkeley and Los Angeles, 1968), 24, 29, and see xiv. 5 γέγραπται.

version of the laws, which fails to mention the lesser penalties for theft other than those kinds listed by Demosthenes (see the preceding paragraph) and the possibility of paying a fine mentioned by Pollux (9. 61), and, instead, implies that death is invariably the penalty for theft, will have served to intimidate his slaves.

Xenophon was neither a legal expert nor an author of forensic orations. In *Mem.* 1. 2. 62 he gives the same abbreviated version of the laws on theft which he gives in the *Oeconomicus*.[277] It was illegal for the Athenian owner to kill a slave, but the consequence of such a homicide may have been nothing more than the necessity to undergo purification.[278] Ischomachus is consistent in his treatment of slaves, in applying the laws of citizens to them. He could have executed his slaves without reference to Draco's and Solon's laws (see Ch. 5, sect. I).

5. διδασκαλία. For the lawgiver as teacher of ethics see also Pl. *Laws*, esp. 811 D, 858 D.

γέγραπται. According to Arist. *Ath. Pol.* 41. 2, Draco's laws were the first in Athens to have been promulgated in written form. Although the reference to Draco in the passage in Aristotle may have been a late addition,[279] the fact that Draco's were the earliest written laws of Athens is not incorrect.

ἀλῷ ποιῶν . . . ἐγχειροῦντας. The concept of *flagrante delicto* appears in Athenian private law in the regulations on theft and adultery. Flagrance is a feature of archaic legal forms.[280]

9–10. ἐλευθέροις . . . χρῶμαι . . . καλούς τε κἀγαθούς. The aristocratic ideal of a gentleman is associated with agriculture (vi. 11) and is usually far removed from the banausic activities of slaves. In Xenophon's extension of the concept of gentleman to slaves Hermann Wankel sees the end of this aristocratic concept.[281] However, not all slaves are engaged in banausic work. In Ischomachus' household some hold positions of authority. Rather than destroying the concept of καλὸς κἀγαθός Xenophon extends it to include those who earn it not by birth, but by meritorious behaviour. In a similar way, in the Hellenistic period, the Hellenic ideal was extended to those who were not necessarily Greek by

---

[277] Cohen, *Theft*, 56, 58–61, awards unwarranted priority to Xenophon's quotations of the laws on theft.
[278] Antiphon 5. 47, 6. 4. and see A. R. W. Harrison, *The Law of Athens*, i. 171–2.
[279] So Rhodes, *A Commentary on the Aristotelian Athenaion Politeia*, 485.
[280] See L. Gernet, *Anthropologie de la Grèce antique* (Paris, 1968), 267–9, and 'Note sur la notion de délit privé en droit grec', in *Droits de l'Antiquité et sociologie juridique: Mélanges H. Lévy-Bruhl* (Paris, 1959), 393–405.
[281] *Kalos kai Agathos* (diss. Würzburg, 1961), 58.

birth, but whose education and behaviour showed them as
Hellenized. See on vi. 12 and Ch. 5, sect. I.

xv. 3. Τὴν τέχνην . . . ἐπισταμένους. Since farming is so central to
Greek life that everyone knows about it, in i. 22 failure in farming
is attributed to enslavement to vice, rather than to ignorance.
Therefore Xenophon does not need to write a detailed manual on
agriculture, and, incidentally becomes indignant at those who do
(xvi. 1). Such manuals would reduce farming to a banausic pursuit,
rendering it inappropriate for the upper-class citizen.

4–5. φιλανθρωπίαν . . . ἀνθρώπους. This paragraph is reminiscent
of the praise of agriculture in c. v. Such recapitulation is characteristic of Xenophon's narrative style in the *Oeconomicus*, and serves
to punctuate and unify the treatise. See on iv. 24, vi. 2, and
Ch. 2, sect. E.

9–10. δίδασκέ . . . γεωργίας. See on xvi. 1.
 λεληθέναι. On μαίευσις, see below, xix. 15.

xvi. 1. ποικιλώτατον . . . λόγῳ . . . ἀκριβέστατα. In *Works and
Days* Hesiod gives advice on farming, but prose monographs on
agriculture did not appear until the fourth century BC. Ps.-Pl.
Minos 316 E, refers to γεωργικὰ συγγράμματα Arist. *Pol.*
1258ᵇ30–1259ᵃ2 reports that Charetides of Paros, Apollodorus of
Lemnos, and several others had written manuals on agriculture.
Theophrastus names Cleidemus (*CP* 1. 10. 3, 5. 9. 10, *HP* 3. 1. 4)
and Androtion (*HP* 2. 7. 3, *CP* 3. 10. 4) among his predecessors
who had written on the subject. Neither Aristotle nor
Theophrastus mentions Xenophon as an agronomist. Whether
the authors they cite are the ones to whom Xenophon is referring
here cannot be established. Although they must be older than or
contemporaries of Aristotle or Theophrastus, they may have been
younger than Xenophon, or at any rate have written their
treatises after the composition of the *Oeconomicus*. If Androtion
and Cleidemus were the Atthidographers of the same name, then
they were younger.[282] The extant fragments of authors such as

---

[282] Whether the Androtion who wrote about agriculture is the Atthidographer
(author of Athenian history) of the same name has been disputed. F. Jacoby (*FGrH*
324 T 17, F 75–82) rejecting the verdicts of F. Susemihl, *Geschichte der griechischen
Literatur in der Alexandrinerzeit* (Leipzig, 1891–2), 1. 833, and of M. Wellmann,
'Androtion 2', *RE*, Suppl. 1 (Stuttgart, 1903), col. 82, argues that the historian is also
the author of the *Georgica*. According to W. Kroll, 'Kleidemos 2', *RE* xi. (Stuttgart,
1922), col. 593, Cleidemus is not the same as the Atthidographer. But there is little
basis for certitude in either case.

Androtion and Cleidemus indicate that they gave straightforward practical information on topics similar to those discussed in *Oec.* xvi–xx. Inasmuch as the works of the classical Greek agronomists are extant only in fragments, the *Oeconomicus* is our earliest extant source for most of the agricultural practices mentioned in it; this accident of preservation has given this material more prominence than Xenophon probably expected. Nevertheless, his advice is correct. As many of the notes to cc. xvi–xx demonstrate, most later writers on agriculture agree with Xenophon's preferences and suggestions. Varro (*RR* i. i. 7–8) states that more than fifty authors had written various agricultural treatises in Greek. But they certainly were not all authors of technical monographs. In the list of such writers he names Xenophon after Democritus[283] and preceding Aristotle.

In ποικιλώτατον and ἀκριβέστατα may be discerned a barb at the writers of technical manuals because their knowledge is merely theoretical and because they turn a simple subject into a complicated one. The true gentleman ought to have sufficient knowledge about agriculture without needing to read about it: just a few suggestions will jog his memory (see also on xv. 3). However, a comparison between the *Oeconomicus* and the more comprehensive agricultural treatises such as those by Varro and Columella and the *Geoponica* shows that Xenophon by no means intended to write an encyclopaedic manual on agriculture. Rather, the advice on agriculture is subordinate, though integral, to the philosophical discussion of οἰκονομία. In contrast, the Pseudo-Aristotelian *Oeconomica* omits specific advice on agriculture, although, in general, it follows the content of Xenophon's *Oeconomicus*.

On reasons for the appearance of treatises on agriculture in the fourth century see on v. i, xx. 22, and Ch. 5.

2–3. φύσιν . . . τῆς γῆς . . . ἀλλοτρίας γῆς. The principle of comparing the soil of adjacent properties appears in a lease from Heraclea of the fourth century BC, R. Dareste, B. Haussoullier, and Th. Reinach, *IJ* 12. 2, ll. 116–19 (repr. F. Sartori, *Archäologische Forschungen in Lukanien*, ii: *Herakleiastudien* (Heidelberg, 1967), 44); see ibid. 225 for the similarities in procedures at Heraclea and Athens.

Cato, *De agr.* 1. 2, Varro, *RR* 1. 5. 3, 1. 9. 7, and Col. *RR* pr. 23 offer similar common-sense advice to someone considering

---

[283] For Democritus see M. Wellmann, *Die Georgika des Demokritos* (Berlin, 1921), and, in general, see Breitenbach, *Xenophon von Athen*, col. 1865.

whether to farm in unfamiliar territory. Some judge soil by colour (Theophr. *CP* 2. 4. 12, Hom. *Od.* 19. 111, Herod. 2. 12, 4. 198, Varro, *RR* 1. 9. 7; see also Pollux 1. 227). Verg. *Georg.* 2. 226–58, gives over-detailed instructions for soil analysis, probably in the tradition of those who farm by word (xvi. 1) rather than by experience.[284]

3. θεομαχεῖν. Hes. *WD* 320, and Theophr. *HP* 1. 9. 2 also recommend taking the gifts offered by the gods. The gods are a source of risk and hazard as well as of bounty in the natural world. (See also xx. 13 and *Revenues* 1. 3 for Xenophon's advice to the farmer to follow the divine will.)

5. χερσεύουσα. Xenophon presumably means different plants, not domestication of the same plant. For the latter and for cultivation changing quantity into quality see Theophr. *HP* 1. 3. 5, 1. 4. 1, 6. 1. 1.

Weed growth in the Mediterranean basin, as elsewhere, is an indication of soil properties, in particular of moisture and moisture retentiveness, and to a lesser extent, of soil nutrients.

7. ἁλιέων . . . ἐπαινοῦσι. Fishermen who can recognize the qualities of soil at a glance are probably only part-time, seasonal fishermen. The rest of their livelihood would have been derived from farming.[285]

9. κριθὰς . . . πυρούς. Xenophon begins his detailed discussion of agriculture with grain, the most important component of the ancient diet (see on ix. 3 τὸν σῖτον and xx. 27 σῖτον).[286] Barley is mentioned before wheat, because the former was more important in Attica. Grain contributed approximately 70–75 per cent of the calories consumed in classical antiquity.[287]

10. νεόν. Fallow ploughing was not strictly necessary, but it was important in Ischomachus' intensive exploitation of the land. It normally took place in spring or summer, but see Theophr. *HP* 8. 6. 5 and *CP* 3. 20. 7 for winter.

11. κινεῖν τῷ ζεύγει. The farmer's year begins in the springtime. The first ploughing takes place at the time of the first spring rain

---

[284] See further Robin Osborne, 'Rural Structure and the Classical Polis: Town–Country Relations in Athenian Society' (Ph.D. diss. Cambridge, 1982), Appendix A: 'Greek Knowledge of the Soil'.

[285] See further T. W. Gallant, *A Fisherman's Tale* (Ghent, 1985), 38, 42, 44.

[286] On the symbolic value of grain as distinguishing human beings from other creatures see Pierre Vidal-Naquet, 'Valeurs religieuses et mythiques de la terre et du sacrifice dans l'Odyssée', *Annales* (*ESC*), 25 (1970), 1278–97, repr. in M. I. Finley (ed.), *Problèmes de la terre en Grèce ancienne* (The Hague, 1973), 269–92.

[287] See further Foxhall–Forbes, 'Σιτομετρεία', 69, 74.

in early March; its purpose is to uproot weeds. The second ploughing is done in midsummer. For the thrice-ploughed field see Hom. *Il.* 18. 542, *Od.* 5. 127, Hes. *WD* 463–4, *Th.* 971, Varro, *RR* 1. 27, and Pausanias 8. 15. 1. Theophr. *CP* 3. 20. 8 recommends four ploughings.

Because Xenophon mentions only two ploughings, spring and summer, P. Guiraud conjectures that there was a third ploughing just before sowing.[288] However, the number of ploughings depended upon variable factors such as the requirements of the soil, the crop to be planted, the weather, and available labour. Thus in xi. 16–17 Ischomachus reports that he makes on-the-spot decisions about fallow ploughing.

Frequent ploughing and periods of fallow helped to compensate for the lack of manure (see xvi. 12 κόπρον). Intensive pulverization by ploughing and digging permits the soil to retain twice as much water as unworked soil.[289] Here and in xx. 3 Xenophon describes the traditional short-fallow system in which grasses and weeds are permitted to grow on the fallow. These are subsequently ploughed under in early summer. Hes. *WD* 461–4 and Theophr. *CP* 3. 20. 8, *HP* 8. 9. 1, also recommend alternating short fallow with the grain crop. (For fallow stipulations in land leases see xvi. 12 κόπρον.) According to Heichelheim the statement in xvi. 12–15 offers further evidence of a more scientific approach to farming and shows that Xenophon understood the 'three-strip economy'.[290] Guiraud more correctly interprets this passage as meaning that the land was sown with grain only every other year and left fallow or planted with pulse in alternate years.[291] This method was customary, although farmers did not always adhere to it. See on xvi. 13 νεός.

12. ἔαρος. The spring ploughing is followed by sowing. The ploughing and fallow regime described by Ischomachus is as set out in Table 1.

κόπρον. Here, and in xvii. 10, xviii. 3, and xx. 12 Ischomachus mentions κόπρος ('fertilizer') composed of vegetable matter, rather than dung, although that mentioned in xviii. 3 may be a mixture (see also on xix. 13 πηλόν). He uses an ecologically sound system

---

[288] *La Propriété foncière en Grèce jusqu'à la conquête romaine* (Paris, 1900), 475, followed by A. Jardé, *Les Céréales dans l'Antiquité grecque*, 23–4, and see on xvi. 14 πλειστάκις.

[289] Courtenay Edward Stevens, 'Agriculture and Rural Life in the Later Roman Empire', in J. H. Clapham and Eileen Power (eds.), *The Cambridge Economic History of Europe*, i (1941, repr. Cambridge, 1942), 93.

[290] *An Ancient Economic History*, tr. J. Stevens, i (Leiden, 1958), 112.

[291] *La Propriété foncière en Grèce jusqu'à la conquête romaine*, 472–3.

TABLE 1. *Ischomachus' ploughing and fallow regime*

	Year 1	Year 2
January February	} fallow	
March	fallow ploughing	
April		
May		
June July	} fallow ploughing	harvest
August		
September		
October November	} simultaneous sowing and ploughing	} leave fallow
December		

designed to make use of the by-products of farming. Ploughing in green fallow creates fertilizer and prevents weed growth by killing weeds before they produce seeds (see Theophr. *HP* 8. 11. 9, *CP* 4. 6. 1).

Because he owns slaves, Ischomachus has the labour available to collect compost, both vegetable and animal waste. The use of animal waste will have been so obvious to readers of the *Oeconomicus* as not to require discussion. Theophr. *HP* 2. 7. 4, *CP* 3. 9. 4–5, Verg. *Georg.* 1. 80, Col. *RR* 2. 14–16, Varro, *RR* 1. 38, and *Geoponica* 2. 21–2 refer specifically to various kinds of animal dung. Bird droppings are mentioned in *IG* ii². 161A. 43, 162A. 39, ix. 287A. 20, 24 (Delos, 3rd c. BC). In addition, human waste would have been used for fertilizer.[292] According to i. 9, v. 3, 6, 18, 20, vii. 20, xx. 23, *Mem.* 2. 3. 9, 3. 11. 4, 4. 3. 10, 7. 13–14, and *Anab.* 5. 3. 9–11, farmers normally kept animals on their agricultural properties. According to v. 3, agriculture and animal husbandry are linked. Ischomachus is engaged primarily in intensive agriculture: such exploitation will have left little arable land free for grazing although he does have some fallow (xvi. 13 νεός). He probably owns cattle or mules or donkeys needed for threshing and ploughing, for his groom to ride, and for heavy transport (xviii. 3–4), at least one horse to ride himself, dogs for hunting, sheep and goats for milk, and possibly a few other animals for domestic consumption and for sacrificial purposes. Given the atten-

[292] See E. J. Owens, 'The Koprologoi at Athens in the Fifth and Fourth Centuries B.C.', *CQ*, NS 33 (1983), 44–50.

tion paid to weaving Ischomachus must own a considerable number of sheep (see vii. 6, 22, 36 and Ch. 5). These may well have been sent to graze on the hills, especially in the hot summer months, so that their droppings were not available for use as fertilizer. Ordinarily, however, they will have been kept at the farmstead, where their droppings would have been collected and used for fertilizer. The scatter of potsherds found in the fields in Greece is a result of the use of such manure from animal stalls. (Xen. *On Horsemanship* 5. 2 describes cleaning out the dung-heap.)

Stephen Hodkinson argues that there were some properties with few animals.[293] For example, the Attic stelai which record the property of those accused of profaning the Mysteries and mutilating the Herms indicate that animals were kept on only two estates.[294] However, the stelai did not give a complete inventory of the property of the Hermocopidae and now they are incomplete as well. Furthermore, raids and other dangers of the Peloponnesian War reduced the numbers of animals in Attica below normal peacetime levels (Thuc. 7. 27. 5, *Hell. Oxy.* 12. 5). Animal husbandry was not uncommon on the estates of the wealthy in the fourth century. For example, the plaintiff of Ps.-Dem. 47 owned 50 sheep, and Theophon left 60 sheep and 100 goats in addition to land valued at two talents (Isaeus 11. 41). Whether or not manure was available, it is apparent from Ischomachus' remarks that some landowners wasted the vegetable matter which would be effective in restoring nutrients to the soil. In underlining the ease and efficiency of arboriculture and agriculture as a system, Ischomachus avoids introducing the element of animal husbandry and instead emphasizes the use of green manure. Theophr. *CP* 3. 208, *HP* 8. 9. 1, Pliny, *NH* 18. 20, *Geoponica* 3. 5. 7, 3. 10. 8, and Pall. 10. 1 discuss the application of green manure. (See further on xix. 13 πηλόν and xviii. 2 μεσοτομῶν.)

13. νεός. Ischomachus is wealthy enough to have sufficient supplies of food stored (see vii. 36 διανεμητέον and ix. 8 κατὰ μῆνα δαπανώμενα). Therefore he can afford to leave some land fallow in alternate years. However, not all farmers followed this system (xx. 3). Although the fallow system was traditional, lessees (in contrast to owners) might wish to exploit land without respite (Xen. *Symp.* 8. 25, *Suda*, s.v. ἐπὶ καλάμῃ ἀροῦν, Pi. *Nem.* 6. 9–11). Thus land leases often stipulate a period of fallow. See e.g. *SIG* iii. 963 (Amorgos, Arkesine: 4th c. BC); *IG* ii². 1241 (Attica, 300 BC),

---

[293] 'Animal Husbandry in the Greek Polis', 42, 62.
[294] See Pritchett, 'The Attic Stelai. Part II', no. 265, 272 (nos. v. 39–40, vi. 68–73).

2492 (Attica, 345 BC), 2493 (Attica, 339 BC), 2494 (Attica, 4th c. BC), and 2498 (Attica, 321 BC).

ὕλης τε καθαράν. Weeds deprive the soil of moisture and nutrients, but they can be useful: sheep may graze on them and when they are ploughed in they restore nutrients to the soil.

ὀπτὴν . . . ἥλιον. Baking is good because it indicates that the land has been ploughed frequently. Sim. Verg. *Georg.* 1. 65–6 *glaebasque iacentes pulverulenta coquat maturis solibus aestas* ('With ripening suns let the dusty summer bake the clods as they lie').

14. πλειστάκις. *IG* ii². 1241 (Attica, 300 BC) prescribes intense cultivation of the land: 20–1 σκάψει τὰς ἀμπέλους δὶς κατὰ πασῶν τῶν ὡρῶν; 24–5 ἐργάσεται δὲ καὶ τἆλλα δένδρα τὰ ἥμερα.

Frequent ploughing and pulverization of the soil demands an abundant source of labour, such as slaves were most likely to supply.

xvii. 2. βρέξας. Col. *RR* 2. 8. 4, mentions that some ancient writers advised making sowing conditional upon rainfall, although he himself does not completely agree with such advice. Pall. 12. 1, recommends sowing grain in November. Nowadays in Greece the time of sowing arable crops depends upon the rains, which generally arrive any time from late October until December.[295] Modern observation has confirmed the wide variation in annual rainfall that was a major concern to Greek farmers and a common cause of crop failure (e.g. in 361/0, Ps.-Dem. 50. 4–6, 61).[296]

In the *Oeconomicus* the various agricultural activities are usually reviewed crop by crop, rather than as they occur in the calendar year. In v. 4–5 Socrates pointed out that the most important operations on a farm must be performed at fixed times.[297] It was necessary for the overseer to schedule chores over the year, especially when farming scattered plots. The overseer had to take account of variations in such influential factors as weather, temperature, and harvest time. In order to employ the labour force most efficiently and keep the workers busy without undue stress it is preferable to distribute the agricultural activities throughout the year, as much as possible. Thus barley is sown first, and then

[295] See further Hamish A. Forbes, 'The "Thrice-Ploughed Field": Cultivation Techniques in Ancient and Modern Greece', *Expedition* 19 1 (1976), 5.

[296] See further Michæl Jameson, 'Famine in the Greek World, in Peter Garnsey and C. R. Whittaker (eds.), *Trade and Famine in Classical Antiquity* (Cambridge, 1983), 7–8.

[297] Land leases may stipulate specific dates for ploughing: see *IG* ii². 2498. 18–19 (Attica, 321 BC), vii. 235. 2–4 (Oropus, 4th c. BC).

wheat. Sowing through the season, as recommended in xvii. 6, will result in a harvest spread over late spring and early summer. Some fruits and vegetables are harvested in the summer. Summer grain crops such as millet are possible too, though Ischomachus does not recommend them. Owing to the heat in Greece, for Ischomachus as for Hesiod (*WD* 582–95) the summer is relatively a time of rest. Figs would be harvested in August (xix. 12). The next major activity on Ischomachus' farm would be the vintage in September or October, followed, in alternate years, by the olive harvest from December to February. After the harvest the autumn ploughing commences, followed by sowing of the winter crops. Cuttings would be planted in March (xix. 12). The less urgent operations such as maintenance, repairs, wood-cutting, wall-construction, digging trenches for vines and irrigation, and food-processing could be performed at slack times.

The role of farm supervisor is, in many respects, analogous to that of a general. The financial success or failure of a family can depend upon his decisions. When urgent tasks must be performed simultaneously, he must decide where to deploy available labour and how to find additional assistance. Through good will, benefactions, or reciprocal arrangements, he must be able to enlist the help of neighbours or relatives. Like the general, the farm supervisor must have multiple strategies for the complex, and constantly changing, requirements of farming (see further on v. 14–15 συμπαιδεύει ... ἡ ἐργασία).[298]

σπείρειν. Pliny, *NH* 18. 224 criticizes (in Cicero's translation) this passage on the grounds that the god's signal would be expressed not through rainfall but through falling leaves. Hes. *WD* 477 advises sowing before the winter solstice. Theophr. *HP* 8. 1. 3, 8. 6. 1 prefers two sowings: barley and wheat, as a rule, should be sown before the rains rather than after. Barley may be sown in either spring or fall (*HP* 8. 1. 4), but spring-sown barley is less reliable.

2–4. πρὸς τὸν θεὸν ... Καὶ ὁ θεός. Once again, Xenophon emphasizes the importance of the gods in creating or averting the hazards and risks of agriculture (see on v. 20 σώφρονες ... τοὺς θεούς and xvi. 3 θεομαχεῖν). Similar sentiments are expressed in Xen. *Mem.* 1. 1. 18 and Ps.-Xen. *Const. of Ath.* 2. 6.

4. ἔτος ἄγει. Sim. Theophr. *HP* 8. 7. 6 ἔτος φέρει οὐχὶ ἄρουρα ('the

---

[298] For current practices in Greece see P. Halstead and G. Jones, 'Agrarian Ecology in the Greek Islands: Time, Stress, Scale and Risk', *JHS* 109 (1989), 41–55.

year, not the field, makes the crop'), and *CP* 2. 1. 2, 3. 23. 4, 3. 24. 2, *HP* 5. 2.

6. παντὸς μετέχειν τοῦ σπόρου. Didymus in *Geoponica* 2. 14. 8 remarks that, ignorant of the future, some farmers do not sow all their seed at once, but distribute it over as many as four sowings as a precaution. See Theophr. *CP* 3. 26. 5, *HP* 8. 6. 1–2, for later, heavier sowing.

7. ῥίπτειν τὸ σπέρμα ποικίλη τέχνη. Casting seed evenly is, in fact, very difficult.

8. λεπτοτέρα ... παχυτέρα. Heavy or fat soil is generally better than sandy or light soil. Theophr. *HP* 8. 6. 2, also discusses the qualities of various types of soil in metaphorical terms, e.g. πίειρα, λεπτῆς ('fat', 'light'). Roman authors use similar descriptive language to describe the fertility of soil: e.g. Col. *RR* 9. 2 *pinguibus vel mediocribus vel macris*; Varro, *RR* 23. 2 *pingui*; Pall. 1. 5 *macer...ieiuna...pinguis*. The source of the metaphor is doubtless the personification of Earth as female (as in c. v).

πότερον ἴσον. Sim. Verg. *Georg.* 2. 274, recommends sowing more thickly if the soil is rich (*pinguis*, i.e. 'fat'). Col. *RR* 2. 9. 1 recommends the opposite.

9–10. καρπὸν ... ὑποζύγια. This remark suggests that some animals became very weak in periods of the year when grazing and fodder were in short supply, for example in mid-winter. Stalled animals, except pigs, could be turned out to graze for wild plants, but oxen need to be grain-fed. For hunger among human beings see on xi. 12 ἐσθίειν ... ἱκανά.

10. τροφήν. τροφή in the *Oeconomicus* refers to both nutriments and moisture.

κόπρου. See on xvi. 12.

συὶ δὲ ἀσθενεῖ. Piglets were frequently sacrificed.[299] The calendar from Erchia (*SEG* 21. 541) lists the sacrifice of piglets on ten occasions. Pigs were prolific and relatively inexpensive. At Erchia the cost of a piglet was 3 dr., whereas a ram or billy-goat cost 12 dr. *Inter alia*, the slaughter of surplus piglets helps to assure that the surviving animals are better nourished.

12. σκαλέας. A wide-bladed hoe here used for digging.[300] A metal tool was expensive. Less wealthy farmers would have weeded by

---

[299] e.g. Xen. *Anab.* 7. 8. 5 to Zeus Meilichios; Ar. *Peace* 387 to Hermes; *FGrH* 334 F 16 = Photius in Suda, sv. περισίαρχος before assembly meetings; *LSCG* 67, for the sacrifice of pigs at the sanctuary of Hera in Tegea (4th c. BC.)

[300] For modern examples of traditional Greek agricultural tools see Benaki Museum Photographic Archive, Παραδοσιακὲς καλλιέργειες (Athens, 1978).

hand. The amount of water present suggests late autumn to mid-winter, a period when the grain is still low and resilient if trampled. Weeding will provide work for the slaves during the winter. Later, when the grain is higher, weeding by hand is appropriate, but Xenophon does not mention this chore.

This word is found only here and in xvii. 15. Hence the definition is not secure. According to LSJ, s.v. σκαλεύς, the word refers to the person who wields the hoe, rather than to the implement. Local variants of words for agricultural activities must have been popular in the spoken language, but appear rarely in literature. For example ξηρολογία and κορμολογία (words for common agricultural chores) had appeared only once before in extant texts and περισκαλισμός (or perhaps περιφιαλισμός) appears for the first time in *P. Columbia* Inv. No. 65 = *SB* viii. 9835 = *P. Columbia* VII. 179, a document of AD 300.[301]

xviii. 1. ἐπιστάμενος ... Τί δ' οὐ μέλλω; Ischomachus leads Socrates through the discussion by the process of ἀνάμνησις (see on xviii. 9–10 and xix. 15). But there is also little doubt that Socrates has personally participated in reaping. This chore had to be performed at a busy time of year. All available labour was enlisted, including women and the wealthy landowners themselves (see on v. 14–15 and xii. 3).

2. μεσοτομῶν. Varro, *RR* 1.50 reviews three methods of reaping: cutting a handful of grain close to the ground with a toothed hook; cutting off the ears of grain with a curved piece of wood which has a small saw attached to the end; and cutting the stalks in the middle, leaving the bottoms as stubble. Ischomachus prefers the third. This method seems wasteful and inconsistent with Ischomachus' intensive exploitation of his resources. That he was not trying to get as much straw as possible suggests that he has so much land under cereal cultivation and thus so much straw to use or sell that he does not need to waste time and labour gathering more. Another possibility is that he has not many animals to feed (see on xvi. 12 κόπρον). Or perhaps both factors play a part in his decision to leave the straw as stubble.

λειφθέν ... κατακαυθέν. Burning stubble was a normal practice in antiquity (Pl. *Laws* 843 E, Verg. *Georg.* 1. 84–93, Pliny, *NH* 18. 300). A variety of benefits resulted from burning: it cleared the land of weeds, insects, and unwanted seeds, and the wood-ash

---

[301] See Sarah B. [Porges] Pomeroy, 'A Lease of an Olive Grove', *TAPhA* 92 (1961), 473–7.

that was produced restored nutrients to the soil. Of course, it was, and still is, a hazardous operation, and best not performed during the summer.

3. ὑποζυγίῳ. Driving draught-animals over the ears of grain was the most common method of threshing in antiquity. Their hooves alone could do the job, but some farmers also used threshing sledges.[302] In addition to the animals listed by Ischomachus, donkeys might be employed by less wealthy farmers. The chaff would be saved. It was stored in baskets (Aen. Tact. 29. 6) and special storerooms (*IG* xi. 2. 287 A. 149). It was used for building (*IG* ii².463. 68, 1672. 73, Arist. *HA* 612ᵇ22, Aen. Tact. 32. 3), and mixed into barleycake (Poliochus fr. 2 Kock, Antiphanes fr. 226 Kassel–Austin). Animals are muzzled while threshing, but the chaff was later used as feed.[303]

5. δῖνον. Cato, *RR* 91, Varro, *RR* 1. 51, Col. *RR* 2. 19, Pall. 1. 36, and Didymus in *Geoponica* 2. 26 give instructions for the construction of a threshing-floor. It was to be a circular platform so oriented that the wind should not blow the chaff on to other crops.

The estate of Phaenippus—the largest estate known from classical Attica—had two large threshing-floors (Ps.-Dem. 42. 6). Grain was grown, threshed, and milled on many country estates. Archaeological evidence for threshing-floors and grain-storage has been found at several sites in Sounion, in Euboea, and in the Kharaka Valley.[304] These floors were probably constructed of pounded earth surrounded by a circle of stones. Threshing-floors may also be paved with stone.

6. λικμῶντες. Winnowing forks and fans were used, though for the best results sufficient wind was needed as well. For fans see Col. *RR* 2. 10. 13–14.[305]

8. ἄχυρα. Usually means chaff, but here and in Theocr. 10. 49 it refers to the mixture of grain and chaff before winnowing.[306]

πόλον. The πόλος was the pivot in the middle of the threshing-

---

[302] Lin Foxhall (pers. comm.) suggests that ὀκίστια in the Attic stelai (*IG* i³. 422. 135) refers to sledges.

[303] For traditional methods of preparing grain, see Halstead–Jones, 'Agrarian Ecology in the Greek Islands'.

[304] See John H. Young, 'Studies in South Attica. Country Estates at Sounion', *Hesperia*, 25 (1956), 124–6, 140; Donald R. Keller, 'Classical Greek Agricultural Sites: The Karystian Evidence', *AJA* 93 (1989), 275; and H. Lohmann, 'Landleben im klassischen Attika', *Jahrbuch Ruhr-Universität Bochum*, 1985, 71–96.

[305] For depictions of winnowing fans and forks in literature and the visual arts see Jane E. Harrison, 'Mystica Vannus Iacchi', *JHS* 23 (1903), 302–3, 24 (1904), 246–9, and A. D. Ure, 'Boeotian Haloa', *JHS* 69 (1949), 18–24.

[306] See A. S. F. Gow, *Theocritus* (Cambridge, 1952), ii. 206.

floor. Grain was swept to the centre, chaff to the rim. LSJ, s.v. πόλος, citing this passage gives '*centre* of circular threshing-floor'. Breitenbach, *Xenophontis Oeconomicus*, ad loc., incorrectly follows Schol. Ar. *Birds* 181 and gives 'extremam lineam, oram, quae ambit et undequaque terminat aream'.

9. ἐννοῶ . . . γεωργεῖν. For a papyrus fragment of this portion of the text see Ch. 7, sect. A. The papyrus does not support Cobet's conjecture εἰ ἄρα for ἄρα εἰ.[307]

9–10. χρυσοχοεῖν . . . γενναιοτάτη ἡ γεωργική. Farming, the noblest occupation, need simply be recalled. In contrast, banausic crafts such as gold-working, flute-playing, and painting must be learnt. Sim. xix. 16–18.

10. ἐπιστάμενος . . . ἐλελήθειν. On anamnesis see on xix. 15.

xix. 1. δένδρων. Whereas the two preceding chapters dealt with agriculture, xix. 1–12 treats of viticulture. Vines were regularly classified as trees as they are nowadays (see e.g. Theophr. *HP* 1. 3. 1, *IG* ii². 2492. 16–17, Pliny, *NH* 14. 2. 9, *Digest* 47. 7. 1–3). In xix. 12, Xenophon makes it clear that he has been discussing vines. However, the methods he describes can be used for other trees as well. Competition among wine-producing areas in the fourth century caused Greek viticulturists to become more scientific. Although Xenophon's instructions for the novice vine-grower appear inadequate, they may be the first, or at least among the earliest such lessons to be written; thus they constitute a pioneering stage in the professionalization of viticulture. The earliest extant detailed discourses on viticulture are found in the encyclopaedic works of Theophrastus, *HP* and *CP*.[308]

Vines are very labour intensive: an enormous amount of energy is expended in digging the trenches (see on xx. 20–1 σκαπτόντων . . . ἀργόν). Some land-leases have stipulations requiring the lessees to perform this chore (*IG* ii². 1241. 19–21, *SIG*³ 963. 9–10). Xenophon uses labour exerted in the vineyard as a criterion for distinguishing the lazy from the industrious farmer (xx. 4). Hoeing vineyards and ditches for irrigation and drainage, more than any other kind of chore, induces farmers in Greece nowadays to abandon agricultural labour.[309] However, the work can be spread throughout the year. Thus vines are especially suitable for farms

---

[307] Cf. Denniston, *The Greek Particles*, 35.

[308] On the science of viticulture, see Forbes, *Studies in Ancient Technology* (Leiden, 1955), iii. 11–37.

[309] See further Stanley Aschenbrenner, *Life in a Changing Greek Village*, 21.

worked by slaves. Vines are subject to risks, e.g. pests (Theophr. *CP* 3. 22. 5), but can produce a high income. Such high-risk, high-yield agriculture is prestigious, and suitable for a wealthy land-owner who has so much land that he can afford to wait for his vines to mature (see on xix. 6 Λυκαβηττόν and xix. 9).

3. τριπόδου. According to Florentinus in *Geoponica* 5. 12. 1 vines ought to be planted in a trench not less than 4 feet deep, although 3 feet is acceptable. Col. *RR* 3. 13. 4, 5. 5. 2, 5. 9. 1–2, asserts that a depth of 3 feet is adequate. In 3. 15. 2 he mentions trenches of 2½ feet on level ground, 2¾ feet on a slope, and 3 feet on a steep slope, but in 11. 2. 17–18 and 3. 13. 2 he admits a minimum of 2 feet. In 4. 1. 1. he recommends 2¾ feet. Later authors considered the depth of 2½ feet (recommended by Ischomachus, in xix. 5) to be a bare minimum. Of course, the deeper the trenches are, the harder the work in digging them. The *Geoponica* (pr. 7), note that in antiquity there was little consensus about precise details of farming. In any case farmers surely judged the depth by eye, not with a measuring-rod. Thus it hardly matters that there were several standards for the foot in Greece and Rome.[310]

6. Λυκαβηττόν. The mountain of Lycabettos (also known today as Hagios Georgios), in north-east Athens. Dryness made the land almost valueless (Ps.-Pl. *Eryx.* 400 B, Pl. *Critias* 112 A) although it could support olive plantations (Statius, *Theb.* 12. 621).[311] Xenophon implies that vines might be planted in such a location as part of his programme to reclaim land that is insufficiently exploited (xx. 22–3). Vines are sensitive to moisture. The amount of moisture present would affect the flavour of the wine. Raising vines in such a location would involve both greater risk and greater profit than usual (see above on xix. 1).

Φαληρικῷ. One of the two coastal demes of Athens, Phaleron was located east of Piraeus (Strabo 9. 1. 21, 398 C). It was named after Phalerus, grandson of Erechtheus, and was of the φυλή Aiantis.[312] In contrast to Lycabettos, the plain of Phaleron was fertile. Phaleron was well suited to market gardens because it was

---

[310] The Roman foot was close to the short Greek foot of 294–6 mm. Without further qualification, we understand the foot in classical Athens to measure 326–8 mm. See W. B. Dinsmoor, *The Architecture of Ancient Greece*, 3rd edn. (New York, 1950), 161 n. 1, 175 n. 1, 199 n. 3.

[311] J. G. Frazer, *Pausanias's Description of Greece* (London, 1898), ii. 428. For additional classical references to Lycabettos see Walther Judeich, *Topographie von Athen*, 2nd edn. (Munich, 1931), 44–5.

[312] See Judeich, *Topographie von Athen*, 426–9.

moist and easily irrigated from the Cephissos.[313] For example, Hesychius, s.v. Φαληρικαί (Schmidt), mentions the ῥάφανος a black radish that evidently was grown there. Herod. 5. 63 implies that Phaleron was fertile, since the Pisistratids had to clear it so as to be able to use cavalry. It may well have supported vines, for vines can be cultivated in wet conditions and on coastal plains (Theophr. *CP* 5. 9. 11, *Geoponica* 5. 5). Aerial photographs also suggest that there was a considerable amount of farming in antiquity on the Attic coastal plain.[314]

8. κλήματος. Ischomachus uses cuttings to propagate vines. They could also be grafted or layered.

9. Πότερα . . . ὀρθὸν . . . πλάγιόν. Col. *RR* 3. 15. 2, 4. 4. 1, *de Arb.* 3. 4, recommends the first method, Florentinus, in *Geoponica* 5. 9. 6, and Pall. 3. 9. 14 prefer the second. Putting the plant in like a reversed gamma (L) encourages the formation of roots. Both methods of planting presuppose the existence of a previous vineyard from which the shoots are taken and assume that the land-owner has other sources of income on which he may depend until the vines mature (see on xix. 1).

10. ὀφθαλμοί. Theophrastus (e.g. *CP* 3. 15. 2, 5. 1. 12) mentions the buds from the eyes of the vine-cuttings. Sim. *oculi* e.g. Verg. *Georg.* 2. 73, Col. *RR* 11. 2. 16, 38, and see *The Oxford Latin Dictionary*, s.v. *oculus*, para. 9. Greek farmers still refer to buds as μάτια.

φυομένων βλαστῶν ⟨κατὰ⟩ τῆς γῆς. Castiglioni conjectures that τῆς γῆς has been interpolated inasmuch as the κατά which should precede does not appear in the manuscripts.[315] However, the case for assuming that κατά has erroneously been omitted is just as strong as that for assuming that τῆς γῆς has been interpolated. The meaning is not affected, for the prepositional phrase can be supplied from the preceding sentence.

11. ἐπαμήσαιο. Col. *RR* 11. 2. 54 also recommends heaping earth around plants. This paragraph shows that Xenophon understood how to avoid the deleterious effects of capillary action.

12. συκῆν. Figs are high in calories and were important in the Greek diet. They were considered delicious and were eaten both fresh and dried. Athen. 74 c–80 e discusses the varieties at length. The

---

[313] See further William M. Leake, *The Topography of Athens*, 2nd edn. (London, 1841), i. 397.

[314] For photographs see John Bradford, *Ancient Landscapes: Studies in Field Archaeology* (London, 1957), 29, 34.

[315] Review of Chantraine's edition, 342.

Athenians enjoyed figs so much that exporting them was prohibited, and Herod. 1. 71 pairs figs with wine as good things. They were often grown along with other plants including olives, vines, and grains as in *IG* ii². 2494, 2493, 1241, *SIG³* 963, *Inscr. Dél.* 503, *The Rhodian Peraea and Islands* nos. 8–10 Fraser–Bean.[316] Figs could be grown in stony ground and did not require irrigation. For methods of cultivation of figs and fig-like fruits see Theophr. *HP* 2, 3, 4, *CP* 1. 2, 5, 6, *et passim.*

12–13. ἀμπέλου . . . ἄλλας φυτείας. Methods that are effective for vines should be useful for other trees, because most other trees are easier to grow than vines. Theophrastus (*CP* 3. 6. 8) observes that there was general consensus that vines and olives should be cultivated in the same way, but he himself differs.

13. μάλιστα πάντων ἐπιστάμενος. Olive culture was so widespread in antiquity, especially in Attica, that everyone who ventured out of doors must have had some understanding of it.

βαθύτερος . . . βόθρος. *Geoponica* 9. 6. 4 and Col. *RR* 5. 9. 1–2 recommend 3 feet, but cf. Theophr. *CP* 3. 6. 8.

παρὰ τὰς ὁδούς. According to *Geoponica* 3. 11. 2 olive-trees and vines thrive when they are planted by the roadside. Olives provide shade; nowadays eucalyptus trees often line the roads.

πρέμνα. The fruit itself produces only wild olive-trees. Olives may be propagated in several ways. Here Ischomachus is probably referring to grafting shoots onto rooting stocks. Theophr. *HP* 2. 1. 4, *CP* 3. 5. 1, and Leontinus in *Geoponica* 9. 11. 1 describe the method of propagating olives from truncheons of old olive-trunks. Varro, *RR* 1. 41 and Verg. *Georg.* 2. 30 observe that olives take root when the trunk of a tree is split. There was a market for stumps: Dem. 43. 69, *IG* ii². 2492. 42–3.

πηλόν. The clay mixture is applied in order to protect the graft. Xenophon, as in his advice for fertilizing, favours the use of vegetable matter (see on *κόπρον* xvi. 12). Col. *RR* 11. 2. 42 recommends smearing olive-cuttings with a mixture of manure and ashes.

14. ὄστρακον. The shard placed on top of the poultice of clay described in the preceding paragraph prevents water from leaking in and causing the wood to rot.

15. ἐρώτησις διδασκαλία. Here Socrates is subjected to the Socratic method of teaching, but of course since he is actually the narrator of the conversation with Ischomachus he is playing the active role. Implicit in the elenctic process enacted here is the theory that the

[316] See further P. M. Fraser and G. E. Bean, *The Rhodian Peraea and Islands* (London, 1954), 6–12.

soul is immortal. Knowledge is recollection and teaching is actually an attempt to regain latent knowledge (see also xv. 10 λεληθέναι and Pl. *Meno* 80 D).

17–18. γεωργία . . . αὐτὴ διδάσκει. Here, as in v. 4, 5, 6, γεωργία is personified as a beneficent female who teaches human beings how to use her gifts. Similarly in v. 12 earth herself teaches (διδάσκει). There is no need to adopt Jacob's suggestion, noted in the apparatus criticus, that αὐτὴ be followed by ἡ φύσις. The antecedent of αὐτὴ is γεωργία.

18. ἄμπελος ἀναβαίνουσα. There are basically two different ways (with many variations) of training vines: on the ground or raised on props or trees (Hom. *Il.* 18. 561, Theophr. *CP* 3. 7. 5, etc.). While it is easier to leave vines lying on the ground, the fruit is vulnerable to theft by mice, foxes, and other predators. The fruit may ripen unevenly, and the vines themselves be rotted by excessive moisture.

Despite the practice of mixing crops that would put some fruit-trees within reach of some vines (Ar. *Ach.* 995–9, *Wasps* 326 with scholia, Dem. 53. 15, *Geoponica* 5. 8, Theophr. *CP* 3. 10. 6), it was preferable to use props made of wood to support the branches of vines which would otherwise lie on the ground. Although wood-cutting was generally forbidden when Greek estates were leased, an exception could be made for wood intended for use as vine props, e.g. on the Rhodian Peraea (Amos, *c.*200 BC) no. 10b. 7–8 Fraser–Bean (p. 12). References to vine-props in literature are numerous (see LSJ, s.v. χάραξ). They were of sufficient value to be listed among the property of the Hermocopidae (*IG* i³. 422 col. iv, ll. 305, 310, 425, col. ii, l. 28).[317] Cato, *De Agr.* 33. 4, and Col. *RR* 4. 12–13, discuss the need to support the vine.

19. ψιλοῦν. Cato, *De Agr.* 33. 4, Varro, *RR* 1. 31. 1–2, Col. *RR* 4. 27. 2, 5. 5. 14, 11. 2. 61, Pall. 9. 3, and Sotion in *Geoponica* 5. 28 recommend stripping excess leaves to allow the fruit to ripen. Stripping leaves reduces the surfaces from which evaporation can take place, but it exposes the fruit itself to burning. This procedure must be carefully followed in the hot days before the vintage. The stripped leaves could be fed to animals or added to the compost-heap.

ἀεί. Diophanes, quoting Democritus and Africanus, states in *Geoponica* 5. 45. 2 that grapes take no more than six days to ripen, turning from green to black. Grapes were usually harvested in mid-September. The vintage procedure recommended by

[317] See further W. Kendrick Pritchett, 'The Attic Stelai: Part II', 305–6.

Ischomachus is labour-intensive. The harvesters go back to the vines several times, as they would in the case of fruit trees, rather than harvesting the grapes all at once.

In the *Oeconomicus* the discussion of agricultural operations ends, as did the Greek farmer's year, with the vintage.

xx. 1. ῥᾳδιά ... μαθεῖν. The same assertion is made in vi. 9, xv. 10, and xxi. 1.

3. ὁμαλῶς ... οὐδ' ... ἠγνόησέ. While it is important to know how to sow evenly and to recognize the proper soil for vines (which are fussy), clever discoveries are not vital to the farmer. Experiments and innovations can lead to disaster. For the same principle, see 5–6 and xx. Arist. *Pol.* 1258^{b}35–8, who points out that nature furnishes nourishment for living creatures.

4. κόπρος. On the necessity for using fertilizer see, e.g. Theophr. *HP* 2. 7. 1, 4, 8. 7. 7, *CP* 3. 6. 1, Varro, *RR* 1. 38, Pall. 10. 1, etc., and see on xvi. 12 κόπρον for green manure. Col. *RR* 2. 1. 7, reiterates Xenophon's moralizing with the same advice.

οὐδὲ οἶνον ἔχει. Agricultural produce is visible. Just as keeping a well-run, clean house gives a clear indication of a woman's moral worth (see on vii. 32 ἡ τῶν μελιττῶν ἡγεμών),[318] so a successful farm with an abundance of food in storage advertises the virtue of the man who owns it. The connection between moral virtue and full storage-jars was traditional. See e.g. i. 19–22, xx. 15–21, and Hes., *WD* 472–8. In *Hiero* 9. 8, Xenophon states that profits increase through σωφροσύνη rather than through inactivity. In modern Greece a carefully tended vineyard yielded nearly twice as much as a neighbouring plot that had received less attention.[319] (For landowners who neglect their property see on xi. 15–16 κατὰ πόλιν ... εἰς ἀγρόν.)

Cicero, in a quotation from what was probably the third book of his translation of the *Oeconomicus*, renders Ischomachus' words *neque serit vitem, neque quae sata est, diligenter colit, oleum, ficus, poma non habet* (Macrob. *Sat.* 3. 20. 4–5 = fr. 25 Garbarino, p. 82).

9. ἐπιμελοῦνται. Knowledge alone is not sufficient. Concern or diligence and the ability to control subordinates are prerequisites for a successful agricultural enterprise. This point is the culmination of the ethical argument of the *Oeconomicus*. Diligence now appears to have been justly emphasized throughout the treatise. In fact, the development of the argument has been most encour-

[318] See further Pomeroy, *Women in Hellenistic Egypt*, 98.
[319] See further Forbes, 'The "Thrice-Ploughed Field"', 9.

aging to the reader: everybody can farm without specialized, professional knowledge. All that is needed in farming, as in other areas of civic life, is diligence.

11. ἐμβάλλοι. Producing liquid manure takes time. Like the exploitation of inferior soil mentioned in the following paragraph, it is suitable for intensified, high-yield agriculture.

12. ὑγροτέρα. Attention to problems posed by coping with waterlogged, sandy, or salty soil suggests that there was pressure to exploit even inferior land in the classical period (see on xx. 22, 27).[320] Greece is not so rich in good soil that bad can be neglected.

14–15. γῆν ... εὖ πάσχουσα εὖ ποιεῖ. Xenophon reiterates the notion of justice on earth expressed in v. 12.

15. ψυχῆς ... κακῆς. A lazy farmer is an unsatisfactory man. This notion is consistent with the idea expressed earlier that material success is evidence of virtue (see i. 19–22 and xx. 4).

16. λυσιτελεῖν. On Ischomachus' methods of accounting see Ch. 5, sect. E, xx. 21, 29, and on vii. 13–14.

Ancient farmers were well aware of the complex relationships between manpower, energy expended, tasks, and yield. Florentinus in *Geoponica* 2. 46 notes that older vineyards require more work than younger ones and that the intensity of work depends on the nature of the plants and soil. His estimates of the number of workers required per πλέθρον vary accordingly. In *Revenues* 4. 5 Xenophon declares that every farmer can calculate the proper number of oxen and labourers for his farm. Col. *RR* 2. 12 estimates the number of specialized labourers and oxen required to cultivate each *iugerum* of particular varieties of grain and legumes and in *RR* 3. 3. 8 he provides calculations of labour required for vineyards.

δέκα Col. *RR* 11. 1. 15 adapts Ischomachus' statement.

20. καλῶς ἐργάζεσθαι. See on xx. 4 οὐδὲ οἶνον ἔχει.

20–1. σκαπτόντων ... ἀργόν. Vinedigging is hard work (see on xix. 1 δένδρων). It is usually done in the autumn. Weeding is probably a spring chore.

22. χῶρον ... ὠνεῖσθαι. Improving land that had been poorly farmed and selling it could be quite profitable, though, like the grain-trade with which Socrates compares it, land-speculation was risky and required a substantial capital outlay. If we take the reference to Ischomachus' father seriously, then there was a market in land before or during the Peloponnesian War. Land was probably the source of the great wealth attributed to the historical Ischomachus (see on vi. 17 Ἰσχόμαχον). As Ischomachus states in

[320] See further Osborne, *Demos*, 41.

xvi. 2–3, a man who was considering whether to farm an unfamiliar piece of land could gauge the potential of a neglected plot by examining the soil and noticing the productivity of neighbouring farms. A plot that had been neglected and been left to lie fallow would have increased its supply of nutrients.

The present passage constitutes evidence for land-speculation in the late fifth and fourth centuries. Xenophon will have witnessed and perhaps even participated in such transactions. In that period land-speculation was not uncommon and the activities of Ischomachus' father were certainly not unique: on the effects of the war on Athenian agriculture see Ch. 5.[321]

23. ἐπίδοσιν. See Isaeus 9. 28 for an assertion that an estate was planted and cultivated in the first quarter of the fourth century with so much care that its value doubled. Attic land-leases of the classical period tend to be concerned to maintain the value of property. Post-classical Greek land-leases may impose on the lessee the obligation to improve the land: such stipulations include constructing buildings, bringing additional land into cultivation, and increasing the number of trees and vines (Pleket, no. 43, cult of Heros Iatros [Athens, 333/2]).[322] Sartori contrasts Roman leases where the lessee is obliged to prevent the land from deteriorating.[323]

27. φιλογέωργον. Socrates humorously intimates that Ischomachus' father and grain-merchants alike are actually motivated by love of profit. On the malicious implications of this remark see on vi. 17 Ἰσχόμαχον and xx. 27 ἔμποροι. In Xen. *Symp.* 8. 25. Socrates suggests that a landowner behaves like a lover who treats his beloved properly. Rather than seeking to exploit the land quickly, he improves it and enjoys a long-term relationship with it.

ἔμποροι. Despite the efforts of farmers such as Ischomachus, domestic grain production in Athens did not suffice to feed the population (see on xi. 12 ἐσθίειν).[324] On agriculture in Attica see

---

[321] However, M. I. Finley, *Studies in Land and Credit in Ancient Athens, 500-200 B.C.*, 270 n. 46, argues that Ischomachus describes his father's real-estate transactions because of their rarity. Consequently, the story should be read as a moralistic tale, rather than used as evidence of widespread land-speculation in the 4th c. This interpretation is consistent with Finley's often-expressed opinion that the Greeks were mere novices in the economic sphere (see Ch. 5, sect. A).

[322] H. W. Pleket, *Texts on the Economic History of the Ancient World* (Textus Minores, 31 = Epigraphica, 1: Leiden, 1964), 63. See Osborne, *Classical Landscape*, 42–3.

[323] *Archäologische Forschungen in Lukanien*, ii. 74.

[324] Recent estimates of the amount of grain produced annually in Athens and the amount that had to be imported differ. For a large amount of imported grain see Signe Isager and Mogens Herman Hansen, *Aspects of Athenian Society in the Fourth Century B.C.* (Odense, 1975), esp. 19. In contrast, Peter Garnsey, 'Grain for Athens',

Ch. 5. Neighbouring states produced only enough for home consumption; imports came by sea from Egypt, Sicily, the eastern Mediterranean, and the Black Sea region.[325]

Because Athens could not produce enough grain to feed its entire population it had to encourage both Athenian and foreign traders to deliver grain to the Piraeus. Traders, of course, were motivated by profit, for, like Ischomachus' father, they loved money. Those who were engaged in land improvement, like merchants in the grain-trade, were involved in ventures running high risk from natural elements, but promising large profits. In the classical period the ἔμποροι were professionals.[326] Yet, according to the prevailing ethical code, the Athenian gentleman (καλὸς κἀγαθός) was supposed to disdain overtly commercial activities and not engage in professions that had money-making as their sole goal. Consequently, the comparison of Ischomachus' father to traders is uncomplimentary. That a wealthy man was influenced only by the law of supply and demand and a quest for profit without concern for the benefit of his fellow citizens would have appeared objectionable.[327] Implied in the denigrating comparison with grain-merchants is a distinction between citizens and metics. Farming was the appropriate pursuit for an Athenian gentleman. Ownership of land in Attica was restricted to citizens. However, commercial ventures including the grain trade were open to metics (Pl. *Laws* 952 E).[328] At Athens grain-dealers were subject to laws designed to prevent the establishment of a monopoly or manipulation of the market which might increase prices, but attempts to circumvent the laws are recorded. (On the control of the grain-market see Demos. 34. 37, 35. 50, 56. 6. 11; Lyc. 26–7; Lys. 22; Arist. *Ath. Pol.* 51.) Non-Athenian dealers, such as Phoenicians, however, were free to make the greatest possible profit. In *Mem.* 3. 7. 6, Xenophon classifies ἔμποροι with workmen such as fullers,

in P. A. Cartledge and F. D. Harvey (eds.), *Crux* (London, 1985), 62–75, and *Famine and Food Supply in the Graeco-Roman World*, 123, 132–49, argues that Athens was less dependent on grain imports than had formerly been supposed, e.g. by Louis Gernet, *L'Approvisionnement d'Athènes en blé au Vᵉ et au IVᵉ siècle* (Paris, 1909), 301. Garnsey agrees that dependency increased in the 4th c.

[325] e.g. Xen. *Hell.* 5. 1. 28–9, Demos. 18. 241, 248; 32, Arist. *Rhet.* 1411ᶜ9–11, and see J. G. Milne, 'Trade between Greece and Egypt before Alexander the Great', *JEA* 25 (1939), 177–8, 181–3.

[326] See Julie Vélissaropoulos, *Les Nauclères grecs* (Geneva, 1980), 36–7.

[327] See further K. J. Dover, *Greek Popular Morality in the Time of Plato and Aristotle*, 171–4, and Hugo Montgomery, '"Merchants Fond of Corn": Citizens and Foreigners in the Athenian Grain Trade', *SO* 61 (1986), 43–61.

[328] Gernet, *L'Approvisionnement d'Athènes en blé*, 328.

shoemakers, carpenters, smiths, and farmers who come to the agora for no reason other than to buy cheap and sell at a profit. In contrast to his father's activities, Ischomachus' quest for gain was laudable, because he shared his resources with his friends and city (see on xi. 9 θεοὺς ... φίλους ... πόλιν).

σῖτον. σῖτος is a general term for grain. Barley was easier to grow in Attica (Theophr. *HP* 8. 8. 2) but Athenian taste preferred wheat; moreover, wheat was less bulky than barley, and thus transport-costs were relatively less. Therefore wheat was the principal grain import (see on ix. 3 τὸν σῖτον).

πλέουσιν. The sailing period was limited to spring till early autumn (thus Hes., *WD* 619–45, 663–84).

28. Σικελικὸν πόντον. Strabo 2. 5. 20 (123 C) applies this name to the sea which stretches from Sicily to the Peloponnese (now called the 'Ionian'), and extends to the southern parts of Epirus, the mouth of the Ionian gulf, and the cliffs of Crete.

ἀργυρίου. The risks of the grain trade, from adverse weather and seizure by pirates or by hostile forces, coupled with the capital outlay and costs of transport meant that a substantial profit was necessary to induce men to practise it (Ps.-Dem. 34. 36–7, 56. 9–10). Such risks are alluded to in the excursus on the Phoenician cargo ship (viii. 12–16). The terms of Greek bottomry loans, which provided a kind of insurance, are an index of the risk. Loans at the rate of almost 20 to 30 per cent are mentioned in the literature, and these are just for the few months when they would be in effect: per annum the rates are much higher.[329]

xxi. 1. ὅλον τόν λόγον. Socrates indicates that the dialogue is coming to an end.

3. δέῃ περᾶν ἡμερινοὺς πλοῦς. This phrase belies the cliché that Greek sailors avoided the open sea and hugged the coast, always keeping land in sight. Unlike a cargo-ship, which carried supplies for many days, a trireme would usually sail for twelve hours at most, then land in order to give the rowers an opportunity to rest, to obtain water, and to cook their food (Thuc. 1. 48. 1, 3. 49. 3, 4. 30. 2, Xen. *Hell.* 6. 2. 28, Ps.-Demos. 50. 47). Here the slow crew takes twice the time to do one day's journey. So they row twenty-four hours, presumably through the night and without

---

[329] Xen. *Revenues* 3. 9, Ps.-Dem. 34. 6, 23, 35. 10–13, and see further G. E. M. de Ste. Croix, 'Ancient Greek and Roman Maritime Loans', in H. Edey and B. S. Yamey (eds.), *Debits, Credits, Finance, and Profits: Essays in Honour of H. T. Baxter* (London, 1974), 41–59.

fresh food and water. Weariness, thirst, and hunger contribute to the men's dislike of their commander. Sometimes, of course, because of the conditions of war the men were obliged to spend any number of consecutive days on board (see Thuc. 6. 34. 4, Ar. *Ach.* 548–50 with schol., Xen. *Hell.* 3. 4. 3, Ps.-Xen. *Const. of Ath.* 2. 4–5, Plut. *de glor. Ath.* 6 = *Mor.* 349 A, and on viii. 8 τριήρης and 11 τὸ μέγα πλοῖον τὸ Φοινικικόν).

κελευστῶν. The κελευστής, or boatswain, exercised authority over the rowers and was responsible for their performance. He passed the orders of the helmsman to the men and by shouting or tapping established a rhythm for their strokes (Xen. *Hell.* 5. 1. 8–9, Ar. *Frogs* 180, 207, 269, 1073, *Suda*, s.v. κελευστής). Thuc. 2. 84. 3 describes how chaos ensued when rowers could not hear their κελευστής.

ἀκονᾶν. Sim. Xen. *Cyrop.* 6. 2. 33 τήν ψυχήν τι παρακονᾳ.

8. χειρὶ ... χεῖρες. There is a play on the word χείρ: the first use means 'band', the second 'hands'. Xenophon alludes to a cliché. χείρ for 'band of fighting men' is also common in Herodotus (2. 137, 7. 20, 157, etc.), found once in Thucydides (3. 96. 3, cf. 2. 77. 3), and only here in Xenophon.

10. κινηθῶσι. Similarly Xerxes' men perform more effectively in his presence (Herod. 8. 69. 2, 86).

μένος. Menos is principally a poetic word, used frequently in Homer, but it does appear elsewhere in classical prose (see LSJ, s.v.). Xenophon uses it of dogs (*On Hunting* 6. 15) as well as people (e.g. *Cyrop.* 3. 3. 61, *Hell.* 7. 1. 31).

11. παιδείας. In contrast to farming, the art of governing is difficult to learn. Moreover, innate aptitude is a prerequisite.

θεῖον. The juxtaposition of θεῖος with ἀνήρ was not uncommon in Greek literature.[330] Significant in this context, however, are the previous occurrences of the two words in Pi. *Ol.* 1. 64, and Eur. *Or.* 8, in reference to Tantalus (see below on xxi. 12 τυραννεῖν ... Τάνταλος ... φοβούμενος).

12. τὸ ἐθελόντων ἄρχειν. The younger Cyrus (iv. 18–19) and Ischomachus' wife (vii. 37) both ruled over willing subjects, and Ischomachus endeavoured to instil good will in his subordinates (xii. 5–6). In the *Cyropaedia*, Xenophon shows how an absolute

---

[330] For examples and discussion see D. Fehling, *Die Wiederholungsfiguren und ihr Gebrauch bei den Griechen vor Gorgias* (Berlin, 1969), 280–5, N. J. Richardson, *The Homeric Hymn to Demeter* (Oxford, 1974), 186, and L. Gernet, *Anthropologie de la Grèce antique*, 421, 428.

monarch may reign beneficently over willing subjects. In *Hiero* he describes the rule of a tyrant over an unwilling populace.

σωφροσύνῃ τετελεσμένοις. σωφροσύνη, or self-control, is essential for those who rule over others (see on vii. 15). In contrast, the following sentence mentions tyrants and Tantalus, who were notorious for the lack of this virtue and/or the greed that resulted.

τυραννεῖν ... Τάνταλος ... φοβούμενος. Tantalus is mentioned in Hom. *Od.* 11. 582–92, but his crime is not indicated. Later sources state that he served the gods the flesh of his son Pelops. He experienced a major change in fortune: from friendship with the gods to punishment in the underworld.

According to Homer, the punishment of Tantalus consisted of eternal hunger and thirst as water and food continually receded from his grasp. Later, the majority of Greek sources show him condemned to lie under a stone or a mountain that continuously threatened to fall on him (*Nostoi*, fr. 9 Davies; Arch. fr. 91. 14–15 West; Alcman fr. 79, Alcaeus fr. 365 L–P; Pi. *Ol.* 1. 8. 9–11, 54–64; Schol. *Ol.* 1. 91a = i. 37–8 Drachmann; Pi. *Isth.* 8. 10–11; Eur. *Or.* 6–8; Schol. Eur. *Or.* 982). The Homeric punishment is combined with the overhanging stone in Apollodorus, *Epit.* 2. 1, and Pausanias 10. 31. 12.[331] The sources agree that his crime was abusing privileges granted by the gods and that his punishment was eternal fear.

The legendary wrongdoer is an appropriate analogue to a bad tyrant of archaic or classical Greece. The wealth of Tantalus (like that of Greek tyrants) was fabulous (cf. Pi. *Ol.* 1. 56 μέγαν ὄλβον). This wealth was god-given, like the gift of ruling over willing subjects, mentioned in xxi. 12. Like Tantalus, the tyrant is the agent of his own downfall. Both lived in eternal fear: Tantalus afraid of being crushed by a stone poised overhead, the tyrant afraid of death at the hands of his unwilling subjects.

Pindar had also paired Tantalus with a 'good' tyrant (Hiero) in *Ol.* 1. The divinity of the good ruler is mentioned in xxi. 11. Pelops was banished from Olympus, and his son Tantalus was immortal but not blessed. In contrast, as Pindar often proclaims, the good tyrant can attain the status of a hero. For example, Hiero was given the honours accorded to heroes at Catana (Diod. Sic. 11. 66. 4, 11. 38. 5). In *Oec.* xxi. 11, the ability to rule with justice renders human beings divine. The Persian

---

[331] For additional sources, especially in the visual arts, see Christiane Sourvinou-Inwood, 'Crime and Punishment: Tityus, Tantalos and Sisyphus in *Odyssey* 11', *BICS* 33 (1986), 40 nn. 19, 21.

king was close to the gods (see on iv. 5 γεωργίας and iv. 21 ἴσου
... ὀρθοὶ ... εὐγώνια). Ischomachus' wife is also close to the divine:
as queen bee she executes obligations assigned by a god (see
on vii. 32).

In the context of *Oec.* xxi, lack of food and water would be an
appropriate punishment for a man in a position of authority and
good fortune who mismanaged his estate, and lived in fear of his
slaves. Those who lack σωφροσύνη can never quench their appetites
(see on ii. 2–4, vii. 6 τά ... γαστέρα). Having enough to eat is a
reward for virtue (see on xx. 4 οὐδὲ οἶνον ἔχει). Furthermore, the
theme that it is impossible to escape punishment from the gods is
repeated throughout the *Oeconomicus*.

δὶς ἀποθάνῃ. Because Tantalus was already in the Underworld,
the stone's blow would be the equivalent of a second death. In
Luc. *Dial. Mort.* 7. 2, the dead Tantalus is accused of being afraid
of dying from thirst. For other denizens of Hell see vii. 40.

The tone of this last speech of Ischomachus is unexpectedly
lofty. Thus the *Oeconomicus* ends like a sermon, with a vivid picture
of the fate awaiting those who ignore its teachings.

BIBLIOGRAPHY

With a few obvious exceptions, journal titles are abbreviated according to the form in *L'Année philologique*. Accepted abbreviations will be used for standard works. Lists of such abbreviations may be found in reference books such as the *Oxford Classical Dictionary*, 2nd edn., and in the major Greek and Latin dictionaries. Where necessary, specific editions of Greek and Latin works are cited within the text.

ADCOCK, F. E., *The Greek and Macedonian Art of War* (Berkeley and Los Angeles, 1957).

ALFONSI, LUIGI, 'La traduzione ciceroniana dell'Economico di Senofonte', *Ciceroniana*, 3–6 (1961–4), 7–17.

AMPOLO, C., 'Οἰκονομία. Tre osservazioni sui rapporti tra la finanza e l'economia greca', *AIΩN (archeol.)*, 1 (1979), 119–30.

AMUNDSEN, D. W., and DIERS, C. J., 'The Age of Menarche in Classical Greece and Rome', *Human Biology*, 41 (1969), 125–32.

AMYX, D. A., 'The Attic Stelai; Part III', *Hesperia*, 27 (1958), 163–310.

ANDERSON, J. K., *Ancient Greek Horsemanship* (Berkeley and Los Angeles, 1961).

—— *Hunting in the Ancient World* (Berkeley, Los Angeles, and London, 1985).

—— *Xenophon* (London and New York, 1974).

ARNIM, H. VON, *Xenophons Memorabilien und Apologie des Sokrates* (Copenhagen, 1923).

ASCHAM, R., *A Report and Discourse of the affaires and state of Germany* (London, c.1570).

—— *The Scholemaster*, 2 (1570; repr. Menston, 1967).

—— *Toxophilus* (1545; repr. Menston, 1971).

ASCHENBRENNER, STANLEY, *Life in a Changing Greek Village: Karpofora and its Reluctant Farmers* (University of Minnesota Publications in Ancient Studies, 2; Dubuque, Iowa, 1986).

AYLMER, J., *An Harborowe for Faithfull and Trewe Subjectes* ('Strasborowe' [London], 1559, repr. The English Experience, 423; Amsterdam, 1972).

AYMARD, ANDRÉ, *Études d'histoire ancienne* (Paris, 1967).

BALDWIN, T. W., *William Shakespere's small Latine & lesse Greeke* (Urbana, Ill., 1944).

BARBARO, FRANCESCO, *De re uxoria*, trans. Benjamin G. Kohl, in Benjamin G. Kohl and Ronald G. Witt (eds.), *The Earthly Republic: Italian Humanists on Society and Government* (Philadelphia, 1978), 179–228.

BAUMANN, HELLMUT, *Die griechische Pflanzenwelt* (Munich, 1982).

BEAUVOIR, SIMONE DE, *Le Deuxième Sexe* (Paris, 1949).

Benaki Museum Photographic Archive, Παραδοσιακὲς καλλιέργειες (Athens, 1978).

BENNETT, H. S., *English Books and Readers* 1475 to 1557 (Cambridge, 1952).

BERGQUIST, BIRGITTA, 'Sympotic Space: A Functional Aspect of Greek Dining-Rooms', in Oswyn Murray (ed.), *Sympotica* (Oxford, 1990), 37–65.

BICKNELL, P. J., 'Axiochos Alkibiadou, Aspasia and Aspasios', *AC* 51 (1982), 240–50.

—— *Studies in Athenian Politics and Genealogy* (Historia Einzelschrift 19; Wiesbaden, 1972).

BILLIGMEIER, JON-CHRISTIAN, 'Studies on the Family in the Aegean Bronze Age and in Homer', *Trends in History*, 3, 3/4 (1985), 9–18.

BINTLIFF, J. L., and SNODGRASS, A. M., 'The Cambridge/Bradford Boeotian Expedition: The First Four Years', *JFA* 12 (1985), 123–61.

BLOOM, ALLAN, *The Republic of Plato* (New York, 1968).

BOLKESTEIN, H., *Economic Life in Greece's Golden Age* (1923), rev. E. J. Jonkers (Leiden, 1958).

BOSANQUET, EUSTACE F., 'Three Little Tudor Books', *Transactions of the Bibliographical Society*, 2nd ser., 14 = *The Library*, 4th ser., 14 (1934), 178–92.

BOURDIEU, P., 'The Berber House', in M. Douglass (ed.), *Rules and Meanings* (Harmondsworth, 1977), 98–110.

BRADFORD, JOHN, *Ancient Landscapes: Studies in Field Archaeology* (London, 1957).

BRADLEY, R. (trans.), *The Science of Good Husbandry: or, The Oeconomics of Xenophon* (London, 1727).

BRADNER, L., 'The Xenophon Translation Attributed to Queen Elizabeth I', *JWI* 7 (1964), 324–6.

BREITENBACH, HANS RUDOLF, *Xenophon von Athen* (Stuttgart, 1966) = *RE*², ixA2 (Stuttgart, 1967), cols. 1567–2052.

BREITENBACH, L. (ed.), *Xenophontis Oeconomicus* (Gotha, 1842).

BREMMER, JAN N., 'The Old Women of Ancient Greece', in Josine

Blok and Peter Mason (eds.), *Sexual Asymmetry* (Amsterdam, 1987), 191–215.

BRIANT, PIERRE, 'Appareils d'État et développement des forces productives au Moyen-Orient ancien: le cas de l'Empire achéménide', *La Pensée*, 217 (1981), 9–23, repr. in *Rois, tributs et paysans*, 475–90.

—— 'Contrainte militaire, dépendance rurale et exploitation des territoires en Asie achéménide', *Index*, 8 (1978–9), 48–98, repr. in *Rois, tributs et paysans*, 175–226.

—— *État et Pasteurs au Moyen-Orient ancien* (Cambridge, 1982).

—— 'Forces productives, dépendance rurale et idéologies religieuses dans l'Empire achéménide', *Table ronde de Besançon, 1977* (Paris, 1980), 16–67, repr. in *Rois, tributs et paysans*, 431–74.

—— *Rois, tributs et paysans: Études sur les formations tributaires du Moyen-Orient ancien* (Centre de Rec. d'Hist. anc. 43; Annales littéraires de l'Université de Besançon, 269; Paris, 1982).

—— 'Sources grecques et histoire achéménide', in *Rois, tributs et paysans*, 491–538.

BROWNE, Sir THOMAS, *The Garden of Cyrus* (1658); repr. *Urne Buriall and The Garden of Cyrus*, ed. John Carter (Cambridge, 1967).

BRUCKER, JACOB, *Historia Critica Philosophiae*, 2nd edn. (Leipzig, 1767).

BRUNO, VINCENT J., *Form and Color in Greek Painting* (New York and London, 1977).

BRYANT, A. A., 'Greek Shoes in the Classical Period', *HSCPh* 10 (1899), 57–102.

BUCK, C. D., 'Is the Suffix of βασίλισσα, etc., of Macedonian Origin?', *CP* 9 (1914), 370–3.

—— and PETERSON, WALTER, *A Reverse Index of Greek Nouns and Adjectives* (Chicago, 1944).

BUGH, G. R., *The Horsemen of Athens* (Princeton, NJ, 1988).

BURKE, PETER, 'A Survey of the Popularity of Ancient Historians, 1450–1700', *History and Theory*, 5 (1966), 135–52.

BURNET, J., *Greek Philosophy: Thales to Plato* (1914; repr. London, 1953).

—— *Plato's Euthyphro, Apology of Socrates, and Crito* (1924; repr. Oxford, 1960).

BUTLER, CHARLES, *The feminine Monarchie, or a Treatise concerning Bees and the due Ordering of Bees* (Oxford, 1609).

CALAME, CLAUDE, *Les Chœurs de jeunes filles en Grèce archaïque* (Rome, 1977).

Cambridge History of Iran, ii, ed. Ilya Gershevitch (Cambridge, 1985).

CARLIER, PIERRE, 'La femme dans la société mycénienne d'après les archives en linéaire B', in E. Lévy (ed.), *La femme dans les sociétés antiques: Actes des colloques de Strasbourg (mai 1980 et mars 1981)* (Strasburg, 1983), 9–32.

CARTLEDGE, P. A., 'Literacy in the Spartan Oligarchy', *JHS* 98 (1978), 25–37.

—— 'The Politics of Spartan Pederasty', *PCPhS*, ns 27 (1981), 17–36.

—— and HARVEY, F. D. (eds.), *Crux: Essays Presented to G. E. M. de Ste. Croix on his 75th Birthday* = *HPTh* 6 (London, 1985).

CASSON, LIONEL, *Ships and Seamanship in the Ancient World* (Princeton, NJ, 1971).

CASTER, MARCEL, 'Sur l'*Économique* de Xénophon', in *Mélanges offerts à A.-M. Desrousseaux* (Paris, 1937), 49–57.

CASTIGLIONI, L., review of *Xenophon: Économique*, ed. and trans. Pierre Chantraine, *Gnomon*, 21 (1949), 339–42.

—— 'Studi senofontei IV: Intorno all'Economico', *Riv. di Fil.* 48 (1920), 321–42.

CATLING, H. W., 'Archaeology in Greece, 1988–89', *AR* 35 (1989), 3–116.

CAWKWELL, G. L., 'ΝΟΜΟΦΥΛΑΚΙΑ and the Areopagus', *JHS* 108 (1988), 1–12.

CHANTRAINE, P., *Xénophon: Économique* (Paris, 1949).

CHARLTON, KENNETH, *Education in Renaissance England* (London, 1965).

CHAUMONT, M. L., 'Chiliarque et curopalate à la cour des Sassanides', *IA* 10 (1973), 139–65.

CHAYANOV, A. V., 'On the Theory of Non-Capitalist Economic Systems', trans., C. Lane in D. Thorner, B. Kerblay, and R. E. F. Smith (eds.), *The Theory of Peasant Economy* (Homewood, Ill., 1966), 1–28. Originally published as 'Zur Frage einer Theorie der nicht-kapitalistischen Wirtschaftssysteme', *Archiv für Wissenschaft und Sozialpolitik*, 51 (1924), 377–613.

CHERICI, ARMANDO, 'Granai o arnie? Considerazioni su una classe fittile attica tra IX e VIII sec. a.C.', *RAL* 44 (1989), 215–30.

CHROUST, ANTON-HERMANN, *Socrates, Man and Myth: The Two Socratic Apologies of Xenophon* (London, 1957).

CLAIRMONT, C. W., *Gravestone and Epigram: Greek Memorials from the Archaic and Classical Period* (Mainz, 1970).

CLARK, DONALD, L., *Rhetoric in Greco-Roman Education* (New York, 1957).

CLARK, PETER, 'The Ownership of Books in England, 1560–1640: The Example of Some Kentish Townsfolk', in Lawrence Stone (ed.), *Schooling and Society* (Baltimore and London, 1976), 95–111.

Bibliography

CLEMEN, C., *Fontes Historiae Religionis Persicae* (Bonn, 1920).

CLOCHÉ P., *La Restauration démocratique à Athènes en 403 avant J.-C.* (Paris, 1915).

COHEN, DAVID, *Theft in Athenian Law* (Münchener Beiträge zur Papyrusforschung und antiken Rechtsgeschichte, 74; Munich, 1983).

COLLON, DOMINIQUE, *First Impressions: Cylinder Seals in the Ancient Near East* (London, 1987).

COOK, ARTHUR, B., 'The Bee in Greek Mythology', *JHS* 15 (1985), 1–24.

COOK, J. M., 'The Rise of the Achaemenids and the Establishment of their Empire', in *The Cambridge History of Iran*, ii, 200–91.

COUSIN, GEORGES, *Kyros le jeune en Asie mineure* (Paris and Nancy, 1905).

CRANE, E., and GRAHAM, A. J., 'Beehives of the Ancient World', *Bee World*, 66 (1985), 23–41, 148–70.

CRESSY, DAVID, *Literacy and the Social Order* (Cambridge, 1980).

CROISET, A., and CROISET, M., *Histoire de la littérature grecque*, 5 vols. (Paris, 1887–99).

CRÖNERT, WILHELM, 'Litterarische Texte mit Ausschluß der christlichen', *Archiv für Papyrusforschung*, 1 (1901), 502–39.

DALL, CAROLINE, H., *The College, the Market, and the Court; or Woman's Relation to Education, Labor, and Law* (1867; repr. New York, 1972).

DANDAMAEV, MUHAMMAD A., and LUKONIN, VLADIMIR G., *The Culture and Social Institutions of Ancient Iran* (Cambridge, 1989).

DAVENPORT, GUY, *The Geography of the Imagination* (San Francisco, 1981).

DAVID, EPHRAIM, *Aristophanes and Athenian Society of the Early Fourth Century B.C.* (Leiden, 1984).

DAVIES, J. K., *Athenian Propertied Families* (Oxford, 1971).

——'Demosthenes on Liturgies: A Note', *JHS* 87 (1967), 33–40.

——*Wealth and the Power of Wealth in Classical Athens* (Salem, NH, 1984).

DAVIES, MALCOLM, and KATHIRITHAMBY, JEYARANEY, *Greek Insects* (London, 1986).

DELEBECQUE, ÉDOUARD, *Essai sur la vie de Xénophon* (Paris, 1957).

——'Sur la date et l'objet de l'*Économique*', *REG* 64 (1951), 21–58.

DENNISTON, J. D., *The Greek Particles*, rev. edn. (Oxford, 1954).

——*Greek Prose Style* (Oxford, 1952).

DINSMOOR, W. B., *The Architecture of Ancient Greece*, 3rd edn. (New York, 1950).

DITTMAR, H., *Aischines von Sphettos: Studien zur Literaturgeschichte der Sokratiker* (Berlin, 1912).

DIXON, SUZANNE, *The Roman Mother* (Norman, Okla., and London, 1988).

DOVER, K. J., *Greek Homosexuality* (London, 1978).

——*Greek Popular Morality in the Time of Plato and Aristotle* (Oxford, 1974).

DREWS, ROBERT, 'Sargon, Cyrus and Mesopotamian Folk History', *JNES* 33 (1974), 387–93.

DU BOULAY, JULIET, *Portrait of a Greek Mountain Village* (Oxford, 1974).

EHLERS, BARBARA, *Eine vorplatonische Deutung des sokratischen Eros: Der Dialog Aspasia des Sokratikers Aeschines* (Zetemata, 41; Munich, 1966).

EHRENBERG, VICTOR, *The People of Aristophanes*, 2nd edn. (1951; pb. repr. New York, 1962).

EHTÉCHAM, MORTÉZA, *L'Iran sous les Achéménides* (Fribourg, 1946).

EICHLER, GUSTAV, *Die Redebilder in den Schriften Xenophons* (Dresden, 1894).

ESPINAS, A., *Histoire des doctrines économiques* (Paris, 1891).

FALLERS, LLOYD A., and FALLERS, MARGARET C., 'Sex Roles in Edremit', in J. G. Peristiany (ed.), *Honour and Shame: The Values of Mediterranean Society* (Chicago, 1966), 243–60.

FAUTH, WOLFGANG, 'Der königliche Gärtner und Jäger im Paradeisos: Beobachtungen zur Rolle des Herrschers in der vorderasiatischen Hortikultur', *Persica*, 8 (1979), 1–53.

FEHLING, D., *Die Wiederholungsfiguren und ihr Gebrauch bei den Griechen vor Gorgias* (Berlin, 1969).

FINLEY, M. I., *The Ancient Economy*, 2nd edn. (Berkeley and Los Angeles, 1985).

——'Aristotle and Economic Analysis', *Past and Present*, 47 (1970), 3–25.

——'Land, Debt, and the Man of Property in Classical Athens', *Political Science Quarterly*, 68 (1953), 249–68.

——Review of *Xenophon: Économique*, ed. and trans., Pierre Chantraine, *CP* 46 (1951), 252–3.

——*Studies in Land and Credit in Ancient Athens, 500–200 B.C.* (New Brunswick, NJ, 1952).

——'The Study of the Ancient Economy: Further Thoughts', *Opus* 3 (1984), 4–11.

——'Was Greek Civilization Based on Slave Labour?' *Historia*, 8 (1959), 145–64, repr. in id. (ed.), *Slavery in Classical Antiquity* (Cambridge, 1960), 33–72.

——(ed.), *Problèmes de la terre en Grèce ancienne* (The Hague, 1973).

Bibliography

FIRESTONE, SHULAMITH, *The Dialectic of Sex* (New York, 1970).

FITZ, LINDA T., *see* Woodbridge, Linda T.

FORBES, CLARENCE A., 'The Education and Training of Slaves in Antiquity', *TAPhA* 86 (1955), 321–60.

FORBES, HAMISH A., 'The "Thrice-Ploughed Field": Cultivation Techniques in Ancient and Modern Greece', *Expedition*, 19 1 (1976), 5–11.

——'"We Have a Little of Everything": The Ecological Basis of Some Agricultural Practices in Methana, Trizinia', in Muriel Dimen and Ernestine Friedl (eds.), *Regional Variation in Modern Greece and Cyprus* (Annals of the New York Academy of Sciences, 268; New York, 1976), 236–50.

FORBES, R. J., *Studies in Ancient Technology*, i–iii (Leiden, 1955–72), iv–ix, 2nd edn. (Leiden, 1964–72).

FOXHALL, LIN, 'Household, Gender, and Property in Classical Athens', *CQ*, ns 39 (1989), 22–44.

—— and FORBES, H. A., '$\Sigma\iota\tau o\mu\epsilon\tau\rho\epsilon\iota\alpha$: The Role of Grain as a Staple Food in Classical Antiquity', *Chiron*, 12 (1982), 41–90.

FRANKE, P. R., and HIRMER, M., *Die griechische Münze* (Munich, 1964).

FRANKLIN, BENJAMIN, *The Papers of Benjamin Franklin*, ed. W. B. Willcox, xxiii (New Haven and London, 1983).

FRARINUS, PETRUS = Peter Frarin, *An Oration against the Unlawfull Insurrection of Protestantes of Our Time*, tr. J. Fowler (Antwerp, 1566; repr. Ilkley, 1975).

FRASER, H. MALCOLM, *Beekeeping in Antiquity*, 2nd edn. (London, 1951).

FRASER, P. M., and BEAN, G. E., *The Rhodian Peraea and Islands* (London, 1954).

FRAZER, J. G., *Pausanias's Description of Greece* 6 vols. (London, 1898).

FRIEDAN, BETTY, *The Feminine Mystique* (New York, 1963).

FRISK, H., *Griechisches Etymologisches Wörterbuch* (Heidelberg, 1960).

FRYE, RICHARD N., *The History of Ancient Iran* (Handbuch der Altertumswissenschaft, iii. 7; Munich, 1983).

GABRIELSEN, VINCENT, 'The Antidosis Procedure in Classical Athens', *C&M* 38 (1987), 7–38.

GALLANT, T. W., *A Fisherman's Tale* (Miscellanea Graeca, 7; Ghent, 1985).

——*Risk and Survival in Ancient Greece* (Stanford, 1991).

GALLO, LUIGI, 'Popolosità e scarsità di popolazione: Contributo allo studio di un *topos*', *ASNP*, 3rd ser., 10 (1980), 1233–70.

GARBARINO, G., *M. Tulli Ciceronis Fragmenta ex libris philosophicis, ex aliis libris deperditis, ex scriptis incertis* (Florence, 1984).

Bibliography

GARNSEY, PETER, *Famine and Food Supply in the Graeco-Roman World* (Cambridge, 1988).

—— 'Grain for Athens', in P. A. Cartledge and F. D. Harvey (eds.), *Crux*, 62–75.

GAUTHIER, PHILIPPE, *Un Commentaire historique des Poroi de Xénophon* (Paris, 1976).

GAUTIER, L., *La Langue de Xénophon* (Geneva, 1911).

GERNET, L., *Anthropologie de la Grèce antique* (Paris, 1968).

—— *L'Approvisionnement d'Athènes en blé au Ve et au IVe siècle* (Paris, 1909).

—— 'Note sur la notion de délit privé en droit grec', in *Droits de l'antiquité et sociologie juridique. Mélanges H. Lévy-Bruhl* (Publications Inst. de Droit rom. de l'Université de Paris, 17; Paris, 1959), 393–405.

GIANNANTONI, G., *Socraticorum reliquiae*, 4 vols. (Naples, 1983–5).

GIGANTE, MARCELLO, *Ricerche filodemee*, 2nd edn. (Bibl. della *Parola del Passato*, 6; Naples, 1983).

GIGON, OLAF, *Kommentar zum ersten Buch von Xenophons Memorabilien* (Schweizerische Beiträge zur Altertumswissenschaft, 5; Basle, 1953).

—— *Sokrates: Sein Bild in Dichtung und Geschichte* (Berne, 1947).

GIL, J., *Jenofonte: Económico* (Madrid, 1966).

GILLIGAN, CAROL, *In A Different Voice* (Cambridge, Mass. and London, 1982).

GLOTZ, GUSTAVE, *Le Travail dans la Grèce ancienne* (Paris, 1920).

GOMME, A. W., ANDREWES, A., and DOVER, K. J., *A Historical Commentary on Thucydides*, 5 vols. (Oxford, 1945–1981).

GOMME, A. W., *The Population of Athens in the Fifth and Fourth Centuries B.C.* (Oxford, 1933).

GOTHEIN, MARIE LUISE, *A History of Garden Art*, trans., [Laura] Archer-Hind (1928, repr. New York, 1979), originally published as *Geschichte der Gartenkunst* (Jena, 1914).

GOTHEIN, PERCY, *Das Buch von der Ehe* (Berlin, 1933).

GOW, A. S. F., *Theocritus*, 2 vols. (Cambridge, 1952).

GRACE, E., 'Athenian Views on What is a Slave and How to Manage People', *VDI* 111 (1970), 49–66.

GRAHAM, J. WALTER, 'Olynthiaka', *Hesperia*, 22 (1953), 196–207.

GRILLET, BERNARD, *Les Femmes et les fards dans l'antiquité grecque* (Lyon, 1975).

GRONINGEN, B. A. VAN, and WARTELLE, ANDRÉ, *Aristote: Économique* (Paris, 1968).

GUIRAUD, P., *La Propriété foncière en Grèce jusqu'à la conquête romaine* (Paris, 1900).

Bibliography

GUTHRIE, W. K. C., *A History of Greek Philosophy*, 6 vols. (Cambridge, 1962–81).

HALLOCK, R. T., 'The Evidence of the Persepolis Tablets', in *The Cambridge History of Iran*, ii. 588–609.

HALSTEAD, P., and JONES, G., 'Agrarian Ecology in the Greek Islands: Time, Stress, Scale and Risk', *JHS* 109 (1989), 41–55.

HALTINNER, D. O., and SCHMOLL, E. A., 'The Older Manuscripts of Xenophon's *Hiero*', *RHT* 10 (1980), 231–6.

HANSEN, MOGENS HERMAN, *Demography and Democracy: The Number of Citizens in Fourth Century Athens* (Herning, 1985).

HANSEN, OVE, 'The Purported Letter of Darius to Gadates', *RhM* 129 (1986), 95–6.

HANSON, VICTOR DAVIS, *Warfare and Agriculture in Classical Greece*, (Biblioteca di Studi Antichi, 40; Pisa, 1983).

HARDY, W. G., 'The *Hellenica Oxyrhynchia* and the Devastation of Attica', *CP* 21 (1926), 346–55.

HARRIS, W. V., *Ancient Literacy* (Cambridge, Mass., 1989).

HARRISON, A. R. W., *The Law of Athens*, 2 vols. (Oxford, 1968, 1971).

HARRISON, JANE E., 'Mystica Vannus Iacchi', *JHS* 23 (1903), 302–3, 24 (1904), 246–9.

HARVEY, F. D., 'The Wicked Wife of Ischomachos', *EMC* 28 NS 3 (1984), 68–70.

HAYDEN, DOLORES, *The Grand Domestic Revolution* (Cambridge, Mass, and London 1981).

HEICHELHEIM, FRITZ M., *An Ancient Economic History*, trans. J. Stevens, 3 vols. (Leiden, 1958–70).

—— 'Σῖτος', *RE*, suppl. vi (Stuttgart, 1935), cols. 819–92.

HEINIMANN, F., *Nomos und Physis* (Schweizerische Beiträge zur Altertumswissenschaft, 1; Basle, 1965).

HENDERSON, KATHERINE USHER, and MCMANUS, BARBARA, *Half Humankind: Contexts and Texts of the Controversy about Women in England 1540–1640* (Urbana, Ill., and Chicago, 1985).

HERFST, P., *Le Travail de la femme dans la Grèce ancienne* (Utrecht, 1922).

HERLIHY, DAVID, and KLAPISCH-ZUBER, CHRISTIANE, *Tuscans and their Families*. (New Haven, Conn., 1985), originally published as *Les Toscans et leurs familles* (Paris, 1978).

HERMAN, GABRIEL, *Ritualised Friendship and the Greek City* (Cambridge, 1987).

HERTER, HANS, 'Soziologie der antiken Prostitution im Lichte des heidnischen und christlichen Schriftums', Jahrbuch für Antike und Christentum, 3 (1960), 70–111.

HERVET, GENTIAN, (trans), *Xenophon's Treatise of Householde* (London, 1532).

355

Bibliography

HIRSCH, STEVEN W., *The Friendship of the Barbarians: Xenophon and the Persian Empire* (Hanover, NH, and London, 1985).

—— '1001 Iranian Nights: History and Fiction in Xenophon's *Cyropaedia*', in M. Jameson (ed.), *The Greek Historians, Literature and History: Papers Presented to A. E. Raubitschek* (Stanford, 1985), 65–85.

HIRZ, W., *Altiranisches Sprachgut der Nebenüberlieferungen* (Wiesbaden, 1975).

HIRZEL, R., *Der Dialog* 2 vols. (Leipzig, 1895; repr. Hildesheim, 1963).

HODKINSON, STEPHEN, 'Animal Husbandry in the Greek Polis', in C. R. Whittaker (ed.), *Pastoral Economies in Classical Antiquity*, (Cambridge Philosophical Soc., supplementary vol. 14; Cambridge, 1988), 35–74.

—— 'Land Tenure and Inheritance in Classical Sparta', *CQ* NS 36 (1986), 378–406.

HOEPFNER, WOLFRAM, and SCHWANDNER, ERNST-LUDWIG, *Haus und Stadt im klassischen Griechenland* (Wohnen in der klassischen Polis, 1; Munich, 1986).

HOLDEN, HUBERT A., *The Oeconomicus of Xenophon* (London, 1884).

HOLFORD-STREVENS, LEOFRANC, *Aulus Gellius* (London, 1988).

HOLLAND, L. B., 'Colophon', *Hesperia*, 13 (1944), 91–171.

HUBBELL, SUE, *A Book of Bees* (New York, 1988).

HUDSON-WILLIAMS, T., 'King Bees and Queen Bees', *CR* 49 (1935), 2–4.

HUGHES, DIANE OWEN, 'From Brideprice to Dowry in Mediterranean Europe', *Journal of Family History*, 3 (1978), 262–96, repr. in *The Marriage Bargain: Women and Dowries in European History* = *Women and History*, 10 (1985), 13–58.

HULL, SUZANNE W., *Chaste, Silent and Obedient: English Books for Women* (San Marino, Calif., 1982).

HUME, DAVID, 'Of the Populousness of Ancient Nations' (1742), in *Essays, Moral, Political and Literary* (Oxford, 1963), 381–451.

HUNGER, H., *et al.*, *Geschichte der Textüberlieferung*, 1 (Zurich, 1961).

ISAGER, SIGNE, and HANSEN, MOGENS HERMAN, *Aspects of Athenian Society in the Fourth Century B.C.* (Odense, 1975).

JACKSON, W. A., FERGUSON, F. S., and PANTZER, KATHARINE F., *A Short-Title Catalogue of Books Printed in England, Scotland, and Ireland and of English Books Printed Abroad, 1475–1640*. rev. edn., 3 vols. (Oxford, 1976–91).

JAEGER, WERNER, *Paideia, Die Formung des griechischen Menschen* (Leipzig, 1939), 2nd edn. 1944; trans., Gilbert Highet from the 2nd German edn. as *Paideia: The Ideals of Greek Culture*, iii: *The Conflict of Cultural Ideals in the Age of Plato* (New York, 1944).

JAMESON, M. H., 'Agriculture and Slavery in Classical Athens', *CJ* 73 (1977–8), 122–45.

—— 'Famine in the Greek World', in Peter Garnsey and C. R. Whittaker (eds.), *Trade and Famine in Classical Antiquity* (Cambridge, 1983), 6–16.

—— 'Private Space and the Greek City', in Oswyn Murray and Simon Price (eds.), *The Greek City: From Homer to Alexander* (Oxford, 1990), 171–95.

JARDÉ A., *Les Céréales dans l'Antiquité grecque* (Paris, 1925).

JENSEN, CHR., *Philodemi Περὶ οἰκονομίας* (Leipzig, 1906).

JOËL, K., *Der echte und der Xenophontische Sokrates* (Berlin, 1893–1901).

JONES, A. H. M., *Athenian Democracy* (Oxford, 1957).

JONES, J. E., 'Town and Country Houses of Attica in Classical Times', in H. Mussche, P. Spitaels, and F. Goemaere-De Poerck (eds.), *Thorikos and the Laurion in Archaic and Classical Times.* (MIGRA, 1; Ghent, 1975), 63–140.

—— GRAHAM, A. J., and SACKETT, L. H., 'An Attic Country House below the Cave of Pan at Vari', *ABSA* 68 (1973), 355–452.

—— SACKETT, L. H., and GRAHAM, A. J., 'The Dema House in Attica', *ABSA* 57 (1962), 75–114.

JONES, JACQUELYN, *Labor of Love, Labor of Sorrow: Black Women, Work, and the Family from Slavery to the Present* (New York, 1985).

JORDAN, BORIMIR, *The Athenian Navy in the Classical Period* (Berkeley, 1975).

—— PERLIN, JOHN, 'Solar Energy Use and Litigation in Ancient Times', *Solar Law Reporter*, 1 (1979), 583–94.

JUDEICH, W., 'Aspasia', *RE* ii (Stuttgart, 1895), cols. 1716–21.

—— *Topographie von Athen*, 2nd edn. (Handbuch der Altertumswissenschaft, iii/2.2; Munich, 1931).

JÜTHNER, J., 'Kalokagathia', in *Charisteria Alois Rzach zum achtzigsten Geburtstag dargebracht* (Reichenberg, 1930), 99–119.

KAHIL, LILLY G., 'L'Artémis de Brauron: Rites et mystère', *AK* 20 (1977), 86–98.

—— 'Auteur de l'Artémis attique', *AK* 8 (1965), 20–33.

KAUFMAN, GLORIA, 'Juan Luis Vives on the Education of Women', *Signs*, 3 (1978), 891–6.

KELLER, DONALD R., 'Classical Greek Agricultural Sites: The Karystian Evidence', paper delivered at the 90th annual meeting of the Archaeological Institute of America; abstract in *AJA* 93 (1989), 275.

—— and RUPP D. W. (eds.), *Archaeological Survey in the Mediterranean Area* (BAR Int. Ser. 155; Oxford, 1983).

KELLY-GADOL, JOAN, 'Did Women Have a Renaissance?', in Renate Bridenthal and Claudia Koonz (eds.), *Becoming Visible* (Boston, Mass., 1977), 137–64.

—— *Leon Battista Alberti: Universal Man of the Early Renaissance* (Chicago, 1969).

KENT, R. G., *Old Persian: Grammar, Texts, Lexicon*, 2nd edn. (New Haven, Conn., 1950).

KEULS, EVA, 'Attic Vase-Painting and the Home Textile Industry', in W. G. Moon (ed.), *Ancient Greek Art and Iconography* (Madison, Wis., 1983), 209–30.

—— *The Reign of the Phallus* (New York, 1985).

—— *The Water Carriers in Hades: A Study of Catharsis through Toil in Classical Antiquity* (Amsterdam, 1974).

KIER, H., *De Laudibus Vitae Rusticae* (Diss. Marburg, 1933).

KILLEN, JOHN T., 'The Textile Industries at Pylos and Knossos', in C. W. Shelmerdine and T. G. Palaima (eds.), *Pylos Comes Alive: Industry and Administration in a Mycenaean Palace* (New York, 1984), 49–63.

—— 'The Wool Industry of Crete in the Late Bronze Age', *ABSA* 59 (1964), 1–15.

KING, MARGARET LEAH, 'Caldiera and the Barbaros on Marriage and the Family: Humanist Reflections of Venetian Realities', *Journal of Medieval and Renaissance Studies*, 6 (1976), 19–50.

KLEVE, KNUT, 'Scurra Atticus: The Epicurean View of Socrates', in G. P. Pugliese-Caratelli (ed.), *Suzetesis: Studi sull'epicureismo greco e romano offerti a Marcello Gigante* (Bibl. della *Parola del Passato*, 16; Naples, 1983), i, 227–53.

KNAUTH, W., *Das altiranische Fürstenideal von Xenophon bis Ferdousi* (Wiesbaden, 1975).

KNECHT, ANDREAS, *Gregor von Nazianz: Gegen die Putzsucht der Frauen* (Wissenschaftliche Kommentare zu griechischen und lateinischen Schriftstellern; Heidelberg, 1972).

KOCH, HEIDEMARIE, 'Götter und ihre Verehrung im achämenidischen Persien', *Zeitschrift für Assyriologie*, 77 (1987), 239–78.

KROLL, W. 'Kleidemos 2', *RE* xi (Stuttgart, 1922), col. 593.

KUHRT, AMÉLIE. 'A Brief Guide to Some Recent Work on the Achaemenid Empire', *LCM* 8 (1983), 146–53.

—— 'The Achaemenid Empire: A Babylonian Perspective', *PCPhS*, NS 34 (1988), 60–76.

LACEY, A. R., 'Our Knowledge of Socrates', in G. Vlastos (ed.), *The Philosophy of Socrates*, (Garden City, NY, 1971), 22–49.

LACEY, W. K., *The Family in Classical Greece* (Ithaca, NY, 1968).

Bibliography

LANGDON, MERLE K., *A Sanctuary of Zeus on Mount Hymettos* (Hesperia, Suppl. 16; Princeton, NJ, 1976).

—— and WATROUS, L. VANCE, 'The Farm of Timesios: Rock-Cut Inscriptions in South Attica', *Hesperia*, 46 (1977), 162–77.

LANGE, GUSTAV, 'Xenophons Verhältnis zur Rhetorik', in *Natalicium Johannes Geffcken* (Heidelberg, 1931), 67–84.

LATHROP, HENRY BURROWES, *Translations from the Classics into English from Caxton to Chapman* (1477–1620) (University of Wisconsin Studies in Language and Literature, 35; Madison, Wis., 1933).

LAURENTI, RENATO, *Filodemo e il pensiero economico degli epicurei* (Milan, 1973).

—— *Le opere socratiche* (Padua, 1961).

—— *Studi sull'Economico attribuito ad Aristotele* (Milan, 1968).

LEAKE, WILLIAM M., *The Topography of Athens*, 2nd edn. (London, 1841).

LEGON, RONALD P., *Megara* (Ithaca, NY, 1981).

LENAERTS, JEAN, 'Un Papyrus de l'*Économique* de Xénophon', *CE* 49 (1974), 354–5.

LEVI, M. A., 'Il dialogo di Critobulo', *Quattro studi spartani e altri scritti di storia greca* (Milan, 1967).

LÉVI-STRAUSS, CLAUDE, *The Elementary Structures of Kinship*, trans., J. H. Bell (London, 1969), originally published as *Les Structures élementaires de la parenté*, 2nd edn. (Paris, 1967).

LEWIS, D. M., 'Attic Manumissions', *Hesperia* 28 (1959), 208–38.

—— 'Dedications of Phialai at Athens', *Hesperia*, 37 (1968), 368–80.

—— *Sparta and Persia* (Leiden, 1977).

LINCKE, K., *De Xenophontis libris Socraticis* (Jena, 1890).

LINDSTAM, SIGFRID, 'Xenofoncitaten hos Lakapenos', *Eranos*, 24 (1926) 100–22.

LLOYD-JONES, HUGH, and PARSONS, PETER, *Supplementum Hellenisticum* (Berlin, 1983).

LOHMANN, H., 'Landleben im klassischen Attika: Ergebnisse und Probleme einer archäologischen Landesaufnahme des Demos Atene', *Jahrbuch Ruhr-Universität Bochum*, 1985, 71–96.

LOUIS, P., *Les Métaphores de Platon* (Paris, 1945).

LOWRY, S. TODD, *The Archaeology of Economic Ideas* (Durham, NC., 1987).

LUCCIONI, J., *Les Idées politiques et sociales de Xénophon* (Paris, 1947).

—— *Xénophon et le socratisme* (Paris, 1953).

LUCE, J. V., 'The Large House at Dystos in Euboea', *G&R*, 2nd ser., 18 (1971), 143–9.

LUNDSTRÖM, V., 'Ciceros öfversättning af Xenophons Oikonomikos', *Eranos*, 12 (1912), 1–31.

McCartney, Eugene S., 'The Couch as a Unit of Measurement', *CP* 29 (1934), 30–5.

McClees, Helen, *A Study of Women in Attic Inscriptions* (New York, 1920).

MacDowell, Douglas, *Andocides: On the Mysteries* (Oxford, 1962).

—— 'The *Oikos* in Athenian Law', *CQ*, NS 39 (1989), 10–21.

MacLaren, Malcolm, Jr., 'On the Composition of Xenophon's *Hellenica*', *AJP* 55 (1934), 121–39.

Macve, Richard H., 'Some Glosses on "Greek and Roman Accounting"', in P. A. Cartledge and F. D. Harvey (eds.), *Crux*, 233–64.

Maier, Heinrich, *Sokrates* (Tübingen, 1913).

Mallowan, Max, 'Cyrus the Great (558–529 B.C.)', in *The Cambridge History of Iran*, ii. 392–419.

Marchant, E. C., *Xenophon: Memorabilia and Oeconomicus* (New York and London, 1923) = vol. iv of Loeb Classical Library, edn., 2 vols. (1914–25).

—— *Xenophontis: Opera Omnia*, ii. 2nd edn. (Oxford, 1921).

Mariolopoulos, E. G., *Étude sur le climat de la Grèce* (Paris, 1925).

Marrou, H. I., *Histoire de l'éducation dans l'Antiquité*, 6th edn. (Paris, 1965).

Marsh, D., 'Xenophon', in Virginia Brown (ed.), *Mediaeval and Renaissance Latin Translations (Catalogus Translationum et Commentariorum)*, vii (Washington, DC, forthcoming).

Marx, Karl, *Das Kapital*, i (1867), repr. in Karl Marx and Friedrich Engels, *Werke*, xxiii (Berlin, DDR, 1969).

Mayrhofer, M., *Onomastica Persepolitana: Das altiranische Namengut der Persepolis-Täfelchen* (*SBÖAW* 286; Vienna, 1973).

Meek, Ronald L., and Skinner, Andrew S., 'The Development of Adam Smith's Ideas on the Division of Labour', *Economic Journal*, 83 (1973), 1094–1116.

Meiggs, R., and Lewis, D. M., *A Selection of Greek Historical Inscriptions*, rev. edn. (Oxford, 1988).

Meikle, Scott, 'Aristotle and the Political Economy of the Polis', *JHS* 99 (1979), 57–73.

Mejer, Jørgen, *Diogenes Laertius and his Hellenistic Background* (Hermes Einzelschriften, 40; Wiesbaden, 1978).

Michell, H., *The Economics of Ancient Greece* (New York, 1957).

Mickwitz, G., 'Economic Rationalism in Graeco-Roman Agriculture', *English Historical Review*, 52 (1937), 577–89.

Miglio, M., 'Birago, Lampugnino', *Dizionario biografico degli italiani*, x (Rome, 1968), 595–7.

Bibliography

MIKALSON, JON D., *Athenian Popular Religion* (Chapel Hill, NC, and London, 1983).

—— *The Sacred and Civil Calendar of the Athenian Year* (Princeton, NJ, 1975).

MILLER, STEPHEN G., *The Prytaneion* (Berkeley, Los Angeles, and London, 1978).

MILNE, J. G., 'Trade between Greece and Egypt before Alexander the Great', *JEA* 25 (1939), 177–83.

MITSCHERLING, J., 'Xenophon and Plato', *CQ* NS 32 (1982), 468–9.

MOMMSEN, TYCHO, *Beiträge zur Lehre der griechischen Präpositionen* (Frankfurt, 1887).

MONTGOMERY, HUGO, '"Merchants Fond of Corn": Citizens and Foreigners in the Athenian Grain Trade', *SO* 61 (1986), 43–61.

MONTUORI, MARIO, *De Socrate iuste Damnato: The Rise of the 'Socratic Problem' in the Eighteenth Century* (London Studies in Classical Philology, 7, Amsterdam, 1981).

MORGAN, GARETH, 'Euphiletos' House: Lysias I', *TAPhA* 112 (1982), 115–23.

MORRISON, DONALD R., *Bibliography of Editions, Translations, and Commentary on Xenophon's Socratic Writings, 1600–Present* (Pittsburgh, 1988).

MORRISON, J. S., and COATES, J. F., *The Ancient Trireme: The History and Reconstruction of an Ancient Greek Warship* (New York, 1986).

—— and WILLIAMS, R. T., *Greek Oared Ships: 900–322 B.C.* (Cambridge, 1968).

MORRISON, TONI, *Beloved* (New York, 1987).

MOSLEY, D. J., 'Xenophon', In *Oxford Classical Dictionary*, 2nd edn. (Oxford, 1970).

MOSSÉ, CLAUDE, 'Xénophon économiste', in J. Bingen, G. Cambier, and G. Nachtergael (eds.), *Le Monde grec: Hommages à Claire Préaux* (Univ. libre de Bruxelles, Fac. de Philos. et Lettres, 62; Brussels, 1975), 69–76.

—— *Athens in Decline* (London, 1973).

—— *La Fin de la démocratie athénienne: Aspects sociaux et politiques du déclin de la cité grecque au IVe siècle av. J.-C.* (Publ. fac. des Lettres de Clermont-Ferrand, 10; Paris, 1962).

—— 'La vie économique d'Athènes au IVe siècle, crise ou renouveau?', in Franco Sartori (ed.), *Praelectiones Patavinae* (Rome, 1972), 135–44.

—— 'Women in the Spartan Revolutions of the Third Century B.C.', in Sarah B. Pomeroy (ed.), *Women's History and Ancient History* (Chapel Hill, NC, 1991), 138–53.

MOYNIHAN, ELIZABETH B., *Paradise as a Garden: In Persia and Mughal India* (New York, 1979).

MULCASTER, RICHARD, *Positions concerning the Training Up of Children* (London, 1581, repr. The English Experience, 339; Amsterdam, 1971).

MÜLLER, WERNER, *Die heilige Stadt* (Stuttgart, 1961).

MÜNSCHER, KARL, *Xenophon in der griechisch-römischen Literatur* (*Philologus*, Supplementband 13 2; Leipzig, 1920).

MURNAGHAN, SHEILA, 'How a Woman can be More Like a Man: The Dialogue between Ischomachus and his Wife in Xenophon's *Oeconomicus*', *Helios*, 15 (1988), 9–22.

MURRAY, PAULI, *Proud Shoes: The Story of an American Family* (1956, repr. New York, 1987).

MUSCARELLA, OSCAR WHITE, review of Walser, *Die Völkerschaften auf den Reliefs von Persepolis*, *JNES* 28 (1969), 280–5.

NAILS, DEBRA, 'The Shrewish Wife of Socrates', *EMC* 29 NS 4 (1985), 97–9.

NATALI, CARLO, *Senofonte: L'amministrazione della casa (Economico)* (Venice, 1988).

NESTLE, W., 'Die Horen des Prodikos', *Hermes*, 71 (1936), 151–70.

NICHOLS, J., *The Progresses and Public Processions of Queen Elizabeth* (London, 1823).

NICKEL, RAINER, *Xenophon*, (Erträge der Forschung, 3; Darmstadt, 1979).

NORDEN, E., *Die antike Kunstprosa vom VI. Jahrhundert vor Chr. bis in die Zeit der Renaissance* (Leipzig and Berlin, 1909).

NORTH, HELEN F., 'The Mare, the Vixen, and the Bee: Sophrosyne as the Virtue of Women in Antiquity', *ICS* 2 (1977), 35–48.

——*Sophrosyne: Self-Knowledge and Self-Restraint in Greek Literature* (Ithaca, NY, 1966).

OBER, JOSIAH, 'Thucydides, Pericles, and the Strategy of Defense', in *The Craft of the Ancient Historian: Studies in Honor of Chester G. Starr* (Lanham, Md., and London, 1985), 171–88.

ORRIEUX, C., 'Les comptes privés de Zénon à Philadelphie', *CE* 56 (1981), 314–40.

OSBORNE, ROBIN, 'Buildings and Residence on the Land in Classical and Hellenistic Greece: The Contribution of Epigraphy', *ABSA* 80 (1985), 119–28.

——*Classical Landscape with Figures: The Ancient Greek City and its Countryside* (London, 1987).

——*Demos: The Discovery of Classical Attika* (Cambridge, 1985).

——'Rural Structure and the Classical Polis: Town–Country

Relations in Athenian Society' (Ph.D. diss. Cambridge Univ., 1982).

OSTWALD, M., *Nomos and the Beginnings of Athenian Democracy* (Oxford, 1969).

OWENS, E. J., 'The Koprologoi at Athens in the Fifth and Fourth Centuries B.C.', *CQ*, NS 33 (1983), 44–50.

PACK, R. A., *The Greek and Latin Literary Texts from Greco-Roman Egypt*, 2nd edn. (Ann Arbor, Mich., 1965).

PATZER, A., *Bibliographia Socratica: Die wissenschaftliche Literatur über Sokrates von den Anfängen bis auf die neueste Zeit in systematisch-chronologischer Anordnung* (Freiburg, 1985).

PEČÍRKA, J., 'The Crisis of the Athenian Polis in the Fourth Century B.C.', *Eirene*, 14 (1976), 5–29.

——'Homestead Farms in Classical and Hellenistic Hellas', in M. I. Finley (ed.), *Problèmes de la terre en Grèce ancienne* (Paris, 1973), 113–47.

PELLETIER, A., 'Les deux Cyrus dans l'*Économique* de Xénophon', *RPh*, NS 18 (1944), 84–93.

PEPPLER, CHARLES W., 'The Termination -κός, as Used by Aristophanes for Comic Effect', *AJP* 31 (1910), 428–44.

PERSSON, AXEL W., *Zur Textgeschichte Xenophons* (Lunds Universitets Årsskrift, N.F., Afd. 1, Bd. 10, 2; Lund, 1915).

PICKARD-CAMBRIDGE, A. W., *The Dramatic Festivals of Athens*, 2nd edn., rev. J. Gould and D. M. Lewis, with supplement (Oxford, 1988).

PLEKET, H. W., *Texts on the Economic History of the Ancient World* (Textus Minores, 31 = Epigraphica, 1; Leiden, 1964).

POLLITT, J. J., *Art and Experience in Classical Greece* (Cambridge, 1972).

POMEROY, SARAH B., *Goddesses, Whores, Wives, and Slaves* (New York, 1975).

——'Plato and the Female Physician', *AJP* 90 (1978), 496–500.

——'Slavery in the Light of Xenophon's *Oeconomicus*', *Index*, 17 (1989), 11–18.

——'The Persian King and the Queen Bee', *AJAH* 9 (1984), 98–108.

——*Women in Hellenistic Egypt from Alexander to Cleopatra* (New York, 1984).

——'Technikai kai Mousikai: The Education of Women in the Fourth Century and in the Hellenistic Period', *AJAH* 2 (1977), 51–68.

——[PORGES], SARAH B., 'A Lease of An Olive Grove', *TAPhA* 92 (1961), 469–80.

Bibliography

PORGES, SARAH B., *see* Pomeroy, Sarah B.

POWELL, CHILTON LATHAM, *English Domestic Relations, 1487–1653* (New York, 1917).

POWELL, J. U., *Collectanea Alexandrina; reliquiae minores poetarum Graecorum aetatis Ptolemaicae* (Oxford, 1925).

PRÉAUX, CLAIRE, 'L'économie lagide: 1933–1958', *Proceedings of the IX International Congress of Papyrology, Oslo, 19th–22nd August, 1958* (Oslo, 1961), 200–32.

PRITCHETT, W. KENDRICK, 'The Attic Stelai: Part II', *Hesperia*, 25 (1956), 178–317.

RAEPSAET, G., 'Sentiments conjugaux à Athènes aux vᵉ et ivᵉ siècles avant notre ère', *AC* 50 (1981), 677–84.

RAHN, PETER J., 'The Date of Xenophon's Exile', in G. S. Shrimpton and D. J. McCargar (eds.), *Classical Contributions: Studies in Honour of Malcolm Francis McGregor* (New York, 1981), 103–19.

RAUBITSCHEK, ANTONY E., *Dedications from the Athenian Akropolis* (Cambridge, Mass., 1949).

RAWSON, ELIZABETH, *The Spartan Tradition in European Thought* (Oxford, 1969).

REEKMANS, T., *La Sitométrie dans les archives de Zénon* (Brussels, 1966).

REILLY, LINDA COLLINS, *Slaves in Ancient Greece: Slaves from Greek Manumission Inscriptions* (Chicago, 1978).

RHODES, P. J., *A Commentary on the Aristotelian Athenaion Politeia* (Oxford, 1981).

—— *The Athenian Boule* (Oxford, 1972).

RICHARDS, H., *Notes on Xenophon and Others* (London, 1907).

RICHARDSON, N. J., *The Homeric Hymn to Demeter* (Oxford, 1974).

RICHTER, E., *Xenophon in der römischen Literatur* (Berlin, 1905).

RICHTER, G. M. A., *The Furniture of the Greeks, Etruscans, and Romans* (London, 1966).

—— *The Portraits of the Greeks*, (London, 1965).

ROBERT, CARL, '"Ονοι πήλινοι', Εφημερὶς Ἀρχαιολογική, 1892, 247–56.

ROBINSON, DAVID M., *Excavations at Olynthus*, xii: *Domestic and Public Architecture* (Baltimore, 1946).

—— and GRAHAM, J. W., *Excavations at Olynthus*, viii: *The Hellenic House* (Baltimore, 1938).

ROHDE, ERWIN, *Psyche*, trans. from the 8th edn. by W. B. Hillis (London, 1925).

ROOT, MARGARET COOL, *The King and Kingship in Achaemenid Art* (Acta Iranica, Textes et Mémoires, 3rd ser., 9; Leiden, 1979).

ROSCALLA, FABIO, *Senofonte: Economico* (Milan, 1991).

ROSE, H. J., 'The Religion of a Greek Household', *Euphrosyne*, 1 (1957), 95–116.

ROSTOVTZEFF, M. I., *The Social and Economic History of the Hellenistic World* (Oxford, 1941).

RUSCHENBUSCH, E., 'Die athenischen Symmorien des 4. Jh. v. Chr', *ZPE* 31 (1978), 275–84.

RUSKIN, JOHN, preface to *The Economist of Xenophon*, trans. A. D. O. Wedderburn and W. G. Collingwood (London, 1876; repr. New York, 1971).

RUTHERFORD, W. G., *The New Phrynichus* (London, 1881).

STE. CROIX, G. E. M. DE, 'Ancient Greek and Roman Maritime Loans', in H. Edey and B. S. Yamey (eds.), *Debits, Credits, Finance, and Profits: Essays in Honour of H. T. Baxter* (London, 1974), 41–59.

—— *The Class Struggle in the Ancient Greek World, from the Archaic Age to the Arab Conquests* (London and Ithaca, NY, 1981).

—— 'Demosthenes' Τίμημα and the Athenian Eisphora in the Fourth Century B.C.', *C&M* 14 (1953), 30–70.

—— 'The Estate of Phaenippus (Ps.-Dem., XLII)', in E. Badian (ed.), *Ancient Society and Institutions: Studies Presented to Victor Ehrenberg* (Oxford, 1966), 109–14.

—— 'Greek and Roman Accounting', in A. C. Littleton and B. S. Yamey (eds.), *Studies in the History of Accounting* (Homewood, Ill., 1956), 14–74.

—— *The Origins of the Peloponnesian War* (London, 1972).

—— 'Slavery and Other Forms of Unfree Labour', in L. J. Archer (ed.), *Slavery and Other Forms of Unfree Labour* (London, 1988), 19–32.

—— 'Some Observations on the Property Rights of Athenian Women', *CR*, NS 20 (1970), 273–8.

SANCISI-WEERDENBURG, HELEEN, 'The Death of Cyrus: Xenophon's *Cyropaedia* as a Source for Iranian History', in H. Bailey *et al.* (eds.), *Papers in Honour of Professor Mary Boyce* (Acta Iranica: Hommages et Opera Minora, 2nd ser., 10–11; Leiden, 1985), 459–71.

SANDBACH, F. H., 'Plato and the Socratic Work of Xenophon', in P. E. Easterling and B. M. Knox, (eds.), *The Cambridge History of Classical Literature*, 2 vols. (Cambridge, 1982–5), i. 478–97.

SARTORI, F., 'Eraclea di Lucania', *Archäologische Forschungen in Lukanien, ii: Herakleiastudien*, (MDAI(R)), Ergänzungsheft 11, ed. Bernhard Neutsch; Heidelberg, 1967), 16–95.

SAUPPE, GUSTAV, *Lexilogus Xenophonteus* (Leipzig, 1869; repr. Hildesheim and New York, 1971).

Bibliography

SCHACHT, HANS, *De Xenophontis studiis rhetoricis* (diss. Berlin, 1890).

SCHAPS, DAVID M., *Economic Rights of Women in Ancient Greece* (Edinburgh, 1979).

——'The Woman Least Mentioned: Etiquette and Women's Names,' *CQ* NS 27 (1977), 323–30.

SCHENKL, KARL, 'Xenophontische Studien, 2: Beiträge zur Kritik der Apomnemoneumata', *SB k. Akad. Wiss.* (Vienna), 80 (1875), 87–182.

——'Xenophontische Studien, 3: Beiträge zur Kritik des Oikonomikos, des Symposion und der Apologie', *SB k. Akad. Wiss.* (Vienna), 83 (1876), 103–78.

SCHLEIERMACHER, F., 'Über den Werth des Sokrates als Philosophen', *Abhandlungen der Berl. Akad. Phil. Kl. aus den Jahren 1814–15* (1818), 50–68.

SCHLESINGER, A. C., 'Draco in the Hearts of his Countrymen', *CP* 19 (1924), 370–3.

SCHNEIDER, JANE, 'Trousseau as Treasure: Some Contradictions of Late Nineteenth-Century Change in Sicily', in Eric Ross (ed.), *Beyond the Myths of Culture* (Orlando, Fla., 1980), 323–56, repr. in *The Marriage Bargain: Women and Dowries in European History* = *Women and History*, 10 (1985), 81–119.

SCHULZE, C. P., *Quaestiones grammaticae ad Xenophontem pertinentes* (Berlin, 1888).

SCHUMPETER, J. A., *History of Economic Analysis* (New York, 1959).

SCHWAB, DIETER, 'Familie', in Otto Brunner, Werner Conze, and Reinhart Koselleck (eds.), *Geschichtliche Grundbegriffe* (Stuttgart, 1975), ii. 253–301.

SEALEY, R., 'Eupatridai', *Historia*, 10 (1961), 512–14, repr. in id., *Essays in Greek Politics* (New York, 1967), 39–41.

SHEAR, T. LESLIE, 'Psimythion', in *Classical Studies Presented to E. Capps* (Princeton, NJ, 1937), 314–16.

SIMON, J. A., *Xenophon-Studien* (Douren, 1887).

SMITH, H. R. W., *Funerary Symbolism in Apulian Vase-Painting* (CSCA, 12; Berkeley, 1976).

SMITH, H. W., *Greek Grammar* (Cambridge, Mass., 1920).

SOKOLOWSKI, F., *Lois sacrées des cités grecques* (Paris, 1969).

SOREL, GEORGES, *Réflexions sur la violence*, 8th edn. (Paris, 1936).

SOUDEK, JOSEF, 'Leonardo Bruni and his Public: A Statistical and Interpretative Study of his Annotated Latin Version of the (Pseudo-) Aristotelian *Economics*', *Studies in Medieval and Renaissance History*, 5 (1968), 49–136.

SOUILHÉ, JOSEPH, *Platon: Œuvres Complètes* (Paris, 1930).

SOURVINOU-INWOOD, CHRISTIANE, 'Crime and Punishment: Tityus, Tantalos and Sisyphus in *Odyssey* 11', *BICS* 33 (1986), 37–58.

—— *Studies in Girls' Transitions: Aspects of the Arkteia and Age Representation in Attic Iconography* (Athens, 1988).

SPARKES, B. A., and TALCOTT, L., *Pots and Pans of Classical Greece* (Excavations of the Athenian Agora, Picture Book no. 1; Princeton, NJ, 1958).

SPENCE, I. G., 'Perikles and the Defence of Attika during the Peloponnesian War', *JHS* 110 (1990), 91–109.

—— *The Cavalry of Classical Athens* (Oxford, 1993).

STARR, CHESTER G., 'Greeks and Persians in the Fourth Century B.C.: A Study in Cultural Contacts before Alexander, I', *IA* 11 (1975), 39–99.

STEVEN, R. G., 'Plato and the Art of his Time,' *CQ* 17 (1933), 149–55.

STEVENS, COURTENAY EDWARD, 'Agriculture and Rural Life in the Later Roman Empire', in J. H. Clapham and Eileen Power (eds.), *The Cambridge Economic History of Europe*, i (1941, repr. Cambridge, 1942), 89–117.

STONE, LAWRENCE, 'The Educational Revolution in England, 1560–1640', *Past and Present*, 28 (1964), 41–80.

—— 'Literacy and Education in England, 1640–1900', *Past and Present*, 42 (1969), 69–139.

—— 'Social Mobility in England, 1500–1700', *Past and Present*, 33 (1966), 16–55.

STOWE, HARRIET BEECHER, *American Woman's Home* (1869; repr. Hartford, Conn., 1975).

STRAUSS, BARRY, *Athens after the Peloponnesian War* (Ithaca, NY, 1987).

STRAUSS, LEO, *Xenophon's Socratic Discourse*, with trans., of the *Oeconomicus* by Carnes Lord and foreword by Allan Bloom (Ithaca, NY, and London, 1970).

STRONACH, DAVID, 'The Royal Garden at Pasargadae: Evolution and Legacy', in L. De Meyer and E. Haerinck (eds.), *Archaeologia Iranica et Orientalis: Miscellanea in honorem Louis Vanden Berghe* (Ghent, 1989), 475–502.

STROUD, R., *Dracon's Law on Homicide* (Berkeley and Los Angeles, 1968).

STURZ, F. W., *Lexicon Xenophonteum*, 4 vols. (Leipzig, 1801; repr. Hildesheim, 1964).

SUMNER, W. M., 'Achaemenid Settlement in the Persepolis Plain', *AJA* 90 (1986), 3–31.

SUSEMIHL, F., *Geschichte der griechischen Literatur in der Alexandrinerzeit*, 2 vols. (Leipzig, 1891–2).

Bibliography

Sutton, Robert, 'The Interaction between Men and Women Portrayed on Attic Red-Figure Pottery' (Ph.D. diss., Univ. of North Carolina at Chapel Hill, 1981).

Tannenbaum, Nicola, 'Chayanov and Economic Anthropology', in P. Durrenberger (ed.), *Chayanov, Peasants, and Economic Anthropology* (Orlando, Fla, 1984), 27–38.

Taragna Novo, Sandra, *Economia ed etica nell'Economico di Senofonte* (Turin, 1968).

Taylor, A. E., *Varia Socratica* (Oxford, 1911).

Thesleff, Holger, *The Pythagorean Texts of the Hellenistic Period* (Åbo, 1965).

Thompson, Homer A., and Wycherley, R. E., *The Athenian Agora*, xiv: *The Agora of Athens* (Princeton, NJ, 1972).

Thompson, W. E., 'The Athenian Entrepreneur', *AC* 51 (1982), 53–85.

Thumb, A., 'Zur neugriechischen Sprachfrage', *NJbb* 17 (1906), 704–12.

Tilly, Louise A., and Scott, Joan W., *Women, Work, and Family* (New York, 1978).

Tilney, Edmund, *A Brief and Pleasant Discourse of Duties in Marriage, Called the Flower of Friendshippe* (London, 1571).

Tod, M. N., *A Selection of Greek Historical Inscriptions*, ii (Oxford, 1948).

Tomlinson, R. A., 'Ancient Macedonian Symposia', in B. Laourdas and C. Makaronas (eds.), *Ancient Macedonia: Papers Read at the First International Symposium Held in Thessaloniki, August 1968* (Thessaloniki, 1970), 308–15.

Trever, Albert Augustus, *A History of Greek Economic Thought* (Chicago, 1916).

Tuplin, Christopher, 'The Administration of the Achaemenid Empire', in *Coinage and Administration in the Athenian and Persian Empires: The Ninth Oxford Symposium on Coinage and Monetary History* (*BAR* Int. Ser. 343; Oxford, 1987), 109–66.

—— 'Persian Garrisons in Xenophon and Other Sources', in Amélie Kuhrt and Heleen Sancisi-Weerdenburg (eds.), *Achaemenid History*, iii: *Method and Theory* (Leiden, 1988), 67–70.

—— 'Xenophon and the Garrisons of the Achaemenid Empire', *AMI* 20 (1987), 167–245.

Untersteiner, M., 'Prodico e Xenoph. *Oec.*, VII', in A. Rostagni *et al.* (eds.), *Studi in onore di Luigi Castiglioni*, 2 vols. (Florence, 1961), ii. 1059–70.

Ure, A. D., 'Boeotian Haloa', *JHS* 69 (1949), 18–24.

Usher, Stephen, *The Historians of Greece and Rome* (Norman, Okla., 1985).

VALLOIS, R., 'Sera', *Dar.-Sag.* (Paris, 1877–1919), iv/2, 1241–8.

VANDERPOOL, EUGENE, 'The Location of the Attic Deme Erchia', *BCH* 89 (1965), 21–6.

VATIN, CLAUDE, *Recherches sur le mariage et la condition de la femme mariée à l'époque hellénistique* (Paris, 1970).

VÉLISSAROPOULOS, JULIE, *Les Nauclères grecs: Recherches sur les institutions maritimes en Grèce et dans l'Orient hellénisé* (Haute études du monde gréco-romain, 9; Geneva, 1980).

VÉRILHAC, ANNE-MARIE, 'L'image de la femme dans les épigrammes funéraires grecques', in ead. (ed.), *La Femme dans le monde méditerranéen* (Collection des Travaux de la Maison de l'Orient, 10; Lyon, 1985), iii. 85–112.

VERMEULE, C. C., 'Socrates and Aspasia', *CJ* 54 (1958), 49–55.

VERNANT, JEAN-PIERRE, *Mythe et pensée chez les Grecs* (Paris, 1985).

VICTOR, ULRICH, *[Aristoteles] Oikonomikos: Das erste Buch der Ökonomik—Handschriften, Text, Übersetzung und Kommentar—und seine Beziehungen zur Ökonomikliteratur* (Beiträge zür klassischen Philologie, 147; Königstein im Taurus, 1983).

VIDAL-NAQUET, PIERRE, 'Valeurs religieuses et mythiques de la terre et du sacrifice dans l'Odyssée', *Annales (ESC)*, 25 (1970), 1278–97, repr. in M. I. Finley (ed.), *Problèmes de la terre en Grèce ancienne* (The Hague, 1973), 269–92.

VLASTOS, G., 'Introduction: The Paradox of Socrates', in id. (ed.), *The Philosophy of Socrates* (Garden City, NY, 1971), 1–21.

VORRENHAGEN, ELISABETH, *De orationibus quae sunt in Xenophontis Hellenicis* (Elberfeld, 1926).

WACKERNAGEL, J., *Hellenistica* (Göttingen, 1907), repr. in *Kleine Schriften* (Göttingen, 1953), ii, 1034–58.

WADE-GERY, H. T., 'Eupatridai, Archons, and Areopagus', *CQ* 25 (1931), 1–11, 77–89, repr. in *Essays in Greek History* (Oxford, 1958), 86–115.

WAGNER-HASEL, BEATE, 'Geschlecht und Gabe: Zum Brautgütersystem bei Homer', *ZRG* 105 (1988), 32–73.

WAGSTAFF, MALCOLM, and AUGUSTSON, SIV, 'Traditional Land Use', in Colin Renfrew and Malcolm Wagstaff (eds.), *An Island Polity* (Cambridge, 1982), 106–33.

WALKER, SUSAN, 'Women and Housing in Classical Greece: The Archaeological Evidence', in Averil Cameron and Amélie Kuhrt (eds.), *Images of Women in Antiquity* (London and Canberra, 1983) 81–91.

WALLON, HENRI, *Histoire de l'esclavage dans l'Antiquité*, 2nd edn., 3 vols. (Paris, 1879).

WALSER, GEROLD, *Audienz beim persischen Großkönig* (Zurich, 1966).
—— 'Die Bedeutung des "Tributzuges" von Persepolis', *AA* 81 (1966), 544–9.
—— *Hellas und Iran* (Erträge der Forschung, 209; Darmstadt, 1984).
—— *Die Völkerschaften auf den Reliefs von Persepolis: Historische Studien über den sogenannten Tributzug an der Apadanatreppe* (Teheraner Forschungen, 2; Berlin, 1966).
WANKEL, H., *Kalos kai Agathos* (diss. Würzburg, 1961).
WATERFIELD, ROBIN, (trans.), *The Estate Manager: Xenophon*, in Hugh Tredennick and Robin Waterfield (trans.), *Conversations of Socrates* (London, 1990), 289–359.
WATSON, FOSTER, *Vives and the Renascence Education of Women* (London, 1912).
WEBSTER, T. B. L., *The Greek Chorus* (London, 1970).
WEDDERBURN, A. D. O., and COLLINGWOOD, W. G. (trans), *The Economist of Xenophon* (London, 1876; repr. New York, 1971).
WELLMAN, ROBERT R., 'Socratic Method in Xenophon', *JHI* 37 (1976), 307–18.
WELLMANN, M., 'Androtion 2', *RE*, Suppl. i (Stuttgart, 1903), col. 82.
—— *Die Georgika des Demokritos* (ADAW, 4; Berlin, 1921).
WESTERMANN, WILLIAM L., *The Slave Systems of Greek and Roman Antiquity* (Philadelphia, 1955).
WHITEHEAD, DAVID, *The Demes of Attica 508/7–ca. 250 B.C.* (Princeton, NJ, 1986).
WILAMOWITZ-MOELLENDORFF, U. VON, *Antigonos von Karystos* (Philol. Untersuch. 4; Berlin, 1881).
—— review of '*The Oxyrhynchus Papyri*. Part II, ed. Grenfell and Hunt', *Göttingische gelehrte Anzeigen*, 162 (1900), 47.
WOOD, ELLEN MEIKSINS, 'Agricultural Slavery in Classical Athens', *AJAH* 8 (1983), 1–47.
—— *Peasant-Citizen and Slave: The Foundations of Athenian Democracy* (London and New York, 1988).
[Woodbridge], FITZ, LINDA T., '"What Says the Married Woman?": Marriage Theory and Feminism in the English Renaissance', *Mosaic*, 13/2 (1980), 1–22.
WOODBRIDGE, LINDA, *Women and the English Renaissance* (Urbana, Ill., 1984).
WRIGHT, LOUIS B., 'Handbook Learning of the Renaissance Middle Class', *Studies in Philology*, 28 (1931), 58–86.
—— *Middle-Class Culture in Elizabethan England* (Chapel Hill, NC, 1935).
WYCHERLEY, R. E., *The Athenian Agora*, iii: *Literary and Epigraphical Testimonia* (Princeton, NJ, 1957).

YOST, JOHN, 'The Value of Married Life for the Social Order in the Early English Renaissance', *Societas*, 6 (1976), 25–39.

YOUNG, JOHN H., 'Studies in South Attica: Country Estates at Sounion', *Hesperia*, 25 (1956), 122–46.

ZELLER, EDUARD, *Die Philosophie der Griechen*, 5th edn., 3 vols. (Leipzig, 1922).

GREEK INDEX TO COMMENTARY

ἀλεξητήρ 237
ἄμπελος 336–7
ἀντίδοσις 226, 265–6
ἀπαρχαί 255
ἀποικίζειν 280
ἀργός 280
ἄριστος 248
αὐλός 220
ἀφροδίσια 317–18

βασίλεια 277
βασίλισσα 303
βάναυσος 235–6

γαστήρ 271, 319
γαῦλος 288
γεωργία 238–40, 254, 337
γεωργικὰ συγγράμματα 322
γεωργός 231
γυμνασιαρχία 227
γυναικωνῖτις 293–7; see also
    θάλαμος

δαπανᾶν 281–2, 301
δέ 216
δεκάκλινος 288–9; see also
    ἑνδεκάκλινος
δένδρα 245, 333–34
δέσποινα 222
δεσπότης 318
διάκονος 308, 316
διαλέγεσθαι 272–3
δῖνος 332
δοκιμασία 302
δοῦλος 221, 241 n. 72, 256, 319;
    see also ἐπίτροπος, οἰκέτης

εἰρεσιώνη 255
εἰσφοραί 228
ἑκοῦσα 308

ἔμποροι 340–2
ἑνδεκάκλινος 288–9
ἐνδογενής 300
ἔνδον 276
ἐπιμέλεια 258, 269–70
ἔπιπλα 301
ἐπίστασθαι 218, 220, 322
ἐπιστήμη 230
ἐπίτροπος 281, 314–17; see also
    δοῦλος, οἰκέτης
ἐργάτης 317
ἔρια 270; see also ταλασία
ἑταίρα 220–2
εὔνοια 317
εὐπατρίδαι 221–2
ἐχθροί 221

θάλαμος 292–7
θεῖος 343
θεός 230, 257–8, 275, 310, 329
θύρα 297

-ικός suffix 214–15
ἱμάτια 319
ἵππος 219, 243–4, 309
ἱπποτροφία 226

καλεῖν 266
καλὸς κἀγαθός 223, 259, 265, 285,
    314, 321–2, 341
κελευστής 343
κλοπή 228–9; see also νόμος
κοινωνός 273
κόπρος 325–6, 338
κρεμαστά 288
κτήματα 218
κύριος 268

μέλισσα 279
μέλιττα 276–80

372

μεσημβρία 293, 295
μίλτος 306

νόμος 275, 319–21; see also κλοπή
νομοφύλακες 302–3

ξένος 224–5, 265
ξυλινά 288
ξυστός 312

οἰκέτης 230–1, 297–300, 316; see
    also διάκονος, ἐπίτροπος
οἰκία 214, 291
οἰκογενής 300
οἰκονομία 216–17, 230, 232, 240,
    283, 291, 323
οἰκονομική 214
οἰκονομικός 213–14
οἶκος 213–14, 217, 230
ὀφθαλμοί 335

παιδικά 229–30, 317–18
παράδεισος 240, 247–8, 252
πατρόθεν 266–7
ποικίλματα 291
πόλος 332–3
πόρνη 220
πρέμνα 336
προστατεία 227
πρωρεύς 289

σῖτος 293, 324, 342
σκαλεύς 330–1
σμῆνος 275, 277–8, 283
στοά 264–5
στρατιά 286–7
συκῆ 335–6
σωφροσύνη 223, 275, 279, 338, 344

ταλασία 284; see also ἔρια
τάξις 286
τέκνα 273–4
τελεῖν 218, 225–6
τριηραρχία 227–8
τριήρης 287

φιλεργία 277 n. 164
φιλία 273
φίλοι 230
φυλή 300–1
φύσις 275, 323–4

χαλαζοφύλακες 258
χειροήθης 272
χιλίαρχος 243
χορηγία 226–7
χορός 286, 291

χρήματα 218–19
χρῆσις 219–20

ψιμύθιον 305

GENERAL INDEX

Page numbers in italic indicate an illustration.

accounts, keeping 55–6, 283, 339
Adler, A. 250 n. 107
Aelian 241, 251, 269, 279, 279–80
Aeschines:
  and skills of women 64
  and wealth 223
Aeschines Socraticus:
  Aspasia 48, 72–3, 233–4
  and Critobulus 229
  and Ischomachus 260
  and Socrates 19, 22, 264
  and wealth 220
Agesilaus 3, 216
Agesilaus, king of Sparta 4, 9, 233,
  318
agriculture 309
  diversification 54–5, 257
  failure in 321
  in fourth-century Attica 46–50,
    254, 256
  and free workers 44, 315–17
  intensive 45, 48, 54, 326–8
  manuals 15, 46–7, 322–3
  and military role 52, 235–7,
    255–6, 276, 317
  and Persian king 238–41, *239*,
    254, 309
  and piety 310
  rituals 257
  slaves in 256, 280–1, 314–17,
    328, 333–4
  as sphere of men 235–7
  'three-strip economy' 325
  and water-supply 257, 313, 328
  and weather 256–8, 328–9
  see also grain; tools; viticulture
Aigeis tribe 2
Alberti, Leon Battista 74, 75, 88
Alcaeus 303

Alcibiades 222, 309
  house 290–1
Alciphron 320
Alcuin 73 n. 11
Alfonsi, Luigi 70 n. 8
alliteration 223, 288
Ampolo, C. 240 n. 70
Anabasis 3, 253, 267
  and agriculture 326
  autobiographical memoir 1 n. 1,
    15
  criticism of prose style 13
  and economy 45
  as historical source 7, 237–8,
    246
  and Parysatis 276
  and piety 258
  portrayal of Cyrus 244,
    248–51
  in Renaissance England 76
  and women 306
anachronisms 7, 18, 73 n. 11, 215,
  250
anamnesis 27, 331, 333
anaphora 17
Anderson, J. K. 5, 292
Andocides 222, 261–2, 267
  trial 4 n. 10, 263
andron 287, 293
Androtion 322
animals:
  analogies with, 231–2
  husbandry 55, 326–7, 330
  waste as fertilizer 325–6
  see also bees, horses
Anthesteria festival 257
anthropomorphization 309–10
Antiphon, and rhetoric 14, 16

374

Antisthenes:
  Aspasia 233
  Oeconomicus 7–8, 25, 68 n. 2,
    213
  and Socrates 19, 22, 25, 271
Apollodorus 344
Apollodorus of Lemnos 322
Apology, Xenophon's 216
  relationship to *Oeconomicus* 93
  and Socrates 22, 216
Araros 261
Arévalo, 74 n. 13
Arginusae, battle of 2
Ariaeus 251
Aristophanes:
  Clouds 22, 26, 28, 29, 217, 231,
    282, 292, 309
  Frogs 64, 312
  Knights 215
  Lysistrata 305
  and Socrates 22, 223
Aristotle 10
  and agriculture 46, 236, 323
  Ath. Pol. 222, 266, 302, 319, 321,
    341
  and definitions 27, 217
  and exercise 307
  and gender 34, 37, 39
  HA 278–9
  Oeconomica see Pseudo-Aristotle
  Pol. 34, 46, 68, 235, 283, 305,
    307, 319, 322, 338
  and slaves 66, 67, 318–19
  and Socratic dialogues 19, 27
  and speech 272–3
army 286–7
Arrian:
  on bees 279
  and Cyrus 249
  and style of Xenophon 13
Artemisia of Halicarnassus 277
Ascham, Roger 76–7
Aspasia 72–3, 220, 282
  and Socrates 81–2, 232–4
assonance 17
Asulanus, edn. of *Oeconomicus* 94

asyndeton 16–17
Athenaeus 82 n. 45, 215, 289, 335
  and Critobulus 229
  and Persians 239, 249–50
  and Plato 23, 26–7
Athenian Constitution 15
Athens:
  and agriculture 46–9, 311
  as setting of *Oeconomicus* 5–6
Atthidographers 322
audience 9–10, 50, 270, 287
authority, and merit 247
Aylmer, Bishop J. 86

bailiff 61, 67
Baldwin, T. W. 77 n. 28
banausic work 28, 235–7, 276, 321
Barbaro, Francesco and
    Ermolao 74–5
barley 324, 328–9, 342
Bean, G. E. 335
Beauvoir, Simone de 89
bedroom 292–3
Beecher, Catherine 89
bees 36
  and divinity 279–80
  hive compared with house 63,
    293
  and Persian king 17, 240–2
  and sexuality 279
  slaves as 63
  swarming 280, 283
  wives as 59–60, 72, 240–2,
    275–80, 283, 302, 344
benefactions, voluntary 225
Berthelet, Thomas 78, 83–4
Bicknell, P. J. 234 n. 48
Billigmeier, Jon-Christian 41 n. 2
Biragus, Lampus 75
bisexuality 306
Bloom, Allan 90
Boeotians, capture of Xenophon 2
Bolkestein, H. 314 n. 262
Bonini, Eufrosino, edn. of
    Oeconomicus 94
Boule 302
Bradley, R. 214

Bradner, L. 78 n. 28
bread 308
Breitenbach, L., edn. of
  Oeconomicus 94, 238, 256, 333
Briant, Pierre 237, 240, 246
bridal chamber 292–3
Browne, Sir Thomas, and
  Cyrus 250, 252
Brucker, Jacob 23–4
Bruni, Leonardo 74
budgeting 57
Busolt, G. 49

Caldiera, Giovanni 74–5
calendar, sacrificial 224–5
Callias 221, 222, 260–2
Camerarius, Joachim 75 n. 19
cargo-ship 288
Castiglioni, Luigi 6–7, 335
Catherine of Aragon 78–81, 83
Cato the elder:
  and agriculture 323, 332, 337
  and *Oeconomicus* 69–71
Cavalry Commander 3, 48, 219, 267,
  302
cavalry service 226
  by Ischomachus 313
  by Xenophon 2, 48
Cawkwell, G. L. 302 n. 240
chaff 332
Chantraine, P., edn. of
  Oeconomicus 95–6, 236, 288
Charetides of Paros 322
Charon of Lampsacus 279
chastity, and bees 279
Chaumont, M. L. 243
Chayanov, A. V. 44–5
Cheke, Sir John 76
children, obligation to maintain
  parents 35, 273–4
choregia 226–7
chorus 286–7, 291
Chroust, Anton-Hermann 24–5, 27
  n. 19
Chrysilla 4 n. 10, 267, 269
  and Callias 261–3
  see also Ischomachus, wife of

Cicero, Marcus Tullius:
  and Cyrus 252
  and Lysander 251
  and *Oeconomicus* 69–70, 72–4,
    213, 290
  trans. of *Oeconomicus* 13, 70, 73,
    91, 99–100, 214, 301, 329, 338
  and women 71
  and Xenophon 13, 15, 22
citizenship:
  and land-ownership 341
  and wealth 256
Cleidemus 322
Cleander of Sparta 224
Cleanthes 271
Cleinias:
  and Critobulus 229, 318
  and Xenophon 229–30
climate 256–7, 328
clothing:
  Persian 253
  of slaves 65–6, 256, 319
Cobet, C. G. 332
Codex Laurentianus 80. 13(E) 92
Codex Reginensis 96(H) 92, 95
Collingwood, W. G. 98, 213
Columella 293
  and agriculture 323, 326, 330,
    332, 338–9
  and bees 279–80
  and Latin version of
    Oeconomicus 70–2, 74, 92, 315
  and olive culture 336
  and slaves 317–18
  and viticulture 334, 336–7
  and Xenophon as philosopher 22
comedies 231
concinnity 17, 230–1
Cook, J. M. 245–6
Corinth, Xenophon resident of 4
Coronea, battle of 4
cosmetics 19, 38, 75, 80, 252, 304–6
Cousin, Georges 248
Cratinus 260
Critobulus 2, 17–18, 50
  and choregia 227

homosexuality 229, 318
marriage 18, 216–17
as profligate 229
and Socrates 216–18
wealth 38, 217, 219, 222–4, 229,
   286, 310
wife 232, 268–9, 272, 281
Croiset, A. and M. 14
Ctesias 251
cults 257, 272, 310
Cunaxa, battle of 3–4, 25, 250–1
Cyropaedia 248, 252, 267
   and army 286
   and criticism of prose style 13, 15
   and division of labour 43
   and economy 45
   and exercise 253, 311
   as historical source 7, 237, 245–6
   and homosexuality 318
   and leadership 3, 231, 244, 278,
      343–4
   and Panthea 276
   and Plato 10, 26
   in Renaissance Europe 76–7
   and women 295
Cyrus the Great 3, 77, 98, 248,
   252–3
   and Cyrus the Younger 248–50
   and oikonomia 239–41, 244, 250
   and virtue 286
Cyrus the Younger:
   clothing 253
   and Cyrus the Great 248–50
   death 18
   and Lysander 238, 251
   mercenary service with 2–3

Dall, Catherine 87–8
Danaides 284
dancing 307
Dandamaev, Muhammad A. 238,
   240 n. 69, 246
date:
   of composition 5, 7–8
   dramatic 18–19, 228, 264–5, 320
David, Ephraim 49

Davies, J. K. 226, 227, n. 33, 261,
   266
Deceleian War 49, 260
definitions 27, 30, 43, 217–18, 258
Delebecque, Édouard 5–6, 7,
   8 n. 18, 16 n. 19, 215 n. 8, 248,
   311–12
Demetrius of Magnesia, biography
   of Xenophon 1, 5 n. 11, 15
Demosthenes 53, 62, 269, 272, 341
   and agriculture 312, 337
   father 46–7, 282
   and slaves 284, 295, 298
   and theft 320
   see also Pseudo-Demosthenes
Denniston, J. D. 14
dialogue 19–20, 22, 24, 26–7, 100
diligence 338–9
Dindorf, L., edn. of
   Oeconomicus 94–5
dining-rooms 287–9, 293
Dio Chrysostom, and style of
   Xenophon 14
Diodora, mother of Xenophon 2
Diodorus, and agriculture 48
Diodorus, son of Xenophon 3
Diogenes Laertius:
   and Antisthenes 271
   biography of Xenophon 1–2, 5,
      213
   and Cyrus 249–50
   and death of Xenophon 4, 5 n. 11
   homosexual affairs 229
   and Plato 23, 26–7
   and prose style of Xenophon 13
   and Socrates 22, 25–6, 223
Dionysius of Halicarnassus, and
   Xenophon as philosopher 22
Dittmar, H. 229, 260
domestication of women 87, 272,
   277, 319
Donatus 73 n. 12
doors 296–7
Dover, K. J. 223
dowries 52–3, 60, 262, 274
Draco, legislation 302, 319–21
dualities 254

economy, domestic *see* oikos
editions:
Renaissance to twentieth-
century 94–5
twentieth-century 95–6
education:
changes in 267
for ideal ruler 77
in *Oeconomicus* 38–9, 51, 68, 70
in Plato 37–9
of slaves 317
for women 34, 58, 60–1, 78–84,
89–90, 232, 267–73, 285–7
Ehrenberg, V. 49
Ehtécham, Mortéza 246
Eichler, Gustav 12 n. 10
eisphorai 228
elenctic method 27, 217–18, 336
Elizabeth I 77
ellipsis 256
embezzlement 228–9
enemies 221
England, knowledge of
Oeconomicus 76–87
Ephialtes, reforms 302
Epilycus 261
Erchia, deme 2
Erinna 270
estate management 9
in classical Athens 51–5
as profession 47
see also agriculture
Eupatrids 221–2
Euphranor 265
Eupolis 309
Autolycus 221
Euripides, *Andromache* 308
exercise 38, 253, 306, 311–12, 317

fables 310
fallow 47, 324–6, *326*, 327, 340
family:
in classical Greece 31–3
in domestic economy 44–5
and gender-roles 32–4, 36–9,
68–9, 74, 87–90, 296–7
in *Oeconomicus* 33–5, 59

and slaves 40, 214
see also oikos
farmer, professional 3
farming *see* agriculture
father, role in marriage 35, 268
Fauth, Wolfgang 238
feminism, and *Oeconomicus* 87–90
fertilizer 47, 325–7, 338
figs 329, 335–6
finances, wife's management of 72,
281–3
Finley, M. I. 42–4, 49, 54 n. 34,
56 n. 42, 57, 62, 96 n. 19, 315 n.
264, 340 n. 321
first-fruits 255
fishermen 324
flute 220
food, storage 282–3, 293, 338
footwear 290
foreman 65, 71–2, 241, 281, 329
as slave/freeman 316–17
Foxhall, Lin 213 n. 2, 332 n. 302
Fraser, P. M. 336
Friedan, Betty 89
Frisk, H. 235
Frye, Richard N. 242, 246

Galen 11–12, 93, 213
Gallant, T. W. 314 n. 262
Garbarino, G. 73 n. 12
gardener-king 238–9, *239*, 249
gardens, Persian 247, 252
Garnsey, Peter 257 n. 126, 340 n.
324
Gauthier, Philippe 230–1
Gautier, L. 14
Gellius, Aulus, and Plato and
Xenophon 22, 27
gender-roles:
and equality 287
in family 32–4, 36–7, 39, 68–9,
74, 87–90, 296
gentleman 97–8, 223
and agriculture 321, 323, 341
and commerce 341
obligations 314
slave as 67, 259, 321

Geoponica:
and agriculture 323, 326, 327,
330, 332
and bees 279
and olive culture 336
and viticulture 334–7, 339
Gigon, Olof 24–5
Gil, J. 101
Glotz, Gustave 41–2
gods, *see* piety; theology
Gomme, A. W. 44
Gorgias, and rhetoric 14, 16, 314
Gortyn, Law Code of 61
Gothein, Percy 75 n. 22
Grace, E. 316
grafting 336
Graham, J. W. 293, 296, 312
grain:
cultivation 49, 50, 324–5,
328–32, 340
imported 314, 340–1
storage 293
Graux, Ch., edn. of
Oeconomicus 94–5
Gregory of Nazianzus 304
Grenfell, B. P. 91
Gryllus, father of Xenophon 2
Gryllus, son of Xenophon 3, 4, 8,
10, 265
'guest-friends' 224–5, 265
Guiraud, P. 325
Gulick, Charles Burton 82 n. 45
gymnasiarchy 227
gynaikonitis 292–7, 317

hail 258
Hallock, R. T. 239
Haloa festival 257
Haltinner, D. O. 93 n. 8
handiwork, Socrates on 235
Hansen, Ove 239 n. 65
Hardy, W. G. 47
Harpocration 264
harvest 255, 329
Harvey, F. D. 263
Heichelheim, Fritz M. 325
height, enhancing 38, 306

Heinimann, F. 275
Helladius 12
Hellenica 7, 46, 216, 229, 244–5,
247, 251, 267, 278
henbane 217, 221
Heraclides Ponticus 260
Herlihy, David 75 n. 22
Hermogenes of Tarsus 11, 13, 22
Herodotus 216, 295, 301, 343
and agriculture 335
and Cyrus and Persians 242, 249,
253
and women 271, 277
Hervet, Gentian 80–5, 87, 98, 214
Hesychius:
and agriculture 254, 322, 324–5,
329
and food storage 282–3
and idleness 280
and marriage 268–9
and slaves 300
Works and Days 268–9, 338
Hesychius 264, 302, 334
hetairai 220–1, 223, 234
see also Aspasia
Hiero:
and homosexuality 318
and leadership 3, 77, 344
and slaves 283, 308, 315
and wealth 224, 338
Hippolytus, and marriage 36
Hirsch, Steven W. 237, 243 n. 77,
249
Hodkinson, Stephen 327
Hoepfner, Wolfram 293, 294, 296,
312
Holden, H. A. 216
edn. of *Oeconomicus* 95
Homer:
influence 16
Odyssey 306, 308, 344
homoioteleuton 17
homosexuality 98, 229–30, 300,
317–18
horses:
in fables 309–10

ownership 2, 219, 226, 231, 243, 312
training 285
house:
  decoration 291, 304
  design 291–6, *294*
  furnishings 230, 297
  women's quarters 292–5
household, *see* oikos
housekeeper 61, 65, 67, 72, 241, 298, 301, 317, 320
Hugo of Saint-Victor 74
Hull, Suzanne W. 85 n. 56
human waste, as fertilizer 326
Hume, David 299
humour 28, 90, 217, 232
hunger 310, 330
Hunt, A. S. 91
Hyrde, Richard 78, 84

idleness, criticized 280
innovation in Xenophon 7, 8, 26
irony 28
Isaeus 261, 266, 274, 282, 327
Ischomachus 1 n. 1, 8, 18
  and agriculture 237, 311–12, 316–17, 324–31, 338–9
  and cavalry 313
  daughter 261
  and domestic economy 45
  identity 259–61, 263
  and law 320–1
  and marriage 33–6, 59–60
  and practical issues 30
  as realist 265
  and rhetoric 15–17
  and slaves 51, 65–7, 321
  and Socrates 218
  and viticulture 334–7
  wealth 51–5, 260, 265–6, 310–12, 327
Ischomachus, wife of 18–19, 232
  authority of 247
  compared with queen bee 59–60, 240–2, 275–8, 283, 303, 345
  contribution to oikos 60–1, 98, 270, 274
  control of slaves 61, 281, 283–5, 297–8, 303
  educated by Ischomachus 34–5, 38, 262, 267–73, 286–7, 313
  feminist views of 87–90
  freedom 6, 295
  identity 261–3
  and judgement of Ischomachus 16, 247, 278, 302
  judicial powers in household 313
  literacy 10, 34, 59
  management of finances 56–7, 281–3
  masculine mind 34, 39, 287, 303
  name not given 233, 263, 267
  and Xenophon 263
  see also Chrysilla; cosmetics
Isidore of Seville 74
Isocrates 10, 255
Italy, knowledge of *Oeconomicus* 74–5

Jacob, A., edn. of *Oeconomicus* 95, 336
Jacoby, F. 302, 322 n. 282
Jameson, Michael 295 n. 220, 315 n. 264
Jardé, A. 55–6
Jerome 73
Jones, A. H. M. 224 n. 25
Jones, Jacquelyn 300
Julian, and Xenophon as philosopher 22
justice 301, 339

Kaufman, Gloria 77 n. 27, 88 n. 69
Kelly-Gadol, Joan 88
Kent, R. G. 241 n. 71
Keuls, Eva 292
king, Persian 238–44, 280, 344
  and agriculture 238–9, *239*, 254
  compared with queen bee 17, 240–2, 276, 278
  wife of Ischomachus compared with 240–2, 276, 301, 343
Klapisch-Zuber, Christiane 75 n. 22

Kleve, Knut 70 n. 6
Knauth, W. 238
Knecht, Andreas 304
koine 11, 15
Kornemann, E. 49
Kroll, W. 322 n. 282
Kuhrt, Amélie 246

labour, division of 35–7, 39, 43,
    45–6, 57, 276–7
Lacey, A. R. 29 n. 25
Lacey, W. K. 214, 269 n. 152
land:
    fragmentation 51, 54–5, 314, 328
    leases 44, 54, 327, 328 n. 297,
        333, 340
    market 339
    ownership 256, 341
language of *Oeconomicus* 10–12
    and gender 98
    see also vocabulary
Laurenti, R. 292
leadership 3, 38, 227
    by wife 278
Lenaerts, Jean 91
'Letter of Darius' 239
Leuctra, battle of 4
Levi, M. A. 224 n. 25
Libanius, and Socrates 28
Lincke, K. 93, 95
Lindstam, Sigfrid 250 n. 107
literacy 215, 283
    of slaves 320
    of women 10, 34, 59, 80, 82–3,
        283
liturgies:
    and challenges 265–6
    costs 47, 52–3, 225–8
    liturgical class 2, 59, 217, 260
    types 226–8
location of *Oeconomicus* 6–7, 18 n. 20
locks 297
Longinus 12, 22
Lord, Carnes, trans. of
    Oeconomicus 97, 100, 292
Luccioni, Jean 50, 216
Lucian:

Dial. Mort. 345
Salt. 233
Ship 288
    and style of Xenophon 14
Lycurgus, legislation 32, 75, 80
Lysander, and Cyrus 238, 251
Lysias 48, 226, 228, 260, 282, 292,
    298, 304, 341

MacDowell, Douglas M. 213 n. 2
Macve, Richard H. 56 n. 42
Maffei, Raphael 75 n. 19
magistrates 301–2
maieutic method 27
Mantinea, battle of 4, 8, 10, 265
Marcellinus, and Plato and
    Xenophon 27
Marchant, E. C. 30, 92, 95–8,
    100–1, 214, 222 n. 22, 230, 236,
    292
Mariolopoulos, E. G. 257 n. 126
Marius Victorinus 73 n. 11
markets 55
marriage 58–61, 71, 74, 242
    age of 3, 232, 268–9, 275
    as economic union 33, 58–9, 84
    as partnership 273, 276
    in Renaissance England 85–6
    in Renaissance Italy 75
    role of parents in 268
    as sexual union 34–6, 234, 306
    of slaves 66, 72
Marx, Karl 43, 57
Maximus of Tyre 82 n. 45
Memorabilia 7
    and agriculture 326, 329
    and army 286
    and Aspasia 233
    and house design and
        decoration 291, 293
    and household management 217
    and merchants 341
    relationship to *Oeconomicus* 93–4,
        213, 216
    and slaves 67, 299, 316–17
    and Socrates 22–3, 27–8, 30,
        215–16, 273, 305, 316

and theft 320
and wealth and poverty 224
and weaving by women 64
and work and idleness 280
men:
  education 267–8
  and household
    management 79–80
  in public sphere 33, 36–7, 57, 74,
    88, 235, 247, 287
  'womanish' 236–7, 276, 303
mercenary, service as 2–3, 5, 9
merchants 55, 340–1
metaphors, recurrent 17, 62, 223,
  287
metics 227, 231, 341
Michell, H. 42, 49
Mickwitz, G. 56
millet 328
misfortune, and impiety 256
Mithra 252–3
Mommsen, Tycho 12 n. 9
Montuori, Mario 23 n. 6
More, Sir Thomas 78, 80
Morgan, Gareth 295 n. 220
Morrison, Toni 300
mother, role in marriage 268
Müller, Werner 252
Münscher, Karl 68 n. 1, 250
Murnaghan, Sheila 302 n. 239
Murray, Pauli 281 n. 175
Muscarella, Oscar White 242 n. 73

Nails, Debra 263
narrative structure 17–18, 98–9,
  215–16, 251–2, 322
neologisms 9, 303
Nepos 293 n. 215
Nestle, W. 219–20
Nicias 309
Norden, E. 14
nostalgia 16, 50, 241, 264

Oeconomicus:
  in Greece 68–9
  as historical source 237–8, 246
  in Middle Ages 73–4

in Renaissance England 76–87
in Renaissance Italy 74–5
in Rome 69–73
Oertel, F. 49
oikos:
  in economic theory 41–5
  and economics of
    patriarchy 57–8, 232
  in fourth-century
    philosophy 33–9, 217
  furnishing 230
  meaning 31, 213–14, 258
  and political structure 52
  in Socrates 29–30
  in Xenophon 45–6, 51
  see also cults; family
olives 47, 49, 329, 334, 336
On Horsemanship 216, 219, 231, 267,
  285, 327
On Hunting 267
oral tradition 215
oratory 17–18
order, necessity for 17, 230–1,
  240–1, 252, 285–90
Osborne, Robin 292
Oschophoria festival 257

P. Columbia VII 179: 331
P. Oxyrhynchus II 227: 91, 95
P. Tebtunis II 682: 91
painting 303–4
Palladius 328, 330, 332, 338
  and viticulture 335, 337
Panaetius, and Xenophon as
    philosopher 22
papyrus fragments 91–2
paradox 28, 232
parents, children's obligation to
    maintain 35, 273, 285
park:
  as model of household 240, 252
  Persian 247, 252
patriarchy 34–5, 39, 57–8, 75, 88,
  98, 231, 271
patronymic, use of 266
Pausanias 265, 344
Pelletier, A. 248

Peloponnesian War 18, 32, 64
  effects on agriculture 46–50, 314,
    327, 339
  effects on families 31, 262, 311
  and guest-friends 225
  Xenophon's cavalry service 2, 48
Peppler, Charles W. 215
Persian Empire 237–53, 273, 276
  division of power 245–7
  personification 16, 98, 222, 254,
    330, 335
Persson, Axel W. 91, 93
Petrarch 74, 214 n. 4
Phocylides 277
Philesia, wife of Xenophon 3
Philochorus 301
Philodemus 22 n. 2, 92
  on *Oeconomica* 68, 70, 213
Philostratus, and Xenophon 2
phrourarchs 246, 301–2
Phrynichus of Bithynia 11, 236
piety 29, 81, 256, 258, 271, 310
pigs 330
Pindar 344
plants, growth 324
Plato:
  Apol. 313
  and Cyrus 10, 26, 240
  and exercise 307
  and gender 37–8, 69, 86, 90, 303
  Gorg. 286
  and homosexuality 230
  Laws 10, 26–7, 39, 69, 90, 268,
    292, 302, 307
  and leadership 278
  and marriage 269
  Menex. 48, 233
  Meno 271, 275, 337
  and oikos 217
  and order 286
  and painting 304
  Phil. 304
  portrayal of Socrates 19, 23–5,
    27–9, 216, 218, 223, 313–14
  Rep. 216, 271, 276, 303, 307
  and reward 298

  and rhetoric 16
  Symposium 20, 215
  and Xenophon 26–9
  see also Pseudo-Plato
Pliny:
  and agriculture 327, 329
  and bees 241, 277, 279
  and Latin version of
    Oeconomicus 70
ploughing 324–5, *326*, 328–9
Plutarch 74, 253, 272
  and adultery 279
  and agriculture 257–8
  and Aspasia 233–4
  and battle of Cunaxa 251
  and estate management 218
  and Eupatrids 222
  and household finances 282
  and Ischomachus 260
  and Lysander 251
  quotes *Oeconomicus* 290
  and theft 319–20
  and women 270, 295
  and Xenophon 13, 221
Pöhlmann, R. von 49
Pole, Sir Geoffrey 81
Pollitt, J. J. 32 n. 3
population levels 49, 244, 280,
    314
Portus, Franciscus 75 n. 19
possessions, categories 300–1
poverty 28, 220, 223–4
power:
  in oikos 247
  separation of 245–7
Priscian 73 n. 12
Prodicus of Ceos 2, 18, 220
profit:
  as aim of estate
    management 51–2, 54–5, 338
  and record-keeping 55–6
  and work 61–5
property:
  exchange of 265–6
  held in common 303
Protagoras, and household
    management 7

Proxenos of Boeotia 224
Pseudo-Aristotle:
  and agriculture 46, 47 n. 21
  and gender-roles 34, 37, 69
  Oeconomica 46, 68, 74–5, 213, 236,
    241, 273, 282, 293, 298, 317,
    323
  and slaves 66, 318
Pseudo-Demosthenes:
  and agriculture 327, 332
  and hetairai 220
  and Ischomachus 261
  and marriage 35, 276, 282, 313
  and wealth 266
Pseudo-Plato:
  Eryxias 219–20
  Minos 322
Pseudo-Xenophon:
  Athenaion Politeia 216, 228, 329
  and slaves 65–6, 283, 319
punishment:
  and reward 241, 244, 285, 319,
    344
  for theft 319–20

queens 276–7
Quintilian 13, 22
  and Latin version of
    Oeconomicus 70, 73

Raepsaet, G. 273
reaping 331
recapitulation 6, 258, 321–2
record-keeping 55–7, 283
Reilly, Linda Collins 299
religion, family as male sphere 271
repetition 6, 99, 240, 288, 322
reproduction, encouragement 244
Revenues 4–5, 216, 218
  and agriculture 256, 339
  and economy 45
  and furnishing of household 230
  and levies 228
  and record-keeping 55
  and slaves 66 n. 61
reviews 6, 17, 258, 321–2

reward:
  for slaves 65–7, 256, 285, 298,
    317, 319
  for subordinates 241, 244
rhetoric 14–17, 254–5, 288, 313
Rhodes, P. J. 302
rhyme 218, 223, 254, 288
Richards, H. 12 n. 9, 101
Richter, G. M. A. 82 n. 45
rising, early 310–11
Robinson, D. M. 292–3, 296, 312
Root, Margaret Cool 242 n. 73
Rostovtzeff, M. I. 42, 315
Rural Dionysia 231
Ruskin, John 87
Rutherford, W. G. 12

Sancisi-Weerdenburg, Heleen
  238 n. 58, 249 n. 102
Sartori, F. 340
Sauppe, G. 12
  edn. of *Oeconomicus* 94–5, 100
Savile, Sir Henry 77 n. 28
Schacht, Hans 12 n. 10
Schenkl, Karl 92, 94, 95, 100, 216,
  221
Schleiermacher, F., and Plato 23–4
Schmoll, E. A. 93 n. 8
Schneider, J. G., edn. of
  Oeconomicus 94, 101
Schulze, C. P. 93 n. 9
Schumpeter, J. A. 42
Schwandner, Ernst-Ludwig 293,
  294, 296, 312
Scillus, estate at 4, 5–6, 7, 247
Sealey, R. 222 n. 21
Second Sophistic, and style of
  Xenophon 11, 13
self-control 59, 271, 275, 313, 318,
  344
Semonides:
  and marriage 36
  and wife as bee 59–60, 277–9
Seneca, and agriculture 258
Servius 70–1
settlements, rural 280–1
Seuthes, king of Thrace 3

sexuality:
  and bees 279
  and marriage 34–6, 234, 305–6,
    308
  and slaves 35, 39, 65, 297–8, 306,
    308, 317
  see also homosexuality
sheep 327
ships 17, 287–9, 301, 342–3
Simon, J. A. 12 n. 10
skin, whitening 305
slaves:
  in agriculture 256, 281, 314–17,
    326, 328, 334
  in authority 66–7, 71, 318, 321
  banausic work 321
  clothing 65–6, 256, 319
  disposition 283
  and estate management 218
  and family 40, 213
  female, productivity 3, 43–4,
    61–2, 64–5, 284
  gluttony 319
  literacy 320
  manumission 256, 285, 298, 300,
    319
  in *Oeconomicus* 65–9, 221
  older 223, 303
  and profit 61
  reproduction 66, 72, 280,
    297–300, 317
  rewards 241, 256, 285, 298, 317,
    319
  and rhetoric 313
  role in domestic economy 44–5,
    53, 230–1
  Roman views 71–2
  sexual access to 35, 39, 65, 297–8,
    306–9, 316–17
  training 317
  treatment 321
  value 61, 284–5
  see also gentleman
Smith, Adam 43 n. 11
Socrates 6–8, 17–18, 309
  and agriculture 331, 340

  and Aspasia 81–2, 232–4
  and dialogues 19–20, 100,
    217–18
  and oikos 29–30, 70, 214
  in Plato and Xenophon 27, 313
  poverty 28, 38, 59, 223–4, 234
  and religious beliefs 258
  and 'Socratic problem' 22–6
  trial and death 3–4, 21, 230, 250
  and use of rhetoric 16
  and wealth 53, 222
  and women 80–2, 90, 232, 234,
    271, 305, 317
  Xenophon as disciple of 21–2,
    215–16
  see also definitions; paradox
soil 323–4, 330, 338–9
Solon, legislation 28, 222, 278, 291,
    319–21
Sophocles, *Trach.* 312–13
Sorel, Georges 5, 43, 57
sowing 325, 328–30
Sparta:
  banausic trades 235–6
  family and state 32, 80
  and Persia 251
  role of women 236, 282
  as setting for *Oeconomicus* 5–6
  and sexuality 318
  Xenophon's familiarity
    with 8–10, 305
Spartan Constitution 7, 32, 216, 244,
    267
spies 242–3
stables 312
Starr, Chester G. 237, 253 n. 118
states, administration 240
Ste. Croix, G. E. M. de 44, 56, 226,
    315
Stephanus, H., edn. of
  Oeconomicus 94
Stoa of Zeus Eleutherius 8, 19, 81,
    264–5, 304
Stobaeus 92, 95, 101, 236
storage:
  of food 282–3, 293, 338

household 72, 230, 287–91, 293
Stowe, Harriet Beecher 89
Strabo 253, 342
Strauss, Barry 224 n. 25
Strauss, Leo 24, 97
stubble, burning 331
Sturz, F. W. 12, 292
style of *Oeconomicus* 6–7, 9, 9–11, 16
  and Attic style 11–15, 93, 99
  see also repetition
Suda 250, 264
  on style of Xenophon 12 n. 7, 13
    n. 11, 15
Sumner, W. M. 244
supervisor, *see* foreman
Sutton, Robert 32–3
Symposium, Xenophon's 215
  and agriculture 255
  and Eupatrids 221
  and land-ownership 340
  and poverty 224
  relationship to *Oeconomicus* 93–4
  and Socrates 22, 222, 271
  and women 39, 232, 304
syntax 12

Tacitus:
  and style of Xenophon 13 n. 11
  and Xenophon as philosopher 22
Tantalus 344–5
taxation 52–3, 226, 228
Ten Thousand, the 3
  see also *Anabasis*
textiles, as women's productive
    task 60–4, 270, 274, 284, 297,
    307, *307*
texts:
  ancient 7, 91–2, 236, 333
  medieval and Renaissance 92–3
  and other works of
    Xenophon 93–4
thalamos 292–3, *294*
Thalheim, Th., edn. of
    Oeconomicus 95–6, 101
Thebes, detention of Xenophon
    in 16
theft 319–21

themes, reiteration 17, 75, 99, 219,
    240, 255, 319
Theocritus 306, 332
Theodote 220–1
theology 230, 258, 275, 280, 329
  of Xenophon 258
Theophrastus:
  and agriculture 257, 313, 322–5,
    327, 329–30, 338
  and literacy 283
  and *Oeconomica* 68
  and viticulture 333, 335–6
Thesmophoria 279
thetes 223–4
Third Sacred War 4–5
Thirty, the 2
Thrasymachus of Chalcedon 10
threshing 332
Thucydides:
  and civilized polis 52 n. 31
  and Peloponnesian War 48, 311
  prose 16
  and ships 342–3
  and slaves 64
Tilney, Edmund 86
time-frame 17, 215, 276
title of *Oeconomicus* 213–15
Tomlinson, R. A. 289 n. 197
tools 330
translation 97–101, 214
  by Cicero 13, 70, 73, 91, 99–100,
    214, 301, 329, 338
trees 245, 252, 285
  vines as 333, 335–6
Trever, Albert Augustus 87 n. 66
tribe 300–1
trierarchy 225, 227–8
trireme 287–8, 342
Tuplin, Christopher 237, 247, n. 91
tyrants 344

unity of *Oeconomicus* 17, 232

variety 17
Varro, Marcus Terentius 280, 293
  and agriculture 323, 325–6,
    330–2, 336–8

and Latin version of
  Oeconomicus 70
Vatin, Claude 69
Vergil, *Georgics* 324, 326, 328, 330,
  335–6
vessels, ceramic 277, n. 163, 290
vice 222–3
Victor, Ulrich 68 n. 2
vilica 71–2, 280
vilicus 71–2
virtue:
  female 80, 275, 301, 303
  and food in storage 338
  of men and women 271, 275, 286,
    303, 317
viticulture 333–7, 339
Vitruvius Pollio 312
  Arch. 292–3
Vives, Juan Luis 78–82, 84,
  88 n. 69, 214
vocabulary 10–12, 93, 302, 330–1,
  343
  abstract 99
  poetic 10, 14, 16, 237
  technical 10

Wackernagel, J. 12 n. 9
Walker, Susan 295 n. 220
Wallon, Henri 298
Walser, Gerold 238, 242 n. 73
Wankel, Hermann 321
water, carrying 283–4
Waterfield, Robin, trans. of
  Oeconomicus 97–8, 100, 213, 230
wealth:
  in Aeschines 220
  and military status 256
  and obligations 224–9, 265–6
  and ostentation 291, 319
  and political life 222
  Socrates on 218–19
  and vice 222–3
weather, and agriculture 256–8,
  328
weaving, *see* textiles
Wedderburn, A. D. O. 98, 213

wheat 324, 328–9, 342
Whitehead, David 225 n. 29
widows, control of 262
Wilamowitz-Moellendorf, U.
  von 92
Willcox, W. B. 86 n. 59
winnowing 332
women:
  in Aristotle 34
  in authority 34, 37–8, 86, 247
  in domestic economy 43–4,
    58–61, 70, 84–5, 274
  and gluttony 36, 59, 271
  literacy 80, 82–3
  names not given 233
  in *Oeconomicus* 34–6, 68–9, 74,
    236–7
  older 39, 60, 223, 285
  and Peloponnesian War 49–50
  in Plato 37–8, 39, 86
  in private sphere 33, 36–8, 71,
    74, 79, 88–9, 247, 287
  quarters for 292–7, 317
  and religion 269, 272
  in Renaissance England 77–86
  seclusion 234, 269, 295–6, 317
  as silent 269–70, 272
  social role 268
  in Socrates 80, 90
  working 316
  see also cosmetics; education;
    feminism; textiles
Wood, Ellen Meiksins 315
wool-working 270, 284
word-play 16–17, 217, 218,
  223
work, and profit 61–5

Xanthippe 81, 234
Xenophon:
  departure from Athens 2–4
  as disciple of Socrates 21–2,
    215–16
  as economist 45–6
  exile 4–5, 7, 32, 45–6
  as historian 24 n. 10

and Plato 26–9
portrayal of Socrates 26–30, 70,
    223
and 'Socratic problem' 22–6
youth 1–2
see Pseudo-Xenophon

Xenophon, grandson of
    Xenophon 5

Zenon 56
Zeune, J. K., edn. of *Oeconomicus* 94
Zeuxis 303–4